D1562845

DATE DUE

The Fate of Reason

The Fate of Reason

German Philosophy from Kant to Fichte

Frederick C. Beiser

Harvard University Press
Cambridge, Massachusetts, and London, England

Copyright © 1987 by the President and Fellows
   of Harvard College
All rights reserved
Printed in the United States of America
10 9 8 7 6 5 4 3 2

Publication of this book has been aided by a grant from
the Andrew W. Mellon Foundation.

This book is printed on acid-free paper, and its binding
materials have been chosen for strength and durability.

Library of Congress Cataloging in Publication Data

Beiser, Frederick C., 1949–
   The fate of reason.

   Bibliography: p.
   Includes index.
   1. Philosophy, German—18th century.   2. Reason—
History—18th century.   I. Title.
B2748.R37B45   1987   193   86-14303
ISBN 0-674-29502-1 (alk. paper)

For Frederick Robert Beiser

Preface

THIS BOOK grew out of the conviction that there is a serious lacuna in our knowledge of the history of philosophy in the English-speaking world. The years between 1781 and 1793—after the publication of Kant's first *Kritik* and before the appearance of Fichte's 1794 *Wissenschaftslehre*—still remain terra incognita for many. This is a grave gap since this period was one of the most revolutionary and fertile in the history of modern philosophy. The philosophers of this time broke with the twin pillars of the modern Cartesian tradition: the authority of reason and the primacy of epistemology. They also witnessed the decline of the *Aufklärung*, the completion of Kant's philosophy, and the beginnings of post-Kantian idealism. All these are events that no history of philosophy can afford to ignore and that deserve examination in the closest detail. Yet, apart from a few studies of individual philosophers, the English-speaking reader will find very little to guide him; there is no general study that concentrates on this period as a whole.

This work intends to be only an introduction, a general survey of the most important thinkers and controversies of the period between Kant and Fichte. I have not attempted to provide a social history of the reception of Kant's or Spinoza's philosophy, and still less a study of the social and political context of late eighteenth-century German philosophy. Rather, I have focused on the philosophical doctrines themselves and have limited myself to the preliminary tasks of textual exegesis and criticism.

The precise subject of this book is definable more by my objectives than by any arbitrary set of dates. My aim has been twofold: to examine the philosophical background of post-Kantian idealism; and to trace the influence of Kant's critics on the development of his philosophy. I have therefore focused on the period between 1781 and 1793, the first decade or so after the publication of the first *Kritik*. At times, however, fulfillment of my objectives has required going beyond this timespan and discussing texts and controversies that precede it. Some texts or disputes that had a decisive influence upon Kant and post-Kantian idealism were written or conducted before the appearance of the first *Kritik*, and it was impossible to ignore them.

While I have been liberal in setting myself a starting point, I have been conservative in laying down a stopping point—at the year 1793. This has meant cutting out important works that belong of necessity in any complete history of post-Kantian philosophy. Thus I do not discuss Beck's *Einzig mögliche Standpunkt*, Nicolai's *Sempronius Grundibert*, or Schiller's *Aesthetische Erziehung*, because they were all published after 1793. In some cases I do not discuss works or controversies because a full discussion of their contents would require taking into account developments after 1793. Hence I have not examined Schiller's early essays, Fichte's first writings, or Kant's theory-practice essay.

Even within these general limits I have had to make difficult, and partly arbitrary, decisions about which author, text, or controversy to discuss. This has been particularly the case in Chapters 6 and 7, where I have examined a few of the many polemical writings directed against Kant's first *Kritik*. In selecting a few texts from a huge mass of material, I decided to discuss only that text or dispute which had philosophical merit *and* which was in some way influential.

Despite these selections, I hope to have illuminated the period as a whole, particularly for those who have read some Kant or Hegel and who want to know more about what happened in between.

I would like to thank the following people for their advice and support: Isaiah Berlin, Robert Brandom, Daniel Brudney, Burton Dreben, Raymond Geuss, Paul Guyer, Peter Hylton, Charles Lewis, Susan Neiman, Thomas Ricketts, Ellen Rosendale, Simon Schaffer, Harriet Strachan, Charles Taylor, Michael Theunissen, Kenneth Westphal, and Allen Wood. I also wish to thank Berneta Burnam for typing a draft of the manuscript.

My interest in the history of German idealism began in 1973–74 at Oxford, where I was motivated by Bill Weinstein, to whom I am grateful. The book was written from 1980 to 1984 in a *Hinterhof* in Berlin, Neukölln. During that time I was fortunate to receive generous financial support from the Fritz Thyssen Stiftung.

Contents

The Fate of Reason

Introduction

DURING the period between Kant's first *Kritik* and Fichte's first *Wissenschaftslehre* (1781–1794), philosophers devoted themselves to a single fundamental problem. They returned again and again to this problem, though it had many guises, and though its presence was not always clearly recognized. If we were to formulate this issue in a single phrase, then we might call it 'the authority of reason'. It arises as soon as we begin to question our apparently healthy and natural faith in reason. Why should I listen to reason? What reason do I have to obey it? We demand that a person's beliefs and actions be rational; to say that they are irrational is to condemn them. But why do we make such a demand? What is the justification for it? Or, in short, whence the authority of reason?

Such were the questions that philosophers began to ask themselves during the last decades of the eighteenth century in Germany.[1] They began to look critically at the fundamental article of faith of the European Enlightenment: the authority of reason. Philosophers loyal to the Enlightenment bestowed enormous authority upon reason, which was the Enlightenment's sovereign standard of truth, its final court of intellectual appeal. They made many bold claims in behalf of reason. Reason had self-evident first principles; it could criticize all our beliefs; it could justify morality, religion, and the state; it was universal and impartial; and it could, at least in theory, explain everything in nature. Toward the close of the eighteenth century, however, all these claims were thrown into question. If the Enlightenment was 'the age of criticism', then the last decades of the eighteenth century marked the beginning of a new age, 'the age of meta-criticism'. Intellectuals began to suffer a crisis of conscience and question their own faith in the powers of criticism.

Philosophers in the late eighteenth century had one very good reason for questioning the authority of reason: it seemed as if modern science and philosophy were undermining morality, religion, and the state. The Enlightenment's reign of reason had become a reign of death and destruction since the mechanistic methods of modern science, and the critical demands of modern philosophy, were leading straight toward atheism, fatalism, and anarchism. The more science advanced, the less room there seemed to be for freedom and God in the universe; and the more philosophy exercised its critical powers, the less authority could be claimed for the Bible and the old proofs of the existence of God, providence, and immortality. Thus the progress of the Enlightenment toward the close of the eighteenth century only seemed to vindicate Rousseau's damning indictment in the first *Discours:* the arts and sciences were not improving but corrupting morals.

The animated discussion surrounding Kant's and Spinoza's philosophies during the 1780s in Germany seemed to give dramatic and decisive evidence in favor of Rousseau's melancholy conclusion. Both Kant's and Spinoza's philosophies were generally regarded as paragons of the Enlightenment, as bulwarks of the authority of reason.[2] Kant's philosophy represented an uncompromising philosophical criticism; and Spinoza's philosophy stood for a radical scientific naturalism. But their philosophies also illustrated the dangerous consequences of rational inquiry and criticism. The consequence of Kant's philosophy, if it were to drop its inconsistent postulate of the thing-in-itself, was solipsism; and the consequence of Spinoza's philosophy, if it were to delete its superfluous religious language, was atheism and fatalism. Thus the two philosophies foremost in the public mind seemed to be destructive of morality, religion, and the state. But this naturally raised a very disturbing question in many minds: why should we listen to our reason if it undermines all those beliefs necessary for the conduct of life?

This question was especially disturbing for philosophers of the Enlightenment. For their faith in reason was largely based upon the assumption that reason could justify morality, religion, and the state. Never would they have dared to trust reason had they imagined that it would destroy these institutions. Rather, they were confident that reason could peel away the mystical shell of our moral, religious, and political beliefs (their supernatural sanction through the Bible) and that it could lay bare their truthful core (the universal and necessary principles of human nature and society). Philosophers predicted that the authority of reason would eventually replace the authority of tradition, revelation, and scripture precisely because they believed that reason was a more effective sanction for moral, religious, and political beliefs.

Yet it was just this belief that had been thrown into question in the late 1780s by the bitter controversies surrounding Kant's and Spinoza's philosophies. Rather than supporting faith, reason now seemed bent on destroying it. Kant's and Spinoza's philosophies represented two very different models of rationality; but both of them seemed to have disastrous consequences for morality, religion, and common sense. The Spinozistic model defined reason in terms of the principle of sufficient reason, which was interpreted in a strictly mechanistic fashion, so that it read 'for any event B there must be some prior event A, such that given A, B occurs of necessity'. If this principle is universalized, however, it leads to atheism and fatalism; for God and freedom must be self-causing agencies, causes that act without a prior cause. The Kantian model explained reason in terms of its a priori activity and declared that reason knows a priori only what it creates or what it makes conform to the laws of its activity.[3] If this principle is generalized, so that knowledge is only possible through reason, then it results in solipsism; for then all we know are the products of our own activity but no reality independent of them.

These models of rationality confronted philosophers with a very painful dilemma. They now had to choose either a rational skepticism or an irrational fideism. If they remained loyal to reason, then they had to doubt all their moral, religious, and political beliefs; but if they clung to these beliefs, then they had to renounce reason. Both of these options were plainly intolerable. They could not renounce reason, which they saw as the foundation of moral and intellectual autonomy and as the only antidote to the dreaded evils of mysticism and dogmatism; but nor could they abandon faith, which they knew to be the basis for moral action and social life. As unacceptable as these options were, there no longer seemed to be a middle path between them in the last decades of the eighteenth century.

This crisis, which became apparent only at the end of the eighteenth century, had been prophesied some fifty years earlier by David Hume at the close of the first book of his *Treatise of Human Nature*.[4] Here Hume saw an irresolvable conflict between the claims of reason and faith, philosophy and life. His reason led him to the skeptical conclusion that he knew nothing more than his own passing impressions; but the demands of practical life compelled him to forget these 'extravagant speculations', whose force mercifully disappeared after a game of backgammon with friends. The conflict Hume posed was the same as that faced by the Enlightenment toward the end of the eighteenth century. It was indeed no accident that many of Kant's early critics—Hamann, Jacobi, Wizenmann, Schulze, Platner, and Maimon—all defended Hume against Kant. They confronted Kant with Hume's dilemma at the end of the *Treatise:* either a rational skepticism or an irrational leap of faith. The history of the early criticism of Kant's philosophy is indeed in large measure a tale of Hume's revenge. The ghost of *le bon David* stood above the twilight of the Enlightenment only to sigh "I told you so."

It was in the revival of Hume's skepticism at the end of the eighteenth century that we find the first glimmerings of a problem which was to haunt philosophy toward the close of the nineteenth century: nihilism.[5] As early as the 1780s, nihilism, "that most uncanny of guests," was already knocking at the door.[6] It was F. H. Jacobi who introduced the term 'nihilism' (Nihilismus) into modern philosophy. To Jacobi, the paradigm case of the nihilist was someone like Hume at the end of the Treatise. The nihilist was a skeptic whose reason told him that he had to doubt the existence of everything—the external world, other minds, God, and even the permanent reality of his own self; the only reality that he could affirm was nothingness itself. In its original sense, then, the word 'nihilism' was used to denote the alleged solipsistic consequences of all rational inquiry and criticism. The fear of nihilism was indeed very widespread toward the end of the eighteenth century. Although many philosophers resisted Jacobi's argument that nihilism was the inevitable consequence of all rational investigation, they agreed with him that it was the chief danger facing any philosophy. Thus the charge of Humean solipsism was the most common criticism among Kant's early opponents—whether they were Lockeans, Wolffians, or Stürmer und Dränger—and it was generally regarded as the reductio ad absurdum of his philosophy.

Nihilism was perceived as a pressing danger around the late 1780s partly because of the decline of the rationalist metaphysics of the Leibnizian-Wolffian school. The great charm of that metaphysics, and the main reason for its persistence on the German intellectual scene, was that it seemed to provide a safe middle path between the extremes of Hume's dilemma: an a priori knowledge of the existence of God, providence, and immortality. Even before the appearance of the Kritik der reinen Vernunft in May 1781, however, this charm began to wear thin. The skepticism of Hume, the empiricism of Crusius, the pragmatism of the Popularphilosophen, and the antirationalism of the French philosophes had all brought metaphysics into disrepute. Kant's attack on rationalism in the Kritik was only the coup de grace to the rotting edifice of the Leibnizian-Wolffian school. The disappearance of rationalist metaphysics did create a very frightening vacuum. Without an a priori knowledge of God, providence, and immortality, how could we justify our moral, religious, and political beliefs?

The main reason for the extraordinary success of Kant's philosophy in the early 1790s was that it seemed to fill this vacuum.[7] Kant's doctrine of 'practical faith', as it was outlined in the "Kanon" of the first Kritik and the "Dialektik" of the second, promised a more reliable middle path between the extremes of Hume's dilemma. It was no longer necessary to demand the quixotic, namely, a priori proofs for our beliefs in God, providence, and immortality. Even if reason could not supply such proofs, it could give a moral justification for these beliefs. They could be shown to be necessary incentives for our moral duty to bring about 'the highest good', that ideal state where happiness and virtue are in perfect harmony. What justified our moral and religious beliefs was thus not the theoretical reason of metaphysics but the practical reason of the moral law. For Kant's early disciples, this doctrine was no mere afterthought, a placebo given to Kant's weeping manservant Lampe, who could not live with the skeptical conclusions of the first *Kritik*.[8] Rather, it was the very spirit of the critical philosophy. Such eminent Kantians as Fichte and Reinhold were converted to the critical philosophy precisely because of the enormous appeal of this doctrine. The crisis of the Enlightenment now seemed to be resolved, thanks to the timely intervention of Kant's practical faith.

But such feelings of relief proved to be short-lived. There were many philosophers who remained unconvinced by Kant's doctrine of practical faith and who pressed his disciples very hard to defend it. Remove the thing-in-itself and admit the emptiness of the categorical imperative, these critics said, and Kant's philosophy collapses into a Humean solipsism. The categorical imperative amounts to nothing more than the demand of consistency; and that can be used to sanction all kinds of beliefs, even beliefs in the *nonexistence* of God, providence, and immortality. And if Kant rids his philosophy of the thing-in-itself—as he must, if he is to remain within his own limits upon knowledge—then we are left with nothing more than the existence of our own fleeting sensations. Since Kant's philosophy turns all reality into a mere dream, the most that it can ever justify is the command to act *as if* God, providence, and immortality exist.

The attacks on Kant's doctrine of practical faith were relentless, only increasing in their intensity in the mid-1790s. Philosophers such as Jacobi, Pistorius, Schulze, Maimon, Flatt, Eberhard, Maass, and Schwab heaped objections upon it. In the end even such an enthusiastic Kantian as Fichte had to admit their force; he then conceded that the entire foundation of the critical philosophy needed a thorough rethinking. But the breakdown of Kant's doctrine of practical faith in the mid-1790s only left a more horrifying vacuum than before. All the options appeared to be exhausted. Neither the theoretical reason of metaphysics nor the practical reason of the moral law could justify faith. The old dilemma of a rational skepticism or an irrational fideism returned with more force than ever. Thus, to many philosophers at the end of the eighteenth century, it seemed as if reason was heading straight toward the abyss and that there was no means of stopping it.

It was not only this conflict between reason and faith that disturbed the Enlightenment trust in reason. Philosophers were beginning to realize that even if reason did support faith, it did not support itself. Toward the close of the eighteenth century, reason seemed bent on destroying itself, "on suffering violence at its own hands," as Hegel later put it. But why was this?

The Enlightenment faith in reason was based first and foremost upon its belief in the powers of criticism. Reason was identified with the faculty of criticism, that is, the power to determine whether we have sufficient evidence for our beliefs.[9] The guidelines of criticism were laid down by the principle of sufficient reason: every belief should have a sufficient reason, such that it follows of necessity from other beliefs known to be true.

The Enlightenment conferred great authority upon its tribunal of criticism. The principle of sufficient reason suffered no exceptions; all beliefs had to submit to its requirements. Nothing was sacred before the criticism of reason, not even the state in its majesty nor religion in its holiness.[10] Nothing, that is, except of course the tribunal of critique itself, which was somehow sacred, holy, and sublime.

But such a conspicuous and dubious exception only created suspicions about the Enlightenment faith in criticism. Some philosophers began to recognize that an unqualified demand for criticism is self-reflexive, applying to reason itself.[11] If it is the duty of reason to criticize *all* our beliefs, then *ipso facto* it must criticize itself; for reason has its own beliefs about itself, and these cannot escape criticism. To refuse to examine these beliefs is to sanction 'dogmatism', the demand that we accept beliefs on trust. But dogmatism, which refuses to give reasons, is clearly the chief enemy of criticism, which demands that we give reasons. So, unless criticism is to betray itself, it must become, in the end, meta-criticism, the critical examination of criticism itself.

Yet if the meta-criticism of reason is necessary, is it not also dangerous? If reason must criticize itself, then it must ask itself the question 'How do I know this?' or 'What reason do I have to believe this?' But then we seem to face a very disturbing dilemma. Either we must ask this question ad infinitum, and embrace skepticism, or we must refuse to answer it, and lapse into dogmatism.

Now Kant thought that he had found a middle path between the extremes of this dilemma, one that rescued reason from its imminent self-destruction. This middle path was nothing less than his project for a critique of pure reason. "The critical path alone remains open," Kant wrote in the penultimate paragraph of the *Kritik*, contrasting his criticism with skepticism and dogmatism.[12] How would the critique steer reason between these dangerous extremes? It would undertake "the most difficult of all reason's tasks": it would bring it to self-awareness of its "eternal laws."[13] Since these laws would be the necessary conditions of any possible experience, they would be immune from skepticism. If the skeptic were to deny them, then he would not be able to describe even his own passing sense impressions. Armed with a knowledge of these laws, the critical philosopher would then have an infallible answer to the question 'How do I know this?' one that would not involve any appeal to authority and that would stop the skeptic's infinite regress dead in its tracks.

Although it was simple and straightforward, Kant's solution to the meta-critical problem left one unanswered question in its wake. Namely, how do we know the necessary conditions of any possible experience? This question is legitimate, pressing, and important; but Kant did not have any clear or explicit answer to it.[14] The sad truth of the matter is that he never developed a general meta-critical theory about how to acquire knowledge of the first principles of criticism.[15] If self-knowledge was the most difficult of all reason's tasks, Kant was still not forthcoming with any advice about how this was to be achieved. But Kant's failure to address the meta-critical problem in any sustained and explicit manner had a very serious consequence: it left the authority of reason hanging in the balance. Although Kant taught that the authority of reason depended upon the possibility of criticism, he had no clear explanation or justification of the possibility of criticism itself.

If the meta-critical problem is the point where Kant's philosophy ends, it is also the point where much post-Kantian philosophy begins. Kant's successors were willing to accept his contention that the authority of reason depends on the possibility of criticism; but, unlike Kant, they looked critically at the possibility of criticism itself. In questioning this possibility, they were taking the criticism of reason a new and important step beyond Kant. They were no longer content to examine the first-order claims of reason as Kant had—the claims of physics to know the laws of nature, or the claims of metaphysics to know things-in-themselves. Rather, they insisted upon questioning its second-order claims—its claims to be a sufficient criterion of truth and to be in possession of self-evident first principles. While philosophy before Kant concerned itself with the question 'How is metaphysics possible?' philosophy after Kant focused upon the question 'How is the critique of knowledge possible?' Hegel's concern with this question in the introduction to his *Phänomenologie des Geistes* was not the beginning, but the end of an era.

All this does not mean, of course, that the post-Kantians collectively denied the possibility of criticism. If some of them attacked its possibility, others defended it. Some argued that consistent criticism ends in skepticism (Schulze, Platner, Garve, and Jacobi), others that it results in dogmatism (Eberhard, Maass, and Schwab), while still others held that it is indeed the middle path between such evils (Reinhold, Maimon, and Fichte). What all these thinkers do have in common, however, is the awareness that criticism is problematic and can no longer be taken for granted.

It is important to recognize the historical significance of this post-Kantian question. To examine the possibility of criticism was to examine the possibility of epistemology itself; in other words, it was to raise the question of whether it is possible to have knowledge of the conditions and limits of knowledge. The post-Kantians were therefore questioning one of the fundamental and characteristic tenets of the modern Cartesian tradition: that epistemology is *philosophia prima*. Descartes, Locke, Berkeley, Hume, and Kant had all embarked upon their philosophical programs in the confident belief that epistemology would provide them with a self-evident starting point. In questioning this belief, the post-Kantians were forcing the entire epistemological tradition to account for itself. That tradition by no means ended with post-Kantian philosophy. It indeed was revitalized in the hands of Reinhold and Fichte. Yet it has now become self-critical and self-reflective. The happy and heady days of the Cartesian legacy were over.

The crisis of confidence at the end of the eighteenth century deepened when another of the Enlightenment's most cherished convictions was thrown into question—that reason is universal and impartial. The tribunal of critique spoke with such awesome authority not only because its principles were self-evident, but also because they were universal and impartial. They were universal in the sense that they were true for every intelligent being, regardless of his culture, education, or philosophy; and they were impartial in the sense that they could arrive at conclusions independent of, and even contrary to, interests and desires.

The Enlightenment faith in the universality and impartiality of reason ultimately rested upon another of its even more fundamental beliefs—the autonomy of reason. Reason was thought to be an autonomous faculty in the sense that it was self-governing, establishing and following its own rules, independent of political interests, cultural traditions, or subconscious desires. If, on the contrary, reason were subject to political, cultural, or subconscious influences, then it would have no guarantee that its conclusions were universal and necessary; they might then turn out to be disguised expressions of political, cultural, or subconscious interests. Perhaps the clearest example of this belief in the autonomy of reason was Kant's noumenal-phenomenal dualism as it was laid down in the first *Kritik* and *Grundlegung*. It is important to see that the purpose of Kant's dualism was to save not only the possibility of freedom, but also the universality and impartiality of reason.

Perhaps the most original, powerful, and influential critic of this belief was J. G. Hamann. In his essay "Metakritik über den Purismum der reinen

Vernunft" (1783), Hamann attacked the main premise behind Kant's belief in the autonomy of reason, his noumenal-phenomenal dualism. A self-styled Aristotelian and critic of Kant's 'Platonism', Hamann vigorously opposed what he called 'the purism of reason': the hypostasis of reason through its abstraction from language, culture, and experience. If we are not to hypostatize reason, Hamann argued, then we have to raise the old Aristotelian question 'Where is reason?' 'In what particular things does it exist?' We can answer such questions, he maintained, only by identifying the embodiment of reason in language and action. Reason is not therefore a special kind of faculty that exists in some noumenal or mental realm; rather, it is only a specific manner of speaking and action, and, more concretely, it is only a manner of speaking and acting in a specific language and culture. Accordingly, Hamann stressed the social and historical dimension of reason, which had been so neglected during the Enlightenment. As he summed up his position, the instrument and criterion of reason is language; but language has no warrant other than the customs and traditions of a nation.[16]

Hamann's emphasis on the social and historical dimension of reason had very clear—and very threatening—relativistic implications. If the language and customs of a culture determine the criteria of reason, and if languages and customs differ from or even oppose one another, then there will be no such thing as a single universal reason. Reason will not be able to stand outside cultures and to judge between them since its criteria will be determined from within them. Such relativistic implications were not explicitly drawn by Hamann; but they were developed in detail by those who came under his influence, most notably Hegel, Herder, and F. Schlegel. In his *Auch eine Philosophie der Gesschichte der Menschheit* (1774), for example, Herder argued that the Enlightenment's tribunal of critique only universalized the values and interests of eighteenth-century Europe. Philosophers of the time therefore had no right to criticize the beliefs and traditions of another culture (namely, the Middle Ages) since that was to judge another culture by Enlightenment standards.

The faith in the autonomy of reason came under fire from another direction by F. H. Jacobi in his *Briefe über Spinoza*.[17] While Hamann and Herder insisted that we cannot abstract reason from society and history, Jacobi stressed that we cannot separate it from desire and instinct. We have to see reason as part of a single living organism, he argued, where it organizes and directs all its vital functions. Reason is not a disinterested power of contemplation, then, but an instrument of the will, which uses it to control and dominate the environment. Reason is under the influence of the will to such a degree, Jacobi further maintained, that even its standards of truth and falsity are dictated by it. What is true or false becomes what is successful or unsuccessful in achieving the ends of life. Not shirking any relativistic implications, Jacobi then insinuated that these ends could differ from one culture to another.

Jacobi's argument that reason is subject to the will found additional support in a prescient insight of Hamann's and Herder's: that conscious and rational activities are expressions of subconscious and irrational urges. Thus Hamann saw sexual energy as the spring of creativity and held that even ratiocination is only its sublimation.[18] And Herder maintained that the source of all our activity lay in "dark powers," which we had to repress for the purposes of daily life.[19] These suggestive and inchoate insights were still far from the more explicit and sophisticated theories of Freud and Nietzsche. Nonetheless, their implications were still the same: they questioned the Enlightenment belief in the autonomy of reason.

The many criticisms of the autonomy of reason that surfaced at the end of the eighteenth century were in part only the bitter harvest of the Enlightenment's own program of scientific explanation. If we accept the dictum that we should explain everything according to natural laws, then we should stop seeing reason as a self-sufficient faculty that exists apart from nature, and we should start explaining it as another part of nature, just like everything else. The attempt to rescue the autonomy of reason by putting it inside a special noumenal sphere inaccessible to scientific study then amounts to nothing more than 'supernaturalism', 'mysticism', or 'obscurantism'—to use the terms that Kant's critics applied to his postulate of a noumenal world. Thus, in the end, the Enlightenment belief in the autonomy of reason became difficult to square with scientific naturalism. Here again the self-reflexivity of reason came into play, undermining its authority. If reason should explain everything according to natural laws, then it should ipso facto explain *itself* according to natural laws; the subject who explains nature stands in no privileged transcendental relation to the nature that he explains. But that means that reason can be shown to be subject to the influence of natural forces (such as instinct and desire) and thus no longer autonomous.

The Enlightenment faith in reason rested last but not least upon naturalism, the belief that reason could, if only in principle, explain everything in nature. This belief, bold though it was, appeared to have all the success of modern science in its favor. To many freethinkers, *Aufklärer*, and philosophes, the new physics of Galileo, Newton, and Huygens had shown that everything in nature is explicable according to a system of mathematical laws, which are transparent to and discovered by reason. Such diverse phenomena as the fall of an apple, the ebb and flow of the tides, and the orbit of a planet around the sun could all be explained by a single universal law, the law of gravitation. This law alone appeared to provide striking evidence for the view that reason had insight into the structure of nature.

Philosophers eagerly embraced the new physics because it seemed to vindicate one of their most precious dogmas: the harmony of reason and nature, the isomorphism of thought and being. The eighteenth century had inherited, and never questioned, this principle of seventeenth-century rationalism.[20] It did indeed break with rationalism; but its quarrel with rationalism concerned not the existence of this unity or harmony, but how to demonstrate or establish it. The Newtonians, the *Aufklärer,* and the philosophes abandoned the deductive method of rationalism in favor of the inductive method of empiricism. To know the logic behind nature, they argued, we could no longer begin with self-evident principles and then descend to specific conclusions; that would merely force our arbitrary constructions upon nature. Rather, we had to begin with observation and experiment and only then ascend to general laws. Yet, whether our method was inductive or deductive, the motivation behind it was the same: to demonstrate the harmony between reason and nature.

The greatest threat to the Enlightenment belief in the harmony of reason and nature came as early as 1739 with Hume's attack on causality in the *Treatise of Human Nature.* According to Hume, there is no empirical justification for the assumption that there are universal and necessary connections between events. If we examine our sense impressions, then all that we find are accidentally repeated sequences and not necessary connections, which are simply the product of our imagination and habits of association. By insisting on a sense impression corresponding to necessary connection, Hume had embarrassed the Enlightenment philosophers in terms of their own empirical standard of knowledge. A close look at experience seemed to falsify, rather than verify, the unity of reason and nature. A disturbing dualism thus arose where the universal and necessary principles of reason stood in stark contrast to the particularity and contingency of experience.

It was the mission of Kant's *Kritik der reinen Vernunft* to counter the threat of Humean skepticism and to rescue the Enlightenment faith in science. In the "Transzendentale Deduktion" and "Zweite Analogie" Kant embarked on his defense of the principle of causality. Here he argued that this principle is a necessary condition of ascribing objectivity to experience, of distinguishing between the subjective order of perceptions and the objective order of events themselves. This objective order is not given to us, however, but created by us. Reason knows the structure of experience only because it creates it, imposing its a priori forms upon it; and among these forms is the principle of causality. In other words, this principle applies to experience only because our a priori activity has made experience conform to it.[21]

But Kant's defense of the principle of causality had a double-edged effect on the faith in the harmony of reason and nature. It showed that harmony held only for appearances, and not things-in-themselves. We could know nature insofar as it conformed to our a priori concepts, but not insofar as it existed apart from and prior to them. The harmony of reason and nature was therefore confined within the realm of consciousness itself. It signified not the correspondence between consciousness and external reality, but the conformity of consciousness with its own self-imposed rules or a priori concepts. So if the challenge of Hume's skepticism had been met, it was only at the price of limiting reason to the realm of appearances.

In spite of their obscurity and difficulty, Kant's "Deduktion" and "Analogie" encountered waves of criticism in the early 1790s. They quickly became the target of a neo-Humean counterattack. Philosophers such as Maimon, Platner, Hamann, and Schulze argued that Kant had only begged the question against Hume. Even if Kant were right that the principle of causality is a necessary condition of the objectivity of experience, there was no reason, if we were Humean skeptics, to accept such objectivity. Why was experience not just a rhapsody of impressions, just as Hume imagined? Furthermore, in arguing that reason is the lawgiver of nature, Kant had simply presupposed the principle of causality, which it was his original purpose to defend. For did not Kant mean that our a priori activity is in some sense the cause of our experience?

Although Kant had limited the principle of causality to experience or appearances, this restriction did not satisfy his critics. They argued that the gap between reason and nature reappeared even within the realm of experience. Two reasons were cited for Kant's failure to close this gap. First, his noumenal-phenomenal dualism forbids any interaction between understanding and sensibility. If the understanding is noumenal and beyond space and time, then how can it impose its order upon appearances, which are phenomenal and within space and time? It does not seem possible for such heterogeneous domains to interact. Second, it is impossible to determine when, and consequently whether, a category applies to experience. A category by itself is so general that it holds for any possible experience; hence it does not tell us how it applies to particular cases in actual experience. The category of causality, for example, is compatible with fire being the cause of smoke and smoke being the cause of fire. But there is nothing within our experience that tells us when a category applies to it; for, as Hume said, all that experience ever reveals is a constant conjunction of impressions. Where, then, is our criterion for applying a category if it does not lie in the categories or in experience itself? We seem to be without guidelines for correlating understanding and experience.[22]

All these neo-Humean doubts about Kant's defense of causality had very damaging consequences for the Enlightenment faith in the harmony between reason and nature. This harmony was threatened not only by the chasm between reason and things-in-themselves, but also by the gap between reason and appearances. Even within the realm of experience, there was still a sharp dualism between the universal and necessary principles of reason and the particular and contingent data of sense impressions. So, to many philosophers at the close of the eighteenth century, it seemed as if reason were spinning a web of its own without any connection to a reality outside it. How, despite all these neo-Humean doubts, would it be possible to defend and restore the unity of reason and nature? This question soon preoccupied Fichte, Schelling, and Hegel.

It was not all gloom and doom around the close of the eighteenth century, however. There was one promising development, which offered some hope for the declining authority of reason. This was the gradual rebirth of teleological models of explanation in the second half of the century. It now seemed as if the Enlightenment rejection of teleology in favor of mechanical or efficient causality was premature. Some of the latest results of the natural sciences seemed to give telling evidence for teleology. Haller's experiments with irritability, Needham's and Maupertuis's theory of spontaneous generation, and Wolf's and Blumenbach's concept of the *nisus formativus* appeared to show that there were organic forces within matter. The essence of matter was not exhausted by dead extension. Rather, it consisted in self-organizing and self-activating forces. Matter appeared to be alive, since, like all living things, it moved and organized itself when no apparent cause pushed it into action. Hence, purposes could be ascribed to matter, even though it was not explicitly conscious. This new vitalistic materialism, which had already been developed by Toland and Priestley in England and Diderot and Holbach in France, was promulgated and defended by Herder and Forster in the 1770s and 1780s in Germany.

The revival of teleology at the close of the eighteenth century seemed to rescue the Enlightenment from the horns of a disturbing dilemma. Since the Enlightenment thinkers had assumed a mechanistic model of explanation, they had only two options in the philosophy of mind: mechanism or dualism. But both of these alternatives were plainly unsatisfactory. Mechanism destroyed freedom and could not account for such sui generis mental phenomena as intentions; and dualism limited scientific explanation to the material world by postulating a supernatural mental realm. Hence there did

not seem to be any nonreductivist yet scientific explanation of mental phenomena. The new vitalistic materialism, however, offered an explanation of
the mind that resolved this dilemma. We could now explain the mind as
the highest degree of organization and development of the forces inherent
in the body. This would avoid mechanism since the body would no longer
be a machine but an organism; and it would escape dualism since there
would be a continuum between the mental and physical worlds where each
consisted in different degrees of organization of the same living force. The
mind would be a highly organized and developed form of the forces inherent
in the body; and the body would be an inchoate form of the forces inherent
in the mind.

Although a vital materialism seemed promising, it could not establish
itself without severe resistance. The question soon arose whether teleology
could indeed provide verifiable natural laws, or whether it amounted to
nothing more than a return to the old scholasticism. In the early 1770s
Hamann had raised just this question when he attacked some of the vitalistic
assumptions behind Herder's theory of the origin of language.[23] According
to Hamann, Herder's postulate of organic forces only reintroduced occult
qualities, which merely redescribed the phenomena to be explained. Furthermore, vitalism still held no answer to Hume's skepticism toward causality. Whether we construe a cause as a purpose or an antecedent event,
there is still no necessary connection between cause and effect.

The issue of the scientific status of teleology came to a head in the mid-
1780s with Kant's attack on Herder and Forster. In his review of Herder's
Ideen (1785) and in his essay "Ueber den Gebrauch teleologischen Prinzipien
in der Philosophie" (1787), Kant argued that teleology amounts of necessity
to metaphysics because its explanations cannot be verified in possible experience. We cannot verify the claim that nonconscious agents act according
to ends, because our only experience of purposive activity is taken from
our own consciousness. We assume that things in nature act according to
ends only by analogy with our conscious activity; but we cannot ever confirm
such an analogy, since we know nothing about the inner world of vegetables,
crystals, and animals. All that we can safely assume, then, is that nature
appears to act *as if* it were purposive. Thus teleology has a strictly regulative,
not a constitutive, role in the sciences.

Hamann's and Kant's attack on Herder's vitalism had raised serious
questions about the prospects for teleology as a model of explanation in
natural science. It seemed that if reason were to remain within the limits of
possible experience, then it had to content itself with a mechanical model
of explanation. But this was not satisfactory either, since it only reinvoked
the old dilemma of dualism or mechanism. Thus philosophers of the Enlightenment had come to an impasse. They had rejected all the options

available to them. Vitalism did not satisfy their demand for verifiability; dualism restricted the frontiers of science; and mechanism could not explain mental phenomena. There was but one route out of this impasse: confronting Kant's objections against teleology and attempting to verify vitalism by the latest scientific results. This course emerged only in the late 1790s with the *Naturphilosophie* of Schelling and Hegel.

Chapter 1

Kant, Hamann, and the Rise of the *Sturm und Drang*

1.1. Hamann's Historical and Philosophical Significance

Although long since recognized in Germany, Johann Georg Hamann, sometimes called "the Wizard of the North," has been almost entirely ignored in the Anglo-American philosophical world. So widespread is the neglect of Hamann that most philosophers do not even know how to spell his name. Yet if we consider Hamann's decisive and abiding influence upon the history of philosophy, then such ignorance appears lamentable. Hamann was the father of the *Sturm und Drang*, the intellectual movement that grew up in Germany during the 1770s in reaction against the *Aufklärung*. His influence on the *Sturm und Drang* is beyond dispute, and indeed readily traceable. Hamann was the teacher of Herder; and Herder, in turn, introduced Hamann's ideas to the young Goethe, who also fell under their spell. In the twelfth book of *Dichtung und Wahrheit* Goethe later recalled the impact Hamann's ideas had upon him and the whole Romantic generation.[1]

It is difficult to exaggerate the many respects in which Hamann influenced the *Sturm und Drang*, and ultimately Romanticism itself. The metaphysical significance of art, the importance of the artist's personal vision, the irreducibility of cultural differences, the value of folk poetry, the social and historical dimension of rationality, and the significance of language for thought—all these themes were prevalent in, or characteristic of, the *Sturm und Drang* and Romanticism. But they were first adumbrated by Hamann, and then elaborated and promulgated by Herder, Goethe, and Jacobi.[2]

We do not need to dwell upon Hamann's role in the *Sturm und Drang*, though, to establish his historical significance. Hamann continued to have an impact on major thinkers well into the nineteenth century. One devotee of Hamann's was F. W. J. Schelling, whose *Positivephilosophie* reflects Hamannian themes.[3] Another avid student of Hamann's was F. Schlegel, who wrote one of the first appreciative essays on Hamann's philosophy.[4] Still another admirer was G. W. F. Hegel, who gave a flattering review of the first edition of Hamann's works.[5] Last but not least, Hamann was a seminal influence upon Søren Kierkegaard, a debt that Kierkegaard readily acknowledged.[6] By way of Kierkegaard, Hamann has had a significant and lasting effect upon twentieth-century existentialism.

Even if we disregard Hamann's influence on the eighteenth and nineteenth centuries, we must admit his stature as a thinker. Judged by twentieth-century standards, Hamann's thought is often striking for its modernity, its foreshadowing of contemporary themes. Thus, like many analytic philosophers, Hamann insists that language is the very criterion of thought and that the philosophy of language should replace epistemology. Anticipating Freud, he puts his finger on the formative role of the subconscious in our intellectual life. And, long before Hegel or Wittgenstein, he stresses the cultural and social dimension of rationality.

If we were to summarize Hamann's significance in the history of philosophy, we would have to stress his role in the revival of Luther. It was Hamann's mission to defend the spirit of Luther when the *Aufklärung* threatened to destroy it. Hamann never made any disguise of his great debt to Luther, and he explicitly affirmed his wish to see a restoration of his master's doctrines.[7] There are indeed many Lutheran themes that reappear in Hamann's writings: the authority of the Bible, the importance of a personal relationship to God, the denial of freedom of will, the superrationality of faith, and the necessity of grace. But it is especially important to note the manner in which Hamann kept Luther's spirit alive. Rather than simply reasserting his doctrines, like so many of the orthodox pietists of his age, Hamann defended Luther by exploiting the latest ideas of modern philosophy, especially the skepticism of David Hume. Using such modern weapons, he made Lutheranism seem not antiquated and superstitious but modern and irrefutable.

One particular tenet of Luther's became a hallmark of Hamann's thought and inspired his fateful attack upon the *Aufklärung:* the doctrine of the frailty of reason and the superrationality of faith. Just as Luther once railed against the scholastics for their claims to a rational knowledge of God, so Hamann assailed the *Aufklärer* for their belief in the authority of reason. Like Luther, then, Hamann was in the Ockhamist tradition, which held that faith transcends the criticism and demonstration of reason.

Hamann's revival of this Lutheran doctrine had an enormous influence upon the history of post-Kantian philosophy. Although he was not an 'irrationalist' in any strict sense of the word, Hamann gave a mighty stimulus to the currents of irrationalism that were present in the *Sturm und Drang* and Romanticism. He attacked the authority of reason in a number of influential ways. Thus he argued that reason is not autonomous, but governed by the subconscious; that it cannot grasp the particular or explain life; that it is inseparable from language, whose only foundation is custom and use; and that it is not universal but relative to a culture.

It is important to recognize that Hamann's critique of reason is the natural competitor to Kant's, and indeed grew up as a reaction against it. Whereas the aim of Kant's critique is to establish the autonomy of reason (that is, its power to determine its principles independent of other faculties), the task of Hamann's critique is to put reason in context, to see it as the product of social and cultural forces. The main principle behind Hamann's critique is his Aristotelian argument that reason exists only in embodied form in particular activities. According to Hamann, the great fallacy of the *Aufklärung*, and Kant's philosophy in particular, is the 'purism' or hypostasis of reason. We hypostatize reason when we become 'Platonists', who postulate a self-sufficient faculty that exists in some special noumenal or intelligible realm of being. Hamann offers us some very sensible methodological advice about how to avoid this fallacy. He enjoins us to examine the particular manifestations, embodiments, or expressions of reason, which consist in ways of speaking, acting, and writing, and more specifically the ways of speaking, acting, and writing in a particular culture. We are justified in seeing reason in such a light, Hamann thinks, since reason exists only in language, and language amounts to nothing more than the customs and conventions of a culture.

Although it is not as well known, Hamann's critique of reason was just as influential as Kant's. Its criticism of the purism of reason proved to be especially important for post-Kantian thought. Herder, Schlegel, and Hegel all accepted Hamann's advice to see reason in its embodiment, in its specific social and historical context. Indeed, the emphasis upon the social and historical dimension of reason, which is so important for post-Kantian thought, can trace its origins back to Hamann.

It is strange but true: Kant, the foremost champion of the *Aufklärung*, and Hamann, the father of the *Sturm und Drang*, knew each other personally and lived only a few miles apart in the provincial Prussian city of Königsberg. Furthermore, in a period stretching over nearly three decades, from 1759 to 1788, there were frequent philosophical exchanges between them. These exchanges were more often than not confrontations, dramatic clashes between contradictory *Weltanschauungen*. Through them the conflict between the *Aufklärung* and *Sturm und Drang* took on a very personal and flesh-and-blood form.

But this is not the end of the matter. The disputes between Kant and

Hamann do not merely illustrate the conflict between the *Aufklärung* and *Sturm und Drang;* they also helped to create it. Hamann developed his philosophy in reaction to Kant; and he introduced Kant to Hume and Rousseau, who had such an impact on him. In the balance of this chapter I will expound the three texts of Hamann's that had such a major influence on the *Sturm und Drang* and post-Kantian philosophy—*Sokratische Denkwürdigkeiten, Aesthetica in nuce,* and "Metakritik über den Purismum der reinen Vernunft"—as well as refer to relevant exchanges between Hamann and Kant.[8]

1.2. The London Conversion and Its Philosophical Consequences

To locate the source of Hamann's philosophy, we have to go back to his early years in London in 1758. What the young Hamann saw during a mystical experience contains the germ of his later philosophy, not to mention the basis for his critique of Kant and the *Aufklärung.* Considering Hamann's formative influence upon the *Sturm und Drang,* his mystical experience acquires a much broader historical significance. It marks one of the starting points of the *Sturm und Drang* and the reaction against the Enlightenment. It is certainly comparable in its historical significance to Rousseau's experience only ten years earlier, when, while walking to Vincennes to see Diderot in prison on that hot summer afternoon in 1749, Rousseau came to the startling conclusion that the arts and sciences had done more to corrupt than improve morals. It was from these two experiences—appropriately, two flashes of insight and inspiration—that *Sturm und Drang* was born.[9]

The story behind Hamann's conversion is dramatic and moving, the stuff of a novel or play. In 1757 the twenty-eight-year-old Hamann, then an enthusiastic student of the French and English Enlightenment, went to London on a diplomatic and business mission for the House of Berens, a merchant firm in Riga.[10] For no fault of his own, his mission proved to be an abject failure. Upon his arrival at the Russian Embassy, where he was supposed to conduct delicate and secret negotiations, he was greeted with derision. This brusque reception humiliated the shy and sensitive Hamann, who then fell into despair. His would-be career as a diplomat was in ruins, and he was lost and lonely in a foreign land. Seeking escape from his misery, he led a life of debauchery, eating, drinking, and whoring his cares away. After quickly squandering all the money entrusted to him—some £300 of the Berens' money, an enormous sum in those days—Hamann attempted to earn his living from his modest skills as a lute player. His search for a lute soon brought him into company with a disreputable character, however, a certain 'nobleman' who became his confidant and companion. The evidence more than suggests that Hamann had a homosexual affair with him.

After nearly nine months of complete indulgence, Hamann made a horrible discovery: his friend was being kept by a rich man. Upon hearing this, Hamann went into a jealous rage, resorting to cajolery and blackmail.[11] But all to no avail.

By this time it was plain that things had gone far enough. Hamann was down to his last guinea, and his health was suffering from all his dissipation; it was time to forget the emotionally disastrous affair. So, in the winter of 1758, he rented a room in the house of a decent family, closeted himself with his books, and adopted a spartan diet. Here he hoped to recover what was left of his body and soul. In his despair he turned to the Bible, which became his sole consolation. He read it in the most personal manner, as if it were God's message to him alone. He saw the history of the Jewish people as a parable about his own sufferings. All that happened to him in London, all his trials and tribulations, seemed to be prefigured in the Bible.

It was during his Bible reading that Hamann had his shattering mystical experience. On the evening of March 31, 1758, he read from the fifth book of Moses: "The earth opened the mouth of Cain to receive the blood of Abel." Reflecting upon this passage, Hamann felt his heart pound, his hands tremble. In a convulsive flood of tears he realized that he was "the murderer of his brother," "the murderer of God's only begotten son," Christ himself. He began to feel the spirit of God working through him, revealing "the mystery of love" and "the blessing of faith in Christ."[12]

After hearing the voice of God inside himself, and after reading the Bible in his personal and allegorical way, Hamann came to believe that God was always communicating with him, if he would only listen. Indeed, he became convinced that everything that happened to him contained a secret message from God, and that it was an allegory like everything else in the Bible. This conviction then led Hamann to a grand and extraordinary metaphysical conclusion: that the creation is the secret language of God, the symbols by which he communicates his message to man. All nature and history therefore consist in hieroglyphs, divine ciphers, secret symbols, and puzzles. Everything that happens is an enigmatic commentary upon the divine word, the physical embodiment and expression of divine thoughts. In Hamann's metaphorical terms, "God is a writer, and his creation is his language."[13]

Although it seems purely personal and imaginary, Hamann's mystical vision had important philosophical consequences. The break with the Enlightenment was now a fait accompli. In his London writings, which were written shortly after his experience, Hamann begins to question some of the fundamental dogmas of the Enlightenment.[14] First of all, he casts doubt upon the 'naturalism' of modern science, its attempt to explain everything according to mechanical laws without reference to supernatural or final causes.[15] If all events are divine signs, then they have a supernatural significance that cannot be fully explained according to natural causes. To understand events, we will also have to consult the Bible. "We are all capable of becoming prophets," he writes. "All appearances of nature are dreams, visions, puzzles, which have a hidden meaning, a secret significance. The books of nature and history are nothing more than ciphers, hidden signs, which require the key of Holy Scripture."[16] In passages like these, Hamann disputes the distinction between the natural and supernatural, which is vital to modern science's attempt to free itself of theology and metaphysics. If all natural events are divine symbols, then the supernatural will not transcend the natural but be embodied in it. All true physics will be religion, and all true religion will be physics.

Second, Hamann becomes suspicious of the Enlightenment's faith in human autonomy, its belief that man attains perfection through his own efforts and not the grace of God.[17] According to his mystical vision, God embodies himself not only in nature, but also in history. What man thinks and does is also what God thinks or does through him, so that all human actions give witness to the divine presence: "Is not the smallest blade of grass a proof of God? If so, then why should the smallest actions of man mean anything less? . . . Nature and history are the two great commentaries upon the divine word."[18] But this only raises the question: if God is co-present in all human thoughts and actions, then how is man the maker of his own destiny? What he achieves will be due not to his own efforts, but to the grace of God alone. As Hamann reminds us, "Let us not forget that we require God's assistance for all our actions, just as we require breath for all our living powers and activities . . . The breath of life in our nose is also the exhalation of God."[19]

Third, Hamann criticizes the assumption common to much post-Cartesian psychology and epistemology that self-consciousness is self-illuminating, the self-evident starting point of philosophy. His mystical vision means that we have no privileged access to ourselves. Since God is the source of all our thoughts and actions, we cannot know ourselves anymore than the unfathomable God within ourselves. Rather than being self-illuminating, self-awareness is problematic, mysterious, and obscure. "Our self is grounded in our creator. We do not have the knowledge of ourselves in our power; and, in order to measure its compass, we must penetrate into the very bosom of God, who alone can determine the whole mystery of our being."[20] If we are to acquire self-knowledge, then we first have to know our position in nature, history, and society, for our identity depends upon our relations to everything else.[21] Hence philosophy should begin not with self-knowledge, but with the knowledge of being.[22]

Last and most important of all, Hamann disputes the Enlightenment's principle of the sovereignty of reason, the right of reason to criticize all our beliefs. He is convinced that his vision is a revelation from God, and that it is incomprehensible to reason, which has no right to judge it. It is necessary to distinguish between the sphere of revelation, where facts are given to us through the grace of God, and the sphere of reason, where we can only draw inferences from given facts. Reason is perfectly within its rights in making deductions from given facts; but it exceeds them in presuming to question or create facts. "It is the greatest contradiction and misuse of our reason if it wants to reveal. A philosopher who, to please his reason, puts the divine word out of our vision is like those Jews who more stubbornly denied the New Testament the more they hung on to the old."[23] We shall soon see how Hamann developed remarks like this into a general critique of reason.

1.3. The Summer of 1759: The Stirrings of the *Sturm und Drang*

After his return to Riga in the summer of 1758, Hamann went back to work for the House of Berens. Despite the failure of his mission and his huge debt, the Berens family still received him as a long lost son. But it was plain that things could not return to normal. Hamann had been hired by the House of Berens to serve as a spokesman for its ideological views. But Christoph Berens, the young director of the firm and a university friend of Hamann's, was a convinced *Aufklärer*. Not surprisingly, he was appalled by Hamann's new faith, which he saw as a betrayal of the *Aufklärung* and as a lapse into the ranks of its worst enemy, *Schwärmerei* or enthusiasm. Relations between Hamann and Berens grew tense. And when Berens absolved Hamann's engagement to his sister, Katherina Berens, Hamann retaliated by quitting the House of Berens. In a fit of pique, he returned to his home in Königsberg in March 1759.

But Berens was still determined to reconvert his friend at all costs. If Hamann was not to be rescued for the House of Berens, he at least was to be saved for the *Aufklärung*. Their correspondence was soon broken off, however, since Hamann insisted upon being left alone in his beliefs. Luther had taught him that faith is a matter of deep personal commitment, an irrevocable decision. As Hamann told J. G. Lindner, a mutual friend who was acting as a mediator in the affair: "If he [Berens] wants to know what I am doing, tell him that I Lutherize. This is what a dear monk said in Augsburg; 'Here I stand; I cannot do otherwise. God help me. Amen.' "[24]

Despite the breakdown of the correspondence, Berens was undaunted. In mid-June 1759, he traveled to Königsberg to see Hamann personally. By July it was almost like old times, as if all their differences were unimportant.

Full of hope, Berens then hit upon a plan to regain his friend's soul. He decided to enlist the support of a forty-five-year-old privatdocent at the University of Königsberg, a promising young philosopher whose reputation was on the rise. This philosopher was also devoted to the cause of the *Aufklärung;* and, even better, Hamann was likely to listen to him since he much admired him.[25] Who was this young philosopher? None other than Immanuel Kant.

Sometime in early July a dramatic meeting between Hamann, Kant, and Berens took place at the Windmill, a rural inn outside Königsberg. Here the distance between Hamann and Berens became all too evident and embarrassing. The atmosphere was tense, especially due to the awkward presence of that third party. Later in the week, Hamann wrote his brother about the evening: "At the beginning of the week I was in the company of Herr Berens and Magister Kant at the Windmill, where we had an evening meal together . . . Since then I have not seen them again. Just between us: our friendship does not have the old intimacy, and we impose the greatest restraint upon ourselves to avoid every appearance of this."[26]

On July 24 Kant visited Hamann in the company of Berens. It was now suggested that Hamann translate some articles from Diderot's *Encyclopedie*. Kant and Berens hoped that a translation of this classic of the Enlightenment would bring Hamann back to his senses. A further colloqia was agreed upon, where Kant and Hamann would discuss philosophy. But this never took place. Instead of coming, Hamann sent Kant a strong letter, rejecting a mediator in the dispute. He felt that a third party could not understand the personal issues between himself and Berens and feared that it would lead to a breach of confidentiality.[27]

Hamann's letter to Kant, dated July 27, 1759, is a significant historical document. It has good claim to be the first clash between the *Aufklärung* and *Sturm und Drang,* the first battle between Kant and his pietistic opponents. Apart from its personal content—the rejection of Kant's mediation—the letter consists mainly in a defense of faith and feeling against the tyranny of reason. Hamann casts himself in the role of a prophet who is persecuted by the 'priests' of the *Aufklärung*.[28] The dramatis personae are now clear to him: if Kant is Socrates, and if Berens is Alcibiades, then Hamann is the genius who speaks through Socrates. This genius represents divine inspiration, the voice of prophecy, which is what "little Socrates" needs if he is to explain "the mystery of faith" to "big Alcibiades." But Hamann fears that Kant, as a mere philosopher, has no understanding of the heart. Hence he tells Kant that he writes to him in epic rather than lyric style since a philosopher cannot comprehend the language of feeling. Hamann then ridicules Berens' use of a philosopher to change his beliefs: "I nearly have to laugh at the choice of a philosopher to change my thinking. I see the best demonstration like a sensible girl sees a love letter, and I see a Baumgartian definition as a fleuret."[29]

In his closing paragraph, however, Hamann cites one philosopher who does understand the need for faith: "the Attic philosopher," David Hume. If Hume is right that reason cannot prove or disprove the existence of ordinary things, then it a fortiori cannot prove or disprove the existence of 'higher things'. If we can only believe in the existence of tables and chairs, then a fortiori we can only believe in the existence of God. Hume is "a Saul among prophets" since he sees that reason cannot make us wise, and that we need faith "to eat an egg or to drink a glass of water."

Hamann's appeal to Hume here is strangely, and perhaps intentionally, ironic. Hume argues that there are no rational grounds for the belief in the existence of God in order to attack faith; but Hamann reverses his argument and uses it to defend faith. The argument is the same; but its uses conflict. To Hamann, the merit of Hume's skepticism is not that it challenges faith, but that it secures it from the criticism of reason.

Whatever the merits of his interpretation, Hamann's citation of Hume in his July 27 letter proved fateful. It is the earliest evidence of Kant's acquaintance with Hume.[30] Here was the spark that later awakened Kant from his "dogmatic slumber." Hume also played a decisive role in the development of Hamann's philosophy, particularly his defense of faith against the attacks of reason.[31] In citing Hume against Kant, Hamann also set a precedent for those philosophers who eventually launched a Humean counterattack upon Kant.

1.4. The *Sokratische Denkwürdigkeiten*

The July 27 letter to Kant was only a prelude, however. Hamann needed a more formal statement of his credo to keep a solicitous Kant and Berens at bay. To stop their tiresome reconversion campaign, he had to show them that his faith was neither enthusiasm nor superstition; he had to convince them it was based on an experience that reason dare not judge. In short, Kant and Berens were going to have to learn that there is more on heaven and earth than was ever dreamed of in their enlightened philosophies. So, in only two weeks, two hectic and inspired weeks from August 18 to 31, Hamann wrote a short apology for his faith, the *Sokratische Denkwürdigkeiten*, which was published at the end of December 1759.

Although it is little read outside Germany, the *Sokratische Denkwürdigkeiten* is a seminal work in the history of modern philosophy. It is the first manifesto of the *Sturm und Drang*, the first influential attack upon the *Aufklärung*'s principle of the sovereignty of reason. It is of the greatest interest, then, that Hamann's work was conceived as a response to "the little Socrates" of Königsberg, Immanuel Kant himself. This goes to show that Kant was anything but a mere spectator of the *Sturm und Drang*. Rather, he was its direct catalyst, a true Socratic gadfly.

The *Sokratische Denkwürdigkeiten* has a strange subtitle and two cryptic dedications, which are important for an understanding of its aims and content. The subtitle runs: "For the Boredom of the Public compiled by a Lover of Boredom." The lover of boredom is of course the author. In so describing himself, Hamann is reacting against the ethic of trade and industry espoused by the political economy of the Enlightenment. To love boredom is to protest against the work ethic, which believes that we justify our existence only through our productivity. In his earlier days Hamann himself was an adherent of this ethic, and he even wrote a short tract singing its praises.[32] But his conversion had taught him that there is something more precious that cannot be acquired through man's own efforts: salvation through grace. Like Luther, Hamann poses an antithesis between the world of spirit, where man finds grace, and the world of work, where he remains caught in this world.[33]

The first dedication, which is purely ironic, is "to the Public, or Nobody, the Well Known." The public here is the *Aufklärung*'s ultimate arbiter of truth, the end of its program of education and reform. Hamann accuses the *Aufklärer* of worshiping an idol, of believing in the reality of a mere abstraction. Another name for the public is therefore nobody since abstractions do not exist by themselves; it is also dubbed the well known since the public is just everybody we know and not some particular person whom we might not know. Underneath Hamann's mockery of the public lies a subtle internal criticism of the *Aufklärung*. Pretending to battle superstition and mysticism, the *Aufklärer* fall prey to them by worshiping abstractions. A common fallacy of the *Aufklärung*, in Hamann's view, is hypostasis. It is indeed no accident that Hamann, like Luther, is a convinced nominalist: just as Luther once used nominalism to attack the scholastics, so Hamann now uses it to criticize the *Aufklärer*.

What Hamann especially condemns in the *Aufklärung*'s reverence for the public is its utilitarian concept of truth. The *Aufklärer* believe that philosophy must be useful and benefit the public; and they make it their business to bring it down from the clouds of speculation and into the marketplace of public life. "But can philosophy be practical or useful?" Hamann asks. He questions whether the search for the truth and the public interest coincide. Philosophy does not necessarily benefit the public; and it might even harm its interests. In his view the history of philosophy is a bitter struggle between the quest for truth and the public interest. Witness the case of his hero, Socrates. Hamann's criticism of the *Aufklärung* here is of historical interest since it was to become a leitmotiv of Jacobi's controversy with Mendelssohn.[34]

The second dedication is "to the Two." The two, though their names are never mentioned, are unmistakably Berens and Kant. Hamann likens them to two alchemists in search of the "stone of wisdom," the faculty of reason. Berens seeks this stone in order to create trade, industry, and prosperity; and Kant looks for it to establish his standard of critique, which will distinguish truth from falsity. Hamann describes Kant as "the Warden of the Mint" because his standard of critique is like a conversion table that determines the gold versus alloy content of coins. This intriguing metaphor plays upon two facts about the young Kant: his desire to explicate "the first principles of knowledge" in his 1755 *Nova Dilucidatio,* and his reverence for Newton, who was once Royal Mintmaster.

The *Sokratische Denkwürdigkeiten* centers on the figure of Socrates, who serves as the mouthpiece for Hamann's views. It is easy to understand Hamann's identification with the Athenian philosopher. Socrates' idleness must have appealed to him as a "lover of boredom." Socrates' martyrdom vindicated his criticism of the *Aufklärung*'s utilitarianism. And Socrates' homosexuality excused his own "sins." Indeed, Hamann asks us to be tolerant of Socrates' notorious trait. "One cannot feel a little friendship without sensuality," he writes, referring to Socrates' "vice."[35]

In another respect, though, Hamann's identification with Socrates appears less comprehensible, even paradoxical. Hamann sees a radical and unrestrained reason as a threat to faith. But did not Socrates take his reason so far that he became impious and "denied the gods"? Is not Socrates the very symbol of reason, the paragon of the examined life? This was indeed the prevalent picture of Socrates in the *Aufklärung.*

It is precisely Hamann's intention to undermine this view. Rather than seeing Socrates as the alternative to Christ, the champion of reason against religion, Hamann regards him as the forerunner of Christ, the pagan apostle of faith against the tyranny of reason. If Hamann could pull off this interpretation of Socrates, then he would deprive the *Aufklärung* of their favorite patron saint. Socrates' wisdom could then be used to sanction Christian, not pagan, values.

There are two facts about Socrates that Hamann cites against the *Aufklärung*'s interpretation. The first is Socrates' confession of his ignorance.[36] This is not only an indictment of the dialectic of the sophists—the ancient equivalent of the reason of the *Aufklärer*—but also a primitive pagan avowal of faith. Socrates' confession is his way of saying that there are some things which we cannot know through reason and which we must simply believe.

The second fact is the role of Socrates' demon or genius.[37] To Hamann it is no accident that Socrates relies upon his genius whenever his reason fails him. That is the most vital clue to the mysterious identity of the genius. He represents nothing less than divine inspiration, the voice of prophecy that we must turn to whenever our reason proves inadequate.

The central concept of the *Sokratische Denkwürdigkeiten* is that of faith *(Glaube)*, and this is Hamann's main counter against the reason of the *Aufklärung*. What Hamann means by faith is especially obscure, however, and even he admitted that he never fully understood his own usage. Sticking to the basics, though, we can analyze Hamann's concept in terms of two simple aspects, one positive and the other negative. The negative aspect consists in the recognition of ignorance, the acquiescence in the limits of reason, and especially its inability to demonstrate the existence of anything. Hamann refers to this aspect of faith when he writes: "Our own existence, and the existence of all things outside us, must be believed and cannot in any way be demonstrated."[38] The positive component of faith consists in a particular kind of experience or what Hamann calls 'sensation' *(Empfindung)*. Sensation is an ineffable feeling, an experience in contrast to an abstract principle. Thus Hamann describes Socrates' ignorance in these terms: "The ignorance of Socrates was sensation. There is a greater difference between sensation and a theorem than between a living animal and its anatomical skeleton."[39]

What kind of sensation characterizes faith? What distinguishes it from other sensations and experiences? That is the crucial question in coming to terms with Hamann's concept of faith. Unfortunately, Hamann becomes vague at just this point. Close consideration of his examples, however, shows that Hamann thinks the sensation of death arises when we sense the incomprehensibility of death. Voltaire and Klopstock both had this sensation, he says, in the face of sudden and tragic death.[40] Voltaire felt it after the Lisbon earthquake, which forced him "to renounce his reason"; and Klopstock felt it after his wife's death, which "robbed him of his muse." These examples suggest, then, that the sensation of faith arises in confronting the incomprehensibility or absurdity of life and death. What we sense or feel in faith therefore seems to be the givenness, mystery, and absurdity of existence itself.

Hamann's insistence that faith is not mere belief but a kind of experience brings him to a novel and provocative conclusion: that faith is a special kind of knowledge.[41] In his view the opposite of faith is not knowledge per se, as is so often assumed, but a particular kind of knowledge, namely, discursive or rational knowledge. The sensation of faith gives us a kind of intuitive knowledge which is not reducible to the discursive. It is even superior to discursive knowledge, since it gives us a direct insight into existence itself, while reason cannot demonstrate or conceive the existence of anything.

Hamann's claim that faith consists in a special kind of knowledge does raise a serious problem, however. Namely, how can we acquire the knowledge of faith? How indeed can we communicate it if it is nondiscursive? Hamann has no clear answer to this difficulty in the *Sokratische Denkwürdigkeiten;* his chief task is to establish only the possibility, not the reality, of such knowledge. At one point, though, he suggests that the medium for such knowledge is art: "The philosopher is as subject to the law of imitation as the poet."[42] This is indeed a promising suggestion since art is after all a nondiscursive form of communication. We shall see how this suggestion eventually led Hamann to a new and exciting theory about the metaphysical significance of art.[43]

The general thesis of the *Sokratische Denkwürdigkeiten* is that faith transcends the province of reason; in other words, it is neither demonstrable nor refutable by it. The main premise behind this thesis is that faith is an *immediate* experience, one whose content is private, ineffable, and just given. According to Hamann, then, the experience of faith is on a par with our perception of simple sense qualities, such as the tangy taste of oranges, the sharpness of a needle, the brightness of a color. We cannot fully describe such qualities, nor can we prove or disprove their existence. If we want to know whether they exist, or what they are like, then we just have to look and see. As Hamann explains, "Faith is not the work of reason, and therefore cannot succumb to its attacks; for faith happens for reasons just as little as tasting and sensing do."[44] In this passage, and others like it in his writings, Hamann questions the universal applicability of the principle of sufficient reason, that is, the demand that we give reasons for *all* our beliefs. We cannot universalize this principle, he contends, because we can give reasons for a belief only when it can be inferred or deduced from other beliefs that act as evidence for it. But there are many beliefs for which this condition just does not hold, for example, 'silk is smooth' or 'yellow is brighter than green'. In these instances we cannot cite other beliefs as evidence and must consult experience. We might sum up Hamann's point like this: it would be *irrational* to universalize the principle of sufficient reason since this would be to ask for reasons in cases where none can be given. So if reason demands the right to criticize all our beliefs—to determine whether they have sufficient reasons—it transcends its proper limits and turns into its opposite, unreason.

Although it has a prima facie plausibility, Hamann's argument is not conclusive. We might admit his point that we cannot universalize the principle of sufficient reason in the case of primitive empirical beliefs. But the question still remains whether religious beliefs are like empirical ones. A skeptic would dispute this analogy on the grounds that religious beliefs do not simply describe experience but interpret it as well. Thus a Buddhist, Moslem, and Christian will all see the same glow of inspiration in a different light. Conceding this much, however, draws the principle of sufficient reason into play again. Although reason cannot quarrel with a simple report about the content of experience, it can do so for an interpretation of that content; for here we have to assess whether the content warrants the conclusions drawn from it. (As we shall soon see, Kant later pressed Hamann and Jacobi on just these lines.)[45]

It is important to distinguish Hamann's thesis from two positions that are often confused with it. First, in claiming that faith consists in a form of immediate experience, Hamann is not postulating the existence of some mystical faculty of knowledge, some sixth sense. This cannot be the case since he doubts the existence of any such faculty.[46] He explicitly affirms that all our knowledge, whether religious or not, comes through our five senses.[47] Nevertheless, though he limits knowledge to the senses, Hamann still thinks that we trivialize the nature of our experience if we assume that it contains nothing more than everyday objects. If we are truly sensitive to what is given, then we will see the underlying religious dimension of experience.

Second, Hamann is also not committing himself to a form of 'irrationalism' or 'antirationalism'. Using these terms precisely, we must attribute them to a position which states that faith *contradicts* reason, in other words, that we ought to make 'a leap of faith' even though our reason proves that God does not exist.[48] This would be to assume, however, that reason has jurisdiction over faith, that it can prove or disprove it. But that reason has no such jurisdiction is the central thesis of the *Sokratische Denkwürdigkeiten*. The whole point of Hamann's argument is indeed that faith is neither rational nor irrational since reason cannot either prove or disprove it. The stumbling block of all irrationalist interpretations of Hamann is therefore nothing less than the central thesis of the *Sokratische Denkwürdigkeiten* itself.

1.5. Kant, Hamann, and the Optimism Controversy

Since the *Sokratische Denkwürdigkeiten* would not be published until Christmas, Hamann had to wait around for his formal explanation to arrive. In the meantime, Berens was still in Königsberg and Kant was still at his side. The net result: Hamann remained under siege. Although the July 27 letter had a chastening effect, Kant and Berens were still solicitous about their friend's soul. Berens continued to visit Hamann in the ever-waning hope of a recantation; and Kant, though he withdrew his services as mediator after receiving the letter, still corresponded with Hamann, trying to start a philosophical dialogue with him. In early October 1759 he sent Hamann a copy of his latest work, the short essay "Versuch einiger Betrachtungen über den Optimismus." Hamann duly replied to Kant's essay, criticizing it most severely. Thus began a whole new chapter in the Kant-Hamann drama. Kant's essay and Hamann's reply to it constitute two opposing responses to one of the great philosophical questions of the age.

The exchange between Kant and Hamann centers on a famous eighteenth-century controversy: the debate concerning Leibniz's optimism, or, whether this is the best of all possible worlds. The controversy began in 1753 when the Berliner Akademie der Wissenschaften made this question the subject of a prize competition; and it became a less academic and more live issue after the Lisbon earthquake of 1755, when the sudden death of thousands of innocent Christians seemed to make a mockery of Leibniz's theory. Sooner or later, nearly every major eighteenth-century thinker would participate in this debate, Voltaire, Rousseau, Lessing, and Mendelssohn, to name a few. Although prima facie the controversy seems to concern nothing more than the truth of Leibniz's optimism, it still raised a much more fundamental issue, namely, the classic problem of evil: how can there be providence, a moral world order governed by a just and benevolent God, if there is evil and suffering? This ancient problem continued to haunt the eighteenth-century mind because it could not renounce the Christian belief in providence. A world without providence was a world without meaning or value. If there were no providence, the universe would be absurd or amoral, indifferent to all moral concerns like life and death, joy and suffering, right and wrong. There would be no reason to be born or die; there would be no purpose to all our struggling and suffering; and there would be no reward for the virtuous or punishment for the vicious. The prospect of such a meaningless existence was the most awesome thought of all. The young Kant called it "the black abyss";[49] and Jacobi summed up a very common sentiment when he wrote in his notebooks: "Nothing frightens man so much, nothing darkens his mind to such a degree, as when God disappears from nature . . . when purpose, wisdom and goodness no longer seem to reign in nature, but only a blind necessity or dumb chance."[50]

But behind the problem of providence there was an even more disturbing question for the eighteenth-century thinker. Suppose for a moment that the pessimist were right, that there is no rational ground for the belief in providence. Suppose that reason does compel us to accept the absurd. What then? This would raise serious doubts about the authority of reason itself. If we cannot accept that our lives are meaningless, and if reason tells us that this is the case, then why should we remain loyal to our reason? Thus, the optimism controversy attracted such widespread and abiding interest in the eighteenth century partly because it disturbed the Enlightenment's faith in reason itself.

Such were the fraught questions that Hamann and Kant were addressing in the autumn of 1759. In "Versuch," one of the most dogmatic of his early writings, the young Kant takes an unambiguous stand in favor of Leibniz's optimism. His confidence in reason appears unshakable. He is convinced that Leibniz's optimism is the only rational position, and that even such tragic events as the Lisbon earthquake give us no reason to doubt providence. Of course, it is necessary to admit that there is unpunished evil, tragic death, and pointless suffering. But that is only from our finite perspective, which does not grasp the universe as a whole. If, however, we had the infinite understanding of God, then we would see the plan behind the whole of things and realize that everything is ultimately for the best. We would then admit that there is a deeper reason, a higher plan behind everything, so that all evil is punished, all death redeemed, and all suffering compensated.

By sending Hamann a copy of his essay, Kant could not fail to start a debate. Hamann's position was the very opposite of Kant's. Reason sanctions not optimism, but pessimism, in Hamann's view. It shows us not that life is meaningful, but that it is meaningless. As Hamann explains in the *Biblische Betrachtungen,* one of his early London writings, "Reason discovers nothing more for us than what Job saw—the misery of our birth—the advantage of the grave—the uselessness and inadequacy of human life."[51]

Both Kant and Hamann affirm the existence of providence, and neither of them is willing for a moment to embrace the absurd. But they are completely at odds about how to know providence and escape the absurd. Whereas Kant thinks that it is reason that gives our life significance, Hamann believes it is faith.

Hamann's differences with Kant became all too apparent and explicit when Hamann replied to Kant's essay in his letter of December 1759.[52] Here Hamann rejects Kant's theodicy for reasons Kant would later appreciate: it transcends the limits of reason. We cannot prove that this is the best of all possible worlds, Hamann says, since we do not know anything about God. We also cannot argue that the evil and suffering in the world are only apparent since we do not know reality as a whole and cannot attain the infinite perspective of God. Reprimanding Kant for his metaphysical pretensions, Hamann tells him in no uncertain terms: "If you want to prove that the world is good, then do not appeal to the world as a whole, for we human beings cannot know it, and do not refer to God, for only a blind man with staring eyes can see him."[53] The whole project of a theodicy is misguided, Hamann claims, because it is anthropomorphic, judging God by the standards of human reason: "The creator and governer of the world is a proud being. He pleases himself with his plans and is not concerned with our judgments."[54] It is not known whether Kant replied to Hamann's letter. But at least one thing is certain: Hamann had given the young Kant reason to reconsider his optimistic rationalism.

1.6. The *Kinderphysik* Fiasco

By late autumn 1759, the drama began to draw to a close. Berens left Königsberg at the end of October, his reconversion mission an evident failure. Kant retreated even further from the scene, weighed down by academic duties. But the drama did not end without its bitter climax, one final clash between Kant and Hamann at the end of 1759.

The occasion of the quarrel was a letter of Kant's, probably written in December 1759.[55] Kant wrote Hamann with a strange request: to collaborate with him in writing a physics book for children. The aim of such a book, at least in Kant's mind, was to bring the *Aufklärung* into the classroom by teaching children the rudiments of Newton.

Hamann replied to Kant's request in three long "love letters" (as Hamann called them), all of them written in late December 1759.[56] Naturally, he treated Kant's project with suspicion. He did show evident interest, but on no account was he willing to pursue the project on Kant's terms. Hamann made suggestions and recommendations that he knew to be at odds with Kant's intentions. Indeed, the tone of his letters is so defensive, querulous, and patronizing that he seems to be spoiling for a fight. It appears as if Hamann saw through Kant's motives—and was determined to sabotage the book from the start.

The main task of Hamann's letters is to define the philosophy of education that should inspire their project. The essence of Hamann's position is straight from Rousseau's *Emile:* the proper method of education is to put oneself in the position of the child. The teacher must understand the language and soul of the child if he is to initiate the child into the adult world. To be master to the child, he first must be a servant; to be leader, he first must be follower. The main difficulty with such a method is that to put ourselves in the position of the child, we first must renounce all age and learning. "This will be especially difficult for you," Hamann tells Kant, "given all your learning and gallantry."

What should the contents be of a physics book for children? What lessons should it contain? Hamann's answer to this question reveals his differences with Kant. The book ought to be based upon Genesis, he insists, and the order of exposition ought to follow the six days of creation. Kant should not be ashamed "to ride the wooden horse of Mosaic history." Hamann does not hesitate to tell Kant of his supernaturalistic vision of nature. Nature is "a book, fable or letter" written by God. It is an equation with unknown quantities, a Hebraic word with missing vowels. Although the task of physics is to spell out the alphabet of nature, that knowledge would no more allow us to decipher its message than knowing the alphabet helps us to understand a book. To grasp the parable behind nature, we eventually must consult its ultimate key: the Bible. Such is Hamann's advice to Kant only four years after his *Allgemeine Naturgeschichte,* in which he aimed to explain the origin of the universe on naturalistic principles.

Hamann sees a great danger in their project, which is indeed the danger involved in all education: corruption. "It is easy for the learned to preach as it is for them to deceive." There is no problem when the learned write for themselves; most of them are so perverse that it is impossible to corrupt them further, which is not the case with children. We must be careful not to offend "the majesty of their innocence," Hamann warns, and we must not corrupt them with "a seductive style" or "the wit of a Fontenelle." Like Rousseau, Hamann sees more wisdom in the innocence of the child than in the learning of the philosopher. The conflict between Kant and Hamann here reflects the earlier struggle between Diderot and Rousseau. Just as Rousseau detested Diderot's *Encyclopedie* for its presumptuous belief that it is possible to improve mankind through art and science, so Hamann was suspicious of Kant's project for educating children by popularizing Newton. Hamann was the Rousseau, Kant the Diderot of Königsberg.

What effect did Hamann's letters have upon Kant? Their provocative tone certainly met with a cool reception. Pointedly, Kant did not reply to Hamann's letters, a silence which deeply insulted Hamann.[57] Kant had learned his lesson: he made no further attempts to have a dialogue with Hamann, or, in effect, to reconvert him. But there was another more important consequence of Hamann's letters: they introduced the young Kant to Rousseau. In 1759 Kant had still not read Rousseau and had a reputation around Königsberg as *der gallante Magister.* Although not yet receptive to such new ideas, Kant had at least become aware of them. Perhaps it was indeed Hamann, then, who laid the ground for Kant's later reception of Rousseau.[58]

1.7. *Aesthetica in nuce* and Eighteenth-Century Aesthetics

Hamann's next major work after the *Sokratische Denkwürdigkeiten* is his *Aesthetica in nuce,* which was published in 1762. Although the *Aesthetica* does not enter into a dispute with Kant—its targets are Lessing, Mendelssohn, and Baumgarten—it is still of the first importance for post-Kantian philosophy. It became the bible for the aesthetics of the *Sturm und Drang*, the holy writ for the epistemology of the *Romantiker*. It was indeed largely due to the *Aesthetica* that Hamann became known as the spokesman for the *Sturm und Drang*.[59] The Romantic apotheosis of art, intuition, and genius also finds its origins in Hamann's classic text.[60]

Although the *Aesthetica* is ostensibly a polemic against naturalistic interpretations of the Bible, it is more fundamentally a manifesto for a revolutionary aesthetic theory. One of its radical objectives is to liberate art from the stranglehold of classical convention and rationalistic norm. The *Aesthetica* is a defense of artistic creativity, a paean to the genius whose art breaks all the rules. According to Hamann, the artist should not comply with moral rules, artistic conventions, and rational principles; and still less should he bother to imitate the Greeks as Winckelmann suggested. Rather, he should express his passions, reveal his feelings, and give vent to his personal visions. What makes a work of art beautiful is its expression, its revelation of the personality of the artist. Hence it is necessary to abolish all rules and conventions, because they only inhibit personal expression.

Hamann's stand against classicism and rationalism was truly revolutionary, pitting him against the great majority of eighteenth-century aestheticians. Almost all his contemporaries, while acknowledging the importance of the passions and the claims of genius, still held that art must conform to some kind of norm, whether that be a moral principle, social convention, logical law, or artistic technique. This is the case not only for such rigid classicists as Boileau, Batteau, and Gottsched, but also for such progressive thinkers as Voltaire, Diderot, and Lessing. The stormy controversy between Gottsched and the Swiss aestheticians Bodmer and Breitinger in the 1740s never really questioned the sanctity of aesthetic norms: the issue was only whether they should be consciously applied, as Gottsched said, or subconsciously expressed, as Bodmer and Breitinger claimed. But Hamann departs from all these trends with his radical demand to overthrow *all* the norms.

Another radical objective of *Aesthetica in nuce* is to reestablish the metaphysical significance of art. Here again Hamann fights against the current. The predominant trend of eighteenth-century aesthetics was toward subjectivism, which denied the classical equation of truth and beauty.[61] Aesthetic experience was seen less and less as the imitation of reality and more and more as a form of illusion. This is the case whether we consider the empiricist tradition in France and Britain or the rationalist tradition in Germany. According to Dubos and Burke, who represent the empiricist tradition, aesthetic experience consists not in learning moral principles or in perceiving metaphysical truths, but in having pleasant sensations. And according to Wolff, Baumgarten, and Mendelssohn, who represent the rationalist tradition, aesthetic experience is either a confused conception of reality (Wolff), a clear perception of appearances (Baumgarten), or a pleasant sensation (Mendelssohn). In both traditions art has lost its claim to metaphysical insight, its power to give knowledge of reality; it is more a form of entertainment than instruction.

Aesthetica in nuce is a protest against this growing subjectivism. Hamann accuses both the empiricists and the rationalists of betraying the metaphysical calling of art. Indeed, in his eyes, these gentlemen are no better than Pontius Pilate: "Yes, you fine critics! You ask for what truth is and reach for the door because you cannot wait for an answer."[62] As Hamann sees it, aesthetic experience does not consist in a confused conception of reality, a clear perception of appearances, or a pleasing sensation. Rather, it is the purest of insights into reality itself. Art is indeed the only instrument to grasp the truth, the only medium to provide knowledge of reality itself. Although the classical aesthetics of Boileau and Batteau also confers metaphysical honors upon art, art is still seen as an inferior, or at best equal, source of knowledge to logic and mathematics. But, to Hamann, art is the highest form of knowledge, one which is far superior to even logic and mathematics.

It is surely not surprising, though, that Hamann gives such pride of place to art. This completes the position that he had already laid down in the *Sokratische Denkwürdigkeiten*. In that earlier work Hamann envisaged "a higher form of knowledge" that provided a pure insight into existence. Such knowledge would be purely immediate, avoiding all the pale abstractions of reason, which cannot apprehend the richness, diversity, and particularity of experience. But Hamann failed to explain how such experience could be acquired. The *Aesthetica in nuce* fills in this gap. Art, and art alone, is in a position to provide us with immediate knowledge, Hamann now tells us, because it is essentially a nondiscursive medium. Its stock-in-trade is not concepts, but images. Rather than dissecting reality into lifeless parts, these images directly reproduce the wholeness and richness of experience. Hence the *Aesthetica in nuce* supplements the *Sokratische Denkwürdigkeiten* in one crucial respect: it provides the organon and criterion for the higher form of knowledge promised in the earlier work.

Bearing in mind the epistemology of the *Sokratische Denkwürdigkeiten*, we are in a better position to understand how Hamann revives the metaphysical stature of art in the *Aesthetica*. This epistemology allows Hamann to build upon a central insight in the critique of the classical tradition, that art cannot be reduced to rational principles, and yet to avoid its damaging conclusion, that art cannot have metaphysical significance. The empiricist and rationalist critics of the classical tradition denied the metaphysical significance of art only because they failed to free themselves from its underlying rationalist criterion of knowledge; they equated knowledge of nature with knowledge of reason. Hence their awareness of the nonrational content of art seemed to imply the loss of its metaphysical status. But, thanks to the epistemology of the *Sokratische Denkwürdigkeiten,* which questions reason's exclusive claim to knowledge of reality, Hamann can accept the critique of the rationalist tradition while reestablishing the metaphysical significance of art.

Ultimately, though, the basis of Hamann's aesthetic theory, like so much in his philosophy, derives from his mystical vision in London. For Hamann, art has first and foremost a religious calling: to translate and decipher the word of God. Such an unconventional view of art has, however, a surprisingly conventional premise: the classical notion of imitation.[63] Hamann accepts Aristotle's notion but then reinterprets it in light of his general religious vision. If art ought to imitate nature, and if nature consists in the secret language of God, then it is the task of art to translate and decipher that language. As Hamann puts it, in his usual declamatory style, "Speak that I may see thee!—This wish was fulfilled through the creation, which is a speech to its creatures through its creatures . . . Speaking is translating—from the language of angels into the language of men, that is from thoughts into words—from things into names—from images into signs."[64]

Although Hamann accepts the ancient notion of imitation, he departs radically from the French and German classical tradition concerning how the artist must imitate nature. The artist imitates nature not by following conventions and applying rules, as Batteau, Boileau, and Gottsched would suggest, but by expressing his feelings and portraying his sensations. This new method of imitation is the direct consequence of Hamann's empiricism. Unlike Batteau, Boileau, and Gottsched, who are influenced by Wolffian and Cartesian rationalism, Hamann is a thoroughgoing empiricist.[65] We acquire knowledge of nature not through reason, he maintains, but through our senses and feelings. Whereas the principles of reason are mere ghostly abstractions from nature, our senses and feelings directly reproduce it in all its richness, particularity, and diversity. To imitate nature the artist must remain true to his senses and feelings and shun all forms of abstraction: "Oh, for a muse like the fire of the goldsmith, and like the soap of the washerwoman! It will dare to purify the natural use of the senses from the unnatural use of abstractions, which cripples our awareness of things as much as it obscures and slanders the name of God."[66]

If we were to sum up *Aesthetica in nuce,* then we would have to single out two doctrines: that art ought to imitate nature and reveal the word of God; and that art ought to express the innermost personality of the artist. What is central to Hamann's aesthetics, however, is precisely the combination or intersection of these doctrines. It is a seemingly paradoxical fusion of an extreme subjectivism, which insists that the artist express his innermost desires and feelings, and an extreme objectivism, which demands that the artist strictly imitate nature and surrender to its effects upon him.

But how is it possible to combine such extreme and apparently conflicting doctrines? How do the artist's personal feelings also reveal the word of God? How do his passions and desires acquire a grand metaphysical significance? For the solution to this problem, we must again go back to Hamann's mystical experience in London, and in particular to his vision of God's presence in man. If God is inside man and reveals himself through man, and if he reveals himself especially through the senses and passions of man (given Hamann's empiricism), then it follows that the artist only has to express his senses and passions if he is to reveal God. What the artist personally senses and feels is therefore also what God senses and feels through him, so that the most inward revelation of his feelings is also the self-revelation of God. Artistic creativity is not only the activity of the artist, then, but also of God, who reveals himself through this activity. As Hamann expresses this point, "Every impression of nature in man is not only a reminder, but a testimonial to the basic truth: who is the Lord. Every reaction of man in his creation is the letter and seal of our participation in the divine nature and our affinity with it."[67]

It was Hamann's belief in the metaphysical significance of artistic self-expression that proved to be so appealing to the *Stürmer und Dränger* and the whole Romantic generation. Such a belief gave the artist his cake and allowed him to eat it too. The artist could express his personal passion and at the same time have a metaphysical insight into reality in itself. The general Romantic faith in the metaphysical significance of artistic creativity, which appears in Schleiermacher's *Reden*, Hölderlin's *Hyperion*, Schelling's *System des transcendentalen Idealismus*, Novalis's *Lehrling zu Sais*, and F. Schlegel's *Vorlesungen über Transcendentalphilosophie*, goes back to the metaphysics of Hamann's *Aesthetica in nuce*. All these thinkers believe that the forces of the universe reveal or manifest themselves in the personal vision of the artist. It is indeed partly due to Hamann's *Aesthetica* that metaphysics regains its wings after the onslaught of the Kantian critique. But these are less the wings of pure reason than those of artistic inspiration. Art has become the new organon and criterion for metaphysical knowledge, avoiding all the pitfalls of pure reason so ruthlessly exposed in the Kantian critique.

1.8. The "Metakritik": Genesis, Contents, and Consequences

The two decades separating the publication of Hamann's *Aesthetica in nuce* (1762) and Kant's *Kritik der reinen Vernunft* (1781) were not especially eventful for the relationship between the two philosophers. Although they often met on social occasions, there were few significant exchanges between them. Hamann wrote a critical review of Kant's *Beobachtungen über das Gefühl des Schönen und Erhabenen* in 1764; and there was a brief correspondence in 1774 concerning Herder's latest work, *Die Aelteste Urkunde des Menschengeschlechts*. Other than this, though, little of significance happened. Kant and Hamann seemed to have finally recognized the immense distance between them and to have become resigned to it.[68]

Nevertheless, during this longueur, Hamann maintained a lively interest in Kant's work. He could not repress his curiosity about Kant's progress with the first *Kritik*. Indeed, such was Hamann's interest in Kant's magnum opus—his "Moral der reinen Vernunft," as he called it—that he helped to arrange a publisher for it, J. F. Hartknoch. Then, through his connections with Hartknoch, and without Kant's consent, he managed to obtain the proof sheets as soon as they came out. In this furtive manner Hamann became the first person to read the *Kritik* apart from Kant himself. He had perused it and formed his judgment upon it even before its publication in mid-May 1781.

Hamann saw Kant's masterpiece as a prime example of many of the vices of the *Aufklärung*. A review of it therefore became a tempting idea, an opportunity to settle differences with the *Aufklärung* in general. By July 1, 1781, only six weeks after its appearance, Hamann had already drafted a short notice of the *Kritik*. Although too short to amount to a proper review, this notice still contains *in nuce* some of Hamann's later themes. It is indeed the first written criticism of Kant's work. But Hamann decided not to publish it, because he feared that its derisory tone would offend a very sensitive Kant.

After setting aside his early review, Hamann still could not resist "breaking a lance against the transcendental philosophy." Later in the summer of 1781 he considered the idea of writing an extensive critique of Kant, a temptation that also tortured him because he felt inadequate to the task: "My poor head is a shattered jug in comparison with Kant's—clay against iron."[69] It took Herder's constant nagging to get him to work on his project; and only in January 1784 did he finally complete it. The finished product was a short essay of some ten pages entitled "Metakritik über den Purismum der reinen Vernunft."[70] Hamann was never satisfied with it—"the whole idea proved abortive," he later told Herder—and till late in his life he intended to rewrite and expand it.[71] Unfortunately, these plans did not come to fruition.

Although the "Metakritik" was not published until 1800, it exercised a considerable subterranean influence. Hamann sent a copy to Herder, who in turn sent one to Jacobi. Through Herder and Jacobi, some of the ideas of the "Metakritik" became common post-Kantian currency.

Hamann's "Metakritik" has a strong claim to be the starting point of post-Kantian philosophy. It is the first writing to raise those meta-critical questions that are so characteristic of the period: What is reason? How can we criticize it? And, how do we know its conditions and limits? Hamann thinks that these questions are inescapable, the necessary consequence of criticism itself.[72] If everything on heaven and earth must submit to criticism, as Kant says, then ipso facto criticism itself must submit to criticism, or what Hamann calls 'meta-criticism'.

The main theme of the "Metakritik," as its full title indicates, is 'the purism of reason'. This is the central fallacy, the reductio ad absurdum of the whole *Kritik,* in Hamann's view. By 'the purism of reason' he means its hypostasis, its abstraction from its necessary embodiment in language, tradition, and experience. According to Hamann, Kant hypostatizes reason by postulating a self-sufficient noumenal realm that exists apart from the phenomenal realms of language, history, and experience. Kant commits a threefold hypostasis or purification of reason. He abstracts it from sense experience, tradition, or custom, and—worst of all—language. What remains after all this abstraction is nothing but the purely formal transcendental "subject = X," "the talisman and rosary of a transcendental superstition which believes in all *ens rationis.*"[73]

The purism of reason is a fallacy, Hamann thinks, because reason exists only in particular activities. There is no special faculty of reason, there are only rational ways of thinking and acting. To identify reason, we must refer to the ways people think and act; and that means, more specifically, how they act, write, and speak in their language and in their culture. Thus the main point behind Hamann's charge of purism is not that reason is inseparable from other faculties, as is often thought,[74] but that it is not a faculty at all. Rather, reason is only a function, a specific way of thinking and acting in a specific cultural and linguistic context.

The foundation of Hamann's critique of Kant in the "Metakritik" is his philosophy of mind, which he had already laid down in his "Philologische Einfälle und Zweifeln" (1772). Here Hamann expounds an Aristotelian philosophy of mind that defines the soul as a form of activity rather than as a kind of entity. The target of this earlier essay is Herder, who Hamann dubs a 'Platonist' for his belief that reason consists in a peculiar faculty. The later critique of Kant simply repeats the earlier critique of Herder. Hamann now accuses Kant, just as he did Herder, of Platonism. As Hamann wrote Herder on May 10, 1781, "I am curious to hear your opinion of Kant's masterpiece . . . He deserves the title of a Prussian Hume . . . Without realizing it, he revels more mischievously than Plato in the intellectual world beyond space and time."[75] Kant is a Platonist, Hamann thinks, because he hypostatizes a self-sufficient noumenal realm that exists apart from the phenomenal realm. By contrast, Hamann sees himself as an Aristotelian, because he maintains that reason exists only in things, in its linguistic and cultural embodiment. In Hamann's view, then, his conflict with Kant repeats the classic conflict between Plato and Aristotle.

Of all Kant's purifications of reason, the most problematic to Hamann is that concerning language. According to Hamann, language is the very "instrument and criterion of reason,"[76] so that to talk about reason without referring to its embodiment in language is only to reify an abstraction.[77] If we are to have a critique of reason, as Kant enjoins us, then we ought to have a critique of language, since language is the source of all the confusions and fallacies of reason.[78] It is indeed "the center point of reason's misunderstanding of itself."[79]

Nevertheless, despite the importance of language, Hamann considers Kant guilty of ignoring it. He neglects language because he is just another victim of a very old error: the belief that thought precedes language, or that concepts precede words, which are only their dispensable signs. Thus the very slogan of Kant's *Kritik* should be "the receptivity of language and the spontaneity of concepts."[80]

But is Kant really guilty of ignoring language? Prima facie Hamann's charge seems to be unjust. A brief glance at the "metaphysical deduction of categories" in the first *Kritik* seems to show that Kant gives supreme importance to language. The key to that deduction is the identification of the power to think with the power to judge. The various forms of the understanding are deduced from the various forms of judgment, which are the syntactic forms of language.

Taking a closer look at the "Metakritik," however, we see that Hamann does consider the metaphysical deduction, and that he is still displeased with it.[81] The source of his displeasure is Kant's noumenal-phenomenal dualism. According to Hamann, this dualism means that Kant cannot explain or justify his assertion that there is an intimate bond between reason and language. If there is a sharp dualism between the noumenal and phenomenal, the rational and sensible, then the sphere of reason is ipso facto cut off from that of language. For the sphere of language is essentially phenomenal, consisting of necessity in sounds and letters. Thus Hamann says that language is "the visible element of reason," "the true aesthetic element of all human knowledge."

Hamann's philosophy of language, as briefly adumbrated in his "Metakritik," is one of his most powerful weapons against Kant and the *Aufklärung* in general. It allows him to question a basic presupposition behind the *Aufklärung*'s faith in reason: that reason is permanent and universal, the same for all intelligent beings at all times and places. While claiming that language is the very instrument and criterion of reason, Hamann also holds that it consists in rules "whose only warrant is custom, tradition and use." It then follows that the very criteria of rationality will be cultural, varying with the different traditions of different cultures. Reason is now in danger of losing its authority since its principles will no longer be universal and impartial, binding for every intelligent being. Rather, they will simply express the values, traditions, and language of a culture.

A central target of the "Metakritik" is Kant's dualisms, in all their forms, whether between understanding and sensibility, noumenon and phenomenon, or a priori concept and form of intuition. Hamann condemns all such dualisms as arbitrary and artificial abstractions, as the reifications of purely intellectual distinctions. All the functions of man form an indivisible unity, he insists, a single whole that is more than the mere sum of its parts. We can understand each function only by investigating its intricate relationships with all the rest. But Kant has violated this simple principle, Hamann maintains. He has divided the indivisible, he has separated the inseparable. Although Kant says that there is a single source for all his faculties,[82] he has destroyed it with all his sharp distinctions. What has been so drastically dissected cannot be so easily reunited. As Hamann complains, "if sensibility and understanding as the two branches of human knowledge spring from one common root, to what end such a violent, unauthorized and willful separation of that which nature has joined together! Will not both branches wither away and die through a dichotomy and division of their common root?"[83]

Hamann believes that the philosophy of mind should move in the very opposite direction from Kant's *Kritik*. Rather than making precise distinctions between intellectual functions, we should seek their unifying principle. It is only when we discover the common source of all the different faculties, Hamann insists, that we will be in a position to explain the interaction between them. If, however, we continue dividing these faculties, giving each a self-sufficient status, then their interaction becomes mysterious and miraculous. But this is just what happens in Kant's *Kritik*, Hamann claims. Although Kant says that knowledge arises from the interaction between understanding and sensibility, he has so sharply divided these faculties that all interchange between them becomes inconceivable. The understanding is intelligible, nontemporal, and nonspatial; but sensibility is phenomenal, temporal, and spatial. How, then, will they coordinate their operations?

Kant's dualistic tendencies have an extremely serious consequence for the *Kritik* as a whole, Hamann thinks. The main problem of the *Kritik*—How are synthetic a priori judgments possible?—becomes unsolvable, since we cannot explain how the a priori concepts of the understanding apply to the completely heterogeneous intuitions of sensibility. If we are to solve this problem, Hamann argues, then it is necessary to raise a much more general question: How is the faculty of thought possible? In the preface to the first edition of the *Kritik,* however, Kant rejects this question as much too speculative.[84] But it is only when we dare to answer it, Hamann replies, that we will be in a position to solve the central problem of the *Kritik.*

Hamann does not hesitate to suggest where an investigation into the faculty of thought should begin. He is convinced that the most fruitful path for epistemology lies in the direction of the philosophy of language. Language, he suggests, is the common root behind Kant's heterogeneous faculties, the unifying point of understanding and sensibility.[85] Words bring together the intelligible and sensible realms since they belong to sensibility, as sounds striking the ear and as letters appearing before the eyes, and the understanding, as signs having a meaning. So if we are to investigate the apparently mysterious connection between the intelligible and sensible, the spiritual and physical, then we should first come to terms with the connection between thought and language.

Along with Kant's dualisms and neglect of language, another target of Hamann's "Metakritik" is Kant's transcendental method. Hamann devotes much attention to Kant's method, which he rightly regards as the foundation of his whole philosophy. "The whole Kantian edifice rests upon the idle trust *ex vi formae,*" he writes to Herder in referring to Kant's method.[86] And he says toward the close of the "Metakritik": "The cornerstone of critical idealism" is the possibility of constructing "the forms of intuition" out of "the pure and empty mind."[87] Hamann's remarks upon Kant's methodology are significant since they reveal his reaction to the implicit—and often ignored—meta-critical theory behind the *Kritik.*

What Hamann objects to in Kant's method is the assumption that it is possible to construct a priori the complete system of reason simply by reflecting upon oneself. Although Kant does not assume that it is possible to construct 'the matter of knowledge' (that is, the content of given intuitions), he does think that it is possible to construct its 'form' (the number, types, and systematic order of the categories of understanding and ideas of reason). But even this modest claim Hamann finds unacceptable. He construes it to mean that it is possible to find 'the form of a word' (the order of its letters and syllables) from its 'mere concept'. To the question whether it is possible to find the 'matter of a word' (the letters and syllables themselves) from its concept, the Kantian answers with a clear and decisive "No"; but to the question whether it is possible to find the form of a word from its concept "he snorts a 'Yes!' as loud as Hansel and Gretal at the altar." In other words, Kant assumes that it is possible to construct a priori the syntax or grammar of a language. He thinks that the ideal philosophical language is purely innate, waiting to be discovered by sheer introspection.[88]

Hamann leaves it to his reader to judge whether or not this assumption is correct. But it ought to be clear from his philosophy of language why he thinks that Kant's method is radically mistaken. Since reason is not prior to language, and in particular the natural languages spoken in different cultures, Kant's a priori construction is a complete delusion. Kant can construct the forms of reason a priori—but only by a surreptitious abstraction from natural languages. The only way to discover the forms of reason, Hamann implies, is through the comparative empirical study of natural languages.[89]

What effect did the "Metakritik" have upon post-Kantian philosophy? The general historical significance of Hamann's critique of reason has already been noted. But Hamann's essay is influential for another reason. It states one of the central goals of all post-Kantian philosophy: the search for the inner unity, the common source of Kant's dualisms. In arguing that the problem of synthetic a priori knowledge is not resolvable until this unity is found, Hamann made it necessary to go beyond the narrow boundaries of the critical philosophy. The history of post-Kantian philosophy largely consists in the quest for the unifying principle behind Kant's dualisms; and there are almost as many principles as there are philosophers: language in Hamann, representation in Reinhold, the will in Fichte, the indifference point in Schelling, religion in Schleiermacher, and spirit in Hegel. But this search begins in Hamann.[90] He is the first to see the problematic nature of Kant's dualism; and he is the first to insist that we must grasp man's faculties as a whole if we are to explain the possibility of knowledge.

It is important to see, however, that Hamann poses this problem anew and in a manner decisive for the generation that follows him. There is now no going back to the one-sided extremes of Leibnizian rationalism or Lockean empiricism. Hamann does not want only "to intellectualize the senses" like Leibniz, or only "to sensualize the intellect" like Locke. Rather, he wants to do both at once. He agrees with Kant that understanding and sensibility play an equal and coordinate role in knowledge; but he strives to find the common source from which both these faculties spring. The problem is to formulate the unifying principle of the intellect and senses *while* accounting for the equal and coordinate role of both. In short, to use the jargon of Schiller, Schelling, and Hegel: it is necessary to find 'a unity amid difference', a whole of which the understanding and sensibility are only parts.[91] It is this search for a unity-in-difference which distinguishes the mind-body problem in post-Kantian philosophy from pre-Kantian philosophy. Whereas pre-Kantian philosophy seeks a reductivist solution by reducing one term to another, post-Kantian philosophy strives for a nonreductivist principle that grants equal status to both terms.

Chapter 2

Jacobi and the Pantheism Controversy

2.1. The Historical Significance of the Pantheism Controversy

Along with the publication of the *Kritik der reinen Vernunft* in May 1781, the most significant intellectual event in late eighteenth-century Germany was the so-called pantheism controversy between F. H. Jacobi and Moses Mendelssohn.[1] The controversy began in the summer of 1783,[2] initially as a private quarrel between Jacobi and Mendelssohn. But, two years later, the dispute became public and engaged almost all the best minds of late eighteenth-century Germany. Among the celebrities who took part in it were Kant, Herder, Goethe, and Hamann. Furthermore, each party to the dispute had a large supporting cast, including such later stars as Thomas Wizenmann, who defended Jacobi, and Karl Leonhard Reinhold, who popularized Kant.

It is difficult to imagine a controversy whose cause was so incidental—Jacobi's disclosure of Lessing's Spinozism—and whose effects were so great. The pantheism controversy completely changed the intellectual map of eighteenth-century Germany; and it continued to preoccupy thinkers well into the nineteenth century. The main problem raised by the controversy—the dilemma of a rational nihilism or an irrational fideism—became a central issue for Fichte, Schelling, Hegel, Kierkegaard, and Nietzsche. It is indeed no exaggeration to say that the pantheism controversy had as great an impact upon nineteenth-century philosophy as Kant's first *Kritik*.[3]

The first and most visible effect of the controversy was the remarkable rise in the fortunes of Spinozism in Germany. Nearly all the major figures of the classical *Goethezeit*—Goethe, Novalis, Hölderlin, Herder, F. Schlegel, Hegel, Schleiermacher, and Schelling—became Spinoza enthusiasts in the wake of the controversy. Apparently overnight, Spinoza's reputation changed from a devil into a saint. The scapegoat of the intellectual establishment in the first three quarters of the eighteenth century became its hero in the last quarter. Thanks to the controversy, pantheism became, as Heine later put it, "the unofficial religion of Germany."[4]

A second striking effect of the controversy was the breakthrough of Kantianism, its final triumphal entry onto the public stage in Germany. Before the controversy reached its height in the winter of 1786, Kant had already made some progress in gaining a reputation. He had a few worthy disciples in various universities, for example, F. G. Born in Leipzig, L. H. Jakob in Halle, and C. G. Schütz in Jena; and the *Jenaische Allgemeine Literaturzeitung* had begun to champion his cause. But the critical philosophy was still far from dominating the philosophical scene and still far from the center of the public eye. Its influence was confined to a few universities, and indeed only a few select circles within them. The pantheism controversy soon changed all this, however. The decisive breakthrough came sometime in the autumn of 1786 with Reinhold's *Briefe über die kantische Philosophie.* In an elegant, popular, and lively style Reinhold had succeeded in making Kant's philosophy intelligible to a wider public. The *Briefe* had created— to quote a friend of Kant's—"a sensation."[5] But it is important to note the secret behind Reinhold's success. He established the relevance of the critical philosophy to that dispute foremost in the public eye: the pantheism controversy.

A third effect of the controversy was that it created a crisis in the *Aufklärung,* one so severe that it accelerated its eventual downfall. The revolt against the *Aufklärung* had already begun in the 1770s with the *Sturm und Drang.* The novels and plays of Goethe, Lenz, and Klinger; the philosophical tracts of Hamann, Herder, and Jacobi; and the religious writings of Lavater, Jung-Stilling, and Claudius had all established a new literary trend and spirit in Germany. The rights of feeling were proclaimed against the cold rules of reason; and the rights of self-expression were asserted against the repressive norms of society. The dawn of Romanticism was already visible as the twilight of the *Aufklärung* grew near. But, in the meantime, the *Aufklärung* still lived on, indeed as the predominant intellectual force. During the 1770s, the natural sciences made further progress; the philological and historical criticism of the Bible gained momentum; and Wolffianism entrenched itself in most of the universities of Protestant Germany. Around the same time, Lessing, Mendelssohn, and Nicolai were still active; the *Popularphilosophie* movement became even more popular; and societies like the *Freimauerer* and *Illuminati* grew in power and numbers. All in all, then, the *Aufklärung* continued to represent the literary and philosophical status quo in the 1770s, even if it was not the latest fashion.

The pantheism controversy threw the *Aufklärung* back on the defensive, forcing it to struggle for its very life. Seventeen eighty-five, the year that Jacobi published his *Briefe über die Lehre von Spinoza,* marks the end of its hegemony. Jacobi had succeeded in casting doubt upon the central dogma of the *Aufklärung*: its faith in reason. The dramatic manner in which he attacked this dogma inflicted nothing short of trauma on the contemporary intellectual scene. Referring to the effect of the *Briefe* on the public, Goethe spoke of "an explosion,"[6] and Hegel wrote of "a thunderbolt out of the blue."[7]

The *Aufklärung's* faith in reason was based on the belief that reason could justify all the essential truths of common sense, morality, and religion. The authority of reason replaced the authority of tradition and revelation because it was a more effective sanction for all moral, religious, and commonsense beliefs. This all-important but vulnerable premise was the main target of Jacobi's attack. Reason, he argued, was not supporting but undermining all the essential truths of morality, religion, and common sense. If we were consistent and pushed our reason to its limits, then we would have to embrace atheism, fatalism, and solipsism. We would have to deny the existence of God, freedom, other minds, the external world, and even the permanent existence of our own selves. In short, we would have to deny the existence of everything, and we would have to become, to use Jacobi's dramatic language, 'nihilists'. There was then only one way to save ourselves from nihilism: 'a leap of faith', a *salto mortale*.

It is important to see that it was Jacobi, and not Kant, who shook the *Aufklärung* to its very foundations. Kant was a typical *Aufklärer* insofar as he never doubted the *Aufklärung's* fundamental postulate of the harmony between reason and faith. Rather than questioning this belief, Kant attempted to give it a new foundation with his doctrine of rational faith. Indeed, the very reason for the success of Kant's philosophy during the pantheism controversy is that Kant seemed to rescue this all-important belief of the *Aufklärung* in the face of Jacobi's provocative criticism. His doctrine of rational faith, already worked out in the "Kanon" of the first edition of the *Kritik*, appeared to silence all of Jacobi's unsettling doubts. Significantly, Reinhold's *Briefe* saw this doctrine as the selling point of Kant's philosophy and stressed that it alone held the solution to the controversy between Jacobi and Mendelssohn.

But Kant's practical faith was at best an ad hoc solution, a finger in the dike of a swelling irrationalism. No sooner did Kant's doctrine become the center of attention than Jacobi and his allies brought it under heavy fire. The ultimate effect of these counterattacks was deeply disturbing: the truce between reason and faith seemed more fragile than ever. While Jacobi and friends picked holes in the wobbly edifice of Kant's practical faith, they also welcomed Kant's destruction of metaphysics, as more fuel to their irrationalist flames. To the German mind at the end of the eighteenth century, reason seemed to be heading toward the abyss, and no one could see any means of stopping it.

Jacobi's attack on the *Aufklärung* in Germany is not accidentally reminiscent of Pascal's and Rousseau's earlier critiques of the *Illumination* in France. The young Jacobi was a student of Pascal and Rousseau, and he deliberately imported their ideas into Germany.[8] He merely repeated Pascal's provocative argument that reason, unaided by revelation, leads to skepticism; and he simply rehearsed, albeit in epistemological guise, Rousseau's radical thesis that the arts and sciences had done more to corrupt than improve morals. Jacobi knew that these arguments had disturbed the philosophes;[9] and he was determined that they would now upset the *Aufklärer* too.

Jacobi's criticism of reason also appears to follow along the lines of another more indigenous precedent: Hamann's *Sokratische Denkwürdigkeiten*. Jacobi was indeed an admirer of Hamann, and, just before the controversy, he entered into a correspondence with him, hoping to gain his support for the forthcoming battle against the *Aufklärung*.[10] Hamann responded warmly to Jacobi's overtures, providing him with all the advice, information, and encouragement that he needed. Despite their alliance, there was still a very important difference between Hamann's and Jacobi's positions. It was Jacobi, and not Hamann, who was the genuine irrationalist. Whereas Hamann held that faith and reason are independent of each other, so that reason neither demonstrates nor refutes faith, Jacobi argued that reason and faith are in conflict, so that reason refutes faith. Thus he said that reason, if consistent, leads to atheism. By contrast, Hamann maintained that reason transcends its limits if it attempts to disprove the existence of God. This difference did not escape Hamann, who confessed to Herder that he never could accept Jacobi's *Pia desiderata*.[11]

Even a single one of the above consequences should be sufficient to establish the historical and philosophical significance of the pantheism controversy. But, surprisingly, for an intellectual event of its magnitude, the controversy has been largely ignored.[12] The reason for this neglect primarily lies with the controversy itself, in that its deceptive appearance masks its underlying significance. It has an outer shell—the biographical issue of Lessing's Spinozism; an inner layer—the exegetical question of the proper interpretation of Spinoza; and a hidden inner core—the problem of the authority of reason. The main difficulty in understanding the controversy is seeing how these outer layers reflect the inner core, how the biographical and exegetical issues reflect and arise from the philosophical problem. It has often been assumed that the main problem was only whether Lessing was a Spinozist,[13] or how we should interpret Spinoza's pantheism.[14] To understand the deeper significance of the pantheism controversy—and indeed the significance that it had for the participants themselves—we must recognize its underlying philosophical dimension. We have to see that Lessing and Spinoza were only symbols, which had a much wider cultural and philosophical meaning.

We have, however, paid a heavy price for our ignorance of the pantheism controversy. We have lost our philosophical orientation in dealing with the speculative systems of post-Kantian philosophy. In no small measure these systems grew up as a response to the fundamental problem raised by the pantheism controversy. What Fichte, Schelling, and Hegel were trying to do was to preserve the authority of reason in the face of Jacobi's provocative criticisms.

Before I proceed to an examination of the pantheism controversy proper, it is important to have some idea of the history of Spinozism in Germany. This history forms part of the essential background to the controversy; and the rise of Spinozism in the late eighteenth century is a phenomenon of no less significance than the emergence of Kantianism itself. By the beginning of the nineteenth century, Spinoza's philosophy had become the main competitor to Kant's, and only Spinoza had as many admirers or adherents as Kant.

2.2. The Rise of Spinozism in Germany, 1680–1786

Until the publication of Jacobi's *Briefe über die Lehre von Spinoza* in 1785, Spinoza was a notorious figure in Germany. For more than a century the academic and ecclesiastical establishment had treated him "like a dead dog," as Lessing later put it. The *Ethica* was published in Germany in 1677, and the *Tractatus theologicus-politicus* in 1670 (though it appeared anonymously, Spinoza was known to be the author). Until the middle of the eighteenth century it was de rigueur for every professor and cleric to prove his orthodoxy before taking office; and proving one's orthodoxy often demanded denouncing Spinoza as a heretic. Since attacks on Spinoza became a virtual ritual, there was an abundance of defamatory and polemical tracts against him. Indeed, by 1710 so many professors and clerics had attacked Spinoza that there was a *Catalogus scriptorum Anti-Spinozanorum* in Leipzig. And in 1759 Trinius counted, probably too modestly, 129 enemies of Spinoza in his *Freydenkerlexicon*. Such was Spinoza's reputation that he was often identified with Satan himself. Spinozism was seen as not only one form of atheism, but as the worst form. Thus Spinoza was dubbed the 'Euclides atheisticus', the 'princips atheorum'.[15]

The reception of Spinoza by the great luminaries of the early *Aufklä-*

rung—Leibniz, Wolff, and Thomasius—was scarcely more favorable. They pretended to write impartial criticisms of his philosophy; but it is plain that Spinoza's unorthodoxy heavily weighed the scales against him. There were the same dire warnings about Spinoza's heretical beliefs, and the same tendentious polemics that we find in the worst *Schmähschriften*. All of them felt obliged to denounce Spinoza and to write lengthy refutations of him. Thus, in 1688 Thomasius went to the trouble of writing an elaborate and involved critique of Spinoza in his *Monatsgespräche*. Deeming the *Ethica* to be a dangerous book, Thomasius warned his students that, of all sects, the Spinozists were the most difficult to combat. For his part, Wolff boasted that his philosophy was a bulwark against Spinozism. In his *Theologica naturalis* (1737) he gave a full-scale refutation of Spinoza, which became the standard line of the Wolffians for generations.[16] Leibniz too warned of the evils of Spinozism, which he condemned as heresy. He considered the *Ethica* "a dangerous book for those who took the pains to master it" and wrote a critical commentary on it.[17] All these thinkers, in true orthodox fashion, saw Spinozism as atheism and fatalism. For more religious than philosophical reasons, they could not accept Spinoza's denial of providence, revelation, freedom of will, and a supernatural and personal God.

Leibniz and Wolff had a special reason to distance themselves from Spinoza, however. 'Spinozism' became a favorite objection of the pietists against the Leibnizian-Wolffian school. It was felt by them that Leibniz's and Wolff's philosophy, with its insistence on strict demonstrative method, was little more than a halfway house on the fatal road to Spinozism. Some of the disciples of Thomasius, notably Joachim Lange and Johann Franz Budde, argued that Wolff's rationalism, if consistent, led straight to the atheism and fatalism of Spinoza.[18] The only way to escape such consequences, they argued, was to recognize the sovereignty of faith over reason, or revelation over demonstration. This line of argument foreshadows the later controversy between Jacobi and Mendelssohn, which in many ways merely continued the debate between the pietists and Wolffians. Jacobi's debate with Mendelssohn was only a more sophisticated version of Budde's and Lange's critique of Wolff.

But why was there such a vehement reaction against Spinoza? The fact that Spinoza was seen as the very incarnation of evil by the academic and ecclesiastical establishment forces us to raise this question. For why single out Spinoza for such abuse, especially when there were other heretics whose doctrines were no less heterodox than Spinoza's, for example, Hobbes or Bruno? Of course, part of the answer lies in Spinoza's Jewish ancestry; it was no accident that Spinoza was called "the accursed Jew of Amsterdam." But there was still another—and more important and interesting—reason why Spinoza was regarded as such a horrible heretic. Namely, Spinoza represented the extreme left wing in seventeenth- and eighteenth-century religious and political conviction. Spinoza's political views were an indictment of the whole academic and ecclesiastical establishment in Germany, and this threat was clearly felt.[19] In his *Tractatus theologicus-politicus* Spinoza not only laid down the basis for the philological and historical criticism of the Bible—the sacred cow of the Lutheran establishment—but he also defended such progressive causes as tolerance, freedom of speech and conscience, democracy, a universal religion, and the separation of church and state. Consider the effect that such a book would have upon the powers that be of seventeenth- and eighteenth-century Germany. Since the "Augsburger Religions-friede" (1555), the princes in Germany had the right to determine the religion of their principality, so that the church became part of the general legal system. Observation of the official religion became a sheer legal necessity. Hence there was no such thing as tolerance, freedom of conscience, and ecclesiastical independence in the principalities—all the causes championed by Spinoza. The professors and clergy, who were little more than glorified civil servants, had to exorcise Spinoza, who had criticized their dubious dependence on the state. Spinoza was biting the hand that was feeding him, and gratitude demanded heaping not a little obloquy upon his cursed head.

Fortunately, the history of Spinoza's reception in Germany is not only a tale of infamy and woe. If Spinoza was passionately denounced by the establishment, he was equally passionately embraced by its opponents. It is an old myth that Spinoza was treated "like a dead dog" long before the end of the eighteenth century. The truth of the matter is that he was in the very vanguard of the *Aufklärung* in the late seventeenth and early eighteenth centuries in Germany, and that he was indeed the patron saint of its extreme left wing. Almost all the radical freethinkers of that time—Gottfried Arnold, Johann Christian Edelmann, Friedrich Wilhelm Stosch, Theodor Ludwig Lau, Johann Lorenz Schmidt—were also covert or overt Spinozists. Those who did not ally themselves with Spinoza—Konrad Dippel and Angelus Silesius—still had metaphysical and political views that were similar to his.[20] These thinkers stood—and suffered—for all the radical ideals of Spinoza's *Tractatus:* tolerance, a universal religion, freedom of conscience, the separation of church and state, and the historical and philological criticism of the Bible. Thus the establishment's harsh condemnation of Spinoza was also a symbolic denunciation of its left-wing opposition.

Almost all the early Spinozists in Germany were the unhappy children of the Protestant Counter-Reformation.[21] Most of them had been, or still were, pietists, and all of them had become bitterly disillusioned with the course of the Reformation. They were fiercely loyal to its original ideals: the universal priesthood of believers, freedom of conscience, the necessity for an immediate relationship to God. But in their eyes the Reformation had gone astray and betrayed its own principles. Since the Lutheran Church had become part of the state, it had developed an authoritarian structure of its own, and had thus become a form of dogmatism and elitism no better than the Roman Catholic Church. What, then, had become of Luther's ideals?

To these discontented radicals and reformers, Spinoza represented the very spirit of rebellion. His criticism of the Bible, his support for democracy, his ideal of a universal religion, and his call for a separation of church and state were just the weapons that they needed to fight the political and ecclesiastical establishment. The *Tractatus theologicus-politicus* thus became the manifesto for all their radical opinions.[22]

If Spinoza's *Tractatus* was important to these early freethinkers and radicals, his *Ethica* was even more so. They eagerly embraced Spinoza's pantheism, which they saw as the foundation for all their radical political convictions. What Heine said of pantheism in the early nineteenth century—that it was the religion of the radicals—was in fact true centuries earlier.[23] During the sixteenth, seventeenth, and early eighteenth centuries, many of the radicals were pantheists.[24]

But whence this connection between pantheism and political radicalism? Why was pantheism so appealing to the early radicals? How did it support their political ideals? This issue is of the utmost importance if we are to understand the rise of Spinozism in the late eighteenth century. For the later enthusiastic acceptance of Spinoza's pantheism was partly conditioned by the increasing strength of liberal political causes. The rise of Spinozism was a reassertion of the political ideals of the Protestant Counter-Reformation.

The answer to the question largely lies in the early radical interpretation of Luther's ideal of an immediate relationship to God. According to Luther's ideal, everyone should have a personal relationship to God where he is directly answerable to God alone and not the church. What made such a relationship possible in orthodox Lutheranism was the Bible, which had been made available to the public through Luther's translation. If one simply read the Bible, which he had rendered into plain German, then one could know God's message by oneself, and it would not be necessary to consult the clergy. Now the early freethinkers eagerly embraced Luther's ideal of an immediate relationship to God, which appealed to their sense of equality and freedom. But, thanks to Spinoza's *Tractatus,* they no longer saw the Bible as an infallible guarantee of that relationship. Spinoza had taught them that the Bible was the product not of divine inspiration, but of history and culture, like any other human document. What, then, could guarantee an immediate relationship to God if the Bible was not a sure means of access to him? Our own immediate experience, our direct awareness of God within ourselves, the early radicals said. All of us could have such an experience, they believed, if we would only reflect upon ourselves and listen to God within us.

Here lies the attraction of pantheism for the early freethinkers: it ensured the possibility of everyone having such an experience, of everyone having direct access to God. The God of pantheism is within me and everyone else, so that, in order to experience him, it is necessary for me only to reflect upon myself. The God of theism, however, is not nearly so accessible. He is a supernatural being who only occasionally makes himself known in nature through the odd miracle. Hence he is accessible only to an elite few, namely, those who are fortunate enough to witness his miracles.

Hence the appeal of pantheism ultimately lay deep in Lutheranism itself. Someone who insisted upon Luther's ideal of an immediate relationship to God, and who at the same time had his doubts about the authority of the Bible, would find pantheism a very appealing doctrine. It is no accident that most of the later Spinozists had Lutheran backgrounds, that they did not accept the authority of the Bible, and that they insisted on the need for an immediate experience of God. Pantheism was thus the secret credo of the heterodox Lutheran.[25]

The first significant step toward a more public recognition of Spinoza in the eighteenth century was taken by—ironically—Moses Mendelssohn.[26] Mendelssohn is usually portrayed as the bitter opponent of Spinozism, and so he was in his *Morgenstunden* (1785). But, in his first published work, the *Philosophische Gespräche* (1755), Mendelssohn wrote a spirited defense of Spinoza. Although Mendelssohn himself was a disciple of the Leibnizian-Wolffian school, he still pleaded for a more serious and impartial examination of Spinoza. Here indeed lies the historical significance of Mendelssohn's little book. It is the first attempt at an objective philosophical treatment of Spinoza.[27] Neither the defenders nor opponents of Spinoza in the early eighteenth century could make any claim to objectivity because they were either too predisposed or too hostile to his views.

The basis for Mendelssohn's sympathy for Spinoza was undoubtedly his Jewish heritage. Both Mendelssohn and Spinoza were ardent students of Moses Maimonides in their youth, and, accordingly, both affirmed a belief in the reconcilability of philosophy and faith, reason and religion. Although sympathetic to Spinoza, who he deeply admired for his nobility of character amid persecution, Mendelssohn was an orthodox Jew who was disturbed by Spinoza's apostasy. He may have dreamt of becoming "a second Spinoza," as Lessing said, [28] but he never wanted to preach a philosophy as controversial as Spinoza's or to break with the religion of his fathers. Mendelssohn's path toward Spinoza was therefore an individual one, and he was never allied with the early Spinozists, who were for the most part nonconformist Christians. As legend has it, Mendelssohn met one of the most notorious of the early Spinozists, Johann Christian Edelmann, whose coarseness sent him hurrying to the door.[29]

The *Philosophische Gespräche* was, true to title, written in dialogue form. The characters in the dialogue, Neophil and Philopon, probably represent Lessing and Mendelssohn; and it is likely that the dialogue reconstructs conversations between Lessing and Mendelssohn during the first year of their friendship.[30] Ironically, there is a complete reversal of the positions later taken by Lessing and Mendelssohn in 1785. In the *Philosophische Gespräche* Lessing is cast in the role of the skeptical anti-Spinozist, and it is Mendelssohn who tries to convince him of the plausibility of Spinoza's philosophy. It was indeed Mendelssohn who first introduced Lessing to Spinoza.

The express aim of the *Gespräche* is to rehabilitate Spinoza. Although Mendelssohn does not intend to convert his readers to Spinozism—that would be going too far even for his more liberal taste—he does want them to consider Spinoza more dispassionately and impartially. In this modest aim Mendelssohn succeeds admirably. There are a number of ways in which he establishes Spinoza's importance and vindicates his reputation. (1) He discredits the popular picture of Spinoza found in Bayle's *Dictionaire historique et critique*. Bayle's criticisms of Spinoza had found wide acceptance in the eighteenth century, although this was based more on Bayle's wit than on his profundity. Mendelssohn has little difficulty in showing that most of Bayle's criticisms rest upon misunderstandings.[31] (2) Mendelssohn reveals that there are many points of similarity between Leibniz and Spinoza, and argues that Leibniz had taken some of his characteristic doctrines from Spinoza. Leibniz's notion of the preestablished harmony, for example, is said to have its source in Spinoza's idea that the mind and body are independent attributes of one and the same substance.[32] (3) Mendelssohn maintains that Leibniz is on weak grounds in some of the respects in which he differs from Spinoza, so that mending Leibniz's system brings him closer to Spinoza. Leibniz's theory that the world arises from God's free will, for instance, suffers from the classic objection that there is no reason why God did not create the world earlier. This difficulty does not arise with Spinoza, Mendelssohn claims, since he admits the infinity of the universe.[33] (4) Last, but most important, Mendelssohn interprets Spinoza's philosophy so that it is consistent with morality and religion. Spinoza's view of the universe becomes perfectly acceptable, Mendelssohn suggests, provided that it applies to the world as it exists in God's mind prior to becoming real through his decrees.[34] The Leibnizians attribute a twofold existence to the world: the world as it exists prior to its creation as a possibility in the mind of God; and the world as it exists in reality outside God and as a product of his decrees. Spinoza fails to recognize this distinction, however, and that is where he goes astray, according to Mendelssohn. What the Leibnizians assert of the ideal world—that it exists in God and is inseparable from his intellect—is what Spinoza also says of the real world. But, provided that we recognize this distinction, Mendelssohn contends, it is possible to be a qualified Spinozist—a Spinozist in the ideal world and a Leibnizian in the real one. This reinterpretation of Spinoza, stressing the ideal existence of the world in the mind of God, is significant in foreshadowing the 'purified pantheism' that Mendelssohn later attributes to Lessing in *Morgenstunden*.[35]

In general, although he sometimes argues in favor of Spinoza against Leibniz, Mendelssohn tries to resurrect Spinoza by showing that he is a mediating figure, the necessary transitional stage, between Descartes and Leibniz. That is a neat reversal of the old pietist argument that Leibniz is only a halfway house on the fatal road to Spinoza. Later, in his *Morgenstunden,* Mendelssohn defends this interpretation of Spinoza against Jacobi, who reasserts the pietistic argument.

In 1763, only eight years after the publication of Mendelssohn's *Gespräche,* someone else made his personal discovery of Spinoza—a discovery that was to prove fateful for the later reception of Spinoza in Germany. This person was none other than F. H. Jacobi himself. The story of Jacobi's discovery of Spinoza is an exciting one, shedding not a little light on Jacobi's early relationship to Kant and his later controversy with Mendelssohn. But the story has a strange and surprising twist: it was Kant who first convinced Jacobi of the necessity of Spinoza's philosophy.

In the first edition of *David Hume* Jacobi himself tells us how he came to Spinoza. While studying all the old protagonists of the ontological argument in 1763, he says, he came across a striking remark of Leibniz's: "Spinozism is nothing more than exaggerated Cartesianism." It was this remark that sparked his interest in Spinoza.[36] Jacobi turned to the *Ethica,* hoping to find a clearer formulation of Descartes's version of the ontological argument. And he was not disappointed. Spinoza clarified Descartes's proof for him; but, even more important, he also taught him "for what God" the proof was valid. Presumably, this God was no less than the God of Spinoza, the single universal substance of which everything else is only a mode. Unfortunately, Jacobi does not explain precisely how he became convinced of this. One significant point is still clear: as early as 1763 Jacobi already held that reason was heading in the direction of Spinozism.

Jacobi recalls that he became totally convinced of this point upon reading Kant's early work *Der einzig mögliche Beweisgrunde zu einer Demonstration des Daseins Gottes*. This work so excited him, he later confessed, that he had to put it down from time to time to stop his heart from beating so wildly. Jacobi enthusiastically endorsed Kant's new proof of the existence of God; but he accepted it with one significant qualification, one that would have horrified Kant: namely, that it was true only for Spinoza's God. Kant, in Jacobi's view, had unwittingly demonstrated the necessity of pantheism.

How could Jacobi arrive at such a remarkable conclusion? It is not difficult to see his point once we understand the thrust of Kant's new proof for the existence of God. According to Kant's proof, the existence of God is prior to his possibility and that of all other things; in other words, if God did not exist, not only would nothing else exist, but nothing else would be even possible.[37] God's existence is prior to the possibility of all things in the sense that all predication, or any possible attribute that we ascribe to a thing, presupposes some existence which is to be qualified or determined. What is it, though, that exists prior to being qualified or determined? Existence pure and simple is the answer, or what Kant calls 'the absolute positing of a thing'. This absolute existence of all things, what exists prior to their being determined in this or that respect, Kant equates with the existence of God himself.

Now, to Jacobi, Kant's proof was tantamount to a demonstration of the existence of Spinoza's God. For what is Spinoza's God, Jacobi asks, other than the concept of existence itself, that being of which everything else is only a limitation? The same proof would not hold for the God of deism, however, which is not existence per se, but a specific kind of existent, a set of properties (omniscience and omnipotence) from which we can never automatically infer existence itself. Of course, Kant himself would not be so hasty in equating God's existence with his essence. In his view, God's existence preceded *his* possibility as well as that of all other things; God had other properties which made him a specific kind of existent. But Jacobi had no such scruples. His tendentious reading of Kant's work had shown him that the only possible demonstration for the existence of God was a demonstration for the existence of Spinoza's God. So, for better or for worse, it was Kant who originally convinced Jacobi that all speculative philosophy ends in Spinozism. During his reading of Kant's book, Jacobi hit upon the central idea that he would later pit against Mendelssohn.[38]

Of course, the most famous Spinozist of them all was Lessing. Around 1763, the same time as Jacobi was discovering Spinoza, Lessing began his first serious study of the *Ethica* and *Tractatus theologicus-politicus*. Mendelssohn had already introduced Lessing to Spinoza as early as 1754, and an early fragment dating back to that time, "Die Christenthum der Vernunft," shows that Lessing was moving toward pantheism, if not downright Spinozism.[39] At this early date, though, Lessing does not seem to have studied Spinoza in depth.[40] It was not until 1763 that his studies began in earnest. Two early fragments from that year, "Ueber die Wirklichkeit der Dinge ausser Gott" and "Durch Spinoza ist Leibniz erst auf die Spur der vorherbestimmten Harmonie gekommen," show Lessing's preoccupation with Spinozist themes.[41]

Lessing is part and parcel of the Spinozist tradition in Germany, and, much more than Mendelssohn or Jacobi, he is in the direct line of succession from the early Spinozists. There is a pantheism which goes hand in hand with liberal political views. Lessing, like all the other early Spinozists, believed in the value of biblical criticism, natural religion, tolerance, and equality. He too was deeply indebted to the *Tractatus,* which probably first fired his interest in Spinoza.[42] *Nathan der Weise* is indeed little more than a dramatic presentation of the philosophical doctrines of Spinoza's *Tractatus.* What completes Lessing's ties with the Spinozist tradition is that he considered himself a Lutheran—if only in spirit—because of his firm conviction that every individual had the right to think for himself.[43] In this respect Lessing preserves the legacy of the Protestant Counter-Reformation, the tradition from which all the early Spinozists sprang.

A crucial chapter in the history of Spinozism in Germany began in 1778, with Lessing's bitter dispute with H. M. Goeze, an orthodox Lutheran pastor in Hamburg. Although this dispute ostensibly did not center on, or even include, Spinoza, the issues that it raised are part of the essential background to Jacobi's later controversy with Mendelssohn. This dispute also laid the ground for the Spinoza renaissance some ten years later.

The occasion for Lessing's dispute with Goeze was Lessing's publication from 1774 to 1778 of the *Wolffenbüttler Fragmente,* a work consisting of a commentary upon, and lengthy extracts from, H. S. Reimarus's *Apologie oder Schützschrift für die vernünftige Verehrer Gottes.* This treatise was so heretical that Reimarus did not dare to publish it in his lifetime. After his death, though, Elise Reimarus, his daughter, handed the manuscript over to Lessing. Lessing then published the manuscript without disclosing the author's name and under the pretense of having found it in the library at Wolffenbüttel.

Reimarus's *Apologie* is essentially a critique of positive religion and a defense of natural religion. It was his general thesis that religion had to be based upon reason alone, and that no rational person could possibly accept the historical record contained in the Bible. Reimarus took his criticism to the most heretical extremes, however. He maintained that many of the stories in the Bible were deliberate fabrications; and he insisted on jettisoning most of the dogmas of orthodox Christianity, namely, the resurrection, original sin, the trinity, and eternal punishment.[44] It should come as no surprise that Reimarus was an avid student of Spinoza's *Tractatus,* and that much in his *Apologie* breathes a Spinozist spirit.[45] In publishing Reimarus's work, Lessing was thus airing Spinoza's views.

Lessing had his own complex philosophical motives for publishing Reimarus's heretical work. He did not agree with everything that Reimarus said, and to make this clear he published his extracts along with a critical commentary. Nonetheless, Reimarus's *Apologie* still provided Lessing with the best opportunity for putting forward his own theological views. It was Lessing's firm belief that the two major theological schools of his day took extreme and implausible views. There were the orthodox, who wanted to base religion upon revelation and the dogmatic truth of the Bible; and there were the neologists, who based religion upon reason and who wanted to demonstrate all the truths contained in the Bible. According to Lessing, the orthodox overextended the sphere of faith in defending beliefs that could not withstand rational criticism, while the neologists overextended the sphere of reason in trying to justify beliefs whose only basis was historical. Now, by publishing Reimarus's *Apologie,* Lessing thought that he could reveal the mistaken beliefs of both the orthodox and the neologists. Reimarus's critique of revelation showed that reason stood in a critical relationship to miracles and prophecy. This would teach the neologists that it is absurd to demonstrate everything contained in revelation; and it would show the orthodox that it is foolish to enjoin a faith that is vulnerable to criticism.

The publication of the *Wolffenbüttler Fragmente* had a sensational effect on the public of the day. Both the neologists and the orthodox theologians were shocked by Reimarus's attack upon positive religion, and they were suspicious of Lessing's motives in publishing such a dangerous book. Such an outspoken attack upon Christianity was to them tantamount to endangering public order. They feared that the book would weaken the faith of the common man, which was the main pillar of civil obedience. As one reviewer complained in the *Allgemeine deutsche Bibliothek:* "What useful purpose can such a book serve in the interests of the Christian public . . . We shall never invent a better religion for men than the religion of Christ, which apart from its inner rationality also has an external positive sanction. Can we want to deprive the people of the latter? Is this not to expose the ship to the open sea without rudder, mast or sail?"[46]

The cause of the orthodox was soon taken up by Pastor Goeze.[47] He felt that Lessing was not only misguided in publishing the work, but also suspiciously lax in criticizing it. Lessing, it seemed, endorsed Reimarus's criticism of the Bible. A pitched battle between Lessing and Goeze then ensued, which produced one of the masterpieces of German polemical literature, Lessing's *Anti-Goeze.*

The main issue between Lessing and Goeze concerned whether or not the truth of the Bible is necessary for Christianity. Goeze defended the orthodox Lutheran position that the Bible is the basis of the Christian faith, an infallible document written under divine inspiration. Lessing maintained, however, that the truth of the Bible is not necessary for faith, so that criticisms like those of Reimarus do not undermine the essence of Christianity. As Lessing summed up his position: "The letter is not the spirit, and the Bible is not religion, so that objections against the letter, or against the Bible, are not ipso facto objections against religion."[48] Lessing used Leibniz's distinction between truths of fact and truths of reason to prove his point. Even assuming that everything in the Bible is true, he argued, it does not follow that any truth of Christianity is also true. For the Bible purports to contain nothing but truths of fact; and from no contingent truth of fact does a necessary truth of reason follow. It does not follow, for example, from the truth of the proposition 'Jesus rose from the dead' that 'Jesus is the son of God'. There is "a wide ugly ditch" between historical and metaphysical truth, Lessing said, and he confessed that he did not know how to cross it. Lessing concluded from this argument that the basis of religion had to be reason, not revelation.[49]

Jacobi's later controversy with Mendelssohn is essentially a continuation of Goeze's debate with Lessing.[50] Jacobi defended the case for positive religion against Lessing and Mendelssohn. This does not mean, however, that Jacobi was willing to defend the infallibility of the Bible, like Goeze, and still less that he was a political reactionary who saw the publication of the *Wolfenbüttler Fragmente* as a danger to public morality.[51] Nevertheless, Jacobi insisted that the basis of religion must be revelation, not reason. Revelation did not necessarily come from the Bible; it could also come from inner experience. Religion had to be based upon historical fact, whether that was the experience of present events or the testimony of past events contained in the Bible. It is interesting to note that Jacobi never disputed Lessing's distinction between the truths of fact and the truths of reason; he only drew the opposite conclusion from it. Namely, that reason could not demonstrate the existence of anything, and in particular the existence of God; hence all evidence for God's existence had to come from revelation.

Lessing's battle with Goeze not only provided the issues for Jacobi's controversy with Mendelssohn; it also paved the way for the later reception of Spinoza. Lessing's devastating polemics against Goeze did much to weaken the position of the orthodox, who had always persecuted the Spinozists. But, much more significant, Lessing had shown that it is possible to be a Lutheran in spirit without accepting the authority of the Bible. There could have been no better restatement of the spirit of the Protestant Counter-Reformation than Lessing's *Anti-Goeze*. In that work Lessing publicly vindicated the cause of Lutheran nonconformity. All the latent pantheistic strains in Lutheranism, which emerge as soon as we divest ourselves of the authority of the Bible, were now free to express themselves.

After 1785 public opinion of Spinoza changed from almost universal contempt to almost universal admiration, largely as a result of the publication of Jacobi's *Briefe*, in which he revealed Lessing's Spinozism. Lessing was the most admired figure of the *Aufklärung*, and his credo automatically gave a stamp of legitimacy to every secret Spinozist. One after another the Spinozists could now come out of their closets and form a file behind Lessing. If Lessing was an honorable man and a Spinozist, then they could be too. Ironically, Jacobi's *Briefe* did not destroy Lessing's reputation, as Mendelssohn feared. It did the very opposite, making him a hero in the eyes of the nonconformists. Lessing made it a fashion to be unorthodox; and to be fashionably unorthodox was to be a Spinozist.

Of course, Lessing's credo explains only how Spinozism became respectable. It accounts for why a Spinozist might go public, but not for why he became a Spinozist in the first place. To understand why Spinozism became the credo of so many other thinkers, we have to consider the new situation of the sciences at the close of the eighteenth century.

The rise in the fortunes of Spinozism resulted in part from the consequence of the decline of theism and deism. By the middle of the eighteenth century theism was suffering at the hands of the sciences. Two of the cardinal tenets of theism—the belief in miracles and the authority of the Bible—were looking less and less plausible. Modern physics had become status quo by the middle of the eighteenth century, and its picture of the necessary order of nature cast doubt upon the possibility of miracles. Around the same time the historical and philological criticism of the Bible, at the hands of J. A. Ernesti in Leipzig and J. D. Michaelis in Göttingen, began to undermine its authority.[52] The Bible seemed to be no longer the product of supernatural inspiration, but of man himself writing under specific historical and cultural circumstances. The main principle behind Spinoza's biblical criticism—that the Bible is the product of nature—had been vindicated.

Although deism seemed to be consistent with modern physics and biblical criticism, it too began its decline. If theism was the victim of science, deism was the victim of philosophical criticism. The mainstays of deism were the ontological and cosmological arguments. But these arguments had become discredited by the 1780s. Hume's *Dialogues concerning Natural Religion,* Butler's *Analogy of Religion,* and Diderot's *Lettre sur les aveugles* had severely damaged the cosmological argument, while Kant's *Kritik* appeared to provide a fatal exposé of the ontological argument.

Whereas theism and deism were vulnerable to the advance of the sciences and philosophical criticism, Spinoza's pantheism seemed to be immune from them both. Indeed, to the eighteenth-century mind, Spinoza was the prophet of modern science. The science of biblical criticism advanced in the *Tractatus* was clearly groundbreaking and far ahead of its time. And the radical naturalism of the *Ethica* seemed to represent the very philosophy of modern science. Spinoza's denial of final causes and providence, his affirmation of determinism and the infinity of the universe, his belief in an impersonal and cosmic God—all these were thought to be the consequences of modern scientific naturalism. Of course, Spinoza's rationalism, and in particular his use of the geometric method in metaphysics, had been largely discredited by the 1780s, and no one was so naive as to believe in its infallibility. But it was more the content of Spinoza's system (its naturalism) than its form (its geometric method) that commanded the respect of the eighteenth century. The belief in Spinoza's cosmic God seemed to be the religion of science itself.

Thus part of the appeal of Spinozism at the end of the eighteenth century was its religious attitude toward the world, an attitude that was still consistent with, if not the result of, modern science. Spinoza's pantheism seemed to be a viable middle path between a discredited theism and deism on the one hand and a ruthless materialism and atheism on the other hand. If the thinkers of the *Goethezeit* were not willing to return to theism or revive deism, neither were they inclined to go as far as Holbach's *System de la nature* and to assert a bald atheism and materialism.

As well as the state of philosophy and science, there were other factors behind the triumph of Spinozism in late eighteenth-century Germany. One of these factors, which cannot be overestimated, is Lutheranism itself, and in particular its ideals of equality and an immediate relationship to God. We have already seen how Luther's ideals lend themselves to pantheism once the authority of the Bible is rejected. For this pantheistic tendency latent within Lutheranism to realize itself, two conditions had to be fulfilled. First, the authority of the Bible had to be discredited; and, second, Luther's ideals had to be maintained. Both of these conditions obtained. The first was satisfied by the growth of biblical criticism and by Lessing's victory over Goeze. The second was fulfilled through the pietistic movement, whose influence was still discernible well into the late eighteenth century. Not a few of the *Goethezeit* pantheists had pietistic backgrounds, which inevitably influenced their thinking.

To understand the rise of Spinozism in late eighteenth-century Germany, it is crucial that we take this Lutheran dimension into account.[53] Luther's ideals were the guiding spirit behind the later Spinozists as well as the early ones. There was indeed a single Spinozist tradition running from the late seventeenth century into the late eighteenth century, one that was constantly under the inspiration of Luther. One characteristic, and indeed conspicuous, feature of *Goethezeit* pantheism betrays his persistent influence. This is the insistence of almost all the later Spinozists upon the importance of having an experience of God, of standing in communion with nature as a whole. We find this expressed time and again in Goethe, Schelling, Schleiermacher, Novalis, Hölderlin, and Herder. It is this mystical strand of *Goethezeit* pantheism that distinguishes it from the rationalism of orthodox Spinozism. It is as if the intellectual love of God were the beginning, not the end, of Spinoza's system. Yet what is this feature of *Goethezeit* pantheism other than a reassertion of Luther's ideal of an immediate relationship to God? What was true of Spinozism in the late seventeenth century did not cease to be true of it in the late eighteenth: it was Lutheranism without the Bible.

2.3. The Dispute over Lessing's Spinozism

On March 25, 1783 Elise Reimarus, friend of Jacobi, Lessing, and Mendelssohn, and daughter of Herman Samuel Reimarus (author of the *Apologie*), wrote Jacobi about the latest news from Berlin.[54] Only the day before, she had paid a visit to Mendelssohn, who had informed her of his latest literary plans. Mendelssohn assured her that he still intended to finish his long-promised work on Lessing's character, a work he had planned to write ever since Lessing's death in February 1781. This tract was to be a tribute to the character of his closest friend, a man whom he had known for thirty years, and with whom he shared all his most intimate thoughts. Reimarus was delighted to hear of Mendelssohn's fresh resolve, and she promptly relayed the happy news to Jacobi.

After hearing of Mendelssohn's plans Jacobi wrote back to Reimarus on July 21, 1783, asking her if Mendelssohn knew about Lessing's final religious views.[55] He had something important to tell her, something so important he could confide it only "under the rose of friendship." It was indeed a shocking piece of news for the orthodox. But Jacobi felt obliged to tell it all the same: "In his last days, Lessing was a committed Spinozist!" Astounding though it was, Jacobi implied that Lessing had made just such a confession to him. And surely this fact should be communicated to Mendelssohn. Surely it was necessary for Mendelssohn to know about Lessing's Spinozism if he was to write a book on Lessing's character. But, plainly, the whole matter was very delicate. How was it possible to disclose Lessing's unorthodox views to an orthodox public? Such was Spinoza's reputation in eighteenth-century Germany that to be a Spinozist was also to be an atheist. Mendelssohn would have to treat Lessing's ultimate religious views with extreme caution. If he openly betrayed Lessing's Spinozism, then he would be bound to shock the public and defame rather than dignify Lessing's character. If, however, he completely repressed the facts, then he could not claim to write anything like an honest or definitive biography. Jacobi told Reimarus that he did not know whether Lessing had imparted his views to others, and Mendelssohn in particular. It was possible that Lessing told Mendelssohn; but it was also possible that he did not, since Lessing had not seen Mendelssohn for a long time before his death and did not like writing letters. Jacobi then left it up to Reimarus's discretion whether or not to tell Mendelssohn of Lessing's Spinozism.

Although it appears to be perfectly honest and well-meaning, Jacobi's letter to Reimarus was in fact disingenuous. Jacobi knew very well that Lessing had not confessed his Spinozism to Mendelssohn.[56] He also was not concerned about discretion or the consequences of revealing Lessing's Spinozism to the public, given that he would publish his intimate conversations with Lessing only two years later. And despite the air of indifference in leaving the matter to Reimarus's discretion, Jacobi wanted nothing more than for her to inform Mendelssohn.

So why the subterfuge? What was Jacobi up to? Simply put, he was laying a trap for Mendelssohn. He knew that his information would alarm Mendelssohn; and he calculated that it would compel Mendelssohn to doubt or deny the claim of Lessing's Spinozism, which was tantamount to calling his best friend an atheist. After Mendelssohn voiced his doubts or suspicions, Jacobi could enter the fray and divulge the contents of his personal conversations with Lessing. Such a tactic would prove his closer friendship to Lessing and expose Mendelssohn's ignorance of their old friend's most intimate opinions. So, prima facie, what was at stake was Mendelssohn's claim to be the sole legitimate heir and spokesman for Lessing. Jacobi wanted that title for himself, and he was willing to resort to underhanded means to get it.

Jacobi's eagerness to contest Mendelssohn's claim was already apparent from a small literary skirmish that he had contrived with Mendelssohn only a year earlier, which foreshadows much of the later controversy. In his *Etwas, das Lessing gesagt hat* (1782) Jacobi cited a statement of Lessing to support his attack on all forms of political and religious authority: "What Febronius and his disciples said was nothing but shameless flattery of the princes; for all their arguments against the rights of the popes were either groundless or applied with double and treble force to the princes themselves."[57] It was significant for Jacobi that Lessing had the courage to criticize the Protestant princes as well as the Catholic popes. This meant that Lessing was not one of the Berlin *Aufklärer*, who were always ready to abandon their intellectual ideals in order to compromise with the moral and political status quo. Lessing, unlike the Berliners, had the integrity to take a point to its logical conclusion, despite the moral and political consequences. Thus

Jacobi felt that Lessing was on his side in the struggle against every form of despotism—and, as will become evident, this included the "despotism of the *Aufklärung*" in Berlin.

After Jacobi's book appeared Mendelssohn made some critical comments on it, a few of which questioned Jacobi's understanding of Lessing.[58] These comments were later forwarded to Jacobi, who then took the extraordinary step of fabricating an article against himself, consisting inter alia of Mendelssohn's remarks. He then published the article anonymously in the January 1783 issue of the *Deutsches Museum*. This remarkable ploy finally gave Jacobi what he wanted: the opportunity to have a public debate with Mendelssohn. In his reply to Mendelssohn's criticisms Jacobi quarreled with Mendelssohn's interpretation of Lessing's irony.[59] Mendelssohn claimed that Lessing's statement against the princes was only an example of his love of paradox and therefore it could not be seriously attributed to him. This love of paradox tended to make Lessing oppose any exaggeration, if it was widely believed, with another exaggeration. But Jacobi countered this interpretation by appealing to his special knowledge of Lessing. Lessing told him personally, he said, that he would never indulge in paradox for its own sake, and that he would never attack a true belief unless it were based upon poor arguments. This interpretation of Lessing's irony was also important for the dispute to come. According to Jacobi, it meant that Lessing did not confess his Spinozism to him merely out of love of paradox.

Despite Jacobi's desperate ploy, Mendelssohn was not to be lured into battle. Mendelssohn only courteously conceded Jacobi's point. He saw Jacobi as a mere literatus, who was not worth his time. Needless to say, Jacobi detected this and was insulted and frustrated by it. The next time he would not let Mendelssohn slip away so easily.

Just as Jacobi expected, Elise Reimarus dutifully passed on the secret about Lessing's Spinozism. On August 4, 1783 she wrote Mendelssohn, giving him Jacobi's news and enclosing a copy of Jacobi's July 21 letter.[60] What was Mendelssohn's reaction to such stunning news? To put it mildly, it was one of puzzlement and annoyance. In his August 16 reply to Reimarus, Mendelssohn asked with some consternation, "What does it mean that Lessing was a Spinozist?"[61] Jacobi would have to explain himself. As it stood, his claim was too bald and too vague for him to cast serious judgment on it. "What precisely did Lessing say?" "How, and under what circumstances, did he say it?" "What did Lessing mean by Spinozism?" "And what particular doctrines of Spinoza did he have in mind?" All these questions, and more, had to be answered before Mendelssohn even began to assess Jacobi's claim. Whatever Jacobi might say, Mendelssohn was suspicious. He dismissed the possibility that Lessing was a Spinozist pure and simple. If Lessing ever said that he held Spinozism to be the only possible system, then he had either lost his senses or was in another of his combative and ironic moods in which he would defend an unpopular view simply for the sake of argument. Assuming, however, that Jacobi were right about Lessing's Spinozism, Mendelssohn said that he saw no reason to suppress this fact. There was no cause for disguise or censorship, as Jacobi imagined. The interests of truth could not be compromised, and they would be served only by frankly revealing Lessing's Spinozism. "Even our best friend's name should not shine in a better light than it deserves," Mendelssohn told Reimarus.

In his readiness to acknowledge and publicize Lessing's Spinozism, provided Jacobi managed to substantiate his allegation, Mendelssohn appeared to have given up his struggle with Jacobi. In fact, he was only playing his cards. Mendelssohn knew that Reimarus would either forward or summarize his letter to Jacobi, so he had to weigh his response carefully. There was an element of disingenuousness in Mendelssohn's reply, just as there was in Jacobi's original letter. What he seemed so willing to acknowledge was precisely what he feared most. If a simple assertion of Lessing's Spinozism were made, it would irreparably damage his friend's reputation. Hence Mendelssohn did not suggest that Jacobi should publish his information, and indeed he was willing to go to great lengths to forestall publication. Why, then, his seeming willingness to acknowledge the bald truth of Jacobi's claim? There were at least two motives for this. First, Mendelssohn sought to remonstrate Jacobi for his suggestion that he might want to suppress the facts and write a less than honest epitaph. That suggestion had put his integrity into question, and he had no choice but to dismiss it. Second, Mendelssohn's apparent willingness was also a sign of his confidence that, if Jacobi should justify his claim, he was in a position to interpret Lessing's Spinozism in an innocuous manner perfectly consistent with the truths of natural religion and morality. In his *An die Freunde Lessings*, written some two years later during the very height of the controversy, Mendelssohn insisted that he had always known of Lessing's sympathy for Spinozism since the earliest days of their friendship. But he associated Lessing's Spinozism with the ideas expounded in the early fragment "Die Christenthum der Vernunft." The strains of Spinozism found in that fragment were, at least in Mendelssohn's eyes, completely compatible with all the essential truths of morality and religion. Thus if Mendelssohn could publish his account of Lessing's Spinozism before Jacobi, that would take the sting out of any bald declaration by Jacobi of Lessing's Spinozism. In that way, Lessing's reputation could easily be saved. All in all, then, Mendelssohn's disingenuousness shows one thing: that he had clearly seen Jacobi's trap—and deftly avoided it.[62]

It was now very clear that a battle between Jacobi and Mendelssohn was imminent. It was only a question of letting events take their natural course. On September 1, 1783 Reimarus duly sent a summary of Mendelssohn's August 16 letter to Jacobi.[63] Upon receiving it, Jacobi felt that he had no choice but to oblige Mendelssohn's request for more information about Lessing's Spinozism.[64] So, only two months later, on November 4, 1783 Jacobi wrote a long letter (of some thirty-six quarto pages), describing his conversations with Lessing, during which Lessing allegedly made his confession of Spinozism. It was this record of his conversations with Lessing that was to have such an enormous impact on the cultural scene of late eighteenth-century Germany.

According to Jacobi, their fateful conversation took place during the summer of 1780, when Jacobi went on his 'great journey' to visit Lessing at Wolffenbüttel. Jacobi first met Lessing on the afternoon of July 5. The next morning, Lessing came into Jacobi's room in preparation for a visit to the famous Wolffenbüttel library. Jacobi was just finishing his correspondence; to entertain Lessing in the meantime, he gave him some things to read, among them the young Goethe's then-unpublished poem *Prometheus*. In commenting on the poem, Lessing made his dramatic confession. As Jacobi recalled, the dialogue went as follows:

> *Lessing:* I find the poem good . . . The point of view in it is also my own. The orthodox concepts of the divinity are no longer for me. "One and All," I know no other. That is the gist of the poem, and I must confess that it pleases me.
> *Jacobi:* Then you would be pretty much in agreement with Spinoza.
> *Lessing:* If I were to name myself after anyone, then I know no one better.
> *Jacobi:* Spinoza is good enough for me; but what a mixed blessing we find in his name!
> *Lessing:* Yes, if that's the way you look at it . . . But do you know anyone better?

At this point, the conversation was interrupted by the arrival of the director of the library. But the next morning Lessing came back to see Jacobi, eager to explain to him what he had meant by the expression "One and All," fearing that he had shocked Jacobi.

> *Lessing:* I've come to talk to you about my "One and All." You were shocked yesterday?
> *Jacobi:* You did surprise me, and I did feel some embarrassment. But you did not shock me. It surely wasn't my expectation to find you a Spinozist or

pantheist; and still less did I think that you would lay down your cards so quickly, bluntly and plainly. I came for the most part with the intention of getting your help against Spinoza.

Lessing: You know Spinoza then?

Jacobi: I believe that I know him like very few others.

Lessing: Then there is no need to help you. You too will become his friend. There is no philosophy other than Spinoza's.

Jacobi: That might well be. For a determinist, if he is to be consistent, must also become a fatalist. Everything else follows from there.

The dialogue came to a stop as Jacobi explained his interpretation of Spinoza's philosophy. His reading stressed Spinoza's denial of free will, providence, and a personal God. Judging from Jacobi's report, Lessing seemed to endorse the salient points of his interpretation. After Jacobi's brief exposition, the dialogue resumed:

Lessing: So we won't be parting company over your *credo* [Spinoza]?

Jacobi: We don't want that on any account. But my *credo* does not rest with Spinoza. I believe in an intelligent and personal cause of the world.

Lessing: Oh, all the better then! Now I'll get to hear something completely new.

Jacobi: I wouldn't get so excited about it. I get myself out of the business with a *salto mortale*. But usually you do not find any special pleasure in standing on your head?

Lessing: Don't say that, as long as I do not have to imitate it. And you will stand on your feet again, won't you? So if it's no mystery, I'll have to see what there is to it.

The conversation then turned into a debate over the problem of freedom. Jacobi confessed that the most important concept to him was that of final causes. If there are no final causes, he explained, then we must deny freedom and embrace a complete fatalism. But the prospect of fatalism was horrible to Jacobi. If fatalism is true, then our thoughts do not direct our actions, but observe them. We do not do what we think, we only think about what we do. Despite Jacobi's passion and conviction, Lessing remained cool and unimpressed. He bluntly replied that the notion of free will meant nothing to him. In true Spinozist fashion he rejected final causes and free will as anthropomorphic. It is only a product of human pride, he said, that we regard our thoughts as the first principle of things. Lessing then taunted Jacobi by asking him how he conceived the personality of God. He doubted that Jacobi could conceive it along the lines of Leibniz's philosophy since this philosophy, in the end, boils down to Spinoza's.[65] Jacobi admitted that there is indeed a correspondence between the philosophy of Leibniz and Spinoza. Because Leibniz is a determinist, he too must become a fatalist like Spinoza.

Here the dialogue reached a crucial point. Having admitted the identity of Spinoza's and Leibniz's philosophy, and having rejected the fatalism inherent in them, Jacobi seemed to be turning his back on all philosophy, or so Lessing suggested. Jacobi's reply was decisive for the dispute to come.

Lessing: With your philosophy, you will have to turn your back on all philosophy.

Jacobi: Why all philosophy?

Lessing: Because you are a complete skeptic.

Jacobi: On the contrary. I withdraw myself from a philosophy that makes skepticism necessary.

Lessing: And withdraw yourself—where?

Jacobi: To the light, the light Spinoza talks about when he says that it illuminates itself and the darkness. I love Spinoza since, more than any other philosopher, he has convinced me that certain things cannot be explained, and that one must not close one's eyes in front of them but simply accept them as one finds them . . . Even the greatest mind will hit upon absurd things when he tries to explain everything and make sense of it according to clear concepts.

Lessing: And he who does not try to explain things?

Jacobi: Whoever does not want to explain what is inconceivable but only wants to know the borderline where it begins: he will gain the largest space for human truth.

Lessing: Words, dear Jacobi, mere words! The borderline you want to fix cannot be determined. And on the other side of it you give free rein to dreaming, nonsense and blindness.

Jacobi: I believe that the borderline can be determined. I want not to draw it, but only to recognize what is already there. And as far as dreaming, nonsense and blindness are concerned . . .

Lessing: They prevail wherever confused ideas are found.

Jacobi: More where false ones are found. Someone who has fallen in love with certain explanations will blindly accept every consequence.

At this point, Jacobi summarized his philosophy in a few famous lines:

Jacobi: As I see it, the first task of the philosopher is to reveal, to disclose existence (*Daseyn zu enthüllen*). Explanation is only a means, a way to this goal: it is the first task, but it is never the last. The last task is what cannot be explained: the irresolvable, immediate and simple.

Here, Jacobi's report quickly concluded. We are left with Lessing's amusing and ironic remarks about Jacobi's philosophy.

Lessing: Good, very good, I can use all that; but I cannot follow it in the same way. In general, your *salto mortale* does not displease me; and I can see how a man with a head on his shoulders will want to stand on his head to get somewhere. Take me along with you if it works.

Jacobi: If you will only step on the elastic spot from which I leap, everything else will follow from there.

Lessing: Even that would demand a leap which I cannot ask of my old legs and heavy head.

What was Mendelssohn's response to Jacobi's remarkable report? Judging from a letter he wrote to Elise and Johann Reimarus on November 18, 1783, it was one of apparent capitulation.[66] Mendelssohn conceded that Jacobi's report had answered his questions "to his complete satisfaction," although he added the important qualification "for the time being" (*vor der Hand*). He praised Jacobi and even sent him his apologies for his previous brusqueness. At first he thought Jacobi a mere literatus; but now he could see that Jacobi was one of the very few who made thinking his chief business. Mendelssohn then made an important concession: such were Jacobi's merits that he could understand why Lessing wanted to confide in him. This concession was tantamount to his recognizing that he alone did not have privileged access to Lessing's character. Having admitted the strength of his opponent, Mendelssohn decided to withdraw from the fray. As he explained, "The knight he had challenged to combat had removed his visor; and upon seeing his worthy foe, he now picked up his gauntlet."[67]

What is even more striking about Mendelssohn's November 18 letter, however, is his apparent willingness to admit that Lessing had fallen into a crude form of Spinozism which was dangerous to morality and religion. He told the Reimaruses that it was necessary to warn philosophers by means of a striking example—namely, Lessing—of the dangers involved in abandoning oneself to speculation without guidelines. He also agreed with Johann Reimarus's diagnosis of Lessing's Spinozism: Lessing's love of paradox and irony, combined with his inclination to take extreme positions in playing the *advocatus diaboli*, had finally gotten the better of him. In any case, in writing an essay on Lessing's character, it never was his intention to make a saint or prophet out of Lessing. His main obligation was to the truth, the truth pure and simple, and that meant portraying Lessing as he was, including all his follies and weaknesses. Attempting to play down Lessing's confession of Spinozism, Mendelssohn claimed that he never put that much importance upon what any great man said in his last days, especially someone as fond of 'leaps' as Lessing. Mendelssohn seemed to be admitting at least the possibility that Lessing's Spinozism was not the same as the Spinozism of his youth, the Spinozism that Lessing espoused in his "Christenthum der Vernunft."

With Mendelssohn's conciliatory November 18 letter, the whole dispute between Jacobi and Mendelssohn seemed to be defused. After apologizing to Jacobi and withdrawing his challenge, Mendelssohn had apparently abandoned the struggle. The general appearance of peace and good will was reinforced by Jacobi's reply to Mendelssohn. On December 24, 1783 Elise Reimarus wrote Mendelssohn to tell him that Jacobi was "completely satisfied" with his letter.[68] Indeed, he had every reason to be satisfied since Mendelssohn had apparently capitulated. Reciprocating the feelings of good will, Jacobi said that Mendelssohn had no need to apologize, and that he found "great joy" in his comment that it was necessary to warn "the devotees of speculation." To Jacobi, this remark was indeed the greatest concession of them all. It was proof of Mendelssohn's readiness to compromise in philosophy, of his willingness to stop short with reason if it threatened morality and religion. Mendelssohn seemed to be admitting that reason, if it were not controlled by moral and religious guidelines, would end in the atheism and fatalism of Spinozism. And that, in essence, was everything that Jacobi ever wanted to say.

The apparent truce between Jacobi and Mendelssohn lasted for the next seven months. But, despite the general tone of capitulation and acquiescence in his November 18 letter, Mendelssohn was only drawing his breath for the struggle to come. His letter was in fact a clever delaying tactic, a way of bargaining for time. Mendelssohn told Elise and Johann Reimarus that he needed more time to consider Jacobi's position. If he appeared to capitulate, that was only because he did not want to challenge Jacobi prematurely and to provoke him into publishing his report. What Mendelssohn wanted more than anything else was the time to prepare his own interpretation of Lessing's Spinozism, an interpretation that would make it consistent with morality and religion. He had to preempt the publication of Jacobi's report with its version of Lessing's Spinozism, which would be sure to damage Lessing's reputation by attributing Spinozism to him.

The die was now cast, and the only question was when Mendelssohn should begin his attack upon Jacobi. The first ominous signs came on July 4, 1785, when Elise Reimarus wrote Jacobi to tell him some exciting news. Referring to Mendelssohn's last letter to her, probably written April 1784,[69] Reimarus said: "He told me that if he has the health and time this summer, he'll set aside the book on Lessing's character in order to risk a contest with the Spinozists."[70]

Without his consent, Elise Reimarus had naively revealed Mendelssohn's battle plans to Jacobi. "A contest against the Spinozists" could mean only one thing: an attack upon Jacobi himself, who claimed that all philosophy ended in Spinozism. A battle was clearly in the offing, then, and Jacobi told Reimarus that he was "delighted" with the news.

A month later the formal declaration of war was finally made. On August

1, 1784 Mendelssohn wrote Jacobi directly for the first time (without the mediation of Reimarus), sending him his objections to the report on Lessing's conversations.[71] Then, in a few dramatic lines, Mendelssohn made his challenge: "You have thrown down the gauntlet in chivalrous fashion; I will pick it up; and now let us fight out our metaphysical tournament in true knightly custom under the eyes of the damsel whom we both esteem."[72]

Jacobi replied directly to Mendelssohn on September 5. He regretted that the delicate state of his health prevented him from making any kind of reply to his objections. But he promised to send him a detailed reply as soon as his health improved. In the meantime he was sending Mendelssohn a copy of his "Lettre a Hemsterhuis," a mock dialogue between Spinoza and himself, setting forth his interpretation of Spinoza. Despite his poor health, Jacobi did manage to make one substantial point: he warned Mendelssohn that his philosophy was *not* that of Spinoza. Rather, it was summed up by the famous lines of Pascal: "La nature confond les Pyrrhoniens, et la raison confond les Dogmatistes."

Jacobi claimed, again disingenuously, that he knew nothing about throwing down the gauntlet. But, if Mendelssohn thought it was thrown, he was not so cowardly as to turn his back. Jacobi accepted the challenge—the challenge he had done so much to provoke—and commended himself to heaven, our lady (Elise Reimarus), and the noble mind of his adversary. With the romantic image of a knightly tournament, the contest began. But it would soon prove to be anything but romantic. It became vicious, and then tragic, for reasons we shall soon see.

The contest was slow in getting started. Little or nothing happened in the autumn and winter of 1784–85. Mendelssohn crept along at a snail's pace with his book. Jacobi's health worsened. And, when it finally improved, he suffered a severe blow: his third son died, and then his wife.[73] All thought of a reply to Mendelssohn's objections was now out of the question.

Only at the end of April 1785, eight months after receiving Mendelssohn's objections, did Jacobi find the strength to write to Mendelssohn. On April 26 he sent Mendelssohn another long manuscript, a summary of his interpretation of Spinoza.[74] But Jacobi did little more than reiterate his position. Rather than making a quid pro quo to Mendelssohn's objections, he told Mendelssohn in no uncertain terms that he had missed the point. This was no basis for a dialogue. Even more ominously, in his covering letter, Jacobi gave a sinister prophecy: "Perhaps we will live to see the day when a dispute will arise over the corpse of Spinoza like that over the corpse of Moses between the archangel and satan."[75] Clearly, the days were over when, as Lessing said, Spinoza was treated like a dead dog.

Jacobi's delay in writing Mendelssohn was as fateful as it was excusable. As Jacobi was summoning his strength to reply to Mendelssohn's objections, Mendelssohn was growing increasingly impatient. Before Jacobi's reply arrived in Berlin, Mendelssohn made a dramatic decision. He wrote Elise Reimarus on April 29, 1785, that he intended to publish the first part of his book without consulting Jacobi or waiting for the reply to his objections.[76] Mendelssohn was tired of waiting for Jacobi's reply, and suspected that it might never come. He also felt that if he stated his views formally and clearly, he could put the whole debate on more substantial footing.

Although this seemed to be a perfectly reasonable decision, it was a questionable move considering Mendelssohn's delicate relationship with Jacobi. It was bound to strain the already weakened trust between them. On the one hand, though Mendelssohn had received permission to cite Jacobi's report, it was still understood that he would not make any use of it before consulting Jacobi. After all, it was Jacobi who was the witness of Lessing's confession, and it was he who provided the information in the first place. But on the other hand, Mendelssohn did think that his decision would not break this tacit agreement. He explained to Elise Reimarus that he would not mention Jacobi's conversations in the first volume of his book. Only the second volume would consider them; but there was still plenty of time for Jacobi to be consulted about that. In this way, Mendelssohn told Reimarus, he could give a formal statement of his position while still keeping his promise to Jacobi.

This is how Mendelssohn put his case to Elise Reimarus. But the truth of the matter was much more complicated. Mendelssohn was in fact acting according to his old strategy.[77] He wanted to beat Jacobi to press, to get his version of events in first. Only in that way could he protect Lessing's reputation against any damaging allegations Jacobi might make about Lessing's Spinozism. Of course, true to his word, Mendelssohn did not mention anything about Jacobi's conversations in the first volume of his book. But he did include a chapter on Lessing's pantheism, where he attributed "a purified pantheism" to Lessing, a pantheism supposedly consistent with the truths of morality and religion. Such a chapter was plainly designed to preempt Jacobi and to deprive him of all the shock value of his revelations about Lessing's Spinozism.

After finally receiving Jacobi's reply to his objections, Mendelssohn only strengthened his resolve to go ahead with the publication of his book. As Mendelssohn explained to Reimarus in a letter written May 24, it was proving impossible to argue with Jacobi.[78] Jacobi dismissed all his objections as misunderstandings; and the more he explained things the more obscure they became. Since they were speaking different philosophical languages, there were no common terms for debate. So it seemed all the more sensible to publish his book without consulting Jacobi. For what difference would it make if Jacobi saw the manuscript? All his criticisms would be unintelligible anyway.

On July 21, 1785, Mendelssohn finally overcame his reluctance and wrote a long overdue letter to Jacobi.[79] It was a delicate business, but he had to go through with it: he had to inform Jacobi of his decision to publish his book, whose title was now firm in his mind, *Morgenstunden*. Despite his wariness, Mendelssohn botched everything. He honestly and bluntly told Jacobi that he found everything he wrote incomprehensible. He then stated that by publishing his book he would be able to establish the *statum controversiae*. This Latin phrase was ambiguous and ill-chosen. Mendelssohn did not explain how he wanted to determine the state of the controversy, leaving Jacobi to guess whether he would refer to his conversations with Lessing. He did not mention his intention of referring to them only in the planned second volume because he reckoned—rightly—that Elise Reimarus had already informed Jacobi of his detailed plans. But she had done so months ago. By leaving his plans so vague, Mendelssohn gave plenty of fuel to Jacobi's febrile and suspicious imagination.

It is not difficult to imagine Jacobi's reaction to Mendelssohn's letter. Jacobi was, to put it mildly, indignant. It seemed as if Mendelssohn had flagrantly violated his trust by publishing his information without consulting him. For all he knew, Mendelssohn would portray him as the *advocatus diaboli*, that is, as a simple Spinozist who knew nothing about the standpoint of faith that transcended all philosophy.[80] In short, Jacobi could see that Mendelssohn was trying to preempt him, and he was furious. What could he do? Jacobi felt that he had no alternative but to publish, and publish soon. He could not sit idly by while Mendelssohn whitewashed all the issues surrounding Lessing's Spinozism. So, in a frantic haste, Jacobi patched together his own book, an odd pastiche containing his letters to Elise Reimarus and Mendelssohn, Mendelssohn's letters to him and Reimarus, and the report of his conversations with Lessing, all embellished with quotations from Hamann, Herder, Lavater, and the Bible. Jacobi threw the book together in a single month, naming it *Ueber die Lehre von Spinoza in Briefen an Herrn Moses Mendelssohn*. Since Jacobi did not want Mendelssohn to get wind of his plans, he did not ask him for permission to publish his correspondence. He knew that this was unethical; but he felt that it was fair, tit for tat, given that Mendelssohn had made unauthorized use of his conversations with Lessing. Although it was a desperate gamble rushing into print, Jacobi's strategy paid off. His *Briefe* appeared as early as the beginning of September, while Mendelssohn's *Morgenstunden*, due to publishing delays, did not come out until the beginning of October. By a narrow margin, Jacobi had won the publishing race.

If Mendelssohn's book angered Jacobi, Jacobi's book so shocked Mendelssohn that he refused to believe in its existence. Mendelssohn had plenty of reasons to be upset. To begin with, Jacobi had beaten him at his own game by rushing into press before him. This had a serious consequence: it meant that he could no longer be sure that *Morgenstunden* would protect Lessing's reputation; for *Morgenstunden,* unlike Jacobi's *Briefe,* did not openly discuss Lessing's confession of Spinozism. Mendelssohn was also indignant that Jacobi had published his private correspondence without his consent.[81] What hurt Mendelssohn most of all, though, was Jacobi's insinuation that there had been no philosophical rapport between him and Lessing. Slyly, Jacobi drove home this point in the cruelest fashion. In the beginning of his *Briefe* he said that he once asked Lessing whether he ever divulged his true philosophical convictions (his Spinozism) to Mendelssohn. "Never" was Lessing's answer, Jacobi claimed.[82] Such a revelation was bound to hurt Mendelssohn by questioning the degree of trust in his thirty-year friendship with Lessing. But Jacobi could not resist. This was his coup de grace to Mendelssohn, his final trump card in his claim to be the legitimate heir and spokesman for Lessing.

The dispute reached a bitter climax—and a tragic close. Eager to wipe out the blemish on Lessing's name created by Jacobi's accusation of Spinozism, and determined to defend the integrity of his friendship with Lessing, Mendelssohn decided to write a riposte to Jacobi's *Briefe.* So, during October and November 1785, in a grim and restless mood, Mendelssohn wrote his final statement on the controversy, his *An die Freunde Lessings.* This brief tract was intended as an appendix to *Morgenstunden* and a replacement for the second volume that Mendelssohn had been planning.

The heart of Mendelssohn's tract is his analysis of Jacobi's intentions in publishing his conversations with Lessing. According to Mendelssohn, Jacobi's aim was to warn people of the dangers involved in all rational speculation—the atheism and fatalism of Spinozism—and to lead them back to "the path of faith." Jacobi held up Lessing as an example to show how reason leads us astray and into the abyss of atheism. The reason Jacobi initiated the conversations with Lessing in the first place, Mendelssohn hypothesized, was that he wanted to convert him to his orthodox and mystical version of Christianity. He wanted to lead Lessing into "the thorny thicket of Spinozism" so that he would recognize the error of his ways, renounce his reason, and make a leap of faith. Lessing, Mendelssohn was convinced, saw through Jacobi's proselytizing zeal but was roguish and waggish enough to play along. Lessing always had more pleasure in seeing a false belief defended competently than a true belief defended incompetently. Since Jacobi was proving to be such a dazzling defender of Spinoza, Lessing simply nodded his consent now and then to spur him on and watch the pyrotechnics. Lessing was therefore not confiding any deep secret to Jacobi in telling him of his Spinozism, but only encouraging him to continue with his dialectical show. The upshot of this interpretation was plain: Jacobi had been taken in by Lessing's love of irony and paradox. By suggesting that Jacobi had been duped, Mendelssohn not only questioned the depth of Jacobi's friendship with Lessing, but he also hoped to establish his superior understanding of Lessing. At the same time Mendelssohn thought that he had cleared Lessing's name. Although Lessing was perhaps guilty of playing with dialectical fire, he was at least not making a serious personal confession when he told Jacobi about his Spinozism. All in all, *An die Freunde Lessings* was a skillful exposé of Jacobi's intentions. But Mendelssohn's defense of Lessing, though well meaning, was very weak. It presupposed precisely that view of Lessing's irony that Jacobi had discredited before the controversy began.

Mendelssohn completed his *An die Freunde Lessings* at the end of December 1785. As far as he was concerned, it was his final word on the matter, and he wanted nothing more to do with "Herr Jacobi."[83] Mendelssohn was so eager to be done with the whole matter that he decided to deliver the manuscript as soon as it was completed. So on December 31, 1785, a bitterly cold day in Berlin, Mendelssohn left his house to hand over the manuscript to his publisher, Voss and Sohn. He was in such a hurry that he even forgot his overcoat, as it turned out, a literally fatal mistake. Upon his return, he fell ill. His condition rapidly declined; and on the morning of January 4, 1786 he died.

News of Mendelssohn's death spread throughout Germany and was met with almost universal regret and dismay. But after tragedy there came farce. Mendelssohn's death became the subject of a huge scandal, which is one reason why the pantheism controversy attracted so much public interest. The scandal arose when some of Mendelssohn's friends suggested,[84] while others baldly asserted,[85] that Jacobi was directly responsible for Mendelssohn's death. According to reliable reports, Mendelssohn was so upset by Jacobi's *Briefe* that his health began to deteriorate. He had suffered from a nervous debility ever since his traumatic dispute with Lavater two decades earlier; but he became much worse after Jacobi's book appeared. So fragile was his health that only the slightest setback, the smallest imbalance, would mean death. It was for this reason that Mendelssohn's chill proved fatal. Even if Jacobi were not the incidental cause of Mendelssohn's death, he certainly had created its essential preconditions. As one report put it, perhaps too dramatically, "He became a victim of his friendship with Lessing and died as a martyr defending the suppressed prerogatives of reason against fanaticism and superstition. Lavater's importunity dealt his life its first blow; Jacobi completed the work."[86] A heated controversy then broke out, debating whether, and to what extent, Jacobi was responsible for Mendels-sohn's death.[87]

Whatever the truth in all these stories about Jacobi's heavy hand in Mendelssohn's death, they are at least good myths. If Jacobi did not literally kill Mendelssohn, he did so figuratively. He delivered the coup de grace to Mendelssohn's tottering philosophy, which Kant had already shaken in the *Kritik*. It was indeed not only Mendelssohn, but the *Aufklärung* itself that died. Mendelssohn was the leading representative of the classical phase of the *Aufklärung*, and when his philosophy collapsed that period too came to an end. Thus Jacobi's 'murder' of Mendelssohn is a fitting metaphor for his destruction of the *Aufklärung* itself.

2.4. The Philosophical Significance of the Controversy

Such was, if only in outline, Jacobi's and Mendelssohn's debate over Les-sing's Spinozism. But what is the philosophical significance of it all? What philosophical problem does it raise? Prima facie the dispute only revolves around the question of Lessing's Spinozism. Yet it would be rash to conclude that only this biographical issue was at stake. Such a conclusion would not explain why Lessing's Spinozism was given such enormous philosophical significance by the disputants themselves. If we are to appreciate the phil-osophical significance of the controversy—and indeed the significance that it had for the participants—then we first have to investigate its underlying symbolism. We have to consider what the parties to the dispute symbolized for one another.

Lessing was a deeply symbolic figure for Jacobi, and indeed a symbol he could use to score important philosophical points. Lessing was essentially a vehicle for Jacobi's criticisms of the Berlin *Aufklärer,* and in particular Mendelssohn, whom he rightly regarded as their leader. Since his early days, Jacobi had been disdainful of the Berlin *Aufklärer,*[88] the circle consisting of Engel, Nicolai, Eberhard, Spalding, Zöllner, and Biester. In his eyes this group represented a form of intellectual tyranny and dogmatism no better than the Catholic Church. It was nothing more than a disguised 'Jesuitism and philosophical papism'. The *morgue berlinoise* set itself up as the highest standard of truth, the final court of intellectual appeal.[89] All views that differed from its own were contemptuously dismissed as falling short of the standards of universal reason. The result was a betrayal of those very values the *Aufklärer* pledged themselves to defend: tolerance and freedom of thought.

Another mortal sin of the Berliners, in Jacobi's view, was their hypocrisy. They were willing to forfeit their intellectual ideals for the sake of compliance with the moral, religious, and political status quo.[90] Although they professed the ideals of radical criticism and free inquiry, they abandoned them as soon as they seemed to lead to unorthodox or dangerous consequences. They stopped short whenever their criticism and inquiry seemed to threaten the foundation of morality, religion, and the state.

Jacobi had an interesting diagnosis of this hypocrisy. The Berliners could not take inquiry and criticism to its limits, he charged, because they were 'utilitarians'.[91] They valued philosophy not for its own sake, but only as a means to an end. This end was nothing more nor less than *Aufklärung:* the education of the public, the promotion of the general welfare, and the achievement of a general culture.[92] Almost all of the Berliners were *Popularphilosophen,* and it was their express aim to make philosophy practical, to bring it into public life, so that it would be not the esoteric possession of an elite, but the common good of the public at large. Such was their devotion to the program of the *Aufklärung,* however, that the Berliners were ready to sacrifice their ideals of free inquiry and criticism for it.

But can philosophy serve two masters? Reason and the public? Can it be both critical and practical, both rational and responsible, both honest and useful? What, indeed, is the purpose of philosophy? Truth or the general happiness? Inquiry for its own sake or the enlightenment of the public? That was Jacobi's question, just as it was Plato's in the *Apology.* And, like Socrates, Jacobi was convinced that this question contained all the material for a tragic conflict. Philosophy, in his view, was intrinsically irresponsible, the pastime for a public nuisance like a Socrates or a Hamann. It is an illusion to think that philosophy supports morality, religion, and the state. Rather, it does the very opposite: it undermines them. If we pursue free inquiry to its limits without imposing any guidelines, then we end up, of necessity, in skepticism. But skepticism erodes the very foundation of morality, religion, and the state. It presents us with a dreadful specter: atheism, fatalism, anarchism.

Thus, as Jacobi saw it, the Berliners were caught in a dilemma. If they remained true to their ideals of free inquiry and criticism, they would have to abandon their program of *Aufklärung;* but if they stuck to their program of *Aufklärung,* they would have to limit free inquiry and criticism. Philosophy could not serve both truth and the public. It was the tragedy of Socrates that he had tried to make it do both. The Berliners were going to have to learn his lesson all over again, Jacobi felt, and he was preparing for them the eighteenth-century equivalent of hemlock: namely, the bitter pill of Lessing's Spinozism.

Lessing became a deeply symbolic figure for Jacobi because he represented the very antithesis of the *Berliner Geist.* Jacobi considered Lessing the only courageous and honest thinker of the *Aufklärung.* He alone had the courage to pursue inquiry for its own sake, despite the consequences; and he alone had the honesty to take criticism to its tragic conclusion without moral or religious scruples. Contrary to popular opinion, it was Lessing, and not Mendelssohn, who was the true Socrates of his time.

Jacobi felt that he had good reason for seeing Lessing in such a light. Was it not Lessing who insisted upon distinguishing between the spheres of truth and utility?[93] Was it not Lessing who despised the shallow attempts to mediate philosophy and religion, and who dismissed rationalist theology as sloppy philosophy and soulless religion?[94] Was it not Lessing who dared to publish the *Wolffenbüttler Fragmente,* even though it threatened the moral and religious status quo?[95] And was it not Lessing who valued the simple faith of the heart over the cold and dead knowledge of reason? It was for all these reasons that Jacobi could so readily identify with Lessing, even though he represented the very epitome of the *Aufklärung,* an ideology that he despised. In using the figure of Lessing to criticize the Berlin establishment, Jacobi had hit on a very potent weapon indeed. For of all the figures admired by the Berliners, Lessing stands out supreme. If Lessing, the most revered thinker of the *Aufklärung,* turned out to be at odds with the moral and religious status quo, then that would make the Berliners think twice about where their reason was taking them.

But, to Jacobi, the most significant fact about Lessing was his Spinozism. Lessing was the most radical and honest thinker of the *Aufklärung* but was also a Spinozist. This connection was certainly not accidental for Jacobi. It meant that Lessing was the only man with the honesty to admit the consequences of all inquiry and criticism: atheism and fatalism. According to Jacobi, all rational speculation, if only consistent and honest, as in the case of Lessing, had to end in Spinozism; but Spinozism amounted to nothing more than atheism and fatalism.[96] Hence Lessing's Spinozism was a symbol—a warning sign—for the dangerous consequences of all rational inquiry and criticism.

Now it was this attack upon the claims of reason, and not merely the biographical sensation of Lessing's Spinozism, that really shocked Mendelssohn and the whole Berlin establishment. This charge was tantamount to the accusation that the rationalist metaphysics, to which Mendelssohn had devoted his entire life, was ultimately Spinozistic and therefore dangerous to morality and religion. It was not only Mendelssohn's knowledge of Lessing that was at stake, then, but more important, his lifelong devotion to metaphysics. The inspiring hope behind that metaphysics—the assumption that we could rationally demonstrate beliefs in God, immortality, and providence—was now thrown into question.

From the very beginning, Mendelssohn knew all too well that his philosophy, not only his knowledge of Lessing, was at stake. Even before his decision to write *Morgenstunden,* Mendelssohn saw his conflict with Jacobi in philosophical terms. He suspected that another contest was brewing between the *Aufklärung* and *Sturm und Drang,* the "flag of reason" and "the party of faith." After reading Jacobi's report of his conversations with Lessing, Mendelssohn wrote to Elise and Johann Reimarus on November 18, 1783: "I still firmly believe that it is necessary and useful to warn the devotees of speculation, and to show them by means of a striking example what dangers they expose themselves to when they engage in speculation without guidelines . . . We certainly do not want to form a party ourselves; we would become traitors to the flag to which we have sworn ourselves as soon as form a party and try to recruit."[97] Here Mendelssohn is insinuating that Jacobi is guilty of proselytizing, of trying to convert Lessing and to win him over to the party of faith; and he is at the same time contrasting Jacobi's proselytizing with his own more liberal and tolerant philosophy. The point that Mendelssohn is making here anticipates his later analysis of Jacobi's intentions in *An die Freunde Lessings.*[98] In this later work Mendelssohn claims that Jacobi's intention in publishing his conversations with Lessing is to convince him (Mendelssohn) of the dangerous consequences of all philosophy and to convert him to the party of faith (Christianity). Jacobi, Mendelssohn suggests, was using the figure of Lessing as a warning against the atheism and fatalism inherent in all rational inquiry. In other words, Mendelssohn had accurately read the writing on the wall and had rightly gauged the symbolic significance of Lessing's Spinozism.

The very decision to write *Morgenstunden* was indeed a victory of the philosophical over the biographical. Although at least one chapter of the book is devoted to the question of Lessing's Spinozism, its primary aim is certainly philosophical. This is evident from Reimarus's letter to Jacobi of July 4, 1785, which explains Mendelssohn's decision to write the book. Referring to Mendelssohn's last letter to her, which was written in April 1784, Reimarus told Jacobi that Mendelssohn was postponing the book on Lessing's character in favor of a battle with the Spinozists.[99] Although Mendelssohn was obviously giving priority to the philosophical issue, it is important to note that it did not entail only the truth or falsity of Spinozism, as the letter itself at first suggests. Rather, what was at stake for Mendelssohn was the very possibility and limits of metaphysics itself, and indeed whether or not reason could offer any justification for essential moral and religious beliefs. Mendelssohn's decision "to risk a contest with the Spinozists" meant he intended to dispute Jacobi's controversial claim that all speculative philosophy ends in Spinozism. Such a claim represented a serious challenge to his allegiance to the Wolffian-Leibnizian philosophy.

If Mendelssohn represented all the vices of the *Aufklärung* to Jacobi, Jacobi symbolized all the dangers of the *Sturm und Drang* to Mendelssohn. From the start, Mendelssohn was convinced that Jacobi was just another

Schwärmer, another pietistic mystic who wanted to debunk reason and to convert him to an irrational form of Christianity, which based religion upon revelation and the Bible alone. Mendelssohn could not help seeing Jacobi in the context of another traumatic affair in his life which occurred some fifteen years earlier. In 1769 Mendelssohn had become involved in a bitter dispute with the Swiss pastor J. C. Lavater, the most notorious *Schwärmer* of them all. Lavater demanded that Mendelssohn refute the defense of Christianity in Bonnet's *La Palingenesie philosophique* or publicly convert.[100] The controversy with Lavater was the most dramatic and trying event in Mendelssohn's life, for it put his deep personal allegiance to Judaism at stake. Mendelssohn could never forget the Lavater affair; and in his weary and suspicious eyes, Jacobi was a front man for Lavater. He was convinced that the forthcoming battle with Jacobi would be a bitter repeat of the Lavater affair.

It is important to see, though, that Jacobi's missionary zeal posed Mendelssohn with not only a personal, but also a philosophical, challenge. Whether or not he should be loyal to Judaism was, as far as he was concerned, the same question as whether or not he should be true to reason itself. For Mendelssohn saw his faith in Judaism as part and parcel of his faith in reason. Like Jacobi, Mendelssohn regarded Christianity as an essentially supernatural religion whose only basis was revelation and the Bible. But Judaism was, in his view, an intrinsically rational religion, which did not contain mere articles of faith, and which insisted on a rational justification of all belief. As Mendelssohn explained to Jacobi in his "Erinnerung," "My religion recognizes no obligation to resolve doubt other than through rational means; and it commands no mere faith in eternal truths."[101] Hence Jacobi's demand that Mendelssohn convert to Christianity was tantamount to the demand that he abandon his reason and take a leap of faith. But that was a step that Mendelssohn was simply not willing to take. He argued that Jacobi's *salto mortale* was conceptually, as well as personally, a meaningless act. Thus he told Jacobi in no uncertain terms: "To doubt if there is something that not only transcends, but also lies completely outside the sphere of our concepts is what I call a leap beyond myself. My *credo* is: doubt about what I cannot conceive does not disturb me. A question that I cannot answer is to me as good as no question at all."[102] Rarely had the rationalist's credo been expressed in such frank and explicit terms. It was now incumbent upon Mendelssohn to defend that credo, a task to which he turned with zeal in his *Morgenstunden.*

It should now be clear why the main issue between Jacobi and Mendelssohn was not simply biographical. The strictly factual question of whether or not Lessing had confessed his Spinozism to Jacobi was seldom at issue.[103] That

Lessing had made such a confession was accepted as a fait accompli by everyone; even Mendelssohn did not question Jacobi's honesty. It was of course more of a problem to determine in what sense Lessing was a Spinozist. But even this issue raised few polemical passions. Indeed, Jacobi had remarkably little interest in plumbing Lessing's mind or quarreling with Mendelssohn's interpretation of his Spinozism.[104] We can understand the significance of Lessing's Spinozism only when we recognize that it was only a symbol— a symbol for the consequences of all rational inquiry and criticism. If Lessing were shown to be a Spinozist, then every self-respecting *Aufklärer* would have to concede that reason was heading toward atheism and fatalism, an admission that in turn would threaten the most important dogma of the *Aufklärung:* the authority of reason. Jacobi was raising the very disturbing question, Why should we be loyal to reason if it pushes us into the abyss? Hence the biographical question of Lessing's Spinozism became weighted with the much larger question of the authority of reason itself. What the historical Lessing said or thought was relevant only insofar as it illustrated something about the general consequences of all rational inquiry.

At this point it should also be plain why the central problem of the controversy was not exegetical. It did not substantially concern the proper interpretation of Spinoza's philosophy, that is, whether or not it is atheistic or fatalistic. Still less did it deal with the truth or falsity of Spinoza's system, as if this were the only philosophical dimension of the controversy. These are indeed problems raised by the dispute; but they are important only in light of Jacobi's general thesis that reason of necessity leads to atheism and fatalism. What is at stake for Jacobi and Mendelssohn is not the specific question of whether *Spinoza*'s metaphysics ends in atheism or fatalism, but the more general question of whether all metaphysics ends in it. Jacobi might have taken some other metaphysical system to illustrate his point (for example, Leibniz's) since he believed that all metaphysical systems are ultimately identical (if they are only consistent), and that they all have damaging consequences for morality and religion.[105]

If, then, we are to distill the fundamental philosophical problem behind the pantheism controversy—and, indeed, the fundamental problem as it was seen by Jacobi and Mendelssohn themselves—we must focus our attention on Jacobi's critique of reason. We might summarize this critique in the form of a dilemma, a dilemma that Jacobi suggests at several points during his conversation with Lessing,[106] and that he explicitly states later on.[107] We are confronted with a difficult and dramatic choice: either we follow our reason and become atheists and fatalists; or we renounce our reason and make a leap of faith in God and freedom. In more general terms, we have to choose either a rational skepticism or an irrational faith. There is simply no comforting middle path between these options, no way to justify morality and religion through reason.

Prima facie it seems as if Jacobi's dilemma is nothing more than a rehash of the old conflict between reason and faith, philosophy and religion. Although this is certainly Jacobi's starting point, he did not stop here. He extended this conflict so that 'faith' covered not only religious, but also moral, political, and commonsense beliefs. The *salto mortale* had to be made apropos not only belief in God, but also the beliefs in freedom, other minds, the external world, and the permanent existence of the human soul.

Seen from a broader perspective, then, Jacobi's dilemma is a perennial one, and as old as philosophy itself. It is the business of philosophy to examine, criticize, and if possible justify our most fundamental principles and beliefs, the principles and beliefs that are the necessary presuppositions of science, religion, morality, and common sense. But in pursuing this task philosophy almost inevitably leads to skepticism: to doubts about induction and freedom, the existence of God, other minds, and the external world. A conflict arises between the standards of a purely critical reason and the demands of religion, morality, science, and common sense. What we find necessary to believe in order to act within our world often proves to be unacceptable when we examine it according to our critical reason. As purely rational philosophers, who stand outside the world, we find it necessary to reject many of our ordinary beliefs; but as simple human beings, who live and act in the world, we find it necessary to cling to them. Now Jacobi's dilemma is merely part and parcel of this eternal conflict between philosophy and ordinary belief. What Jacobi is trying to say is that this conflict is in principle irresolvable. He is claiming that the very hope that motivates us to pursue philosophy—the hope that we can rationally justify the beliefs of religion, morality, and common sense—is nothing more than an illusion. Hence Jacobi's attack upon reason forces us to reexamine our motives for doing philosophy in the first place.

Jacobi has a striking word to designate the skeptical consequences of all philosophical investigation: 'nihilism' (*Nihilismus*). He is indeed responsible for bringing this word into general use in modern philosophy.[108] What is indeed remarkable about Jacobi's use of this term, which has all the weight of precedence in its favor, is that it makes nihilism into the fundamental problem of all philosophy. If 'nihilism' is an appropriate word to denote the skeptical consequences of all philosophical inquiry, and if philosophy is trying to stave off the consequences of skepticism, then philosophy is indeed a desperate struggle against nihilism. If the philosopher cannot escape skepticism, then, by Jacobi's criterion, he ipso facto cannot avoid nihilism. Hence nihilism is Jacobi's final indictment and chief criticism of all philosophy.

What, more precisely, does Jacobi mean by 'nihilism'? Why does he use the word in the sense he does? Jacobi's use of the term is important if only because he is the first to introduce it into modern philosophy. Understanding Jacobi's usage should help us to define this notoriously nebulous word at its very source. But, as we might expect of an antisystematic thinker like Jacobi, he never gives an explicit or general definition. Nevertheless, his use of the word is much more technical, philosophical, and literal than what one might at first glance assume. The most important point to note about Jacobi's use of the term is that he uses it to designate a specific epistemological position. The term is virtually synonymous with, although slightly broader than, another term of Jacobi's: 'egoism' (*Egoismus*). According to the early Jacobi, the egoist is a radical idealist who denies the existence of all reality independent of his own sensations.[109] He is indeed a solipsist, but a solipsist who disputes the permanent reality of his own self as much as the external world and other minds. In his later writings, however, Jacobi tends to replace the term 'egoist' with 'nihilist'.[110] Like the egoist, the nihilist is someone who denies the existence of everything independent of the immediate contents of his own consciousness, whether external objects, other minds, God, or even his own self. All that exists for the nihilist is therefore his own momentary conscious states, his fleeting impressions or representations; but these representations represent, it is necessary to add, nothing. Hence the nihilist is, true to the Latin root, someone who denies the existence of everything, someone who affirms nothingness. Or, as Jacobi puts it, the nihilist lives in a world "out of nothing, to nothing, for nothing and in nothing."[111]

The antithesis to nihilism, in Jacobi's sense, is realism, where 'realism' is defined in a broad sense as the belief in the independent existence of all kinds of entities, whether these be material things, other minds, or God. According to Jacobi, the only escape from nihilism, and indeed the only basis for realism, is the immediate perception of an external reality. This immediate perception is an intuitive grasp of existence, an intuition whose certainty cannot be demonstrated, and which has to be accepted as a mere article of faith. To try to demonstrate the truth of these intuitions, Jacobi contends, is to reinvite the danger of nihilism.

But 'nihilism', it is important to note, does not have a strictly epistemological meaning for Jacobi.[112] It also has an ethical meaning—a meaning that is not accidentally related to the modern sense of the word. Jacobi's use of the word provides all the stuff for the fiction of a Dostoyevsky or the anarchism of a Stirner. The ethical element of Jacobi's usage becomes perfectly explicit when he says that the nihilist denies the existence not only of things, but also of values.[113] Since he denies the existence of an external world, other minds, a soul, and God, the nihilist discharges himself from all obligations to such pseudo-entities. Since all that exists are his own momentary states of consciousness, he cares only for them. He finds the only source of value within himself and believes that what he wills to be right is right—and just because he wills it. The nihilist is indeed such an egomaniac that he is convinced that he is God.[114]

2.5. Jacobi's First Critique of Reason

Having extracted the main philosophical problem behind the pantheism controversy, we are still left with the difficult task of explaining why Jacobi thinks that it is a problem. Or, to put the question more precisely: Why does Jacobi think that his dilemma is inescapable? Why does he believe that we have but two options, a rational nihilism or an irrational faith?

To appreciate Jacobi's position, we first have to come to terms with his interpretation of Spinoza. We have to uncover the rationale behind some of his apparently extravagant claims about Spinoza's philosophy. There are two claims in particular that deserve our attention: (1) that Spinoza's philosophy is the paradigm of metaphysics, the model of speculation; and (2) that Spinozism is atheism and fatalism. These two claims are important since they support the main premise behind Jacobi's dilemma: that reason of necessity ends in nihilism.

The key to Jacobi's later interpretation of Spinoza—the interpretation found in the first and second editions of the *Briefe*—is that Jacobi sees Spinoza as the prophet of modern science.[115] Spinoza represents not the apotheosis of a dying metaphysical rationalism, but the forefront of an emerging scientific naturalism. According to Jacobi's "Brief a Mr. Hemsterhuis" and the seventh "Beylage" to the *Briefe,* the aim of Spinoza's philosophy is to find a mechanistic explanation of the origin of the universe.[116] Spinoza's philosophy continues the ancient Epicurean and modern Cartesian traditions, both of which attempt to explain the origin of the universe in strictly mechanical and naturalistic terms. What Jacobi sees as the paradigm of rationality is not the syllogistic reasoning of Wolff's, Leibniz's, or even Spinoza's metaphysics, but the mechanistic principles of modern science.

The guiding principle behind Spinoza's philosophy, Jacobi tells us, is the governing principle behind all mechanistic or naturalistic philosophy: the principle of sufficient reason. This principle states, at least on Jacobi's reading,[117] that there must be some condition or set of conditions for everything that happens, such that given this condition or set of conditions, the thing occurs of necessity. It is this simple principle that Jacobi sees as the very heart of Spinoza's philosophy. Thus, during his conversations with Lessing, Jacobi sums up "the spirit of Spinozism" with the old scholastic maxim *ex nihilo nihil fit.*[118] This maxim is only a slogan for the principle of sufficient reason, which says, to put it crudely, that something always comes from something else. Of course, Jacobi admits that there are many other philosophers who adhere to this principle. But what distinguishes Spinoza from them, Jacobi thinks, is that he so consistently and ruthlessly applies it.[119] Hence, unlike most philosophers, Spinoza affirms the infinity of the world and a system of complete necessity.

Now, to Jacobi, Spinoza's philosophy is the paradigm of metaphysics, the model of speculation, precisely because it consistently and universally applies the principle of sufficient reason, which is the basis of all rationality and discursive thought. We conceive or understand something, he says, only insofar as we grasp the conditions of its existence. If we want to explain something, then we have to know its conditions, the 'mechanism' behind it. As Jacobi explains, "We conceive a thing if we can derive it from its proximate causes, or if we can grasp its immediate conditions in a series; what we grasp or derive in this manner gives us a mechanical connection."[120] If, then, we consistently and universally apply the principle of sufficient reason, we also assume that everything which exists is explicable or conceivable according to reason. In other words, we are thoroughgoing metaphysicians or speculative philosophers. Jacobi therefore identifies a thoroughgoing rationalism with a complete and consistent naturalism or mechanism.

It is this radical naturalism, this uncompromising mechanism, that Jacobi sees as the source of Spinoza's atheism and fatalism. According to Jacobi, if we believe in the existence of God, then we must assume that God is the cause of his own existence and everything else that exists.[121] Similarly, if we believe in freedom, then we must suppose that the will is spontaneous, acting as a cause without any prior cause to compel it into action.[122] In both cases, then, it is necessary to assume the existence of some unconditional or spontaneous cause, that is, a cause that acts without any prior cause to compel it into action. But this is of course just the assumption that we cannot make if we universally apply the principle of sufficient reason. If universally applied, this principle states that for every cause there is some prior cause that compels it into action.

Assuming, then, this reading of the principle of sufficient reason along with Jacobi's interpretation of the concepts of freedom and God, we are again caught in a dilemma. If we universally apply the principle of sufficient reason, assuming a thoroughgoing naturalism, then we have to accept atheism and fatalism. If, however, we assume that God and freedom exist, committing ourselves to the existence of unconditional causes, then we have to admit that they are completely inexplicable and incomprehensible. We cannot explain or conceive them since that is tantamount to assuming that there is some condition for the unconditioned, which is absurd. If we believe in God and freedom, then, we have no choice but to admit that they are a mystery.[123]

It should now be clear that Jacobi's theory of the nihilism of reason is not simply an attack on the methods of dogmatic pre-Kantian metaphysics.[124] Jacobi thinks that Spinoza's philosophy is the paradigm of reason not because of its geometric method or its a priori reasoning, but because of its rigorous use of the principle of sufficient reason. What this means, then, is that Jacobi's dilemma still retains its force *despite the demise of metaphysical rationalism* at the hands of Kant. Though Kant eventually argues against Jacobi that Spinozism has gone the way of all dogmatic metaphysics,[125] his argument does not affect Jacobi's main point. His point is that the radical application of the principle of sufficient reason is incompatible with the beliefs in God and freedom—and Kant himself would fully endorse this.

This sketch of Jacobi's interpretation of Spinoza also provides another general perspective in which to view his attack on reason. Accepting two of Jacobi's theses—that reason leads to nihilism, and that natural science is the paradigm of reason—we are bound to conclude that natural science is the source of nihilism. The target of Jacobi's attack on reason is therefore natural science itself. In order to undermine reason, Jacobi is raising some unsettling doubts about the consequences of scientific progress. He is preying upon a worry that many philosophers were beginning to have in the eighteenth century, and that many philosophers continue to have in the twentieth: namely, that the progress of the sciences is leading to the destruction of our essential moral and religious beliefs. The mechanism by which this happens is as familiar as it is frightening. The more the sciences progress, the more they discover the causes of life, human action, and the origin of the universe; but the more they find these causes, the more they support materialism, determinism, and atheism. In attacking reason, it is inter alia this scenario that Jacobi had in mind.[126] One explanation for his extraordinary success is that not a few people in the late eighteenth century feared that the sciences were heading in just this direction.

2.6. Jacobi's Second Critique of Reason

Despite all the time and effort that he spends on its elaboration and defense, Jacobi's interpretation of Spinoza is not his only weapon in his battle against the *Aufklärung*. He has other arguments against the hegemony of reason, which are no less challenging. In the concluding section of the first edition of the *Briefe*, Jacobi begins to attack reason from another—and even more vulnerable—direction.[127] Here Jacobi's line of approach is to consider not the consequences of rational inquiry and criticism, but the motives behind it. It is not only the *terminus ad quem* of reason—the atheism and fatalism of Spinoza—but its *terminus a quo* that interests him. In a long and rambling disquisition, whose intent is unclear but whose purport is unmistakable, Jacobi casts doubt upon one of the most fundamental beliefs of the *Aufklärung:* that there is such a thing as purely objective inquiry, through which it is possible to determine truth and falsity apart from all our interests. If he could prove this belief to be false, then the *Aufklärung* would truly have met its end. There would no longer be an impartial and universal reason to destroy the prejudice, superstition, and ignorance protecting vested interests (the Church and aristocracy). For what motivates reason will prove to be nothing more than a prejudice and vested interest of its own.

This belief is an illusion, Jacobi argues, because it presupposes a false relationship between reason and the will. It is not the case that reason governs our interests and desires, he says; rather, our interests and desires govern our reason.[128] "Reason is not the master, but the servant of the will," as the old adage goes. Such a doctrine is of course anything but new, and it can even be found in such apostles of the Enlightenment as Hume and Helvetius. But Jacobi extends this doctrine in a new and dangerous direction. Reason is subordinate to the will not only in the realm of practice, he says, but also in that of theory. The will determines not only the ends of action—what is good and evil—but also the goals and standards of inquiry—what is true and false. It is Jacobi's chief contention that we cannot separate the realms of theory and practice, because knowledge is the consequence of right action, truth the result of the proper interests.

But why is this the case? What could possibly justify Jacobi in making such a radical and apparently reckless claim? We can find no satisfactory answer to this question in the first edition of the *Briefe.* It is only in *David Hume,* and in the much enlarged second edition of the *Briefe,* that Jacobi states the general theory behind his position.[129] There are two important points that bring Jacobi to this radical conclusion. First, reason knows only what it creates, or only that which conforms to the laws of its own activity. Such a claim is not meant as a criticism of reason, but only as a restatement of a definition of reason that is often found in the *Aufklärung.* It is found in Kant, for example, and it is possible that Jacobi has Kant in mind here.[130] Second, the creative activity of reason is not purely disinterested or an end in itself; it is governed by a more basic interest and desire, one that is beyond its control, and one that it does not even understand, namely, the sheer need for survival.[131] The task of reason is to control, organize, and dominate our environment for the sake of the survival of the species. Reason develops hand in hand with language, Jacobi contends, and the purpose of language is to transmit information from one generation to the next about the means for its survival.[132]

Added together, these points seriously undermine the possibility of objective inquiry in the sense assumed by Mendelssohn and the *Aufklärer*.[133] They bring into question any sense in which we can talk about purely 'objective' standards of truth. The first point implies that there is no such thing as objective truth in the sense of an external object in nature to which all our knowledge somehow corresponds. Reason does not conform to nature, but nature conforms to it. In other words, reason does not comply with given standards of truth but creates them. This point still leaves open the possibility of a Kantian notion of objectivity, however, where objectivity consists in conformity to universal and necessary rules. The only question then is whether or not there can be such rules. Jacobi answers this question with a very firm "No." His second point is directed against this Kantian position, bringing into question even its more modest concept of objectivity. Jacobi denies that there is any such thing as objectivity in the Kantian sense of conformity to disinterested, impartial, and autonomous rational criteria. The problem is that reason is not a completely self-governing faculty; it is controlled by our needs and desires as living beings. We cannot separate reason from our needs and functions as living beings because its task is to do nothing more than organize and satisfy them. Of course, it is the business of reason to create laws, Jacobi happily concedes to Kant. But he then adds: in doing so, reason is governed by our interests as living beings, which are not in turn subject to rational control and appraisal. Rather, they determine the very criteria of rational appraisal.

Prima facie this position does not seem to be dangerously relativistic. There still appears to be a plausible antirelativistic line of reply to Jacobi even if we admit his premises. We might concede to him that it is our interests that determine our standards of truth. But then we might argue that our interests are universal. This is indeed the case for such biological interests as self-preservation. Hence there could still be objectivity in the sense that there is a single objective behind all discourse, namely, self-preservation. We can then evaluate all the different criteria of truth in terms of one more general criterion, which asks whether adopting a criterion is an efficient means for survival.

In essence, however, Jacobi's position is much more relativistic than it appears. If we look closer, we find that Jacobi does not have a merely biological notion of interest. He also recognizes the role of culture in the formation of interests, and—even more ominously—he notes that cultural standards are frequently incommensurable with one another. In an early essay, for example, Jacobi writes that the philosophy and religion of one age are often complete nonsense when they are judged by the standards of another.[134] Thus, daring though it might be, Jacobi does take the plunge into relativism. He insists that the interests which determine our reason are conflicting, and that these are incommensurable with one another. There is no rational standard to mediate between them since rationality is defined within the terms of each.

Jacobi does not conclude from this argument that we should drop the concept of truth from our vocabulary. But he does think that we should at least revise our notion of how truth is attained. We do not attain knowledge through disinterested contemplation, he maintains, but through having the right disposition and doing the right actions. "Knowledge of the eternal," Jacobi claims, "is given only to the heart that seeks it." As he sums up his general position in the *Briefe,* "We find ourselves placed upon this earth; and what our actions become there also determines our knowledge; what happens to our moral disposition also determines our insight into things."[135]

But Jacobi's hard-won position inevitably raises the question, How do we know how to act? How do we know what our dispositions should be? It seems that there must be some knowledge before acting in order to make the right choice between all the options available. Jacobi does not evade this question. But neither does he make any concessions about the necessity of having some prior knowledge. If we are to know how to act, he says, then all we need is faith, faith in the promises of Christ.[136] What does it mean to have faith in Christ, though, other than being willing to act upon his commandments? Once we obey his commandments, we can rest assured: we will then act in the right manner and acquire knowledge of the eternal as a result. It is pointless trying to examine and criticize Christ's word before we act, however, because we have knowledge only at the end of action. If we have faith, then we will act; and if we act, then we will have knowledge. But all criticism before acting is nothing more than a *petitio principii.* It is like a blind man denying that colors exist.

Jacobi claims that his epistemology of action represents the spirit of Christianity. "The spirit of my religion," he tells Mendelssohn, contrasting his Christianity with Mendelssohn's Judaism, "is that man comes to know God through leading the life of God."[137] Jacobi then elaborates this statement in the context of the Gospel of John. The God of Christianity is the God of love, he says, and such a God reveals himself only to those who love him and who act in his spirit.[138] To have faith is to love God and one's fellowmen; and the reward of such a life is the knowledge of God.

On the basis of this new epistemology, Jacobi develops a general theory about the nature and limits of philosophy itself. Since our actions determine our knowledge and, furthermore, our actions are determined by the general culture in which we live, it follows that philosophy is nothing more than the product of its time. "Can philosophy ever be anything more than history?" Jacobi asks. And he answers in the negative. Philosophy is nothing more than the self-reflection of an age. Some twenty years before Hegel's *Phänomenologie,* and some fifteen years before Schlegel's *Vorlesungen über*

Transcendentalphilosophie, Jacobi writes, "Every age has its own truth, just as it has its own living philosophy, which describes in its progress the predominant manner of acting in the age."[139]

Jacobi does not hesitate to draw an apparently radical political conclusion from all this. "If we are to improve the philosophy of an age," he argues, "then we must first change its history, its manner of acting, its way of life."[140] But the conclusion only appears to be radical and political. Jacobi does not envisage anything as revolutionary as Marx. The problems of the present age can be resolved, he thinks, only through the reform of its morals. The great problem of the present age is its increasing materialism, its preference for wealth and comfort above everything else, which is leading to a decline in such moral values as patriotism, justice, and community. The only way to remedy this sorry state of affairs is to revive morality, and this can only be accomplished by returning to religion, the good old Christian religion of our fathers. To Jacobi, it is an old and proven truth: "Religion is the only means to rescue the miserable plight of man."[141]

2.7. Jacobi's Defense of Faith

A central task of Jacobi's attack upon reason is to convince us of the necessity and omnipresence of faith. Faith is to Jacobi what reason is to Mendelssohn: the ultimate touchstone of truth. If Mendelssohn argues that we must examine every belief according to reason, Jacobi replies that any such examination in the end rests upon a *salto mortale*. Faith is inescapable, a necessary act of commitment. As Jacobi swore to Mendelssohn in response to his rationalist credo, "My dear Mendelssohn, we were all born in faith, and we must remain in faith, just as we were all born in society and must remain in it."[142]

Why is faith inescapable? We cannot avoid it, Jacobi tells us in the *Briefe,* because even our allegiance to reason is an act of faith.[143] All demonstration has to stop somewhere because the first principles of demonstration are themselves indemonstrable. Then what is our belief in the certainty of these principles, other than faith? All belief that cannot be demonstrated is faith; but these principles cannot be demonstrated; hence belief in them amounts to faith. Thus Jacobi's reply to Mendelssohn's credo is that it is just that: a simple act of faith. Mendelssohn cannot demonstrate his faith in reason without presupposing it.

Mendelssohn could reply to this argument, however, by exploiting a simple point that Jacobi himself admits: that the first principles of reason are self-evident, possessing an intuitive or immediate certainty. If they are self-evident, then we do not just *believe* that they are true; we *know* that they are true. But what we know is not just what we believe. So how is belief in the first principles a simple act of faith? Jacobi's argument derives its plausibility from conflating two very different kinds of indemonstrable belief: that which is indemonstrable because it is self-evident and axiomatic; and that which is indemonstrable because it is uncertain or unverifiable. Mendelssohn could then disarm Jacobi's objection by replying that his belief in the first principles of reason belongs to the first and not the second kind of belief.

What allows Jacobi to conflate these two very different kinds of belief is his technical use of the word 'faith'. In the usual sense faith opposes all forms of knowledge, whether self-evident or demonstrable. But, like Hamann, Jacobi deliberately expands the use of the word, so that it opposes not all knowledge, but only demonstrable knowledge. All belief that does not permit rational justification or demonstration is faith, he argues, and that includes beliefs that are self-evidently true.[144] Hence Jacobi considers the belief in the first principles of demonstration just as much an act of faith as the belief in the existence of God.

Jacobi's broad use of the word 'faith' is clearly tendentious, serving to justify religious and moral belief. Since it conflates these two kinds of indemonstrable belief, it makes religious and moral beliefs seem as certain as the axioms of arithmetic and the axioms of arithmetic as uncertain as religious beliefs. And the palpable difference between these two kinds of belief is reason for rejecting rather than accepting Jacobi's usage. Indeed, Goethe and Herder dismissed Jacobi's concept of faith on just these grounds.[145]

Apparently, Jacobi's broad use of the word 'faith' is perfectly defensible, a strict consequence of the common definition of knowledge as *justifiable* true belief. If we stick to this definition, then beliefs that we regard as certain, but that we still cannot justify, cannot amount to knowledge. Hence even our belief in the first principles of reason can only be an act of faith. Such an interpretation does not excuse Jacobi for confusing two kinds of indemonstrable belief; but at least it makes his usage more understandable. The only problem with this reading is that Jacobi does not always abide by this definition. Thus he sometimes calls *indemonstrable* beliefs knowledge. Whereas the common definition contrasts faith with all forms of knowledge, Jacobi contrasts it only with discursive or demonstrable knowledge.

If Jacobi's attempt to persuade us of the necessity of faith is dubious, resting upon a tendentious use of the word 'faith', his attempt to persuade us of its omnipresence is plausible. Like Hamann, Jacobi thinks that we must limit the principle of sufficient reason, so that we cannot demand a justification or demonstration for all our beliefs. It is just a fact, he argues, that most of our commonsense beliefs cannot be demonstrated.[146] Take the belief in the existence of the external world. It cannot be demonstrated since, from all the evidence of our senses, we cannot infer that objects continue to exist when we do not perceive them. For similar reasons, we cannot prove our belief in the existence of other minds or in the reliability of induction. If, then, we are not to lapse into skepticism, rejecting all beliefs that cannot be demonstrated, we have to restrict the demand for rational justification. We have to recognize that the sphere of faith is much wider than we at first thought. It encompasses all beliefs that are not capable of strict demonstration, and that includes not only our moral and religious beliefs, but also the most basic beliefs of common sense.

While arguing for the omnipresence of faith, Jacobi frequently appeals to the arguments of another philosopher he greatly admires: David Hume. Like Hamann, he admits that he owes a great debt to the Scottish skeptic.[147] It is Hume who taught him that the beliefs of common sense are not demonstrable by reason and that the sphere of faith extends into all the corners of life. In gratitude, Jacobi entitled one of his most important works *David Hume*.

But Jacobi's use of Hume's skepticism, much like Hamann's, was self-serving. Although Jacobi was happy to invoke Hume's skepticism to limit the province of reason, he was not willing to accept Hume's skeptical conclusion that all everyday beliefs are unfounded. Indeed, he used Hume's arguments for the opposite purpose of that intended. Whereas Hume argued that commonsense beliefs are indemonstrable in order to cast doubt upon them, Jacobi used the same point to show that they enjoy an immediate certainty that does not require demonstration. This is precisely where Jacobi betrayed his claim to be the legitimate heir of Hume. He retreated from the challenge of Hume's skepticism by granting an immediate certainty to the realm of faith. Insisting that this certainty is ineffable and inexplicable, Jacobi refused to answer Hume's skeptical question, How do I know this? It is difficult to resist the conclusion, then, that Hume would have dubbed his pietistic follower an 'enthusiast'.

· *Chapter 3* ·

Mendelssohn and the Pantheism Controversy

3.1. Mendelssohn's Place in the History of Philosophy

It is a sad legacy of our nonhistorical age that Moses Mendelssohn is now remembered only as the philosopher 'refuted' by Kant in the "Paralogismus" chapter of the first *Kritik*. This is no reputation for a thinker who was called "the Socrates of his age," and who was regarded as the leading light of the *Aufklärung* in Berlin. Mendelssohn's pivotal role in the *Aufklärung* is indisputable. Consider his famous friendship with Lessing and Nicolai, his influential essay "Was heisst aufklären?" his pioneering contributions to literary criticism in the *Allgemeine deutsche Bibliothek,* and his classic defense of religious freedom and tolerance, *Jerusalem*. Lessing had good reason for using Mendelssohn as the model for the character Nathan in his famous play *Nathan der Weise;* Mendelssohn was indeed a fitting symbol for his whole age.

The injustice of our contemporary image of Mendelssohn is all the more glaring, given Mendelssohn's influential role as a mediator between Judaism and modern secular culture. More than anyone before him, Mendelssohn deserves credit for bringing the Jew out of the ghetto and into the mainstream of modern culture.[1] In this respect Mendelssohn's impact on Jewish life has been compared to Luther's influence on the Germans.[2] Both Mendelssohn and Luther, it has been said, freed their people from the yoke of tradition and authority. What Luther did for the Germans vis-à-vis the Roman Catholic Church, Mendelssohn did for the Jews vis-à-vis Talmudism. An orthodox Jew himself, Mendelssohn was no apostle of assimilation. He wanted Jews to preserve their identity, to maintain their traditions, and to remain loyal to their religion. Nevertheless, he supported dialogue and symbiosis between German and Jew where each could learn from the other. Mendelssohn took two important steps toward this goal. First, he defended religious tolerance and freedom in his *Jerusalem,* a book that achieved widespread recognition.[3] And, second, he made the German language more accessible to Jews through his German translation of the Hebrew Bible. For Jewish life, Mendelssohn's translation is an achievement comparable in its consequences to Luther's translation two centuries before.[4]

Even granting Mendelssohn's historical importance, we might ask why Mendelssohn is important in the history of philosophy per se. Literary criticism, a translation of the Bible, and a defense of political causes do not amount to philosophy in a strict sense, some might say, and a contribution to the culture of a nation does not necessarily amount to a contribution to the history of philosophy. Is there really any reason for granting Mendelssohn a more exalted place in the history of philosophy proper, other than as the hapless thinker ruined by Kant?

If we consider the field of aesthetics and political philosophy alone, Mendelssohn deserves a small but secure place in the history of philosophy. Mendelssohn's aesthetics, often seen as his most important contribution to philosophy,[5] was a significant step away from Baumgarten and toward Kant and Schiller.[6] And Mendelssohn's political theory, as a defense of the liberal values of the *Aufklärung,* is comparable in stature to Kant's. As an apology for religious tolerance, Mendelssohn's *Jerusalem* is indeed on par with Locke's *Letter on Tolerance* and Spinoza's *Tractatus theologicus-politicus.*[7]

Paradoxically, however, Mendelssohn is remembered least in the field in which he originally made his reputation and which was most important to him: metaphysics. Most of his time and energy was devoted to metaphysics, and almost all of his main philosophical works were in this field. Mendelssohn is indeed the last figure in the rationalist metaphysical tradition, the tradition of Descartes, Spinoza, Leibniz, and Wolff. His metaphysical writings are among the very best in that tradition. They are stylistically impressive, displaying clarity, rigor, and elegance—Kant considered Mendelssohn's works to be "a model of philosophical precision"—and they are philosophically illuminating, explaining many of the fundamental ideas of the rationalist tradition.[8] What is left unsaid or vague by Leibniz or Wolff is often articulated and defended by Mendelssohn.[9] All too often, though, Mendelssohn has been reduced to a minor disciple of the Leibnizian-Wolffian school, to a mere *Popularphilosoph* who simply popularized Leibniz's esoteric and Wolff's academic philosophies.[10]

But Mendelssohn was not just another rationalist, one figure among others in a common school of thought. Rather, he deserves a special place within the rationalist tradition. He was the most modern of all the rationalists because he was aware of, and responded to, 'the crisis of metaphysics', its struggle to maintain its credentials as a science. Descartes and Spinoza, Leibniz and Wolff were writing at a time when metaphysics still had authority, largely due to the continuing influence of the scholastic tradition.

But Mendelssohn had to write for a later generation that had lost its faith in metaphysics. Toward the third quarter of the eighteenth century, even before the appearance of Kant's *Kritik,* metaphysics was coming under increasing criticism from several quarters: the skepticism of Hume and the French philosophes; the empiricism of Crusius's and Locke's followers in Germany; and the whole horde of *Popularphilosophen,* who simply had no time for rationalistic *Gründlichkeit.* Mendelssohn's reactions to these criticisms are interesting and important because they put forward the case for the metaphysical tradition itself. Indeed, Mendelssohn was not only aware of the problem of metaphysics: it was his lifelong preoccupation. The main goal of his "Prize Essay" (1763) was precisely to show that metaphysics is capable of attaining the scientific status of mathematics. Mendelssohn's last metaphysical work, his *Morgenstunden* (1785), was a continuation of his earlier concerns, a rehabilitated "Prize Essay" whose purpose was to meet two new threats to the metaphysical tradition: Kant and Jacobi.

The task of the present chapter is, of course, not to examine the length and breadth of Mendelssohn's achievement, but to focus on one phase and aspect of it: his defense of reason and the metaphysical tradition in *Morgenstunden.* Although the history of philosophy usually classifies Mendelssohn under the pre-Kantian tradition, seeing him as the last rationalist in the series from Leibniz to Wolff to Baumgarten, his *Morgenstunden* forms a necessary chapter in the history of post-Kantian philosophy. History itself forces us to make this classification. *Morgenstunden* was published after the first *Kritik;* and it was a reaction against Kant's and Jacobi's criticisms of the rationalist tradition. More important, though, philosophical justice demands that we present the case for the defense as well as the prosecution. We cannot evaluate Kant's and Jacobi's criticisms fairly unless we first see how the rationalist tradition was defended. Both historically and philosophically, then, we are obliged to treat Mendelssohn's *Morgenstunden* in the history of post-Kantian thought.

3.2. In Defense of Reason

The primary aim of *Morgenstunden* is to defend Mendelssohn's credo, his allegiance to reason as the final standard of truth in philosophy. *Morgenstunden* is more ostensibly an exposition and defense of the metaphysical tradition of Leibniz and Wolff. But it is important to see that these issues were inseparable for Mendelssohn. A defense of reason was for him tantamount to a defense of the possibility of Leibnizian-Wolffian metaphysics. Without demonstrative knowledge of God, the soul, providence, and immortality, the case for reason would collapse. Jacobi would be right: we would have to turn our back upon reason to keep our faith.

The foundation of Mendelssohn's faith in reason, the basis of his confidence in it as a standard of truth, is nothing less than his theory of judgment.[11] Like Leibniz and Wolff, Mendelssohn supports the theory that all judgments are in principle identical, so that their truth or falsity ultimately rests on the principle of contradiction. According to this theory, the predicate of a judgment only makes explicit what is already contained in 'the notion of the subject'. Although most judgments appear to be nonidentical from the standpoint of our ordinary knowledge, where we have only a confused knowledge of things, they would prove to be identical if we could sufficiently analyze what is involved in the notion of the subject. If we had the infinite understanding of God, who has a clear and complete knowledge of all things, then we would know everything as a necessary and eternal truth. Thus Mendelssohn likens the analysis of a judgment to the use of a magnifying glass: it makes clear and distinct what is obscure and confused; but it does not add anything new.

This theory of judgment has an extremely important consequence for the general theory of knowledge. Namely, it is possible, at least in principle, for reason to determine the truth or falsity of all metaphysical judgments. In order to do this, it only has to analyze the notion of the subject to see whether the predicate follows from it. Through this simple procedure, reason will provide a sufficient criterion of truth in metaphysics.

Although simple and beautiful, Mendelssohn's theory of judgment is also problematic. In his *David Hume* (1787), which is a reply to *Morgenstunden,* Jacobi raised one of the classical objections to Mendelssohn's theory: that it fails to distinguish between conceptual and real connection.[12] It assumes that the connection between subject and predicate is also a connection between cause and effect in nature, so that it appears as if reason gives us insight into the real connections of things. But this assumption is a delusion, Jacobi argues, since it conceals a fundamental difference between these two kinds of connection. The conceptual connection between subject and predicate is nontemporal because the subject is logically prior to the predicate. But all real connection between cause and effect is temporal because the cause is temporally prior to the effect. We cannot assume that the connection between cause and effect corresponds to that between subject and predicate, Jacobi further maintains, because it is logically possible to affirm the cause and to deny the effect. Hence Jacobi concludes that real succession, the connection between things in time, is incomprehensible to reason. To assume that everything is comprehensible according to reason, we have to deny the reality of time entirely, just as Spinoza does in the *Ethica*.

Jacobi's objection to Mendelssohn's theory had a noble ancestry behind it. The same point had been made against Wolff by Crusius in his *Ver-*

nunftwahrheiten (1745) and by Kant in his *Negativen Grössen* (1763).[13] The problem of causality had indeed become a powerful challenge to the rationalist tradition ever since Hume first raised the matter in his *Treatise* in 1739. 'If something is, then why should there be something else?'—that is how Kant in 1763 formulated the problem that would continue to preoccupy him until the first *Kritik*'s completion in 1781. Despite the age and gravity of the problem, Mendelssohn fails to address it in *Morgenstunden*. Here he restates more than he defends the classical theory of judgment. His failure to deal with this problem is indeed a grave weakness in his defense of reason in *Morgenstunden*.

In addition to the problem of causality, there is another difficulty in Mendelssohn's theory of judgment: what Lessing calls "the broad ugly ditch between possibility and reality, concept and existence." All truths found through the analysis of judgment are only hypothetical in form, Mendelssohn concedes, such that they tell us nothing about existence itself.[14] They are of the form 'If S, then P' where it is still an open question whether there is an S. Mendelssohn recognizes that the philosopher, unlike the mathematician, has to determine not only the relationships between concepts, but also whether these concepts have objects. The transition from concept to reality is indeed "the most difficult knot the philosopher has to untie"; unless he unties it, he runs the risk of playing with concepts that have no reference to reality.

Having seen Lessing's ditch, Mendelssohn still attempts to hurdle it. He thinks that reason can cross it, though only at definite points, namely, those where a concept is self-validating, or where it would be absurd to deny its referent.[15] We are told that there are only two such concepts. The first is the concept of a thinking being; and the second is the concept of the most perfect being, God. Here Mendelssohn has in mind Descartes's *cogito* and Anselm's ontological argument. Like Wolff, he adheres to modified versions of both these arguments.

Rather than strengthening his position, Mendelssohn's response to this difficulty only betrays its underlying weakness. Mendelssohn's defense of reason depends inter alia upon the claim that reason provides conclusions of existential import; but that claim in turn depends upon two very disputable arguments, the *cogito* and ontological argument. When Kant and Jacobi attack these arguments, Mendelssohn is forced to defend his position by engaging in scholastic subtleties. Such niceties, however, are not likely to convince a *Stürmer und Dränger* who questions the authority of all demonstrations in the first place.

An integral part of Mendelssohn's defense of reason is chapter 7 of *Morgenstunden*. It is here that Mendelssohn defends the *Aufklärung*'s ideal of objective inquiry—the need to investigate the truth regardless of interests and despite the consequences.

Mendelssohn's defense of objective inquiry takes the form of an attack on J. B. Basedow, an influential eighteenth-century educational theorist, whose philosophical claim to fame was his notion of 'the duty to believe' (*Glaubenspflicht*). According to Basedow, if a principle is necessary to moral conduct or human happiness, then we have a duty to believe it, even if we cannot establish its truth by purely rational means.[16] There is a patent similarity between Basedow's position and Kant's and Jacobi's; thus in criticizing Basedow, Mendelssohn was probably criticizing Kant and Jacobi as well.[17]

Mendelssohn makes the standard reply to all ideas like Basedow's: that they fail to distinguish between moral and intellectual standards.[18] He argues that all such ideas confuse moral and intellectual assent, that is, the reasons for accepting a belief as true (*Erkenntnisgründe*) and the reasons for morally approving and acting upon it (*Billigungsgründe*). In fact, these are completely distinct from each other. We cannot have a moral duty to believe in God, immortality, and providence, because we cannot be responsible for the truth or falsity of these beliefs. They are true or false apart from our will, so that it might be necessary to admit their falsity despite the moral consequences. The necessity of assenting to a belief is not 'moral' (*sittlich*) but 'physical' (*physisch*), in Mendelssohn's terms, since we have no choice concerning its truth or falsity. The sole duty of the philosopher with respect to belief, Mendelssohn declares, is the duty to investigate.

This argument is Mendelssohn's defense of metaphysics, or his way of saying that metaphysics is indispensable. According to this argument, to justify our moral and religious beliefs, we have to establish that they are true, or we have to acquire knowledge that they correspond to reality. It is not enough to establish that they are morally good or conducive to happiness. But the business of demonstrating our moral and religious beliefs—of acquiring knowledge of God, providence, and immortality—is metaphysics. Of course, Kant rejects metaphysics as too speculative. But, Mendelssohn would reply, if metaphysics is speculative, is it necessarily avoidable? The notion of a duty to believe is only an escape from the arduous task of investigation.

Mendelssohn admits that our investigation might not come to any definite conclusions. But he still thinks that there are more advantages to investigating truth without acquiring knowledge than to clinging to true beliefs without investigating them.[19] The problem with stubbornly adhering to beliefs—even true ones—without investigating the reasons for their truth is that it eventually leads to superstition, intolerance, and fanaticism. According to the natural cycle of things, Mendelssohn says, knowledge leads to contentment, contentment to laziness, and laziness to a failure to inquire;

but that neglect of inquiry ultimately results in superstition, intolerance, and fanaticism. If, then, we are to be cured of these vices, we have to revive the spirit of doubt and free inquiry.

What is important to Mendelssohn, then, is not so much what we believe, but how we believe—the reasons we give for our beliefs, our willingness to admit error, to consider opposing viewpoints and to continue investigation even though we are sure we are right. This is of course a cardinal principle of the *Aufklärung,* and especially of the Berlin circle centering on Lessing, Nicolai, and Mendelssohn. Lessing gave classic expression to it in the famous lines: "If God were holding all truth in his right hand and the erring search for it in his left, and then said 'Choose!' I would humbly fall upon his left hand and say, 'Father give! Pure truth is for thee alone.' "[20] In Mendelssohn's view the problem with a philosophy like Jacobi's is that it values what we believe more than how we believe, thus leading to all the dangers of intolerance, despotism, and dogmatism. A government that values dogma over freedom of thought will be likely to use coercion to maintain the moral and religious status quo.[21]

There is, however, an apparent circle in Mendelssohn's defense of objective inquiry. Mendelssohn is able to justify value-free inquiry only by using certain moral and political values, namely, those of liberalism. Hence it seems as if he has quit objective inquiry in order to justify it, or as if he has abandoned reason in order to defend it. This is of course precisely where Jacobi wants Mendelssohn, having to admit that his belief in reason is in the end only a *salto mortale* of its own.

But the question is whether this circle is a vicious one. And here the answer is not clear-cut. The problem has been thrown back another step. It now depends on whether or not we can determine the right or wrong, the good or evil, of Mendelssohn's political values by a process of sheer rational argument and objective inquiry. If not, Mendelssohn has to admit that his defense of objective inquiry is anything but objective. But if so, then the whole case for objective inquiry has moved into a new and hitherto unexpected field: that of political philosophy. In this case, Mendelssohn's defense of reason in *Morgenstunden* ultimately rests upon his defense of liberalism in *Jerusalem.*

3.3. Mendelssohn's Nightmare, or, the Method of Orientation

Although Mendelssohn disputes the validity of Jacobi's dilemma between reason and faith, he admits there is a prima facie conflict between philosophy and ordinary belief. He sees this as a conflict between 'common sense' (*Gemeinsinn*) and 'speculation' (*Spekulation*), however, and does not use the terms 'faith' (*Glaube*) or 'reason' (*Vernunft*).[22] Nevertheless, though the terms are different, the conflict is the same. Mendelssohn thinks that speculation stands in the same critical relationship to common sense as reason does to faith. Even the extension of Mendelssohn's 'common sense' and Jacobi's 'faith' is the same. Both terms are used in a broad sense, so that they refer to all the fundamental beliefs of morality, religion, and everyday life.[23]

Where Jacobi and Mendelssohn part company, of course, is over whether the conflict between philosophy and ordinary belief is resolvable. Mendelssohn affirms and Jacobi denies that the conflict is in principle resolvable. If philosophy leads to skepticism, then to Mendelssohn that means philosophy has gone astray somewhere in its speculations. According to him, common sense and speculation derive from a single source, and they are merely two forms of a single faculty: the faculty of reason (*Vernunft*). Whereas common sense is the intuitive form of reason, speculation is its discursive form. What common sense sees at a glance, speculation accounts for step by step through a syllogistic analysis into premise and conclusion. Although common sense is essentially rational, it is not self-conscious of the reasons for its beliefs. It is the task of speculation to bring these reasons to self-consciousness and to produce a discursive justification of the intuitions of common sense.

What happens, though, if the claims of common sense and speculation happen to contradict one another? What if philosophy fails to find a rationale for a belief of common sense and tells us to be skeptical about a belief that is necessary for the conduct of life? Mendelssohn is deeply worried by this question, so worried that he devotes an entire chapter to it in *Morgenstunden*.[24] His answer takes the form of an allegory.

After listening one evening to a tale about a journey through the Alps, Mendelssohn tells us, he had a strange dream. He dreamt that he too was traveling through the Alps, and that he had the aid of two guides. One guide was a Swiss rustic, who was strong and robust, but who had no subtle intellect; the other was an angel, who was gaunt and delicate, introspective and morbid. The guides came to a crossroads and went off in opposite directions, leaving poor Moses standing there completely confused. But he was soon rescued by the arrival of an elderly matron, who assured him that he would soon know the way. The matron revealed the identity of his two guides. The rustic went by the name of 'common sense' (*Gemeinsinn*), and the angel by the name of 'contemplation' (*Beschauung*). She then told him that it often happens that these characters disagree with each other and go off in opposite directions. But, she consoled him, they eventually return to the crossroads to have their conflicts settled by her. "So who are you?" Mendelssohn asked the matron. She said that on earth she went by the name of 'reason' (*Vernunft*), while in heaven she was called . . . At this point their conversation was interrupted by the arrival of a fanatical horde who had rallied around the angel of contemplation and who were threatening to overpower common sense and reason. They attacked with horrible screams. Mendelssohn then woke up in terror.

Mendelssohn thinks his dream contains some useful advice for the philosopher. If he wanders too far from the path of common sense, the philosopher ought to reorient himself. He should return to the crossroads where common sense and speculation part and compare their conflicting claims in the light of reason. Experience teaches the philosopher that right is usually on the side of common sense, and that speculation contradicts it only because of some error in its reasoning. Hence the philosopher should retrace his steps and find the error, so that there is agreement between common sense and speculation. This is Mendelssohn's famous 'method of orientation', which was later appropriated by Kant.

Although the method of orientation puts the burden of proof on the philosopher, Mendelssohn admits that there are times when speculation has right on its side. When reason cannot find any error in the demonstrations of speculation, no matter how carefully it retraces its steps, and when speculation is in a position to explain how the error of common sense arose, then Mendelssohn is willing to concede the argument to speculation. He recognizes that there are times when common sense will err because it is too hasty or careless in its judgment. Although common sense is a subconscious and intuitive form of reason, it does not follow that it is infallible. Indeed, it is precisely because common sense reasons in an intuitive and subconscious manner that it is so liable to go astray.

Looking at Mendelssohn's dream more closely, we find that it is really a confusing nightmare, concealing Mendelssohn's deep anxiety about the powerlessness of reason. The manifest content of Mendelssohn's dream, the method of orientation, conceals the horrors of its latent content, the fragile truce between philosophy and ordinary belief. The truth of the matter is that Mendelssohn subconsciously concedes a lot to Jacobi. By admitting that there can be a conflict between common sense and speculation where reason is on the side of speculation, Mendelssohn grants that Jacobi's dilemma is valid, if only in some cases.[25] Thus, the only difference between Jacobi and Mendelssohn is that Jacobi says reason always leads to nihilism, whereas Mendelssohn admits it sometimes results in it. What are we to do, though, in those cases where reason commands us to surrender a belief of common sense, and indeed a belief that is indispensable to morality and religion? What should I do, for example, if reason agrees with speculation that there are no grounds for the belief in the existence of other minds? If I am to act according to my reason, then I do not have to treat other beings with the same respect as I treat myself; but common sense, and indeed morality, vigorously protests against this policy. But if Mendelssohn is not willing to accept some of the nihilistic consequences of speculation—and consequences that have been examined and certified by reason—then does that not show that his commitment to common sense is nothing more than an irrational leap of faith in the manner of Jacobi? And, indeed, does not sticking with common sense against the better judgment of reason invite the very charges of fanaticism, dogmatism, and superstition that Mendelssohn levels against Jacobi?

There is yet another aspect to Mendelssohn's nightmare, which becomes apparent as soon as we raise the question, what is this figure of reason that so blithely settles the conflicts between speculation and common sense? If it is a faculty of criticism, a faculty that demands to know the reasons for our beliefs, then it amounts to nothing more than speculation. If, however, it is an intuitive faculty, a faculty that judges all issues according to "a natural light," then it is little more than common sense. We therefore do not seem to have any criterion for the identity of this mysterious faculty, a criterion that does not boil down to either of the very faculties whose disputes are to be settled. We are then left with a difficult question on our hands: on whose side is reason? That of common sense or speculation? This is an especially embarrassing question, given that reason is supposed to arbitrate the disputes between these faculties.

Assuming there is no third faculty of reason to mediate between common sense and speculation, we have to decide which faculty to follow in the case of a conflict. But here Mendelssohn offers us only the most confusing advice. He cannot decide which faculty deserves priority. Sometimes he says that we must trust our common sense and silence our reason until it returns to the fold of our ordinary beliefs.[26] The truths of natural religion remain unshakable to him, he confesses in his *An die Freunde Lessings,* even though all the demonstrations of the existence of God should fail.[27] We must not let the beliefs of morality and religion rest upon speculation or metaphysical argument, he insists, for that is to leave them dangling perilously, on the thinnest of threads. But is not this faith in common sense, and this mistrust in the demonstrations of reason, a betrayal of Mendelssohn's credo? At other times Mendelssohn says that the task of reason is 'to correct' common sense,[28] and he recognizes the possibility that common sense can err by not sufficiently investigating the reasons for its beliefs.[29] Indeed, in arguing against Basedow, Mendelssohn unequivocally takes his stand with speculation, steadfastly maintaining the necessity of pursuing an investigation despite the moral and religious consequences.

Mendelssohn's ambivalence here only reflects his awareness of the serious consequences of following one faculty at the expense of the other. He is trapped by the old dilemma of dogmatism or skepticism. If he follows his speculation alone, then he could arrive at skepticism, rejecting some of the essential beliefs of common sense, morality, and religion; but if he follows his common sense alone, then he might lapse into dogmatism, dismissing all inquiry and criticism as sophistry. In the case of a persistent conflict between speculation and common sense, Mendelssohn's method of orientation leaves us with no means of steering between these two dangerous extremes.

Predictably, Mendelssohn's ambivalence became a source of widespread dissatisfaction with his handling of the debate. There was the general feeling that, for better or worse, Mendelssohn had not unambiguously supported the sovereignty of reason. Kant argued that Mendelssohn, by sometimes siding with common sense against speculation, had betrayed his declared allegiance to reason. And Wizenmann pointed out that Mendelssohn's belief in common sense was not unlike Jacobi's leap of faith. So, for those who had cast their lot with reason, the problem still remained of how to defend its sovereignty while not making fatal concessions to common sense. We shall soon see how Kant tried to resolve this thorniest of problems.

3.4. The Critique of Spinozism and Purified Pantheism

An essential part of *Morgenstunden* is Mendelssohn's refutation of the Spinozists, his attack on the *Alleiner* in lectures 12, 14, and 15. The critique of the Spinozists has great importance for Mendelssohn because Jacobi uses Spinozism to threaten the authority of reason. Since Jacobi equates Spinozism with atheism and fatalism, his claim that all reason leads to Spinozism is tantamount to the claim that all reason ends in atheism and fatalism. Mendelssohn does not dispute Jacobi's point that Spinozism amounts to fatalism and atheism. Hence it is all the more imperative for him to refute Spinozism if he is to uphold the authority of reason. Only that will show that reason does not lead to atheism and fatalism.

Mendelssohn begins his refutation by defining Spinozism and pinpointing its differences from the deism of Leibniz and Wolff. Seeing Spinozism as a form of pantheism, Mendelssohn defines it as the doctrine that God is the only possible and necessary substance, and that everything else is a mere mode of him.[30] The Spinozist therefore believes that we and the world outside us have no substantial reality, that we are only modifications of the single infinite substance, God. Hence Mendelssohn sums up Spinozism with the pantheistic slogan used by Lessing during his conversations with Jacobi: *Hen kai pan*, 'One and All'.

Using the method of orientation that he outlined in an earlier lecture, Mendelssohn then raises the question "Where did we start from?"[31] Where did the pantheist and deist start from, and where do they part? Where do they agree with each other, and what is the source of the conflict between them? According to Mendelssohn, the pantheist and deist both agree to several propositions: (1) that the necessary being has self-knowledge, that is, it knows itself as a necessary being; (2) that finite things form an infinite series without beginning or end; and (3) that finite beings depend for their existence on God, and that their essence cannot be conceived apart from him. But where the pantheist and deist part company, Mendelssohn says, is over the question whether finite things have a substantial existence apart from God. The deist affirms and the pantheist denies that finite things are distinct substances apart from God. What the deist sees as distinct substances, the pantheist regards as modes of a single substance. Hence Mendelssohn sees the issue between the deist and the pantheist as a conflict between monism and pluralism.

Mendelssohn's first strategy against the Spinozist is therefore to examine Spinoza's argument for the necessity of monism.[32] Borrowing a point from Wolff's critique of Spinoza,[33] Mendelssohn claims that this argument rests upon an arbitrary definition of substance. We can readily agree with Spinoza, he says, that if independent existence is a necessary condition of substance, then there can be only one substance, the infinite being itself; for only that which is infinite cannot depend on anything else in order to exist. But it is arbitrary, Mendelssohn then insists, to consider independence as a necessary condition of substance. What we normally mean by substance is simply some being with a permanent essence or nature that remains the same despite changes in its accidents. And it is consistent with the permanent nature of such a being that it still depends on things in order to exist. It is therefore necessary to distinguish between the independent (*das Selbständige*) and the subsistent (*das Fürsichbestehende*). Although there can be only one entity that is independent, since only the infinite does not depend on anything else in order to exist, there can be many entities that are subsistent.

Mendelssohn admits that this objection still falls short of a refutation of Spinoza. It affects only Spinoza's demonstrations, but none of his main doctrines.[34] To refute these doctrines, we must show their incapacity to explain some indisputable features of our ordinary experience. But Mendelssohn thinks that he has an argument that establishes just that.[35] He asks the reader to consider the following points. Spinoza makes thought and extension into the two attributes of divine substance. He sees extension as the essence of matter and thought as the essence of mind. But, Mendelssohn retorts, there is more to matter than extension, and there is more to mind than thought. Matter also consists in motion; and the mind also consists in will and judgment.[36] Now Spinoza cannot explain these additional features of the mind and body, Mendelssohn argues, because they cannot have their origin in his single infinite substance. This substance cannot be the source of motion since it is the universe as a whole, and the universe as a whole cannot change its place and therefore cannot be in motion. Similarly, this substance cannot be the source of desire or judgment, since Spinoza expressly denies that we can attribute such human characteristics as will, desire, and judgment to God. Hence, Mendelssohn concludes, we have to reject Spinozism because of its failure to account for two fundamental features of experience: the motion of matter, and the presence of the faculties of desire and judgment in the mind. We cannot simply dismiss these aspects of our experience as illusions of the imagination, as Spinoza wishes to, because we would still have to explain the origin of such illusions.

At this point, just as the deist seems to be overwhelming the pantheist with objections, Mendelssohn allows the argument to take a surprising turn against himself. At the beginning of lecture 14 he introduces his friend Lessing to defend a new and more powerful version of pantheism, or what Mendelssohn calls 'purified pantheism'. "What you have at most refuted is Spinoza, but not Spinozism," Mendelssohn has Lessing say. In the ensuing imaginary dialogue between Lessing and Mendelssohn, Lessing happily concedes all of Mendelssohn's earlier objections. But he insists that a Spinozist can admit these points and still maintain his essential thesis: that all things exist in God. Purified pantheism avoids two of Spinoza's mistakes: it does not deny volition to God, and it does not attribute extension to him. The God of the purified pantheist is a strictly spiritual being, having both intellect and will but no extension. He is indeed extremely similar to the God of Leibniz and Wolff: he has an infinite intellect, which conceives all possible worlds in the clearest possible manner; and he chooses that world which is the best possible. Despite this similarity, there is still a serious point of disagreement between the deist and pantheist. Whereas the deist asserts that God, having chosen the best of all possible worlds, grants an independent existence to it outside the divine mind, the pantheist denies it such existence. According to the purified pantheist, all things exist only in the infinite intellect of God and have no existence other than as objects of his ideas. "If I understand you correctly," Mendelssohn asks Lessing, "then you admit a God outside the world, but deny a world outside God, making God as it were into an infinite egoist." Lessing admits that this is indeed his view.

Although Mendelssohn believes that Lessing's purified pantheism does not have the morally damaging consequences of Spinozism, he is not ready to embrace it.[37] He spends the rest of lecture 14 expounding his objections against it. The fatal weakness of purified pantheism, Mendelssohn argues, is that it fails to distinguish between God's concept of a thing and that thing itself. It is necessary to make such a distinction, however, since God's concept of a finite thing is infinite and perfect while the thing itself is finite and imperfect. To refuse to make this distinction is to deny God's perfection by putting finite and imperfect things inside his mind. As Mendelssohn summarizes his point, "It is one thing to have a limitation, to be limited; and it is another thing to know the limitation possessed by a being distinct from us. The most perfect being knows my weaknesses; but he does not have them."[38]

The wider problem that Mendelssohn has in mind here is fundamental for any form of pantheism. Namely, if God is perfect and infinite, and if the world is imperfect and finite, then how can God be in the world or the world in God? This problem was to haunt the pantheistic generation after Mendelssohn. Herder, Schelling, and Hegel all struggled to find a solution to it.[39] Even the most purified of pantheists could not come away from *Morgenstunden* without some nagging doubts on his philosophical conscience.

3.5. Mendelssohn's Covert Critique of Kant

Mendelssohn's critique of pantheism in *Morgenstunden* is of course a disguised attack on Jacobi. But there is someone else behind the lines in *Morgenstunden,* someone who is just as important to Mendelssohn as Jacobi, though his name is also never mentioned. This figure is none other than Kant. Although Mendelssohn admits in his preface that he has not been able to study the *Kritik,*[40] it is still evident from many passages—either from the use of Kantian language or from the Kantian nature of the position—that he has Kant in mind.[41] It is not difficult to understand why Mendelssohn wants to discuss Kant, who is as much a threat to his metaphysics as Jacobi. Indeed, to Mendelssohn, Kant and Jacobi each represent the two horns of a dilemma: dogmatism versus skepticism, or mysticism versus nihilism. Jacobi is a dogmatist or mystic since his *salto mortale* evades the demands of criticism; Kant is the skeptic or nihilist since he destroys the metaphysics necessary to justify moral and religious belief.[42] To vindicate his rationalist metaphysics, Mendelssohn has to show that it is the only middle path between these extremes; but that means he must settle his accounts with Kant as well as Jacobi. The struggle with Kant would have to be a silent one, though, since Mendelssohn was already too old and frail to risk a contest with Jacobi, let alone such a formidable opponent as Kant.

Mendelssohn's hidden quarrel with Kant occupies a place of central importance in *Morgenstunden:* the discussion of idealism in the first seven chapters, which is the very heart of the book.[43] Kant's idealism is the main danger of his philosophy, in Mendelssohn's view. It is an affront to common sense and a threat to morality and religion. How can we act in the world, how can we perform our obligations, and how can we worship a God, if we think everything consists only in representations? Mendelssohn's interpretation of Kant's idealism is typical of the *Popularphilosophie* of his day.[44] Like Garve, Feder, and Weishaupt, Mendelssohn sees no essential difference between Kant's and Berkeley's idealism. Whether Kantian or Berkeleyan, the idealist maintains that nothing exists but spiritual substances; and he denies the existence of an external object corresponding to his representations.[45] Mendelssohn also wrongly assumes—again with Garve, Feder, and Weishaupt—that Kant does not affirm but denies the existence of things-in-themselves.

Mendelssohn's case against idealism largely consists in inductive arguments for the reality of the external world. There cannot be a logically certain inference from all the evidence of the senses to the existence of the external world, Mendelssohn realizes, but he thinks that such inferences are capable of "a high degree of probability."[46] All our inductive inferences about the existence of the external world rest upon evidence from the correspondence or agreement of perceptions. If all the senses agree with one another, and if the experiences of several observers agree with one another, and if, finally, observers with different sense organs also agree with one another, then it is probable, even if not logically certain, that the object of perceptions continues to exist. The more often we perceive something the more likely that it is in fact the case.

Although Kant, despite early plans, did not write a reply to *Morgenstunden*, it is not difficult to imagine his reaction to Mendelssohn's arguments.[47] Resting upon the legitimacy of inductive inference, they beg the question against Hume's skepticism. According to Hume, the fact that we have always perceived something in the past gives us no reason to assume that we will continue to perceive it in the future.[48] Although Kant attempts to reply to this point in the transcendental deduction of the first *Kritik*, Mendelssohn simply ignores it in *Morgenstunden*. Kant's readiness to reply to Hume is indeed one of the major strengths of his philosophy over Mendelssohn's.[49]

The last lecture of *Morgenstunden*, lecture 17, also silently takes issue with Kant. Here Mendelssohn makes a brave attempt to rescue the ontological argument after Kant's attack on it in the *Kritik*. In his 1763 "Prize Essay" Mendelssohn presented a new version of the ontological argument by avoiding the concept of existence and using instead the concepts of nonexistence and dependence, which he felt were not so fraught with difficulties.[50] Although many of his contemporaries, notably Kant and Jacobi, were unconvinced in 1763, Mendelssohn still thinks in 1785 that his argument is as valid as ever. His confidence in the argument remains unshaken because he thinks that it avoids Kant's objections to the concept of existence.[51]

Mendelssohn does not simply restate his old argument, however; he also makes two replies to Kant's criticisms. His first reply is that the inference from possibility to reality, from essence to existence, is valid in one case only, and that is with the one and only infinite being, God.[52] There is a difference in kind between the nature of finite and infinite being, such that existence is necessary to the essence of a perfect and infinite being, but is not necessary to the essence of an imperfect and finite being. Now Kant ignores this point in his critique of the ontological argument, Mendelssohn suggests, because he surreptitiously assumes that the distinction between possibility and reality in the case of a finite being applies *mutatis mutandis* in the case of an infinite being. Hence all his examples that are to prove the distinction between essence and existence are taken from finite beings, for example, the notorious case of the one hundred talers. But while the essence of one hundred measly talers does not involve its existence, as Kant argues, the essence of God does involve his existence, for his essence is incomparably more perfect than that of one hundred talers.

Mendelssohn's second reply to Kant's criticisms claims the ontological argument is not affected by Kant's argument that existence is not a predicate. Assuming that existence is not a predicate but only the affirmation or positing of all the properties of a thing, it is impossible to think of the essence of the infinite being without positing or affirming all its properties. There is indeed still a difference between the contingent existence of the finite and the necessary existence of the infinite. Namely, the infinite is that which of necessity posits all its properties, while the finite is that which might not posit all its properties.[53] In Mendelssohn's view, then, the inference from the infinite or most perfect being to existence is not affected by how we analyze the concept of existence.

If we look back over his contribution to the pantheism controversy, it is difficult to resist the conclusion that, despite his noble intentions, Mendelssohn had weakened the case for reason more than he had strengthened it. He made the case for reason dependent on the claims of rationalist metaphysics; but these claims were, to say the least, very disputable. He assumed that reason could be a sufficient criterion of truth in metaphysics only if the rationalist theory of judgment were correct; but that theory had serious weaknesses, namely, it could not explain real connection or guarantee conclusions of existential significance. Mendelssohn had also based some central moral and religious beliefs—the beliefs in God, providence, and immortality—upon a priori demonstrations. But these demonstrations were severely criticized by Kant in the first *Kritik;* and Mendelssohn's failure to reply to Kant in any thorough and rigorous fashion left his entire position exposed. So, in the end, it seemed as if Mendelssohn had imperiled, rather than defended, two fundamental claims of reason: its claim to be a sufficient criterion of truth in metaphysics; and its claim to justify our essential moral and religious beliefs.

Another serious weakness of Mendelssohn's defense of reason was that, at bottom, it failed to address the deeper problem that Jacobi had raised. In summoning the ghost of Spinoza, Jacobi was alluding to the apparent fatalistic and atheistic consequences of modern science. It was indeed these consequences of modern science that so deeply disturbed late eighteenth-century thinkers. Mendelssohn did little to allay these fears, however, with his antique Wolffian-style refutation of Spinoza. For what was at stake was not the geometric demonstrations of Spinoza's system, but the naturalistic spirit behind it.

There was also the nagging suspicion that Mendelssohn had betrayed the very credo he set out to defend. His moral and religious beliefs meant more to him than his reason, which he was willing to abandon should it continue to contradict them. That, at any rate, was the sad lesson to be learned from his method of orientation. It seemed that, when the going got rough, Mendelssohn was really on Jacobi's side. Who, then, was going to defend the cause of reason?

Given Mendelssohn's poor showing, it was crucial that someone else enter into the fray to defend the crumbling authority of reason. A new defense was needed that did not repeat Mendelssohn's mistakes. It would have to separate the case for reason from the claims of metaphysics; it would have to respond to the deeper challenge behind Jacobi's Spinozism; and it would have to take an unambiguous stand in favor of reason. It was the destiny of Kant to undertake just such a defense. We shall soon see how his defense fared at the hands of Jacobi and his allies.

· *Chapter 4* ·

Kant, Jacobi, and Wizenmann in Battle

4.1. Thomas Wizenmann's *Resultate*

In May 1786, six months after the publication of Mendelssohn's *Morgenstunden* and Jacobi's *Briefe*, a strange anonymous tract appeared that was to have an important effect upon the course of the pantheism controversy. Its title was striking and cryptic: *Die Resultate der Jacobischer und Mendelssohnischer Philosophie von einem Freywilligen.* This tract created a stir through its passionate and provocative tone, and it helped to convince a wider public of the importance of the controversy.[1] Who, though, was this 'volunteer' *(Freywilligen)*? There was much speculation about his identity, and for a while rumor had it that he was none other than Herder.[2] But in a short time the truth came out: the author was the little-known, but extremely gifted friend of Jacobi, Thomas Wizenmann.

On many points, though certainly not all, Wizenmann sided with Jacobi in the pantheism controversy. He agreed with Jacobi that all philosophy ends in Spinozism, and that we can avoid atheism and fatalism only through a *salto mortale*.[3] Nonetheless, Wizenmann still insisted—rightly—that he was no mere disciple of Jacobi, and that he arrived at his position through independent reflection.[4] This is surely the clue to the term 'volunteer' that appears in his title. Wizenmann chose this term in order to stress that he was not a recruit of Jacobi's.[5] And, indeed, his claim to independence vindicates itself time and again in his work. Wizenmann often came forward with new ideas, and he frequently defended Jacobi with fresh arguments. At times, furthermore, he was sharply critical of Jacobi on several points, as we shall soon see.

Wizenmann made several important contributions to the pantheism controversy. First, he clarified the state of the controversy, explaining the similarities and differences between Jacobi and Mendelssohn. It was particularly helpful that he pointed out the hidden irrationalism in Mendelssohn's position. Second, he did much to give Jacobi's position a fairer hearing. This was necessary since the Berliners were all too keen on dismissing Jacobi as a mere *Schwärmer* along the lines of Lavater. Third, he raised the whole tone of the controversy by ignoring the personal, biographical, and exegetical issues and by concentrating on the philosophical ones. This too was a timely deed since, during the spring of 1786, Jacobi's and Mendelssohn's friends were hurling mud at one another at an alarming rate and losing sight of all their original philosophical interests.

What, more than anything else, ensures Wizenmann a short but safe place in the history of philosophy is his impact on Kant. The *Resultate* was the starting point for Kant's reflections on the pantheism controversy. It was indeed Wizenmann who convinced Kant that Jacobi and Mendelssohn were both heading in the dangerous direction of irrationalism, and that something had to be done about it.[6] Wizenmann's later dispute with Kant was also important for Kant because it forced him to clarify his doctrine of practical faith for the second *Kritik*.[7] If one bothers to read behind the lines of the second *Kritik*, then it becomes clear that several of its concluding sections are covert polemics against Wizenmann. Kant himself recognized Wizenmann's merits, his rare combination of honesty, clarity, and philosophical depth. When Wizenmann died tragically at the age of twenty-seven, at the very height of the controversy, Kant paid him a generous and deserved tribute. "The death of such a fine and clear mind is to be regretted," he wrote in the second *Kritik*.[8] It has even been said that Wizenmann's untimely death was "a serious loss to German philosophy."[9]

The central polemical result of the *Resultate* is that, ultimately, there is no essential difference between Jacobi's and Mendelssohn's views on the authority of reason.[10] All that prevents these philosophers from agreeing with each other, Wizenmann argues, is a serious inconsistency in Mendelssohn's position. Although Mendelssohn declares that he recognizes no standard of truth other than reason, he also says that reason must orient itself according to common sense. But how is it possible, Wizenmann asks, for reason to be the supreme authority in metaphysics *and* for common sense to be its guide?

According to Wizenmann, there is a fatal ambiguity in Mendelssohn's position concerning the relationship between common sense and reason.[11] Sometimes Mendelssohn assumes that the knowledge of common sense is identical with reason, so that it is only an intuitive form of reason; but at other times he supposes that it is distinct from reason, so that it guides and corrects reason in its speculation. But both of these options are unsatisfactory. In the first case we can no longer use common sense to direct and discipline reason when it goes astray in speculation; for by definition reason only explains and demonstrates the intuitions of common sense. In the second case we can continue to use common sense to guide and correct reason; but then we forfeit the sovereignty of reason. We will be forced to endorse beliefs that are contrary to reason in those cases where speculation contradicts common sense. Assuming that Mendelssohn plumps for the latter of these uncomfortable options, as he seems to do in *Morgenstunden,* then there is indeed little difference between his notion of common sense and Jacobi's concept of faith. Both Jacobi's faith and Mendelssohn's common sense give intuitive insights that transcend the explication and demonstration of reason, and that demand assent even when reason contradicts them.

Having shown the inconsistency in Mendelssohn's position, Wizenmann then proceeds to attack Mendelssohn's method of orientation. He rejects this method because, like Kant, he cannot accept its underlying standard of truth, common sense. Wizenmann makes all the usual objections against common sense: that it is full of contradictions, that it is often mistaken, and that it does not go beyond mere appearances to explain the cause of things.[12] Although he is in general eager to limit the powers of reason, particularly with regard to religion, Wizenmann still insists upon granting reason sovereignty over common sense. In this respect he feels that he is more loyal to reason than Mendelssohn. Rather than guiding reason by common sense, Mendelssohn should allow reason to guide it, Wizenmann contends,[13] for does he not claim that he recognizes no standard of truth higher than reason? By giving priority to common sense, however, Mendelssohn lays himself open to the same charge that he makes against Jacobi: he admits a 'blind faith' that is beyond all criticism. This critical stance toward common sense is one of Wizenmann's more important differences from Jacobi, who always puts the beliefs of common sense on a par with the certainties of faith.

Wizenmann's criticism of common sense does raise a serious problem for his general polemic against Mendelssohn. Namely, if reason has the right to criticize common sense, and if it is true that Mendelssohn's common sense and Jacobi's faith are essentially the same, then why should not reason also have the right to criticize faith? Why should faith be immune from criticism when common sense is not? All this raises the even more basic question: what is wrong with Mendelssohn's claim that reason has the right to criticize faith?

It is to Wizenmann's credit that he squarely faces this difficulty, and his answer to it is interesting because it resembles Kant's position in the pantheism controversy. Wizenmann claims that there is an important difference between Jacobi and Mendelssohn concerning their justification of moral and religious belief.[14] Whereas Mendelssohn attempts to give a theoretical justification of belief by attributing immediate knowledge to common sense, Jacobi tries to prove a practical justification by showing the genesis of belief in the will. It is the essence of Jacobi's position, Wizenmann asserts, that faith is not a claim to knowledge, but a demand of the heart.[15] According to Jacobi, we acquire faith not by gaining knowledge, but by having the right disposition and performing the right actions.

Now Wizenmann thinks that this practical concept of faith solves the problem at hand, clearing away the apparent inconsistency involved in demanding a criticism of common sense but not faith. It is unfair to criticize faith but not common sense, Wizenmann contends, because it is the task of reason to criticize claims to knowledge, while it is certainly not its province to criticize the demands of the will. A practical demand about what ought to be the case is just not subject to verification or falsification like theoretical claims about what is the case.[16]

It is one of the merits of the *Resultate* that Wizenmann puts forward a simple and powerful argument in favor of positive religion. Where Jacobi is vague and merely suggestive, Wizenmann is clear and bluntly argumentative. His argument is especially interesting since it begins with Kantian premises and then draws fideistic conclusions from them. In the hands of the pietists an essentially Kantian-style epistemology becomes a powerful weapon in humbling the claims of reason and uplifting those of faith.

The main premise of Wizenmann's argument is his definition of reason, which he explicitly states at the very beginning. According to this definition, which is truly Kantian in spirit, the task of reason is *to relate* facts, that is, to compare and contrast them, or to infer them from one another. But it cannot create or reveal facts, which must be given to it. Appealing to Kant's criticism of the ontological argument,[17] Wizenmann advances the general thesis that it is not possible for reason to demonstrate the existence of anything. If we are to know that something exists, then it has to be given to us in experience. Of course, it is possible *to infer* the existence of something, but only when the existence of something else is already known. All inferences are only hypothetical in form, Wizenmann explains, such that we can infer the existence of one thing only if another is already given. Hence Wizenmann concludes in the manner of Kant that there is a twofold source of knowledge: experience, which gives us knowledge of matters of fact; and reason, which relates these facts through inference.[18]

On the basis of this Kantian definition and distinction, Wizenmann builds his case for positive religion. If we know that God exists, then we cannot know it through reason, which cannot demonstrate the existence of anything. Rather, we must know it through experience. But what kind of experience gives us knowledge of God? There is only one kind that gives us such knowledge, Wizenmann insists, and that is revelation. The basis of all religion is therefore positive, resting upon the belief in God's revelation.[19] Thus Wizenmann comes to the dramatic conclusion that there is either positive religion or no religion. As he puts it in these stirring lines: "Either no religion or positive religion. Men of Germany! I challenge you to find a more correct and impartial judgment of reason. Is from my side another relationship to God possible other than through faith, trust and obedience? And can from God's side another relationship to me be possible other than through revelation, command and promise?"[20]

The *Resultate* is particularly interesting since it introduces a new note of skepticism into the pantheism controversy. While Mendelssohn rests his case with reason, and while Jacobi makes his stand with intuition, Wizenmann accepts neither of these standards of truth. He questions not only Mendelssohn's trust in reason, but also Jacobi's faith in intuition. In a remarkably candid passage in the *Resultate*, Wizenmann doubts whether there are any intuitions or feelings that give us an immediate knowledge of the existence of God.[21] Although he admits the possibility of such intuitions, he argues that they will never provide sufficient proof for the existence of God. They will never completely reveal the nature of God, he maintains, because any experience of a human being is finite and therefore inadequate to the infinitude of God.[22] Rather than attempting, like Jacobi, to justify faith as a peculiar form of immediate knowledge, Wizenmann insists that we have to rest content with mere belief, and in particular the belief in God's revelation in history.[23] This is a belief that has to be accepted on trust, the trust in those who first witnessed such supernatural events.

Sadly, this skeptical strand in Wizenmann's philosophy remained largely unexplored due to his untimely death in February 1787. Nevertheless, Wizenmann lived long enough to articulate explicitly the skeptical direction of his thought. In a letter to Jacobi written just six months before his death, Wizenmann expressly declared that the best philosophy is not Spinozism but skepticism: "Spinoza's philosophy is the only consistent one, if one must have a naturalistic philosophy of God. But much better is skepticism, which makes no claim to such knowledge. Skepticism is my proper and explicit position."[24]

4.2. Kant's Contribution to the Pantheism Controversy

It was not easy for Kant to stay out of the pantheism controversy. Both sides to the dispute saw Kant as their ally, and both did their best to cajole him into fighting for their cause. Hamann and Jacobi were especially eager to gain Kant for their 'party of faith'. In his *Wider Mendelssohns Beschuldigungen,* Jacobi had already surreptitiously attempted to enlist Kant on his side by citing him as another philosopher of faith.[25] And during the autumn of 1785, Hamann encouraged Kant in his plans to launch an attack on Mendelssohn's *Morgenstunden.*[26] But Mendelssohn and his sympathizers were no less active in soliciting his support. On October 16, 1785 Mendelssohn himself wrote Kant, summarizing his version of events and insinuating that he was on Kant's side in the struggle against "intolerance and fanaticism."[27] Then in February 1786, only a month after Mendelssohn's death, two of his allies, Marcus Herz and Johann Biester, pushed Kant to enter the fray against Jacobi and to avenge poor Moses' death. As if this was not enough pressure, two of Kant's young disciples, C. G. Schütz and L. H. Jakob, wrote Kant in the spring of 1786 also urging him to join battle.[28] Interestingly enough, they saw Mendelssohn, not Jacobi, as Kant's great foe. They warned Kant that the Wolffians were closing ranks around Mendelssohn and 'singing a song of triumph' over the defeat of criticism.

What was Kant's attitude toward the controversy raging around him? Initially, it was one of ambivalence, reflecting Kant's desire to support and refute both Mendelssohn and Jacobi. Vis-à-vis Mendelssohn, Kant had good reason to feel ambivalent. He could neither accept Mendelssohn's dogmatic metaphysics nor reject his defense of reason. These mixed feelings toward Mendelssohn then led to some wavering in his plans. In November 1785 Kant intended to attack *Morgenstunden,* which he regarded as a "masterpiece of dogmatic metaphysics."[29] But by April 1786 Kant's plans were not to bury Mendelssohn but to praise him. Kant decided to write a piece for the *Berlinische Monatsschrift* in honor of Mendelssohn and his *Jerusalem.*[30] A tribute to *Jerusalem* could mean only one thing: that Kant was siding with Mendelssohn on the point that reason is the ultimate arbiter of truth in metaphysics and religion.

Vis-à-vis Jacobi, Kant's attitude was no less ambivalent. He felt some affinity with Jacobi, given their common disenchantment with metaphysics. He told Hamann, for example, that he was "perfectly satisfied" with Jacobi's *Briefe* and that he had nothing against Jacobi using his name in *Wider Mendelssohns Beschuldigungen.*[31] But Kant was still no 'silent admirer' of Jacobi and had plans to attack him just as he did Mendelssohn.[32] Thus he wrote Herz on April 7, 1786 that he might write an essay for the *Berlinische Monatsschrift* exposing Jacobi's 'chicanery'.[33]

Kant was finally goaded into action on June 11, 1786, when Biester wrote him with another of his entreaties.[34] On the face of it, there is not much new in Biester's June 11 appeal, which again warns Kant of the dangers of the new *Schwärmerei,* and which again begs him to say a word against it.

Kant had heard this refrain before, and indeed on two occasions from Biester alone.[35] But this time Biester hit upon a new tactic. He insinuated that Kant had a grave political responsibility to enter the controversy. A 'change' was likely to take place soon, Biester said, referring to the sad state of Frederick II's health and the imminent succession of Frederick Wilhelm II. There was a great deal of anxiety in liberal circles in Berlin and Prussia at this time about whether freedom of the press would be maintained or a new censorship imposed. Kant shared in this anxiety. He always appreciated the liberal policies of Frederick II—the age of Enlightenment was the age of Frederick, in his opinion—and any reimposition of censorship would be bound to affect a professor of philosophy who was holding a public office. Now Biester knew about Kant's anxiety and exploited it. What would the public think—and, more to the point, Frederick II and his ministers—if 'the first philosopher of the land' were accused of supporting 'a dogmatic fanatical atheism'? That was the accusation that the Berliners were hurling against Jacobi, and many people thought that Kant was on Jacobi's side after Jacobi cited him in *Wider Mendelssohns Beschuldigungen*. So if Kant did not say something soon, then he would be tarred with Jacobi's brush. Even worse, remaining silent certainly would not give the new monarch a good opinion of the consequences of a free press. The die had now been cast. Kant had to enter the controversy to uphold the dignity of the free press, "the only treasure that remains for us amid all civil burdens."[36]

In October 1786 the *Berlinische Monatsschrift* finally came out with Kant's contribution to the pantheism controversy, the short essay "Was heisst: Sich im Denken orientiren?" Although it is little read, this essay is extremely important for a general understanding of Kant's philosophy. It provides us with what we find almost nowhere else in Kant's writings: a settling of accounts with mysticism and the philosophy of common sense. To locate Kant's philosophy in relation to competing contemporary systems, it is necessary to consider it as the alternative not only to Hume's skepticism and Leibniz's rationalism, but also to Jacobi's mysticism and Mendelssohn's philosophy of common sense. When Kant challenged Hume and Leibniz, he could always take for granted one important assumption: that reason is the final standard of truth in philosophy. But when he took issue with Jacobi and Mendelssohn, he was forced to examine and justify just this assumption. Hence the importance of Kant's essay is that it reveals the motivation and justification behind his allegiance to reason.

In this essay Kant takes a middle position between Jacobi and Mendelssohn. He accepts some of their principles but refuses to draw such drastic conclusions from them. On the one hand, he agrees with Jacobi that knowledge cannot justify faith; but he disagrees with his conclusion that reason cannot justify it. On the other hand, he concurs with Mendelssohn that it is necessary to justify faith through reason; but he does not accept the conclusion that to justify faith through reason demands knowledge.

What allows Kant to steer a middle path between Jacobi and Mendelssohn is his denial of one of their common premises: that reason is a faculty of knowledge, a theoretical faculty whose purpose is to know things-in-themselves or the unconditioned. Resting his case upon the central thesis of the second *Kritik,* which would appear only fourteen months later in January 1788, Kant assumes that reason is a practical faculty: it does not describe the unconditioned, but prescribes it as an end of conduct. Reason prescribes the unconditioned in either of two senses: when it commands us to seek the final condition for a series of conditions in nature; or when it commands us categorically to perform certain actions, regardless of our interests and circumstances. In both these cases the unconditioned is not an entity that we know, but an ideal for our conduct, whether that be scientific inquiry or moral action. By thus separating reason from knowledge, Kant creates the opportunity for a rational justification of faith independent of metaphysics.

At the very heart of Kant's essay is his concept of 'rational faith' *(Vernunftglaube).* This he defines as faith based solely on reason.[37] All faith is rational in the minimal sense that it must not contradict reason, Kant states, but rational faith is peculiar in that it is based only on reason (as opposed to tradition or revelation). It is based on reason alone because it requires nothing more for its assent than the categorical imperative, the logical consistency of a maxim as a universal law. Here Kant implies that the categorical imperative provides a sufficient foundation for our belief in God, providence, and immortality, although it is only in the second *Kritik* that he actually engages in the details of such a deduction.[38]

Even though Kant, like Jacobi, denies that faith must be justified by knowledge, it is important to see that his rational faith is the diametrical opposite of Jacobi's *salto mortale.* While Kant's rational faith is based on reason alone, Jacobi's *salto mortale* is contrary to reason. Noting just this point, Kant flatly dismisses Jacobi's *salto mortale.*[39] He argues that it is absurd, not to say perverse, to believe that P when reason demonstrates that not-P.

Although based on reason alone, Kant still insists that rational faith amounts not to knowledge, but only to belief *(Fürwahrhalten).* He expresses this point by saying that 'faith' is 'subjectively' sufficient, but 'objectively' insufficient, belief.[40] It is 'subjectively' sufficient in the sense that it is based upon the universality and necessity of the categorical imperative, which holds for every rational being; but it is 'objectively' insufficient in the sense that it is not based on knowledge of things-in-themselves.

Armed with this concept of rational faith, Kant walks down his middle path between Mendelssohn's dogmatism and Jacobi's mysticism. Since rational faith does not presuppose knowledge of things-in-themselves, it avoids Mendelssohn's dogmatism; and since it is based on the rationality of the categorical imperative, it escapes Jacobi's irrational mysticism.

Kant's essay not only outlines his position in relation to Jacobi's and Mendelssohn's but also subjects their positions to severe criticism. Kant makes one basic point against both Jacobi and Mendelssohn: that they are both guilty of undermining reason, which must remain the final criterion of truth in philosophy. What Jacobi does intentionally against reason Mendelssohn does unintentionally. But the effect is the same: they advocate a faculty of knowledge whose insights stand above all the criticism of reason. The choice between Jacobi and Mendelssohn is therefore a choice between two species of irrationalism, one of common sense and another of faith. Thus Kant implies that the critical philosophy alone upholds the authority of reason.

In Kant's eyes there can be no question that Jacobi is guilty of irrationalism.[41] Jacobi tells us that Spinozism is the only consistent philosophy; but then he advocates a *salto mortale* to avoid its atheism and fatalism. It is not so plain, however, that Mendelssohn is guilty of this charge. Indeed, is it not his intention to defend reason? Kant notes Mendelssohn's intentions, and duly praises them.[42] But, like Wizenmann, he thinks that Mendelssohn unwittingly betrays his own ideals. The ambiguities of his concept of common sense lead him astray, so that he sometimes sees common sense as a special faculty of knowledge that has the power to correct reason. But to attribute a power of intuition to common sense, and then to give it priority over reason in cases of conflict, is to sanction irrationalism.

Assuming, however, that Kant is correct in charging Jacobi and Mendelssohn with irrationalism, the question still remains: what is wrong with irrationalism? Why cannot common sense or intuition be the criterion of truth in philosophy? Why must reason be our guide?

In the course of his essay, Kant advances two arguments in behalf of reason. His first argument makes a simple but basic point: that reason is inescapable.[43] It is not simply that we ought to follow reason: we must follow it. According to Kant, the general rules or abstract concepts of reason are a necessary condition of all knowledge. An immediate intuition by itself cannot be a sufficient source of knowledge, since it is necessary to justify the conclusions drawn from it, and such justification demands the application of concepts. If, for example, we want to know that we intuit God, then we must apply some general concept of him. Otherwise, how do we know that what we intuit is God and not something else? Hence the mere demand that we justify our intuitions forces us to admit that reason is at least a necessary condition of truth.

Kant's second argument defends reason on liberal political grounds. We must make reason into our standard of truth, he argues, if we are to guarantee freedom of thought.[44] Reason is a bulwark against dogmatism—the demand that we accept a belief on mere authority—because it requires that we question all beliefs and accept only those which agree with our critical reflection. With reason, no one stands above anyone else since everyone has the power to ask questions, draw inferences, and assess evidence. The same cannot be said for intuition, however. If we make it our standard of truth, then we sanction dogmatism. Only an elite few can have an intuition of God, so that those who cannot have such intuitions will have to accept the elite's word for it. In other words, they will have to bow to intellectual authority.

Kant has a striking way of summing up his case against Jacobi's and Wizenmann's irrationalism: complete intellectual freedom destroys itself.[45] Jacobi and Wizenmann want such freedom because they overthrow the constraints of reason in order to explore their intuitions and feelings; but, in doing so, they also sanction despotism since only an elite few can have such intuitions and feelings. Here Kant applies a general theme of his whole philosophy: that freedom demands the restraint of law. Intellectual freedom requires the rule of reason just as moral freedom demands the moral law.

Kant closes his essay with a stern warning to Jacobi and Wizenmann: they are undermining the very freedom necessary for their philosophy. In a few stirring lines, which are a direct response to Wizenmann's address to "the young men of Germany," Kant begs them to consider this consequence of their irrationalism: "Men of intellect and broad dispositions! I honor your talent and love your feeling for humanity. But have you thought of where your attacks upon reason are heading? Surely you too want freedom of thought to be maintained inviolate; for without this even the free fancies of your imagination will soon come to an end."[46] Without doubt, this was a timely entreaty given the imminent succession of Frederick Wilhelm II.

4.3. Wizenmann's Reply to Kant

In his *Berlinische Monatsschrift* essay, Kant praised "the perspicuous author of the *Resultate*," whose identity was still unknown to him, for so clearly pointing out the similarities in Jacobi's and Mendelssohn's views. But he also suggested that Wizenmann had embarked on "a dangerous course," one leading to *Schwärmerei* and "the complete dethronement of reason."

Wizenmann was so deeply offended by Kant's insinuation that, despite failing health, he resolved to write a reply to Kant. His reply, "An den Herrn Professor Kant von dem Verfasser der *Resultate*," appeared in the *Deutsches Museum* of February 1787, only four months after the publication of Kant's essay. Wizenmann's essay took the form of an open letter to Kant, which finally revealed his authorship to the public at large. In this long, dense, and obscure piece Wizenmann sets himself two objectives: first, to rebut Kant's charge of irrationalism; and, second, to demonstrate the incoherencies of Kant's concept of practical faith.

To clear himself of the charge of irrationalism, Wizenmann denies that he ever held the Jacobian position that Kant attributes to him.[47] He agrees with Kant that it would be irrationalist to enjoin a leap of faith if reason could prove the nonexistence of God. But Wizenmann protests that he never said that reason has such powers. Rather, all that he said is that reason neither proves nor disproves the existence of God. In that case, belief in God cannot be described as 'irrational' but only as 'extra-rational' or 'non-rational'.

Yet honesty forces Wizenmann to qualify these disclaimers. He admits that he did say at one point that reason proves the nonexistence of God; but he then quickly adds that this is the God of the deists, that is, an abstract, impersonal, and transcendent entity. But he still insists that he did not say that reason proves the nonexistence of the God of the theists, the personal God who reveals himself to man in history. In other words, faith in the deistic God is irrational, while faith in the theistic God is not. With this distinction Wizenmann deftly avoids Kant's charge of irrationalism and lays it on the doorstep of the Berliners, who were one and all deists.

However clever, Wizenmann's reply escapes Kant's accusation only by abandoning the original standpoint of the *Resultate*. There Wizenmann's position was indeed perfectly Jacobian, despite all his disclaimers. Thus he said that Spinoza's philosophy is the only consistent one, and that it proves the nonexistence of God precisely in the theist's sense of a personal being.[48] At the same time, however, Wizenmann enjoined us to have faith in this theistic God. This is surely irrationalism, and not only by Kant's, but also by Wizenmann's, own criterion. At least in the *Resultate*, then, Wizenmann is guilty as charged.

But if Wizenmann's self-defense fails, his counterattack on Kant is more successful. He goes on the offensive against Kant by throwing the charge of *Schwärmerei* back in his face. He argues that Kant's defense of faith as "a need of practical reason" itself leads to all kinds of *Schwärmerei*, since it moves from the presence of a need to the existence of an object that will satisfy it. But is it not the very essence of *Schwärmerei*, Wizenmann asks, that it mistakes a wish for reality? On Kant's reasoning it is proper for a man in love to dream that the woman of his desires also loves him simply because he has a need to be loved.[49]

In the second *Kritik* Kant explicitly addresses himself to this objection, mentioning Wizenmann by name.[50] He agrees with Wizenmann that it is illegitimate to infer the existence of something from a need when that need arises from sensibility, as in the case of a man in love. But it is another matter when that need arises from reason and is justified by a universal and necessary law. In other words, there is a difference between believing something because one wants to and because one ought to.

Although Kant's reply is effective against the charge of arbitrariness—it puts severe restrictions upon the kinds of need that justify faith—it still does not reply to Wizenmann's main point: that it is illegitimate to infer the existence of something from *any* need, whether of sensibility or reason. According to Wizenmann, it makes no difference whether one wants to believe or ought to believe; in either case there is an illegitimate inference from a need to the existence of the object that satisfies it.

After defending himself against the charge of *Schwärmerei*, Wizenmann engages in an elaborate and subtle polemic against Kant's notion of 'rational faith'.[51] His polemic is of historical as well as philosophical interest: it marks the first critical response to Kant's notion and makes several classic objections to it. Wizenmann's arguments may be summarized as follows: (1) Kant cannot infer that God exists from the need of reason. All he can infer is that we ought to think and act *as if* God exists. In more Kantian terms, the need of reason justifies a regulative, but not a constitutive, principle. It cannot justify a constitutive principle, for it is a glaring non sequitur to infer that God exists simply because we have a moral obligation to believe in his existence. (2) If Kant does attempt to justify a constitutive principle, then he reenters the sphere of speculation where it is necessary to determine the truth or falsity of a belief on theoretical grounds. But this would trespass the Kantian limits on knowledge. (3) Kant is caught in a vicious circle: he bases faith upon morality, in that he says we have a moral duty to believe in God; but he also bases the moral law upon faith, in that he claims morality would not be possible without it. (4) If, as Kant claims, morality is independent of religion, such that neither its incentive nor rationale requires belief in God, providence, or immortality, then how is there a need to have such belief? (5) The notion of a 'need of reason' is a *contradictio in adjecto*. If one justifies a belief by a need, then all rational argument comes to a stop, for the only task of reason is to consider whether a belief is true or false, not whether it is good or bad. On this issue Wizenmann finds an unexpected ally in Mendelssohn, who also holds that the only rational justification for a belief must be theoretical.

Kant attempts to answer Wizenmann's objections at various places in the "Dialektik" of the second *Kritik*. Although, except in a footnote, Kant omits direct reference to Wizenmann, it is not difficult to detect his counterarguments beneath the surface. The second *Kritik* is indeed a palimpsest, revealing Kant's earlier intention to write a polemic against his critics.[52]

Of all Wizenmann's objections, Kant is especially worried by the first and second, devoting two whole sections in reply to them.[53] The third and fourth objections are dealt with in a few odd paragraphs, while the fifth finds no explicit reply. Let us consider Kant's replies to the first four objections, taking each objection in turn. (1) A regulative principle does not satisfy the need of reason, since it demands that there be not a hypothetical but an actual harmony between nature and freedom, happiness and virtue. The condition of such harmony, however, is that God exists, and not only that we think and act as if he exists. Hence we are justified in inferring a constitutive principle from the need of reason.[54] (2) In giving practical reason a right to constitutive principles not possessed by theoretical reason, one is not reopening the door to all kinds of speculation. For all that practical reason has a right to assume is *that* God exists; it has no license to make further judgments about *how* he exists.[55] (3) Although the moral law is indeed necessary to justify faith, the converse does not hold, and thus there is no vicious circle. The beliefs in God and immortality are not necessary either to justify the moral law or to act upon it. Rather, they are necessary only as an incentive to act upon the ideal of the highest good, that ideal where happiness is received in direct proportion to virtue. Wizenmann thinks that there is a circularity only because he confuses two senses of the term 'highest good': 'the supreme good', which is the unconditional good or the absolute standard of goodness, the moral law; and 'the consummate good', which is the greatest possible degree of goodness, the harmony between happiness and virtue. In these terms faith is not a necessary condition of the justification or realization of the supreme good; but it is a necessary condition for the realization of the consummate good.[56] (4) Although morality in the sense of an obligation toward the supreme good is independent of faith, morality in the sense of an obligation toward the consummate good is not. But the obligation toward the consummate good depends upon faith only for its realization, not its normative rationale. In other words, faith provides only an incentive for a finite being to act upon his obligation toward the consummate good.[57]

Sadly, despite a promising beginning, Kant's controversy with Wizenmann came to a premature and tragic close in early 1787. Wizenmann's reply to Kant proved to be his last burst of strength, and indeed his epitaph.

Wizenmann had been suffering from tuberculosis for many years, and the slightest exertion always became a heavy setback for his health. Working on the *Resultate* severely weakened him; and writing his reply to Kant literally killed him.[58] Shortly after Wizenmann finished the reply, his health worsened dramatically; and on the twenty-first of February, the very month it appeared in print, he died. The pantheism controversy had thus claimed its second victim and, tragically, its most promising contestant.

4.4. Jacobi's Attack on Kant

In the spring of 1786, during the very height of the pantheism controversy, Jacobi was still hoping for Kant's support in his struggle against Mendelssohn and the Berliners. In his *Wider Mendelssohns Beschuldigungen,* which appeared in April of that year, he invoked the name of Kant to defend himself against the charge of *Schwärmerei*.[59] Kant, "that Hercules among thinkers," had a position broadly similar to his own, Jacobi claimed. He too denied the demonstrability of God's existence, and he too thought that knowledge cannot justify faith. "So if no one dares to call Kant a '*Schwärmer*'," Jacobi asked, "then why should they dare to call me one?" He was modest and cautious enough to add that he did not mean to lower Kant's philosophy to the level of his, or to raise his to the level of Kant's. But it was still evident that Jacobi was making a bid for Kant's support, and that certainly alarmed Mendelssohn's friends.

As late as autumn 1786, Jacobi nurtured hopes for Kant's support. His expectations were raised by some promising news from Königsberg: Hamann told him that Kant was pleased with the *Briefe* and that he planned to attack Mendelssohn.[60] So, when Kant's essay finally appeared in October, Jacobi was naturally disappointed. It was now clear to him that Kant wanted to found 'a sect' of his own by taking a middle position between himself and Mendelssohn. Eager for a fight, Jacobi immediately drew up his battle plans. In a letter written on October 31, 1786 to Hamann,[61] the very letter that voices his disappointment with Kant's essay, Jacobi sketched the criticism of Kant that he would later append to his *David Hume*. This criticism, destined to become famous in the history of post-Kantian philosophy, is one of the most influential criticisms of Kant ever written, particularly considering its effects upon the development of post-Kantian idealism. So let us see what Jacobi had to say.

Jacobi's critique of Kant grew out of his controversy with Mendelssohn, and it is indeed only part and parcel of his general critique of the *Aufklärung*. His chief objection to Kant's philosophy is the same as his objection to all philosophy: it leads to the abyss of nihilism. Kant's philosophy, if it were made consistent, proves to be "a philosophy of nothingness."

Furthermore Kant begins to acquire a special symbolic significance for Jacobi. He is not just another philosopher, like Leibniz or Spinoza, whose philosophy happens to end in nihilism. Rather, starting in 1799 with his *Brief an Fichte*,[62] Jacobi sees Kant's philosophy, especially as it is consistently and systematically developed by Fichte, as the paradigm of all philosophy—and hence as the very epitome of nihilism. Jacobi's attack on philosophy has now become first and foremost an attack on Kant, and in particular on Fichte, whom Jacobi sees as nothing more than a radical Kantian.

The supreme importance of Kant, his pivotal position in the history of philosophy, rests upon a single fact, in Jacobi's view. Namely, Kant is the first thinker to discover the principle of all knowledge, or what Jacobi calls "the principle of subject-object identity." Although it is not explicit, what Jacobi is referring to is nothing less than the principle behind Kant's 'new method of thought', the foundation stone of his Copernican revolution as explained in the prefaces of the first *Kritik*.[63] This principle states that reason knows a priori only what it creates according to its own laws. Since it implies that the self knows only the products of its own activity, it makes self-knowledge into the paradigm of all knowledge. Jacobi's term 'subject-object identity' refers to that self-knowledge where the subject makes the object into the mirror of its own activity.

Jacobi's main objection to Kant is that this principle results in nihilism. If it is universalized (as Fichte would have it), so that knowledge through reason is made into the paradigm of all knowledge, then it leads straight to 'speculative egoism', that is, a solipsism that dissolves all reality into my own representations. This solipsism is a direct consequence of Kant's principle, Jacobi contends, because it implies that all we know is our own representations, the products of our intellectual activity.[64] We do not know any reality that exists apart from and prior to this activity, something that is not created by it, whether that be nature, other minds, God, or the very self that is the source of this activity. Hence we are caught inside the circle of our own consciousness, a circle consisting of nothing but representations, which represent nothing.

Jacobi now confronts us with another of his dilemmas. Either I assume that knowledge is in principle infinite—and dissolve all reality into nothingness—or I suppose that it is limited—and admit that the reality outside my consciousness is unknowable to me. So I know either myself or nothing. There is no middle option, though, where I know something that exists apart from me. This dilemma soon became a formidable challenge to Schelling and Hegel, whose objective idealism was designed to escape it.[65]

Jacobi's famous argument against the thing-in-itself has to be understood in the light of his general critique of Kant. Jacobi regards the thing-in-itself as Kant's final, desperate measure to prevent his philosophy from collapsing into nihilism. If this expedient fails—and it does of necessity, Jacobi argues—then Kant has to admit that he reduces all reality to the contents of our consciousness. It was the sad destiny of Fichte, Jacobi says, to develop Kant's philosophy in just this direction. Fichte rid Kant's philosophy of the thing-in-itself; but in doing so he revealed its true tendency and inner spirit: nihilism.

Jacobi's argument against the thing-in-itself proceeds in two steps.[66] The first step accuses Kant of an inconsistency in assuming that objects are the causes of representation. According to Jacobi, Kant cannot assume that *empirical* objects are the causes of representations; for he explicitly states that they are nothing but representations, and so they cannot be the cause of representations. But Kant also cannot hold that the *transcendental* object is the cause of representations. For he expressly teaches that we cannot have any knowledge of it; and if we cannot know it, then we a fortiori cannot know that it is the cause of our representations.

The second step of Jacobi's argument makes the added claim that this inconsistency is inevitable. In other words, if it is contradictory for Kant to postulate objects that are the causes of representation, it is also *necessary* for him to do so. It is necessary, Jacobi argues, because Kant assumes that we have a passive sensibility, and to talk about a passive sensibility implies that there is something to act upon it. Kant postulates a passive sensibility in the first place because he wants to maintain a semblance of realism in his system.

Hence the assumption of things-in-themselves is incompatible with, but necessary to, Kant's system. As Jacobi sums up Kant's predicament in a famous epigram: "I need the assumption of things-in-themselves to enter the Kantian system; but with this assumption it is not possible for me to remain inside it."[67]

In 1787, when Jacobi first made his charge of nihilism against Kant in his *David Hume,* he was not yet aware of Kant's second *Kritik,* which was published only one year later. Little did he know that Kant would soon devote his second *Kritik* to an explanation and defense of his practical faith in freedom, God, and immortality. Prima facie the notion of practical faith rescued Kant from nihilism because it justified belief in things beyond one's own consciousness (namely, God, providence, and immortality).

Even after the second *Kritik* appeared, however, Jacobi did not retract his charge of nihilism. Rather, he pressed his point home. He saw Kant's practical faith as nothing more than another ad hoc device to stave off nihilism. In his later writings Jacobi makes two objections against Kant's notion of practical faith.[68] (1) Since Kant denies that faith is a form of knowledge, and since he also forbids the possibility of an intellectual intuition of things-in-themselves, his faith remains 'subjectivistic', that is, it does not give us any knowledge of a reality independent of our representations. All that we ever know from our practical faith is that *we* must postulate some ideas of reason, and that we must think and act *as if* they are true. In other words, we only know something more about ourselves, and nothing about reality itself. (2) Kant's attempt to establish faith on the basis of practical reason fails because his categorical imperative provides only a necessary, but not a sufficient, condition of the morality of a maxim. But if the categorical imperative is empty, there is no reason to believe that faith in God, providence, and immortality is moral.

These criticisms show that Jacobi had become aware of the very important differences between his and Kant's concepts of faith. Indeed, Jacobi had begun to compare Kant's concept unfavorably to his own. In his *Brief an Fichte* of 1799 Jacobi sees his 'natural faith', which stems from the heart, as the antidote to Kant's 'rational faith', which allegedly comes from pure reason.[69] "Nothing more fills me with disgust," he writes, "than Kant's attempt to introduce reason into morality." That this attempt is bankrupt is clear to him from the emptiness of the categorical imperative. Kant, in Jacobi's view, fails to grasp the proper relationship between reason and interest. He rightly sees that interests determine belief—on that score Jacobi and Kant agree—but he goes astray in assuming that reason can in any way determine or limit these interests. The emptiness of the categorical imperative shows us that the very opposite is the case: interest determines rationality, and not conversely.

Jacobi's and Wizenmann's counterattack on Kant had apparently given them a winning edge in their battle against the *Aufklärung*. It was Kant's philosophy alone that made an unequivocal stand in behalf of reason during the pantheism controversy. But Kant's philosophy seemed to be heading straight toward the abyss. To be consistent, it had to drop its thing-in-itself, and then become a thoroughgoing nihilism, which denied the existence of anything beyond momentary states of consciousness. Kant's moral faith was no escape from this solipsistic nightmare, since, even if consistent, it could at best allow us to think and act *as if* God, providence, and immortality existed.

After Jacobi's and Wizenmann's counterattack, the burden of proof was on the *Aufklärer* to defend the holy name of reason. To uphold the authority of reason, the *Aufklärer* had to show—somehow—that reason could justify faith. Yet the prospects looked bleak, very bleak indeed. It was clearly no longer feasible to give a theoretical justification of faith as Mendelssohn had. The Kantian critique of rationalism seemed to bar that option. But at the same time it was also plain that Kant's practical justification of faith was extremely problematic. It rested upon the categorical imperative, which was empty; and it could at best secure regulative ideas, which were not sufficient to satisfy belief. Thus, in the end, it seemed as if reason had drawn a blank. There did not seem to be any solution to Jacobi's dilemma. Either we forswore our reason to save our faith, or we abandoned our faith to uphold our reason.

losophy of Mind

iighteenth-Century Philosophy of Mind

.ee-quarters of the eighteenth century philosophers
ught in the grip of a dilemma. They continued to be
.e old questions whenever they pondered the Cartesian
.em. 'Is the mind part of nature because it is explicable
physical laws?' 'Or is the mind outside nature because it is
ле according to physical laws?' To the orthodox *Aufklärer* or
.ophe, who was not willing to abandon his common sense for Berkeley's
.dealism or Malebranche's occasionalism, these questions appeared to ex-
haust the options. It seemed to him as if he had to choose between materialism or dualism—a materialism that explained the mind by reducing it
to a machine, or a dualism that put the mind in a supernatural realm
inaccessible to scientific study. He did not see any middle path between
these extremes: a naturalistic explanation of the mind that was neither
reductivistic nor materialistic.

The eighteenth-century philosophers of the mind suffered under this dilemma largely because they could not shake off the hold of an old Cartesian
assumption—that the paradigm of naturalistic explanation is mechanism.
They continued to believe that to explain a phenomenon is to subsume it
under cause-effect laws. This was the procedure that had been used with
such success by modern science in its explanation of the physical universe;
and the apparently inevitable progress of modern science held out the promise that all natural events could be explained in a similar manner. But the
very method that had proved so successful in physics had stranded philosophers on the horns of a dilemma. If they explained the mind according to
natural laws, then they reduced it to a machine; but if they insisted upon
its sui generis traits, then they hid the mind in a mysterious supernatural
realm. Hence they seemed to turn the mind into either a machine or a ghost.

This predicament was indeed one of the underlying issues behind the pantheism controversy itself. If we accept the premise that mechanism is the paradigm of naturalistic and scientific explanation, then the authority of reason is thrown into doubt; for it then seems as if reason itself, and not merely mechanism, leads to materialism and determinism. The only escape from these evils is then to curtail the power of reason and to postulate a supernatural mental realm. Such reasoning, as we have already seen, was particularly apparent during the pantheism controversy.[1] The dilemma of knowledge versus faith, which is at the very heart of that controversy, tacitly presupposes that mechanism is the only form of explanation or knowledge. Jacobi, Wizenmann, and Kant considered this dilemma valid because they all committed themselves to this very presupposition. Since they assumed that mechanism is the paradigm of knowledge, they felt compelled "to deny knowledge in order to make room for faith"; hence they postulated an unknowable supernatural realm to preserve freedom and immortality from the encroachments of natural science.

The philosopher who deserves most credit for reviving the philosophy of mind in eighteenth-century Germany is Johann Gottfried Herder. By questioning the hegemony of mechanism, his vitalist theory of mind promised a middle path between the extremes of a reductivist materialism and a supernaturalistic dualism. Rather than seeing mechanism as the only paradigm of explanation, Herder reinstated the old Aristotelian paradigms, teleology and holism. According to Herder's vitalism, the mind is neither a machine nor a ghost, but a living organism. To explain the mind is not to subsume it under causal laws, but to know the ends for which it acts and the whole of which it is a part.

It is important to recognize, though, that Herder did not simply reassert the old Aristotelian models of explanation. Rather, he reinterpreted them in light of the growing biological sciences, which seemed to give them a new lease on life. The advance of the biological sciences around the middle of the eighteenth century appeared to confirm the principles of a vitalistic philosophy of mind. Haller's theory of irritation, Needham's and Maupertuis's criticisms of the preformation theory, and Boerhaave's revival of the concept of *vis viva* all seemed to offer strong evidence for a vitalist theory.[2] They appeared to vindicate the vitalist claims that there is a continuity between the mental and physical realms and that living force is the essence of both of them. Herder, who always kept a keen eye on the latest biological developments, therefore saw his theory as strictly modern and scientific. Thus it was no longer necessary to fight an uphill battle against mechanism since its death knell was being rung by the biological sciences.

Herder's theory of mind drastically changed the state of play in the pantheism controversy, pushing it in a new and promising direction. The problem of the authority of reason came to be seen as involving the thorny issue of the legitimacy of teleology and holism as models of explanation. Here indeed was an issue that Kant, Jacobi, Wizenmann, and Mendelssohn had all failed to consider. If these are equally legitimate paradigms, if they too are capable of attaining scientific status, then they could support the crumbling authority of reason. There would be no danger of reason leading to determinism and materialism, and there would be no need to postulate a supernatural mental realm. We would then have naturalistic explanations of the mind that did justice to its sui generis characteristics. The middle path between the dilemma of faith and knowledge would at last be clear: a vitalist theory of mind.

Although Herder is usually remembered for his philosophy of history, the philosophy of mind was ultimately his central concern. His interest in history derived from his preoccupation with the mind, for he saw history as the key to the mind. He was convinced that he could understand the mind only by observing its growth and development, which could only be traced through history.

Throughout his philosophical career, Herder's ambition was to explain the genesis of characteristic human activities—art, language, science, religion, and philosophy—according to natural laws. Hence the need arose for a philosophy of mind that was neither reductivistic nor supernaturalistic. (A reductivist theory would not explain the sui generis features of the mind, and a supernaturalist one would not explain it all.) Herder's early philosophical writings represent several progressive stages toward the development of such a philosophy of mind. The *Fragmente* (1767–68) sketches its method and suggests its goals; the *Ueber den Ursprung der Sprache* (1772) defines and defends its goals on a more general level; the *Auch eine Philosophie der Geschichte der Menschheit* (1774) formulates its methodology; and the *Vom Erkennen und Empfinden der menschlichen Seele* (1778) articulates its general principles. Herder's magnum opus, the *Ideen zur Philosophie der Geschichte der Menschheit* (1784), is the final realization and elaboration of the philosophical program that Herder had conceived in his earlier works.

Herder achieved his ambition, though, only after a long and difficult struggle. Who, of all people, should be his most bitter and outspoken opponents? None other than his two former teachers, Kant and Hamann. Although Kant and Hamann are essentially opposed over the philosophy of mind—Hamann's holism is the diametrical opposite of Kant's dualism— they were strange bedfellows concerning one fundamental point: their antinaturalism; they both denied the possibility of explaining the sui generis characteristics of the mind according to natural laws. It was this belief that drove Hamann to write a harsh review of Herder's *Ueber den Ursprung der Sprache;* and it was the same belief that led Kant to write a hostile review of Herder's *Ideen zur Philosophie der Geschichte der Menschheit.* Herder's subsequent disputes with Hamann and Kant are of considerable philosophical interest since they concern the crucial issue of the possibility of a naturalistic yet nonreductivistic philosophy of mind.

This chapter has three tasks, all of them relating to the above themes. The first aim is to trace the development of Herder's theory of mind, its aims (5.2), principles (5.5), and methods (5.4). The second aim is to analyze the reaction of Kant and Hamann to Herder's theory, and to determine how Kant, Hamann, and Herder reformulated their ideas in the light of their exchanges (5.3, 5.6–5.8). The third and final aim is to describe in greater detail Herder's contribution to the pantheism controversy.

5.2. Herder on the Origin of Language

In 1769 the Akademie der Wissenschaften in Berlin announced a prize competition for the best essay on the questions "If human beings were left with their natural faculties, would they be able to invent language? And by what means could they invent it?" These questions invited competitors to disagree with a recent work by a late member of the Akademie, J. P. Süss-milch's *Versuch eines Beweises, dass die erste Sprache ihren Ursprung nicht vom Menschen, sondern allein vom Schöpfer erhalten habe.* Herder, who had been thinking for several years about just these questions, jumped at the opportunity to enter the competition.[3] "A splendid, great and truly philosophical question," "a question written for me," he wrote his friend Hartknoch in December 1770.[4] So, in the last days of December, Herder hastily wrote his contribution to meet the January 1 deadline. He was duly and justly awarded the first prize for his provocative and original contribution, *Ueber den Ursprung der Sprache,* which was eventually published in 1772 under the auspices of the Akademie. This tract is a milestone in Herder's development, marking the starting point of his philosophical program. It is here that Herder first explicitly defines and defends his naturalistic yet nonreductivistic philosophy of mind.

The problem to which Herder's treatise is devoted—the question whether the origin of language is divine or human—now seems to be hopelessly antiquated, of mere historical interest. But it is important to see that this problem is only the surface issue and that it raises a more general issue which still concerns us: the limits of naturalistic or scientific explanation. It was clear to Herder and the Akademie that if one could develop a naturalistic explanation of the origin of language, then that would be a significant step toward bringing the mind itself within the naturalistic worldview.

Language was commonly held to be the necessary instrument of reason, so that a naturalistic explanation of the origin of language amounted to such an explanation of the genesis of reason. It would then be possible to view reason, our innermost thinking processes, as just as much a natural phenomenon as the velocity of a ball dropped from the leaning tower of Pisa.

Concerning this general issue, Herder takes an uncompromising stand in favor of naturalism. The primary aim of his treatise is to sketch a naturalistic theory of the origin of language. This theory consists in two theses, each of which is necessary for a complete and convincing naturalism. The first thesis states that it is not necessary to postulate a supernatural cause of language since human reason by itself has the power to create language. Or, as Herder puts it: "If the use of reason is natural to man, and if the use of reason requires language, then the creation of language will also be natural to man."[5] This thesis is still insufficient for a complete naturalism, however, since it presupposes the existence of reason itself, which of course opens the door to all kinds of speculation about the supernatural genesis of reason, and thus ultimately language itself. The second thesis closes this gap, providing an explanation of the origin of reason itself.[6] Roughly, it states that man develops a faculty of reason because, unlike animals who are guided by instinct, he has to learn general facts in order to survive; and language is his means of storing these facts, so that what is learned in one generation can be handed down to the next as a lesson for survival.

Paving the way for his naturalism, Herder begins his treatise with a polemic against supernaturalistic theories of the origin of language. His main target is Süssmilch's theory. According to Süssmilch, man does not have the power to create language by himself, but depends on God to do this for him. Although such a theory obviously has a religious motivation, Süssmilch insists that it is based on reason and experience alone and not the Bible.[7] Indeed, his main argument is perfectly plausible, resting upon two apparently faultless premises. The first premise is that language is the necessary instrument of reason, without which it remains inchoate and dormant; and the second is that language is the product of not an animal but a rational nature. It follows from these two premises alone, Süssmilch thinks, that man cannot create language. For, given that human reason is inchoate and inert without language, how can man create it? We are driven in a vicious circle, where man supposedly creates through his reason the very instrument that makes it possible. To escape this circle, then, we must invoke a *deus ex machina*: a superhuman cause that has an all-powerful intellect; but such an intellect is, of course, the possession of God alone.

Such, in sum, is the argument of Süssmilch's notorious and ill-fated treatise. But it is not reasoning that impresses Herder, who dismisses it with a heavy dose of scorn. Herder deftly turns Süssmilch's argument against him, so that it proves the very opposite of what he intends. He raises the question: if language is necessary for the development of reason, as Süssmilch claims, and if the use of reason is natural to man, as Süssmilch also admits, then should not the creation of language also be natural to man?[8] According to Herder, Süssmilch is caught in his own vicious circle, which is indeed the reductio ad absurdum of his whole theory. If human reason develops only through language, then how is it possible for man to understand the instruction that God gives him in the use of language? To comprehend God's instruction, man must already possess a well-developed reason, that is, he must already have language.

However shrewd, Herder's polemic is still not decisive against Süssmilch, who might well reply: "If reason is only a potentiality, a mere latent capacity, then that is enough for man to understand God, although it is not enough for him to create language." This notion of reason as a mere potentiality gives Herder a good deal of trouble in his treatise, and he never formulates an unambiguous reply to it. Thus he admits that reason is initially a mere potentiality; but he also insists that it is a spontaneous self-activating 'tendency' *(Tendenz)*.[9] It is only this added assumption that gets Herder out of Süssmilch's circle—but, of course, it is just this assumption that Süssmilch rejects. Thus, far from refuting Süssmilch, Herder's polemics beg the question. This is a point that Herder himself had to admit later on, much to his embarrassment.[10]

In the end, though, the validity of Herder's naturalism does not rest upon his polemics. It is his new approach to the problem of language that is ultimately decisive. Herder insists on the need for a 'genetic' investigation of the origin of language. The main principle behind such an investigation is that language, like all things in nature, has a history and undergoes gradual change and development, evolving from the simple to the complex, the inchoate to the differentiated. It is in arguing for this principle that Herder finally settles his score with Süssmilch. He is able to question one of Süssmilch's basic presuppositions: that language is given and eternal, a complex, systematic, and perfectly rational structure from time immemorial.[11] Of course, if this were so, then Süssmilch's argument for the divine origin of language would become perfectly plausible. God would have to create language, since man, having a finite intelligence, could not create a perfectly rational structure all at once. But such a picture of language is completely contrary to the facts, Herder assures us, since we can see from experience that language undergoes change and development. Witness, for example, how many abstract words began as metaphors. Thus the true Achilles' heel of Süssmilch's theory is not any a priori argument but its simple failure to do justice to the empirical facts.

Developing a naturalistic theory of the origin of language is only the general aim of Herder's treatise. It is by no means Herder's specific aim, and still less is it an original endeavor. Naturalistic theories had been formulated before him, and indeed by such eminent thinkers as Rousseau and Condillac. Their theories had already aroused a strong debate, and Süssmilch's tract was in fact one reaction against them. It is important to see, however, that Herder disagrees with Rousseau's and Condillac's naturalism as much as Süssmilch's supernaturalism. The specific aim of his treatise is to formulate a new kind of naturalistic theory, one that avoids all the pitfalls of Rousseau's and Condillac's.

What, more precisely, were these naturalistic theories that Herder was reacting against? And what was wrong with them? Although they are both naturalistic in principle, Rousseau's and Condillac's theories are completely different. According to Rousseau, language first came into being with the spontaneous expression of emotion. Man had a need to express his feelings (for example, love, anger, and fear), and hence he uttered sounds. These sounds were of course nothing more than cries; but they were also the first words. Language therefore begins with the primitive expression of emotion.[12] According to Condillac, however, language originates not with natural cries, but with arbitrary conventions. The purpose of language is to communicate; but, in order to do this, it is first necessary to agree upon the meaning of sounds. Since people react the same way to the same stimuli, they have no difficulty in agreeing upon the meaning that they attach to sounds.[13]

According to Herder, Rousseau's and Condillac's theories illustrate opposing weaknesses, two extremes that any satisfactory naturalistic theory must avoid. He sums up their difficulties in a single sentence: "If Rousseau reduces man to an animal, Condillac elevates an animal into man."[14] Rousseau reduces man to an animal, because he assumes that his language, like the language of all animals, consists in cries alone. But he fails to recognize the conspicuous feature of human language: namely, its cognitive content. The vast majority of words do not express emotions, but describe things. We cannot explain the origin of these words, though, if we consider only man's animal nature. Conversely, Condillac elevates an animal into man since he assumes that man must already possess the idea of language in the state of nature. In order to have the idea of a sound designating a thing, or in order to understand the purpose of a convention, we must already have a sophisticated idea of language. Condillac therefore presupposes what he attempts to explain: the origin of language.

Although they illustrate opposing errors, Herder thinks that Rousseau's and Condillac's theories suffer from a single mistake. They both lose sight of the characteristic nature of man. Either they reduce his rationality to his animal nature, as in the case of Rousseau, or they presuppose it without explaining it, as in the case of Condillac. Yet it is rationality, Herder insists, that holds the key to the origin of language. Since man is the only creature who possesses language, are we not justified in seeking its origin in his characteristic nature? That is the guiding assumption behind Herder's whole investigation.[15]

True to his methodological guidelines, Herder begins his investigation with an examination of the concept of reason. He stresses the integrative and unifying function of reason. It is not one faculty in addition to others, as if man were mainly an animal with the extra power of reason. Rather, reason is the power that directs, organizes, and controls all his other faculties. All the powers of man are distinctively human in virtue of the direction given to them by reason. Such indeed is the unity which reason bestows upon these powers that if man were an animal in one of them, then he would be an animal in them all.

Borrowing a term from Locke, Herder sometimes calls reason 'reflection' (Besonnenheit).[16] He chooses this term to refer to man's characteristic self-consciousness. Whence, though, this connection between reason and self-consciousness? The answer lies with Herder's general definition of reason, which he presupposes in his treatise but makes explicit later on.[17] In his Ideen he contrasts reason with instinct and defines it as the power to learn, to acquire knowledge of general facts. Self-consciousness is clearly essential to reason in this sense because it is the precondition of all learning. We could not even remember or verify our experiences, for example, if we could not be conscious of them.

Why is it that reason must give birth to language? Why is the creation of language so natural to it? Although these questions are crucial to his theory, Herder gives only vague and sketchy answers.[18] The crux of his argument is that reason controls and organizes our experience only in virtue of language. To order and classify our experience, reason must be able to reidentify precise aspects of it and to distinguish them from other aspects. But to reidentify these aspects it is necessary to give them signs, signs that refer to them and nothing else. A sign is necessary since, without it, we could not remember or verify that this is the same aspect. But in giving signs to distinct aspects of our experience, we are already using language. Thus Herder exclaims: "The first distinguishing feature of our reflection was a word of the soul. With this word human language is discovered!"[19]

Assuming, then, that reason gives birth to language, how does reason itself come into being? Now we come to the second thesis of Herder's theory, which takes up nearly all of the second half of his treatise. Here Herder develops an interesting proto-Darwinian account of why reason, and indeed language, is necessary for the survival of man. Unlike animals and insects, Herder observes, man has few instincts and innate skills to guide him. These are useful for the animal and insect, who have limited environments, and who need to perform only a limited number of activities in order to survive. But they are useless for man, who not only must live in every kind of environment from the desert to the arctic, but who also has to engage in almost every kind of activity in order to survive. What this means, however, is that man has *to learn* how to survive. Now if every generation is not to be exposed to the perils of past generations, threatening the chances of survival, then it is necessary for man to generalize and memorize facts about his environment (that this kind of plant is cultivatable in this way, and that this kind of animal is dangerous). In other words, man must have reason if he is to learn how to survive. But, more to the point, he also must have language, for the only means of remembering and communicating these facts to future generations is language. Without language, each new generation would commit the same mistakes as past ones, exposing itself to the same dangers and thus diminishing its chances for survival. Language is therefore the medium by which an older generation instructs a younger one about the means for its survival.

5.3. Hamann and Herder's Debate over the Origin of Language

Having a long-standing and deep interest in the nature of language, Hamann was anything but indifferent to the problem of its origin.[20] In the December 27, 1771, issue of the *Königsbergische gelehrte und politische Zeitungen,* he reviewed one of the contributions to the Akademie competition, Dietrich Tiedemann's *Versuch einer Erklärung des Ursprungs der Sprache.*

Tiedemann's treatise is a neglected but noteworthy contribution to the origin of language debate.[21] Tiedemann takes a position that is in many respects strikingly similar to Herder's. Like Herder, he attempts to find a middle path between the extremes of reductivism and supernaturalism. He too argues against Süssmilch and Rousseau, and he too advocates a historical approach to the problem of the origin of language. The main difference between Tiedemann and Herder is that Tiedemann affirms and Herder denies the possibility of prelinguistic knowledge. According to Tiedemann, who is a convinced empiricist, we first have representations and only later give names to them.[22]

Whatever the merits of Tiedemann's work, Hamann gave it a damning review. He passionately rejected Tiedemann's naturalism, which he felt ignored the divine element in language; and he bitterly denounced Tiedemann's empiricism, which he saw as reductivistic. It is hard to imagine a more searing indictment of any philosophical work: "We shall leave it to those readers who are more than mere primates, or indeed more than corrupt reviewers, to judge how shallow and empty the author's philosophy is."[23]

Despite such invective, Hamann did have some substantive objections to Tiedemann's treatise. He criticized Tiedemann's mechanistic view of language, in which language is nothing more than an assemblage of grammatical parts. We cannot explain the origin of language simply by accounting for the origin of the various parts of speech, according to Hamann, since language is no more reducible to the *partium orationis* than reason to the forms of syllogism. Hamann also chastised Tiedemann for not explaining the connection between sign and representation; an account of this connection is necessary to offer some insight into the origin of language. Least of all was Hamann willing to accept Tiedemann's thesis of prelinguistic knowledge, which clashed with his own view that language is the necessary instrument of reason.

Although he had not yet seen it, Hamann could not help preferring Herder's contribution to the Akademie competition. Herder had not only won the prize but was also Hamann's protégé, an old student of his during his university days.[24] Thus, at the close of his review, Hamann promises the public that "the Herderian Prize Essay" will give them more occasion to think about the problems at hand. But Hamann's optimism was based on a false premise. He was confident that Herder's essay would provide an antidote to Tiedemann's naturalism. His harsh judgment of Tiedemann's treatise was therefore prophetic of the storm to come.

When Herder's prize essay finally appeared, Hamann was, not surprisingly, deeply disappointed. He saw it as a betrayal of their common principles, and he even threatened to disown his former student.[25] What he expected was a refutation of naturalism and a more sophisticated divine origin theory than Süssmilch's; but all he got instead was a defense of naturalism and an attack on the divine origin theory that declared it to be "the most hideous nonsense." In a brief review of Herder's treatise in the *Königsbergische Zeitungen* of March 20, 1772, Hamann let his disappointment be known and avowed "revenge for the higher hypothesis."[26]

This was no idle threat. In three later essays, his "Beylage" to the first review, "Des Ritters von Rosenkreuz letzte Willensmeynung über den göttlichen und menschlichen Ursprung der Sprache," and "Philologische Einfälle und Zweifel," Hamann launched a bitter polemic against Herder and the whole Akademie der Wissenschaften with Frederick II at the helm.[27] Although these essays have often been dismissed as the work of a mystic,[28] they deserve our closest attention. They not only make interesting criticisms of Herder and the *Aufklärung*, they also raise important questions for the philosophy of language in general.

Where lay the fatal flaw of Herder's prize essay, in Hamann's view? After reflecting upon this question for several months, Hamann tells us in "Philologische Einfälle und Zweifel," he came to the disturbing conclusion that Herder was never serious about answering the Akademie's question.[29] His theory is more a joke than an explanation. Why? Because it is so hopelessly circular and tautological that it does not begin to explain anything at all. According to Hamann, Herder's so-called proof of the human origin of language depends on his introduction of the vague term 'reflection' (*Besonnenheit*). What is this mysterious capacity, though, but another name for reason? Herder's whole theory therefore boils down to the simple assertion that reason creates language. But, Hamann asks, is this not the very phenomenon that is to be explained? Why does reason create language? All that Herder ever says to answer this question is that it is 'natural' for reason to express itself in language. But that only pushes the question back another step: for what is natural?

But is Hamann fair in condemning Herder's whole theory on these grounds? Undeniably, Herder creates more problems than he solves by introducing his vague concept of reflection. Yet his theory does not rest upon this concept alone. The heart of Herder's theory comes in the second half of the treatise when he explains the origin of language from the need for survival. However speculative this explanation might be, it is neither circular nor tautological.

Although his polemic against Herder is not fair, Hamann makes some interesting general criticisms of the human origin theory. He attacks the very possibility of naturalism itself, and thus by implication any explanation like that given in the second half of Herder's treatise. In "Ritter von Rosenkreuz" Hamann regrets the revival of the doctrines of Epicurus at the hands of such figures as La Mettrie and Holbach, and indeed Kant himself.[30] The genesis of the mind out of "a bog or slime" appears impossible to him. It could at best produce "a pretty mask," but nothing like "a fiery spirit" or "breathing energy." The doubts of Voltaire and Hume have led him to suspect "the evangelical certanty" of Newton, Galileo, and Kepler. Voltaire has shown him that the essence of the mind and body are unknowable; and Hume has taught him that the very possibility of natural law is questionable since there is no necessary connection between cause and effect.

In addition to citing Hume and Voltaire, Hamann brings forward a powerful argument of his own against any form of naturalism. The great obstacle to any naturalistic explanation of the genesis of life or reason, he argues, is the mind-body problem.[31] The connection between mind and body is essentially mysterious, so that it is impossible to explain the genesis of the mind according to natural laws. Anyone who doubts that the connection is mysterious only has to be reminded of Hume's scruples about causality. Since Hume has shown that there cannot be a necessary connection between any events, it follows a fortiori that there cannot be a necessary connection between such heterogeneous events as a mental intention and a physical movement. In raising the specter of the mind-body problem, here, Hamann goes to the very heart of the matter and poses a formidable challenge to naturalism. We shall soon see, though, that Herder has a reply to this challenge.

In his essays on the origin of language Hamann not only criticizes naturalistic theories but also outlines his own supernaturalistic theory. The basis of Hamann's theory is his mystical vision of the union of the divine and human. As he explains in the very first paragraph of "Ritter von Rosenkreuz": "This *communion* of divine and human idioms is the first principle of, and the main key to, all our knowledge and its whole visible economy."[32] According to Hamann, this principle means that the origin of language cannot be exclusively divine or human. Rather, it must be both divine *and* human, supernatural *and* natural. Since God acts through man, what man creates through his natural capacities is also what God creates through him.

Hamann's principle of the coexistence of the divine and human commits him to a dual-aspect theory of the origin of language. This theory assumes that there are two causes of language, one divine and the other human, and that each is sufficient to explain the origin of language. They are both equally valid explanations or descriptions of one and the same process of creation. So even if we assume with Herder that the natural powers of man are sufficient to create language, we may not exclude a divine origin. Rather, it is still possible for there to be a divine origin, namely, one where God creates language through the natural capacities of man. This seems to be at least one version of the divine origin theory that Hamann wants to defend. As he writes in "Ritter von Rosenkreuz," "If a higher being, or an angel, as in the case of Bileams ass, was to act through our tongue, then all such actions, like the speaking animals in Aesop's fables, would manifest themselves according to the analogy of human nature; even in this respect, the origin of language . . . can appear and be something else than the merely human."[33]

According to this version of the divine origin theory, there is no need to retreat to Süssmilch's supernaturalism and to assume that the origin of language requires some miracle contrary to the normal course of nature.[34] We simply have to assume that language is created through natural means, but that God is coactive through these means. Here indeed is a bitter lesson for a naturalist like Herder or Tiedemann. Prove ever so cogently that a phenomenon arises through natural laws, and that still does not disprove the presence of the supernatural which might be copresent in the working of these laws.

It is important to see, however, that Hamann was not always loyal to his dual-aspect theory. In expounding his account of the origin of language he sometimes borrows ideas from Süssmilch and the biblical tradition— ideas that defy all translation into a naturalistic idiom. In the "Beylage" to his review of Herder, for example, he revives Süssmilch's idea that language is learned from divine instruction.[35] Then, at the close of "Ritter von Rosenkreuz," he sketches an account of the origin of language that is supernaturalistic in the extreme. It is essentially a reworking of Genesis interpreted according to his own mystical vision. This is how Hamann describes the genesis of language immediately after the creation: "Every appearance of nature was a word—the sign, image and pledge of a new secret and inexpressible communion of divine energies and ideas. Everything that man at first heard, saw and touched with his hands was a living word. With this word in his mouth and heart, the origin of language was so natural, obvious and easy as the game of a child."[36]

In the end it is doubtful that Hamann does have a single consistent theory of the origin of language. He adopts several incompatible positions toward naturalism, so that it becomes impossible to determine to what extent his theory is either supernaturalistic or naturalistic. At first, Hamann takes a purely defensive stand against naturalism.[37] He appears to admit that naturalism might be able to provide a sufficient account of the origin of language; but he only wants to argue that a naturalistic account does not exclude a supernaturalistic one. This is the standpoint of the dual-aspect theory. Later on, however, Hamann assumes a weaker position.[38] He seems to hold that a naturalistic account is not sufficient, but only necessary. It is not sufficient since it is also necessary to consider such supernatural factors as God's creation of the faculty of speech. Finally, Hamann goes on the offensive and attacks the very possibility of naturalism,[39] arguing that naturalism provides neither a necessary nor sufficient account of the origin of language. Hence he feels that it is safe to resort to his own mystical version of Genesis.

All these inconsistencies and mystical speculations aside, Hamann's theory of the origin of language remains of great philosophical value. The most significant aspect of the theory comes at the very beginning of "Philologische Einfälle und Zweifel" when Hamann explains the philosophical anthropology behind his theory. Hamann begins from the same starting point as Herder: that the characteristic nature of man consists in freedom and reason; and that reason does not consist in instinct or innate ideas, but in man's power to learn.[40] But he gives the concepts of freedom and reason a completely different reading from Herder. Whereas Herder sees human nature in asocial and ahistorical terms in his treatise,[41] Hamann insists on putting it in its social and historical context. According to Hamann, the first principle of philosophical anthropology has been already laid down by Aristotle in the *Politics:* "Man is a political animal; only a beast or god can live outside the polis." Hamann thinks that if we take this principle seriously, then we have to interpret the concepts of freedom and reason in social and historical terms. It means that freedom consists not in some special faculty inherent in the individual alone, but in the distinctive manner in which an individual directs his life in a community. More precisely, freedom is "the republican privilege" to govern others and to be governed by them. Similarly, Aristotle's principle implies that reason is much more than the general capacity to learn, or the manner in which the individual responds to his experience. Rather, we have to see learning in its social and historical setting: it is the manner in which someone assimilates a cultural tradition. What is crucial for the formation of our rationality, Hamann insists, is the internalization of the traditions of a culture: "The stamina and menstrua of our reason are revelation and tradition, which we make into our own property and transform into our powers and vital juices."[42]

Hamann's Aristotelian anthropology is the basis for his social and historical view of language. We completely fail to understand language, Hamann maintains, if we do not understand it as a means of communication. Language, like all essentially human creations, has to be understood in its social and historical context; it is not the product of discrete individuals but of an entire nation. What is language but a verbal custom, a cultural tradition embodied in words? It is the repository of all the characteristic ways of thinking of a nation, both shaping its thought and in turn being shaped by it.

The "Anthropologie in nuce" contained in the first few pages of "Philologische Einfälle und Zweifel" is of great historical significance. It is one of the first reactions against the individualistic anthropology of the Enlightenment, and the beginning of the social and historical concepts of freedom and reason that eventually acquired predominance in post-Kantian philosophy. Ironically, it was the fate of Herder, who was Hamann's original target, to transmit Hamann's teachings to the post-Kantian generation. In his *Ideen zur Philosophie der Geschichte der Menschheit* Herder admitted the point behind Hamann's criticisms and assimilated Hamann's teaching into his own philosophy of history. Through this work, Hamann's ideas were handed down to the next generation.[43]

5.4. Herder's Genetic Method

Although Herder formulates the general goals of his philosophical program in his treatise on the origin of language, he does not explain how they are to be achieved. We are told that philosophy must seek naturalistic yet nonreductivistic explanations of characteristic human activities; but we are still left in the dark as to how to acquire such explanations. In other words, Herder fails to consider the all-important problem of method.

It would be a mistake to infer, however, that Herder was not aware of this problem. Although in the treatise on language he ignores it, Herder had begun to think about the issue as early as 1767, three years before he even wrote his treatise. In the introduction to the first, and in the preliminary discourse to the second "Sammlung" of his *Fragmente,* he had already sketched the outlines of his philosophical method, the so-called genetic method for which he later became famous.[44]

The starting point for Herder's reflections in the *Fragmente* are some problems of literary criticism. Herder raises the question of the proper method for understanding and appraising a literary work. He maintains that the true critic does not apply preconceived principles or standards to a work, but understands it from within, according to the intention of the author. But understanding an author's intention is no simple task, Herder realizes. It imposes difficult demands upon the critic, who must consider all the factors that go into the creation of a work, in particular, the social and historical conditions necessary for its composition, factors such as the language, customs, religion, and political institutions of a culture. The fundamental task of the critic is therefore to put himself in the position of the author, sympathizing with his purposes and identifying with his cultural background. He should then criticize the work internally, according to the author's own purposes and values. Does the author succeed in his plans? Does he express the characteristic life of his culture? And does he exploit the natural riches of his own language? These are the kinds of questions the critic must ask, in Herder's view. Should the critic persist in applying his own preconceived standards, then his criticisms eventually beg the question. He ceases to be an impartial judge and does nothing more than pit his own cultural standards against those of the author.

In the second and revised edition of the *Fragmente,* which appeared in 1768, Herder took another step forward in the development of his methodology.[45] Here he began to apply a lesson that he had learned from Kant's

Allgemeine Naturgeschichte und Theorie des Himmels: that all natural things have a history.[46] It is significant that Herder immediately generalizes Kant's principle, so that it is true not only of all natural things, but of all human creations as well. Language, art, science, and religion are all seen as subject to the same processes of growth and decay as natural things. To understand human creations, Herder argues, we must resist the temptation to see them as eternal or anatural. Rather, we must regard them as the products of history. It is necessary to explain them 'genetically' since their genesis makes them what they are. As Herder explains in one pregnant passage: "With the origin of a thing one part of its history escapes us which can explain so much of the thing, and indeed its most important part. Just as a tree grows from its roots, so art, language and science grow from their origins. In the seed there lies the creature with all its members; and in the origin of a phenomenon there lies all the treasure of its interpretation, through which our explanation of it becomes genetic."[47]

Some seven years later, in his *Auch eine Philosophie der Geschichte der Menschheit* (1774), Herder returns to the problem of method, putting it into the very forefront of his concerns. The aim of this passionate and declamatory tract is to expose some of the abuses of the historical methodology of the *Aufklärung*. Herder's main targets are such historians as Voltaire, Lessing, and Hume. It is indeed fitting to call this work Herder's *Discourse on Method*. The irony of the title stems from the fact that it is meant to be not just another philosophy of history, but the methodological prolegomenon to any future one.

In *Auch eine Philosophie der Geschichte* Herder simply extends the genetic method of the *Fragmente* into the fields of history and anthropology. He generalizes the demand for an internal understanding, so that it applies not only to literature, but to all human activities. How can we understand the actions of the Amazon Indian, an ancient Greek, or a medieval monk? Here again the same methodological dictates apply. It is necessary for the observer to suspend his a priori principles and moral standards. Just as a critic must judge a work according to the purpose of the author, so the historian must understand an action according to the intention of the agent. He must know not only the causes of the action (the conditions that make it necessary according to natural laws), but also the reasons for it (the values and beliefs that justify it in the eyes of the agent himself). No less than the critic, then, the historian must sympathize with the agent and identify with the language, customs, and values of his culture. The fundamental precept of the critic now becomes that of the historian: ". . . go into the age, into the region, into the whole of history, feel yourself into everything—only now are you on the path toward understanding an utterance."[48]

Why is it necessary, though, to have such an internal understanding of a culture? Why not apply a priori principles or absolute standards? Herder has a simple answer to this question—but one that shakes the very foundations of the *Aufklärung*. It is misleading to apply universal or absolute principles, he argues, because at bottom there really are none. The standards applied by the philosophical historians of the *Aufklärung* are only apparently universal, natural, or rational; but ultimately they are nothing more than the standards of their own culture and time, illicitly universalized as if they held for all cultures and times. Hence to judge a culture from an apparently absolute or universal standard is to commit a fundamental fallacy: ethnocentrism.[49] It is to judge covertly one culture in terms of another. It is this fallacy that Herder regards as the main shortcoming of the philosophy of history of the *Aufklärung*. Rather than seeing other cultures as ends in themselves having their own sui generis values, the *Aufklärer* consider the values of eighteenth-century Europe to be the purpose of history itself; they then appraise all other cultures according to the degree that they contribute to these ends. Later, in 1785, Herder begins to see Kant's philosophy of history as a paradigm case of this abuse.

The rationale for Herder's genetic method is thus his doctrine of historical and cultural relativity. This new and radical theory, which Herder is the first to articulate in such daring general terms,[50] is perfectly explicit in *Auch eine Philosophie der Geschichte*. At several points Herder openly states that the values of different cultures are incommensurable, and that there are no absolute standards to judge between them.[51] As he sums up his doctrine in an oft-cited metaphor: "Every nation has the center of its happiness within itself just as every ball has its own center of gravity."[52]

There is, however, a deeper rationale for Herder's method, and indeed for the doctrine of cultural relativity itself. This is nothing less than Hamann's philosophical anthropology, which Herder acquired from Hamann. According to this anthropology, there is not a single, permanent human essence that remains the same for all epochs and cultures. Rather, the nature of man depends upon his culture, so that there are as many forms of humanity as there are different cultures. The only natural essence of man is his plasticity, his ability to adapt to the most diverse circumstances, whether these be his climate and topography or his cultural conditioning. There is not a Hobbesian natural man, then, who has some fixed needs in the state of nature, which then provide the criteria for appraising all social and political institutions. On the contrary: the nature of man is shaped by these institutions, so that there is no absolute standpoint outside them from which they can be judged. Hence, given the formative role of society and history, a genetic method becomes a sheer necessity. Since culture determines the very identity of man, the philosopher has no option but to understand him from within, according to the norms, beliefs, and traditions of his culture.

To sum up the essence of Herder's genetic method, it is necessary to stress two fundamental guidelines. The first is that characteristic human activities (language, religion, art, philosophy, science) are not innate, eternal, or supernatural, but the product of social, historical, and cultural forces. Hence to explain these activities is to describe their social-historical genesis since this genesis makes them what they are. Furthermore, according to the second guideline, it is necessary to understand an action according to the intention of the agent and not only according to its conformity to causal laws. To understand an action is therefore to know not only its causes, but also its reasons. With the first guideline, Herder rules out not only the supernaturalist, who believes these activities are God-given, but also the rationalist, who thinks that they are innate, universal, or eternal. With the second guideline, he proposes a new teleological paradigm of explanation against the mechanistic paradigm of the materialist. In other words, the first guideline is the maxim of naturalistic explanation; and the second is the maxim of nonreductivistic explanation. Taken together, then, these guidelines secure Herder's objective: a naturalistic, yet nonreductivistic account of characteristic human activities.

Of course, Herder's method is easier to explain than to practice. There are obvious difficulties in achieving an internal understanding of another culture. How can we adopt the standpoint of another culture without covertly allowing the values and beliefs of our own culture to influence our perception and judgment? Herder does see that there is a problem here.[53] But his solution is still a weak one: to make a more thorough study of the facts, to examine with greater patience and precision all the data about the language, customs, and traditions of other cultures. The more we examine these data, he argues, the more we will creep outside our own cultural-epistemological shell.

Such optimism is bound to leave the skeptic cold, however. For what are these facts? And how do we know them, especially when our own judgment is culturally conditioned? Herder is simply restating the need for objectivity—when its very possibility is in question. Indeed, a strong version of Herder's doctrine of cultural relativity undermines the possibility of all objectivity. If our perception and judgment is completely conditioned by our culture, then it is not possible to get outside it and to understand another culture on its own terms. The conclusion of a radical relativity therefore seems to be a total skepticism about the possibility of knowledge of other cultures. So, unless Herder carefully defines and qualifies his doctrine, it will not support but undermine his methodology.

Whatever its difficulties, Herder's method proved to be a historical success. It had a visible influence upon the post-Kantian generation, and especially Fichte, Schelling, and Hegel. This method was applied by Fichte in the "Pragmatische Geschichte" section of the *Wissenschaftslehre* (1794), by Schelling in the *System des transcendentalen Idealismus* (1800), and by Hegel in the *Phänomenologie des Geistes* (1807). All three agreed with Herder that characteristic human activities are the products of culture, and that to understand them is to trace their genesis in history.

5.5. The Principles of Herder's Vitalism

In December 1774 Herder submitted another treatise for an academic prize, his *Vom Erkennen und Empfinden der menschlichen Seele*. This work was rewritten several times and eventually published in 1778.[54] The question posed by the Akademie was "What is the nature of, and the relationship between, the two basic faculties of the soul, knowledge (*erkennen*) and feeling (*empfinden*)?" This time, however, Herder did not win the prize. The reason was that he could not agree with the main assumption behind the Akademie's question: that there are two separate faculties of the soul that somehow interact with one another. Siding with his former teacher, Hamann, Herder saw all the faculties of the soul as inseparable, as indivisibly united in a single, living whole. One purpose of his treatise was to explicate just this old Hamannian theme. Herder knew all too well that his disagreement with the Akademie would cost him the prize. But that did not diminish his own view of the work. Herder considered *Vom Erkennen und Empfinden* his best book; and he thought its themes were so important that all philosophy rested upon them.[55]

Vom Erkennen und Empfinden marks an important stage in the development of Herder's thought. While *Ueber den Ursprung der Sprache* initiates his philosophical program, and while the *Fragmente* and *Auch eine Philosophie der Geschichte* formulate its methodology, *Vom Erkennen und Empfinden* sets forth its general metaphysical principles. It is here that Herder first elaborates his theory of organic powers, which he applies in almost all of his later philosophical works. The purpose of this theory is to resolve one formidable issue still facing Herder: the mind-body problem. How is it possible for the mind and body to interact when they appear to be such heterogeneous entities? Some answer to this question is clearly necessary if Herder is to achieve his goal of finding naturalistic explanations of characteristic human activities. If the relationship between mind and body is intrinsically mysterious, or if the mind is independent of the body and nature as a whole, then plainly such explanations will be out of the question.

It was probably Hamann who alerted Herder to the importance of the mind-body problem. Hamann's claim in "Ritter von Rosenkreuz" and "Philologische Einfälle und Zweifel," that the mind-body relationship is essentially mysterious, must have presented a powerful challenge to Herder. *Vom Erkennen und Empfinden* is Herder's reply to that challenge, his attempt to defend his naturalism against Hamann's objection.

Herder's treatise is also a critique of the psychology of the *Aufklärung*. A faculty psychology that divides the soul into compartments, a crude materialism that reduces the mind to a machine, and a narrow intellectualism that sees the intellect as the predominant power of the soul—all these trends of eighteenth-century psychology are brought under fire. Herder rejects all these theories for two reasons: they are either too reductivistic or too dualistic. The problem with both reductivism and dualism, Herder maintains, is that they fail to do justice to some basic facts. If we are reductivists, who reduce the mind to a machine, then we cannot explain its sui generis features; and if we are dualists, who divide the mind from the body and all the faculties of the mind from one another, then we cannot account for the fact that they interact. What we need, then, is some new theory of mind that is neither reductivistic nor dualistic. This theory will have to account for both the dependence *and* independence of mind and body. A central task of *Vom Erkennen und Empfinden* is to sketch just such a theory.

The guiding assumption behind Herder's theory of mind is that mind and body are not distinct kinds of substance, but different degrees of organization and development of a single living power. According to this theory, the body is not a mere machine, a system that acts only upon the imposition of some external force. Rather, it is an organism, a system that spontaneously generates its activity and organizes itself. Conversely, the mind is not a disembodied spirit, but only the highest degree of organization and development of the physical powers of the body. It is important to see that this theory does not define the mind by what kind of thing or entity it is, but only by its distinctive purpose or function, which is to integrate, control, and organize all the various functions of the body.[56]

Herder's theory postulates a single principle, a single concept to unite our notions of mind and body: the concept of power *(Kraft)*. The essence of power is defined as self-generating, self-organizing activity, activity that gradually develops from simpler to higher degrees of organization. The difference between mind and body is not a difference in kind, then, but only one in degree: the body is amorphous power, the mind organized power. It also follows from this theory that we can treat both mind and body in either mental or physical terms: the mind is a higher degree of organization of the body, or the body is a lower degree of organization of the mind, depending on our perspective.

It is a great advantage of this theory, Herder maintains, that it avoids the pitfalls of dualism and reductivism. The theory is clearly not dualistic since it defines the mind by its purpose, the control and organization of the various functions of the body.[57] But it is also not reductivistic because it states that the mind is the unity of the various functions of the body, and such a unity is seen as a whole that is not reducible to the mere sum of its parts. Even more to the point, however, the whole question of reducibility is now irrelevant since Herder breaks with the central principle behind materialism: that the body is a machine. According to Herder, the body is not a dead machine, but a living organism. Hence the materialist and the mechanist are deprived of the terms of their reductive explanations. They cannot explain the body, let alone the mind.

Another important advantage of the theory, Herder argues, is that it easily explains the interaction between mind and body.[58] Since they are not heterogeneous substances and are instead only different aspects of a single living force, there is no problem in accounting for the interaction between them. Indeed, the theory accounts for not only the possibility, but even the necessity of mental-physical interaction. The mind not only can but must interact with the body since its very nature is to organize and control the various functions of the body. Conversely, the body would cease to function and live if it were not organized and directed by the mind.

Herder finds added confirmation for his theory in the new biological sciences, and in particular in the physiological research of Albrecht von Haller. Indeed, the final draft of *Vom Erkennen und Empfinden* gives pride of place to a discussion of the implications of Haller's works.[59] It is not difficult to see why Herder is so enthusiastic about Haller's discoveries. According to Herder, Haller's observations of the phenomenon of 'irritability' *(Reizbarkeit)*—the contraction of muscle tissue upon the application of a stimulus and its relaxation upon removal of the stimulus—show that there is one and the same living force in the mental and the physical. An apparent piece of matter (the muscle tissue) seems to be alive, reacting to the stimuli with a force of its own. On the basis of these observations Herder felt justified in concluding that irritability is the missing link between the material and the mental, the essential transition in the *lex continui* leading from matter up to mind. If thought is the power of organizing and controlling sensation, sensation in turn consists in nothing more than irritation.[60] Hence thought itself appears to be a function of the physical-physiological forces at work in irritability. Thanks to Haller, Herder sees physiology as the basis for a new philosophy of mind that will investigate the continuity between the mental and the physical. As Herder declares at one point: "In my humble opinion, no psychology is possible that is not physiology at every step."[61]

Whatever its advantages, Herder's theory is also open to some serious objections. Aware of these objections, Herder tries to reply to them.

'What are these organic powers but *qualitates occultae* that simply redescribe what they are to explain?' That is one of Kant's main objections against Herder in 1785; but Herder raised it himself some ten years earlier. What is his reply? Herder admits that we do not know the inner essence of power, and he also recognizes that we do not explain anything just by postulating some general force. Nevertheless, he maintains that we know the effects of a power from experience, and that we are therefore justified in assuming some organic powers as the causes of these effects. Herder is intent on giving the concept of power a strictly tentative or hypothetical, though by no means regulative, status. He treats the problem of the nature of power as an empirical and not metaphysical issue; and he expects that the growing biological sciences, which are always discovering new forces in the body (namely, animal magnetism), will gradually come closer to solving this problem. Yet the question still remains: can the concept of power be given such empirical or scientific status? Is Herder not transcending the limits of experience in postulating such forces? That is the question. And, as we shall soon see, Kant never tired of pursuing Herder along just these lines.

'We attribute ends to external objects only by analogy with our own activity, so that any organic theory is anthropomorphic'. This is another of Kant's later objections to Herder; but again Herder already has a reply to it in 1778. His reply is as frank as it is brash. Herder openly admits that our knowledge of organic objects is analogical, derived from likening things outside us to ourselves. A pure insight into things-in-themselves is impossible for us; hence we have to content ourselves with a knowledge of how things appear to us or how they are like us. That is to say: we have to resign ourselves to analogy. Thus Herder confesses, "I am not ashamed of myself . . . I run after images, after analogies . . . because I do not know any other game for my thinking powers."[62]

This recognition of the role of analogy brings Herder to a striking conclusion about the importance of literature. Literature, he argues, is more important than philosophy for an understanding of life. It is the great strength of literature that it can grasp life through analogy. A Homer or a Sophocles, a Dante or a Shakespeare, is more helpful for an understanding of life than an Aristotle or a Leibniz, a Locke or a Shaftesbury.

But does not Herder's frank and daring position concerning analogical explanation leave him out on a limb? In admitting the literary quality of his theory, does he not also forfeit its claim to scientific status? Has he not simply traded supernaturalistic explanations for anthropomorphic ones? These too are questions that Kant did not fail to raise in his later controversy with Herder.

5.6. Kant's Quarrel with Herder

During his formative university years in Königsberg, 1762 to 1764, Herder had been one of Kant's most talented and devoted students.[63] He had a great debt to Kant, who he considered his best teacher. And Kant was equally impressed with the talents of his young pupil. He allowed him to attend his lectures gratis and followed his career with interest and admiration. But as the years grew so did the distance between teacher and student. Kant became suspicious of Herder's intimate relationship with Hamann, which had been quickly restored after the debate over the origin of language.[64] He saw Herder's *Aelteste Urkunde des Menschengeschlechts,* a work which Hamann explained to him,[65] as a relapse into Hamannian mysticism. For his part, Herder had little inclination to study the *Kritik,* which he found "a hard bone to chew," and which he admitted was contrary to his own way of thinking.[66] Despite these tensions, Kant and Herder maintained the semblance of friendship. At least Kant never let his misgivings be known; and, through Hamann, Herder sent his regards to his former teacher.

The storm clouds broke sometime in the summer of 1783. At a salon, Herder heard some very disturbing news: Kant held him responsible for the poor reception of the *Kritik.* Herder could hardly believe his ears. But that, at any rate, is what J. F. Hartknoch, Kant's and Herder's publisher, whispered into them.[67] Herder was shocked by the news. How could Kant, his best teacher, expect that of him, one of his best students? Herder admitted that the *Kritik* was not to his liking; but he protested that he never said or wrote anything against it.

Although these disavowals are probably ingenuous, it is not difficult to see the source of Kant's suspicions. He had been distressed by the poor reception of the *Kritik* ever since its publication in May 1781. If the *Kritik* were to make an impact, it was important that it receive a sympathetic hearing in Weimar and Jena, which were rapidly becoming the cultural centers of Germany. But Herder was in Weimar, where he enjoyed the limelight and had close ties with nearly everyone on the literary scene. And Kant was already convinced that Herder was on Hamann's side in the ideological struggle between *Aufklärung* and *Sturm und Drang.* Hence, Herder must have seemed a grave obstacle to the reception of the *Kritik.*[68]

A quarrel with Herder was clearly in the offing then. Kant probably felt that if he were to secure a public for the *Kritik* he would have to combat Herder's influence. The only question then was how? The answer to that question finally came on July 10, 1784, when C. G. Schütz, the editor of the *Allgemeine Literatur Zeitung,* asked Kant to review Herder's latest work, *Ideen zur Philosophie der Geschichte der Menschheit.* Kant jumped at the opportunity, even waiving the royalties. Here was a chance to settle scores with Herder and to check the forces holding back the reception of the *Kritik.* Kant's review of the first part of the *Ideen* duly appeared in January 1785; a review of the second part followed in November of the same year.

Kant's review of Herder's *Ideen* has been accurately described as "a masterpiece of personal attack veiled under an appearance of objectivity."[69] It is full of ironic compliments, snide criticisms, and schoolmasterly advice— all smoothed over with a dry and proper academic style. Kant's disparaging remarks about Herder's clerical vocation, and his unfair claim that his book cannot be judged by customary standards, show that he was aiming at the author.

Despite such invective, Kant's review remains of great philosophical importance. It contains, if only *in nuce,* Kant's response to almost every major aspect of Herder's philosophy. Herder's naturalism, historicism, vitalism, and methodology all come in for a brief but brutal bombardment. If we take the view that Herder's philosophy is the main alternative to Kant's,[70] then Kant's review becomes all the more important for stating his reactions to that alternative. A short examination of the issues and arguments behind Kant's review should then provide us with a little more insight into why Kant took the position he did.

Kant's review of the *Ideen* is primarily a criticism of the attempt to justify metaphysics through natural science. It is indeed surprisingly modern and positivistic in spirit, an all-out attack on 'pseudo-science'. The main issues raised by the review, and the subsequent controversy surrounding it, concern the methods and limits of scientific explanation. What is the proper method of science? What, indeed, is explanation? And what is the boundary line between the natural and metaphysical? Such are the questions at dispute.

The controversy immediately becomes more complicated, however, as soon as we recall that Kant and Herder share roughly similar ideals of science. They both agree on the necessity of naturalism, and they both use the same criterion to distinguish between science and metaphysics, namely, possible experience. Nevertheless, they disagree with each other concerning the limits of naturalism, or where to draw the boundary line between the natural and the metaphysical. This line is 'possible experience', to be sure. But what is that? Where does experience begin and where does it end? There is indeed a very serious problem here. If we make the boundaries of experience too large, then we permit all kinds of metaphysics; but if we make them too small, then we make the explicable inexplicable and unduly restrict the frontiers of science. This problem soon became a sticking point in the controversy between Kant and Herder. While Kant accuses Herder of going beyond the limits of experience, Herder charges Kant with arbitrarily limiting this sphere and rendering the comprehensible incomprehensible. So who is guilty of metaphysics—Kant or Herder?

It is a new breed of metaphysics that Kant confronts in the *Ideen*—one that he does not even consider in the *Kritik*. This metaphysics does not proceed a priori, applying the Wolffian syllogistic apparatus so ruthlessly exposed in the *Kritik*. Rather, it operates a posteriori, using the methods and results of natural science. It sees metaphysics as nothing more than a general system of all the various sciences. All in all, it is metaphysics on the model of Kant's "Prize Essay" of 1763: ontology in the manner of Newton. Herder had been influenced by Kant's early work and continued to apply its methodology in his later philosophy.[71] So, ironically, in criticizing the metaphysics of Herder's *Ideen*, Kant is sparring with his own precritical shadow.

Kant's review of the *Ideen* is a sharp attack on Herder's new metaphysics. Kant regards this metaphysics as pseudo-science, the misconceived effort to verify empirically the empirically unverifiable. He repeatedly accuses Herder of trying to sneak metaphysics in through the back door of natural science. Thus he criticizes Herder time and again for drawing grand metaphysical conclusions from weak empirical premises; and at one point he is perfectly explicit: "though Herder denounces metaphysics in the usual fashionable manner he still practices it all the time."[72] So Kant had not only personal, but also philosophical motives for writing a hostile review of the *Ideen*. If the negative teaching of the *Kritik* were not to be in vain, then Kant had to strike—and strike hard—to nip this new metaphysics in the bud. The dragon born of his own "Prize Essay" had to be slain before it devoured the *Kritik*.

The prime example of Herder's covert metaphysics, in Kant's view, is his concept of organic power. What does this concept amount to, he asks, but the attempt to explain the little known through the completely unknown? Since all that we know from experience is the effect of organic powers, knowledge of the powers themselves cannot be given in possible experience. So whether Herder admits it or not, in postulating organic powers he is transcending the limits of possible experience and thus indulging in metaphysics.[73] In making this objection, Kant is of course only repeating the old criticism of the scholastic substantial forms, which Descartes, Bacon, and Hobbes all repudiated as *qualitates occultae*.

As discussed in the previous section, Herder tries to anticipate this old criticism. He argues that the assumption of organic powers does not postulate occult qualities since their effects are known from experience. But this reply only begs Kant's question: if we do not know the powers themselves, then how do we know that what we see in experience is their effect?

No less metaphysical in Kant's eyes is Herder's naturalistic explanation of the origin of reason. In the fourth book of the *Ideen* Herder speculates about the anatomical and physiological preconditions of rationality, stressing the importance of such factors as the structure of the brain and the upright posture of man.[74] Ironically, some of these speculations were inspired by Kant's theorizing at the close of the *Allgemeine Naturgeschichte*,[75] another work of the young Kant much admired by Herder. But now Kant flatly dismisses such speculations as metaphysical. What effect such gross material factors have upon human rationality obviously transcends the limits of reason, he says, though without giving any justification.[76] Kant then asks: if we are to use the concept of power to explain the origin of reason, then why not just invoke a distinct kind of power for reason itself? Why bother explaining reason on the basis of simpler powers, as if it were the effect of the forces inherent in matter? Thus the old problem about the identification of substantial forms rears its ugly head.

Along with all the hidden metaphysics in the *Ideen*, Kant also takes strong exception to Herder's philosophical method. He finds Herder's method no less pseudo-scientific than his metaphysics. In his *Ideen* Herder employs a method of analogy, making inferences about the unknown on the assumption that it is similar to the known. In using this method he again follows the young Kant, who had drawn analogies between our solar system and the rest of the cosmos in his *Allgemeine Naturgeschichte*.[77] But Kant protests that, however useful this method in the natural sciences, it is the very opposite of a proper philosophical method. Rather, it confuses the boundaries between philosophy and poetry, sacrificing the clarity and rigor of the understanding for the vagueness and caprice of the imagination. Such a method permits metaphor to replace explanation, allegory to supplant observation, and speculation to oust demonstration. What a philosophy of history requires above all, Kant insists, is "logical exactitude in the determination of concepts," "careful analysis and verification of principles."[78] At the close of his review Kant even suggests that Herder "impose some restraints upon his genius" before writing the next part of his work. He ought to discipline his "bold imagination" for the sake of "the cautious use of his reason."

Although Herder undoubtedly makes some hasty analogies, Kant's criticism of his methodology is not entirely fair. The method recommended by Kant is in fact explicitly rejected by Herder.[79] The standards of rigor, clarity, and precision that Kant demands are unattainable in studying life and history, Herder contends. But, even more to the point, he would say that Kant's scholastic procedure of definition and proof does not grasp life from within, according to the purposes of the agent. Herder also has a much more sophisticated defense of analogy than Kant assumes. In *Vom Erkennen und Empfinden* he argues that our only guide in history is analogy since we cannot understand the actions of others except by analogy with our own actions. So rather than unintentionally confusing philosophy with literature, as Kant charges, Herder is intentionally pushing philosophy in the direction of literature. It is supposedly literature that, with all its images and metaphors, provides us with the deepest understanding of life. Better a Shakespeare than a Leibniz—and, by the same token, a Herder than a Kant.

5.7. The Kant-Herder Controversy and the Origins of the Third *Kritik*

After his review of the second part of the *Ideen* appeared, Kant's quarrel with Herder seemed to end abruptly. In his letter of June 25, 1787, to C. G. Schütz, Kant formally called off all further hostilities.[80] Pleading that he had no more time, Kant declined Schütz's offer to review the third part of the *Ideen*. It was time to put polemics aside and turn to the pressing task of completing the critical philosophy. Hence Kant informed Schütz that he planned to devote himself to the "Grundlage der Kritik des Geschmacks," which later became known as the first part of the third *Kritik*, the "Kritik der aesthetischen Urteilskraft."

Despite his formal cessation of hostilities, Kant's struggle with Herder was really only beginning. Herder's allies were now preparing a counterattack, which would force Kant to reply.[81] But, much more significant, and even more ominous, the controversy with Herder had raised some serious questions—questions that posed a formidable challenge to the critical philosophy; Kant had seen this challenge and knew that he could not ignore it. His decision to work on the "Kritik des Geschmacks" is only an apparent closure of his debate with Herder; it is more a resolve to reflect upon the deeper questions raised by the debate.

What were these questions facing Kant? They all revolved around the thorny issue of teleology. Is it possible to attribute final causes to things in nature? Are final causes reducible to efficient ones? And, if not, are they equally capable of formulation into scientific laws? These questions were always lying underneath the surface of the controversy with Herder. The legitimacy of Herder's concept of power, one of the issues raised by the debate, ultimately depends upon the issue of teleology. If it is possible to attribute final causes to things in nature, and if these are not reducible to mechanical causes, then the concept of power does have its own sui generis explanatory value. In his review of the *Ideen*, however, Kant fails to consider this deeper issue. He simply dismisses Herder's concept as an occult quality, a refuge of ignorance that simply re-describes what it is to explain. Yet, as Leibniz pointed out long ago, this objection against the idea of a *vis viva* begs important questions, gratuitously supposing that mechanical causality is the only form of natural explanation.[82]

So it was now incumbent upon Kant to examine the ticklish problem of teleology. But it was much more than his criticism of the concept of power that was at stake: the fate of the critical philosophy itself hung in the balance. If teleological explanations are capable of becoming natural laws, then the door is open for a new kind of naturalistic explanation of the origin of human rationality, an explanation on the basis not of mechanical but teleological laws. All our rationality then amounts to nothing more than a manifestation of organic force, so that reason no longer belongs to an autonomous noumenal realm. Assuming, then, that such an explanation is possible, the noumenal-phenomenal dualism of the first *Kritik*, and the entire moral philosophy of the second *Kritik* that rests upon it, is in danger of collapse. This form of explanation is indeed a possibility that Kant does not fully consider in the first *Kritik*.[83] There Kant limits the category of causality to the phenomenal world; but he still does not have a consistent or detailed theory of teleology. And, in any case, his restrictions upon the category of causality would not bother Herder, who agrees that reason is not explicable according to mechanical laws, but who advances another possibility in suggesting teleological ones.

Despite its importance, teleology would probably have remained a dead issue for Kant if it were not for a provocative article that appeared in the October-November 1786 issue of the *Teutsche Merkur*, "Noch etwas über die Menschenrassen: An Herrn Dr. Biester."[84] This curious piece was, of all things, a critique of Kant's theory of race, and in particular of a recent essay of Kant's that appeared in the November 1785 issue of the *Berlinische Monatsschrift*, "Bestimmung des Begriffs einer Menschenrasse." Its author was a renowned biologist and anthropologist, Georg Forster.[85] All of this seems to be of little interest for the problem at hand, and indeed it has usually been ignored.[86] We too could happily forget about it if one stubborn little fact did not catch our eye: Forster was an admirer of Herder's *Ideen* and, moreover, had just formed an alliance with Herder.[87] Like many people in Jena and Weimar, Forster thought that Kant's review of the *Ideen* had not done Herder justice. So, as we might expect, his *Teutsche Merkur* article continues Herder's debate with Kant. Although Forster's main purpose in his article is to attack Kant's theory of race, he now and then makes a few remarks to defend some patently Herderian ideas. Forster's defense of Herder is largely covert, never mentioning Herder by name. But Kant was suspicious and easily blew Forster's cover, exposing his polemical intent in a few telling lines.[88]

Although the details of Kant's and Forster's debate over race do not concern us here,[89] there is one major issue underlying the debate that does deserve our attention, given its philosophical significance. This is the fact that Kant and Forster have opposing theories about the origin of life, each of them representing the two main competing theories of eighteenth-century biology. Kant is an advocate of the 'preformation' theory, which explains the origin of life from the presence of preformed hereditary factors. The origin of these factors is usually ascribed to divine creation; but Kant dismisses all such speculation as metaphysics. All that natural science can explain, he argues, is the transmission of the preformed factors from one generation to the next; but it cannot explain the origin of these factors themselves. By contrast, Forster, like Herder, is an adherent of the theory of spontaneous generation. This theory explains the origin of life from the presence of spontaneous forces in matter that adapt and react to their surroundings (climate, topography, and so on). Unlike Kant, Forster affirms that it is in principle possible to explain the origin of life itself if we assume that there are organic powers in matter. According to Forster, the concept of an organic power is not metaphysical, as Kant charges, but a valid inference from empirical facts. In an especially provocative passage of his *Teutsche Merkur* essay Forster accuses Kant of "an unmanly fear" in not allowing such an inference.[90]

Judging from the little historical evidence available, Forster's essay appears to have been the catalyst for Kant's reflection upon the problem of teleology. It is at least noteworthy that, in his few remarks about the third *Kritik* prior to the appearance of Forster's article, Kant never mentions a critique of teleology, but speaks of only a "Kritik des Geschmacks." But only a year after Forster's article was published, and indeed at the same time as Kant was preparing his reply to it, Kant refers to 'Teleologie' as a necessary part of his system. In his letter of December 27, 1787, to Reinhold, Kant announces the final structure of his system of philosophy, stating explicitly that 'Teleologie' is the middle point of his system, the connecting link between the theoretical philosophy of the first *Kritik* and the practical philosophy of the second.[91]

Kant eventually replied to Forster with an article in the January-February 1788 issue of the *Teutsche Merkur*. The very title of his reply reveals his newfound preoccupation with the problem of teleology: "Ueber den Gebrauch der teleologischen Prinzipien in der Philosophie." This essay is indeed the preparatory study for the "Kritik der teleologischen Urteilskraft" of the third *Kritik*. In its concluding paragraphs Kant grapples with the problem of teleology and proclaims a 'natürliche Teleologie', which soon became the second half of the third *Kritik*.

Kant's reply to Forster unmasks the motive behind his treatment of the problem of teleology. When Forster accuses Kant of his "unmanly fear" in not permitting the inference in the existence of organic powers, Kant retaliates with his argument against teleology.[92] The motive behind Kant's argument is therefore plain: to debunk the scientific status of Herder's concept of organic power, and in doing so to ward off the threat to the noumenal-phenomenal dualism of the first *Kritik*. Kant's strategy against Forster—and ultimately Herder—is to expose the pseudo-scientific status of the concept of organic power by revealing the metaphysical dimension inherent in all teleological judgment. Kant now sees that he can argue successfully against Herder's concept only by considering the deeper issue of teleology. In the face of Forster's defense of organic power as an empirical concept, it simply would not do to reiterate the old charge of occult qualities.

At this point, then, our investigation comes to a surprising conclusion. The origin of Kant's theory of teleology in the third *Kritik* runs counter to all our expectations and the usual explanations.[93] The catalyst for Kant's theory is *not* the problem of bridging the gap between the noumenal and phenomenal worlds. Rather, the very opposite is the case: the stimulus is the problem of how to defend and preserve that dualism.

Of course, Kant has both of these concerns in the third *Kritik*. His aim is not only to preserve, but also to overcome the noumenal-phenomenal dualism.[94] If teleology threatens to destroy that dualism, it also promises to bridge it. Hence Kant faces the delicate task in the third *Kritik* of both limiting and preserving teleology. His solution to this problem is his regulative theory of teleological judgment, which establishes both the necessity and the regulative status of teleology.

Although Kant certainly faced both these problems, the fact still remains that the immediate stimulus and incentive for his theory came from Forster's essay; and the motive for Kant's attack upon Forster was not to bridge, but to defend that dualism. In using Herder's concept of power to explain the origin of life, Forster renews Herder's threat to Kant's dualism. Kant saw that threat, and knew that he could not ward it off by simple gerrymandering, that is, by replying that the explanation of the origin of life fell into the phenomenal realm and posed no danger to the noumenal realm. He recognized all too clearly that the very legitimacy of a noumenal-phenomenal borderline was being thrown into question by Forster and Herder, who wanted to explain the genesis of rationality itself. Hence if Kant was to protect that dualism, he had to limit the teleological claims implicit in the concept of organic power. This became a central task of the second half of the third *Kritik*.

Kant's argument against Forster in the "Teleologie" is the foundation for his critical theory of judgment in the third *Kritik*. Kant begins his argument by defining a basic principle which serves as its premise. According to this principle, everything in natural science must be explained naturalistically, that is, without appeal to metaphysical principles or supernatural causes.[95] Since Forster and Herder also endorse this principle, Kant feels confident that his argument begins from a common premise. The next problem is then to define the limits of naturalistic explanation. To Kant, these limits are clear: they are the boundaries of possible experience. If we postulate fundamental forces that cannot be verified in experience, then "we quit the fruitful field of natural investigation and go astray in the desert of metaphysics." Concerning these boundaries, Kant again thinks that he can rely upon Forster's and Herder's assent, given that they are both champions of observation against metaphysics. So given that Herder and Forster agree with the principle of naturalism, and given that they also concur about its limits in possible experience, the source of their conflict with Kant concerns only whether they stick to this principle and whether they remain within these limits. In other words, Kant is raising the question, Are Forster and Herder true to their naturalistic ideals?

Predictably, Kant's answer to this question is an emphatic "No." Herder and Forster violate their naturalistic ideals, he argues, because they postulate organic powers within matter, whose existence cannot be confirmed by any possible experience. The concept of an organic power is utterly metaphysical, Kant claims, because it attributes purposes to things in nature.[96] But why is the concept of a purpose metaphysical? That is the crucial question concerning the legitimacy of teleological explanation. But Kant comes forward with a clear answer to it. According to Kant, if we attribute purposes to things in nature, then we are going beyond the limits of possible experience, since we can understand purposive activity only through our own experience, where we act according to ends and for the sake of ideas or principles. But, so far as we know, nothing in nature itself acts according to such ends or for the sake of ideas, for we have no evidence that anything in it possesses rationality as human beings do. Though plants and animals all appear to act purposively, they also do not seem to have conscious intentions or rational ends; to put it paradoxically, they act purposively but without a purpose *(zweckmässig ohne Zweck)*. We therefore attribute purposes to natural things only by analogy with our own activity. There is no possible case, though, in which we can verify such an analogy. It is no more possible for us to confirm the analogy than it is for us to jump outside ourselves and become a plant or animal. Hence the attribution of purposes to nature goes beyond the limits of possible experience; and it is therefore, according to the general criterion of naturalistic explanation, completely metaphysical.

In pointing out the analogical status of teleological judgment, Kant is of course only repeating an old thesis of Herder's *Vom Erkennen und Empfinden*. Herder therefore would have to agree with Kant all along the line. Like Kant, he too affirms the necessity of naturalism; he too claims that the limits of naturalism are the limits of experience; and he too insists that teleological explanation is analogical. What Kant's argument against Herder amounts to, then, is the simple charge of inconsistency. According to Kant, Herder is inconsistent because he admits that teleological explanations are analogical; but then he also pretends that they have a naturalistic or scientific status (as constitutive principles). This is a palpable inconsistency because Herder admits that analogical judgments transcend the limits of possible experience, and that the limits of possible experience are those of naturalistic explanation.

Of course, Kant would not dispute Herder's claim in *Vom Erkennen und Empfinden* that the best understanding of life is to be found in literature. His only bone of contention with Herder is his claim that teleological explanations can be analogical *and* scientific. As Herder at times admits, the proper realm of analogy is literature. But, in Kant's eyes, we cannot do good natural science and good literature at the same time. It is the fatal flaw of Herder's philosophy that it tries to do both.

5.8. Herder and the Pantheism Controversy

Herder's entry into the pantheism controversy came as a surprise to no one, least of all Herder himself. The ghost of Spinoza had haunted him for a long time, much as it had Lessing, Mendelssohn, and Jacobi.[97] As early as 1775 Herder had planned to write a work on the triumvirate of Leibniz, Shaftesbury, and Spinoza, defending the views of each philosopher and explaining the parallels between them. There were also Spinozist themes strewn throughout Herder's early writings, a debt that he was acutely aware of and eager to acknowledge. But, for one reason or another, the work on Spinoza was always postponed.[98]

The opportunity for Herder to collect and clarify his thoughts on Spinoza finally came, however, on November 22, 1783, when Jacobi sent him the account of his conversations with Lessing. Jacobi was eager to gain Herder's support for his forthcoming battle with Mendelssohn; and, in the hope of an alliance, he had even cited Herder approvingly in his *Briefe über Spinoza*.[99] But Jacobi was to be disappointed. Herder was delighted to find that such an eminent figure as Lessing also had Spinozist sympathies. That supported his own convictions and gave him the courage to express his own views. So, when Herder eventually replied to Jacobi, on February 6, 1784, he too declared his Spinozism, making a confession no less dramatic and startling than Lessing's: "In all seriousness, my dear Jacobi, since I've moved into the sphere of philosophy, I continue to become aware of the truth of Lessing's proposition that really only the philosophy of Spinoza is at one with itself."[100]

After such a declaration, Herder's role in the pantheism controversy was clearly cut out for him. It was his task to be the spokesman for Spinoza. Now that Mendelssohn, Kant, Jacobi, and Wizenmann had all turned their backs on Spinoza, Herder felt called upon to defend him.[101] In April 1787 he duly completed his contribution to the controversy, *Gott, Einige Gespräche*. With this work, the debate took on a new and interesting dimension.

The significance of *Gott, Einige Gespräche* for the pantheism controversy primarily lies in Herder's creative reinterpretation of Spinoza. Herder completely reverses Jacobi's, Mendelssohn's, and Wizenmann's picture of Spinozism. Rather than seeing it as a danger to morality and religion, Herder regards it as their only foundation. Spinozism is not atheism or fatalism, but the only philosophy that provides us with a tenable concept of God and freedom. The great strength of Spinoza's philosophy, in Herder's view, is that it makes our moral and religious convictions consistent with reason and scientific naturalism.

Of course, such a reappraisal of the moral and religious dimension of Spinoza's philosophy goes hand in hand with some rather unorthodox concepts of morality and religion. But Herder frankly confesses with Lessing: "the orthodox concepts of the divinity are no longer for me." According to Herder, God is neither transcendent nor personal, but omnipresent and impersonal; and freedom is not arbitrary choice, but acting according to the necessity of one's own nature and the beneficent designs of providence. Herder insists, however, that embracing these less orthodox concepts does not mean abandoning Christianity. On the contrary, it merely means reinterpreting our faith in a new and profound manner. The gospel of John and the moral philosophy of Spinoza, the Christian agape and the intellectual love of God, are for Herder one and the same.[102] Hence we can have our faith and our philosophy at the same time. Jacobi's dilemma is valid only if we accept his orthodox concepts of God and freedom. If, however, we reinterpret them in a less orthodox manner, then we find that Spinoza's philosophy does not undermine but supports morality and religion. Jacobi's leap of faith is therefore superfluous. As Herder explained to Jacobi: "If it is not necessary to make a *salto mortale,* then why should we bother? Certainly we do not need to do it; for we are on even ground on God's creation."[103]

Behind Herder's reassessment of the moral and religious implications of Spinoza's philosophy lies his reinterpretation of Spinoza's naturalism. Like Jacobi, Herder sees Spinoza's philosophy as the paradigm of scientific naturalism, not as the relic of metaphysical dogmatism. But Herder construes this naturalism in completely different terms. It does not mean materialism or mechanism, as it does for Jacobi, but something entirely different: vitalism. In Herder's eyes, Spinoza's universe is not a machine, but an organism.

Prima facie it seems absurd to read Spinoza as a vitalist, especially when he denies final causes. And, indeed, at one point, Herder virtually admits that his reading of Spinoza is more a modification than an interpretation of him.[104] Yet Herder does think that he is only updating Spinoza's naturalism so that it is consistent with all the new advances in the biological sciences. Unlike Jacobi, who believes that science is leading toward materialism, Herder maintains that it is moving toward vitalism. To prove his point, Herder refers to the new discoveries in physics and biology which show that the body consists in various forces (for instance, electricity and magnetism).[105] If Spinoza had lived only a century later, free from the mechanistic preconceptions of Descartes's physics, then he would have made force rather than substance his first principle.

With this vitalist reading of Spinoza Herder is able to reassess the moral and religious implications of his philosophy. There is now room for life and providence in Spinoza's otherwise barren and gloomy universe. On Herder's reading Spinoza's God is not a dead, static substance, but a living, active force; and it acts not according to blind necessity, but with intelligent ends.

As part of his campaign to rehabilitate the moral and religious dimension of Spinoza's philosophy, Herder attempts to clear Spinoza of the charges of atheism and fatalism. He has little difficulty in showing the injustice of the accusation of atheism. We cannot say that Spinoza is an atheist, Herder argues, because an atheist is someone who denies the existence of God, no matter how he is conceived.[106] Rather than denying God's existence, Spinoza makes him into his first principle, his *ens realisimum.* Such a position deserves to be called 'pantheism', but not 'atheism'.

One of Herder's contributions to the pantheism controversy is that he advances a more sophisticated interpretation of Spinoza's pantheism than Jacobi or Mendelssohn. He rightly reinstates Spinoza's distinction between the *natura naturans* and the *natura naturata.*[107] According to Herder, Jacobi and Mendelssohn accuse Spinoza of atheism because they wrongly equate his God with the sum total of finite things. Understandably, they balk at the suggestion that belief in God amounts to nothing more than a belief in the totality of things. But Herder then points out that Spinoza's God is not simply the sum of all things; rather, he is the self-sufficient substance in which they all exist. So, although Spinoza's God cannot exist without the world, neither is he identical with it.

The charge of fatalism creates more problems for Herder than that of atheism. To clear Spinoza of this charge, Herder must, as he admits, deviate from the 'letter' of Spinoza's system; but he insists that this involves no change in its 'spirit'. According to Herder, the spirit of Spinoza's system is not fatalistic (that is, it does not hold that everything is determined by blind necessity without purpose or intelligent cause) since it is necessary for Spinoza to attribute will and understanding to God.[108] There are of course passages in the *Ethica* where Spinoza appears to deny will and understanding to God.[109] But Herder explains away these passages as either inconsistent with, or not necessary to, his system as a whole. Given his general principles, Herder says, Spinoza not only can but must attribute understanding to God. For if, as he says, God possesses all perfections, then surely he must possess thought, which is the greatest of perfections. And there is also nothing preventing Spinoza from attributing will to God, that is, from assuming that God acts for specific ends. Although Spinoza denies final causes, he does so only because they appear to impute arbitrariness to God's actions. But this does not mean we cannot attribute ends or design to God's activity, Herder insists.[110] For even though God acts from the necessity of his own nature alone, it is still possible for him to act for the sake of some end. Acting of necessity and acting for some end are, at least in Herder's eyes, perfectly compatible. We therefore can regard God's activity as purposive without introducing arbitrariness or contingency into Spinoza's system.

Herder's entry into the pantheism controversy forced him to clarify his position vis-à-vis Jacobi and Mendelssohn. Of Jacobi, Herder is sharply critical. He not only defends Spinoza against Jacobi's charges of atheism and fatalism, but he also attacks Jacobi's concept of a personal and supernatural God. We cannot attribute personality to God, Herder tells Jacobi, since that is patently anthropomorphic.[111] To have personality is to have wishes, desires, and attitudes, and these are characteristic of a finite being or man alone. We also cannot conceive of God as a supernatural entity 'above' and 'beyond' the world, for such a supernatural God is unknowable and therefore irrelevant to us.

Herder's critique of Jacobi's concept of God, though apparently of only polemical value, is significant for the pantheism controversy as a whole. For it brings into question Jacobi's all too questionable assumption that faith demands belief in a supernatural and personal God. By making this strict demand on faith, Jacobi obviously puts faith in a weak position vis-à-vis reason and easily draws his conclusions about the irrationality of faith. But in questioning these arbitrary requirements, Herder helps to close the gap between reason and faith.

Siding with Mendelssohn, Herder defends the right of reason to criticize religious belief.[112] He chastens Jacobi for assuming that faith transcends criticism.[113] Religious belief is based upon historical testimony, and such testimony has to be weighed in the light of the available evidence. Like Mendelssohn, Herder holds that reason has the power not only to criticize, but also to demonstrate religious belief. But it is important to note the considerable differences in their views on how reason can justify faith. Unlike Mendelssohn, Herder does not think that reason can provide us with a priori demonstrations of God's existence, having long since rejected the scholastic style of demonstration found in *Morgenstunden*.[114] In his view the only possible demonstration of God's existence is a posteriori and not a priori. Reason has the power to uncover facts about the order and harmony of the universe; and these make it probable, if not a priori certain, that there is a wise and benevolent creator.

The aim of Herder's *Gott, Einige Gespräche* is not only to reinterpret Spinoza's philosophy, but also to change it. Herder remains true to two essential Spinozist doctrines: pantheism and naturalism. But he freely combines these doctrines with those of other philosophers, creating his own eclectic mixture. Thus Herder is by no means a strict Spinozist, and he even refuses to call himself one.[115] Indeed, he argues that there are grave weaknesses in Spinoza's philosophy, and that these demand its inner transformation.

According to Herder, the most serious problems in Spinoza's philosophy stem from his theory of divine attributes.[116] This theory has two major flaws, in his view. First, Spinoza makes extension into an attribute of the divine substance. This not only makes God exist in space, as if he were a hunk of matter, but it also ensnares Spinoza in an inconsistency. Namely, Spinoza sharply distinguishes between eternity and time, but extension cannot be an attribute of the single eternal substance any more than time; for both time and extension share the essential properties of being complex, divisible, and destructible. Second, Spinoza makes thought and extension into the only attributes of God. This contradicts Spinoza's own statement that the infinite God manifests himself in infinite ways;[117] but, even more seriously, it creates an irreconcilable dualism between mind and body. According to Herder, both of these difficulties in Spinoza's theory arise from his Cartesian inheritance. Though they are alien to his own thinking, Spinoza never freed himself from the Cartesian doctrines that the essence of body is extension and that mind and body are heterogeneous.

Given these weaknesses in Spinoza's philosophy, how do we surmount them? How can we change Spinoza's system to give it the inner unity that it lacks? At this crucial point, Herder maintains, Leibniz comes to Spinoza's rescue.[118] The Leibnizian notion of power, of organic or substantial force, solves these problems in Spinoza's system. Rather than seeing Spinoza's God as a substance with two heterogeneous attributes (thought and extension), we should regard it as a power with an infinity of manifestations. Spinoza's dead substance then becomes an active, living force, and his God becomes the monad of monads, the *Urkraft aller Kräfte*. This notion of power not only replaces extension as the essence of matter, but it also mediates between mind and body, so that they are no longer distinct attributes, but different degrees of organization of one and the same primal force.

This synthesis of Leibniz and Spinoza—a pantheistic vitalism or a vitalistic pantheism—remains the central achievement of Herder's *Gott, Einige Gespräche*. By injecting life into Spinoza's static universe, Herder made Spinozism into an appealing doctrine for the post-Kantian generation. It thus seemed possible to combine one's scientific naturalism and one's moral and religious beliefs. It was largely for this reason that Herder's vitalistic pantheism became the inspiration for Schelling's and Hegel's *Naturphilosophie*. The revival of Spinozism in late eighteenth-century Germany is indeed more a flowering of Herder's vitalistic pantheism than Spinozism proper; and that vitalistic pantheism ultimately has its roots in *Gott, Einige Gespräche*.[119]

Despite its contributions to the pantheism controversy—a vitalistic pantheism, a more sophisticated interpretation of Spinoza's pantheism, a needed defense of Spinoza against the charges of atheism and fatalism—Herder's *Gott, Einige Gespräche* still has to be judged a failure. It does little or no justice to Herder's more original and profound contribution to that controversy: his vitalist theory of mind, which promises to resolve the crisis of reason. If it is possible to have a naturalistic yet nonreductivistic theory of mind, then we can expand the realm of reason with no fear of the moral consequences, namely, the atheism and fatalism of mechanism. But the fatal flaw of Herder's book is that it fails to vindicate the crucial presupposition behind his theory: that teleology, no less than mechanism, is capable of providing naturalistic or scientific explanations. Kant had strongly criticized just this presupposition in his essay "Teleologie," developing powerful arguments to the effect that no teleological explanations could claim naturalistic status. But Herder does nothing to reply to them in *Gott, Einige Gespräche*. We are then left with the unsettling feeling that Herder's theory of mind rests upon a metaphysics no more defensible than Mendelssohn's.

With Herder's theory of mind stranded in a vulnerable position, the whole problem of the authority of reason appears more unsolvable than ever. The three possible solutions to Jacobi's dilemma appear to lead nowhere. Mendelssohn's metaphysics is crippled by Kant's criticisms; Kant's moral theology is weakened by Jacobi's and Wizenmann's counterattack; and Herder's theory of mind is vulnerable to Kant's objections against teleology. There still does not seem to be any prospect, then, of justifying moral and religious beliefs through reason.

Chapter 6

The Attack of the Lockeans

6.1. *Popularphilosophie:* A Sketch of a Movement

Around the third quarter of the eighteenth century, particularly in Berlin under the enlightened despotism of Frederick II, but also at the University of Göttingen under the liberal policies of its first chancellor, A. Münchhaussen, a new philosophical movement began to flourish. This movement represented the popular philosophy of the German Enlightenment, and accordingly went by the name *Popularphilosophie*. Among its leading members were J. A. Biester, J. A. Eberhard, J. Engel, J. F. Feder, C. Garve, F. Nicolai, E. Platner, and A. Weishaupt. Although most of these figures are now obscure, they were all famous in their day. The *Popularphilosophen* were the German counterparts of the philosophes in France, and they were as important for Germany as Voltaire, Diderot, and D'Alembert were for France.

The *Popularphilosophen* shared the same goal as the philosophes: the spread of enlightenment (*Aufklärung*). Enlightenment was understood as the education of the general public; its liberation from superstition, ignorance, and servitude; and the cultivation of its taste, manners, and reason.[1] *Popularphilosophie* was therefore not only an intellectual but also a political movement. Its primary aims were practical: to break down the barriers between philosophy and life, speculation and action, so that the principles of reason were not locked away in an ivory tower, but practiced by church and state.[2]

Although modeled on the French and British Enlightenment, *Popularphilosophie* was also a response to trends within Germany itself. While the French and British Enlightenment took its inspiration from the philosophies of Locke and Newton, the German Enlightenment had its own resources to draw on, in the philosophy of Leibniz and Wolff. The *Popularphilosophen* did for Leibniz and Wolff what the philosophes did for Newton and Locke:

they popularized their doctrines, making them part of the public consciousness. Although many of the *Popularphilosophen* were loyal to Leibniz and Wolff, they still reacted against one disturbing tendency in the Leibnizian-Wolffian school: its increasing scholasticism. In the eyes of the *Popularphilosophen* the Wolffian methodology, with all its pedantic definitions, strict proofs, and painstaking system building, was turning philosophy into an elite and esoteric discipline. And this elitism and esotericism reminded them of medieval scholasticism, which was one of the chief enemies of enlightenment. Hence the *Popularphilosophen* rejected the esoteric form as they affirmed the exoteric content of the Leibnizian-Wolffian philosophy.

Attempting to spread enlightenment by the most effective means, the *Popularphilosophen* devoted themselves to literary as well as philosophical pursuits. Rather than grinding out technical treatises according to numbered Wolffian paragraphs, they wrote articles, epigrams, and popular textbooks. Anything that educated the public was a means to their ends. They were indeed very successful in editing literary reviews. There was Nicolai's *Allgemeine deutsche Bibliothek,* Biester's *Berliner Monatsschrift,* Wieland's *Teutsche Merkur,* and Heyne's *Göttinger gelehrte Anzeige.* Thanks to these journals, literary criticism attained a high standard, and many philosophical works found a much wider public. The *Popularphilosophen* were also effective in introducing the philosophy of the French and British Enlightenment into Germany. They translated Hume, Locke, Beattie, and Reid, not to mention Rousseau, Condillac, Voltaire, and Diderot.[3]

Although many of them were influenced by Leibniz and Wolff, the *Popularphilosophen* were not the disciples of any particular philosopher. They were indeed self-conscious eclectics. Ideas from the most antithetical philosophers were combined by them, even at the price of consistency; for example, it was not uncommon to find Locke's empiricism mixed with Leibniz's metaphysics. According to the *Popularphilosophen,* however, such eclecticism was not the betrayal of critical and independent thought, but its very affirmation. It was their firm belief that the philosopher must free himself from the sectarian spirit of the schools, and that he must develop his own personal philosophy. The rational man judged each system according to its merits, and he took from each according to the outcome of his critical evaluation.

The politics of the *Popularphilosophen* were liberal and reformist, but not revolutionary or radical. They pleaded for freedom of thought, religious tolerance, and educational reform; but they disapproved of democracy. They believed in equality before the law and natural rights; but they never questioned the need for elite rule. Although they wanted to enlighten the public, they did not want it to question the state. Indeed, most of the *Popularphilosophen* welcomed the benevolent despotism of Frederick II, and much of their intellectual and political activity—whether in the Royal Academy or in clandestine societies like the Freimauer—went on under royal patronage. Unlike the philosophes, then, the *Popularphilosophen* were more agents than critics of their government.

As committed *Aufklärer,* the *Popularphilosophen* naturally wanted to maintain the authority of reason at all costs. They saw reason as the only effective sanction for moral and religious belief, and they held it to be the most potent weapon against superstition and ignorance. Accordingly, during the pantheism controversy they were as sympathetic to Kant and Mendelssohn as they were hostile to Hamann and Jacobi. Jacobi's criticism of reason had deeply disturbed them, since it questioned the value of their entire program of enlightenment. If reason did lead to atheism and fatalism, as Jacobi taught, then enlightenment would be bound to corrupt rather than improve morals.

Although they were on his side during the pantheism controversy, the *Popularphilosophen* were normally among Kant's most bitter opponents. For more than two decades they attacked his philosophy in countless tracts, reviews, and articles. There were even journals devoted to the criticism of Kant, such as Feder's *Philosophische Bibliothek* and Eberhard's *Philosophisches Magazin.* Why, though, was there such hostility toward Kant? The *Popularphilosophen* thought that Kant's intentions were as noble as his philosophy was dangerous. Although Kant intended to defend the authority of reason, his philosophy threatened to undermine it. It was the general theme of the *Popularphilosophen*'s campaign against Kant that his philosophy ended in a Humean skepticism, which denied knowledge of anything beyond our passing impressions. In their eyes Kant's practical faith was only a ploy to conceal these skeptical consequences. It at best justified the regulative maxim that we should think and act *as if* God, immortality, and providence existed; but in truth all that we could know was the confines of our consciousness. Like Mendelssohn, then, the *Popularphilosophen* insisted on a theoretical defense of faith, because only such a defense could satisfy the belief in the existence of God, immortality, and providence.

In making these criticisms of Kant, the *Popularphilosophen* proved themselves unwitting allies of Jacobi and Wizenmann, whom they otherwise bitterly opposed. In the 1780s and 1790s the *Popularphilosophen* and *Glaubensphilosophen* composed a single chorus united in accusing Kant of a single charge: Humean solipsism or nihilism. There was, however, one very important note of discord in this chorus. While the *Glaubensphilosophen* held that Kant's philosophy was the paradigm of reason and therefore illustrated the dangerous consequences of all rational inquiry, the *Popularphilosophen* held that Kant's philosophy misrepresented the nature of reason. Reason was not "the principle of subject-object identity," as Jacobi formulated it, but common sense (*der gesunde Menschenverstand*).

Although the *Popularphilosophen* were desperate to defend the *Aufklärung*, in the end they contributed more to its decline than survival. Their criticism of Kant had moved the burden of proof onto themselves. To maintain the authority of reason, they had to come forward with a new theoretical defense of moral, religious, and commonsense beliefs. What they usually had to offer, however, was nothing more than worn Leibnizian-Wolffian arguments, which were vulnerable to Hume's and Kant's criticisms. Otherwise, the *Popularphilosophen* were content to appeal to common sense as the final sanction of morality and religion. But, in doing so, they betrayed rather than served the cause of reason. For, as Kant and Wizenmann argued, if common sense has no reply to Hume's skepticism, then it amounts to nothing more than a refuge of ignorance and a Jacobian *salto mortale*.

Though the burden of proof was on them, the *Popularphilosophen* were not prepared to provide a new defense of reason. Such a defense went beyond the goal of their movement, which was not to discover the principles of reason, but only to implement them. In limiting themselves to this objective, however, the *Popularphilosophen* had already begged the main philosophical question: whether reason is worthy of such implementation. They failed to see that the fundamental question was really not practical—*How* do we act according to reason? Rather, it was philosophical—*Should* we act according to reason? By failing to address this question, the *Popularphilosophen* contributed to the extinction of their movement and the decline of the *Aufklärung* itself.

Although the *Popularphilosophen* had no original or profound defense of reason, they made one important contribution to the discussion of the authority of reason in the late eighteenth century: their criticism of Kant. They often raised acute objections that questioned Kant's claim to uphold the authority of reason. These objections were also influential because they sometimes led Kant to rethink and reformulate his position. Indeed, no history of Kant's philosophy after the first *Kritik* can afford to ignore the *Popularphilosophen*. They made up the vast majority of Kant's early opponents, and most of his early polemics were directed against them.

Any treatment of the *Popularphilosophen*'s battles immediately runs up against an obstacle, however. Namely, how to organize and classify the vast amount of material (polemics, articles, and reviews). Since there were so many of them, and since they were eclectics, the *Popularphilosophen* are especially difficult to group or categorize.

Despite this diversity, we can distinguish some rough groupings among the *Popularphilosophen*. Examining their writings, interests, and educational backgrounds, we discover that there is at least one basic dividing line between most, if not all, of them. Although almost all of the *Popularphilosophen* were influenced by Leibniz and Wolff, some of them were empiricists and more loyal to the tradition of Locke, while others were rationalists and more true to the tradition of Wolff.[4] Among the former were J. G. Feder, C. Garve, J. F. Lossius, C. Meiners, F. Nicolai, H. A. Pistorius, C. G. Selle, D. Tiedemann, G. Tittel, and A. Weishaupt; among the latter were J. A. Eberhard, J. F. Flatt, J. G. E. Maass, E. Platner, J. G. Schwab, and J. A. Ulrich. These two groups naturally shared many of the same concerns and beliefs, but there was still one fundamental difference between them: the empiricists or Lockeans denied the possibility of a priori ideas, while the rationalists or Wolffians affirmed such a possibility.

This difference between the empiricist and rationalist *Popularphilosophen* inevitably led to a basic divergence in their reactions toward Kant. Both parties were quick to recognize Kant's attempt to synthesize rationalism and empiricism. But, just as we might expect, the empiricists thought that Kant leaned too far to rationalism, while the rationalists held that he surrendered too much to empiricism. According to the empiricists, Kant was excessively rationalistic in assuming the existence of the a priori and in postulating a noumenal realm apart from experience. According to the rationalists, however, Kant was inordinately empiricist in demanding that ideas be verified in experience and in denying the possibility of knowledge through pure reason. In the following discussion these differences will emerge again and again.

6.2. Highlights of the Lockean Campaign against Kant

The Lockeans were not exactly amused by the appearance of the *Kritik der reinen Vernunft*. Their first reaction to Kant's imposing tome was one of disappointment. Not a few of them were admirers of the early precritical Kant.[5] They loved the skeptical tone of the *Träume eines Geistessehers;* they enjoyed the playful observations of the *Beobachtungen;* and they praised the subtle dialectic of the *Beweisgrund*. Kant, it seemed, was one of them. He appeared to have the same empiricist tendencies, the same metaphysical interests, and the same desire for popularity. But the *Kritik* cruelly shattered these illusions, these shallow feelings of bonhomie. Now the wolf in sheep's clothing had finally appeared—and with all teeth bared.

The Lockeans' second reaction to the *Kritic* was therefore one of alarm, and indeed defiance. The *Kritic* attacked almost everything they stood for, and it stood for almost everything they attacked. Kant's idealism was an affront to their common sense; his critique of metaphysics was a threat to their natural religion; his a priori ideas were reminiscent of pre-Lockean epistemology; and his technical terminology and dogmatic method smacked of a new scholasticism. Almost overnight, Kant became the Lockeans' most formidable foe, and, moreover, one whom they could barely comprehend. They had a confused, conflicting image of Kant. In their eyes Kant was both a dangerous skeptic and a dogmatic metaphysician—a skeptic for having denounced religion and common sense, and a metaphysician for having revived a priori ideas and the dogmatic method.

Although the Lockeans were sharply critical of the *Kritik*, they were the first to recognize its stature and significance, and they were indeed the first to respond to the challenge it posed. Their campaign against Kant began in January 1782 with Garve's infamous review of the *Kritik*. This review provoked a hostile reply from Kant in the *Prolegomena*—a reply so effective that it frightened off all would-be reviewers for years to come. After a lull lasting nearly two years, from early 1782 to early 1784, the Lockean campaign was reopened by Dietrich Tiedemann in his cautious and sober review of the *Kritik*. It was followed in the same year with an essay by C. G. Selle and a review of the *Prolegomena* by H. A. Pistorius. By the year 1786 the Lockean offensive had spread on a wide front. Kant was under attack in several reviews, essays, and books. The years 1787–1788 mark the height of this campaign. In these years alone the Lockeans published more than ten books exclusively devoted to criticism of Kant. The Lockean offensive continued into the 1790s with Tiedemann's *Theäet;* and it persisted even into the 1800s with Nicolai's relentless parodies and tirades.

Although it is difficult to summarize a polemical campaign of this magnitude, duration, and diversity, it is possible to discern general themes and recurrent leitmotivs in the Lockean campaign against Kant. These themes are either found with more frequency among the Lockeans than the Wolffians, or they are characteristic of their campaign in the sense that no Wolffian would ever in principle hold them. Let us briefly consider each of these themes.

(1) One of the central issues between Kant and his empiricist opponents concerned the possibility of a priori knowledge. Every Lockean maintained that all synthetic knowledge is a posteriori, derived from and justified through experience. Some of them, however, were daring enough to argue that even analytic knowledge is a posteriori.[6]

(2) Another basic conflict centered on the proper method of epistemology. The Lockeans advocated a purely naturalistic epistemology, that is, one which explains the origins and conditions of knowledge according to natural laws alone. Such an epistemology was obviously modeled upon the natural sciences; its prototype was "the plain historical method" of Locke's *Essay* or "the principles of observation and experiment" of Hume's *Treatise*. The Lockeans therefore rejected Kant's a priori method. They saw it as meta-

physical and condemned it for forfeiting the ideal of a scientific epistemology.[7]

(3) Yet another controversy surrounded the legitimacy of Kant's sharp dualism between reason and the senses, his radical dichotomy between the *homo noumenon* and *homo phenomenon*. The Lockeans regarded this distinction as arbitrary and artificial, as the reification of a purely intellectual distinction. Reason and sensibility were, in their view, inseparably united, different not in kind but only in degree. Of course, the Wolffians also attacked Kant's dualism; but there was still an important difference between the Lockeans and Wolffians on this score. While the Woffians saw sensibility as a confused form of the understanding, the Lockeans regarded the understanding as a derivative form of sensibility.[8]

The Lockeans most often objected to Kant's dualism on the ground that it is antinaturalistic. It postulates a mysterious Platonic realm, the world of noumena, which is inexplicable according to natural laws. Kant's noumenal world makes the origin of our ideas and intentions obscure to us; and it renders the interchange between reason and sensibility unintelligible. Hence the Lockeans frequently accused Kant of 'mysticism', 'obscurantism', or 'superstition'.[9]

(4) The most notorious and controversial issue between Kant and the Lockeans concerned whether there is any essential difference between Kant's and Berkeley's idealism. Feder was the first to deny such a difference; and all the Lockeans, and most of the Wolffians, seconded him.[10] The charge of Berkeleyan idealism was tantamount to the charge of solipsism, which was generally regarded as the reductio ad absurdum of the critical philosophy.[11]

(5) The Lockeans were sharp critics of the "Aesthetik," and in particular Kant's theory that space and time are a priori. They argued that space and time are not a priori intuitions, but a posteriori concepts, which are abstracted from particular distances and intervals.[12] Almost all of their early examinations of the *Kritik* focused upon the "Aesthetik," because it was seen as the test case for Kant's idealism and theory of the synthetic a priori. On the whole the Lockeans, like the Wolffians, ignored the "Analytik," passing it over in silence.[13]

(6) The Lockeans criticized the way Kant classified concepts of the understanding as completely arbitrary and artificial. The Wolffians too made such objections to Kant. But the Lockeans, unlike the Wolffians, regarded any such classification as in principle mistaken. Maintaining that all concepts are abstractions from experience, they denied that there could ever be any complete list of all the possible concepts of the understanding.[14]

(7) The Lockeans were the first to argue that the categorical imperative is empty, and that duty for duty's sake is in conflict with human nature.

Against Kant, they defended eudaemonism as the only moral philosophy that can provide a sufficient criterion of morality and be in harmony with human needs.[15]

6.3. The Garve Affair

The *Kritik der reinen Vernunft* was born into an indifferent world. The first seven months after its publication it seemed to suffer the same fate as Hume's *Treatise:* "to fall still born from the press." Although the *Kritik* appeared in May 1781, there were no reviews of it for the rest of that year. Even worse, Kant knew that he could not expect to hear from anyone qualified to appraise it. Lambert, who Kant said would have been his best critic, was already dead.[16] Mendelssohn, whose judgment Kant had always admired, was too old and frail.[17] And Tetens, having retired from the sphere of philosophy altogether in 1777, after the publication of his *Versuche,* said nothing.[18] To add insult to injury, Marcus Herz, Kant's most loyal student, was also slow to respond, and in any case was still devoted to the precritical "Inaugural Dissertation." All that Kant did hear were complaints about unintelligibility and obscurity. Thus Johann Schultz, the first expositor of the *Kritik,* wrote that the public in those days saw the *Kritik* as "a sealed book," consisting in nothing but "hieroglyphics."[19] It was in these depressing circumstances that Kant grumbled that the *Kritik* had been "honored by silence."[20]

This disappointing silence was finally broken, however, in the beginning of 1782. On January 19 of that year an anonymous review of the *Kritik* appeared in the *Zugaben zu den Göttinger gelehrte Anzeigen.*[21] Such an obscure journal turned out to be the setting for an extremely important article. This was the first review of the *Kritik,* and it became the most notorious. No review so succeeded in arousing Kant's indignation; and none had a greater effect upon him in making him reargue and reformulate his position. It was largely thanks to the "Göttingen review" that Kant redefined his transcendental idealism in the *Prolegomena* and the second edition of the *Kritik.* In addition to its impact on Kant, the review became a cause célèbre among Kant's empiricist opponents, who defended it with as much fervor as Kant denounced it. All in all, if only in retrospect, it was not a bad start. The review created a controversy, which attracted attention to the *Kritik.* Kant got a little of the publicity he was looking for—though certainly not in the manner he wished.

What was the controversy created by the review? What did it say that sparked off such a scandal? The main issue raised by the review concerns the nature of Kant's idealism. Here for the first time the classic problem is posed of the distinction between Kant's and Berkeley's idealism. The review flatly denies that there is any such distinction—a thesis that soon became a rallying cry of the empiricist campaign against Kant.

The strategy behind this thesis was indeed very threatening to Kant. If the empiricists could whitewash Kant's idealism as nothing more than a disguised form of Berkeley's, which no one took seriously in eighteenth-century Germany, then they could safely disarm the whole threat of the *Kritik* under the you-have-seen-it-all-before rubric. Hence Kant had no choice but to clarify his idealism and to distinguish it from Berkeley's. Simply put, it was a question of survival.

The Göttingen review sums up the *Kritik* as "a system of higher or transcendental idealism."[22] This is defined as an idealism that reduces not only matter but also spirit to mere representations. The main principle of Kant's idealism is then said to be the same as Berkeley's and Hume's: that perception consists in nothing but representations, which are only "modifications of ourselves." In attributing this principle to Kant, the reviewer sees Kant's idealism through the eyes of Thomas Reid, whose philosophy of common sense was much in favor among the Göttingen *Popularphilosophen*.[23] Just as Reid accuses Berkeley of confusing the object of perception with the act of perception, so the reviewer insinuates that Kant has made the same error.

According to the review, Kant's idealism has the same difficulty as Berkeley's: it reduces experience to a dream or illusion.[24] Kant is caught in this predicament we are told, because he does not have a sufficient criterion to distinguish between reality and illusion. Kant thinks that the criterion of reality consists in nothing more than conformity to the rules of the understanding; but this is not sufficient to distinguish reality from illusion, given that a dream can also have the order and regularity of a rule-governed experience. The criterion of reality therefore has to be found not in the rules of the understanding, but in some characteristic of sensation itself.[25] The reviewer then concludes his case against Kant by saying that the *Kritik* fails to devise a middle path between skepticism and dogmatism. This middle path is identified with "the common human understanding" (*der gemeine Menschenverstand*), "the most natural manner of thinking" (*das natürlichste Denkart*), that is, the common sense favored by the *Popularphilosophen*. The *Kritik* is accused of undermining this path and leaning toward skepticism since it destroys our beliefs in the reality of the external world.

Predictably, and justifiably, Kant's reaction to the Göttingen review was indignant, not to say downright hostile. Kant felt that the review was completely biased, and that he had been deliberately misunderstood. Accordingly, in the *Prolegomena* Kant devoted an entire appendix and several explanatory sections to a refutation of the review.[26] The "Widerlegung des Idealismus" in the second edition of the *Kritik* can also be seen as a reply to it.

The appendix to the *Prolegomena* is a bitter reproach against the standards and procedures of the review. Kant accuses the reviewer of judging the *Kritik* according to the standards of his own metaphysics—an approach that begs the question since the main task of the *Kritik* is to investigate the possibility of metaphysics.[27] Rather than impartially examining the principles of the *Kritik*, the reviewer merely reacts against their consequences, dismissing them as absurd without telling us why. Worst of all, the reviewer has not understood, or even stated, the main problem addressed in the *Kritik*: the possibility of synthetic a priori judgments.[28] In no way has he tried to show that the *Kritik* has failed to solve its problem or that it is not genuine. If, however, the reviewer had seen the *Kritik* in light of this issue, then he would have realized that transcendental idealism is not the first principle but the consequence of the *Kritik*'s solution to the problem of synthetic a priori knowledge.[29]

The thrust of Kant's reply to the review is his distinction between transcendental and Berkeleyan idealism. In the appendix and in two explanatory sections of the *Prolegomena* Kant states that there are two fundamental differences between his idealism and Berkeley's.[30]

(1) While Berkeley's idealism denies, transcendental idealism affirms, the existence of things-in-themselves. Alternatively, Berkeley's idealism holds that experience consists in nothing but perceptions or ideas; but transcendental idealism claims that it consists in appearances of things-in-themselves. In making this distinction, Kant rebuts the claim that the principle of his idealism is that the objects of perception are ideas; they are not only ideas, but appearances of things-in-themselves.

(2) While transcendental idealism is in a position to maintain that experience is real, Berkeley's idealism has to hold that it is illusory. Although Kant puts forward this distinction as if it were basic, it is important to see that it is a consequence of a much more fundamental difference, which is not fully explored. The more fundamental difference is this: Kant affirms and Berkeley denies that there are synthetic a priori principles.[31] Now given Kant's argument that synthetic a priori principles are a necessary condition of the objectivity of experience, it follows that Berkeley is guilty of transforming experience into an illusion. For Berkeley's empiricism commits him to denying one of the necessary conditions of the objectivity of experience: the synthetic a priori. So, although Kant states that it is a principle of Berkeley's idealism that experience is illusory, he in fact should argue that

it is a consequence of Berkeley's empiricism. The difference between transcendental and Berkeleyan idealism therefore turns out to be the difference between a rationalist and empiricist idealism.

These distinctions between transcendental and Berkeleyian idealism, which are not at all apparent in the first edition of the *Kritik,* are the direct result of the Göttingen review. Along with these distinctions, though, it is possible to detect a new general formulation of transcendental idealism in the *Prolegomena* that is not evident in the first edition of the *Kritik* and that is also a reaction to the Göttingen review.[32] Namely, while the first edition of the *Kritik* defines transcendental idealism as the claim that the objects of the senses are only appearances and not things-in-themselves,[33] the *Prolegomena* identifies it with the claim that the objects of the senses are appearances of things-in-themselves. This redefinition of the sphere of appearances, which is not even implied in the first edition of the *Kritik,* is explicitly affirmed in the *Prolegomena.*[34]

Who was the author of the Göttingen review? Who could have stirred up so much trouble for the ruffled Kant? Kant himself did not know when he wrote his *Prolegomena.* But, at the close of his reply to the review, he demanded that the author reveal himself, arguing that his anonymity was only an escape from responsibility and public debate. Only a few months later, Kant's demand was duly met. In July 1783, several months after the publication of the *Prolegomena,* Kant received a letter from someone who took responsibility for the review.[35] The letter was from none other than Christian Garve (1742–1798), one of the foremost *Popularphilosophen,* and one of the most celebrated thinkers of his day. Along with Mendelssohn, Garve was then generally regarded as the leading figure of the *Aufklärung.* More than anyone else, he was responsible for introducing British thought, especially British political economy, into the mainstream of the *Aufklärung.* Garve was the translator of several British classics, among them Smith's *Wealth of Nations,* Burke's *Observations on the Sublime and Beautiful,* and Ferguson's *Principles of Moral Philosophy.* Even Kant had the highest respect for Garve, whom he classed with Baumgarten and Mendelssohn as "one of the great analysts of his age."[36] It therefore must have come as a surprise to Kant that Garve was behind the Göttingen review. How could such an eminent thinker be the author of such a base review?

In his letter to Kant Garve admitted responsibility for the review of the *Kritik.* He wrote the original manuscript; and he permitted the editor of the *Göttinger Anzeige* to edit it as he saw fit. But Garve, in a move that has never ceased to trouble Kant-scholars, still disowned the published version of the review. "I would be inconsolable if it were completely from my own hand," he told Kant. Without mentioning names, Garve protested that the editor had "mutilated" his original review. The manuscript was much too long for a customary review, so the editor omitted many passages, compressed others, and even added some of his own. According to Garve's estimate, the degree of distortion was indeed very great. He wrote Kant that "only some phrases" from his original remained in the published version, and that they made up only one-tenth of his original and only one-third of the published version.

Garve's disclaimers naturally raise very serious questions of authorship. Who was responsible for the notorious criticisms of Kant in the Göttingen review, Garve or the editor, J. G. Feder? Did Feder drastically distort Garve's views in editing the manuscript or did he merely compress them?[37] These questions are of some interest, given the historical and philosophical significance of the review.

To begin with, it is necessary to point out that Garve's claim to have written only one-third of the edited review is a gross exaggeration. A comparison of the edited version with Garve's original, which was later published in Nicolai's *Allgemeine deutsche Bibliothek*,[38] leads to the opposite conclusion. Even including compressed sentences and minor stylistic changes, only one-third of the review stems from Feder.[39] Of course, besides giving us some idea of the extent of the editing, such numbers mean little or nothing. The crucial question still remains about the quality of the editing: even if Feder did write only one-third of the review, was he substantially faithful to Garve's views?

Although the answer to this question is complex, permitting no straightforward answer, to a certain extent it must be "no." For one thing, the tone of the edited review is completely different from the original. Where Feder's edition damns Kant, Garve's original praises him. Whereas Feder's review is a heated polemic, Garve's is a sober summary, cautiously suggesting its criticisms rather than baldly asserting them. But, much more significant, Feder suppresses some of Garve's more interesting critical remarks.[40] Garve rejects the artificiality of Kant's architechtonic; he questions Kant's solution to the third antinomy; and he argues against the notion of space and time as a priori forms of intuition. Not a trace of this appears in the Feder edition, however. On these grounds alone, then, Garve had some excuse for disowning the review.

If, however, we abstract from the tone of the review and Garve's omitted remarks, then it is necessary to admit that the critical standpoint of both reviews is broadly the same. Although there are many criticisms in Garve's original that are not in Feder's edition, the converse is not the case. On the whole Feder reproduces philosophically, if not stylistically, Garve's basic line of criticism. The problematic distinction between transcendental and empirical idealism, the insufficiency of Kant's criterion of truth, and the claim that Kant equates the object of sensation with "a modification of ourselves"—all these criticisms are explicit in Garve's original.[41] All that Feder does is put them in a more polemical dress. It is hardly surprising, then, that Kant was little more pleased with the original than with Feder's doctored version.[42]

Despite these similarities, there is still one important difference between the two versions. Although both find Kant's distinction between transcendental and empirical idealism dubious, it is Feder who identifies empirical idealism with Berkeley's idealism. Hence the most provocative and notorious thesis of the Göttingen review—the identity of Kantian and Berkeleyan idealism—stems from Feder's and not Garve's hand. There is not a single reference to Berkeley in Garve's original; and Feder himself confessed that he added the passages about Berkeley.[43]

What makes Feder's addition a serious distortion of Garve's original is that neither Garve's 'empirical idealism' nor his 'transcendental idealism' is anything like Berkeley's idealism. His 'transcendental idealism' states that mind is as unknowable as matter; and his 'empirical idealism' holds that the existence of objects that cause sensation is uncertain. Both of these positions are plainly far removed from Berkeley's idealism. What Garve means by 'empirical idealism' is in fact what Kant calls 'problematic idealism', that is, skeptical doubt about the existence of external objects. But what Feder means by 'empirical idealism' is what Kant calls 'dogmatic idealism', the denial of the existence of external objects. Hence there is a fundamental difference between Garve's and Feder's arguments concerning the identity of transcendental and empirical idealism: namely, while Garve maintains that transcendental idealism makes the existence of things uncertain, Feder claims that it denies their existence.

6.4. Two Early Critics: C. G. Selle and D. Tiedemann

After the Garve affair, the *Kritik* still seemed to be "honored by silence." Apart from a brief notice, there were no further reviews in 1782; and there were no reviews at all in 1783.[44] It seemed as if no one had the time, energy, or interest to read, let alone review, such an imposing tome. Kant grew even more pessimistic. In a letter to his disciple Johann Schultz he complained that he had been "understood by no one," and he expressed the fear that all his work had been in vain.[45]

It was only in 1784 that the silence hanging over the *Kritik* was finally broken. There were indeed a few propitious signs. The *Prolegomena* received a thorough and sympathetic review in the *Allgemeine deutsche Bibliothek,* the most influential journal of the day.[46] And Schultz published his commentary on the *Kritik,* which promised to allay some of the charges of obscurity and unintelligibility.[47] Although this commentary was not a popular success,[48] it at least received favorable notices and reviews.[49]

It was also in 1784, in the *Hessische Beyträge zur Gelehrsamkeit und Kunst,* that the first substantial review of the *Kritik* appeared, "Ueber die Natur der Metaphysik: Zur Prüfung Herrn Professor Kants Grundsätzen."[50] The author of this review was none other than Dietrich Tiedemann (1748–1803), the most eminent historian of philosophy of his age, and one of the worthier contestants in the origin of language debate. Tiedemann had been professor of classical languages at Kassell since 1776, but was then named professor of philosophy at Marburg in 1786. Like Garve and Feder, Tiedemann was essentially an empiricist, even if he leaned more to Leibniz and Wolff than his cohorts. He was indeed intimately associated with the Göttingen empiricists—he was a student at Göttingen and a friend of Feder's and Meiners's—so it is not unlikely that he collaborated with them in their campaign against Kant.

Although it is full of misunderstandings, Tiedemann's review of the *Kritik* is at least thorough, rigorous, and fair, and it does succeed in raising a few interesting objections. Tiedemann has two essential aims in his review, both of them characteristic of an empiricist *Popularphilosoph:* to attack the possibility of the synthetic a priori, and to defend the possibility of metaphysics. Against the synthetic a priori, Tiedemann is the first to doubt the synthetic status of mathematic judgments. They are one and all analytic, he says, if we analyze the subject term in all its detail.[51] Tiedemann also raises a difficult question for Kant's theory of the a priori nature of space: how do we distinguish one place from another?[52] Since the parts of absolute space are perfectly identical in themselves, it is necessary to distinguish places by referring to the things that occupy them; but that involves a posteriori knowledge. In defense of metaphysics, Tiedemann focuses upon Kant's claim in the "Antinomien" that he can discredit any metaphysical proof, no matter how cogent, with an equally cogent proof of the antithesis. Kant's proofs are themselves subject to metaphysical dispute, Tiedemann remarks, so that the antinomies cannot be construed as indisputable proof of the breakdown of metaphysics.[53]

What was Kant's reaction to the Tiedemann review? His official reaction was hostile, and indeed downright contemptuous.[54] Kant complained that Tiedemann had "no idea" of the problems facing the critical philosophy. But, significantly, Kant's private reaction was much less dismissive and much more serious. He had written some crude notes for a reply to the review,[55] all of them attacking Tiedemann's defense of metaphysics.

Shortly after Tiedemann's review appeared, another empiricist critic made his debut against Kant, Christian Gottlieb Selle (1748–1800). Along with Feder and Tiedemann, Selle was connected with Göttingen: he was a student there and imbibed its empiricist spirit at an early age. Like his mentor, John Locke, Selle was a doctor by vocation, a philosopher by inclination. He was highly respected for his medical writings and was the personal physician of Frederick II. Selle was also associated with the Berlin *Aufklärer*. He was a friend of Nicolai and Mendelssohn, a fellow of the Akademie, and a member of the Mittwochgesellschaft, the Berliners' debating club. Kant himself seems to have had a high opinion of Selle as he sent him one of the very few complimentary copies of the *Kritik*.[56]

Like Garve and Feder, Selle admired the precritical Kant as much as he condemned the critical Kant. The *Kritik* was a great disappointment to him. It seemed to be a betrayal of Kant's earlier 'empiricism' and a conversion to rationalism and scholasticism. "I was beside myself to hear from you that there is a philosophy independent of experience," Selle wrote Kant on December 29, 1787.[57] In his view Kant's doctrine of the synthetic a priori revived ideas of innate rationalism and thus opened the door for a new scholasticism. Determined to fight any relapse into rationalism or scholasticism, Selle in 1784 embarked upon a vigorous polemical campaign against Kant.[58]

Although Selle cannot be credited with a profound understanding of Kant, his polemical writings did receive widespread attention. They provoked a heated discussion in contemporary literature, and sparked off one of the first controversies surrounding Kant's philosophy. In 1787 one of the major questions of the day became whether to accept 'Selleian empiricism' or 'Kantian purism'.[59] Although Selle had his detractors, he also had his disciples;[60] and he had one powerful advocate in H. A. Pistorius.[61] Kant himself considered writing a reply to Selle, though age and academic duties prevented him from doing so.[62]

Selle's campaign against Kant had the same objectives as Tiedemann's: to discredit the possibility of the synthetic a priori and to vindicate the possibility of metaphysics. In his first objective Selle was much more radical than Tiedemann, however. He argued against the possibility of *all* a priori knowledge, not only synthetic a priori knowledge. According to Selle, all knowledge is derived from, and justified through, experience; even analytic propositions owe their truth to experience, because they are based upon the law of contradiction, which is an abstraction from it.[63] In an early essay directed against Kant Selle attempted to defend his radical empiricism with a proof that all knowledge derives from experience.[64] Kant was quick to point out the self-defeating nature of such an enterprise: it was like proving through reason that there is no reason.

Eager to wipe out every vestige of innate ideas, Selle attacked not only a priori knowledge in general, but also synthetic a priori knowledge in particular.[65] He criticized the synthetic a priori on two grounds. First, as Tiedemann argued, the synthetic a priori can be made analytic if we sufficiently analyze the subject term. And, second, the basic premise behind the synthetic a priori—that there are judgments possessing universality and necessity—is simply false. Selle admitted that if there is universality and necessity, then Kant has every right to infer the existence of the synthetic a priori; but he still denied this premise. All synthetic knowledge is based upon experience, he maintained, and for this reason it lacks universality and necessity.

Although Selle was an empiricist, he was still eager to defend the possibility of metaphysics against Kant's criticisms. Like most of the *Popularphilosophen,* he saw metaphysics as the foundation for natural morality and religion and was therefore not willing to abandon it without a struggle. Selle agreed with Kant's demand that all claims to knowledge have to be justified in experience; but he still thought that such justification is possible in metaphysics. Kant prematurely excludes the possibility of empirical verification in metaphysics, he complained, only because he artificially restricts its boundaries, limiting it to simple sense perception, that is, what is given to the senses without reflection.[66] But, Selle insisted, experience consists in much more than bare sense perception. There is also our self-awareness or reflection, which is not neatly separable from perception, but a constitutive element of it. Hence, in Selle's view, there is no firm dividing line between the empirical and metaphysical, the transcendental and transcendent. To justify our metaphysical ideas, we only have to show how they are constitutive elements of our experience.

6.5. The Lockean Ringleader, J. G. Feder

The leader of the empiricist *Popularphilosophen* was J. G. Feder (1740–1821), the editor of the notorious Göttingen review. Although he has been almost completely forgotten, Feder was a celebrity in his day. He played a pioneering role in the *Aufklärung* as one of the founders of *Popularphilosophie.* He also enjoyed power and reputation as professor of philosophy at Göttingen, then the most progressive and prestigious university in Germany. Not a few *Aufklärer* came under his influence: Garve, Tittel, Meiners, Tiedemann, and Weishaupt. Feder was well connected with many of the leading figures of the *Aufklärung:* he was the friend of Nicolai, Mendelssohn, and Tetens; and was much praised by Lessing and Lambert for his services in discrediting Wolffian scholasticism. And thanks to his lively and popular style, his textbooks became very successful, going through many editions and finding their way to the pulpits of almost every university in Germany.[67] Like Garve, Feder also played an important role in introducing the French and British Enlightenment into Germany. He wrote *Neuer Emil*, which was designed to make Rousseau's classic more practicable for the *Hofmeister*;[68] and he also penned the first German review of Adam Smith's *Wealth of Nations*, a work which he immediately recognized as a classic.

It was inevitable that Feder would have a quarrel with Kant. After Kant's bitter attack on the Göttingen review, and after Garve's disavowal of its authorship, the pressure was on Feder to argue his case openly before Kant. Kant had already guessed that Feder was responsible for editing the review;[69] and his surmise was soon confirmed when his close ally C. G. Schütz disclosed the whole matter to him.[70] Thus, the stage was set for a public dispute; and, sure enough, both sides duly took up their positions. Kant planned to write a polemic against Feder for the *Berliner Monatsschrift*,[71] though the advice of friends and the pressing need to complete the second *Kritik* stopped him. For his part, Feder decided to launch an all-out campaign against the critical philosophy. He began by writing a general polemic against the *Kritik* in 1788, his *Ueber Raum und Causalität: Zur Prüfung der kantischen Philosophie;* and then, with the collaboration of his friend Christian Meiners, he edited a new journal, the *Philosophische Bibliothek*, whose main aim was to stem the swelling tide of Kantianism.[72]

Despite such efforts, Feder's campaign against Kant was a miserable failure. *Raum und Causalität* had none of the effect on Kant that Feder imagined;[73] and, due to lack of demand, the *Bibliothek* folded after only a few issues. Because of Kant's increasing popularity, Feder's reputation drastically declined.[74] The students quit his lectures; and he was even compelled to abandon his post at Göttingen. It was sad but true: Kant's reputation could rise only at the expense of his opponents.

Feder's *Raum und Causalität* is a classic in the empiricist *Popularphilosophen*'s campaign against Kant. Its preface provides a good summary of the empiricist's general attitude toward Kant. Feder's chief complaint against Kant is his "dogmatic method." According to Feder, Kant's philosophy is no better than any full-blown metaphysics. Although Kant is indeed a sharp critic of the conclusions of rationalist metaphysics, he never succeeds in freeing himself from its methodology. He simply transfers these methods to his own transcendental philosophy, so that, like any metaphysics, it transcends the limits of possible experience. Kant's fatal error, in Feder's view, is his contempt for 'empirical philosophy'. An empirical philosophy does not apply a demonstrative method to the faculty of knowledge, but explains it according to the laws of nature and the principles of observation and experiment.

Raum und Causalität was indeed the central text in the empiricists' campaign against Kant's "Aesthetik." It assembles and clearly presents all their arguments against Kant's theory of space and time and was at the very center of the early controversy surrounding Kant's "Aesthetik."[75]

Feder's attack upon the "Aesthetik" concentrates on Kant's arguments for the a priori status of space. Since these arguments are especially clear and apparently plausible, Feder regards them as a test case for Kant's general theory of a priori ideas. The refutation of Kant's theory would, so Feder hoped, prove the superiority of his own empiricism.

Feder has essentially three objections against Kant's theory of the a priori nature of space.[76] (1) Kant's argument that space is a priori because it is a necessary condition of perceiving things outside us confuses judgment and perception. It is indeed necessary to have the representation of space before we judge size, shape, and position; but it is not necessary to have it before we have any visual experience. Consider the perception of a child, who cannot judge distances or even distinguish himself from external objects. This example suggests that the representation of space arises from experience, before we have learned how to judge size, shape, and position.[77] (2) Kant's claim that space is a priori because it is impossible to have a representation of no space is a non sequitur. What cannot be thought, or that which is necessary to our representations, is not necessarily a priori. Words are a perfect case in point: they are necessary to all thinking; but they are learned and not innate.[78] (3) Kant's contention that space must be a priori if the propositions of geometry are to have universality and necessity suffers from a false premise: that all empirical propositions are only probable and contingent. If we accept this premise, then we must indeed accept the a priori status of space to ensure the certainty of geometry. We must reject it, however, because, in some cases, it is possible to derive a universal and necessary proposition from experience. This is the case where I feel that something cannot be otherwise, and everyone else has the same feeling under the same circumstances.[79]

What are we to make of Feder's criticisms? His third objection is weak because it rests upon his implausible attempt to derive universal and necessary conclusions from empirical premises. Kant would reply to Feder: just because I and everyone else have the feeling that an event is necessary, it does not follow that the event itself is necessary. His other objections miss their target because they are directed against an assumption that Kant does not hold: that space is an a priori representation or innate idea.[80] It is important to see that Kant does not think that space is a representation or idea, as if it were one kind of intuition on a par with others. He explicitly calls space "the form of intuition" in order to distinguish it from sensation or intuition proper; and such "a form of representation" is not a representation, but "the power to relate representations to one another."[81] Had Feder recognized this point, he would never have quarreled with Kant in the first place, since he admits that space is innate in the sense of a capacity to receive representations.[82]

Raum und Causalität is not only an attack on Kant's "Aesthetik," but also a defense of the Göttingen review. Feder now attempts to vindicate his equation of Kantian and Berkeleyan idealism. After considering Kant's reply to the Göttingen review in the *Prolegomena,* he still insists that it does not affect the main point at issue.[83] Although Kant wants to grant 'empirical reality' to objects in experience by saying that they exist 'outside us' or 'external to us', this does not clear him of the charge of idealism. All that he means by objects existing 'outside us' or 'external to us' is that they exist in space; but, Feder insists, no idealist would ever dispute this. Indeed, on Kant's own reckoning, 'existence in space' cannot mean 'existence independent of consciousness' because Kant himself says that space is nothing but a form of consciousness. So, merely by admitting the existence of objects in space, Kant fails to distinguish his idealism from Berkeley's.

Pressing home his attack, Feder argues that it is useless for Kant to distinguish his idealism from Berkeley's on the grounds that his idealism does not reduce experience to an illusion. This is said to be unfair to Berkeley, who also insists that experience is not an illusion. All idealists distinguish between reality and illusion within consciousness by some criterion of conformity to law. Hence there is no difference between Kant's and Berkeley's idealism on this score either.

Although these are fair points, they fail to do full justice to Kant's reply in the *Prolegomena.* Feder does not pay sufficient attention to Kant's point that his idealism, unlike Berkeley's, affirms the existence of the thing-in-itself. Only in a footnote does Feder admit the obvious discrepancy between Kant's and Berkeley's idealism on this matter;[84] and then it is embarrassing to find him expressing complete agreement with Kant that we can know nothing more than appearances of things-in-themselves. Feder does not even attempt to reconflate Kant's and Berkeley's idealism by arguing that Kant has no right to affirm the existence of the thing-in-itself. The reader is again left with the impression that, had Feder been more careful in examining Kant's position, he would never have picked a quarrel with him in the first place. It comes as no surprise when Feder says that he has nothing more to complain about than Kant's careless language: "Kant should not say that appearances are nothing more than representations 'in us' if he means that they are appearances of things-in-themselves."[85] That is a point well taken; but it does not affect the substance of Kant's position.

Feder also ignores Kant's argument that Berkeley's empiricism forbids him to distinguish between reality and illusion. Of course, Berkeley wants to distinguish between reality and illusion within consciousness, and he attempts to do so by some criterion of regularity, just as Feder says. But Kant's point is that Berkeley's empiricism foils his good intentions because it forces him to admit that the regularity of experience consists in nothing more than habit and association, which does not give the necessity required for objectivity.

In the end, then, Feder's charge of idealism does not stand up to Kant's reply in the *Prolegomena*. But, as we shall soon see, this was not the end of the matter. There were other empiricists who were willing to pick up where Feder left off, and who had stronger arguments. Kant was not to be let off the hook so easily.

6.6. Feder's Circle: A. G. Tittel and A. Weishaupt

Feder's most powerful ally in his battle against Kant was Gottlob August Tittel (1739–1816), professor of philosophy in Karlsruhe and then of theology in Jena.[86] Although Tittel received his philosophical education in Jena, a bastion of Wolffianism before 1780, he eventually came under the spell of Feder's empiricism.[87] But Tittel's great hero was Locke, whom he went to great pains to defend against Kant. As late as 1790 he published *Locke vom menschlichen Verstande,* an exposition of Locke designed to combat the dangerous popularity of Kant's 'rationalism'.

If he was no original thinker, Tittel was certainly a sharp critic. His two polemics against Kant—the *Ueber Herrn Kants Moralreform* (1786) and the *Kantische Denkformen oder Kategorien* (1787)—rank among some of the best of the early anti-Kantian tracts. Kant was worried by the criticisms in *Kants Moralreform,* so worried that he even intended to write a reply for the *Berliner Monatsschrift.*[88] But, due to advancing age and the pressing need to complete the critical project—the second and third *Kritiken* were still to be written—Kant eventually decided to abandon polemics.[89] As a result, Tittel was relegated to a footnote in the preface to the second *Kritik.*[90] A history of post-Kantian philosophy cannot so easily ignore Tittel, however. He was among the first to formulate some of the classic criticisms of Kant: the artificiality of the table of categories, the emptiness of the categorical imperative, and the inapplicability of the categories to experience.

Tittel's *Kants Moralreform* is a polemic against the *Grundlegung zur Metaphysik der Sitten,* which appeared one year earlier. The aim of Tittel's vitriolic tract is to defend eudaemonism against *die kantische Mystik,* which is accused of sacrificing the straightforward principle of happiness for some 'mystical' ideal of pure duty.[91] Tittel's thesis is that Kant's notion of duty for duty's sake is not only empty, but also contrary to human nature, which demands sensible motives for its actions.[92] This is surely a pregnant theme, anticipating some of Schiller's and Hegel's later criticisms of Kant.

The main target of Tittel's criticism is Kant's division of man into noumenon and phenomenon. Like Hamann and Herder, Tittel rejects this dualism as a reification of a purely intellectual distinction. But he also finds it untenable for other interesting reasons. This dualism is the source of Kant's 'mysticism', he says, in that it compels him to put reason in a mysterious inexplicable realm above and beyond experience.[93] Kant destroys the possibility of a scientific explanation of the development of our rationality— for example, one according to Locke's 'plain historical method'—when he banishes all naturalistic explanation to the realm of appearances.

Tittel's defense of eudaemonism essentially consists in the now classic argument that the categorical imperative is empty. The categorical imperative determines the morality of a maxim, he claims, only by covertly introducing considerations of utility.[94] The principle to will only that maxim which can be a universal law of nature presupposes an evaluation of the consequences of everyone acting according to such a maxim. In other words, Kant is nothing but a rule utilitarian in disguise. To prove his point, Tittel goes through all of Kant's famous examples and argues that the morality of the maxim is determined by the value of its consequences. For example, 'I ought to borrow money with false promises of repayment' cannot be a moral maxim according to Kant's criterion simply because its universalization would destroy the institution of money lending.[95] The whole Kantian moral reform rests upon a mere formula, Tittel concludes, because Kant's categorical imperative can be only a reformulation of the already present and perfectly adequate criterion of utility.[96] The categorical imperative, if it has any significance at all, boils down to the formula to act only on those maxims whose consequences would be beneficial as universal laws of nature.

It was this charge of 'formalism' that irked Kant and provoked him to reply to Tittel in the preface to the second *Kritik.* But Kant, it must be said, missed the point of Tittel's criticism. He trivialized it by interpreting it as the claim that the categorical imperative cannot *discover* the principles of morality; Kant then had an easy time of it explaining that the aim of his criterion is not to discover but only to justify these already well-known principles. The point of Tittel's criticism, however, is precisely that the categorical imperative cannot *justify* the principles of morality. This is surely a much more serious objection, which Kant conveniently chose to ignore.

In 1787, only a year after *Kants Moralreform* appeared, Tittel published his *Kantische Denkformen oder Kategorien*. The main targets of this short, clear, and well-argued tract are two very difficult and controversial parts of the first *Kritik:* the metaphysical and transcendental deductions.

Tittel abruptly dismisses the metaphysical deduction, the derivation of the categories from the forms of judgment. Like many later critics, he finds Kant's organization of the categories, and his architechtonic in general, completely arbitrary and artificial.[97] Although Kant claims to derive the categories systematically from the forms of judgment, his method is still 'rhapsodic' since his organization of the forms of judgment is itself arbitrary. While Kant pretends that he is finding the objective order of reason in his classification of the categories, he is in fact only rediscovering the order that he imposes upon them. Tittel especially objects to Kant's claim that his list of categories comprises all possible forms of thought. We cannot exhaustively list all the possible forms of thought, he argues, because a concept is nothing but an abstraction from experience, and we cannot predict what that will bring.[98]

Tittel makes only two critical remarks against the transcendental deduction, but both of them are worthy of serious attention. First, he observes that the categories are so general that there cannot be a criterion to tell how they apply to experience.[99] There is nothing in the category itself which determines how it applies to particular cases; and there is nothing in experience that shows whether the category applies to it, since perception reveals nothing more than a constant conjunction of events. So how can we ever know that the categories are necessary conditions of our experience? How can they be constitutive of it? Second, Tittel sees an inconsistency which he does not know how to resolve. Namely, Kant states that a priori concepts have significance only within the field of possible experience; but he also says that nothing in our perception ever reveals the universality and necessity of an a priori concept. That raises the question: how do these concepts get their significance from experience if there is such a discrepancy between them and perception? The skeptic would have to conclude that they have no significance at all.

Another notable figure in Feder's circle was Adam Weishaupt (1748–1830). Weishaupt is best known as the founder and leader of the *Illuminati*—a secret society devoted to the cause of political reform and *Aufklärung*—but he was also one of the more influential empiricist *Popularphilosophen*.[100] Although educated as a Jesuit, Weishaupt soon converted to the cause of the *Aufklärung*, largely due to the influence of the practical philosophy of Feder. Weishaupt generously admitted that Feder delivered him from "the darkness of monasticism" and that he owed his whole manner of thinking to him.

When the Garve scandal broke and Feder declared war on Kant, Weishaupt rallied around the flag of his master. In 1788, the same year Feder's *Raum und Causalität* appeared, Weishaupt unleashed a broadside against Kant, publishing no less than three polemics against him, including *Zweifel über die kantische Begriffe von Zeit und Raum, Gründe und Gewissheit des menschlichen Erkennens,* and *Kantische Anschauungen und Erscheinungen.* Weishaupt's polemic created a stir in its day, disturbing Kant's friends and delighting his foes.[101] Kant was warned from various quarters of the threat posed by Weishaupt, though his embargo against polemics prevented him from launching a counterattack.

The aim of Weishaupt's attack on Kant is to defend the charge of idealism in the Göttingen review. Weishaupt's central thesis is that Kant's philosophy ends in a complete 'subjectivism', that is, the denial of all reality independent of our passing states of consciousness. This subjectivism is, in Weishaupt's estimation, the *Grundfehler,* or the reductio ad absurdum of Kant's philosophy.[102]

Why does Weishaupt think that Kant's system is guilty of subjectivism? He goes to great lengths to establish his case, but in the end his entire polemic boils down to the following points. (1) Kant states that we know nothing but appearances; but he also says that these appearances are only representations "in us."[103] (2) Kant's belief in the existence of the thing-in-itself is incompatible with his critical principles, so that to remain true to these principles, he must embrace a total idealism.[104] (3) Kant thinks that objectivity consists in nothing more than the conformity of a representation to a rule; but, even if this condition is fulfilled, it is possible that the representation does not correspond to reality itself.[105] (4) Kant maintains that the principle of causality is only a subjective rule of the understanding which is inapplicable to things-in-themselves; but this implies that we cannot ever get outside our representations to know their causes or origins.[106]

Assuming that all these points are correct and that Kant is guilty as charged, that still leaves the question, what is wrong with subjectivism? Weishaupt usually points out the moral and religious consequences of accepting subjectivism. But he also has a more philosophical objection: that complete subjectivism is self-refuting.[107] A radical subjectivist who maintains that all knowledge is true only for appearances will have to say the same about his own theory.

In general, Weishaupt's campaign against Kant's idealism was an advance over Garve and Feder. While Garve resorted to casual remarks and Feder to careless polemic, Weishaupt engaged in a systematic and rigorous investigation. Considering the history of post-Kantian philosophy as a whole,

Weishaupt's writings occupy a very definite, and indeed conspicuous, position: they represent the most determined and painstaking attempt to prove the charge of idealism against Kant.

Yet there are some serious shortcomings in Weishaupt's polemic against Kant. He repeatedly insisted that knowledge requires nothing less than correspondence with things-in-themselves; but then he ignored Kant's argument that such a demand cannot possibly be fulfilled.[108] He swore his allegiance to empiricism; but then he castigated Kant for not permitting inferences beyond experience. Worst of all, though, Weishaupt never closely examined Kant's reply to the charge of idealism in the *Prolegomena* and second edition of the *Kritik*.

6.7. The Good Pastor Pistorius

Perhaps the most acute of Kant's empiricist critics, and certainly the most respected by Kant himself, was Herman Andreas Pistorius (1730–1795), the pastor of Pöserwitz on the island of Rügen in northern Germany. Although Kant had nothing but contempt for Tittel and Tiedemann, he had the highest respect for Pistorius.[109] In the preface to the second *Kritik* he paid handsome tribute to the wise pastor. Unlike his other critics, Kant said, Pistorius was "truth-loving and acute, and therefore worthy of respect."[110] It was indeed Pistorius who, in Kant's view, had made some of "the most weighty objections to the *Kritik*."[111] Kant took these criticisms so seriously that he was convinced "nothing less than a detailed critique of practical reason could set aside the misconceptions behind them." Indeed, many of the sections of the second *Kritik* are disguised polemics against Pistorius. What Feder and Garve were to the second edition of the first *Kritik*, Pistorius was to the second *Kritik*.

Although he was an obscure figure even to his contemporaries, Pistorius had an influential position as a reviewer for Nicolai's *Allgemeine deutsche Bibliothek*. From 1784 to 1794 Pistorius reviewed almost all of Kant's works for this journal, not to mention many works of Kant's friends and enemies. Since these reviews were anonymous—they were signed merely by the initials "Rg," "Sg," "Zk," or "Wo"[112]—Pistorius failed to receive all the recognition that he deserved.[113] Thus we rarely find mention of him in the works or correspondence of Kant's contemporaries.

Pistorius's reaction to the first *Kritik* was in most respects typical of the empiricist *Popularphilosophen*. All that is untypical about it is his greater understanding of Kant's position, and his greater subtlety in attacking it.

Like Garve, Feder, and Weishaupt, Pistorius accuses Kant of idealism, of dissolving all reality into a dream, a mere play of representations.[114] He avoids Feder's mistake of blankly equating Kant's and Berkeley's idealism; but he still maintains that, if consistent, Kant's idealism would indeed be no better than Berkeley's. According to Pistorius, there are nothing but appearances in the Kantian system—though they are not appearances *of* anything real or *for* anything real. They are not of anything real, since to assume that they represent a thing-in-itself is to violate Kant's teaching about the limits of knowledge. And they are not appearances for anyone real, because the Kantian transcendental *Ich* denotes not an existent substance, but only a purely formal unity of representations. All that Kant leaves us with then are representations—representations without a subject that represents or an object that is represented.

Pistorius finds it especially paradoxical that, in the *Kritik*, inner sense is on a par with outer sense in giving us knowledge only of appearances.[115] If we do not know ourselves as things-in-ourselves, he argues, then we know our representations only as appearances; but since these representations are in turn only appearances of things-in-themselves, all that we ever know are appearances of appearances. Pistorius frankly confesses that he does not understand Kant here; and he begs him to explain how appearances are possible if all knowledge of them is also only an appearance.[116]

It is significant that Pistorius, unlike Feder and Weishaupt, defends his charge of idealism against the "Widerlegung des Idealismus" in the second edition of the *Kritik*. For the first time the empiricists confront Kant's most important attempt to avoid the accusation of idealism. In his review of the second edition of the *Kritik* Pistorius attacks the "Widerlegung" as inconsistent with the central doctrines of the *Kritik*.[117] He immediately confronts Kant with a dilemma. What, he asks, does Kant mean by 'the reality of objects in space'? If he means only their existence in space, the simple fact that they are 'outside' and not 'inside' us, then he has not refuted the idealist, who does not deny the existence of objects in space anymore than the existence of Dr. Johnson's stone. If, however, Kant means the existence of objects independent of consciousness, then he flatly contradicts the *Kritik*. This clashes not only with his critical strictures, which forbid knowledge of things-in-themselves, but also with the "Aesthetik," which maintains that space is nothing more than an appearance, an a priori form of intuition. According to Pistorius, there is a blatant contradiction between the "Widerlegung" and the "Aesthetik." While the "Widerlegung" asserts that our consciousness of ourselves in time has an objective foundation in things outside us, the "Aesthetik" holds that all representations of time are subjective, having no basis in reality itself.

Although Pistorius was a sharp critic of the first *Kritik,* he is mainly re-membered for his criticism of Kant's ethics. It was in particular his review (published in 1786) of the *Grundlegung* which had such a striking effect upon Kant, forcing him to defend himself in many parts of the second *Kritik.* Pistorius outlined many objections to the *Grundlegung,* and four of them were weighty enough to receive a reply from Kant. Let us consider each of these objections along with Kant's replies.

(1) Pistorius first questions the sufficiency of a purely formal criterion of morality (namely, universalizability).[118] We must first specify what is good, the object of the will, Pistorius says, before we can know whether or not the will is good. The pure form of the will—acting for the sake of the law, fulfilling duty for duty's sake—is not sufficient to establish the morality of the will, because someone might act for the sake of the law and still act according to a morally evil law. Hence it is necessary also to know the material of the law, whether it is conducive to happiness, before judging the morality of the will.

In the preface to the second *Kritik,* Kant explicitly mentions this objection and hopes that he has given a sufficient answer to it.[119] He responds to this objection extensively, devoting the second section of the "Analytik" to the problem raised by it.[120] In his reply Kant admits that he does determine the criterion of morality before deciding what is good or evil, and he concedes that this must appear paradoxical in light of conventional moral theory. He even calls his procedure "the paradox of method in a critical examination of practical reason." Nevertheless, Kant is able to defend himself on the following grounds. If he began his investigation with an analysis of the concept of good and derived his criterion of morality from it, then he would have already abandoned his case to the eudaemonist. For to determine what is good or evil prior to the moral law is merely to discern what is pleasant or painful, and that is a strictly utilitarian consideration. But the very aim of his investigation, Kant tells us, is to discover the possibility of a purely formal criterion of morality; and it would be against all rules of philo-sophical method to foreclose that whose very possibility is to be determined.

It is necessary to admit, however, that Kant's reply to Pistorius misses the point. Pistorius does not doubt that beginning with the concept of good imports utilitarian calculations; his point is that it is necessary to introduce such calculations given that a formal criterion is not sufficient. Kant brings nothing to bear against this point, merely reiterating his conviction that the moral law can be determined apart from all utilitarian considerations. This is, however, just the belief that Pistorius questions.

(2) Pistorius's second objection raises the hoary and difficult question of

whether reason alone can provide incentives or motives for action.[121] He insists that we must have motives and incentives for action, but he denies that reason can provide us with any. According to Pistorius, a completely rational being who has no sensible desires or interests will not act at all. There must be some 'third representation' between the will and the law, as he puts it, which motivates the will to act according to the law; and such a third representation must be the object of desire.

Kant's reply to this objection is nothing less than his theory of moral incentives, the third section of the "Analytik."[122] Kant concedes that there must be some motive or incentive for action; but he denies that admitting motives for action is ipso facto to grant sensible motives. The moral law provides its own incentive for action, Kant argues, since it gives rise to a sui generis moral feeling. This respect for the law is derived not from sensibility, but from the moral law itself.

(3) Pistorius's third objection claims that the Kantian categorical imperative, unlike the principle of happiness, is neither comprehensible to, nor applicable by, everyone alike. It can be understood and applied only by an elite few, namely professional philosophers. The principle of happiness avoids these problems, however. Everyone understands it and knows how to apply it in particular cases.[123]

This kind of objection worried Kant, who was as eager to surmount the gap between theory and practice as the *Popularphilosophen*. If Pistorius's objection were valid, then Kant's principle of morality would be completely ineffective as a means of *Aufklärung,* that is, as a guide to rational action for the public at large. Kant's reply to Pistorius, which appears in the "Anmerkung" to the third proposition of the "Analytik," is that whether or not a maxim is universalizable is a simple matter "that can be distinguished without instruction by the most common understanding."[124] Kant then throws this criticism back in Pistorius's face. It is the principle of happiness that is incomprehensible and inapplicable, he argues, because all the differences between people's desires, and the different consequences of action under different circumstances, make it impossible to develop a universal imperative.

(4) It was undoubtedly Pistorius's fourth objection that disturbed Kant most. Pistorius argues that Kant's moral theory demands a knowledge of things-in-themselves, which should be impossible according to the first *Kritik*.[125] There are two respects in which Kant presupposes such knowledge. First, he assumes that man is a noumenal agent, a *causa noumenon,* whose power to act is not determined by the natural causality of the phenomenal order. But, Pistorius asks, if all we know are phenomena, then how do we know that man even exists as a noumenon? All our self-knowledge is supposedly only of ourselves as appearances. Second, Kant defines the concept

of freedom as the power to begin a causal series without determination by a prior cause. But such a definition, Pistorius insists, already exceeds the Kantian limits on knowledge. For the notion of a power is a causal concept; and the notion of a beginning is a temporal one. Hence the definition requires the application to noumena of the category of causality and the form of inner sense, time; but that is expressly forbidden according to the first *Kritik*.

Kant devotes a full section of the second *Kritik* to a reply to this objection.[126] The right of practical reason to extend the categories beyond experience is dubbed "the enigma of the critique." But Kant still insists that the inconsistency here is only apparent. Although the *Kritik* excludes the possibility of knowing noumena according to the categories, it does not forbid the possibility of thinking or conceiving them according to the categories. Now when practical reason extends the categories beyond experience, it does not pretend to give us knowledge of noumena; it only leads us to think or conceive them.

Assuming that we do have a right to think the possibility of freedom, how do we establish its reality? Pistorius might grant us such a right, although he would then insist that any method of establishing the reality of freedom will be theoretical, thus violating the *Kritik*'s strictures upon knowledge. But Kant is ready with a reply to this objection, which is indeed one of the central teachings of the second *Kritik*.[127] According to Kant, we know the reality of freedom not through applying the categories to intuitions, but through our awareness of the moral law, which gives us a consciousness of ourselves as beings who belong to a different order than the phenomenal order of nature. While the categories give us knowledge of only what *is* the case, the moral law tells us what *ought* to be the case; and the mere fact that we ought to do something shows that we have a power to act not limited to the natural order.

Chapter 7

The Revenge of the Wolffians

7.1. Leitmotivs of the Wolffian Campaign

Although seven long and eventful years had passed since the publication of the *Kritik der reinen Vernunft*, the Wolffians had yet to wake from their dogmatic slumber and launch a counterattack upon Kant. By the year 1787 Kant was an established figure on the intellectual scene. He had influential disciples in various universities; Reinhold's popular *Briefe über die kantische Philosophie* had appeared; and the *Allgemeine Literatur Zeitung,* a pro-Kantian journal, had been in circulation for years. Kant, who criticized almost everything the Wolffians stood for, was becoming popular, dangerously popular. But, by the year 1787, the Wolffians had still done very little to counter this looming threat. A few critical remarks appeared appended to this textbook or that, but little more.[1]

The Wolffian alarm bells went off some time in 1788. It was in this year that the Wolffians began to publish their polemics against Kant. In 1788 there appeared J. G. E. Maass's *Briefe über die Antinomie der Vernunft,* J. F. Flatt's *Fragmentarische Beyträge,* and J. A. Ulrich's *Eleutheriologie,* all of which were potent weapons in the Wolffian counterattack. But something else happened in 1788, something of greater significance for the Wolffian campaign as a whole. This was the publication of J. A. Eberhard's *Philosophisches Magazin,* a journal devoted entirely to the defense of fortress Wolffiana.[2] The declared aim of the *Magazin* was to counter the pro-Kantian sentiments of the *Allgemeine Literatur Zeitung.*[3] In the four years of its existence, the *Magazin* quarreled tirelessly with the *Zeitung.* Abuse was met with abuse, reviews with counter-reviews, and objections with rejoinders.

If the *Zeitung* had considerable talent behind it—K. L. Reinhold, C. Schmid, J. Schultz, and C. G. Shütz—the *Magazin* could boast of equal resources. Supporting Eberhard were men of no mean intellects: J. G. E. Maass, J. S. Schwab, J. F. Flatt, and G. U. Brastberger. And from time to time the *Magazin* recruited such eminent mathematicians as L. Ben David and K. G. Kästner to add authority to its critique of Kant's theory of mathematics. Thus two equally matched phalanxes opposed one another, ready for battle.

The Wolffian campaign against Kant, no less than its Lockean counterpart, has its general themes, its recurrent leitmotivs, its common criticisms. These themes and criticisms are either found with much greater frequency and clarity among the Wolffians than the Lockeans, or they are characteristic of the Wolffian campaign in the sense that no empiricist would even in principle state them. Despite exceptions to these generalizations, it is less difficult to generalize about the Wolffians than the Lockeans, for the simple reason that the Wolffians acted much more in unison through the *Magazin*.

Let me, then, for the sake of a general overview, briefly summarize these common themes. We should bear in mind that these themes are found particularly in the *Magazin*, though they are also found in other writings of the Wolffians.

(1) Perhaps the general theme of the whole Wolffian campaign against Kant is that criticism, if thorough and consistent, results of necessity in dogmatism. There is no middle path between skepticism and dogmatism; and if we are to escape skepticism, then we have to defend dogmatism.[4]

Although the Wolffians held that true criticism leads to dogmatism, they also argued that, in Kant's hands, criticism ends of necessity in skepticism. Kant's false analysis of the conditions and limits of reason implies, if consistently developed, that we cannot know anything. The Wolffians had a whole battery of arguments for the skeptical consequences of Kantian criticism. But the most common of them is that Kant's criticism leads to solipsism because it limits all knowledge to appearances, which consist in nothing more than our representations. Kant's criticism therefore traps us inside the circle of our own consciousness, so that we know nothing but our own momentary representations.[5]

So, like the Lockeans, the Wolffians also wanted to escape the alleged solipsistic consequences of Kant's idealism. But it is important to see that the Wolffians chose a different route of escape. Rather than arguing for some form of realism in the sensible world, like the Lockeans, the Wolffians advocated a rational knowledge of the supersensible world. Only such knowledge avoids solipsism, they maintained, since empiricism, if consistent, denies all knowledge of the external world and other minds. The Wolffians therefore praised Hume for demonstrating the skeptical consequences of empiricism.[6] It is interesting to note that, on the whole, they were much more appreciative of the challenge of Hume's skepticism than the Lockeans.

(2) Kant's criterion to distinguish between the analytic and synthetic is ancient, psychologistic, and useless. It is ancient, and not a new discovery, as Kant pretends, since Leibniz was already well aware of it. It is psychologistic because it is based upon whether a predicate "expands" or "explicates" "the thought contained in the subject." And it is useless in that it is too vague to determine which judgments are analytic or synthetic in specific cases. Whether a judgment is analytic or synthetic will also be, on Kant's criterion, a relative matter, for everything depends upon the thought someone happens to have of the subject.[7]

Rather than a psychologistic criterion, a strictly logical criterion is necessary to distinguish between the analytic and synthetic a priori. The distinction between these judgments ought to be a distinction between the logical principles that govern their truth. Analytic a priori judgments are governed by the principle of contradiction; and synthetic a priori judgments are determined by the principle of sufficient reason. The distinction between analytic and synthetic a priori judgments therefore should not be seen as a distinction between logical and nonlogical truth; for both kinds of judgment are forms of logical truth.

The Wolffians' attack upon Kant's analytic-synthetic criteria is one of their more valuable contributions to post-Kantian philosophy. They deserve credit for bringing this issue into the open for the first time. A bitter controversy broke out between them and the Kantians over the purpose, originality, and adequacy of Kant's criterion.[8]

(3) The propositions of mathematics are not synthetic, but analytic a priori. They do not require a priori intuitions for their truth, but are in principle reducible to statements of identity, which are true in virtue of the principle of contradiction. Although mathematics, particularly geometry, sometimes does have recourse to intuitions, these are never necessary to the truth of its propositions. Rather, they are only aids for our limited understanding, which cannot immediately comprehend the truth of a deductive chain. If, however, we had the infinite understanding of God, then we would not require any a priori intuitions.[9]

(4) While the propositions of mathematics are analytic a priori, those of metaphysics are synthetic a priori. But the synthetic a priori status of metaphysical propositions does not mean that their truth is undecidable by reason. The connecting link between the distinct terms of a synthetic a priori judgment does not have to be an a priori intuition, as Kant assumes; it can be a higher law of the understanding, namely, the principle of sufficient reason.[10]

(5) Metaphysics is capable of attaining the same degree of certainty as mathematics. Mathematics is not in a superior position to demonstrate its

truths because it has access to a priori intuitions. The truth of both meta-physics and mathematics rests upon pure reason alone.[11]

(6) Kant's empirical criterion of significance is inappropriate in meta-physics. The significance of any abstract concept is inexplicable in empirical terms, though it is perfectly definable through other abstract concepts. All that follows from the empirical indefinability of abstract concepts is that they do not have *empirical* significance; it does not follow that they have no significance at all.[12]

(7) It is not only permissible but also necessary to grant the categories a transcendent validity. To explain the conditions of experience, it is nec-essary to extend the categories beyond it; thus Kant has to apply the category of causality to things-in-themselves in order to explain the origin of expe-rience. This means that there cannot be a firm dividing line between the transcendent and the transcendental.[13]

(8) The principles of reason are not only laws of thought, and they are not only universal and necessary forms of consciousness, as Kant implies. Rather, they are much more: they are laws of being, laws that are true not only for all possible consciousness, but all possible things, whether these be representations in consciousness or things-in-themselves outside it.[14]

It is therefore wrong to assume that we have to choose between idealism, where objects conform to concepts, and realism, where concepts conform to objects. These are the only options that Kant seriously considers in the *Kritik*. But there is a third and middle option, which happens to be the true one: that concepts and objects, though independent of one another, conform to one another in virtue of some common structure or general laws. These general laws are the laws of logic, which are neither purely subjective nor purely objective, but general laws of all being. Thus our thinking corre-sponds to things, and conversely, because it and they both conform to the same common structure and the same general laws, namely, the laws of logic.[15]

The Wolffians saw their insistence upon the ontological status of logical laws as their fundamental difference with Kant. According to Eberhard, for example, criticism and dogmatism are at one in denying empiricism and in affirming the a priori origin of the principles of reason; the only difference between them is that according to criticism, these principles are valid only for consciousness, while according to dogmatism, they are valid for things-in-general.[16]

(9) There is no such thing as 'a natural illusion of reason'. If reason deludes itself, then we cannot even discover its own delusions. The an-tinomies are not a conflict of reason with itself, but of reason with the imagination.[17]

(10) It is not necessary to postulate transcendental freedom in order to

escape fatalism. Freedom and determinism are perfectly compatible with each other. Furthermore, Kant's theory of transcendental freedom is incompatible with his restrictions upon the categories, because it demands the application of the category of causality to things-in-themselves.[18]

(11) Practical reason has no primacy over theoretical reason. We have no right to believe in the existence of something simply because we ought to believe in its existence. Kant's practical faith is subjectivistic, for it permits a belief in God that is valid for us and not for things-in-themselves.[19]

7.2. Revolution versus Reaction

Although the Wolffians fought against Kant with much cunning, passion, and energy, it was clear from the start that they were engaged in a losing battle. They began their campaign against Kant on a defensive footing, for one thing. Even worse, they were vainly struggling against the spirit of the times. The sad truth of the matter is that the Wolffians were relics of a passing age—and they knew it in their heart of hearts.[20] They were the aging sentinels of the old order, the Europe of the ancien régime where monarchy, clergy, and aristocracy still held sway.[21] Of course, the Wolffians were reformers and *Aufklärer*; but they were also shameless elitists. They firmly believed in the need for rule from above; and they deeply feared the will of the masses below. Democracy was an anathema to them, and revolution a crime. Their very model of government was the old status quo: the benevolent despotism of Frederick II.[22]

Now metaphysics played a vital role in the Wolffians' defense of the status quo. They saw metaphysics as the theoretical precondition for political order and stability, for it provided the necessary justification for the beliefs in God, providence, and immortality. These beliefs were regarded as necessary incentives and guarantees of all moral and political conduct.[23] Although the elite of course knew better and would do their duty for its own sake, the masses needed the fear of supernatural punishment, and the hope of supernatural reward, to stay in the political harness. Without such hopes and fears, they would lose all inner motivation to obey the law, and the eventual result would be anarchism. Thus the possibility of metaphysics was not merely a philosophical issue: it was also a political one. To attack the possibility of metaphysics was therefore to undermine the very foundation of public order; it was indeed to license anarchism itself.

The fatal blow to the already moribund Leibnizian-Wolffian school came not with Kant's *Kritik*, but with the French Revolution. The younger generation, which was filled with enthusiasm for the Revolution, dismissed the old metaphysics as little more than a prop for the ancien régime.[24] It was not so much that the old metaphysics had been proven wrong, whether by

Kant or any other philosopher. Rather, it was that political events had shown that there was no longer any need for such a metaphysics. The beliefs in God, providence, and immortality were beginning to lose their hold as political sanctions. If all men could govern themselves, then what need was there for a God to govern them? If men could make the world conform to their moral ends, what need was there for providence? And if they could make themselves happy in this life, what need was there for immortality, which only promised happiness in some afterlife? Once the political necessity of these beliefs had been questioned, the very motivation to do metaphysics disappeared. Anyone who insisted upon the need for Wolffian-style dem-onstrations after 1789 immediately revealed his political colors: he was a lackey of the old guard, a defender of the ancien régime.

It is indeed significant, and surely not surprising, that the Wolffians as-sociated Kant with the French Revolution, which "the old Jacobin" was known to support.[25] Their critique of Kant therefore became part and parcel of their reaction against events in France. The Wolffians were convinced that Kant's critique of metaphysics would lead to skepticism and atheism, which would ultimately result in the complete collapse of social order. After the chaos and bloodshed of the terror, the Wolffians felt themselves totally vindicated.[26] Here was living proof that democracy meant mob rule and that metaphysics was necessary to prevent mankind from sinking into bar-barism. The most burning question to the Wolffian mind in the early 1790s was whether Germany would follow the bloody path of France.[27] The Wolf-fians were adamant that it should not. Hence their campaign against Kant acquired new energy and earnestness well into the 1790s.[28] After all, it was not only a philosophical school, but also the very fabric of society, that was at stake.

If there is any single factor that explains Kant's decisive victory over the Wolffians, it is indisputably the French Revolution.[29] What Kant's pen could not do, the guillotine did for him. The association between Kant's philos-ophy and the Revolution proved to be an extremely strong selling point for the younger generation.[30] The political revolution in France seemed to find its abstract formulation with the philosophical revolution in Germany. The principle of autonomy, which plays such a conspicuous role in Kant's ethics, appeared not only to express but also to justify the egalitarian demands behind the Revolution. By contrast, however, the Wolffians acted like a bunch of stuffy reactionaries. Rather than promoting the march of freedom, they seemed intent on obstructing it. Their attempt to revive metaphysics appeared to be nothing less than a conspiracy to restore the ancien régime. So, given this contrast, the decision was already made for any young man of liberal disposition in the 1790s. The choice between Kantianism and Wolffianism was a choice between revolution and reaction.

7.3. The Wolffian Defense of Metaphysics

The unpopularity of metaphysics around the 1790s, the Wolffians' painful self-awareness of their forthcoming extinction, and the many formidable objections hurled against them in Kant's *Kritik,* all lead us to an interesting and important question. Namely, how did the Wolffians attempt to vindicate themselves against such overwhelming odds? How did they attempt to defend the possibility of metaphysics? How indeed did they reply to Kant's many criticisms?

The answer to this question is naturally complex, admitting of no easy generalizations. Each of the Wolffians naturally had his own arguments for the possibility of metaphysics and his own replies to Kant's objections. Nevertheless, there were two general theories shared by several prominent Wolffians that played a fundamental role in their attempt to revive metaphysics: their theories of the synthetic a priori and the objectivity of logic, doctrines advanced by Eberhard, Maass, and Schwab in the *Magazin* and *Archiv.*[31] Since these theories were so important to them, and since they also occupied pride of place in the *Magazin* and *Archiv,* the central organs of the Wolffian reaction, they deserve separate consideration here.

According to Kant, the fate of metaphysics hinges upon the issue of the possibility of the synthetic a priori: How is it possible to make universal and necessary judgments about the world if there is no empirical evidence for them? How is it possible for there to be a necessary connection between the distinct terms of a synthetic a priori judgment? These questions are the starting point for Kant's investigation into the possibility of metaphysics. But, somewhat surprisingly, they are also the starting point for the Wolffians, who never question Kant's formulation of the problem.[32] The Wolffians agree with Kant that, if they are to have ontological significance, metaphysical judgments must be synthetic.[33] (Otherwise, if analytic, these judgments would be empty and formal truths.) They also concur with Kant that metaphysical judgments are a priori, that they are universal and necessary and therefore unjustifiable through experience. The Wolffians do not attempt to base metaphysics upon the natural sciences, like Herder; and still less do they try to derive universality and necessity from experience, like the Lockeans. Hence for the Wolffians, no less than the Kantians, the problem of metaphysics is the problem of the synthetic a priori.

Despite this point of agreement, the Wolffians disagree with the Kantians on one fundamental point: the truth conditions of the synthetic a priori. In their view these conditions are to be found not in a priori intuitions, as the Kantians assume, but in pure reason alone. In other words, both mathematics *and* metaphysics, insofar as they employ pure reason, provide valid synthetic a priori judgments.

The Wolffians arrived at this bold and comforting conclusion through their own theory of the synthetic a priori, based on their distinction between analytic and synthetic a priori judgments. According to Eberhard, Maass, and Schwab, the distinction between these judgments is basically a distinction between the different principles that govern their truth.[34] The truth of analytic a priori judgments is governed by the principle of contradiction, while the truth of synthetic a priori judgments is determined by the principle of sufficient reason. This is also formulated as a distinction between the kinds of predicate of an a priori judgment.[35] While the predicate of an analytic a priori judgment 'expresses' or is 'contained in' the essence of the subject, the predicate of a synthetic a priori judgment is 'grounded in' or 'determined by' it.

Now it is a general feature of all a priori judgments, Eberhard, Maass, and Schwab maintain, that their truth is determinable by reason alone. This is plain from the case of analytic a priori judgments. But Eberhard, Maass, and Schwab insist that it is no less true for synthetic a priori judgments. To see whether the connection between subject and predicate holds, we have to see if the subject is 'a sufficient reason' for the predicate. We do this through further analysis of the subject, which should suffice to tell us whether or not it implies its predicate.[36] What brings together the distinct terms of a synthetic a priori judgment is thus not an a priori intuition, but a higher principle of reason, namely, the principle of sufficient reason.[37] This principle states that the predicate is true *of necessity* of the subject if the subject is the sufficient reason for the predicate, that is, if the notion of the subject entails the predicate, and not conversely.

The strategic value of this theory of the synthetic a priori is considerable. It ensures that metaphysical judgments have both ontological significance and a priori decidability. Since it does not reduce their truth down to the principle of contradiction, the theory gives synthetic status to metaphysical judgments. Hence their ontological significance is guaranteed. But at the same time, since it connects the distinct terms according to the principle of sufficient reason, a higher principle of reason, it also provides for the a priori decidability of metaphysical judgments. According to this theory, to determine the truth of a synthetic a priori judgment, it is necessary only to see if the subject is a sufficient reason for the predicate; and to do this, it is necessary merely to analyze the subject term—all in all, then, an extremely convenient doctrine. It means that the Wolffians can know the truth about things by sheer a priori excogitation.

This theory of the synthetic a priori is necessary to, but not sufficient for, the Wolffian defense of metaphysics. By itself, it does not justify the transcendent dimension of metaphysical judgments, their claim to be true not only for consciousness, but also for things-in-themselves. As it stands, it is still possible that the principle of sufficient reason, the main principle of synthetic a priori judgments, is true only for us, for appearances, but not for things-in-themselves. So, even admitting the Wolffian theory of the synthetic a priori, Kant's limits upon knowledge might still apply.

It is at just this point that the Wolffian theory of logic comes to the rescue. The Wolffians are ardent defenders of the objectivity of logic—and equally ardent critics of Kant's apparent psychologism and subjectivism. It is self-refuting to maintain that the principles of logic are true only for appearances, they argue, for such a proof has to be true of us not only as appearances but also as things-in-ourselves.[38] As already discussed, the Wolffians maintain that the principles of logic are not 'laws of thought', but laws of all being; and these laws are true for 'things-in-general', whether these things be appearances or things-in-themselves, noumena or phenomena. An a priori judgment is true not in virtue of how we think, but in virtue of the essences or possibilities of things. It is true if the essence of the subject entails the predicate; and such an entailment is true or false no matter how we happen to think. Using this theory as a premise, the Wolffians then argue that there is no problem in our thought corresponding to reality. Since both thought and reality have to conform to the laws of logic, we can rest assured that thought conforms to reality (and conversely); for both concept and object share a common logical structure.

Adding this theory of logic to the theory of the synthetic a priori appears to secure the transcendent significance of metaphysical judgments. Consider the following points. Since, according to the theory of the synthetic a priori, the truth of metaphysical judgments is based upon the principles of logic, and since, according to the theory of logic, the principles of logic are true of things-in-general, it follows that metaphysical judgments are true of things-in-general. Such, at any rate, is the general line of reasoning that the Wolffians hurled against Kant.

However strategic, and however important, it is still doubtful, in the end, that this combined theory gives the Wolffians everything they want. Even if we admit their theory of the synthetic a priori, and even if we concede the theory of logic that supports it, we are far from providing a sufficient foundation for metaphysics. In the final analysis this theory suffers from the same difficulty as the classical rationalist theory of judgment: it cannot leap Lessing's broad, ugly ditch between possibility and reality, concept and existence.[39] Assuming that we can know the truth of synthetic a priori judgments through sheer analysis of their subject terms, and assuming that the connection between subject and predicate is an eternal truth that holds not only for appearances but also for things-in-themselves, we are still left with the question of whether the synthetic a priori judgment applies to reality. The problem at hand here is as simple as it is insuperable. In order to know whether a synthetic a priori judgment is true, it is (according to the theory) necessary only to analyze the subject term to see if it involves the predicate; the inference is true or false whether or not the subject refers to anything that exists. But if we are to know whether this inference holds between things in reality and not only between abstract essences or possibilities, then it is necessary to know whether the subject exists in the first place. It is necessary to know, in other words, whether or not the subject term has a reference. But how are we to determine whether this is the case? This is an important question, clearly, but it is also one for which Eberhard, Maass, and Schwab have no straightforward answer.[40] And the more we try to respond to this question, the more we begin to see the force of Kant's original point that we have to consult experience.

Another basic difficulty attached to the Wolffian theory of the synthetic a priori concerns its main premise, its distinction between the analytic and synthetic a priori. This distinction was aggressively attacked by Kant himself, who argued that the principle of sufficient reason alone cannot distinguish between these two classes of judgment.[41] The mere stipulation that the predicate is 'a consequence' of the subject, or that the subject is 'the ground' of the predicate, is insufficient, in Kant's view. It is necessary to ask *in what sense* the predicate is the consequence of the subject, or *in what sense* the subject is the ground of the predicate. If the predicate is a consequence of the subject in the sense that to posit the subject and to deny the predicate results in a contradiction, then we are again back with the principle of contradiction and have another analytic judgment on our hands. If, however, the predicate does not follow from the subject according to the principle of contradiction, then the judgment is indeed synthetic, just as Eberhard says. But in that case we are still left with the embarrassing questions, in what sense is the predicate a consequence of the subject, and in what sense is the judgment valid if not in virtue of the principle of contradiction? This is, of course, the problem of the synthetic a priori all over again—the very problem that Eberhard's theory is designed to resolve.

The difficulties with the Wolffian theory of the synthetic a priori begin to multiply as soon as we realize that Eberhard and his cohort are only nominally loyal to it. In several instances Eberhard, Maass, and Schwab blur their distinction between the analytic and synthetic a priori. They unwittingly undermine the synthetic status of the synthetic a priori, so that it ultimately boils down to nothing more than an implicit form of the analytic a priori. Thus at one place Eberhard works hard to deduce the principle of sufficient reason from the principle of contradiction.[42] If, however, such a deduction succeeds, then it means that the synthetic a priori is also reducible to the principle of contradiction. Elsewhere, Eberhard says explicitly that the propositions of metaphysics are in principle derivable from higher axioms, which are nothing more than instances of the law of identity.[43] And at still another place, he states clearly that both mathematics and philosophy are capable of attaining the same degree of certainty because they are both governed by the principle of contradiction.[44]

The Wolffians' disloyalty to their own theory is easily explicable, however, once we consider the dilemma facing them. On the one hand, they wanted to deduce the principle of sufficient reason from the law of contradiction, so that they could give this principle an incontrovertible foundation immune to all Kantian and Humean objections. Such a deduction would also substantiate a favorite rationalist theme that the Wolffians could never bring themselves to abandon: the identity of philosophical and mathematical truth. On the other hand, they did not want to deduce the principle of sufficient reason because they recognized, if only vaguely, that such a deduction reduces the synthetic to the analytic a priori. All metaphysical judgments then become analytic, losing their ontological significance. Hence the Wolffians faced a difficult and painful choice: either certainty and emptiness, or uncertainty and nonemptiness. When they inclined toward the first option, they betrayed their theory of the synthetic a priori; when they leaned toward the second option, they remained loyal to it. But never did the Wolffians dare to face the consequences of making a firm decision one way or the other.

7.4. The Thorn in Kant's Side, J. A. Ulrich

One of the most influential—and certainly one of the most controversial—Wolffian critics of Kant was J. A. Ulrich (1746–1813). Throughout the last three decades of the eighteenth century, Ulrich held the important post of professor of philosophy at Jena, the center of German cultural life. Like so many philosophers of his generation, Ulrich was raised in the Leibnizian-Wolffian school, and his early writings reveal a clear sympathy for Leibniz.[45] Although he was not an orthodox Wolffian, Ulrich never shook off the influence of his schooling. During the 1790s, those heady days when Jena was overtaken by its wave of enthusiasm for Kant, Ulrich became a dissenting and reactionary figure, the last solitary representative of the old guard.

It is surprising to learn, therefore, that Ulrich was one of Kant's first spokesmen. When the first *Kritik* appeared, he underwent a conversion. "The *Kritik* contains," he is alleged to have proclaimed,[46] "the true and only code of genuine philosophy." Ulrich was indeed one of the first philosophers to lecture on Kant in Germany, and he was certainly the first to do so in Jena.[47] As early as the autumn of 1785, and long before Reinhold arrived on the scene, Ulrich incorporated the *Kritik* into his lectures on metaphysics. Kant duly recognized Ulrich's efforts in his behalf. He was so pleased to have such a senior and respectable professor lecture on his philosophy that he went out of his way to encourage Ulrich, sending him one of the very few complimentary copies of the *Grundlegung*.[48] So great were Ulrich's early leanings toward Kant that many mistook one of his textbooks for a long-awaited work of Kant's.

It is extremely doubtful, however, that Ulrich ever completely converted to Kant's philosophy. His major work concerning Kant, *Institutiones logicae et metaphysicae* (1785), is so critical of Kant, and so critical of him over so many points, that it cannot be considered the work of a disciple. If we examine this work closely, it is difficult to resist the conclusion that Ulrich's conversion to Kant was partly selfish and tactical. In the *Institutiones* he used Kant for his own metaphysical ends. Ulrich considered the *Kritik* a prolegomenon to any future metaphysics—in particular, the neo-Leibnizian metaphysics he had just developed.

Ulrich's approval of Kant was indeed very short-lived. Reinhold's extremely popular *Briefe über die kantische Philosophie,* and his hugely successful introductory lectures on the first *Kritik,* stole the limelight from Ulrich. It now appeared as if the up-and-coming authority on Kant was no longer going to be Ulrich, but Reinhold. Ulrich became so envious of Reinhold's meteoric success, so embittered by his own loss of audience, and so skeptical of the uncritical allegiance of Kant's devotees, that he soon turned into Kant's avowed enemy.[49] He then did everything in his power to combat Kant's growing influence in Jena. He had to give six lectures a day—and he devoted every one to a refutation of Kant. Judging from contemporary reports, the tone of these lectures was vitriolic and defamatory.[50] At the conclusion of one of them Ulrich defiantly proclaimed: "Kant, I will be the thorn in your side, I will be your pestilence. What Hercules promises that he will do."[51]

These were not empty threats. Whatever the merits of Hercules' labors, they at least did not fail to spurn Kant into retaliatory measures.

Ulrich's *Institutiones logicae et metaphysicae* is an attempt to reconcile and synthesize Kant's critique with Leibniz's metaphysics. In Ulrich's view the Kantian critique has not destroyed metaphysics; rather, it promises metaphysics a new and more secure foundation. What Ulrich has in mind, however, is certainly not the kind of metaphysics Kant would approve of.

It is not the regulative architechtonic that Kant recommends in the "Methodenlehre," but the dogmatic speculation that he condemns in the "Dialektik."

The thrust of Ulrich's criticism of Kant is that the critical philosophy is consistent and complete only if it incorporates a thoroughgoing dogmatic metaphysics within itself. Ulrich adopts much of the conceptual apparatus of the *Kritik;* and he agrees with many of its central doctrines, such as, Kant's theory of space and time, and the distinctions between noumena and phenomena and mathematical and philosophical knowledge. But he departs from Kant in one significant respect, which reveals his underlying metaphysical intentions: he insists that the categories of the understanding, and the ideas of reason, are not limited to experience but are extendable to, and give us knowledge of, things-in-themselves. This is Ulrich's main point of contention with Kant, which he defends from many different angles in the *Institutiones*.

Ulrich's main argument against restriction of the categories to experience concentrates not upon the transcendental deduction, as we might expect, but upon the analogies of experience. Apropos the second analogy, Ulrich argues that the category of causality has a much broader application than to experience alone.[52] It applies not only to events in time, but also to anything that exists, be it noumenal or phenomenal. The category must have this wider significance, since we ask not only why something happens in time, but also why it exists as it does, whether it is in time or not. Indeed, we could not ask for the cause of events in time if we could not also ask for the cause of everything that exists. Because the category of causality has this wider significance, it is permissible to assume that things-in-themselves are the causes of experience.

Concerning the first analogy, Ulrich also defends the transcendent use of the category of substance.[53] He argues that to explain the origin of experience we have no choice but to permit such usage. Since the realm of appearances consists in changing representations, there must be some cause of their changes; and that cause must be a substance, the permanent subject of these changes. Ulrich seems to countenance the view that this substance is nothing less than the 'I' of the unity of apperception.[54] But he insists that we know this 'I' as a thing-in-itself. The 'I think' gives us consciousness of ourselves not as appearances, he says, but as things-in-ourselves; for the 'I' is that for whom all representations are appearances, and it too cannot be only an appearance without incurring an infinite regress.[55]

Ulrich's *Institutiones* would probably have been ignored by Kant if it were not for a favorable review of it that appeared in the *Allgemeine Literatur*

Zeitung.[56] Although the review was anonymous, Kant knew the author was Johann Schultz, his close friend and disciple, and the author of the first commentary on the *Kritik.*[57] Aware that Schultz was the author, Kant had to pay attention to the review and the *Institutiones.*

In his review Schultz praises Ulrich for his patient and impartial criticisms of Kant, stating that he shares many of Ulrich's doubts. Yet he observes that Ulrich has failed on one very important score: he has not considered the transcendental deduction. This is the very heart of the *Kritik,* Schultz rightly stresses, and Ulrich would have done well to examine it in order to prove his case against limiting the categories to experience. It is the deduction that lays down the principles behind Kant's limitation of the categories to experience, and it is necessary for Ulrich to examine these principles. Despite such a serious shortcoming, Schultz exonerates Ulrich. His failure to consider the deduction is deemed all too understandable, given the difficulty of this part of the *Kritik.* Although the deduction is the most important part of the *Kritik,* it is also the most obscure. Schultz thus insinuates that the deduction was in serious need of a rewrite—a hint that Kant was not to ignore.

Although Schultz admits that a proper treatment of the deduction goes well beyond the confines of a single review, he cannot resist making one criticism en passant. The aim of the deduction, he writes, is to show that synthetic a priori concepts are a necessary condition of experience. "But what does experience mean here?" he asks impatiently. Schultz accuses Kant of equivocation. Sometimes experience comprises what Kant calls 'judgments of perception', and sometimes it consists in what he calls 'judgments of experience'. Yet, in either case, the deduction does not prove its point. If, on the one hand, Kant thinks that synthetic a priori concepts are a necessary condition of judgments of perception, then he states a falsehood. For it is possible to make empirical judgments without applying synthetic a priori concepts: If we simply say 'the stone is warm when the sun shines', we do not commit ourselves to the claim that there is a universal and necessary connection between the heat of the sun and the warmth of the stone. If, on the other hand, Kant thinks that synthetic a priori concepts are a necessary condition of judgments of experience, then he utters a tautology. It is difficult to deny that a judgment stating a universal and necessary connection between events (for example, 'the heat of the sun is the cause of the warmth of the stone') requires synthetic a priori concepts. But it is important to note that this more modest point does not help Kant against the skeptic who denies that our perception gives us any evidence for attributing universal and necessary connections to experience. So the deduction appears to be either false or trivial. Such, in Schultz's eyes, is the dilemma facing the deduction. Schultz is still careful to say, however, that this dilemma need not be fatal. Nevertheless, he begs Kant for clarification.

Kant eventually took cognizance of the *Allgemeine Literatur Zeitung* review in a rather unpromising and inconspicuous place: a footnote to the preface of his *Metaphysische Anfangsgründe der Naturwissenschaften* (1786).[58] Such an obscure corner of the Kantian corpus is in fact of some significance, though, for here Kant reflects upon the aims and claims of the transcendental deduction. Kant begins by focusing on Schultz's claim that, without a clear and convincing deduction, the critical philosophy is built upon a weak foundation. This claim is met with a surprising response, however. In order to avoid the objection, Kant seems to demote the importance of the deduction. He states explicitly that the deduction is not necessary to establish "the fundamental proposition of the *Kritik*": "that the speculative use of our reason cannot extend beyond possible experience." According to Kant, the deduction tells us not *that,* but only *how,* synthetic a priori concepts are necessary conditions of experience. The problem of the deduction— *How* do synthetic a priori concepts apply to experience?—is therefore not necessary to the general result of the *Kritik, that* synthetic a priori concepts apply only to possible experience. Although the deduction is useful in explaining this result, it is still not necessary to establish it.

Rather than putting the burden of the entire *Kritik* upon the transcendental deduction, Kant claims that its fundamental principle can be established independently. He argues that it can be proven from three propositions: (1) that the table of categories exhausts all the concepts of the understanding; (2) that the concepts of the understanding apply to experience only through the mediation of the a priori forms of intuition, namely, space and time; and (3) that these a priori intuitions are nothing more than forms of appearances, that is, forms of possible experience. It follows from these three points alone, Kant claims, that all the concepts of the understanding are applicable only to possible experience.[59]

Having constructed this new proof, and having argued that the deduction is not necessary to establish such a conclusion, Kant still resolves to rewrite the deduction. It is as if he has seen Schultz's point but is not willing to admit it. He says that he now has a simpler and more powerful exposition of the deduction in mind, one that requires nothing more than the definition of judgment.[60] Kant vows to take "the nearest opportunity" "to rectify the lacks" of the first version of the deduction. Here, then, we have Kant's fateful resolve to write the second version of the deduction—a direct response to the *Allgemeine Literatur Zeitung* review.

Kant's apparent demotion of the deduction in the *Anfangsgründe* did create problems for him, however. It now seemed as if he had no consistent position toward the deduction. If he states explicitly in the *Anfangsgründe* that the deduction is not necessary to the foundation of the critical philosophy, he declares expressly in the *Kritik* that the deduction is "indispensably necessary."[61] This apparent contradiction was drawn to Kant's attention by Reinhold, who begged him to clear up the matter.[62]

Kant addresses himself to this contradiction at the close of his essay "Ueber den Gebrauch teleologischen Prinzipien in der Philosophie."[63] Here Kant makes a neat and tidy distinction between the two senses in which the deduction is 'necessary'. It is necessary for the positive purpose of demonstrating the possibility of synthetic a priori knowledge within experience. It is not necessary, however, for the negative purpose of showing that the categories do not give us knowledge beyond possible experience. For this latter purpose, we are told, it suffices merely to explain what is involved in the notion of a category. Supposedly, it follows from this notion that a category cannot give us knowledge without a given object in sense experience.

We can leave aside the questions whether this distinction avoids Reinhold's contradiction, and whether the deduction is necessary for such a negative purpose. Even if Kant is correct about these matters, he is still demoting the importance of the deduction. For why should the negative purpose be more important to the foundation of the critical philosophy than the positive one? What is so surprising about Kant's evasive move in the *Anfangsgründe* is that he identifies the 'foundation' of the critical philosophy with its negative teaching about metaphysics. But in doing so he underplays the importance of another central task of his philosophy: namely, the justification of natural science against Humean skepticism. That task is undeniably important to Kant, and the deduction is undeniably necessary to it. Under pressure from his critics, then, Kant has conceived the critical philosophy as the negative enterprise of limiting metaphysics; it is not the positive business of defending the possibility of natural science against skepticism.

The *Institutiones* was not the only work of Ulrich's to provoke a response from Kant. No less provocative was a polemic that Ulrich wrote some two years later, in 1788, at the height of his anti-Kantian frenzy. This was his *Eleutheriologie oder über Freiheit und Nothwendigkeit,* a tract reviewed by Kant's friend and ally C. J. Kraus in the *Allgemeine Literatur Zeitung.*[64] Kraus, in fact, wrote the review under Kant's direction and on the basis of a manuscript of Kant's.[65]

The review of the *Eleutheriologie* is an interesting document since it defends and clarifies Kant's difficult doctrine of transcendental freedom. It contains Kant's retort to compatibilism, a position often seen as the correct alternative to his own more uncompromising views.

Ulrich's *Eleutheriologie* is basically a defense of the classical Wolffian position that freedom and determinism are compatible. Against Kant's concept of transcendental freedom, Ulrich pits his own 'system of necessity'. In his view freedom does not transcend the natural world, but is continuous with it; it is indeed the direct product of organic, mechanical, and chemical forces.[66] But such a natural necessity does not destroy freedom, Ulrich says. We can be determined in our actions, and still want to do them; we are free because we have the power to act according to our wants.[67]

Having made the common point that a determined action is compatible with a wanted one, Ulrich avoids the common mistake of simply equating freedom with the power to act according to our wants. He insists that freedom also includes the power to improve and perfect ourselves in light of our moral awareness, so that we can control our immediate wants and act for higher moral ends. Freedom includes "the perfectibility of our practical knowledge," so that, though we might act wrongly today, we can still act rightly tomorrow if we resolve to do good and exert ourselves.[68]

In tune with his general position, Ulrich maintains that determinism is compatible with morality and religion. The determinist reinterprets rather than annuls our moral obligations. Our obligations are still valid, Ulrich argues, even if, at the time of acting, we could not have done otherwise. 'Ought' implies the possibility of doing otherwise to be sure, but it does not imply the possibility of doing otherwise in the present or at the time of action; it implies only the possibility of acting otherwise in the future when we have resolved to do better and have improved our character. The proper interpretation of phrases like 'You could have done otherwise' is therefore 'You will have to do better in the future'.[69]

The thrust of Kant's reply to Ulrich is that his determinism, like all determinism, reduces to fatalism: that is, it must deny all moral obligations because it cannot permit any intelligible reading of the phrase 'he could have done otherwise'.[70] What Ulrich fails to see, Kant argues, is that a strict determinism destroys not only the power to act otherwise now, at the moment duty calls, but also the power to act otherwise in the future. In other words, there is no distinction between the necessity of present and future actions. Kant asks Ulrich a pointed question: how is it possible to become different and to do otherwise in the future if everything in the past determines the future? The perfectibility of character, which is so important for Ulrich's explanation of moral obligation, is no less a victim of determinism than the power to act here and now with a present imperfect character. Whether or not we perfect our character depends on the causes that act upon us. All self-improvement must begin with some resolve of character;

but that resolve will be determined by further causes ad infinitum. Hence what right do we have to praise or blame?

In stressing the need for a transcendental concept of freedom, Kant is eager to point out that he is not ignoring the difference between instinctual compulsion and long-term self-interest.[71] He is not postulating a transcendental freedom simply because he fails to take this commonplace distinction into account. Rather, he insists that the critical philosophy can accommodate the phenomenon that Ulrich is referring to when he talks about our ability to restrain ourselves and to act according to our higher interests. This is what Kant calls 'comparative freedom', that is, not the 'absolute freedom' of a first cause, but the power to act according to enlightened self-interest rather than instinct. Nevertheless, having acknowledged such freedom, Kant insists that it is not sufficient for our moral obligations. The power to act according to our enlightened self-interest does not imply the power to act otherwise, whether in the future or in the present.

There is one objection of Ulrich's that is especially troublesome for Kant. This is Ulrich's argument that it is necessary to distinguish between the power to begin a series of events and the application of that power at specific times.[72] Although it might well be, Ulrich says, that we cannot ask the reason why the series begins, we must be able to ask the reason why our power is applied at one point in time rather than another. But this is just enough, he thinks, to give the determinist a foothold. If we deny that there is any reason for the application of the power, then the act of will is arbitrary, a matter of chance; but if we affirm that there is a reason for its application, then we return to determinism.

Admitting Ulrich's distinction between the power to begin a series and its application, Kant still thinks that it is illicit to ask for the explanation of why the power applies itself in some cases rather than others. Such a demand would confuse the border between the phenomenal and noumenal worlds and seek explanations where none are to be had. Kant admits that his own theory introduces a large element of mystery into the concept of freedom. But he thinks that this is the price that we must pay if we are to save morality. Indeed, in Kant's view the compatibilist theory introduces more mysteries than his own. The inconceivability of the compatibility of freedom and necessity is much worse than the simple inconceivability of freedom.

7.5. The Scrooge of Tübingen, J. F. Flatt

J. F. Flatt (1759–1827), professor of metaphysics (from 1785) and then theology (from 1792) at Tübingen, has not occupied an enviable place in philosophical history. He has gone down in the annals as something of a fuddy-duddy or reactionary. Flatt has been remembered most for his intransigent stand in behalf of positive religion at a time when the natural religion of the *Aufklärung* had long since become status quo. As a disciple of C. G. Storr, senior professor of theology at Tübingen and the founder of the so-called old Tübingen school of biblical criticism,[73] Flatt conducted a subtle and sophisticated last-ditch defense of the literal truth of the Bible and the authority of revelation. He turned the new tools of historical research and philological criticism on their head, using them not to undermine but to support the supernatural content of the Bible. Kant's doctrine of practical faith was exploited in a similar way.[74] All the basic dogmas of positive religion—the trinity, resurrection, and incarnation—were proclaimed necessary postulates of practical reason. Such a defense of positive religion was regarded as hopelessly anachronistic in the 1790s; and many critics saw this use of modern philological and historical methods as a perversion of their original intention.

Flatt would never have acquired such an unflattering reputation if it were not for the fact that he was the hapless teacher of three very disgruntled students at the Tübinger Stift. They reacted bitterly to his compulsory lectures,[75] and they were unsparing in their later judgments,[76] casting a dark shadow over their old teacher's name. Who could these students be that they had such power to make or break a reputation? None other than Schelling, Hegel, and Hölderlin. A very formidable tribunal indeed! From 1788 to 1793, Schelling, Hegel, and Hölderlin dutifully but begrudgingly attended Flatt's lectures on metaphysics, theology, and psychology, lectures that frequently contained criticisms of Kant and defenses of positive theology. It is no wonder, then, that the three students began to see their teacher as a reactionary, as indeed an obstacle to the new philosophical ideas of Kant, Reinhold, and Fichte. They particularly disliked Flatt's tendentious use of Kant's moral theology, which seemed to them to be a perversion of Kant's critical aims and a cowardly attempt to sneak dogmatism in through the back door.[77] Schelling's *Briefe über Dogmatismus und Kriticismus* (1795) was a covert attack upon Storr's and Flatt's pseudo-Kantian moral theology.

But if the elder Flatt deserves this reputation, the same cannot be said for the younger Flatt. Before his days in service of Storr's anachronistic moral theology, which did so much to blacken his name, Flatt was an acute and much respected critic of Kant.[78] He wrote numerous reviews concerning Kant for the *Tübingen gelehrte Anzeige* and two much respected and discussed polemics, the *Fragmentarische Beyträge zur Bestimmung und Deduktion des Begriffs und Grundsätze der Causalität* (1788) and the *Briefe über den moralischen Erkenntnisgrund der Religion* (1789). Rather than using Kant's practical reason to defend religion, these early works attack the very attempt to justify faith on practical grounds.[79] The young Flatt's aim was to revive a Wolffian natural theology, and in particular to defend the cosmological argument against Kant's criticisms.[80] This earlier anti-Kantian phase of Flatt's career made its mark in the history of post-Kantian philosophy, and, if only because it has been so ignored, deserves our attention here.

Flatt's reviews of Kant in the *Tübinger Anzeige* were a persistent annoyance to Kant, who had no great respect for his pesky critic.[81] It was Flatt's habit to accuse Kant of inconsistency; and, as if to remind his critic that he could not be so guilty of such a simple and dire failing, Kant wrote in the second *Kritik:* "consistency is the highest obligation of the philosopher."[82] In his reviews Flatt made two notorious criticisms of Kant.[83] First, he argued that Kant is caught in a vicious circle where he deduces the moral law from freedom and then freedom from the moral law. Second, he maintained that Kant, contrary to his restrictions upon the categories, has to apply the category of causality to the noumenal self if he is to have an intelligible account of noumenal agency.

Both of these criticisms worried Kant, who replied to them in the second *Kritik.*[84] Kant's reply to the first criticism is that, though freedom is indeed the *ratio essendi* of the moral law, the moral law is the *ratio cognoscendi* of freedom. His reply to the second criticism is his distinction between thinking and knowing an object according to the categories.

Flatt's *Fragmentarische Beyträge* is a defense of the transcendent use of the principle of causality in natural theology. The point of this exercise is to rescue the cosmological argument from Kant's criticism. Like Ulrich, Flatt argues that the principle of causality has a logical significance which justifies its extension beyond experience.[85] Kant maintains that its significance is empirical on the grounds that there would be no distinction between cause and effect if all idea of antecedence and succession in time were taken away.[86] But, Flatt replies, even if we abstract from time, we can still distinguish between cause and effect: the cause is the ground from which the effect follows, and not conversely.[87] We can use the principle of sufficient reason to distinguish between cause and effect; and this principle applies not only to events in time, but to things-in-general.

The *Briefe über den Erkenntnisgrund der Religion* is a sharp attack on Kant's moral theology. Here Flatt criticizes the fundamental premise behind Kant's moral theory: that it is possible to justify beliefs on the basis of moral interests or 'needs of reason'. No interest or need, no matter how moral or rational, is ever sufficient to justify a belief, Flatt argues, since it is always compatible with the falsity of the belief.[88] We might have an interest or need to believe what is not true. To justify our religious beliefs, we must restore to theoretical reason all the old rights Kant took away. As Flatt sums up the main lesson of his book: "Practical reason cannot stretch its wings and fly to the supersensible if those of theoretical reason have been clipped."[89]

According to Flatt, Kant's moral theology rests upon two propositions, both of which Kant fails to establish.[90] (1) Morality demands that we believe in not only the possibility but also the reality of the highest good, that is, the harmony between happiness and moral deserts. (2) The highest good is possible only if we believe in God, who creates and maintains it. Flatt argues that these propositions are either incompatible with or do not follow from Kant's system as a whole.

Flatt makes two objections to the first proposition. First, it is incompatible with Kant's claim that the moral law is binding only upon human beings with their peculiar sensibility.[91] If this claim is true, then the moral law is valid only for us, and we have no right to infer the objective existence of anything from it. All that we can say is that we are so constituted as finite beings that the moral law, and all the beliefs that follow from it, are necessary for us; but we cannot infer from this that the beliefs are true of reality itself. Second, Kant's argument for this proposition is a *petitio principii*. He argues that since we have a duty to realize the highest good, we also have a duty to believe in its existence, such a belief being a necessary condition of the fulfillment of our duty. But the premise of the argument presupposes the truth of its conclusion. We cannot assume that we have a duty to realize the highest good unless we already know that the conditions for its realization prevail.[92]

The second proposition of Kant's moral theology is also inconsistent with his system as a whole, Flatt argues. It is not permissible on Kantian principles to think of God as the governing agent behind the highest good, for that would demand applying the category of causality to the noumenal world, which Kant expressly forbids.[93] And it is not necessary on Kantian principles to think of God as the cause of the harmony between morality and happiness in the highest good; for the highest good might be the result of the activity of the finite agents themselves.[94] Thus Kant himself says in the first *Kritik* that if everyone did what morality demanded of him, he would be the creator of his and everyone else's happiness.[95] Even assuming that God is the cause of the highest good, it is still not possible for Kant to infer that he is an unconditioned and independent being.[96] For that would be to infer the unconditioned from the series of conditions, which is also not permissible according to Kant's system. All Kant's arguments against the physicotheological argument apply *mutatis mutandi* to his own practical proof.[97]

Such, if only very roughly, is the gist of Flatt's early polemic against Kant.

Undoubtedly, his polemic leaves much to be desired. The *Beyträge* purports to be a critical examination of Kant's treatment of causality; but it does not even analyze the argument of the second analogy, and it ignores Kant's all-important distinction between thinking and knowing an object according to the categories. The *Briefe* suffers from a crude formulation of Kant's position; and, having set up a paper dragon, it has an easy time smashing it. Still, when all is said and done, Flatt deserves credit for an acute and cautious examination of then two much neglected areas of Kant's philosophy. No one before him had examined Kant's moral theology or theory of causality in such detail and with such care and precision. Flatt's polemics are by no means on a par with the later works of Schulze and Maimon; but they were at least a step in the right direction. So, as far as his early polemic against Kant is concerned, Flatt was not that much of a reactionary after all.[98]

7.6. Platner's Meta-Critical Skepticism

Among the most eminent of the rationalist critics of Kant was Ernst Platner (1744–1818), professor of medicine and physiology at the University of Leipzig. Before Kant's rise to fame, Platner was regarded as one of the foremost philosophers in Germany.[99] He was often mentioned in the same breath as Lambert, Kant, and Tetens.[100] Platner was in the very vanguard of the *Popularphilosophie* movement, and his *Anthropologie* and *Aphorismen* were among its classics. He was famous for his polished, witty, and urbane lectures, which were popular and influential. Among his early students was K. L. Reinhold, who first learned of Kant through him.[101] Platner's reputation suffered, however, when Kant's philosophy became so popular during the early 1790s. Platner fought hard against Kant's influence by developing a new meta-critical skepticism. But this brought him none of his former glory.

The early Platner definitely belongs to the rationalist rather than empiricist wing of the *Popularphilosophie* movement. His early writings show a marked debt to Leibniz, and he was even regarded as "one of the foremost improvers of the Leibnizian system."[102] In an early edition of the *Aphorismen* (1782–1784), for example, Platner expounds a Leibnizian epistemology and psychology and defends it against Kant's objections.[103] He also maintains the possibility of metaphysics becoming a science,[104] and even attempts a refutation of skepticism.[105] But partly, if not entirely, under Kant's stimulus Platner began to move toward a more skeptical position.[106] Kant had convinced him of the impossibility of knowledge of things-in-themselves, causing him to modify and rethink much of his earlier position. In the later edition of the *Aphorismen* (1793) Platner renounces the possibility of metaphysics and maintains the necessity of skepticism, which he declares to be "the only consistent point of view in philosophy." Despite this movement toward skepticism, Platner never fully foreswore many of his earlier Leibnizian allegiances. His later philosophy still retained those features of Leibniz's philosophy that were compatible with his new skepticism, for example, a rationalist psychology almost identical to Leibniz's.

Platner's philosophical reputation was largely based upon a single book, his famous *Aphorismen*. This is in reality not one book, but many under a single title, since it underwent so many drastic revisions in its various editions.[107] While the earlier editions expound a Leibnizian epistemology and psychology, the later editions advance a neo-Kantian skepticism. Platner brought out a third, completely revised edition of the *Aphorismen* in 1793 in order to take the critical philosophy into account. This third edition provoked wide discussion among Kant's friends and enemies.[108] Platner's criticisms of Kant won him great respect, and he was generally regarded as a figure to be reckoned with.[109] Reinhold wrote a counterattack on Platner's new skepticism,[110] and F. G. Born, another prominent Kantian, made a point of replying to Platner's objections.[111] Most important, though, the *Aphorismen* became a virtual textbook in Jena during the last decade of the eighteenth century. It became an established tradition to criticize and comment upon the *Aphorismen* in introductory lectures. Fichte, Schmid, and Reinhold all used the *Aphorismen*. Of course, as we might expect from such avid Kantians, the *Aphorismen* was used more for target practice than exposition. Nonetheless, it remains an important text in post-Kantian philosophy if only because it forms the backdrop for Fichte's and Reinhold's lucubrations.[112]

Platner's main contribution to post-Kantian philosophy is his new skepticism, or what he calls his 'skeptical criticism'. Along with his two skeptical contemporaries, Maimon and Schulze, Platner deserves a great deal of credit for the rehabilitation of skepticism after Kant. It has often been said that the revival of skepticism after Kant was due to the triumvirate of Maimon, Schulze, and Platner.[113]

Platner's new skepticism consists in two essential theses, both of them directed against Kant: (1) that Kant has not refuted, but only begged the question against Hume;[114] and (2) that all the criticisms Kant makes against metaphysics apply in equal measure to his own epistemology. In attempting to revive skepticism, Platner does not simply hark back to Hume, however. Rather, he builds his skepticism upon a new foundation, the Kantian critique. Platner's skepticism, like Maimon's and Schulze's is meta-critical. Its starting point is Kant's critique; but it then goes a step further in turning the critique against itself. Thus Platner distinguishes between a 'dogmatic' and 'skeptical' critique of knowledge.[115] A skeptical critique, unlike Kant's dogmatic critique, examines and criticizes the limits and powers of criticism itself. According to Platner, Kant has completely misunderstood the nature of skepticism. He defines it as the mistrust in reason without a preceding criticism of its powers.[116] But, Platner retorts, true skepticism is based upon criticism; it is a necessary conclusion of a consistent criticism that does not shirk before the criticism of its own powers.

Although his skepticism is decidedly anti-Kantian in tone and spirit, Platner is still eager to plead that he does not consider himself Kant's enemy.[117] He is indeed at pains to stress that he agrees with the fundamentals of Kant's philosophy. The two main principles of Kant's philosophy are also the two main principles of his own, Platner writes.[118] These principles are first, that there cannot be knowledge of things-in-themselves, and second, that all philosophy must return to its foundation in common sense, morality, and experience. Platner, no less than Kant, affirms that we must deny knowledge in order to make room for faith.[119]

Yet if Platner is keen to agree with what he calls Kant's 'philosophy', he also does not hesitate to disagree with what he calls Kant's 'system' or 'doctrine'.[120] He defines Kant's 'system' or 'doctrine' as the methods and arguments by which he attempts to prove his main principles. According to Platner, these methods and arguments are just as dogmatic as those of the metaphysician. Kant's dogmatism is especially evident, Platner maintains, when he presumes to know the whole faculty of knowledge and to determine its powers and limits with complete certainty. But a true critique of knowledge is skeptical, Platner argues, since it recognizes that we cannot know our faculty of knowledge with any more certainty than things-in-themselves. As Platner summed up his critique of Kant in his letter of May 19, 1792, to Prince Christian Frederick Augustenberg: "When it comes down to it, is it not wiser and more temperate to admit that human thought is just as much a puzzle as the world which it should explain? . . . Kant flatters himself that he knows the inner essence of the human mind—thus he can prove that it knows nothing. But which presumption is greater? Wanting to fathom the human mind or the world?"[121]

Platner's polemic against Kant is indeed at its best when he attempts to expose Kant's 'dogmatism'. We might summarize his most interesting objections as follows. (1) Kant's negative statements about things-in-themselves are just as dogmatic as the positive statements of the metaphysician. The negative statement that things-in-themselves do not exist in space and time, for example, trespasses against Kant's limits upon knowledge as well as the positive statement that they do exist in space and time. For if, as Kant says, we do not know anything about things-in-themselves, then it is indeed possible that they do exist in space and time; from the mere fact that space and time are a priori forms of sensibility it does not of necessity follow that they are not also properties of things-in-themselves.[122] (2) Kant is much too hasty and dogmatic in his attempt to demonstrate that all our knowledge is limited to experience. Such a demonstration, if not carefully qualified, is self-refuting, for it cannot be justified through experience.[123] (3) We cannot say with certainty that our a priori concepts are the product of the understanding and that our moral actions are the product of noumenal freedom. For all we know, it is possible that they are the effect of things-in-themselves acting upon us. The rigid causality of the phenomenal world might indeed have its counterpart in the noumenal world.[124] (4) Kant is mistaken if he thinks that he has refuted Hume. All that his transcendental deduction proves is that *if* we have a regular and orderly experience, then it is necessary that it conform to the categories; but that still leaves it open for Hume to deny that we have such an experience.[125]

After hearing this litany of complaints against Kant's 'dogmatic' critique, we might well ask Platner how he justifies his own 'skeptical' critique. What is it that steers his skepticism between the Scylla of self-refutation and the Charybdis of dogmatism? Platner has a striking and radical answer to this question.[126] Skepticism is completely irrefutable, he maintains, because the skeptic does not affirm or deny anything. Since he has no beliefs, he cannot refute himself or be dogmatic. It would be a great misunderstanding of skepticism, Platner says, to assume that it consists in a set of beliefs or that it is a particular theoretical position. Skepticism is not a doctrine or theory, but only an attitude or disposition. It is that frame of mind in which we look upon all beliefs with complete indifference and detachment. The skeptic knows that he cannot justify his attitude other than in a strictly personal and subjective manner. Skepticism gives him independence and imperturbability of mind, and that is sufficient justification for him.

Platner's personal skepticism represents one of the most radical answers to the problem of the authority of reason in eighteenth-century philosophy. If, for Platner, all criticism ends in skepticism, all skepticism ends in a total subjectivism. He claims his skepticism is nothing more than the attitude of the individual, *die Denkart des einzelnen Mannes*. The critical direction given to philosophy by Kant thus concludes in a radical subjectivism. In the end, one can only admire Platner's courage and consistency in advocating such extreme skepticism—and then wonder if this was indeed where criticism was heading.

7.7. The Eberhard Controversy

The year 1788 marks a new phase in the history of Kantian philosophy. Now that Kant, thanks largely to Reinhold's *Briefe* and Schütz's *Zeitung*, had achieved public recognition, the problem arose of defending the critical philosophy on a much wider scale. Nothing breeds enemies more than success. In this respect, 1788 was a crucial year. This was the year of reaction, the beginning of the spirited polemical campaigns against Kant. Strangely, as if by design, all the forces opposing Kant began to organize themselves in one and the same year. Seventeen eighty-eight is the year that Feder and Meiners started their *Philosophische Bibliothek,* the mouthpiece of the Lockeans. But it is also the year Eberhard began his *Philosophisches Magazin,* the organ of the Wolffians. The avowed aim of both of these journals was to combat the growing influence of the critical philosophy. Appearing in the same year, they represented a serious challenge to Kant, who now faced a war on two fronts.

Of these two journals, Kant felt threatened more by the *Magazin* than the *Bibliothek.* While he did not bother to reply to the *Bibliothek,* he went out of his way to attack the *Magazin.* Against the advice of friends,[127] and against his own resolve not to engage in polemics,[128] Kant went to the trouble of writing a weighty polemic against Eberhard. This is his *Ueber eine Entdeckung, nach der alle neue Kritik der Vernunft durch eine aeltere entbehrlich gemacht werden soll,* which was published in April 1790, simultaneously with the third *Kritik.* The *Entdeckung* is indeed the largest polemical work of Kant's later years. But Kant's fury did not stop here. In addition to writing his polemic, Kant encouraged his allies, Reinhold and Schulz, to attack Eberhard, sending them detailed instructions.[129] Kant's passionate engagement against the *Magazin* was surprising even to his friends, who did not expect such a surge of activity from such an old and busy man.

Why did Kant go to such pains to attack the *Magazin*? Although this journal represented an obvious threat to him, and although it made a very serious charge against him in accusing him of a lack of originality, such factors were still not sufficient to draw Kant into battle. Thus when the *Magazin* first appeared Kant declined to fight it, assigning this task to his disciples. Why, then, did Kant change his mind? The answer probably lies in the losing battle that Kant's disciples were waging against the Wolffians.[130] Neither of Kant's allies, A. W. Rehberg and K. L. Reinhold, had come forward with devastating replies to the Wolffians.[131] On the contrary, Eberhard and his clever associates, Maass and Schwab, had succeeded in mounting a convincing counterattack that put the Kantians back on the defensive.[132] Indeed, Rehberg, in desperation, had sent out a distress signal, begging for Kant's assistance.[133] The Wolffians, it seemed, were beginning to gain the upper hand. So, given this dismal news from the battlefront, Kant had good reason to break his earlier resolve not to engage in polemics. Now that the third *Kritik* was virtually complete, he also had the time and energy to enter the fray.[134]

Kant's response to the *Magazin* is a milestone in the history of the critical philosophy. This was Kant's last attack upon the Leibnizian-Wolffian school, his final settling of accounts with his oldest foe.[135] After the smoke cleared from the battleground, Kant had emerged the obvious victor in the eyes of his contemporaries. The Wolffians were well and truly routed, if only in the mind of the public.[136]

So let us briefly tell the tale of Kant's victory and the Wolffians' defeat. That demands that we first take a look at the tactics and arguments of his most formidable opponent, J. A. Eberhard.

Eberhard, the editor of the *Magazin,* was the figurehead of the Wolffian reaction against Kant. The rationalist *Popularphilosophen* rallied around Eberhard just as the empiricists stood behind Feder. What gave Eberhard such a commanding role among the Wolffians was not his philosophical acumen—he was a second-rate Wolffian, at best—but his social position. Eberhard was professor of metaphysics at Halle, the birthplace and bastion of Wolffianism in Germany. He was also a prominent figure in the Berlin *Aufklärung,* having all the right friends and connections. Two of Eberhard's works attracted much attention and gave him a little fame: the *Neue Apologie des Sokrates* (1772) and the *Allgemeine Theorie des Denkens und Empfindens* (1776), which won the prize of a Berlin Akademie competition. In his day, then, Eberhard was a celebrity. When he attacked Kant, people were bound to listen.[137]

Although he did not possess any great philosophical talent, Eberhard did have one indisputable skill: he knew how to give an academic dispute the added air of scandal. It was Eberhard's aim not merely to refute Kant, but to discredit him. He wanted to puncture Kant's claim to originality, and thus darken the glow of novelty surrounding the critical philosophy, which was proving to be one of its strongest selling points. In order to undercut Kant in this way, Eberhard put forward a striking and provocative claim: that the project of a critique of pure reason was already to be found in Leibniz.[138] "The Leibnizian critique contains everything in the Kantian critique," he blustered, "and it offers us much more besides."[139] Interpreting a critique of reason in the broadest sense as any analysis of the powers and limits of reason, Eberhard insisted that Leibniz had long since embarked upon such an enterprise. He specifically had in mind Leibniz's *Nouveaux Essais,* where Leibniz does engage in broadly epistemological, if not strictly critical, tasks. We cannot dispute Leibniz's right to the title of a critical philosopher, Eberhard argued, unless we first identify the project of critique with certain specific results and conclusions about the limits of reason; but such an identification would be nothing more than a crude *petitio principii.*[140] In Eberhard's view the Kantian and Leibnizian critiques are distinct from each other not in their aims or methods, but in their results only. And the important difference in their results is simply that Kant's critique denies, while Leibniz's affirms, the possibility of knowledge of things-in-themselves. Knowledge of things-in-themselves is that tempting extra that Leibniz's critique offers us over Kant's.

Prima facie Eberhard, in disputing Kant's originality, seems to be making only an ad hominem point. But, on a deeper level, his argument contains the central message of the entire Wolffian campaign against Kant: that criticism, if consistent and thorough, does not undermine but supports metaphysics. Eberhard is saying, in other words, that Kant represents no advance over Leibniz. The Wolffians were plainly worried by Kant's charge of 'dogmatism' since it implied they were too complacent to examine their own premises. The critical philosophy, Kant had insinuated, stood on a higher and more sophisticated level of self-reflection, having a self-awareness of the limits and powers of reason that Leibniz in his dogmatic slumbers would never have dreamed of. By claiming that Leibniz too had a critique of reason, Eberhard deftly counters that suggestion. Leibniz, he implies, was just as self-reflective as Kant. Indeed, in Eberhard's view, Leibniz is more self-reflective than Kant since he arrives at his conclusion about the possibility of knowledge of things-in-themselves through a more painstaking and accurate examination of reason. So, neatly reversing Kant's claim to be an advance over Leibniz, Eberhard retorts that Leibniz is an advance over Kant.

Having argued his case for the existence of a Leibnizian critique of reason, Eberhard then poses the question of which critique we should prefer, Leibniz's or Kant's. Of course, just as we expect, Eberhard comes down heavily on the side of Leibniz. But it is the rationale that he gives for this choice that is so interesting. The crucial question in choosing between these critiques, he says, is which one avoids Hume's idealism.[141] Eberhard sees Hume's idealism as the central challenge to all philosophy. A philosophy is successful, he thinks, only insofar as it avoids the dangerous consequence of Hume's empiricism: solipsism. This consequence is not so easy to avoid, however, once we accept the Lockean principle that the immediate objects of perception are ideas. According to Eberhard, Hume alone had the courage to bring this principle to its ultimate conclusion: the denial of all reality independent of our ideas, whether that be the external world, God, other minds, or even the self. It is indeed interesting that Eberhard, like Jacobi, portrays Hume's idealism in nihilistic terms. Hume, he writes, has taken the *salto mortale* into "the kingdom of absolute nothingness."[142] So for a Wolffian like Eberhard, and not only a pietist like Jacobi, the reductio ad absurdum of philosophy is nihilism.

Given this criterion, Eberhard thinks that our choice has already been made for us. We cannot opt for Kant since he does not avoid, but embraces Hume's idealism. Because Kant limits all knowledge to appearances and because he understands these appearances as nothing more than "subjective modifications of ourselves," he has explicitly endorsed Hume's solipsism.[143] Now the great advantage of Leibniz's critique, Eberhard assures us, is that it avoids such a drastic conclusion. Leibniz breaks out of the Humean circle of consciousness since he has uncovered the sphere of pure a priori concepts, which give us knowledge of a noumenal reality transcending the sphere of the senses.[144] So even if all the knowledge that we receive from the senses is nothing more than appearances, as Kant and Hume maintain, we are still left with a priori concepts, which take us beyond this veil of maya and which penetrate into the realm of the purely intelligible things-in-themselves.

The main aim of Eberhard's *Magazin* was to defend the heritage of Leibniz and Wolff against the attack of the Kantian critique. What this meant is that Eberhard had to defend the possibility of metaphysics, or, as he defined it, the possibility of rational knowledge of noumena or things-in-themselves. But the hasty and sloppy manner in which Eberhard executed this delicate and difficult task only damaged the case for the tradition he was trying to vindicate.

Apart from his theory of the synthetic a priori (examined in section 7.3), Eberhard's defense of metaphysics consists in little more than two tired arguments from the Leibnizian-Wolffian tradition. The first argument indulges in a popular Wolffian pastime: proving the principle of sufficient reason from the principle of contradiction. Like Leibniz, Eberhard regards the principle of sufficient reason as part of the foundation of metaphysics. Without this principle, he says, it would be impossible to know anything more than the immediate objects of our senses; it would be illegitimate to make inferences about the existence of God, the soul, and the universe as a whole.[145] But since this principle is not an obvious analytic truth, and since it has been attacked by skeptics like Hume, Eberhard has to admit that there is a problem in justifying it. Nevertheless, he maintains that this problem is surmountable by constructing a proper proof. If we can show that the denial of this principle entails a contradiction, then someone who disputes it will also have to admit the contradiction. So, like Wolff, Eberhard proceeds to construct such a proof, using a textbook Wolffian argument.[146] If we deny that something has a reason, the argument goes, then we have to assume that it could have the property P just as well as the property not-P at one and the same time; but to admit that it could be both P and not-P at the same time is to contradict oneself.[147]

Eberhard's second argument is essentially a rehash of Leibniz's monadology. Eberhard attempts to argue that a monadology is an internal necessity of the transcendental philosophy itself. If we are to be good transcendental philosophers and to determine the necessary conditions of experience, he argues, then we have to analyze our sensations, dissecting them into their ultimate constituents, which are indivisible points. Since these points are the necessary conditions of anything appearing to the senses, they are not phenomenal but noumenal entities. Thus, when reason has analyzed the grounds of its experience, it has effectively passed from the realm of phenomena into that of noumena. Hence, to Eberhard, there is no firm dividing line between the transcendental and the transcendent. Any analysis of the conditions of sensation immediately becomes metaphysics. The ability of reason to analyze its sensations into its ultimate noumenal constituents proves that it can know things-in-themselves, and thus the possibility of metaphysics.

Kant's reply to Eberhard, his *Ueber eine Entdeckung* (1790), is a masterpiece of philosophical polemic. Rhetorically, Kant's work does not compare with the brilliant fireworks of Lessing's *Anti-Goeze*, a work in a similar genre. The same involved, prolix, and dense prose of the *Kritik* still prevails. Nonetheless, as a polemical exposé of sloppy and tendentious reasoning, Kant's work is peerless, revealing the weaknesses of Eberhard's argument with matchless skill.

The bulk of Kant's polemic is taken up with a reply to Eberhard's arguments for the possibility of metaphysics. Kant has an easy time of it dispatching Eberhard's proof of the principle of sufficient reason.[148] He accuses Eberhard of deliberately conflating two senses of this principle. There is a logical sense that reads 'Every proposition has a reason'; and there is a transcendental sense that states 'Everything has a cause'. Although it is possible to prove the first sense from the principle of contradiction, it is not possible to do so for the second. Eberhard tries to get around this difference through an intentionally vague formulation of the principle, which reads 'Everything has a reason' where 'everything' could refer to either propositions with reasons or things with causes. Commenting on the details of Eberhard's proof, Kant then points out that it is an obvious non sequitur. The denial of the principle of sufficient reason implies not that something could be *both* A and not-A at the same time, but only that it could be A *instead of* not-A or conversely. It is only the first option, though, not the second, that is self-contradictory.

Kant thinks that Eberhard's return to the monadology suffers from similar ambiguities in argument.[149] In trying to prove the existence of noumenal entities through the analysis of sensation, Eberhard confuses two different senses of the word 'nonsensible' (*nichtsinnlich*). The nonsensible can be something phenomenal, which we cannot discern or be conscious of given the present state of our sensory powers; or it can be something noumenal, which cannot be given in any possible experience, even if our conscious and sensible powers were infinitely magnified. Now Eberhard is right to claim that we can analyze sensation into nonsensible entities of the first kind; but he is wrong to infer that this is a proof of nonsensible entities of the second kind. All that we ever discover through the analysis of phenomena, Kant insists, is more phenomena. We never arrive at the noumena behind the phenomena, even if our present sensory powers were magnified to infinity. It is important to note here that Kant does not deny the possibility of analyzing phenomena into simpler units, and that he is in no way restricting the boundaries of science; thus he refers approvingly to Newton's analysis of light into particles.[150] What Kant disputes is that any such scientific analysis provides us with noumenal entities.

The remainder of Kant's polemic consists in a brisk reply to various objections of Eberhard. Kant is particularly quick in dismissing Eberhard's suggestion that his empirical criterion of significance is arbitrary.[151] It is anything but arbitrary, he maintains, because it is a conclusion and not a premise of the transcendental deduction.[152] So if Eberhard wants to dispute this criterion, then he must find fault with the reasoning of the deduction. But here Kant ignores his own demotion of the deduction in the *Metaphysische Anfangsgründe*,[153] where he said that it is not necessary for such a result. Kant's reply to Eberhard on this point again leaves us wondering whether he had a consistent attitude toward the deduction at all.

Responding to Eberhard's criticisms of his criterion of the synthetic a priori,[154] Kant simply argues that his criterion avoids the problems of Eberhard's. Eberhard's criterion of analyticity—that the predicate asserts something that belongs of necessity to the essence of the subject—is rejected on the grounds that it is insufficient.[155] Both analytic and synthetic a priori judgments have predicates that assert something that belongs to the essence of the subject, Kant says. Hence it is necessary to add another factor to distinguish between the analytic and synthetic, and that is the criterion already laid down in the *Kritik*: whether or not the predicate already contains more than is thought in the notion of the subject.

What did Kant have to say about Eberhard's provocative claim that Leibniz already had a critique of reason? Kant's reply to this charge is a stroke of tactical genius. He does not bother to wade through Leibniz's texts with the intention of showing that *der berühmte Weltweisen* had no such objective. That would only reveal his consternation—and, even worse, his anxiety. Rather, Kant does the very opposite: he shows that in many ways Leibniz's ideas indeed do anticipate the *Kritik*.[156] Thus Leibniz's principle of sufficient reason is interpreted as a regulative idea; and his preestablished harmony is seen as a heuristic principle to explain the interaction between understanding and sensibility. Such a volte-face immediately puts

Eberhard on the defensive. Now Leibniz is on Kant's side, not Eberhard's. At the same time, Kant does not have to worry about Eberhard's charge of unoriginality. Although Kant happily admits that Leibniz foreshadows his ideas, he implies that Leibniz does nothing more than crudely anticipate them.

In the end, though, Kant's victory over Eberhard is strictly eristic. If *Ueber eine Entdeckung* is a success as a polemic, it is still a failure as philosophy. Whoever bothers to wade through it will not find much illumination of puzzling patches of the *Kritik*. There are a few interesting and instructive passages, to be sure.[157] But on the whole the work is disappointing because it does not clarify the *Kritik* in light of Eberhard's objections. Thus Kant does not explicate his criterion of the synthetic a priori; nor does he defend his criterion of significance. In each case we are simply referred back to the *Kritik* when we are hoping for a clarification of it. This is all too understandable given Kant's aim in writing his polemic. His top priority was not to clarify the *Kritik*, but to disgrace his opponent. Kant achieved his end; but only at the expense of his philosophy.

7.8. The Consequences of the Wolffian Campaign

Although the Wolffians lost their battle against Kant and although they disappeared from the philosophical scene after their defeat, their struggle had not been in vain. They had thrown the Kantians back on the defensive in the early 1790s, a time when Kant's philosophy seemed ready to steamroll all opposition. The Kantians could no longer dismiss all criticisms as misunderstandings, a common tactic before the Wolffian campaign; and they were forced to clarify and define their views in response to Wolffian objections.[158] This particularly applies to the criterion of the synthetic a priori, and the theories of space and time.[159]

Apart from this general effect, we can also detect the impact of the Wolffian campaign on particular thinkers. The most important of these thinkers was Kant himself. The controversy with Eberhard affected him far more than the polemic against Eberhard suggests. If we look at the retrospective *Fortschritte*, for example, we find Kant criticizing a conception of metaphysics that is decidedly Eberhardian in spirit.[160] All throughout this work Kant wrestles with Eberhard's sly insinuation that there is no difference between his epistemology and Leibniz's.

Another thinker affected by the Wolffian campaign was Reinhold. Although he loyally stood by Kant during his controversy with the Wolffians, Reinhold also had his nagging doubts about the strength of Kant's defense. Thus in 1790 he argues in his *Beyträge* that the critical philosophy as it stands is vulnerable to a number of criticisms—and the criticisms he has in mind come straight from the pages of the *Magazin*.[161] Although Reinhold does not believe these criticisms are fatal, he holds that an adequate reply to them demands rethinking the whole foundation of the critical philosophy. But perhaps the thinker most struck by the Wolffian campaign was C. G. Bardili, whose 'logical realism' became the subject of much controversy around 1800. The inspiration for Bardili's doctrine came from the Wolffians' critique of Kant's psychologism.[162] Eberhard's argument that logic alone provides us with the path out of the Kantian circle of consciousness is indeed the central thrust of Bardili's later attack upon Kant. Reinhold was so persuaded by this argument that he eventually completely abandoned the critical philosophy and formed an alliance with Bardili.[163]

The Wolffians' most significant contribution to post-Kantian philosophy ultimately lay in their pugnacious reassertion of the classical metaphysical tradition. This kept the spirit of metaphysics alive when it seemed near extinction after the spread of Kantianism. The Wolffians had indeed prepared the ground for the revival of metaphysics after Kant. Some of their most important doctrines reappear in the metaphysical systems of Schelling, Hegel, and Schopenhauer. Their dissatisfaction with Kant's practical faith and their insistence on a theoretical justification of faith; their argument that the critical philosophy is consistent and complete only if it transcends its critical limits and becomes metaphysical; and their contention that only a rational knowledge of things-in-themselves avoids the solipsistic consequences of Kant's idealism—all these themes recur in the early writings of Hegel and Schelling and the later writings of Reinhold. The most important doctrine the Wolffians handed down to the post-Kantian generation, however, was their theory of logic. Their claim that the principles of logic are neither subjective nor objective but valid of things-in-general anticipates Hegel's *Logik* and Schelling's *Identitätssystem*.

· *Chapter 8* ·

Reinhold's *Elementarphilosophie*

8.1. Reinhold's Historical Significance

One of the most important, and certainly influential, figures in the history of post-Kantian philosophy is Karl Leonhard Reinhold (1758–1823). Although his influence was felt largely within the post-Kantian period, and even then only during the early 1790s, it is important to see that his historical significance transcends these narrow boundaries. Reinhold occupies a central, if little recognized, place in the history of modern philosophy: he is the first philosopher to rethink and rebuild epistemology upon a meta-epistemological foundation; he is indeed the first thinker to develop a general and systematic meta-epistemological theory.

What we find in Reinhold for the first time in the history of modern philosophy is the acute awareness that the epistemological tradition is problematic. Reinhold raised one very important question: why had the epistemology of Kant, like that of Descartes, Locke, and Hume, so palpably failed in its ideal of becoming the *philosophia prima*? Why indeed had the entire epistemological tradition not succeeded in its grand ambition of making philosophy into a science? According to Reinhold, Descartes, Locke, Hume, and Kant were themselves largely to blame. They had simply taken the possibility of epistemology for granted; they had not been sufficiently self-reflective about its problems, methods, and presuppositions. As a result epistemology had become confused with psychology and metaphysics and thus became committed to assumptions its very purpose was to investigate.

Reinhold's response to the crisis of epistemology was his famous *Elementarphilosophie*, his so-called philosophy without a nickname (*Philosophie ohne Beynamen*). In the *Elementarphilosophie* Reinhold set out to rebuild epistemology on a firm meta-epistemological foundation, so that it could finally realize its ideal of a *philosophia prima*.

Why, though, was an *Elementarphilosophie* so important to Reinhold? Why did it matter that epistemology was built upon a firm foundation?

Reinhold saw his *Elementarphilosophie* as the only means of saving the *Aufklärung* from its imminent collapse. It alone, he believed, could restore the *Aufklärung*'s flagging confidence in the authority of reason. Although Reinhold began his philosophical career as a *Popularphilosoph*, he soon realized that the central problem facing the *Aufklärung* lay not in implementing the principles of reason but in discovering them. Only if these principles were clear and established beyond doubt could reason provide a firm foundation for morality, religion, and the state. The only means of discovering these principles was, of course, through epistemology, through a rigorous and thorough investigation into the faculty of reason. But Reinhold was convinced that the corrupt practices of the old epistemology had only hindered rather than promoted this goal. Rather than finding the first principles of reason, it had become bogged down in metaphysical disputes and psychological speculations. Hence a reform of epistemology seemed to be a dire necessity. Only that would ensure the discovery of the first principles of reason; and only that would provide a firm foundation for morality, religion, and the state.

Reinhold's main step beyond Kant is his insistence that the critical philosophy has to be reestablished upon a meta-critical foundation. The source of Reinhold's dissatisfaction with Kant, and the sum of his criticisms against him, is that Kant is not sufficiently self-reflective and self-critical. Kant, in Reinhold's eyes, has failed to investigate the principles and procedures by which he acquires transcendental knowledge. But Reinhold warns us that this failure has a very serious consequence for the critical enterprise as a whole: it means that the very foundation of the critical philosophy hangs in the balance. Without consciousness of the principles and procedures of transcendental reflection, we have no guarantee of the truth of the theory based upon them. We proceed in no less blind and dogmatic a fashion than the old metaphysicians. Kant's philosophy therefore needs to be built upon a new foundation, Reinhold concludes, and it will acquire that foundation only through a general meta-critical theory of the conditions and limits of transcendental knowledge.

Reinhold's call for a new meta-critical foundation had a decisive impact on the course of post-Kantian philosophy. It created a new center of concern, a new problematic. If one were a Kantian in the early 1790s, the main question was no longer how to defend Kant against his enemies, but how to rebuild the critical philosophy from within upon a new foundation. The center of interest thus shifted from external defense toward inner reform. Reinhold's demand for a new foundation was indeed the starting point for Fichte, Schelling, and Hegel. Although they disagreed with Reinhold concerning the nature of that foundation, they accepted his contention that it was a necessity.

Reinhold's meta-critical methodology—his ideas concerning the proper method of transcendental philosophy—gained wide influence and became virtually canonical for the post-Kantian generation. Three ideas of his in particular were assimilated by Fichte, Schelling, and Hegel: (1) the demand that philosophy be systematic; (2) the insistence that philosophy begin with a single, self-evident first principle; and (3) the claim that only a phenomenology can realize the ideal of a *philosophia prima*. Although the first theme is already implicit in Kant, Reinhold made it explicit and lay great stress on it. The second theme appears in the early methodological writings of Fichte and Schelling;[1] Hegel, however, broke from this tradition in his *Differenzschrift*.[2] And the third theme bore fruit in Schelling's *System des transcedentalen Idealismus* and Hegel's *Phänomenologie des Geistes*. Following Reinhold's precedent, both of these works practice a phenomenological methodology, that is, they attempt to lay aside all presuppositions and to describe consciousness. Indeed, it has sometimes been said that Reinhold is the father of modern phenomenology.[3]

To understand the history of the critical philosophy in the early 1790s, then, we must first consider Reinhold. In the period from 1789 to 1793 Reinhold had virtually supplanted Kant as the definitive spokesman for the critical philosophy. It was indeed Reinhold, and not Kant, who made the critical philosophy so popular. His *Briefe über die kantische Philosophie* had done almost overnight what Kant's *Prolegomena* had not been able to do in years. After Kant gave his imprimatur to the *Briefe,* Reinhold began to acquire a reputation as the definitive expositor of Kant. But, even more important, Reinhold was also successful in his claim to have established a firm foundation for the critical philosophy. In the early 1790s it was generally accepted that the *Elementarphilosophie* was indeed the final, rigorous, and systematic form of the critical philosophy. It seemed as if Reinhold had truly grasped the principles behind the Copernican revolution, principles that Kant had only vaguely sensed.

The signs of Reinhold's success were as dazzling as they were plentiful. His lectures in Jena were always filled to capacity, and a large number of works by his disciples appeared, defending and developing his *Elementarphilosophie*.[4] The *Allgemeine Literatur Zeitung* gradually evolved from a pro-Kantian into a pro-Reinholdian journal. All Reinhold's works were given favorable reviews, and the defense and discussion of his philosophy took precedence over Kant's. Around the same time, a disciple of Reinhold's, F. G. Fuelleborn, founded another pro-Reinholdian journal, the *Beyträge zur Geschichte der Philosophie,* which portrayed the *Elementarphilosophie* as the culmination of philosophical history, the final realization of the *philosophia prima et perennis*. Even Reinhold's enemies paid him due respect, though in their own negative fashion. In the early 1790s they began to attack Reinhold more than Kant.[5] Criticism of Reinhold was given priority since it was regarded as an attack upon the critical philosophy at its strongest point.

Reinhold's rise continued unabated until the middle of the 1790s, when his star fell as quickly as it rose. The turning point was 1794. It was in this year that the cumulative force of the many criticisms of the *Elementarphilosophie* began to strike home, sowing doubts among Reinhold's most faithful students. It was in the same year that Fichte arrived on the scene in Jena, stealing the limelight from Reinhold. As if he knew his heyday was over, Reinhold retired from Jena to Kiel, where he was no longer at the center of the philosophical stage.

8.2. Reinhold's Early Quarrel with Kant

Although Reinhold achieved his fame as a disciple of Kant, his first encounter with his later teacher was, interestingly enough, almost entirely hostile. In an anonymous article in the February 1785 issue of the *Teutsche Merkur,* "Schreiben des Pfarrers zu *** an den Herausgeber des T. M.," Reinhold wrote a counter-review to Kant's adverse review of the first part of Herder's *Ideen*.[6] A new member of the Weimar circle, which then consisted of Goethe, Wieland, and Herder,[7] Reinhold identified with some of its interests and ideals. He found Herder's *Ideen* "an extraordinary appearance on the literary horizon" and thought that Herder had even discovered "a new science" with his "unique philosophy of history." Like many people in Weimar, though, Reinhold felt that Kant's review had done Herder a grave injustice. So, vowing to right a wrong, Reinhold took it upon himself to defend Herder against Kant. His counter-review is an interesting chapter in the history of the controversy between Kant and Herder, representing the reaction of the Weimar circle to Kant's criticisms.

Reinhold's chief complaint against Kant's review is that Kant ineptly and unfairly evaluates Herder's book according to the standards of proof and rigor of traditional metaphysics.[8] According to Reinhold, who was to begin his study of the *Kritik* only eight months later, Kant is a typical representative of the metaphysical tradition, a dryasdust Wolffian. He expects a philosophy of history to apply the a priori method of definition and proof that is used in metaphysics. Hence he complains about "the lack of precision and rigor" in the *Ideen*. In Reinhold's view, however, such standards are completely inapplicable to the study of history. History consists in a mass of contingent facts, which can be known not by a priori proof and definition but only by a posteriori observation and research. It is precisely because Herder is aware of this point, Reinhold says, that he shuns the methods and concepts of traditional metaphysics. Rather than deductively applying concepts to the facts, so that they are forced into some Procrustean bed, Herder has gone to the facts themselves and inductively derived his concepts from them. Of course, as Kant complains, Herder often does resort to analogies and conjectures. But, Reinhold retorts, that is to be expected in any empirical discipline.

Kant's failure to appreciate Herder's empirical method is especially apparent, Reinhold notes, in his objection to the concept of 'power'.[9] Kant's claim that this concept posits an occult quality ignores its hypothetical and heuristic function. Like Herder's other advocate, Forster, Reinhold argues that the purpose of this concept is to indicate the sui generis vital causes of certain phenomena, which would be otherwise explained in purely mechanistic terms.[10] Hence Herder's concept has a real value in guiding empirical research, for it tells us that our mechanistic explanations have come to an end. En passant Reinhold then shrewdly insinuates that Kant attacks Herder's concept in the first place only because he adheres to the orthodox dualistic model of the mind-body relationship.

Reinhold's defense of Herder's methodology in the *Ideen* is all part and parcel of his wider concern with the methodology of metaphysics in general. He rejects the a priori method of traditional metaphysics, which allegedly forces experience into preconceived molds. And he advocates instead an a posteriori method, which should examine experience for its own sake and then derive its concepts from them. It is only such an a posteriori method, Reinhold insists, that will overcome the gap between thought and experience, speculation and life.

The "Schreiben des Pfarrers" is an interesting document in Reinhold's philosophical development largely because it reveals the influence of the Weimar circle upon him. In his early years in Vienna Reinhold was a *Popularphilosoph,* a champion of the *Aufklärung,* writing scores of articles in defense of its cause.[11] After his arrival in Weimar, though, Reinhold began to fall under the spell of the Weimar circle, many of whose ideas laid the ground for the Romantic movement. Some of the Romantic themes that Reinhold learned from this group played an important role in his later transformation of the critical philosophy.

There are two respects in which Reinhold's early essay reveals the influence of the Weimar circle. First, Reinhold shares its striving for unity, its concern to see all the aspects of man as a whole, and its contempt for all dualistic conceptions of human nature. Reinhold's sympathy for this theme is apparent from his defense of Herder's concept of force, whose purpose is to find a unifying concept of the mental and physical. Although Reinhold later heeds Kant's warnings about the metaphysical implications of this concept,[12] he never abandons his holistic ideals.[13] Second, Reinhold's criticism of traditional metaphysics, and his demand for a new metaphysics that surmounts the gap between thought and experience, are not original and merely repeat a favorite theme of Goethe, Herder, and Schelling.

Both of these debts to the Weimar circle are apparent in the development of the *Elementarphilosophie*. Reinhold's holistic ideals led him to search for the single source, the common root of all Kant's divided faculties. And his critique of traditional metaphysics provided the foundation for the phenomenological method of the *Elementarphilosophie*, which demands bracketing all metaphysical concepts in favor of a description of the facts of immediate experience. Thus both of Reinhold's debts to the Weimar circle illustrate how Romanticism became a potent force in the transformation of the critical philosophy.

Kant was quick to reply to Reinhold's counter-review. Only a month after the "Schreiben des Pfarrers" appeared, the *Allgemeine Literatur Zeitung* published his brief and brisk riposte to Reinhold. In writing his response, Kant was well aware that his opponent was Reinhold, whom he associated with Herder's Weimar circle.[14] Little did he know, however, that this 'pastor' was soon to become his foremost disciple.

Kant's reply to Reinhold is a defense of the standards and procedures applied in his review. Kant denies Reinhold's insinuation that he is an orthodox Wolffian, and he assures him that they are agreed about the uselessness of a metaphysics that quits the field of experience. He insists that he was not demanding scholastic standards of proof and definition in history. He did demand rigor, care, and precision, to be sure; but these are also virtues of an empirical investigation. If the materials for a history of mankind cannot be provided by metaphysics, Kant says, neither can they be supplied by Herder's wild speculations about human anatomy.[15] Rather, they are to be found only through the careful and rigorous study of human action, which alone reveals human character. Kant also protests that he did not mean to disparage the use of conjecture and analogy in empirical inquiries. What he did object to, however, was the metaphysical conclusions drawn from such conjectures and analogies.

Kant's swift reply to Reinhold suggests that he took his charges very seriously. It was indeed important for Kant's general campaign against Herder that he dispel all charges of metaphysical orthodoxy. For they distorted his position vis-à-vis Herder: that *every* metaphysics, not only the Herderian but also the Wolffian variety, is impossible. Kant was addressing himself to a very real danger. There was in fact a general impression amid the Weimar circle that Kant was a recidivistic Wolffian, a rationalist of the old school who wanted to straitjacket everything into syllogistic form.[16] Kant's quick response to Reinhold was therefore a timely and strategic move, preventing his opponents from whitewashing his critique of Herder.

8.3. Reinhold's *Briefe* and Conversion to the Critical Philosophy

In the autumn of 1785, only six months after Kant's reply to Reinhold, and during the very height of the pantheism controversy, Reinhold began his fateful study of the *Kritik der reinen Vernunft*. His interest in Kant's masterpiece was stimulated by an extract of the *Kritik* published in the *Allgemeine Literatur Zeitung*.[17] The effect of Reinhold's study of the *Kritik* could not have been more dramatic: a complete conversion to the critical philosophy. The sharp critic of Kant had become his ardent disciple. Such indeed was the ardor of Reinhold's conversion that he felt called upon "to become a voice in the wilderness to prepare the way for the second Immanuel." Reinhold resolved to write a defense of the critical philosophy, an apology that would prepare the public for the forthcoming revolution in philosophy. This resolve soon took concrete form: the *Briefe über die kantische Philosophie*, which appeared in installments in the *Teutsche Merkur*, starting August 1786.

What brought about Reinhold's sudden conversion to the critical philosophy? Why this abrupt volte-face, so that an antagonist of Kant became a protagonist almost overnight? In a short essay,[18] and in a letter to Kant,[19] Reinhold himself explained the reasons for his conversion. In that gloomy autumn of 1785 he was suffering from a severe intellectual crisis, which he was desperate to resolve at any price. His head and heart were in conflict. His heart led him to faith in the existence of God, immortality, and providence; but his head forced him to doubt these cherished beliefs. What Reinhold was looking for was some middle path between rational disbelief and irrational belief. He was thus caught in the very dilemma portrayed by Jacobi in his *Briefe über Spinoza*.

Now what Reinhold saw in Kant's philosophy was a middle path between the extremes of this dilemma. The Kantian doctrine of practical faith offered a rational justification for the beliefs in God, immortality, and providence, one that was based not on the insecure, speculative reason of metaphysics, but on the secure, practical reason of the moral law. Kant's practical faith satisfied the demands of his heart since it justified his religious beliefs as a necessity of the moral law; and at the same time it fulfilled the demands of his head because it established that the moral law was a requirement of pure reason itself.

The primary aim of Reinhold's *Briefe* appears modest enough: "to invite, encourage and prepare the reader to study the critical philosophy for himself."[20] It consists of only letters, not a system of philosophy, Reinhold warns us, so that we must not expect 'demonstrations' but only 'suggestions'. Furthermore, the *Briefe* is not an exposition of, or commentary upon, the main principles of Kant's *Kritik*. All Reinhold intends to do is to explain some of the *Kritik*'s results and to show their relevance for recent philosophy, theology, and ethics. This procedure will prepare the ground for a better public reception of the *Kritik*, Reinhold thinks, since it will show the relevance of the critical philosophy to the problems of contemporary culture. It is important to note, however, that such an apparently modest aim is in fact part of Reinhold's grand strategy as a *Popularphilosoph*: to close the gap between theory and practice, philosophy and public life.[21]

Although the *Briefe* is not explicitly autobiographical, it is at bottom a deeply personal document, stating Reinhold's reasons for his conversion to the critical philosophy. Its main concern is with just that problem which motivated Reinhold to study Kant in the first place: whether reason can justify belief in the existence of God, providence, and immortality. Reinhold's aim is to explain and defend Kant's doctrine of practical faith as the only satisfactory answer to this question. In one form or another, almost all eight of the original letters center on this theme.[22]

In making the question of the limits of reason in religion into the main concern of the *Briefe*, Reinhold had certainly hit upon a topical issue. Since the 1750s, this issue had dominated philosophical discussion in Germany.[23] The philosophical scene was split into two opposing camps over just this question. One camp consisted in the 'rationalists' or 'neologists', who held that reason could demonstrate the existence of God, providence, and immortality, and that revelation and scripture were only allegories or myths. The other camp consisted in the 'pietists' or 'fideists', who maintained that the existence of God, providence, and immortality was only a matter of faith, and that faith could be based only upon revelation and scripture, which were either contrary to or independent of reason. This dispute finally came to a head in the summer of 1785 with the pantheism controversy. All the issues between the rationalists and pietists were dramatized in the scandal surrounding Mendelssohn's death and Jacobi's revelations. It was surely a stroke of tactical genius on Reinhold's part that he chose just the right moment and just the right issue to demonstrate the strengths of the critical philosophy. No one in the later half of the eighteenth century, especially in the stormy summer of 1785, could afford to ignore a new solution to the heated dispute between rationalism and pietism—even if that solution were proposed by a nearly forgotten professor in Königsberg.

Reinhold's apology for Kant begins with a defense of his program for a critique of pure reason. Only a critique of pure reason is in a position to resolve the dispute between rationalists and pietists, Reinhold contends. To prove his point he shows that the dispute has reached a stalemate.[24] The rationalist cannot convince the pietist, since the pietist can always pick holes in his most elaborate and subtle demonstrations. Conversely, the pietist cannot persuade the rationalist, because the rationalist will always be able to question the authority of revelation and scripture through the latest philological and historical research. This deadlock has now made the fundamental issue plain to see, Reinhold thinks. The pietist accuses the rationalist of expecting too much of reason, and the rationalist charges the pietist of expecting too little of it. Because each side maintains that the other fails to understand the true nature of reason, the whole dispute turns into the question, What are the limits of reason? The only way to settle the dispute, then, is through an investigation into the faculty of reason itself.[25] Such an inquiry is the only step forward in the dispute. To seek to resolve it by arguing for and against particular demonstrations of God's existence is only to go backward, since such arguments only presuppose the more important second-order question, whether such demonstrations are even possible.

Now this project for a critique of pure reason is not a mere ideal, a pious hope, Reinhold tells his readers.[26] In fact, it has been realized by a book published five years ago, which has still not received much recognition. Reinhold calls this book "the greatest masterpiece of the philosophical spirit" and declares that it has solved his doubts in a manner that satisfies both his head and heart. This remarkable book—*das Evangelium der reinen Vernunft*—is entitled *Kritik der reinen Vernunft*.

After defending Kant's program for a critique of pure reason, Reinhold takes his apology for Kant one daring step further. Thanks to his investigation of the faculty of reason, he argues, Kant has discovered the only possible solution to the conflict between rationalism and pietism. He has found a middle path between these extremes, a compromise that satisfies the legitimate demands of both parties while destroying their pretensions. The novelty of Kant's solution becomes apparent, Reinhold says, when we analyze the question, What role does reason play in the belief in God's existence?[27] This question divides into two further questions. First, is God's existence knowable through reason and through demonstrations that make faith superfluous? And, second, if God's existence is not knowable, can there be faith in God that is not justified by reason? The rationalist answers the first question in the affirmative, as does the pietist the second. But the new middle path of the critical philosophy replies to both questions in the negative. Against the rationalist, the critical philosophy shows that theoretical reason cannot prove the existence of God; and against the pietist, it shows that only practical reason, and not faith or feeling, permits belief in the existence of God. This solution destroys the groundless pretensions of both parties: the rationalist must surrender his demonstrations of God's existence and accept the necessity of faith; and the pietist must abandon his demand for a *salto mortale* and submit to the discipline of reason. But at the same time it does justice to their rightful claims: the rationalist is correct that the belief in God is rational; and the pietist is right that this belief cannot be demonstrated through metaphysics. Where both the rationalist and pietist go astray, however, is in their common premise that reason is only a theoretical faculty, that the role of reason in religion is limited to demonstrations of God's existence. They both fail to see that the true foundation for belief in the existence of God lies in practical reason.[28]

Having set forth Kant's contribution to the controversy between rationalism and pietism, Reinhold is confident enough to declare that Kant solved the dispute between Jacobi and Mendelssohn four years before it broke out.[29] Both Jacobi's and Mendelssohn's positions are now antiquated, Reinhold writes, since they both presuppose nothing but the possibility of metaphysical dogmatism. Mendelssohn thinks that reason demonstrates the existence of God, while Jacobi thinks that it proves his nonexistence; but in each case, whether they accept or reject these conclusions, reason is equated with the demonstration of a Leibnizian or Spinozistic metaphysics. The conflict between Jacobi and Mendelssohn is indeed precisely what we expect according to the critical philosophy, Reinhold claims, since the critique shows that theoretical reason traps itself in antinomies whenever it transcends the limits of reason, so that it can equally well prove (with Mendelssohn) or disprove (with Jacobi) the existence of God.[30] What Jacobi and Mendelssohn both fail to see, however, is that there is a rational faith that is based not upon theoretical reason but the practical reason of the moral law. They wrongly believe that reason is exhausted by theoretical reason, and so they falsely conclude that belief in God has to amount to either blind faith or dogmatism.

Thanks to his graceful and lively style, and his strategy of explaining the relevance of the critical philosophy to the then raging pantheism controversy, Reinhold's *Briefe* became a success. Almost immediately, Reinhold had achieved his end: public recognition of the critical philosophy. Judging from the testimony of a friend of Kant's, the effect of the *Briefe* upon the general public was very great indeed: "The letters on your philosophy in the *Merkur* have created the most stunning sensation. Since Jacobi's doings, the *Resultate* and these letters, all the philosophical heads of Germany seemed to be awakened to the most lively sympathy for you, my Herr Professor."[31]

On the strength of the *Briefe,* Reinhold won himself a professorship at the University of Jena. He then began to hold introductory lectures on the critical philosophy, which attracted large audiences. Largely due to Reinhold, the University of Jena began to acquire its reputation as the center of Kantianism in Germany.

Given his efforts in behalf of the critical philosophy, Reinhold naturally desired friendly relations with Kant. But after Reinhold's sharp criticism of Kant in the "Schreiben des Pfarrers," it was not easy to break the ice with his old adversary. Nonetheless, Reinhold overcame his inhibitions, swallowed his pride, and duly wrote to Kant on October 12, 1787.[32] In his letter Reinhold confessed his authorship of the counter-review, apologizing for the "unphilosophical philosophizing" of "the solicitous pastor." But at the same time Reinhold was proud to reveal his authorship of the *Briefe.* Assuming that Kant was satisfied with this tract, Reinhold had a delicate request to make: would Kant publicly state that Reinhold had understood him? Such a statement would give the needed imprimatur to Reinhold's claim to be the legitimate heir and spokesman for Kant.

Kant, of course, could not be anything but pleased with the *Briefe,* and he was all too happy to forgive the erring pastor. On December 28 and 31, 1787, Kant replied to Reinhold, encouraging, praising, and thanking him.[33] He found the *Briefe* "beautiful" and "splendid," "insurpassable in their combination of thoroughness and grace." With satisfaction, Kant told Reinhold that the *Briefe* "had not failed to have every desired effect in our region." He was indeed perfectly willing to oblige Reinhold's request. At the close of his *Ueber den Gebrauch teleologischer Prinzipien in Philosophie,* which appeared in the January 1788 issue of the *Merkur,* Kant gave his official blessing to the *Briefe.*[34] He acknowledged Reinhold's "contribution to the common cause of a speculative and practical reason," and welcomed his appointment at Jena, "an acquisition that could not be anything but advantageous to that famous university."

These were the halcyon days of their relationship, when Reinhold was content to be an eloquent and popular expositor of Kant. But these days were not to last.

8.4. The Path toward the *Elementarphilosophie*

Reinhold could not remain content for long as a mere spokesman for Kant. Some two years after his conversion, his relationship to Kant underwent another dramatic change. In the *Briefe* Reinhold was happy to be only the loyal expositor of Kant. By the autumn of 1787, however, he felt that it was necessary for him to become Kant's creative reinterpreter. He now declared that he understood the 'spirit' of the critical philosophy better than Kant himself. Indeed, Reinhold had even moved beyond the confines of the critical philosophy. He had conceived a philosophical program of his own, one of which the critique of pure reason was to be only a result. Reinhold became convinced that the critical philosophy had to be rebuilt upon a new foundation, and, moreover, a foundation that Kant had never imagined.

Why this change in Reinhold's relationship to Kant? Why did Reinhold think that the critical philosophy was in need of drastic reform? What had gone wrong with it that it required a completely new foundation? In a retrospective essay written in 1789, Reinhold recounted the train of reasoning which led him to his fateful conclusion.[35]

After assuming his professorship in Jena in the autumn of 1787, he decided to give some introductory lectures on the *Kritik*. Reflecting upon the best method to explain the basics of Kant's philosophy, Reinhold consulted all the writings of Kant's defenders and detractors. But an extensive reading of these works proved to be disappointing. Reinhold could find no consensus on the interpretation or truth of some of Kant's most important ideas. On the one hand, Kant's opponents had completely misunderstood him; and all their objections were directed against difficulties of their own making. On the other hand, Kant's exponents committed themselves to presuppositions that their opponents would never allow; and they clothed all their explanations in technical terminology that was intelligible only to a few specialists. The more he studied the writings of Kant's allies and enemies, the more Reinhold became convinced that the conflict between them was no more resolvable than the old disputes between the dogmatists.

Reinhold's concern with the 'fate' of the critical philosophy was perfectly justified. The bitter dispute between Kant's friends and foes, their complete lack of agreement about his most basic concepts, raised some very serious questions about the critical philosophy. If, as Kant claimed, the critique was in possession of the universal principles of reason, then why was there no consensus or unanimity about it? And if, as Kant also claimed, the critique could resolve the disputes between philosophers, then why had it created nothing but dissension? Toward the late 1780s, then, it seemed that the grand claims Kant had made for his philosophy were contradicted by its public reception. The philosophical millennium that Kant had prophesied had not appeared.

Now it was this crisis that Reinhold faced in the autumn of 1787 and that convinced him that the critical philosophy was in serious need of reform. The ultimate source of this crisis lay with the critical philosophy itself, he believed, and not with an unsympathetic public.[36] It was not only the dry exposition and tortured style of the *Kritik* that was to blame, though that obviously played a damaging role. What was much more at fault, Reinhold argued, was the vagueness of Kant's principles. Kant had presupposed some fundamental concepts that he had not yet defined. The disputes over the truth and meaning of the *Kritik* arose only because opposed meanings had been read into these undefined and fundamental concepts. So, if these disputes were to cease, then it was necessary to go back to the fundamental concepts of the *Kritik* and to give explicit definitions of them. Thus Reinhold's task was no longer one of merely expounding the critical philosophy but rethinking its very foundation.

There was one concept in particular, Reinhold held, that was responsible for all the disputes surrounding the critical philosophy: the concept of representation (*Vorstellung*).[37] Kant had not defined this concept, and the reader was left to guess its sense from the few scattered occasions of its use. But it is of the most fundamental importance, Reinhold insisted, since the *Kritik* presupposes it in basic ways. First, it is the genus of the various kinds of representation, namely, the concepts of understanding, the ideas of reason, the intuitions of sensibility. Second, the aim of the critique is to analyze the conditions and limits of knowledge; but the concept of knowledge depends upon that of representation. Hence, the many disputes about the conditions and limits of knowledge are resolvable only through a prior analysis of the concept of representation.

It was for this reason that, sometime in the autumn of 1787, Reinhold decided to develop "a new theory of the faculty of representation." His main concern was to analyze the concept of representation assumed but never defined in the *Kritik*. Since the concept of representation is more general than, and presupposed by, the concept of knowledge, Reinhold held that his theory of representation preceded any theory of knowledge—and, in particular, the theory of synthetic a priori knowledge laid down in Kant's *Kritik*. Hence Reinhold believed that his new theory would provide the foundation of the critical philosophy, justifying its presuppositions, supplying its premises, and defining its terms. One of Kant's most eloquent spokesmen had thus become one of his boldest interpreters.

Reinhold's resolve to develop a new theory of representation soon bore fruit: his *Versuch einer neuen Theorie des menschlichen Vorstellungsvermögens*. Of all Reinhold's works, the *Versuch* is perhaps the most important. It is here that Reinhold explains the ideals behind his philosophy, and it is here that he so painstakingly deduces all the results of the *Kritik*. Although many of its doctrines underwent revision or expansion, the *Versuch* sets forth the body of Reinhold's theory.

Despite its importance, the *Versuch* is not the definitive or official state-ment of Reinhold's early philosophy. It does not contain Reinhold's first principle, the famous 'proposition of consciousness' (*Satz des Bewusstseins*). It also does not formulate the conception of an *Elementarphilosophie*, which is so characteristic of the Kantian phase of Reinhold's thought. Reinhold worked out this idea, and set forth his first principle, only in his *Beyträge zur Berichtigung der bisherigen Missverständnisse der Philosophen* (1790), in which he revised most of the doctrines in the *Versuch*. The *Beyträge* contains Reinhold's official and final statement of the theory of represen-tation, the "Neue Darstellung der Hauptmomente der Elementarphiloso-phie."

Reinhold's major writings concerning the *Elementarphilosophie* stretch over a period of only five years, 1789 to 1794.[38] His other main works on the *Elementarphilosophie* are *Ueber das Fundament des philosophischen Wissens* (1791), the second volume of the *Briefe* (1792), and the second volume of the *Beyträge* (1794). The *Fundament* is Reinhold's manifesto for the *Elementarphilosophie* and the best introduction to his work; the second volume of the *Briefe* is an excursion into the realm of moral and political philosophy, revising and explaining Kant's moral theory in light of the *Elementarphilosophie*.

What was Kant's reaction to Reinhold's *Elementarphilosophie?* What did he think of Reinhold's attempt to provide a new foundation for his philos-ophy? Such questions are important for understanding not only Kant's relationship to Reinhold, but also Kant's later attitude toward the *Kritik* itself. If we can answer them, they should shed some light on whether the older Kant was satisfied with the foundation of the *Kritik*.

Unfortunately, these questions permit no straightforward answer. Delib-erately, Kant never explicitly or formally stated his views on Reinhold's project. Reinhold, again hoping to obtain Kant's imprimatur, made repeated requests to get his opinion.[39] But these requests fell on deaf ears. Kant was always evasive, forever postponing judgment. He pleaded that he did not have the strength or time to study Reinhold's work, and that this prevented him from forming a reliable judgment.[40]

The reasons for Kant's elusiveness are not hard to fathom. It was one thing to approve of the *Briefe,* which was only a popular exposition of the *Kritik;* but it was another thing to endorse the *Elementarphilosophie,* which claimed to be its new foundation. If Kant gave his official approval to Reinhold's project, then his philosophy would be overshadowed by Rein-hold's. Reinhold would then acquire the authority to speak for Kant, even if he said things that Kant could not fully understand or approve. Yet Kant could not simply disapprove of Reinhold's enterprise. If he turned his back on Reinhold, denying him all support, that would mean a break with one of his most devoted and talented allies.[41] So Kant did what everyone does in such a predicament: he procrastinated; judgment upon Reinhold's work was deferred time and again.

Despite Kant's evasiveness, there are strong indications that he did not welcome Reinhold's project. In his letter of September 21, 1791, to Reinhold, Kant threw cold water on his over-eager friend.[42] Although he did not reject out of hand the attempt to analyze the current foundation of the *Kritik,* he did not think it necessary; and even less did he believe that the *Kritik* needed a new foundation. He admitted that he wanted to see a clearer development of the *consequences* of his principles; but he did not wish his followers "to undertake abstract revisions" of the principles themselves. Kant, it seems, was content with the foundations of the critique.

8.5. Reinhold's Critique of Kant and the Aims of the *Elementarphilosophie*

Although Reinhold constantly sought Kant's approval, he did not hesitate to criticize him. Indeed, the more Reinhold developed his own *Elementarphilosophie* the more his critical distance from Kant grew. The 1789 *Versuch* contains few criticisms of Kant; but the 1790 *Beyträge* includes a comprehensive critique of Kant;[43] and the 1791 *Fundament* persistently stresses the weaknesses of Kant's position in comparison with the *Elementarphilosophie.* So, if in 1786 Reinhold could only write a popular exposition of Kant, in 1790 he had written virtual polemics against him. Of course, without this critical stance, Reinhold could not insist on his originality and independence from Kant.

All of Reinhold's criticisms of Kant revolve around two main charges: that Kant does not fulfill his own ideal of science (*Wissenschaft*) or his own ideal of critique (*Kritik*). We can condense both of these points into a single sentence: Kant has not put his philosophy upon a firm scientific and critical foundation. Reinhold's critique of Kant is therefore strictly immanent; he evaluates him in the light of his own ideals. The basic problem with the critical philosophy, in Reinhold's view, is the discrepancy between its ideals and practices, its goals and performance.

The ideal of science that Reinhold presupposes in his critique of Kant is articulated by Kant himself. According to the first *Kritik,* science consists in a complete system organized around and derived from a single idea.[44] Such a system will be completely a priori, where every proposition is deduced from one principle.

A major theme of both the *Beyträge* and *Fundament* is that the critical philosophy fails to realize this ideal. It is anything but systematic, Reinhold charges, because its method is not 'synthetic', that is, it does not begin with the ideal of the whole and then determine the necessary order of its parts through a rigorous a priori deduction.[45] Rather, its method is 'analytic'; it begins from the parts and then arrives at the idea of the whole through a random induction.

Reinhold cites Kant's metaphysical deduction of the categories as a striking case in point of Kant's haphazard methodology. He complains that Kant fails to deduce the categories from a single principle, and that he simply picks them up from the various forms of judgment. There is nothing in the deduction, he alleges, to tell us why the table of categories is complete and why it must be organized into the forms of quality, quantity, and relation.[46]

According to Reinhold, it is not only the method of the critical philosophy that betrays its ideal of science: it is also its narrow scope or limited subject matter. The critical philosophy is not truly systematic simply because it is not sufficiently comprehensive. It does not even conceive the idea of the whole that would organize its investigation into the various faculties of knowledge. It examines only the specific kinds of representation—the intuitions of sensibility, the concepts of the understanding, and the ideas of reason—but it fails to consider the concept of representation as such. Since the critique does not investigate the genus of its various species of representation, it also does not grasp their systematic structure or how they relate to one another in a whole.[47] Even worse, the critique has so disastrously divided the faculty of representation into faculties of knowledge and desire that it has lost sight of their common source or unity.[48]

Kant comes no nearer to satisfying his ideal of critique than his ideal of science, in Reinhold's view. Kant's ideal of critique is a *philosophia prima*, a presuppositionless epistemology that does not commit itself to claims to knowledge without prior examination of such claims.[49] But, Reinhold maintains, Kant betrays this ideal from the start. He commits himself to presuppositions that he has not examined, and that he then uses to determine the conditions and limits of knowledge.

The most important unexamined presupposition of the critical philosophy, Reinhold believes, is Kant's concept of experience.[50] This concept consists in the assumption that there are laws governing events, or that there are necessary connections between perceptions. According to Reinhold's reading, the transcendental deduction presupposes this concept but does not demonstrate it. It begins with the concept of experience and then shows that synthetic a priori concepts are a necessary condition of it; but it does not prove that there is such an experience. This argument is significant, Reinhold remarks, only if we accept the Kantian concept of experience in the first place. But it is just this concept that the skeptic denies. Although he may agree that a priori concepts are a condition of the necessary connections between perceptions, the skeptic doubts that there are such connections and assumes instead that perception consists of nothing more than constant conjunctions. A justification of the Kantian concept of experience, Reinhold then concludes, requires going beyond the limited boundaries of the critical philosophy and deducing its first principle from an even higher one.

Another basic presupposition of the critical philosophy, Reinhold argues, is its dualism between understanding and sensibility.[51] Although Reinhold thinks that this dualism happens to be correct, he complains that Kant provides no convincing grounds for its acceptance. The diehard Wolffian, who holds that there is only a difference in degree between understanding and sensibility, will have an easy time picking holes in Kant's main argument for this dualism—the presence of synthetic a priori judgments in mathematics. He will deny that there are any synthetic a priori mathematical judgments, and hence he will dismiss the claim that there are sui generis forms of intuition which are not reducible to the law of contradiction. According to the Wolffian, the judgments of mathematics are only apparently synthetic; their analyticity becomes evident through a more careful definition of their terms.

Still another unjustified presupposition of the critical philosophy, Reinhold maintains, is its doctrine that reason cannot know things-in-themselves.[52] A Wolffian who insists that reason can know things-in-themselves beyond appearances cannot be refuted by any *general* argument in the *Kritik*. The "Analytik" and "Aesthetik" at most restrict the forms of understanding and sensibility to possible experience; but they do not prove that a similar restriction also holds for reason. A Wolffian will readily admit Kant's point that no idea of reason is presentable within possible experience.[53] But he will not accept Kant's conclusion that these ideas are therefore without content. Rather, he will insist that experience is an inappropriate standard to measure the truth or falsity of such ideas. The "Dialektik" provides nothing more than an inductive survey of the ideas of reason and a random polemic against some arguments of rationalism. However convincing Kant's polemic in the antinomies, amphibolies, and paralogisms, it at best shows only the weaknesses of individual arguments, not the failure of the rationalistic enterprise as a whole.

The aim of Reinhold's *Elementarphilosophie* is to overcome the discrepancies between Kant's ideals and practice. It attempts to realize Kant's ideals of science and criticism, so that the critical philosophy will be put upon a firm scientific and critical foundation.

The *Elementarphilosophie* realizes these ideals by following a simple but bold procedure: it suspends all beliefs and presuppositions and begins with a single self-evident first principle that is based upon a datum of consciousness. All the presuppositions of the *Kritik*—the sui generis nature of the synthetic a priori, the unknowability of the thing-in-itself, the necessity of twelve categories, and the distinction between the forms of understanding and sensibility—are then rigorously deduced from this principle. The *Elementarphilosophie* will therefore begin where the *Kritik* left off. What is a premise in the *Kritik* is a conclusion in the *Elementarphilosophie*.[54]

Reinhold is confident that this radical procedure satisfies Kant's ideals of criticism and science. It fulfills his ideal of criticism since it accepts a belief into its system only if it has been shown to be a necessary condition of the first principle, which is self-evident. It also satisfies the ideal of science because such a principle organizes all the results of the critical philosophy into a single unified system.

Although the aim of the *Elementarphilosophie* is to realize Kant's ideals, it does not follow that Reinhold only wants to carry out Kant's original program for a critique of pure reason. The program of the *Elementarphilosophie* is not the same as the critique; and the mere fact that Reinhold attempts to realize Kant's ideals in such an uncompromising fashion compels him to expand his original program for a critique of pure reason. Throughout the *Fundament* and *Beyträge,* Reinhold insists upon the differences between the *Elementarphilosophie* and Kant's critique. Kant has not even conceived the undertaking of the *Elementarphilosophie,* Reinhold insists, and still less has he provided a foundation for it.[55]

What, then, are the basic differences between the *Elementarphilosophie* and Kant's critique? If we reduce Reinhold's involved and lengthy discussion down to its barest essentials, two important differences emerge.[56] First, the *Elementarphilosophie* is more general than the critique. Its aims are broader and its subject matter more extensive. While the main aim of the critique is to lay the foundation for only one part of philosophy—namely, metaphysics—the central concern of the *Elementarphilosophie* is to establish a foundation for all the parts of philosophy. Moreover, if the aim of the critique is to investigate the possibility of synthetic a priori knowledge, the goal of the *Elementarphilosophie* is to investigate not only the possibility of knowledge in general, but also the possibility of representation or consciousness as such. Second, the critique employs an analytic-inductive method while the *Elementarphilosophie* applies a synthetic-deductive one. Kant provides an inductive survey of all the a priori forms of sensibility, understanding, and reason; but he never derives them from a single first principle or from the possibility of consciousness in general. The critical philosophy thus supplies all the material or data for the *Elementarphilosophie;* but it does not provide it with its method or form.

In general, Reinhold regards the critical philosophy as the last step of philosophy on its analytic path where it has been slowly gathering all the materials for a single universal system of philosophy. With the *Elementarphilosophie,* though, a new epoch of philosophical history begins. Philosophy is finally in a position to discover the idea of the whole for such a system, and to deduce all its parts that have been gradually collected through the ages. This new synthetic starting point, Reinhold proclaims, is the true beginning of the Copernican revolution. Of course, Kant promises this revolution; but he never truly achieves it because of his haphazard analytic method. Only the *Elementarphilosophie* with its synthetic method can claim to inaugurate this long-awaited revolution.[57]

8.6. Reinhold's Methodology

Reinhold intends the *Elementarphilosophie* to be above all the philosophy of first principles, not only of philosophy, but of all human knowledge. Reinhold himself considers this to be the definitive feature of the *Elementarphilosophie.* In his *Beyträge,* for example, he states explicitly that the *Elementarphilosophie* is not ontology, logic, or psychology, but the system of principles that is the foundation for all philosophy and human knowledge.[58] Indeed, the very term *Elementar* implies a philosophy of first principles. According to Kantian usage, a principle or concept is *elementar* if it is not derivable from any other principle or concept.[59] The *Kritik* is divided into an "Elementarlehre" and "Methodenlehre," where the "Elementarlehre" treats the first principles of the various faculties of knowledge, reason, sensibility, and understanding.

What conditions must the first principle satisfy if it is to be the first principle of all knowledge? This question preoccupied Reinhold a great deal, and most of his methodological writings center on this theme.[60] Reinhold thinks that the most important step toward finding the first principle of philosophy is accurately specifying its necessary conditions.

If we reduce Reinhold's scattered and involved discussion to its essential points, there are four chief conditions of the first principle (*Grundsatz*). (1) It must be the foundation, the sufficient and necessary reason, for all other true propositions. All true propositions will be derivable from it or its consequences. (2) Its terms must be precise and self-explanatory. Otherwise, if they have to be defined through other propositions, an infinite regress occurs where the terms of the definiens will also have to be defined, and so on ad infinitum. (3) The first principle must be of the highest generality, so that its terms are the most universal concepts of which all others are only species. If its terms are not the most universal, then there will be some higher concept that they stand under and that determines their common or generic meaning. Hence, the principle will not be the first principle (since its terms will be explicable by those of some higher-order principle). (4) The first principle must also be a self-evident or immediate truth. More precisely, it cannot require any reasoning to be found true; for, as the first principle of all demonstration, it cannot itself be demonstrated. The proof of the first principle must therefore lie outside the science that it is to demonstrate.

On the basis of this last property, Reinhold draws an important conclusion about the nature of the first principle.[61] Namely, it cannot be a logical formula, concept, or definition. All conceptualization or definition destroys immediate truth, for it introduces the possibility of mistakes and conflicting interpretations about the phenomenon to be explained or defined. Rather than a concept, definition, or formula, then, the first principle of philosophy must be the *description* of a self-revealing fact, an immediate fact that does not require any further explication or definition.

Assuming that we have discovered the first principle that satisfies all these conditions, we are still left with a very serious problem on our hands. How does the first principle 'derive' or 'deduce' all the other propositions of philosophy? What is the method of deduction, and how indeed is it possible?

Unfortunately, Reinhold does not devote sufficient attention to his method of deduction, offering only a few brief explanations in his *Beyträge*.[62] Here he blithely assumes that it is possible to set up a chain of deduction where the first principle deduces propositions, and so on. All propositions are then immediately or mediately derived from the first principle. Reinhold views this chain of deduction as a gradual progression down a hierarchy of genera and species, where the first level of propositions are species of the highest genus, and where the second level are differentia of these species, and so on. He stresses the importance of consecutively proceeding down this hierarchy, so that no level is reached before going through all the preceding levels. Disobeying this rule means allowing unnecessary vagueness into the system.

But this simple and apparently faultless method in fact raises a very difficult problem. It appears as if the first principle, which contains the most universal concept, cannot deduce any lower-order propositions, which contain more specific concepts. It is a simple, logical point—but a crucial one for Kant's battle against rationalism—that a universal and indeterminate premise cannot have a specific and determinate conclusion.[63] In other words, the species of a genus cannot be inferred from the genus itself. Reinhold cannot afford to ignore this point since he agrees with Kant that it is a fallacy to derive the particular from the universal or the concrete from the abstract.[64] Nevertheless, Reinhold insists that the first principle has to be of the highest universality *and* the basis for the deduction of all other propositions. Reinhold therefore faces a dilemma: either he abandons the attempt to construct a rigorous system where every term is deduced from higher terms, or he commits the simple fallacy of inferring the particular from the universal.

So how does Reinhold attempt to escape this dilemma? It is to his credit that he recognizes this problem and that he attempts to find a solution to it.[65] Admitting that it is not possible to derive the species of a genus from the genus itself, Reinhold states that it would be ridiculous to assume that his first principle contains the propositions under it "as an acorn contains the oak." These propositions are *subsumed* under the first principle, he says, but they are not *within* it. After making this point, Reinhold tries to resolve the difficulty by distinguishing between the 'matter' and 'form' of a proposition. The matter of a proposition is defined as the meaning of its terms, while the form is understood as their connection in a judgment. Now although the first principle cannot deduce the matter of a proposition, it can deduce its form. Reinhold is confident that this distinction solves his dilemma. Since the first principle does not derive the matter of the proposition, there is no fallacy of deducing the specific from the universal; and since the first principle does derive the form, systematic unity and rigor are guaranteed.

Although it has an initial plausibility, Reinhold's solution does not really escape the problem at hand. The old fallacy of deducing the specific from the generic—of squeezing blood from a turnip, as Kant calls it—recurs even if the first principle deduces only the form of a proposition. Assuming that the concepts of the first principle are of the highest universality, it still cannot determine the form (that is, the proper connection between subject and predicate) of those lower-order propositions where some more specific property is attributed to a thing, for example, from the form of the higher-order proposition 'red is a color' it will not be possible to deduce the form of the lower-order proposition 'red is the color at the least refracted end of the spectrum'. Here again the old genus-species rule comes into play: although everything true of the genus is also true of the species, it is not the case that everything true of the species is also true of the genus, for a species is distinguished from the genus precisely because there are many facts true of it but not of the genus. There will therefore be a large number of propositions whose form cannot be deduced from the first principle, namely, all those that attribute some more specific property to a thing.

What complicates matters is that Reinhold makes another demand upon the system of philosophy which is inconsistent with his rule that the first principle cannot deduce anything about the content of a proposition. This is his demand that the system of philosophy must not admit concepts whose meaning is not completely determined and dependent upon the first principle.[66] He makes this demand because it is the only guarantee that the concepts of the system will have a perfectly precise meaning. If they are not definable through the first principle, or the propositions derived from it, then their meaning will be vague and open to conflicting interpretations; hence all rigor, and the possibility of acquiring universal consent for the system of philosophy, will be sacrificed. So the old dilemma reasserts itself in a new guise. If the first principle does not determine the content of a proposition, then the system of philosophy will be vague and nonrigorous; but if the first principle does determine the content, then it is guilty of the logical fallacy of deriving specific conclusions from general premises.

8.7. Reinhold's Phenomenological Project

The *Elementarphilosophie* is not only a philosophy of first principles. This is a necessary, but not sufficient, description of it. To describe completely the characteristic features of the *Elementarphilosophie*, we must consider not only its form, the methodology of first principles, but also its content, the specific nature of its first principles. After all, Wolff's ontology is also supposed to be a philosophy of first principles; but Reinhold insists that it is still far from his own idea of an *Elementarphilosophie*.[67]

The *Elementarphilosophie* is also, to use a modern term, 'a phenomenology of consciousness'. It began its career as "a new theory of representation," whose main task was to describe and analyze "consciousness in general" or "representation as such." This new theory of representation was a 'phenomenology' in the strict sense of the word: it renounced all psychological and metaphysical speculation about the origins of consciousness and restricted itself to describing the phenomenon of consciousness itself. In 1790, in his *Beyträge*, Reinhold incorporates this phenomenology into the *Elementarphilosophie*. According to the *Beyträge*, the first principle of philosophy is not a definition or concept but a fact of consciousness.[68] The *Elementarphilosophie* must begin with a neutral and presuppositionless description of what appears in consciousness.

Why, though, a phenomenology of consciousness? Why does Reinhold think that philosophy can have a presuppositionless and self-evident starting point only as a phenomenology? Reinhold's argument for a phenomenology begins with a defense of the modern Cartesian tradition. Like Descartes, Locke, Berkeley, and Hume before him, Reinhold sees the starting point of philosophy in consciousness.[69] His argument for this position is more or less the classical one. He insists that the only fact immune from skeptical doubt is that I have representations. Although the skeptic can doubt that his representations belong to a single self-identical subject, and although he can also doubt that they correspond with an external object, there is still one fact that he cannot doubt: that he has representations. His denial of the existence of representations is self-defeating—for such a denial amounts to a representation itself. The starting point of philosophy therefore cannot be found in the subject and object in themselves, as they exist apart from and prior to consciousness; for all that we have an immediate knowledge of is our own consciousness of them. All our knowledge of the subject and object in themselves is only mediate, an inference from our conscious states or representations.

Although Reinhold accepts the argument of the Cartesian tradition that the starting point of philosophy lies within consciousness, he departs from that tradition in significant respects. Indeed, Reinhold came to his conclusion that first philosophy is phenomenology only after long reflection upon the failures of traditional epistemology. A phenomenology seemed to him to be the only solution to all the shortcomings of traditional epistemology.[70] In many of the earlier sections of the *Versuch* Reinhold subjects classical epistemology to a thoroughgoing critique.[71] This critique is indeed one of the most fruitful and interesting aspects of the entire book. Reinhold's great strength and virtue—despite the weaknesses of his theory of representation—is the sophisticated level of his meta-epistemological or meta-critical awareness. In the true spirit of post-Kantian philosophy, Reinhold insists that epistemology must examine its own methods and presuppositions. What Descartes, Locke, and Kant presuppose in their investigation of the conditions of knowledge becomes a problem for Reinhold and the subject matter of a new higher-order inquiry.

Reinhold criticizes traditional epistemology, beginning with an attack on its precise starting point.[72] If Reinhold agrees with the tradition that the starting point lies within consciousness, he still disagrees with it concerning where it should begin in consciousness. Reinhold maintains that philosophy, rather than restricting itself to an examination of the conditions and limits of *knowledge,* should begin with an investigation into the conditions and limits of *consciousness in general.* If philosophy is to begin somewhere within consciousness, then it must start with the general and common principle behind all conscious states, and that is the concept of representation. Traditional epistemology commits a grave blunder, Reinhold asserts, when it investigates the concept of knowledge before that of representation. This leaves its concept of knowledge vague and without foundation, since that concept presupposes the more general concept of representation. The concept of representation ought to be investigated before that of knowledge, given that all knowledge is representation but not conversely. Hence the *Elementarphilosopie* is primarily a theory of representation and only secondarily a theory of knowledge. It is indeed this concern with the nature of consciousness as such that makes the *Elementarphilosophie* a phenomenology as opposed to just another epistemology.

The failure of traditional epistemology to investigate consciousness in general is only one of its flaws, in Reinhold's view. Another serious short-coming is that it prematurely commits itself to metaphysics—even though it claims to avoid all metaphysics and to investigate its very possibility.[73] Rather than beginning with an inquiry into the faculty of representation and then determining the possibility of a metaphysical knowledge of the subject and object, it begins with metaphysical theories about the subject and object—for example, whether they are mental or physical—and then uses these theories to determine the nature of the faculty of knowledge. Hence, traditional epistemology is caught in a vicious circle, where it pre-supposes precisely what it ought to investigate.

In a remarkably prescient passage in the *Versuch* that anticipates modern notions of 'semantic ascent', Reinhold states that traditional epistemology's premature commitment to metaphysics arises from its failure to distinguish two completely distinct questions.[74] The first question, 'What are the con-ditions of knowledge?' is a strictly logical question about the truth conditions of our judgments, Reinhold says. It is not about the laws under which something exists, but about the laws which govern the knowledge of what exists. To talk about a faculty of knowledge in this sense is only a metaphor for the laws that govern a specific kind of knowledge. The second question, 'What is the subject of knowledge?' is a metaphysical question about the nature of the subject who has knowledge, Reinhold explains, and is not about the laws which govern the knowledge of reality but about those which govern something in reality itself. To talk about a faculty of knowledge in this sense is to refer literally to some property or disposition of the subject. The confusion of these questions, Reinhold maintains, has resulted in a serious fallacy: the hypostatization of the laws of knowledge, the reification of the truth conditions of judgment.[75]

Another basic error of traditional epistemology, according to Reinhold, is that it has not carefully defined its terms, such as, 'reason', 'understanding', 'knowledge', and 'representation'.[76] Rather than determining the precise sense of its terms, it simply relies on their loose meanings as found in ordinary language. A dispute then arises about the conditions and limits of reason, understanding, or representation simply because opposing parties assign a different sense to these concepts. In general, following the precedent of Locke, Reinhold sees the source of philosophical disputes in the vagueness and ambiguity of ordinary language.[77]

In order to put his phenomenology upon a firm foundation, Reinhold begins the second book of his *Versuch* by carefully defining the subject matter of his investigation. He wants to specify precisely the pure phenomenon of consciousness, so that it can be distinguished from all metaphysical and psychological speculation. Only an exact definition of its subject matter, Reinhold thinks, will ensure that phenomenology is rid once and for all of all groundless metaphysical presuppositions.

Reinhold initially defines his subject matter as 'the faculty of representation' (*Vorstellungsvermögen*).[78] A phenomenology of consciousness is an investigation into the faculty of representation understood as the faculty of consciousness in general. But what, exactly, is meant by 'the faculty of representation', or for that matter 'consciousness in general'? Before answering this all-important question, Reinhold finds it necessary to make two basic distinctions concerning the concept of representation itself.[79] The first distinction is between the internal and external conditions of representation. The internal conditions appear within the representation and are inseparable from its appearance; the external conditions do not appear within the representation and are separable from its appearance. Reinhold includes the subject and object among the external conditions because they do not appear within the representation and are inseparable from it. The second distinction is between the narrower and broader sense of representation. The narrower sense is only the general concept of representation, what all representations have in common, excluding all the differences between the specific classes of representation; the broader sense is the general concept of representation, including all the differences between the specific classes of representation.

Reinhold then distinguishes three senses of the term 'faculty of representation', all of them making use of these distinctions.[80] First, there is the 'faculty of representation' in the wider sense: this comprehends the internal and external conditions of representation in the broader sense, that is, both conditions for all kinds of representation. This is the sense in which this term has been traditionally used, where an investigation into the faculty of representation has meant studying the subject and object of some of the specific kinds of representation. Second, there is the 'faculty of representation' in the narrower sense: this comprehends only the internal conditions of representation in the wider sense, what appears of necessity in the specific kinds of representation. Third, there is the 'faculty of representation' in the narrowest sense: this covers only the internal conditions of representation in the narrower sense; it refers to what appears of necessity in representation in general or as such, abstracting from all the specific kinds of representation.

Reinhold states that the subject matter of his phenomenology is the narrowest sense of the faculty of representation.[81] In other words, its subject matter is the inner conditions of representation as such. His investigation does not concern itself with the external conditions of a representation or with any specific form of representation. Rather, its subject matter is only the necessary conditions of what is present within consciousness—and not only this or that form of consciousness but consciousness as such. As Reinhold sometimes puts it: he wants to examine the nature of 'mere representation' (*blosse Vorstellung*), representation in itself apart from its external conditions, and representation in general, apart from the specific nature of particular representations.

By thus limiting his theory to the internal conditions of representation, Reinhold aims to exclude the metaphysical questions about the nature of the subject and object from his inquiry.[82] The subject and object are only external conditions of representation, he says, since a representation might occur even if its object does not exist, and even if it belongs to a different subject. A theory of representation goes seriously astray, Reinhold insists, if it attempts to determine the nature of representation from the subject and object. We know the subject and object only from the representations that we have of them, so that to infer the nature of representation from the nature of the subject and object is to put the less certain and mediately known before the more certain and immediately known. Further, knowledge of the subject and object consists in a distinct class of representations, and these cannot be sufficient for explaining the concept of representation in general, which is not reducible to this or that species of representation.

Reinhold also thinks that by restricting his theory to the internal conditions of a representation he does not have to bother with the problem of the origin or genesis of representation. The causes of a representation also belong to its external conditions, since what appears in consciousness might be the same even if its causes were different. The subject matter of the new theory of representation is thus not the cause of representation, but its content.

Reinhold often insists on the purely logical nature of his phenomenological inquiry. What he is investigating, he stresses, is the *concept* of representation, and that has nothing to do with a metaphysical or psychological inquiry into the subject or causes of a representation.[83] The question 'What is the nature of a representation?' means for him what must be thought about the concept of representation in the narrowest sense, that is, he wants to know the logically necessary conditions of that which appears in consciousness. A major error in traditional epistemology, Reinhold contends, is its failure to disentangle logical from genetic questions. It hypostatizes the logical properties of the concept of representation into metaphysical properties of the soul. The new theory of representation is a conceptual investigation dealing with the logical not the causal conditions of representations. Thus Reinhold writes, "Our concern here is not at all with what the representation *is*, but what must be thought in our possible and necessary concepts of representation."[84]

Reinhold's careful definition of his subject matter, painstaking and perfunctory though it might seem, plays an extremely important role in transcendental philosophy in general. Reinhold's phenomenological program, as it is so precisely explained in the *Versuch,* should be seen as a solution to a serious methodological problem of Kant's transcendental philosophy. This is the problem of how a transcendental philosophy investigates the conditions and limits of possible experience without transcending them. A transcendental philosophy always runs the risk of relapsing into metaphysics since the boundary between the transcendental (an investigation into the necessary conditions of possible experience) and the transcendent (metaphysical speculation that cannot be confirmed in any possible experience) is very fine. Kant himself stresses that his transcendental philosophy must remain within the critical limits of possible experience, and must strictly limit itself to analyzing its necessary conditions; and yet he never specifies how it is to do this, and how it is to avoid relapsing into metaphysics.

This is precisely the methodological lacuna that Reinhold wants to fill with his phenomenology. A transcendental philosophy remains within its proper limits, he argues, only if it confines itself to an explication of the necessary conditions of what appears in consciousness. Such is indeed the point of all Reinhold's labored distinctions in the second book of the *Versuch.* These distinctions should be seen as a careful specification of the Kantian distinction between the transcendental and the transcendent. Reinhold is saying that transcendental philosophy remains nontranscendent only if it becomes a phenomenology that investigates the inner conditions of representation as such.

At this point, the general strategy behind Reinhold's *Elementarphilosophie* comes clearly into view. His aim is to build nothing less than a phenomenological foundation for the critical philosophy. Reinhold wants to deduce and systematize all the results and presuppositions of the critical philosophy by beginning with the logical analysis of what appears within consciousness. The critical philosophy will find a secure foundation, he asserts, only to the extent that its results prove to be necessary conditions of consciousness in general or representation as such.

The only question before us now is whether Reinhold succeeds in this grand ambition. Let us turn, then, to an examination of the *Elementarphilosophie* proper. We shall soon see whether Reinhold achieved the high ideals he set for himself.

8.8. Reinhold's Proposition of Consciousness and the New Theory of Representation

Reinhold baldly states his first principle in the very first sentence of the "Neue Darstellung" in the *Beyträge:* "In consciousness, the representation is distinguished from, and related to, the subject and object, by the subject."[85] This banal and puzzling statement, which is grandly baptized 'the proposition of consciousness' (*der Satz des Bewusstseins*), is nothing less than the first principle of philosophy, Reinhold assures us.

No sooner is this principle stated, though, then serious questions arise about its meaning. What does it mean to say that the subject 'relates' the representation to, and 'distinguishes it from', the subject and object? In particular, *how* does the subject relate the representation to, and distinguish it from, itself and the object? The terms 'relate' and 'distinguish' are anything but self-explanatory, and certainly not as precise as Reinhold says that the terms of the first principle ought to be. Even worse, Reinhold offers little or no explanation of their meaning, considering his point as self-evident and in no need of further explication.

Although Reinhold's principle is intolerably vague upon first reading, it is possible to give it a tolerably precise meaning by examining some of his earlier texts. The sketchy formulation of the theory of representation in the *Beyträge* presupposes the earlier formulation in the *Versuch*, which is clearer and more detailed.[86] What Reinhold means by 'relate' (*beziehen*), for example, becomes much more intelligible in light of his earlier analysis. The subject 'relates' the representation to itself in the sense that the representation is possible only if there is someone who has it. A representation without a subject is impossible since the concept of representation implies that something is represented *for* someone, or that there is someone who represents something; in other words, there cannot be ownerless representations. Conversely, the subject 'relates' the representation to its object because the representation is possible only if there is something that it represents. Without having an object, a representation cannot represent anything, and hence it is not a representation at all. Indeed, representations are identified and distinguished from one another only by their different objects.

What Reinhold means by 'distinguish' (*unterscheiden*) also becomes clearer after looking at the earlier analysis of representation.[87] The subject 'distinguishes' the representation from its object in the sense that the representation itself cannot be only what is represented. There must be something that makes the representation of an object into a representation. A representation that is indistinguishable from its object ceases to represent it. Conversely, the subject 'distinguishes' the representation from itself since it knows that the representer is not the same as the representation itself. Even if the subject is a philosophical egoist who believes that everything he represents is only himself, he still has to distinguish his representation of himself from himself. Hence by 'relating' and 'distinguishing' Reinhold means that the subject finds that it is logically connected to, or separable from, the representation and its object. The proposition of consciousness therefore states that there are three terms of any act of consciousness—representation, representer, and thing represented—and that these are logically distinct but inseparable from one another.

But what do the dreadfully vague terms 'subject', 'object', and 'representation' mean? These words too have to be precisely defined if the first principle is to be completely self-explanatory. Reinhold does come forward with an explicit definition of his terms in the *Beyträge*.[88] Strictly adhering to his phenomenological guidelines, he insists that he presupposes no specific concepts of the subject, object, or representation, and that he defines these terms through their relations to one another as expressed in the proposition of consciousness. Thus the representation is nothing more than that which is distinguished from and related to the subject and object by the subject. The subject is nothing more than the representer, or that which distinguishes itself from and relates itself to the representation and its object. And the object is nothing more than that which is represented, or that which is distinguished from and related to the representation and its subject by the subject.

It is important to recognize that Reinhold, again true to his phenomenological principles, regards his first principle not as a definition of representation, but only as a description of a fact of consciousness.[89] This fact consists in the subject performing two activities: relating the representation to, and distinguishing it from, itself and the object. What does it mean, though, to call these activities a 'fact' (*Tatsache*)? Reinhold cannot mean that they are actual events, as if they really do occur, whether consciously or subconsciously, for every representation. Such a claim is either false or unverifiable. It is false if it is said that these acts consciously occur; and it is unverifiable if it is said that they subconsciously occur. What Reinhold must mean, then, is that they are possible events, so that they must be able to occur for the possibility of consciousness, much like Kant's 'I think' must be able to accompany any representation. It is of course not an empirical but a logical necessity that the subject must be able to perform these activities. In sum, the fact of consciousness is not an actual but a possible event; and its possibility is not an empirical but a logical necessity. The proposition of consciousness therefore states that a representation is (logically) possible only if the subject is (logically) able to distinguish the representation from, and relate it to, himself and the object.

Seen in a more historical context, Reinhold's proposition of consciousness is an attempt to develop or explicate Kant's principle of the unity of apperception. Like Kant, Reinhold believes that representation requires the possibility of self-consciousness. In the *Beyträge* he even concedes that Kant's unity of apperception is *in nuce* the first principle of philosophy (although he thinks that Kant limits it to sense intuitions when he should extend it to representations in general).[90] But Reinhold attempts to go a step further than Kant since he wants to specify *the manner* in which the subject must be able to be self-conscious of his representations. In other words, he wants to know the conditions under which the 'I think' can accompany any possible representation. Reinhold's thesis is therefore this: if the subject cannot be conscious of how his representation is inseparable and distinct from himself and its object, then his representation is "nothing to him, or at best a dream" (to use Kant's language).[91]

After stating his first principle and defining the subject, object, and representation in terms of it, Reinhold then begins to dissect the nature of a representation. His first basic proposition is that a representation consists in two constituents, whose unification and separation make up its essential nature.[92] These constituents are the form (*Form*) and content (*Stoff*) of the representation. The form is that which makes the representation 'relate to' (be inseparable from) its subject; and the content is that which makes it 'relate to' its object.

To summarize, Reinhold's argument for a representation consisting in two distinct constituents takes the following form: since a representation is that which is related to and distinct from the subject and object, and since the subject and object are distinct from one another, the representation has to consist in two elements, one relating it to and distinguishing it from the subject, the other relating it to and distinguishing it from the object.[93]

This argument is not in the slightest convincing, however, and puts Reinhold's whole analysis of representation upon a weak foundation. Although the representation stands in distinct relation to distinct things, it does not follow that it has to consist in distinct constituents; for one indivisible thing can stand in distinct relations to distinct things, for example, a mathematical point located east of one point and west of another. It does not even follow from Reinhold's argument that the representation stands in different relations to the subject and object, because one and the same relation might be between distinct things. For better or worse, though, it is from this terribly weak argument that Reinhold claims to have already deduced an important presupposition of the critical philosophy: the distinction between form and content of synthetic a priori knowledge. But where Kant limits this distinction to synthetic a priori knowledge, Reinhold thinks that it is a necessary condition of representation as such.

What, more precisely, are the form and content of a representation according to Reinhold? The content of a representation, he explains, is what it represents. It is also what distinguishes one representation from another, since representations that represent distinct things are never identical.[94] Conversely, the form of a representation is what makes all the different representations with their different contents into representations.[95] It is what makes their content into a representation, so that it represents something, and so that it is not only the object itself. Reinhold also contrasts form and content by stating that the form is that which 'relates' the representation to the subject while the content is that which 'relates' it to the object. Only now he begins to go beyond the original sense of this word where it means only logically 'depends' or 'requires'. Now the content 'relates' to the object in the sense that it 'represents' or 'corresponds' to it; and the form relates to the subject in the sense that it is 'produced' or 'made' by it.

Reinhold stresses the importance of distinguishing between the content and the object of a representation.[96] The content cannot exist without the representation, while the object can exist without it. Since the content is that which 'corresponds' to or 'represents' the object, it cannot be identical with the object itself. This distinction between content and object becomes apparent, Reinhold argues, by considering some examples from ordinary perception. If I perceive a tree from a distance, the content of my representation is vague since I do not know its species or the number of its branches; but when I approach the tree, the content becomes more precise so that I know its species and the number of its branches. Hence the content of the representation varies even though the object remains the same. This distinction between the content and object of a representation is of the first significance, Reinhold insists, for to confuse the content of a representation with its object is to disregard the all-important distinction between representations of things and things themselves.

Reinhold's distinction between content and object creates more difficulties than it solves, however. It renders the nature of a representation ambiguous by forming two levels of representation. Since the content of a representation has been already described as 'what it represents', the representation has to represent its content. But Reinhold also states that the content of a representation represents its object. There are, then, two levels of representation, where the representation represents its content, and where the content in turn represents its object.

What is even worse, though, is that Reinhold is caught in a serious inconsistency where he maintains that the content of a representation 'represents' or 'corresponds' to its object.[97] For he argues along the lines of Kant's transcendental deduction that it is a great fallacy to talk about representations 'mirroring', 'resembling', or 'picturing' their objects.[98] Such language falsely suggests, he writes, that it is possible to get outside our representations to see if they correspond to the object that exists apart from them. Yet Reinhold himself falls prey to this fallacy by stating that the content of a representation 'corresponds' to or 'represents' its object. This implies that the representation in some sense resembles its object; but the only way in which we could know this is by *per impossibile* getting outside our representations and comparing them with the object itself. So rather than deducing the epistemology of the transcendental deduction from some higher principle, the *Elementarphilosophie* violates its very spirit by assuming that representations somehow represent or mirror things-in-themselves.

Already at this point, through the simple analysis of a representation into its form and content, Reinhold prides himself on deducing another of Kant's conclusions in the *Kritik:* that there cannot be knowledge of the thing-in-itself.[99] But Reinhold considers Kant's claim that there cannot be knowledge of the thing-in-itself as only a special case of the more general claim that there cannot be a representation of the thing-in-itself. According to Reinhold, the very nature of representation excludes the possibility of even representing the thing-in-itself, let alone knowing it.

Reinhold quickly dismisses the objection that there must be a representation of the thing-in-itself since the mere concept of the thing-in-itself is also a representation.[100] This objection plays upon an ambiguity in the term 'representation', he argues. The mere concept of a thing-in-itself is not a representation in the sense that it represents a determinate, individual existing thing. It is indeed a representation, but only a general concept of the understanding, which does not represent any determinate thing but only things in general. This objection therefore conflates this general concept of the understanding with the representation of a determinate, existing thing, so that it appears to be self-defeating to talk about the unrepresentability of the thing-in-itself. But in denying the representability of the thing-in-itself, Reinhold insists that he is excluding only the representations of determinate existing things. It is only this sense of representation which is in question, since it is only these representations which could possibly give us knowledge of something that exists.

After removing this objection from his path, Reinhold advances his argument for the unrepresentability of the thing-in-itself. We might paraphrase his argument as follows. The content of a representation has to conform to its form if the content is to enter into consciousness. By conforming to the form of a representation, though, the content acquires an identity that it does not have on its own, so that it becomes inseparable from the form. Hence the content can no longer represent the object in itself, that is, the object as it exists prior to appearing in consciousness and prior to the application of the form.[101] In other words, the thing-in-itself is a formless something; but all representation requires a form; hence it cannot represent that which is formless, the thing-in-itself.

This argument is not compelling, though, if one strictly follows Reinhold's definition of the 'form of a representation'. If, according to his earlier definition, the form is only that which distinguishes the conscious from the nonconscious, the representation of something from the thing itself, then it does not follow that in conforming to the form the content can no longer represent the object in itself; for 'to conform to the form' here means only that the content enters into consciousness; and merely to enter into consciousness does not prevent the content from representing the object in itself. As pure consciousness in general, the form of a representation does not necessarily change any of the determinate features of its content. There must be something about the form in particular, then, which makes it change or condition the content of a representation; but Reinhold's earlier definition does not specify what that must be.

Reinhold's argument therefore requires an extra premise to the effect that the form changes the determinate features of the content. This premise is indeed provided by Reinhold when he covertly assumes that the representing subject is active, creating and conditioning what it represents.[102] Since the subject is active, the content of a representation undergoes a change in conforming to the form. This is the basic reason why the content of the representation cannot resemble or represent the thing-in-itself. It has to conform to the form, which is contributed by the active subject, which changes, determines, and conditions the content.

It is questionable, though, if Reinhold's extra premise is permissible according to his own phenomenological guidelines. These guidelines state that the epistemologist cannot make any assumptions about the subject, and still less any about the origins of a representation. But, in order to prove the unrepresentability of the thing-in-itself, Reinhold has to assume that the subject is active and not passive, and that it is the source or cause of the form of representation. He has thus already gone beyond the original strictly phenomenological bounds of his theory in that these assumptions go far beyond the analysis of the inner conditions of representation.

Having introduced the thing-in-itself into the *Elementarphilosophie*, Reinhold assigns it the same tasks it performs in the critical philosophy. Like Kant, Reinhold postulates the thing-in-itself to explain the origin of the content of representations. He argues that, because the faculty of representation cannot create the content of its representation, there must be some cause which acts upon it to give it this content, and that cause is the thing-in-itself.[103] But, in retaining the traditional role of the thing-in-itself, Reinhold appears to be unaware of its serious inconsistencies with his and

Kant's critical teaching about the limits of knowledge and representation. If we cannot know the thing-in-itself, as Kant says, and if indeed we cannot represent it, as Reinhold says, then how is it possible for us to know or even represent the alleged fact that the thing-in-itself is the cause of the content of our representations? So rather than having a reply to Jacobi's criticism of the thing-in-itself, Reinhold only repeats Kant's mistake. This will soon prove to be one of the deepest sources of dissatisfaction with the *Elementarphilosophie*.

After arguing for the unrepresentability of the thing-in-itself, Reinhold proceeds with his analysis of the nature of representation. He now asks: given that a representation consists in a form and content, what are the necessary conditions of its having a form and content?

For a representation to have a distinct form and content, Reinhold argues, they must derive from distinct sources.[104] The distinction between form and content is impossible if they both arise from a common source. The form of a representation has to be produced by the subject; and the content has to be produced by the object. The content has to be given because the representing subject cannot create its representations out of nothing; like Kant, Reinhold thinks that the subject has a limited creative capacity, which means the source of its representations must be outside itself.[105] Reinhold also argues that if the subject creates everything it represents, then it will be nothing but a projection of itself, so that there will no longer be a distinction between subject and object;[106] this distinction, as we have already seen, is a necessary condition of representation as such. Conversely, the form of the representation has to be produced by the subject; for, if the form were given along with the content, then the representation *per impossibile* would be able to exist outside the consciousness, so that there would be ownerless representation.[107]

Here again it seems as if Reinhold is violating his phenomenological principles. When he says that the form of a representation is produced and the content given, he appears to transcend the limits of consciousness itself by speculating about its origins or causes. But Reinhold is ready with a reply to this objection.[108] He insists that the givenness of the content and the production of the form are inner conditions of a representation, that is, they are logically necessary conditions of its appearance within consciousness. To talk about 'production' and 'givenness' is admittedly to introduce causal concepts; but it is necessary to use these concepts to conceive the possibility of representation.

But if these are conceptual connections, the question remains whether they are valid ones. We might well ask here why the form must be produced by the subject. If the object creates the form of the representation, that does not imply that the representation has to exist, *per impossibile,* outside consciousness; every property of the form might be produced by the object, even though it appears only within consciousness. And why must the content be produced by the object? At this stage, Reinhold has not developed any knockdown argument against idealism. Moreover, idealism is perfectly compatible with the subject-object dualism established thus far by him. That dualism simply states that every representation consists in a representer and a thing represented; but an idealist would admit this distinction and deny only that the thing represented corresponds to some external reality.

Having determined, at least to his own satisfaction, that the form of a representation is produced and that the content is given, Reinhold makes some more general deductions about the faculty of representation as a whole.[109] These deductions are very important to him since they supposedly yield some further conclusions of the critical philosophy.

Reinhold first deduces that the faculty of representation has to consist in an active and a passive capacity. Since the content of a representation is given, the faculty of representation has to consist in a capacity of receptivity, the power to receive the content of a representation. This capacity of receptivity has to act in a passive manner since it merely receives what is given. Conversely, since the form of the representation is produced, the faculty of representation has to consist in a capacity of spontaneity, an active power that produces the form without a prior cause acting upon it.

Reinhold then goes on to deduce some further features that are necessary to these passive and active capacities. He attempts to describe what he calls the 'form' of these capacities, that is, what is characteristic of their activity.[110] The form of receptivity consists in the capacity to receive a manifold, since the content of a representation consists in a number of distinct objects. This content has to be a manifold because representations differ from one another only through their content; but their content is distinguishable only if it corresponds to a number of distinct objects having features that distinguish them from one another.[111] At the same time, the form of activity has to be the capacity to produce a unity, since the form of representations is the same for all consciousness, no matter what its content. In other words, the form of spontaneity consists in a synthesis because the form of a representation is its unity; and this unity can be created in a manifold only through synthesis, which is the activity of unifying its multiplicity.[112]

In arguing that the faculty of representation is necessarily divided into a passive faculty that receives a manifold and an active faculty that produces a synthetic unity, Reinhold is of course attempting to justify some of Kant's own dualistic premises in the first *Kritik,* and in particular his dualism between sensibility and understanding. It is important to note, however, that Reinhold's receptive and spontaneous faculties are supposedly valid for representation in general, and not only for specific kinds of representation, namely, concepts in the case of the understanding and intuitions in the case of sensibility.

While elaborating upon some of the necessary features of spontaneity and receptivity, Reinhold turns to another important objection to his whole theory of representation. This objection states that the theory of representation forbids and yet demands the representation of the thing-in-itself.[113] One of the alleged selling points of the theory of representation is that, by carefully defining the nature of representation, it prevents the confusion between representations of things and things themselves. Indeed, in the preface to the *Versuch,* Reinhold explains that his desire to expose the source of this confusion is the underlying motivation behind his whole theory.[114] But the question inevitably arises, How is it possible to distinguish between what belongs to a representation and what belongs to the object itself without *per impossible* getting outside our representations and having a pure view of the object in itself? By criticizing hypostasis, the theory of representations remains true to the spirit of Kant's criticism; but by demanding a representation of the thing-in-itself to prevent this fallacy, it relapses into the crudest dogmatism.

To this objection Reinhold replies that, in order to distinguish between what belongs to the representation and what belongs to the object itself, it is indeed necessary to have a representation of what is proper to the object as distinct from the representation itself; but he immediately adds that such a representation need not be of the thing-in-itself.[115] Rather, it is necessary to have only a *pure* representation of the forms of receptivity and spontaneity, that is, a representation of these forms themselves, apart from any given object. By subtracting everything that is not necessary to the pure representation of the forms of receptivity and spontaneity, it is then possible to distinguish what belongs to the faculty of representation and what belongs to the object itself. Everything that is not necessary to the pure representation of spontaneity and receptivity then belongs to the object itself. There is thus a distinction between the 'subjective' and 'objective' content of a representation: the subjective content is that which belongs to the forms of understanding and sensibility; and the objective content is that which belongs to the given object.

Attempting to defend his concept of objective content, Reinhold argues that the objective content of a representation is indispensable to the faculty of representation as a whole.[116] It plays several important roles. First, it is necessary to stimulate the faculty of representation into activity. Mere empty forms by themselves, the faculties of spontaneity and receptivity represent something only if they have something given to act upon; and that is the objective content of a representation. Second, the objective content is also necessary for the subject to become self-conscious of its faculty of representation. The subject is aware of its spontaneity and receptivity only through its products; but to have products, it must have a given material to act upon, and that is again the objective content. Third, the objective content of a representation convinces us of the reality of an external world apart from our faculty of representations. In all these respects Reinhold's concept of objective content is the ancestor of Fichte's concept of an 'obstacle' *(Anstoss)*, which plays such an important role in the *Wissenschaftslehre* of 1794.

By appealing to this notion of objective content, Reinhold attempts to bolster Kant's refutation of idealism.[117] He contends that we can be as certain of the existence of objects external to ourselves as we can be of our own representations. This is because there is an objective content to our representation, which is a necessary condition of self-awareness.

Despite all these alleged advantages, it is doubtful that Reinhold's concept of objective matter gets him out of his original difficulty. It is easy to see that such a concept is dogmatic, transcending all the limits that Reinhold imposes on representation. For if the form of a representation is necessary to any possible representation, as Reinhold states, then even the representation of the objective content has to conform to the form, so that there simply cannot be a representation of what the object alone contributes to the representation. It is just not possible to abstract from the form of a representation to see the objective content in itself; for such an abstraction could not conform to the forms of representation, which Reinhold maintains are universally valid of all possible consciousness. Indeed, on just these grounds Reinhold himself has already argued that there cannot be a representation of the pure content of representation.[118] This pure representation of the objective content—supposing it is truly formless, as it must be—then amounts to nothing more than the impossible: the representation of the unrepresentable thing-in-itself. Hence Reinhold is now caught in a serious dilemma. Either he admits that there are formless representations, or he surrenders the attempt to distinguish the objective from the subjective matter of a representation. The first option permits representation of the thing-in-itself; and the second surrenders the attempt to find the source of the hypostasis of representations. In either case, though, the *Elementarphilosophie* fails in its campaign against metaphysical dogmatism.

We have now arrived at the close of the second book of Reinhold's *Versuch*, the 'theory of representation' proper. By beginning with the concept of representation and deriving its necessary conditions, Reinhold thinks that he has deduced some of the most significant conclusions of the critical philosophy: the unknowability of the thing-in-itself, the distinction between form and content, the dualism between a spontaneous and a receptive faculty, and the refutation of idealism. Nonetheless, we have seen that Reinhold obtains these results only by going beyond his phenomenological starting point and transcending the limits of consciousness. In assuming that the objective content of a representation corresponds to its object, in postulating an active subject and object that are the causes of representation, and in applying the category of cause to the thing-in-itself, Reinhold commits himself to assumptions which are not verifiable within consciousness itself. Hence there arises a serious gap between the ideals and the practices of the *Elementarphilosophie*: its specific deductions betray its phenomenological guidelines on point after point. In the *Elementarphilosophie* Reinhold intends to surmount the discrepancy between ideal and practice in Kant's work; but the irony is that he does so only by positing another equally disturbing discrepancy of his own.

8.9. The Crisis of the *Elementarphilosophie*

At the close of the third book of the *Versuch,* Reinhold moves into a new and dangerous field for his theory of representation. He now begins to consider a faculty of mind that appears to go beyond the confines of his theory of representation; the faculty of desire *(Begehrungsvermögen)*.[119] The presence of the faculty of desire poses a serious problem for Reinhold's theory of representation—a problem so severe that it virtually forces Reinhold to abandon his theory. The theory of representation is essentially a single-faculty theory, stating that the faculty of representation is the single faculty of the mind, of which all other faculties are only manifestations. But this single-faculty theory has difficulty in accommodating the faculty of desire, which appears distinct from the faculty of representation. There are two conspicuous difficulties in explaining desire on the premises of Reinhold's theory. First, the faculty of representation does not entail the power to act according to representations. But desire is such a power; hence desire cannot be reduced to some species of representation. Second, desire is not a faculty subsequent to representation, since there is the possibility of weakness of will, where we are conscious of the good but do not choose to act according to it.[120]

In addition to these difficulties, the problem of explaining the faculty of desire is especially embarrassing for Reinhold. The truth of the matter is that as a good Kantian he does not even want to reduce the faculty of desire to that of representation. If he is to be true to the 'spirit' of the Kantian philosophy—the doctrine of the primacy of practical reason—then he has to affirm the autonomy of practical reason, its power to be a determining ground of the will apart from theoretical reason. And, indeed, in the second volume of the *Briefe,* Reinhold himself vehemently argues that the will is free in the sense that it can choose to act or not to act according to the moral law, independent of its knowledge of the good.[121]

So Reinhold is again caught in a serious dilemma. If he reduces desire to the faculty of representation, then he denies the autonomy of practical reason, betraying the 'spirit' of the critical philosophy; but if he does not reduce desire to the faculty of representation, then he has to surrender his single-faculty theory and admit Kant's dualism between practical and theoretical reason, the will and understanding. The point of the theory of representation, though, was precisely to overcome such dualisms in a single all-embracing theory. Hence the general problem facing Reinhold is this: how is it possible to maintain a single-faculty theory as well as the autonomy of practical reason?

This is the problem that Reinhold faces at the close of his *Versuch,* and that he attempts to solve in its concluding section, "Grundlinien des Begehrungsvermögens." Here Reinhold struggles to preserve his single-faculty theory without reducing the will to a faculty of representation. His solution marks an extraordinary volte-face, and its consequences are of the first importance, not only for the *Elementarphilosophie* but also for Fichte's *Wissenschaftslehre.* Rather than 'intellectualizing desire', like Wolff, so that desire arises from the faculty of representation, Reinhold takes the very opposite course: he 'vitalizes representation' so that it stems from the faculty of desire. Thus he states that the faculty of desire is the power that creates all representations. The faculty of representation by itself gives only the conditions for the *possibility* of representation; but the faculty of desire supplies the conditions for their *existence.* The faculty of desire consists in two drives *(Triebe)* that correspond to the two constituents of representation: the drive for matter or content *(Trieb nach Stoff),* and the drive for form *(Trieb nach Form).*[122] Hence, to Reinhold, the faculty of desire is the basis for the faculty of representation, creating the essential constituents of all representation. This daring thesis permits him to preserve his single-faculty theory and to maintain the autonomy of desire simply by making desire into the basic single faculty of the soul.

Although Reinhold's new theory of desire does get him around his dilemma, it also compels him to abandon his original theory of representation. If Reinhold manages to maintain his single-faculty theory and the independence of desire, his single faculty is no longer representation, as previously thought, but desire. The question then arises: why not investigate the faculty of desire rather than the faculty of representation as the foundation of the *Elementarphilosophie?* Why not begin the *Elementarphilosophie* with an investigation of practical rather than theoretical reason, the will rather than representation? This is precisely the direction in which Fichte was to push the *Elementarphilosophie;* his *Wissenschaftslehre* is an *Elementar-philosophie* that begins with the faculty of desire.

What Reinhold discovered at the close of his *Versuch* is the fundamental incompatibility of his theory of representation with the 'spirit' of the critical philosophy. Reinhold's single-faculty theory contradicts the Kantian doctrine of practical reason, which is the very heart of Kant's philosophy. But this is not the only respect in which Reinhold betrays Kant's philosophy. There are indeed good reasons for thinking that the inspiration for Reinhold's theory comes from the rationalist tradition—the very tradition which Kant fought tooth and nail. In positing the faculty of representation as the single basic faculty of the mind, Reinhold follows—probably subconsciously—in the footsteps of his rationalist predecessor, Wolff. According to Wolff, the mind consists in a single active force, the *vis repraesentativa,* or power of representation.[123] Wolff refers every activity of the mind back to its power of representation, which manifests itself in every mental function, whether perception, imagination, memory, understanding, or will. Wolff's single-faculty theory is of course all part and parcel of his rationalist epistemology. If all the powers of the mind are so many forms of representation, then they all have an intellectual content, which could be, at least in principle, analyzable by reason.

Reinhold's hidden debt to Wolff raises the serious question whether he is relapsing into Wolff's rationalism—and hence the very dogmatism that Kant condemns. Such suspicions are indeed difficult to avoid. It is important to recall that Kant was a bitter opponent of the Wolffian single-faculty theory.[124] He arrived at his own trichotomous division of the mind—understanding, will, and judgment—only after a long and bitter struggle against Wolff's psychology.

A reductivistic psychology like Wolff's certainly does seem to destroy the independence of mental functions, which Kant was so eager to maintain. If the will and aesthetic pleasure are nothing but forms of the faculty of representation, then practical reason and judgment cannot be autonomous, but reduce to only a few forms of the intellect or understanding. Hence it appears to be impossible to unify and systematize all the results of the critical philosophy on the basis of a single-faculty theory like Reinhold's. Such a systematization succeeds only by erasing all those distinctions between faculties that Kant saw as crucial for the critical philosophy.

· *Chapter 9* ·

Schulze's Skepticism

9.1. Schulze's Historical Significance and Influence

The *Elementarphilosophie* was doomed to a short, if brilliant, career. Although it dominated the philosophical scene in Jena from 1789 to 1794, the year of Reinhold's departure and Fichte's arrival, its fate was sealed even before it reached the height of its fame. While Reinhold was busy putting the finishing touches upon the *Elementarphilosophie* in the second volume of the *Beyträge,* its entire foundation was thrown into question by the publication of a curious polemical work. This work appeared anonymously in the spring of 1792 under the odd title *Aenesidemus, oder Ueber die Fundamente der von dem Herrn Professor Reinhold in Jena gelieferten Elementarphilosophie.* As the lengthy title suggests, *Aenesidemus* was mainly an examination of Reinhold's *Elementarphilosophie,* especially its new exposition in the third essay of the first volume of the *Beyträge.* But it was also a sustained and savage attack upon Kant himself. *Aenesidemus* was indeed a general declaration of war against the critical philosophy in general, whether in its Kantian or Reinholdian form. It preached the gospel of a new and radical skepticism, which claimed to destroy all the "dogmatic pretensions" of the critical philosophy.

The author of *Aenesidemus* remained a mystery for some time, indeed for at least a year after the book achieved acclaim. Some readers indulged in wild speculation about the identity of the author. Thus K. G. Hausius, the first bibliographer of post-Kantian philosophy, surmised that the author was "the famous and acute Reimarus."[1] Other readers simply resigned themselves to ignorance. In his famous review of *Aenesidemus,* for instance, Fichte had to refer to the author by the title of his book. For a while, he was known to the public only as "Aenesidemus."

It eventually transpired that the author of *Aenesidemus* was a then little-known professor of philosophy at the University of Helmstadt, Gottlob Ernst Schulze (1761–1833). Obscure though he was, Schulze had a perfectly respectable career behind him. As a student at the University of Wittemberg, he studied under F. V. Reinhard, a close disciple of Crusius.[2] Schulze's debt to Reinard, and ultimately to Crusius, is significant since it places Schulze firmly within the German voluntarist tradition, which springs from Crusius. Schulze was also associated with Feder's circle in Göttingen, and indeed to a very intimate degree: he married Feder's daughter.[3] In 1810, when the University of Helmstadt was disbanded, Schulze became professor at Göttingen, where he taught until the end of his life.

Schulze's main claim to fame was, and still remains, his *Aenesidemus*. This book had a remarkable impact upon the philosophical scene in the early 1790s. It became a succès de scandale, the first generally recognized threat to the apparently impregnable critical fortress. All but the most hidebound Kantians were challenged by it; and for the first time they were forced to respect one of their critics.[4]

Almost everyone in the 1790s—whether friend or foe of Kant—paid handsome tribute to *Aenesidemus*. Hausius wrote that, of all anti-Kantian tracts, *Aenesidemus* was "indisputably the best."[5] G. G. Fuelleborn, a prominent disciple of Reinhold, stated that the book was "an honor to German philosophy," and he even doubted whether his teacher would ever muster a convincing reply to it.[6] Writing to J. F. Flatt in the autumn of 1793, Fichte called *Aenesidemus* "one of the most remarkable products of our century."[7] The book had completely confounded him, and indeed convinced him that neither Kant nor Reinhold had established philosophy upon a firm foundation. J. H. Abicht, Reinhold's most able defender, also praised *Aenesidemus* and admitted that it would be necessary to revise his master's doctrines.[8] And Salomon Maimon took Schulze's book so seriously that he wrote a detailed reply to it, *Philalethes an Aenesidemus*. Only Reinhold was not impressed. He protested that Schulze had willfully misunderstood him.[9] But Reinhold stood alone as the dam burst around him. It was largely due to *Aenesidemus* that the *Elementarphilosophie* disappeared from the philosophical scene in Germany.

Schulze's historical influence went far beyond Reinhold's contemporaries, however. In 1803 Hegel wrote an extensive re-review of Schulze's *Kritik der theoretischen Philosophie,* a work that refined and systematized the criticisms of Kant in *Aenesidemus*. Of course, as is well known, Hegel's review was a damning one. Hegel saw through many of the weaknesses in Schulze's crude interpretation of Kant and was ruthlessly unforgiving. In a few notorious lines he said that Schulze could understand the thing-in-itself only as "a rock underneath the snow." And he added with his characteristic sarcasm: "If Christ transformed stone into bread, then Schulze transformed the living bread of reason into stone."[10] Nevertheless, such sharp criticisms should not blind us to the valuable dialectical function that Schulze performed for Hegel. Like many philosophers who were heavily indebted to Kant, Hegel felt challenged by Schulze's skepticism; and in taking issue with it, he was forced to define the proper relationship between philosophy and skepticism in general. The conclusion of these reflections—that a true skepticism plays a positive role in every system of philosophy—was an important step toward the development of Hegel's dialectic in the *Phänomenologie*.[11]

Schulze had a more positive influence on another famous philosopher: Arthur Schopenhauer. A student of Schulze's at the University of Göttingen in 1810, Schopenhauer was inspired by Schulze's lectures to abandon his study of natural science and to devote himself to philosophy. It is true that the young Schopenhauer quickly became critical of his teacher. The marginalia of his lecture notes abound in such epithets as "Gewäsch," "Unsinn," "Sophist," and even "Rindvieh-Schulze." But such outbursts were the product of Schopenhauer's youth, of his need to assert his independence from a more established and powerful figure. In his later years, when he had gained self-confidence, Schopenhauer gratefully acknowledged Schulze's influence on him. He was especially thankful for Schulze's advice to read Plato and Kant before Aristotle and Spinoza—a debt that tells us not a little about the spiritual allegiances of Schopenhauer's own philosophy. In *Die Welt als Wille und Vorstellung* Schopenhauer always considers Schulze's criticisms of Kant; and at one point he praises his old teacher as "the most acute of Kant's opponents."[12] There are indeed marked signs of Schulze's influence throughout Schopenhauer's philosophy. Schulze's insistence on clarity and rigor, his emphasis on the primacy of the will over the intellect, and his view of philosophical systems as forms of *Weltanschauungen,* all had their effect.

9.2. Schulze's Meta-Critical Skepticism

Schulze's *Aenesidemus* introduces a new and radical form of skepticism into modern philosophy,[13] the essence of which is succinctly stated by Schulze at the very beginning of his book.[14] Schulze sums up his position in two propositions: first, that nothing has been known or demonstrated with certainty about the existence or properties of things-in-themselves; and, second, that nothing has been known or demonstrated with certainty about the origins and conditions of knowledge.

It is the second proposition that is new to, and characteristic of, Schulze's skepticism. What now falls under skeptical doubt is not only the claim of metaphysics to know the thing-in-itself, but also the claim of epistemology to know the origins and conditions of knowledge. Schulze radicalizes skeptical doubt, so that it becomes meta-critical, applying to not only our first-order but also our second-order beliefs.

Schulze's meta-critical skepticism gives a new twist to modern skepticism since its inception in Descartes's and Hume's writings. While Descartes and Hume use epistemology as an instrument of their skepticism, examining the conditions of knowledge in order to expose unfounded claims to it, Schulze brings this very instrument into question. The skeptic is now forced to be self-reflective, self-critical of the tools of his trade.

Although *Aenesidemus* pushes modern skepticism in a new and radical direction by attacking epistemology, Schulze thinks he is only reintroducing an ancient form of skepticism into the modern philosophical world.[15] His choice of the title *Aenesidemus* is indeed singularly appropriate. Aenesidemus was the foremost renewer of Pyrrhonism around the first century A.D. According to Sextus Empiricus, the ancient historian of skepticism, Aenesidemus criticized the academic skeptics as dogmatists in disguise because they dogmatically taught that knowledge is impossible.[16] His ten tropes argued that sensation cannot provide objective knowledge of things themselves; and his eight tropes set forth objections against the concept of cause, claiming that it cannot give us an objective knowledge of things. All this anticipates Schulze's own position. The dogmatism of denying the possibility of knowledge, the difficulty of knowing things-in-themselves, and the unreliability of the concept of cause—these are all cardinal tenets of Schulze's own skepticism. Just as Aenesidemus once renewed Pyrrhonism to combat the academic skeptics, so Schulze attempts to resurrect Aenesidemus to attack the critical philosophy.

Although Schulze makes a great deal of his allegiance to Aenesidemus, there is another philosopher who also inspires Schulze's skepticism: David Hume. Like Hamann and Jacobi, Schulze sees Hume as the great destroyer of the pretensions of reason and indeed of the lofty claims of *Vernunftkritik*. In a review of Eberhard's *Magazin,* for instance, Schulze defends Hume against his recent opponents, claiming that none of them—Tetens, Feder, Eberhard, and Kant himself—have managed to meet the challenge of Hume's skepticism.[17] And in *Aenesidemus* Schulze argues at length that Kant has not refuted Hume, but has only begged the question against him.[18] With Schulze, then, the revival of Hume in post-Kantian philosophy gains momentum. Now it is not only Hamann and Jacobi, but also Schulze, who adds weight to the campaign. When Maimon jumps on the bandwagon, Hume is fully reinstated, posing as great a threat after Kant as before him.

Although Schulze's skepticism is directed against Kant, it would be misleading to describe it as 'anticritical'.[19] It is important to recognize that Schulze's skepticism and Kant's criticism begin from the same point. Schulze's guiding principle is taken straight from the first *Kritik:* "that all our beliefs must submit to the free and open examination of reason."[20] Schulze sees this principle as the very heart of his own skepticism, making it the motto of his examination of Reinhold's *Elementarphilosophie*. Like Kant, then, and unlike Hamann and Jacobi, Schulze believes in the sovereignty of reason, its right to be the final arbiter of any claim to knowledge. Thus in the preface to *Aenesidemus*, Schulze declares that the skeptic's sole authority is reason and that the highest excellence of man consists in the perfection of this faculty.[21] Schulze is indeed at pains to stress that skepticism is not at odds with reason, but is reason's only consistent position.

Rather than expressing hostility toward the critical philosophy, like so many of Kant's critics, Schulze praises and defends it. He admires the critical philosophy for bringing reason a step further on the road toward self-consciousness, and he realizes that, thanks to Kant, there cannot be a relapse into the dogmatic metaphysical rationalism of Leibniz and Wolff.[22] This praise of Kant is not a mere *Höflichkeitsformel*, as is sometimes assumed,[23] since it stems from Schulze's deep allegiance to the main principle of the *Kritik*. But nowhere is Schulze's sympathy for Kant more apparent than in his harsh review of Eberhard's *Magazin*, which appeared in the *Allgemeine deutsche Bibliothek*.[24] Reviewing almost all the articles in the first issue of the *Magazin*, Schulze finds gaping holes in virtually every anti-Kantian argument. He defends Kant's theory of the synthetic a priori, his concepts of space and time, and his arguments for the unknowability of the thing-in-itself. Like a true Kantian, Schulze stresses the originality of Kant's critique and insists that it is an advance over Leibniz's and Wolff's rationalism.

It is precisely because Schulze is an adherent of the Kantian critique that he undertakes his meta-critique of Kant in *Aenesidemus*. Schulze sees his meta-critique as the necessary consequence of Kant's critique. Since the critique demands that all beliefs submit to the examination of reason, it too must subject its aims, methods, and arguments to a thoroughgoing meta-critique. If the critique refuses to investigate its own powers, then it lapses into a dogmatism as bad as that of the rationalist metaphysician.[25]

Schulze maintains that the inevitable and ultimate result of Kantian criticism is his own skepticism. If there is indeed a single central thesis of *Aenesidemus*, then it is that criticism must become skepticism. In essence, Schulze's argument is that if all criticism must become meta-criticism, then all meta-criticism must become skepticism.

Schulze's skepticism is not a little reminiscent of the snake who swallowed his own tail: it is in serious danger of self-destruction. All the meta-critical questions that Schulze raises against Kant's criticism prima facie apply to his own skepticism. How, indeed, does Schulze know that nothing has been known or demonstrated with certainty about the origins and limits of knowledge? If nothing has been known about them, then ipso facto Schulze should know nothing about the lack of knowledge about them. Just as the critical philosopher has to find the middle path between dogmatism and skepticism, so the skeptic must walk the fine line between self-refutation and dogmatism.

Schulze is deeply—and rightly—worried about the problem of justifying his radical skepticism. It is to avoid this very danger that he says in the beginning of *Aenesidemus* that the skeptic does not deny the possibility of knowledge, whether of things-in-themselves or the faculty of knowledge.[26] The true skeptic does not make this denial, Schulze explains, because he recognizes that it too is a dogmatic assertion. He sees that he cannot claim knowledge of the impossibility of knowledge without refuting himself. So rather than affirming the impossibility of knowledge, the skeptic simply keeps an open mind about its possibility. He is perfectly willing to admit that, with the progress of inquiry, there might someday be knowledge about things-in-themselves and the faculty of knowledge.

The next question for Schulze, then, is why is he a skeptic at all? If the skeptic admits the possibility of knowledge, then how does his position differ from the nonskeptic's? In answering this question, Schulze first takes refuge in history. He replies that his skepticism rests upon a simple historical fact: that there is not now, and there so far has never been, any knowledge or successful demonstration of things-in-themselves or the faculty of knowledge.[27] Hence Schulze formulates the main theses of his skepticism so that they are historical propositions: they state 'there *has not been* knowledge' and not 'there *cannot* be knowledge . . .'. The skeptic therefore differs from the dogmatist in one significant respect: the dogmatist affirms, and the skeptic denies, that we are *now* (and not only will be sometime in the future) in possession of infallible knowledge. According to Schulze, the main lesson of the history of philosophy is that no system or school has ever been successful in acquiring indisputable knowledge. No matter how rigorous and conscientious philosophers have been, holes have always been found in their demonstrations. Although experience teaches us to be wary, Schulze insists that there are no a priori grounds for dismissing all philosophical claims to knowledge. The only basis for our skepticism is the poor track record of philosophical history.

It is doubtful, however, that Schulze's initial efforts to avoid self-refutation succeed. The appeal to history is a desperate move, which raises more questions than it answers. One basic question is how Schulze knows that no philosophical system has been successful. This is not a simple 'fact', as Schulze pretends. Whether a system is a success or failure is not a straightforward historical issue about whether people have in fact accepted or rejected the system; for no number of facts about its acceptance or rejection determines its truth or falsity. So the issue is at bottom a philosophical one. But then the question is inescapable: what are the criteria that so indisputably determine the lack of success of past philosophical systems? Here Schulze is extremely short on answers. And it is in any case extremely dogmatic to claim that no system of philosophy has ever been successful. Do we now know what is wrong with Plato and Aristotle any more than with Kant and Reinhold? If the history of philosophy has taught us anything, then it is surely that no system has been successfully judged successful or unsuccessful.

On a deeper level, though, Schulze does not rest that much importance on his historical defense of skepticism. His ultimate justification of skepticism is a moral one. What justifies skeptical doubt for him is neither history nor pure reason, but a moral imperative: the demand that we perfect our cognitive faculties.[28] The fundamental article of faith for the skeptic, he writes in the preface to *Aenesidemus,* is the perfectibility of human reason.[29] This perfectibility is infinite, however, requiring nothing less than infinite striving, the ceaseless effort of inquiry. Now, to Schulze, the main aim of skepticism is precisely to promote such striving. Through his questions and doubts, the skeptic maintains and stimulates the spirit of inquiry. He remorselessly attacks dogmatism since it threatens to suppress inquiry with its presumption that it is already in full possession of the truth. It is indeed just this moral obligation to perfect our reason that compels the skeptic to doubt the claim that there cannot be knowledge as much as the claim that there already must be knowledge. He must deny both of these claims—that of the 'dogmatic skeptic' and that of the 'dogmatic metaphysician'—simply because they pose a serious threat to the progress of inquiry. They presume either that knowledge is already attained or that it never will be attained. In either case there is no point to further inquiry and reason loses all motivation to perfect itself. What we have to avoid above all, Schulze warns us, is a doctrine that sanctions *die Faulheit der Vernunft*—and that doctrine is espoused just as much by the dogmatic skeptic as by the dogmatic metaphysician.

9.3. The Critique of Reinhold

True to its long-winded subtitle—*Ueber die Fundamente der von dem Herrn Professor Reinhold in Jena gelieferten Elementarphilosophie*—Schulze's *Aenesidemus* is primarily a critique of Reinhold's *Elementarphilosophie.* Nearly two-thirds of the book is devoted to a detailed examination of Reinhold's *Beyträge,* in particular, the third essay of the first volume, where Reinhold reformulates the first principles of his *Elementarphilosophie.* Schulze pays more attention to Reinhold than Kant because he accepts Reinhold's claim that the *Elementarphilosophie* provides the foundation for the critical philosophy. He agrees fully with Reinhold that Kant does not examine some of his basic presuppositions, and that he fails to make his first principles explicit. Hence Schulze regards an attack on the *Elementarphilosophie* as an attack on the critical philosophy at its strongest point: if the *Elementarphilosophie* collapses, so a fortiori does the critical philosophy.

Schulze's critique of Reinhold has never failed to arouse controversy, having provoked opposing reactions among Schulze's contemporaries and modern historians alike. There are those who claim that Schulze completely destroyed Reinhold,[30] as well as those who maintain that he completely missed the point.[31] But the only accurate, fair, and balanced view lies between these extremes.[32] Although Schulze's objections often stem from a misunderstanding of Reinhold's general program, they are usually telling against Reinhold's analysis of representation, in fact so telling that they demand nothing less than a complete revision of the *Elementarphilosophie*. This more moderate view of Schulze's achievements should emerge from the following review of some of his most important arguments.

Although Schulze is far from a penetrating interpreter of the aims of the *Elementarphilosophie*, he makes a serious attempt to criticize Reinhold internally, evaluating his practice according to his own ideals. Schulze declares at the outset that he agrees with Reinhold on several fundamental points: (1) philosophy has to be based upon a single first principle if it is to realize its ideal of science; (2) this first principle must express the concept of representation, which is the most general concept of all philosophy; and (3) there are immediate and indisputable facts of consciousness.[33] Schulze then raises three questions corresponding to each of these points: Is the proposition of consciousness really the first principle of philosophy? Has Reinhold accurately, thoroughly, and unambiguously analyzed the concept of representation? And does Reinhold strictly describe the facts of consciousness and truly remain within the phenomenological limits of his own theory?

In order to ensure an open and impartial examination of the *Elementarphilosophie*, Schulze explicitly lays down the standards of his critique.[34] He maintains that only two standards are necessary to guarantee him a powerful yet non-question-begging critique: the facts of consciousness and the general laws of logic. Applying these standards commits Schulze to two propositions, which he explicitly states. The first proposition is that there are representations within us, which have characteristics that relate them to, and distinguish them from, one another. The second proposition is that a necessary criterion of truth is logic, that all reasoning over matters of fact has a claim to correctness only if it conforms to these rules. According to Schulze, these propositions are indisputable and every skeptic has to affirm them if his own skepticism is not to be self-defeating. Hence they can safely serve as a certain and impartial basis for the evaluation of the *Elementarphilosophie*.

After setting forth these preliminary points, Schulze immediately proceeds to his detailed review of the *Elementarphilosophie*.[35] He begins with a careful examination of Reinhold's first principle, the proposition of consciousness. With his first main objection, Schulze makes a bold but simple claim: even if it is true, the proposition of consciousness cannot be the first principle of philosophy. It cannot attain such status, Schulze argues, because it is of necessity subordinate to a still higher principle, namely, the law of contradiction. It is subordinate to this law, since, like any proposition, it cannot be both affirmed and denied. On this basis alone Schulze concludes that the proposition of consciousness cannot be the first principle of philosophy. For, according to Reinhold himself, the first principle of philosophy must be completely 'self-determining', that is, its truth cannot depend upon any other principle. We have just seen, however, that the proposition of consciousness depends upon the truth of the principle of contradiction.

Even before the publication of *Aenesidemus* in 1792, Reinhold was long aware of this objection. Indeed, he had already formulated his reply to it in 1791 in the *Fundament*,[36] a response that Fichte found so convincing that he repeated it in his review of *Aenesidemus*.[37] In his reply Reinhold admits that the proposition of consciousness is subordinate to the law of contradiction in the negative sense that it must comply with it and cannot contradict it; but he denies that it is subordinate to it in the positive sense that its truth follows from it. In other words, only the possibility, but not the reality, of the proposition depends upon the law of contradiction. To determine its truth or reality, we have to consult our immediate experience. Now, in Reinhold's view this qualification is not at all damaging to the proposition's claim to be the first principle of philosophy. The first principle needs to be self-determining or independent only in its truth or reality, but not in its possibility. This is for the simple reason that it has to act as the basis for only the reality, and not also the possibility, of knowledge. Thus Schulze misses the point of the first principle: it is the foundation for all *knowledge* or *true belief*, not for any belief whatsoever, whether true or false.

Admitting Reinhold's distinction between the possibility and reality of the proposition of consciousness, Schulze still has an interesting, if little noticed, reply to Reinhold.[38] This proposition cannot be the first principle even of the reality of knowledge, he contends, since it contains only the generic concept of representation, which cannot determine or deduce any of the specific kinds of representation that fall under it. Here Schulze is relying upon the incontestable logical point that we cannot infer the truth of the species (for example, 'this is red') from the truth of the genus ('this has a color'). This is indeed a weighty objection, not only to the proposition of consciousness, but also to Reinhold's whole deductive method. Later on, Kant himself makes just this point in his denunciation of Fichte's *Wissenschaftslehre*.

Schulze's second major objection to the proposition of consciousness is even more difficult to deny: he claims that it is hopelessly vague and ambiguous.[39] Rather than being self-explanatory and precise, as Reinhold says a first principle should be, it permits a number of different, and even conflicting, interpretations. This is especially the case, Schulze contends, with the terms 'relate' and 'distinguish'. The subject can 'relate' the representation to itself and the object in a variety of ways: as a whole to its parts, as an effect to its cause, as matter to its form, as a sign to what it signifies. It can 'distinguish' the representation from itself and the object in all these respects too. Reinhold's usage gives no indication, however, of what particular sense is to be read into these terms.

Schulze's third objection to the proposition of consciousness is that it is not universal, valid for every possible state of consciousness.[40] There are some states of consciousness that do not conform to it, he claims, citing intuition *(Anschauung)* as a counterexample. An intuition is a representation where the subject is not self-conscious and where he focuses all his attention upon his object, 'getting lost in it', so to speak. According to the proposition of consciousness, however, the subject has to distinguish himself from his representation and his object. But this palpably does not hold in the case of intuition, Schulze insists, since the subject cannot distinguish his representation of the object from the object itself; as soon as he reflects on his intuition, he destroys it, because he ceases to be in an immediate relationship to the object. Hence Schulze concludes that the proposition of consciousness is at best valid of many, but by no means of all, states of consciousness.

After raising these three objections, Schulze makes two closing critical remarks about the general logical status of the proposition of consciousness.[41] He first points out that the proposition is synthetic, its truth resting upon a 'fact of consciousness', as Reinhold says. Since its truth is based upon experience, it follows that it cannot be either necessary or certain. Like all empirical generalizations, it must be prone to possible falsification. In his second remark Schulze states that the proposition is an abstraction, a generalization from similar but irreducibly particular cases of experience. Hence we always find the subject, object, and representation in some determinate relation that is omitted or not precisely expressed by the proposition. Furthermore, since abstraction is always an arbitrary business, a selection of this or that aspect of a thing rather than another, it is necessary to admit that the proposition of consciousness is also arbitrary. These two remarks then bring Schulze to the sweeping and damning conclusion that the foundation of the *Elementarphilosophie* is not certain and necessary, but merely probable and arbitrary.

But Schulze's closing remarks only betray his superficial and implausible interpretation of the proposition of consciousness. He reads it as a mere empirical generalization. Yet a more profound and plausible interpretation, and indeed one that avoids all of Schulze's damaging conclusions, is possible. To recognize the philosophical point of Reinhold's proposition, we must construe it not as a description of empirical facts, but as a logical analysis of the conditions of consciousness. According to this more logical reading, the proposition does not describe what happens in consciousness; rather, it analyzes what must be able to happen if a representation is to be (logically) possible. As Reinhold himself insists in his *Versuch*, the task of his theory of representation is not to discover facts about representations but to analyze the concept of representation.[42] Of course, as Schulze observes, Reinhold does say that his first principle is about 'a fact of consciousness'; but there is no need to interpret 'a fact' as an actual event; it might also be a possible one, that is, what must be able to happen if a representation is to be possible. This more logical reading of the proposition of consciousness completely obviates Schulze's criticisms about its being merely probable and arbitrary. In fact, it is no more probable and arbitrary than any logical analysis.

After the proposition of consciousness, the next target of Schulze's polemic is Reinhold's argument for the existence of a faculty of representation *(Vorstellungsvermögen)*. According to Schulze's interpretation of Reinhold's theory, which is largely based upon the shorter exposition of the *Beyträge* and which ignores the more careful and lengthy exposition in the *Versuch*, Reinhold argues that it is necessary to postulate the existence of a faculty of representation in order to explain the existence of the representations themselves. There must be some cause for their existence, and that is formulated by the concept of a 'faculty of representation'.

Armed with this crude interpretation, Schulze has no trouble finding defects in Reinhold's postulate of a faculty of representation. He puts forward the following objections: (1) When Reinhold postulates the existence of a faculty of representation that is the cause of the representations themselves, he is guilty of violating a cardinal principle of the critical philosophy: that the categories are applicable only within possible experience. He applies the categories of 'causality' and 'reality' to the faculty of representation, which he admits cannot be given in experience itself; and yet at the same time he attempts to deduce Kant's claim that the concepts of the understanding are valid only within the realm of possible experience. So, just by postulating the existence of a faculty of representation, the *Elementarphilosophie* is guilty of transcending its own phenomenological limits.[43] (2) Reinhold's procedure of inferring the properties of the faculty of representation from those of the representations themselves is illicit. Since the faculty is the cause and the representations its effects, this procedure rests upon inferring the nature of the cause from that of its effects. But all such inferences are uncertain, since the nature of the effect never logically entails anything about the nature of the cause. Furthermore, in this case there is not even any basis for inductive inference because there cannot be any experience of the faculty itself to see if it is indeed connected with the representations.[44] (3) Reinhold's postulate of a faculty of representation has no explanatory value since it simply renames what it is to explain. It is only a collective term for the conditions of representation, which does not state what these conditions are. Introducing this concept to explain representations is like saying that what makes water cling to a sponge is the sponge's power of absorption.[45] (4) Even granting Reinhold's argument that representations cannot be thought without a faculty that creates them, it does not follow that such a faculty *exists*. What we must think is no evidence for what must exist since it is necessary to distinguish a necessity in reason from a necessity in existence.[46] This is indeed Kant's teaching in the "Dialektik," though Reinhold simply ignores it when it comes to his theory of representations. Like the dogmatic metaphysician, he hypostatizes the conditions of thought. Just as the metaphysician infers the existence of the unconditioned because the series of conditions cannot be conceived without it, so Reinhold deduces the existence of the faculty of representation because representations cannot be conceived without it. According to Schulze, the skeptic does not deny that it is necessary to conceive the faculty of representation in order to make the existence of representations intelligible; but he does refuse to draw the conclusion that such a faculty exists simply because it is necessary to conceive it. In general, the skeptic draws a rigid line between what we must think and what exists; and his task is to prevent philosophers—especially hypocritical critical philosophers—from carelessly trespassing it.

But Reinhold still has a plausible line of defense against this array of objections. He can reply that they rest upon another crude empiricist interpretation of the theory of representations. They wrongly presuppose that this theory is a first-order investigation into the causes of the existence of representations. Yet this again goes against the express warnings in the *Versuch* that it is a strictly second-order examination of the logical conditions of the concept of representation. The faculty of representation is not the cause of the existence of representations, but a construct to express the conditions of their possibility. Schulze is therefore guilty of construing a metaphor as if it were a literal truth. All the objections that he raises against a first-order theory might be perfectly correct—but it is precisely because Reinhold is aware of these difficulties that he rules out a first-order theory in the first place.

It is a token of the thoroughness of Schulze's examination of Reinhold that he anticipates this reply and prepares a counterattack upon it.[47] If the task of the *Elementarphilosophie* is only to analyze the concept of representation, he writes, then it forfeits all interest in truth and becomes a mere *Begriffsspiel*. It might well be the case that the concept of representation has the implications that Reinhold presents; his analysis of this concept might well be accurate and exhaustive; but that still leaves open the question of whether it has a reference. Simple analysis of concepts never suffices in philosophy, Schulze insists, since the task of philosophy is to know reality, not merely our conceptualization of it. Schulze then confronts Reinhold with a painful choice. If his theory is second-order, then it is a mere play on words; but if it is first-order, then all his earlier objections apply to it. Thus Reinhold faces either irrelevance or incoherence.

Schulze next begins to consider the details of Reinhold's theory of representation, commenting upon each of the propositions deduced by Reinhold in the third essay of the *Beyträge*. It is here that Schulze's polemic indisputably hits his target. It is no longer a question of criticizing Reinhold's general project, which Schulze arguably misinterprets, but of finding the weak spots in Reinhold's reasoning. This is a task which Schulze dispatches with great dialectical skill. Although his polemic against Reinhold's first principle and general project does light damage, his attack upon the details of Reinhold's theory leaves very little standing.

Schulze first criticizes Reinhold for thinking that a representation consists in two distinct elements, matter and form.[48] Reinhold argues that what relates to distinct things must consist in distinct constituents; hence a representation consists in two constituents because it relates to two things, subject and object. According to Schulze, however, the premise behind this argument is simply false. What relates to distinct things does not necessarily consist in distinct constituents, for example, one side of a triangle relates to its other two sides, but it does not ipso facto consist in two distinct components since it is the whole side that relates to the other two.

In order to give Reinhold his full due, Schulze proposes another more plausible formulation of his argument.[49] He suggests construing Reinhold's vague concept of 'relation' as a causal connection. The representation then 'relates' to the subject and object in the sense that it is the effect of their causal activity. Such a reading of the concept of relation provides Reinhold with an apparently more tenable premise: what is the effect of distinct causes consists in distinct aspects or components. But, not surprisingly, Schulze also rejects this version of Reinhold's argument. Upon closer inspection, the new premise turns out to be equally false, because the same component or aspect of a thing might be the effect of distinct causes. Furthermore, even assuming that the premise were correct, Reinhold has no right to introduce it at this stage of his theory, given that none of his preceding propositions demonstrate that subject and object are causes of representation.

Assuming, however, that Reinhold were correct in dividing a representation into two components, calling them matter and form would be arbitrary, Schulze asserts.[50] What relates the representation to the subject is the form, and what relates it to the object is the matter, Reinhold says. "But why should this be so?" Schulze asks. Introduction of the distinction between form and matter to describe these relations is so arbitrary that Reinhold could have just as well put these terms to the opposite use. If he defines 'form' as what relates to the object and 'matter' as what relates to the subject, there is still no contradiction. Admittedly, it is more plausible to say that the form relates to the subject since it is a fact of common sense that the subject cannot create the content of his experience. But Schulze rightly points out that the *Elementarphilosophie* has no right to rest its reasoning upon a mere 'fact' of common sense. Reinhold claims that the *Elementarphilosophie* admits only those propositions which it has deduced from its first principle. Whence then the reliance upon common sense?

What seduces Reinhold into dividing a representation into form and content in the first place, Schulze suggests, is nothing more than his sloppy language.[51] He thinks that a representation has to consist in two constituents since it 'relates' to two things, subject and object. If, however, he more carefully examined the sense in which a representation 'relates' to subject and object, he would find that it does not relate to them in the same sense at all. The representation relates to the subject as a property to a substance (hence we speak about the subject 'having' a representation), while it relates to the object as a sign to a thing signified (hence we talk about the representation 'representing' or 'symbolizing' the thing itself). It is extremely important to specify these senses, Schulze maintains, since this makes it plain that it is the *whole* representation, not only one part or aspect of it, that relates to the subject and object. It is the whole representation (form and matter) that is the property of the subject, and it is the whole representation that is the sign of the object. It is completely otiose to introduce the distinction between form and matter to explain these different relations; for both form and matter are properties of the subject and signs of the thing signified.

9.4. The Meta-Critique of Kant

Although *Aenesidemus* is primarily a polemic against Reinhold, it still contains a large battery of objections against Kant. These are in fact the most important objections in Schulze's arsenal. While the polemic against Reinhold deals with only a single formulation of the critical philosophy, and a rather weak one at that, the arguments against Kant concern the enterprise of the critical philosophy as a whole. Schulze is under no illusion that, ultimately, Kant is the most important figure, both historically and philosophically.[52] He knows all too well that Kant is the guiding spirit behind Reinhold and that he is the genuine father of the critical philosophy.

Schulze's polemic hardly spells the end of the critical philosophy. Although he raises some interesting questions that should not go unanswered, most of his objections miss the point, being based upon a crude psychologistic interpretation of the critical philosophy. Nevertheless, Schulze's misreading of Kant is instructive. His gauntlet of objections, however misaimed, provides a necessary ordeal for the critical philosopher if he is to be clear about the aims, methods, and discourse of transcendental philosophy. If a student of Kant does not know how to reply to Schulze, then chances are that he does not understand the idea of transcendental philosophy itself.

We can easily summarize Schulze's arguments against Kant by setting them in 'tropes', short polemical paragraphs containing a single argument. Schulze himself would heartily endorse such an exposition, which was favored by the ancient skeptics, especially Aenesidemus himself.

(1) Any explanation of the origins and conditions of experience must violate the critique's own standard of knowledge. For these origins and conditions cannot appear within experience itself when they must be prior to it. According to the critique's standard of knowledge, however, there is knowledge only within possible experience. Hence the very nature of transcendental inquiry—an investigation into the origins and conditions of experience—infracts the critique's standard of knowledge. Thus, Kant must choose between his standard of knowledge and his transcendental inquiry.[53]

(2) There is a grave discrepancy between the aim and means of the critical philosophy. Its aim is to acquire universal and necessary knowledge of the conditions and limits of reason; but its means are observation and reflection upon one's inner experience. This must be its means if it is to remain within its own self-imposed limits of possible experience. But such means are completely inadequate to the ambitious aim of the critical philosophy. Since Hume, it is a commonplace that it is not possible to derive universal and necessary knowledge from experience, which is always particular and contingent. What I observe in my inner experience is not necessarily in that of others.[54]

(3) Kant's restriction of knowledge to appearances also applies *mutatis mutandis* to his own transcendental inquiry. This restriction is self-reflexive because an inquiry into the origins of knowledge has to employ the category of causality, which *ex hypothesi* is applicable only to appearances. Hence Kant's transcendental inquiry is valid for the faculty of knowledge only as an appearance and not as a thing-in-itself. Here again, then, a conflict arises between Kant's inquiry and his standard of knowledge.[55]

(4) Kant's transcendental deduction does not refute Hume, but only presupposes what he brings into question: the principle of causality. The deduction proves that the categories apply to experience only by assuming that the transcendental subject is the lawgiver of nature. But to assume that this subject is the lawgiver of nature, that it creates the laws to which nature conforms, presupposes the application of the principle of causality, which only begs the question against Hume.[56]

It is important to note that Schulze sees this as a general problem of all epistemology. In his view epistemology is caught in a vicious circle. It pretends to be the presuppositionless first philosophy; but it has to presuppose the principle of causality in order to investigate the origins of knowledge. Hence the whole enterprise of epistemology cannot get off the ground because of Hume's skepticism about causality.[57]

(5) Kant's concept of the transcendental subject is ambiguous; and in whatever sense one construes it—whether as thing-in-itself, noumenon, or transcendental idea—it makes no sense to think of it as the origin or source of knowledge. If it is the thing-in-itself, then we cannot apply the category of causality to it. If, however, it is a noumenon, then it is either a purely intelligible entity or the formal unity of experience (that is, the unity of apperception); but in the first case, we again apply the category of causality beyond experience; and in the second we assume that a mere concept or abstract unity creates the order of experience. If, finally, it is only a transcendental idea, then we cannot claim constitutive value for it; for Kant himself insists that all ideas have only a regulative validity.[58]

(6) Kant's reasoning about the conditions of experience creates a transcendental illusion of its own. According to Kant, a transcendental illusion occurs when a necessary condition of our thought is hypostatized and confused with a necessary condition of things-in-themselves. But Kant's own transcendental deduction commits just this fallacy; for it reasons that the mind must be the lawgiver of nature since it is necessary to think of it as the lawgiver of nature. This is of course a non sequitur; but it is also just the fallacy that Kant imputes to rationalist metaphysics. What Kant regards as the main error of metaphysics is thus a *Grundfehler* of the *Kritik*.[59]

(7) Kant's philosophy, at least when consistent, amounts to 'formalism'; that is, it reduces all reality to nothing but "an aggregate of forms and

effects of the mind." Of course, in the second edition of the first *Kritik* Kant adds a "Widerlegung des Idealismus," where he attempts to distinguish his philosophy from Berkeley's. But this attempt fails, and for two reasons. First, it shows at most that there are permanent things existing in space; but that does not amount to a demonstration of the existence of material objects. And, second, if Kant rids his philosophy of the thing-in-itself—as he must to be consistent—then it is identical to Berkeley's in placing all reality within the sphere of consciousness.[60]

(8) Kant's moral theology, his practical faith in the existence of God and immortality, is built upon an extremely weak foundation, a *petitio principii*. Kant argues that *if* it is a moral duty to realize the highest good, then it is also necessary to believe in the existence of God, providence, and immortality, since they are necessary conditions for the realization of this ideal. Resting his case upon the simple point that 'ought' implies 'can', Kant infers the conditions for the fulfillment of a duty (the beliefs in God, providence, and immortality) from the duty itself (the obligation to act on the highest good). Now even granting that the ideal of the highest good requires these conditions, Kant's argument begs the question. Of course, it is the case that *if* it is a duty to realize the highest good, then the conditions for acting according to the duty must also prevail. What is in question, however, is whether there is a duty to realize the highest good in the first place. This is in question precisely because it is doubtful that these conditions (God, providence, and immortality) prevail.[61]

There is an important lesson to be learned from the failure of this argument: practical reason has no right to make decrees to theoretical reason. We must not believe in God, providence, and immortality simply because practical reason commands it. A command does not necessarily amount to an obligation, at least when it is possible to doubt that the conditions for its fulfillment exist. So rather than practical reason having primacy over theoretical reason, the converse is the case. Theoretical reason has primacy over practical because it determines whether the conditions for fulfillment of a command prevail, and hence whether the command really does amount to an obligation.[62]

9.5. Strengths and Weaknesses of Schulze's Skepticism

What are we to make of this veritable phalanx of arguments? Upon reflection, they are not as imposing as they appear. Almost all of them suffer from a psychologistic interpretation of the critical philosophy. The main premise behind this interpretation is that Kant's transcendental inquiry is only a first-order psychological investigation into the cognitive faculties of the mind, whose ontological status is on a par with other ordinary things (such as ships, shoes, and sealing wax). Thus to know 'the conditions of knowledge' is to know the causes or origins of the various kinds of representation, just as explaining any natural event is a question of knowing its causes. What distinguishes epistemology from metaphysics, therefore, is not its type of discourse, but only its subject matter.

Such an interpretation, however, is surely a simplification of Kant's transcendental enterprise. However important the 'subjective deduction' might be, Kant's primary aim in the *Kritik* is to conduct a second-order investigation into our synthetic a priori judgments about things, not a first-order investigation into the faculty of mind.[63] He does not want to know the causal conditions of representation as much as the truth conditions of synthetic a priori judgments. This intention is evident not only from Kant's distinction between transcendental and empirical deduction, but also from his distinction between the *quid juris* and *quid facti*.

The second-order status of Kant's transcendental enterprise invalidates most of Schulze's polemic, however. Since there is a fundamental logical difference between a first- and a second-order investigation, it does not necessarily follow that all the restrictions which Kant applies to first-order propositions also hold for second-order ones. Furthermore, an analysis of synthetic a priori judgments does not require the principle of causality, so that Kant is not guilty of begging the question against Hume. So, in the end, it is Schulze and not Kant who is guilty of hypostasis: he sees Kant's second-order discourse as if it were first-order, and thus confuses truth conditions with causal ones.

Despite his misunderstanding of Kant, many of Schulze's arguments have their point. If we follow a psychologistic reading of Kant, then almost all of them are perfectly valid. Hence the value of Schulze's polemic is precisely that it points out the consequences of such a reading of the transcendental enterprise. They are indeed a strong antidote to the self-hypostasis of the critical philosophy.

But Schulze's psychologistic interpretation of Kant is only one of the serious weaknesses in his skepticism. Schulze also commits himself to some very dogmatic presuppositions, which a radical skeptic should call into question. The first of these is his correspondence criterion of truth, which states that a representation is true only if it corresponds to an object as it exists apart from consciousness. This criterion is one of the general premises of Schulze's skepticism, providing the basis for his conclusion that we cannot have knowledge of things-in-themselves. Thus Schulze argues that since we cannot get outside our own representations to compare them against the object in itself, we cannot know reality. Schulze also applies this criterion in his critique of Kant and Reinhold, accusing them of 'formalism' and 'subjectivism' because they cannot satisfy it. But it is just this criterion of truth that Kant questions in the transcendental deduction. One of the central arguments of the deduction is that there is no room for skepticism if the correspondence criterion is replaced by that of synthesis. It is a major weakness of Schulze's polemic, and his skepticism in general, that he fails to treat this argument.

A second dogmatic presupposition of Schulze's skepticism is his belief in the existence of things-in-themselves. A radical skeptic, or a consistent critical philosopher, should question this belief, however. But this would render absurd one of the main articles of Schulze's skepticism—that there has not been knowledge of things-in-themselves—simply because there would not be any things-in-themselves to know.

Yet a third unwarranted presupposition of Schulze's skepticism is that there are immediate facts of consciousness. A critical philosopher will want to question this naive assumption on the grounds that all representations must be conceptualized before they even enter consciousness. Indeed, all the arguments that Kant brings against Jacobi's immediate intuitions apply *mutatis mutandis* to Schulze's so-called facts.

The weaknesses of Schulze's skepticism left the philosopher succeeding him at a fateful crossroads. Either he could develop a more rigorous critical philosophy, defining its second-order discourse, eliminating transcendent entities, and banishing all psychologistic language; or he could advance a more radical skepticism, which would question the existence of things-in-themselves and deny the immediacy of the facts of consciousness, and which would challenge the applicability of the Kantian concept to experience. Of course, the most daring—and paradoxical—step forward would be to follow both these paths to their bitter end. Such was the destiny of Schulze's successor, Salomon Maimon.

Chapter 10

Maimon's Critical Philosophy

10.1. Maimon's Historical Significance and the Question of the Unity of His Thought

On April 7, 1789, only one day before Reinhold completed his *Versuch,* and nearly one year before the publication of Kant's third *Kritik,* Marcus Herz, an old student and friend of Kant, sent his former teacher a weighty parcel. The parcel contained a large manuscript written by a friend of Herz's, which purported to be a critical commentary on the first *Kritik.* This manuscript was undoubtedly curious: written in crude German, it had no systematic order; it was also self-reflexive, containing a large commentary upon itself. Nonetheless, Herz had the greatest confidence in its contents. In a covering letter Herz asked Kant to read the manuscript, recommending it to him and hoping it would receive his blessing before publication. Kant, who was sixty-six, in failing health, and eager to finish the third *Kritik,* nearly returned the parcel, citing his age and health as an excuse. After a glance, however, he was so convinced of the quality of the manuscript that he felt compelled to read through several sections and to write a lengthy reply. In his return letter to Herz, written May 26, 1789, Kant gave this verdict on the manuscript: "... but a glance soon enabled me to recognize its merits and to see not only that none of my opponents had understood me so well, but that very few could claim so much penetration and subtlety of mind in profound inquiries of this sort."[1]

The author of this strange manuscript was himself a very strange character. A Polish-Russian Jew, in fact, a rabbi, he came from the most humble circumstances and was then leading a precarious existence in Berlin. Having never received a university education, his only philosophical training came from the Talmudic tradition. His native language was an almost incomprehensible combination of Hebrew, Lithuanian, Yiddish, and Polish, so that upon his arrival in Berlin only such a skilled linguist as Mendelssohn could understand him. His life had been a long tale of woe: he had lived in constant poverty; he had a broken marriage behind him; he was exiled from his community because of his unorthodoxy; and for several years he was even a wandering beggar. Understandably, he was a man of few social graces. He was crude, naive, and simple, and frequently embarrassingly outspoken in expressing his radical views. Since he often drank away his misery, he spent most of his time in taverns, where he would write his philosophy on wobbly tables, and where anyone could buy his amusing conversation for a few drinks. In short, this character was the Rameau's nephew of eighteenth-century Berlin. But we must not forget: he was also the man whom Kant regarded as his best critic. This was Salomon ben Joshua, or as he liked to call himself in honor of Moses Maimonides, the twelfth-century Spanish-Jewish philosopher, Salomon Maimon.

The title of Maimon's extraordinary manuscript is *Versuch über die Transcendentalphilosophie*, a work of the first importance for the history of post-Kantian idealism. To study Fichte, Schelling, or Hegel without having read Maimon's *Versuch* is like studying Kant without having read Hume's *Treatise*. Just as Kant was awakened by Hume's skepticism, so Fichte, Schelling, and Hegel were challenged by Maimon's skepticism. What shook them out of their Kantian slumbers was Maimon's attack upon the transcendental deduction. According to Maimon, the central question behind the deduction—How do synthetic a priori concepts apply to experience?—could not be resolved on Kantian premises. Kant had created such an unbridgeable dualism between understanding and sensibility that it became impossible for synthetic a priori concepts to correspond to experience. This argument created a new and daunting task for Fichte, Schelling, and Hegel: to find a more plausible solution to the problem of the deduction. Like Kant, they were eager to defend the possibility of synthetic a priori knowledge; but they had to admit Maimon's point that such knowledge is not possible given Kant's dualism.[2]

But Maimon not only raised one of the fundamental problems of post-Kantian idealism: he also proposed the generally accepted solution to that problem. According to his *Versuch*, the critical philosophy can resolve the problem of the deduction only if it incorporates some of the basic themes of the metaphysical tradition. If synthetic a priori concepts are to apply to experience, then it is necessary to postulate Leibniz's and Malebranche's idea of an infinite understanding that is present within our finite understanding and that creates not only the form but also the content of experience. Only such an idea resolves the problem of the deduction, Maimon argues, because it alone surmounts Kant's problematic dualism.

This theory of Maimon's had a remarkable impact upon Fichte, Schelling, and Hegel, who all accepted the main principle behind it. Thanks to Maimon, the Kantian transcendental ego acquired a new metaphysical status: it became a single universal subject present within the consciousness of every individual, unifying the finite subject and object. Maimon's infinite understanding is thus the forerunner of Fichte's *Ich* and Hegel's *Geist.*

Maimon's defense of the metaphysical tradition in his *Versuch* began a new chapter in the history of post-Kantian philosophy. It marks the decisive transition from critical to speculative idealism.[3] What characterizes Fichte's, Schelling's, and Hegel's speculative idealism in contrast to Kant's critical idealism is the recurrence of metaphysical ideas from the rationalist tradition. What Kant forbade as a violation of the limits of human knowledge, Fichte, Schelling, and Hegel saw as a necessity of the critical philosophy itself. Now Maimon was the crucial figure behind this transformation. By reviving metaphysical ideas from within the problematic of the critical philosophy, he gave them a new legitimacy and opened up the possibility for a critical resurrection of metaphysics.

Although Maimon's historical importance is generally recognized and is a matter beyond dispute, the same cannot be said about the proper interpretation of his philosophy. Maimon's philosophy is notoriously obscure, and, despite generations of interpretation, there is no unanimity on the most basic issues. The difficulty of interpreting Maimon stems in part from his obscurity, in part from some important changes in his views, and most of all from the very structure of his philosophy. In his *Lebensgeschichte* Maimon describes the *Versuch* as a *Koalitionsystem,* which is indeed a fitting description of his thought as a whole.[4] His philosophy is an apparently paradoxical coalition of rationalism, skepticism, and criticism. Whether these seemingly conflicting elements cohere, and if so how, is the central problem of interpreting Maimon.

The problem of the coherence of Maimon's thought largely boils down to the issue of whether he finds a critical middle path between the extremes of skepticism and dogmatism or in the end is caught in this familiar dilemma. This issue is plainly vital to understanding the general aim of Maimon's philosophy. If it ends with this dilemma, then its purpose is to attack Kant; but if it finds a middle path, then its aim is to reconstruct Kant. Despite the importance of this issue, there is very little agreement about the interpretation of Maimon.[5] It is still an unsolved question whether Maimon wanted to destroy Kant or to save him.

While providing the reader with a general introduction into each aspect of Maimon's *Koalitionsystem,* I will also attempt in the present chapter to sketch a solution to the problem of the inner unity of Maimon's thought. I shall argue that there is indeed a coherence to Maimon's philosophy, and that he does formulate a critical middle path between skepticism and dogmatism. It is necessary to acknowledge, however, that Maimon never carefully elaborated the pivotal ideas that gave his thought its consistency and systematic structure. Like so much in his philosophy, these ideas remained little more than suggestions. It fell to Fichte, Maimon's great successor, to develop their full implications.

10.2. Maimon's Skepticism

In his *Philosophischer Briefwechsel* Maimon makes a revealing statement about his central concern in philosophy.[6] Replying to Reinhold's demand for a first principle, Maimon declares that his primary interest in philosophy is not in finding principles that systematize all our knowledge, but in determining whether these principles are true. What matters to him is not 'the formal excellence' of a principle, whether it is clear, distinct, and systematizes all our knowledge, but its 'material truth', whether it applies to or corresponds with the facts. Thus the most important question the philosopher can raise is, in Maimon's view, *quid facti?*—What fact makes a principle true?

Maimon's skepticism is the direct result of this philosophical concern. According to Maimon, the skeptic is a philosopher whose primary interest is the truth rather than the formal virtues of a principle. What distinguishes the skeptic from the critical philosopher, he writes in his *Streifereien*, is the fact that the skeptic always raises the question *quid facti?*[7] Whereas the task of the critical philosopher is to discover the necessary conditions under which synthetic a priori concepts apply to experience, the job of the skeptic is to determine whether these conditions in fact obtain.

The central thesis of Maimon's skepticism is that there cannot be synthetic a priori knowledge of experience. Applying his skeptical *quid facti* to the critical philosophy, Maimon raises the question of whether there is any evidence that Kant's synthetic a priori principles apply to sense intuitions. He answers this question with a clear and decisive "No." All the evidence of our senses, he argues as did Hume, shows us only a constant conjunction between distinct events but never any universal and necessary connections. Like Schulze, Maimon falls under the spell of Hume's skepticism, doubting whether Kant ever rescues the possibility of natural science from Hume's doubts. His skepticism, no less than Schulze's, is a Humean counterattack on Kant.

The main target of Maimon's skepticism is Kant's transcendental deduction. Like Schulze, Maimon maintains that the deduction is a *petitio principii*, presupposing precisely what Hume calls into question.[8] According to Maimon's interpretation, the deduction attempts to demonstrate that synthetic a priori principles are a necessary condition of possible experience, where 'experience' is understood as the universal and necessary connection between distinct representations and not only as the contingent constant conjunction between them. Although Maimon is willing to admit the argument of the deduction, that possible experience requires the application of the categories, he still disputes its premise, that there is possible experience. If we closely examine our sense impressions, he claims, then all we find are contingent constant conjunctions. Maimon puts the problem this way: Kant answers the question *quid juris?* Under what conditions do synthetic a priori principles apply to nature? But that still leaves the question *quid facti?* Are these conditions in fact the case?

Maimon's argument that the transcendental deduction is a *petitio principii* still leaves open the possibility that synthetic a priori principles apply to experience. Maimon has only questioned this premise of the deduction; but he has not refuted it. Nevertheless, his skepticism does not stop here. He has additional arguments that are designed to show that it is impossible to apply synthetic a priori principles to experience. Maimon's main argument is that Kant cannot have a criterion to determine when his synthetic a priori concepts apply to a posteriori intuitions. In other words, he can have no way of knowing when these concepts apply because he has no means to distinguish cases where they apply from those where they do not. Without this criterion, there is no basis for the belief that these concepts ever do apply. For if it is doubtful that they apply in any particular case, it is also doubtful that they apply in general.

To prove his point, Maimon argues that neither experience nor understanding provides a criterion for the application of a priori concepts to a posteriori intuitions.[9] On the one hand, there is nothing in experience itself that tells us when an a priori concept applies to it. A contingent constant conjunction of perceptions is identical in its empirical content to a universal and necessary connection between them; or, as Hume puts it, all the evidence of our senses justifies only the belief that there is a contingent conjunction between events. On the other hand, there is nothing in an a priori concept that tells us when it applies to experience. An a priori concept holds for 'objects in general', to use Kant's terms, and that means that it might apply to any possible object. Since it is so general, the concept simply does not specify which object in particular it applies to in our actual experience. The category of causality, for instance, states only that for any event B there must be some prior event A that precedes it according to a universal and necessary rule. We are left with the problem, however, of determining which events in our actual experience are causes and thus fill the role of the empty variable A. Although any event will have some cause according to the category of causality, it is indeterminate what that cause is. This category leaves open an infinite number of causes for any event, for example, it is as compatible with smoke being the cause of fire as with fire being the cause of smoke.

To consolidate his position, Maimon also argues that Kant has no solution to the problem of applying the categories in the "Schematismus" chapter of the *Kritik*.[10] What allows us to apply a priori concepts to an a posteriori intuition, Kant believes, is the a priori form of inner sense, time. This faculty determines the concept's application by assigning it a temporal significance; for example, the category of cause applies to temporal sequences where the cause is that which precedes and the effect that which follows. Assigned such a temporal significance, the category of causality becomes compatible only with certain sequences, such as, fire is the cause of smoke, and not conversely, since fire always precedes smoke in time. But Maimon replies that this is still not a sufficient criterion. The problem is that all the evidence of my senses does not warrant the application of this category. If I constantly observe fire preceding smoke, this still does not justify applying the category of causality, which attributes a universal and necessary connection between fire and smoke. There is no means, then, of distinguishing cases where there is only a contingent constant conjunction from those where there is a universal and necessary connection. Although Kant is right to think that the application of a category requires knowing its temporal schema, he is wrong to conclude that this is a sufficient condition of its application, since knowing the temporal schema does not justify applying the category.

Closing off all possible escape routes, Maimon claims that Kant's deduction of the individual categories in the "Analogien" brings him no closer to providing a criterion for the application of the categories to experience.[11] In the second analogy, for example, Kant attempts to establish a criterion to distinguish an objective sequence of perceptions from a subjective sequence, where the objective sequence conforms to the category of causality and the subjective sequence does not. This criterion is the irreversibility of a sequence of perceptions. If a sequence of perceptions (A,B) is irreversible, so that perception B must follow A, then it is possible to attribute objectivity to that sequence, so that (A,B) is not only the contingent order of my perceptions, but the order of the events themselves. Kant's argument is then that the irreversible sequence (A,B) conforms to the category of causality. But Maimon points out that this only pushes the problem back another step. Although Kant's argument might be correct—an objective sequence of perceptions is irreversible and falls under the category of causality—that does not solve the problem of how to tell when a sequence of perceptions is irreversible. There is nothing in our experience itself which shows that a sequence of perceptions is irreversible in the sense that representation B *must always* follow A. Again, all that our experience shows us is the constant conjunction of B after A, and that is not sufficient to subsume the sequence under the category of causality. Maimon therefore concludes that the "Analogien" leaves the faculty of judgment without a rule for determining when the category of causality applies to a sequence of perceptions.

In addition to his argument that Kant has no criterion for the application of synthetic a priori concepts to particular cases in experience, Maimon has another important, and much more influential, argument against the possibility of a transcendental deduction. What also prevents the application of a priori concepts to experience, he contends, is Kant's radical dualism between understanding and sensibility.[12] I have already noted the historical significance of this argument; but let us now turn to its logical detail.

It is notorious that Kant divides the understanding and sensibility into two completely independent and heterogeneous faculties. These faculties are independent of each other because the understanding creates a priori concepts that do not derive from sensibility, whereas sensibility receives intuitions that do not come from the understanding. They are also heterogeneous since the understanding is purely intellectual, active, and beyond space and time, while sensibility is purely empirical, passive, and within space and time. According to Maimon, Kant's understanding-sensibility dualism is analogous to Descartes's mind-body dualism, and all the problems of the latter hold *mutatis mutandis* for the former. Although there is no longer a dualism between distinct kinds of being or substance—a thinking mind and an extended body—there is now an equally sharp dualism between faculties within the sphere of consciousness itself. And just as Descartes cannot explain how such independent and heterogeneous substances as the mind and body interact with each other, so Kant cannot account for how such independent and heterogeneous faculties interact with each other.

Now Maimon argues that if understanding and sensibility cannot interact with one another, then it is hardly possible for the a priori concepts of the understanding to apply to the a posteriori intuitions of sensibility. According to Kant himself, a priori concepts apply to experience only if there is the most intimate interaction between understanding and sensibility. Understanding has to act upon sensibility to produce the form of experience ("intuitions without concepts are blind"), while sensibility has to supply its intuitions to give content to the concepts of the understanding ("concepts without intuitions are empty"). But, Maimon asks, how can understanding and sensibility interact with each other in this manner if they are such completely independent and heterogeneous faculties? How can the understanding create an intelligible form out of that which is nonintelligible and formless? How can it bring what is not under its control (the given) under its control? How indeed can its purely spaceless and timeless activity act upon the spatial and temporal world created by the forms of sensibility? All these questions are unanswerable, Maimon claims, given Kant's original dualism. There would be no problem of applying a priori concepts to sensible intuitions if either the understanding created the intuitions of sensibility according to its laws or if sensibility produced the concepts of understanding according to its laws. But Kant rules out both these options at the very beginning. He says that it is as wrong for Leibniz to intellectualize intuitions as it is for Locke to sensualize concepts. If either of these options were correct, though, the whole problem of applying a priori concepts to a posteriori intuitions would not arise in the first place, for the problem is created by the understanding-sensibility dualism. Thus the very dualism that creates the problem of the transcendental deduction, Maimon remarks, prevents the possibility of its solution.

The main result of Maimon's skepticism is that it renews the challenge of skeptical doubt within the context of the critical philosophy itself. According to traditional skepticism, we have reason to doubt our knowledge of the external world because we cannot get outside our own representations to see if they ever correspond to reality as it exists apart from and prior to them. Unlike Schulze, Maimon rightly sees that this standard of truth—the correspondence of a representation with an external object—cannot be applied against the critical philosophy, which expressly denies it, and which places the standard of truth within consciousness itself.[13] Nonetheless, Maimon shows that a new basis for skeptical doubt arises *even if* we adhere to the spirit of the critical philosophy, eliminating all talk of representations corresponding to objects and putting the standard of truth within consciousness itself. Assuming that truth is not the correspondence of representations with an external object but the correspondence between distinct representations, the problem still arises of how such heterogeneous representations as the a priori concepts of understanding and the a priori intuitions of sensibility ever correspond to one another. According to Maimon, the skeptical problem returns simply because there is such an unbridgeable dualism between these kinds of representation. This dualism is insurmountable either because we do not have a criterion for how such distinct representations correspond to one another, or because they derive from such heterogeneous and independent faculties that they cannot interact with one another. As Maimon sums up Kant's predicament in one striking passage from the *Streifereien:* "Philosophy has not been able to build a bridge which makes the transition from the transcendental to the particular possible."[14] It is important to see that Maimon arrives at this pessimistic conclusion by an internal critique of Kant, by remaining true to the standard of knowledge of the critical philosophy. Thus the ultimate—and very threatening—message of Maimon's skepticism is that the critical philosophy cannot solve the problem of knowledge even when formulated in its own terms.[15]

10.3. The Idea of an Infinite Understanding

Now that we have examined one side of Maimon's *Koalitionsystem,* its Humean skepticism, it is time to turn to its other side, its Leibnizian rationalism. This aspect of Maimon's philosophy presents just as great a challenge to Kant as its skepticism. Maimon argues that some of the basic themes of the metaphysical tradition, which Kant tried so hard to discredit, are in fact necessary to the critical philosophy itself. But why does Maimon ever make such a daring claim? Why does he believe that metaphysical themes are necessary to the critical philosophy?

Maimon's defense of the metaphysical tradition begins from where his skepticism left off. According to his skepticism, the whole problem behind the deduction—how can synthetic a priori concepts apply to experience— arises only if we admit Kant's dualism between understanding and sensibility. If, however, we deny this dualism, the problem disappears, since then there will be no need to postulate some mysterious preestablished harmony between totally heterogeneous faculties. Assuming, then, that we deny this dualism, we are left with only two alternatives: either to "sensualize the intellect" with Locke's empiricism or to "intellectualize the senses" with Leibniz's rationalism. Since the first option fails to account for the presence of synthetic a priori principles, which cannot be reduced to mere empirical generalizations, we have no choice but to accept the second.[16] It is therefore necessary to assume with Leibniz and Wolff that the understanding is completely active, the source of the form *and* content of experience. This means that sensibility is not a distinct source of knowledge, as Kant believes, but only a confused form of understanding, as Wolff asserts. This assumption completely resolves the problem of the transcendental deduction, Maimon argues, since a purely active understanding has a complete a priori knowledge of his experience.[17] He is ensured such knowledge because (1) he creates his experience, and (2) the products of his own intellectual activity are perfectly transparent to himself. Hence, Maimon concludes, the only possible solution to the problem of the transcendental deduction comes from Leibnizian-Wolffian metaphysics.

After setting forth this argument, Maimon makes an even more radical move, introducing a daring speculative idea into the critical philosophy. This is the classical idea of the infinite understanding, the *intellectus archetypus,* which creates all objects in the very act of knowing them.[18] It is necessary to postulate such an idea, Maimon claims, as soon as we accept a rationalistic solution to the problem of the transcendental deduction. Once we assume that the understanding creates not only the form, but also the content of experience, then we also have to postulate the existence of an infinite understanding that is present within our finite understanding. For it is only an infinite understanding that has the power to create everything that it knows; experience is plainly given to the finite understanding. So, strictly speaking, it is not we who know things in sense experience, but it is God who knows them through us. This is just a reworking, of course, of the classical metaphysical idea that we know all things in God. Maimon attributes this idea to Plato,[19] but its more immediate sources are Spinoza, Leibniz, and Malebranche.

This postulate of an infinite understanding—provided that it is read as a constitutive principle—commits Maimon to a thoroughgoing metaphysical rationalism. Since this postulate states that all reality is created by an infinite intelligence according to rational laws, it follows that everything will be governed by a rigorous logical necessity. The essence of each particular thing will be perfectly rational, such that all its properties will follow of necessity from it. Although these properties appear to be contingent, they are so only from the limited standpoint of our own finite understanding, which cannot perfectly grasp the essence of things. If, however, we had the infinite understanding of God, then we would see that all these properties follow from the essence of each thing.

This extreme rationalism makes Maimon reconsider the Kantian classification of judgment.[20] If the essence of things is completely rational, then there are ultimately no synthetic a priori judgments and all true judgments will be analytic. Although some a priori judgments will appear to be synthetic, that will be only because we have not fully analyzed their subject terms. If, however, we do completely analyze them, then their predicates will follow of necessity. In other words, for the infinite understanding of God, who creates and perfectly grasps the essence of all things, all judgments will be analytic.

According to Maimon, this new classification of judgments completely solves the Kantian problem of the synthetic a priori—How is there a necessary connection between distinct terms?—by assuming that the syntheticity of certain a priori judgments is ultimately nothing more than their implicit and obscure analyticity. The mysterious X of the transcendental deduction—what binds together the distinct terms into a necessary connection—is then dissolved into a straightforward analytic connection.

One of the more troublesome questions concerning the interpretation of Maimon's philosophy is whether Maimon confers regulative or constitutive status upon the idea of an infinite understanding. Maimon gives vague and conflicting answers to this question, reflecting his own reluctance to make grand metaphysical commitments. In his early *Versuch* (1789) Maimon is ambivalent. At first he says that it is necessary to assume an infinite understanding "at least as a regulative idea."[21] This phrase, enclosed within parentheses, shows his hesitation to commit himself to the existence of an infinite understanding. In the remark to this passage, however, Maimon explicitly states that he attributes 'objective reality' to this idea.[22] But no sooner does he say this than he again becomes plagued by doubts. We must attribute reality not to the idea "considered by itself," he writes, but only to the idea as a "condition of intuition." Maimon then explains that just as it is necessary to attribute reality to the concepts of understanding as conditions of intuition, so it is necessary to do the same to the idea of the infinite understanding insofar as it is a condition of intuition. What he appears to be saying in this obscure passage, then, is that we have no right to attribute reality to the idea itself insofar as it would be a transcendent entity beyond experience, but that we have every right to do so insofar as it is a transcendental condition of experience itself. In this guarded fashion the *Versuch* seems to bestow a constitutive status upon the idea of an infinite understanding.

But a little later, in his *Wörterbuch* (1791), Maimon begins to underplay the constitutive status of the idea.[23] It takes on a more regulative role as a goal of inquiry. The infinite understanding represents that ideal of knowledge where the object is no longer given but completely created. Maimon prescribes such an ideal as a goal of inquiry; but he admits that it is a goal we approach but never attain.

10.4. The Theory of Differentials

Although Maimon's postulate of an infinite understanding provides an interesting solution to the transcendental deduction, it also raises serious problems of its own. The fundamental claim behind the postulate—that the transcendental ego creates not only the form, but also the content of experience—appears to be straightforwardly false. All our ordinary experience seems to belie this claim. What we perceive in our experience, and when we perceive it, seems to be given, independent of our conscious activity. If I open my eyes, for example, then I have no choice in my perception of this desk, this window, these trees and buildings. Everything I see has these qualities and no others quite apart from my will and imagination.

This givenness of my sense experience appears to be confirmed especially by the sui generis nature of sensible phenomena. All the sense qualities of my experience seem to be simple and primitive, irreducible to any intellectual analysis. What distinguishes one sense quality from another—red from blue, sweet from sour, rough from soft—appears to be discernible by the senses alone. The *principium individuationis* of these sense qualities is incomprehensible to the understanding, and so a fortiori cannot be a creation of it. It is indeed precisely this given and irreducible dimension of sense experience that drove Kant away from rationalism in the first place. So if Maimon is to develop a plausible form of metaphysical rationalism, then he has to find some means of resolving this problem.

To Maimon's credit, he is aware of this difficulty and has an answer to it. This is his famous theory of differentials, which is surely one of the most difficult and obscure aspects of Maimon's philosophy. Nonetheless, this theory deserves our closest attention. It is here that Maimon confronts the classical problem of the apparent givenness and irreducibility of sense experience—the stumbling block of all rationalism and idealism—and attempts to resolve it according to idealist and rationalist principles. Clearly, it is only when Maimon has solved this problem that he can claim to have completely closed the gap between understanding and sensibility, and thus to have satisfactorily solved the problem of the transcendental deduction.

The starting point of Maimon's theory of differentials is Kant's discussion of intensive magnitude in the first *Kritik*.[24] According to Kant, the pure matter of sensation, its purely a posteriori element in contrast to its a priori one, consists in an intensive magnitude, which is defined as the degree of intensity with which it affects the senses. This magnitude can be measured on a continuum from zero to infinity, where zero is the pure a priori form and infinity matter apart from all form. Such intensive magnitude, Kant maintains, has to be conceived apart from all extensive magnitude in space and time. Extensive magnitude derives from the a priori forms of intuition, space, and time, and hence does not apply to the purely a posteriori element of sensation. A pure case of intensive magnitude therefore consists in an extensionless point. The matter of sensation is analyzable into such points, which can be augmented or diminished on a continuum to produce a given intensity.

Taking off from Kant's discussion, Maimon suggests that sense qualities are not simple but complex, that is, capable of analysis into more basic units. These units consist in the lowest possible degree of intensity of a sensation, which is the basic element of all consciousness. The addition of these units increases the degree of consciousness, and their subtraction decreases it. We approach such units, Maimon says, by continually diminishing the degree of consciousness of sensation. Since these units are infinitely small, however, the analysis of sensation only approaches but never reaches them. Thus Maimon calls them 'limiting concepts' *(Gränzbegriffe)*.[25]

Although these infinitesimal units are no longer determinable by the senses themselves, they are still exactly determinable by the understanding, Maimon thinks.[26] They are so determinable because it is possible to fix their relationships to one another. It is even possible to set up a differential equation to express their relationship, an equation of the form dx:dy = a:b, which states that x varies with y as a varies with b no matter what the magnitude of x and y. What distinguishes one sense quality from another, Maimon then claims, is the rule for its production or genesis, the rule for the combination or aggregation of its basic units. All the differences between the various sense properties will then be determinable from the differences between their rules of production; and, furthermore, all the relations between sense properties will be determinable from the relations between their rules of production.

What is specific to a sense quality, its *principium individuationis,* is perfectly intelligible to the understanding, then, provided that it can specify 'the rule for its production'. But, Maimon declares, this is what is characteristic of all understanding.[27] To understand an object is to know how it is produced from its simpler elements, or how it becomes what it is through the law of combination of its constituents. Such a concept of the understanding comes straight out of the rationalist tradition that Maimon wants to revive. In his *Von den Kräften des menschlichen Verstandes,* for example, Wolff himself defines the understanding in just such terms: "Nothing more can be thought of a thing other than how it has originated or how it has become what it is. For this reason one understands the essence of a thing when one distinctly conceives how it has become what it is."[28] In adhering to this Wolffian definition of the understanding, Maimon does not surrender Kant's own concept of the understanding: he simply redefines it in Wolffian terms. The Kantian rule of synthesis now becomes the rule of production of an intuition.

Maimon has two uses of the term 'differential', and these two senses are partly responsible for some of the difficulty and confusion surrounding his theory. In one sense the differential is simply the smallest unit of analysis of sensation.[29] In another sense, however, it is the relationship between these units, the rule of their combination.[30] This second sense obviously rests upon a mathematical analogy, and Maimon does not hesitate to bring out these similarities. He likens the differential to the general formula for a differential equation (given above). Just as this equation expresses the precise properties of a specific curve through its analysis into lines and points, so the differential for a sensation expresses its distinguishing characteristic through the rule for its production from simpler units.

What, though, does the theory of differentials have to say about the rational origin and structure of experience? How does it explain the givenness of experience? The differentials or rules for the genesis of a sense quality are not merely comprehensible by the understanding, Maimon says, they are also posited by it. All the various sense qualities are therefore so many products of the laws of the understanding. Hence Maimon writes in a significant passage, "the understanding has the capacity not only *to think* the general relationships between determinate objects of intuition, but also *to determine* objects through relationships."[31] Here Maimon takes a decisive step beyond Kant. The understanding becomes not only a faculty of concepts, but also of intuitions. Despite all Kant's strictures, Maimon has in effect attributed a power of intellectual intuition to the Kantian transcendental ego.

In his *Versuch* Maimon explicitly uses his concept of the differential to explain the genesis of experience. As he states in another important passage, "the understanding brings forth from the relationships between the various differentials the relationships between the sensible objects deriving from them. These differentials of the objects are the so-called *noumena,* and the objects springing from them are the *phenomena.*"[32] Here the concept of the differential takes on the role of the Kantian thing-in-itself: it is the cause of the sensible manifold. But at the same time Maimon reinterprets Kant's distinction between the noumenal and phenomenal. He specifies that these noumena are not entities but principles for the explanation of the origin of sensation: "These noumena are ideas of reason that, as principles for the explanation of the genesis of objects, act according to the rules of the understanding."[33] Hence noumena are, on Maimon's reading, no longer unknowable entities beyond phenomena, but the very laws that govern them.

Of course, in maintaining that sense experience is a construction of the understanding, Maimon does not mean to deny that it still *appears* given and contingent. He wants to explain this phenomena, but without drawing Kant's dualistic conclusions from it. He therefore makes the assumption that sense experience is indeed given and contingent for our conscious sensibility, although it is in fact posited by the subconscious activity of the understanding. We do not see our experience as produced by our understanding, then, simply because we are not conscious of its activity. As Maimon puts this point in the *Versuch:* intuition is *regelmässig* but it is not *regelverständig.*[34] In other words, the given and contingent experience of sensibility is nothing but a confused representation of the understanding. If, however, the philosopher analyzes experience, he will find that its apparently given sense qualities disappear, leaving nothing but the clear and distinct ideas of the understanding. Here Maimon adumbrates the distinction between the empirical standpoint of ordinary consciousness and the transcendental standpoint of the philosopher, a distinction that became the stock-in-trade of Fichte, Schelling, and Hegel.

The theory of differentials expands the role of the Kantian understanding in another direction. The understanding is now not only a faculty of intuition but also of ideas. In more Kantian terms, not only reason but also the understanding seeks the unconditioned for the series of conditions. Hence, deliberately increasing the number and kind of Kantian ideas, Maimon calls his differentials 'ideas of the understanding' *(Verstandesideen)*.[35] These are not only ideas of reason *(Vernunftideen)* that seek the unconditioned for concepts of understanding, he says, but there are also ideas of the understanding that seek the unconditioned for elements of sensation. Whereas the ideas of reason strive for the most complete *synthesis* of representations, and thus begin with concepts of the understanding, the ideas of the understanding strive for the most complete *analysis* of representation, and thus begin with the intuitions of sensibility.[36] We are allowed to make this distinction in ideas, Maimon argues, since there is a plain difference between the totality of conditions of thought and the totality of intuitions that can be subsumed under thought.[37]

Maimon maintains that this expanded role of the understanding, both as a faculty of perception and as a faculty of ideas, provides the answer to the problem of applying synthetic a priori concepts to a posteriori intuitions. A priori concepts need no longer *per impossible* directly apply to a posteriori intuitions; rather, they apply to their differentials, which are themselves ideas of the understanding.[38] The judgment 'red is different from green', for example, does not directly apply the category of difference to the sensations of red and green, but applies to their differentials, which mediate the category and the sensations. There is, then, no need to invent a preestablished harmony between completely heterogeneous faculties, since the understanding is applying its a priori concepts only to its own subconscious productions. Hence Maimon sees his theory of differentials as a solution to the schematism problem of the first *Kritik*.[39]

One of the persistent problems with Maimon's theory of differentials is that it is difficult to determine whether Maimon thinks that differentials (understood as infinitesimal units) are real entities or mere fictions of thought. Again, he is ambivalent, just as in the case of the infinite understanding. In the remarks to the *Versuch*, he tends toward the view that they are real entities.[40] Thus he distinguishes between the 'symbolic' and 'real' infinite, stating that the differential is a case of the latter. The symbolic infinite denotes a state an object can approach but never attain unless it destroys itself, for example, the point of intersection of two parallel lines. But this concept is only a mathematical fiction, Maimon asserts, so that it does not have any ontological significance. The real infinite, however, signifies an 'indeterminate but determinable' condition which is always smaller or greater than any given magnitude. As an instance of the real infinite the differential does have ontological status, for although it is not presentable in intuition, the real infinite can be thought of as an existing object. Elsewhere in the *Versuch,* Maimon explicitly assumes the existence of the infinitely small, claiming that such an assumption is necessary to avoid the mathematical antinomies.[41] Yet if Maimon commits himself to the existence of differentials in the earlier *Versuch,* he avoids all such ontological commitments in his later writings. According to the *Logik* and *Wörterbuch,* for example, a rigorous transcendental philosophy shuns all transcendent entities, especially infinitesimal ones.

10.5. The New Theory of Space and Time

Although the theory of differentials posits an intelligible structure behind sense qualities, it does not completely close the gap between understanding and experience. There is still another fundamental dimension of experience that Maimon has failed to consider: its appearance in space and time. If, however, Maimon wants to hold that *all* aspects of experience are in principle intelligible, if he wants to develop a transcendental idealism that totally overcomes the dualism between understanding and sensibility, then he has to formulate a theory of space and time that is as rationalistic as it is idealistic. This theory has to defend the following two theses: (1) the idealistic thesis that space and time are a priori forms of consciousness and not objective things; and (2) the rationalistic thesis that they are a priori forms of understanding and not sensibility. Maimon sketches just such a theory in his *Logik* (1794) and *Kritische Untersuchungen* (1797).

Maimon's theory of space and time is a marriage of Kant and Leibniz, a synthesis of Kant's transcendental idealism and Leibniz's rationalism. It accepts Kant's idealistic thesis that space and time are not properties of things-in-themselves, but a priori forms of consciousness, transcendental conditions of experience. But it also upholds Leibniz's rationalistic thesis that space and time are in principle analyzable, reducible to an assemblage of relations, the distances or intervals between things. Hence Maimon rejects Kant's argument that space and time are nondiscursive, forms of sensibility rather than understanding.

Although Maimon adopts Kant's theory that space and time are a priori forms of consciousness, he drastically limits the extent to which they can be a priori. Space and time are not necessary conditions of *any* possible experience, he argues, because it is possible for us to have spaceless sensations.[42] To prove his point, Maimon devises an interesting counterexample to show the possibility of such sensations. Suppose that our visual field consists of nothing more than a perfectly continuous and homogeneous sensation, for example, an infinite expanse of a single tone of red. Such a sensation would not appear in space, Maimon claims, because it lacks the diversity that is required to see things apart from one another. All its points would be utterly identical with one another, so that its extensive magnitude would shrink to nothing. If we do think of a homogeneous and continuous object as existing in space, that is only because we unconsciously think of its relations to other objects outside itself; for instance, we see a river, all of whose segments are alike, as in space only because we relate it to distinct objects on the bank, which enable us to divide it into distinct sections. Assuming, though, that there were no objects beyond the river, all its segments would be indistinguishable, so that it would not appear in space. Maimon then draws a significant anti-Kantian conclusion from this counterexample: since there can be spaceless sensations, space cannot be an a priori form of sensation or perception.

With this counterexample, Maimon does not abandon but merely qualifies Kant's theory about the a priori status of space and time. In his view they are necessary conditions not of sheer *sensation* but of the objectivity of experience.[43] Space and time are necessary to distinguish the private and changing order of our sensations from the order of events themselves. We represent an object as external to us, as independent of our sensations, only because we see it in space as something apart from our body. Thus the role that Kant assigns to the categories in creating an objective framework of experience Maimon also confers upon space and time. Not only the categories, but also space and time are necessary for the analysis and measurement of experience.

In expounding the idealistic component of his theory, Maimon basically reiterates Kant's arguments for the a priori nature of space and time. Although he qualifies the conclusions of these arguments, he only rarely questions them. In defending the rationalistic component of his theory, however, Maimon comes into direct conflict with Kant. Indeed, the greatest challenge to his attempt to revive a rationalistic theory of space and time is Kant's "Aesthetik." One of the main aims of the "Aesthetik" is to refute Leibniz's theory of the conceptual nature of space and time—the very theory that Maimon wants to rehabilitate.

According to Kant's "Aesthetik," space and time are not forms of rational knowledge but limits upon it. They prevent us from acquiring a purely intellectual knowledge not only of things-in-themselves, but also of the form of experience itself. They prohibit such knowledge because they are not categories of the understanding, which are valid for any rational being, but forms of intuition, which are valid only for human beings who possess a passive sensibility. So if all sensibility were removed, space and time would also disappear; a purely rational being, such as Leibniz's God, would thus not know anything of space and time.

In defending his theory of space and time as forms of intuition, Kant advances the following two arguments in the *Kritik* and *Prolegomena*.[44] (1) Space is an irreducibly simple representation that cannot be analyzed into its parts, its particular places. The idea of the whole of space is prior to its parts, since every place has to be recognized and identified in space. This idea must therefore be an intuition or form of sensibility; for if, on the contrary, it were conceptual, then it would be divisible, analyzable into its parts, each of which would be logically prior to it. (2) There are distinctions within space that are apparent only to the senses, and that cannot be expressed through the understanding. Such distinctions are especially evident in the case of incongruous counterparts. Here two objects are completely identical in all their properties, but they are not spatially congruent with one another, for example, my right hand and its image in the mirror. The only distinctions that are expressible through the understanding, though, are distinctions in properties.

In resurrecting Leibniz's theory of space and time, Maimon duly replies to both of these arguments. He attacks Kant's first argument by questioning its underlying premise that space and time are absolute. According to Kant, space and time are absolute in the sense that it is possible to represent them to ourselves even if there is nothing in them; it is for this reason alone that they must be prior to all partial spaces and times and thus not reducible to them.[45] Maimon attacks this premise by invoking the identity of indiscernibles, the very principle that Leibniz once cited against Newton.[46] If space and time were absolute, the argument goes, then they would be perfectly continuous and homogeneous, consisting in nothing but indistinguishable parts, such as points or instants. According to the identity of indiscernibles, however, if two things are indistinguishable—if all their properties are identical—then they really are identical. Hence all the points of space and all the instants of time would collapse into a single point and single instant.[47]

In replying to Kant's argument for incongruous counterparts, Maimon falls back upon another Leibnizian defense: the principle of sufficient reason. This principle simply states, to use Leibniz's words, "that nothing happens without a reason why it should be so rather than otherwise."[48] Just as Leibniz once used this principle against Newton, Maimon now wields it against Kant. The crux of Maimon's reply to Kant is that this principle is violated if two objects differ from each other only spatially and temporally.[49] There must be a sufficient reason for an object having its spatial and temporal position, and that reason consists in either some intrinsic property or its relations to other objects. It contradicts the principle of sufficient reason to postulate two identical objects with identical relations to other objects in two different points of space and time; for there cannot be any reason for them to be in these different spaces and times. Since, however, there must be some property (intrinsic or relational) to account for spatial and temporal position, and since that property is a universal comprehensible by the understanding, it follows that there will always be some conceptual explanation for spatial and temporal position.

According to Maimon, space and time act as signs to show us that our empirical knowledge is still incomplete.[50] If there are two apparently identical objects that appear to differ only spatially and temporally, then that means that we have an insufficient knowledge of their inner nature and that we ought to extend our inquiry. To take their spatial and temporal positions as primitive, as Kant bids us, is to stop the progress of inquiry. It is to admit ignorance precisely when we ought to extend our research. There is indeed a deep irony in Maimon's message here. In his solution to the antinomies in the first *Kritik*, Kant sees the great value of his regulative reading of the principle of pure reason as its prescription to the understanding to expand the limits of empirical inquiry. But, Maimon asks, does not the spirit of Kant's teaching here also demand extending such inquiry into space and time, so that they too become consequences of the properties of objects?

10.6. The Critical Middle Path

Now that we have examined the skeptical and rationalist sides of Maimon's *Koalitionsystem,* it might seem as if his sole aim is to attack Kant. For these two sides of his system confront Kant with a double challenge. His skepticism claims that Kant has no solution to the problem of how synthetic a priori concepts apply to experience; and his rationalism maintains that this problem is resolvable only by the metaphysical idea of an infinite understanding. Hence Kant appears to be presented with the dilemma of skepticism or dogmatism, as if there were no critical middle path between these extremes.

Such an impression would be gravely misleading, however, if it were generalized for all of Maimon's philosophical development. In his later works Maimon's aim is not to criticize Kant's philosophy, but to transform it from within, so that it is purged of all transcendent entities (for example, the thing-in-itself) and remains within its self-imposed limits of possible experience. Although Maimon's philosophy is not visibly critical in its earlier stages, it soon moves in a more critical direction. This movement toward a more thoroughgoing criticism is indeed the most fundamental change in Maimon's thought from 1789 to 1797, the years marking the beginning and end of his works concerning transcendental philosophy. In the *Versuch*

(1789) he presents his *Koalitionsystem* in its straightforward and uncompromising form. We are left with the dilemma of skepticism or dogmatism; and many metaphysical ideas are given a constitutive status. Shortly thereafter, however, in the *Wörterbuch* (1791) and *Streifereien* (1793) Maimon shows a more critical spirit. He eliminates all transcendent entities; he assigns his metaphysical ideas a regulative status; and, most important, he formulates a critical solution to the dilemma of skepticism or dogmatism.

It is in his *Wörterbuch* that Maimon first sketches his critical middle path. Here Maimon sees the notion of the infinite progress of inquiry—the very notion formulated by Kant in the first *Kritik*—as the solution to "a universal antinomy of thought."[51] According to this antinomy, there are two conflicting but necessary requirements of all human thought. On the one hand, thought must have something given, a matter in contrast to its form, since thought essentially consists in the application of a form (a rule of the understanding) to a matter (the given). On the other hand, the perfection of thought demands that nothing be given and material, and that everything is created and pure form. In other words, we human beings have to recognize that our understanding is finite and that something must be given to it; but we are also obliged to perfect our understanding so that it creates everything that it knows like the infinite understanding. Since both of these conflicting demands are inescapable, the only solution is for us *to seek* constantly the perfection of our thought. Reason commands "a progress toward the infinite," Maimon says, where the given continually decreases as thought continually increases. Here the idea of an infinite understanding becomes a goal of inquiry, an ideal that we can approach but never attain. This idea now acquires a strictly regulative status: it does not describe the existence of the *intellectus archetypus,* but it prescribes it as a task for our understanding.

If we more closely examine this passage from the *Wörterbuch*, then we discover that the thesis and antithesis of this antinomy represent dogmatism and skepticism, while the solution, the notion of the infinite progress of inquiry, represents the standpoint of criticism. Assuming that the idea of the infinite understanding resolves the *quid juris* (under what conditions do synthetic a priori concepts apply to experience?), the answer to the *quid facti* (do these conditions in fact hold?) then depends upon whether the infinite understanding exists. This is indeed the main point at issue between the dogmatist and skeptic. The skeptic denies while the dogmatist affirms its existence. This is also, however, the main bone of contention in Maimon's antinomy. Whereas the 'dogmatic' thesis affirms the existence of the infinite understanding by demanding completely active thought, the 'skeptical' antithesis denies its existence by maintaining that there is an unbridgeable gap between understanding and sensibility.

Now Maimon's solution to this antinomy is 'critical' in the classic sense of the word: it denies a common assumption of both the thesis and antithesis by regarding the principle under dispute as regulative and not constitutive. Such, indeed, was Kant's strategy in dealing with the 'mathematical' antinomies in the first *Kritik*. Maimon simply extends Kant's strategy to the *quid facti*, applying it to the idea of the infinite understanding, which here plays a role similar to the Kantian principle of reason. Both dogmatism and skepticism assume that the idea of an infinite understanding has constitutive status; the conflict between them is only whether this idea is true or false. So, in true Kantian fashion, Maimon settles this antinomy by seeing the infinite understanding as a regulative principle, that is, a principle that does not state what exists, but that prescribes it as a task of inquiry. This task is nothing less than the complete explanation of experience, whereby all contingency and givenness disappear—the explanation we would have if our understanding were in fact infinite.

Maimon's notion of the infinite progress of inquiry does successfully avoid the extremes of skepticism and dogmatism. It escapes skepticism since it maintains that, even though we never completely attain our goal of an infinite understanding, we at least gradually and continually approach it. Although the skeptic is of course right to claim that there is an eternal dualism between understanding and sensibility, he fails to realize that the progress of inquiry constantly diminishes, even though it never completely closes, the gap between them. Where the skeptic goes astray, then, is in concluding that if the conditions for the understanding of experience do not exist in toto, they cannot be partially created through the striving of inquiry. Conversely, this concept also avoids the pitfalls of dogmatism. It does not transcend ordinary experience by postulating the existence of the infinite understanding; it simply transforms it into a task of inquiry. Maimon fully admits, therefore, that we finite beings never do attain the status of an infinite understanding, no matter how far we progress in inquiry. So if the error of the skeptic is in thinking that the goal is totally unrealizable, the mistake of the dogmatist is in assuming that it is already achieved. But the truth lies somewhere in the middle: we gradually approach the goal, provided that we continually strive to expand the boundaries of inquiry. Whether we avoid the extremes of skepticism and dogmatism, then, ultimately rests upon our will, our constant efforts to extend inquiry.

Although Maimon's concept of the infinite progress of inquiry does suggest a middle path between dogmatism and skepticism, it is important to see that it also demands a fundamental alteration to the Kantian system. This concept implies that there is only a quantitative, and not a qualitative, dualism between understanding and sensibility, that is, the distinction between them is not in kind, but in degree. The border between them is no longer fixed, but moving, so that one increases as the other decreases. It is even possible to set up a scale from zero to infinity, where zero is the confused and subconscious awareness of sensibility and infinity the clear and self-conscious awareness of the understanding. This is certainly a basic deviation from Kantian principles since, in the first *Kritik,* Kant explicitly maintains that sensibility is a sui generis source of knowledge.[52] Thus, in the end, the Kantian system pays a dear price for the resolution of its outstanding *quid facti:* the abandonment of its absolute dualism between understanding and sensibility. Ironically, it is only by reintroducing the old Leibnizian quantitative dualism into the critical philosophy that Maimon saves it from the dangers of skepticism and dogmatism.

Whatever its merits, Maimon's critical path did not go unnoticed. It is not improbable that it influenced one of the most important post-Kantian idealists: Fichte. Thus in his *Wissenschaftslehre* (1794) Fichte constructs a similar antinomy and resolves it in a similar manner.[53] The only difference between these thinkers is that Maimon sees the infinite understanding as a goal of inquiry, a theoretical ideal, whereas Fichte regards it as a goal of action, a practical or ethical ideal. This similarity raises the question, was Fichte's famous concept of infinite striving a borrowing from Maimon?

10.7. The Elimination of the Thing-in-itself

Nothing better illustrates Maimon's critical spirit than his attempt to eliminate transcendent entities from Kant's philosophy. Maimon never tires of insisting on the purely immanent status of transcendental philosophy, which must refrain from all metaphysical speculation. He stresses that it must remain true to its own standards of knowledge; and that means, simply put, that it must stay within the limits of possible experience, avoiding all commitment to transcendent entities.

But Maimon's ideal of a purely immanent transcendental philosophy soon ran up against a formidable problem: the thing-in-itself. After Jacobi's famous criticism, the specter of the thing-in-itself continued to haunt the critical philosophy. It seemed necessary both to affirm and deny its existence. It was necessary to affirm it in order to explain the origins of experience; and it was necessary to deny it in order to remain within possible experience. Neither Reinhold nor Schulze came close to rescuing Kant from this dire dilemma. Reinhold fell victim to it; and Schulze exploited it as a debating point. It was the destiny of Maimon to disarm the force of Jacobi's criticism and to restore the immanent status of the critical philosophy.

Maimon is in perfect agreement with Jacobi that the thing-in-itself is incompatible with Kant's critical principles.[54] But he even goes a step further than Jacobi: he argues that the thing-in-itself really has no explanatory value, so that it is useless to postulate it in the first place.[55] If the thing-in-itself does explain the origin of experience, then it should explain why just these representations and no others are given to sensibility. Thus if we perceive a house of a specific color and size that is because there is a thing-in-itself that acts upon us in such a manner that it produces a representation of this color and size. But such an explanation is ultimately empty, Maimon claims. It only pushes the problem back another step; for the same question arises all over again for the thing-in-itself: why does it act in just this manner to produce these representations and no others?

What is the critical philosophy to say about the origin of experience, then, if the postulate of the thing-in-itself is empty? Maimon has a firm and simple answer to this question: it should say nothing, nothing at all.[56] If Kant is to stick to his critical principles, then all he may say is that experience is the given and nothing more. He cannot speculate about its cause since that would amount to a transcendent application of the category of causality.

It would also be a serious mistake, Maimon argues, to postulate the thing-in-itself as the object of our representations, as if they are true only if they correspond to it. He accuses Reinhold of making just this mistake when he claims that the thing-in-itself is 'the objective correlate' of the content of representation.[57] Such an assumption is condemned as a deep betrayal of Kant's critical principles. According to Maimon, the spirit of the transcendental deduction requires that truth be explained *within* the realm of consciousness. Truth cannot consist in a representation corresponding to a thing-in-itself, for, as Kant teaches, we cannot get outside our representations to see if such a correspondence holds. It is surely correct in a broad sense to see truth as "the correspondence of a representation with something outside itself." But Maimon insists that we must interpret this phrase according to critical principles. What is 'outside' the representation is not a thing-in-itself, but only a synthesis of representations that are connected according to a rule. The whole is 'outside' particular representations in the sense that it is a whole of which they are only parts. A representation then 'corresponds' with an object when it belongs to a synthesis of representations that are necessarily connected according to a rule.

Maimon's elimination of the thing-in-itself then compels him to reinterpret the subject-object dualism of experience. It is just a fact that there is such a dualism, he says, since there are two kinds of representation in experience: those that are universal and necessary, appearing for everyone alike and apart from our will and imagination; and those that are private and arbitrary, differing from one perceiver to the next and according to will and imagination. The problem is to interpret this dualism according to critical principles without invoking the thing-in-itself as the cause or correlate of the universal and necessary representations. If we strictly adhere to critical principles, Maimon claims, then it is necessary to explain this dualism from within consciousness itself.[58] Rather than placing the subject-object dualism between distinct kinds of entity—a representation and thing-in-itself—it is necessary to place it within consciousness itself, so that it is between distinct kinds of representation. As Maimon sums up this point in his *Logik:* "the *Fundamentum divisionis* is not in the source, but the content of our knowledge."[59] Following this rubric, Maimon then reinterprets the meaning of objectivity and subjectivity. What is 'objective' in our experience is not the thing-in-itself, but the universal and necessary structure imposed upon it by the categories. And what is 'subjective' is not the mind-dependency of all representations, but the variability and arbitrariness of some of them.

Although Maimon is eager to eliminate the thing-in-itself as a transcendent entity, he does recognize that there is a legitimate critical use of this concept. It is possible to use it to determine the limits of our understanding, he thinks, *without* committing ourselves to the existence of some entity.[60] In its critical use the thing-in-itself serves as a regulative principle that prescribes an infinite task for our understanding. This task is nothing less than the complete explanation of experience, or, as Kant understands it in the third *Kritik,* the organization of all specific laws of nature into a complete system. The goal of our understanding is to make all experience conform to its activity, Maimon says, so that nothing is given and contingent, and so that everything conforms to its laws. Construed as such a regulative principle, the thing-in-itself amounts to the noumenon, the purely intelligible entity that would result if this goal were achieved and everything conformed to the activity of the understanding. Hence, in Maimon's terms, knowledge of the thing-in-itself is not knowledge of some mysterious entity behind appearances, but only "the complete knowledge of appearances."

According to Maimon, when Kant talks about the unknowability of the thing-in-itself all that he really means is that the ideal of our understanding—complete knowledge of appearances—is unattainable.[61] To say that we cannot know the thing-in-itself is only to admit that our finite human understanding cannot make all of experience conform to its laws. In one of his frequent mathematical analogies, Maimon compares the thing-in-itself to the imaginary numbers of algebra, such as $\sqrt{2}$. Just as $\sqrt{2}$ does not denote a specific number, so the thing-in-itself does not refer to a specific entity; and just as it is possible to approach but never attain the complete analysis of $\sqrt{2}$ into specific numbers, so it is possible to approach but never attain the complete knowledge of appearances.

In construing the concept of the thing-in-itself as a regulative principle, Maimon is simply keeping to the spirit, if not the letter, of the critical philosophy. According to Kant's transcendental dialectic, dialectical illusion consists in the hypostasis of a regulative principle, that is, the assumption that an ideal of the understanding denotes an entity. In the case of the mathematical antinomies, for example, the regulative principle 'if the conditioned is given, seek the entire series of conditions *as a task*' is read 'if the conditioned is given, then the entire series of conditions is also *given*'. Maimon simply turns this critical doctrine against Kant himself. He thinks that it is no less a dialectical illusion to assume that the thing-in-itself denotes an entity. This too would be to hypostatize a regulative principle, namely the understanding's ideal of the complete explanation of experience.

10.8. Maimon's Transcendental Logic

Maimon's attempt to reconstruct the critical philosophy does not end with his elimination of the thing-in-itself, his postulate of an infinite understanding, or his concept of the infinite progress of inquiry. There is still another area where Maimon struggles to build the critical philosophy upon a new foundation. This is the sphere of logic itself. According to Maimon, the critical philosophy can no longer rely upon traditional Aristotelian logic, which Kant wrongly sees as a perfect and complete science, and which he mistakenly uses as the model for his transcendental logic.[62] Rather, traditional logic is far from the status of a science and has to be brought under the examination of the critique no less than metaphysics.[63] The critical philosophy has to develop nothing less than a new logic, a 'new theory of thought', which is strictly based upon critical principles. Accordingly, Maimon devotes much of his energy to the development of such a logic. Two of his major works, the *Kategorien des Aristoteles* and the *Versuch einer neuen Logik oder Theorie des Denkens,* both of 1794, expound the guidelines of his new theory of thought.

Why, though, a new logic? What has gone wrong with the traditional logic that it stands in such urgent need of reform? Reversing the Kantian picture of logic as a complete and perfect science, Maimon maintains that it is in fact nothing but a shambles. He points out that it is still very far from realizing Kant's own ideal of science in the first *Kritik:* a complete system, organized around and derived from a single principle. Maimon shares Kant's faith in the systematic unity of reason; but he differs from Kant in thinking that the traditional logic does not typify that unity. This failure of the traditional logic is especially apparent from its haphazard method, Maimon says.[64] Rather than deriving all the forms of judgment and syllogism from a single principle, traditional logicians simply abstract these forms from their use in ordinary language. They thus forfeit systematic deduction for an inductive survey, and they surrender the ideal of a system to all the vagaries and contingencies of ordinary language. After abstracting all these forms from ordinary language, all traditional logicians do to organize them is to subsume them under certain general rubrics—although that is no more scientific than the organization of a compendium into chapters and paragraphs. The parts of a systematic whole must not merely be arranged next to one another under general headings, they must also depend on one another in their essential meaning.

The lack of scientific rigor in traditional logic becomes even more evident, Maimon suggests, from its faulty classification of the forms of judgment.[65] While some derivative forms are wrongly seen as basic, some basic forms are falsely regarded as derivative. The hypothetical form is a perfect example of a derivative form that is falsely considered basic. A hypothetical judgment is not a distinct form of judgment, Maimon argues, since it is perfectly reducible to a set of categorical judgments, for example: 'If A is B, then C' is only a shorter version of 'The A that is B is also C'. Another case in point is the disjunctive judgment. This is again nothing more than a single formula to express a number of categorical judgments; hence to say 'A is B, C, or D' is only to say in simplified form 'A can be B, C, or D'. By contrast, the infinite judgment is a good example of a basic form that is wrongly seen as derivative.[66] Infinite judgments are often classified as a form of negative judgments; but they are in fact a form of judgment of their own. Although they have a similar grammatical form, negative and infinite judgments have different logical forms. An infinite judgment is of the form 'A is not B' where neither B nor the negation of B is attributable to A; 'Virtue is not square' where virtue does not fall under the genus of square or nonsquare things (the round and rectangular). A negative judgment is of the same grammatical form 'A is not B'; but here the negation of B is attributable to A, for instance, 'A triangle is not square'.

Maimon's attack on the traditional logic makes him, not surprisingly, extremely critical of Kant's 'metaphysical deduction' in the first *Kritik*.[67] According to Maimon, it is wrong to derive the categories from the forms of judgment since the traditional logic lacks a systematic classification of the forms of judgment. Kant's deduction of the categories is therefore no less 'rhapsodic' than Aristotle's; the mere fact that it is based upon logic does not make it systematic and rigorous since this very logic is neither systematic nor rigorous.

Maimon asserts that the problems of traditional logic—its lack of systematic unity and its sloppy classification of the forms of judgment—arise from a single fundamental error. This is the belief that logic is a completely autonomous science, a science whose principles and concepts have a self-sufficient meaning that does not require explanation in the terms of some other science. Both the Kantian and the Leibnizian-Wolffian schools share this belief, and it is indeed fundamental to the *Aufklärung*'s faith in reason. What makes it so questionable, in Maimon's view, is the fact that logical forms have a latent or hidden metaphysical significance, which cannot be explained within logic itself. This metaphysical dimension is apparent in either of two ways.[68] (1) It is not possible to explain the meaning or function of logical forms without employing metaphysical terms. To affirm or negate, for example, is to posit or not posit the 'truth' or 'reality' of some state of affairs; but 'truth' and 'reality' are obviously metaphysical concepts. (2) The forms of judgment are sometimes misleading, tempting us to make false ontological commitments, such as the hypothetical form of judgment, which suggests that there is some necessary connection between events in experience.

Maimon's insistence on the metaphysical dimension of logical form compels him to reverse the Kantian picture of the relationship between pure and transcendental logic.[69] It is not transcendental logic that presupposes formal logic, but the converse. Transcendental logic should precede formal logic since it explains and criticizes the metaphysical terms and commitments of logical form. Such prior explanation and justification is necessary, Maimon claims, since it alone guarantees that logic does not canonize ontologically misleading forms and incorporate problematic metaphysical definitions of its terms.

Maimon's belief in the priority of transcendental over pure logic had some significant consequences for the development of post-Kantian thought. This belief proved to be one of the basic tenets of Fichte's and Schelling's early methodological writings; and it was indeed one of the presuppositions of Hegel's *Wissenschaft der Logik*. Of course, Maimon was not the first post-Kantian to maintain the priority of transcendental over pure logic. Reinhold also thought that pure logic ought to be derived from transcendental logic.[70] Nonetheless, it is much more likely that it was Maimon, and not Reinhold, who was the greater influence upon his three idealist successors, Fichte, Schelling, and Hegel. Reinhold never goes beyond a few programmatic remarks; but Maimon criticizes the traditional logic in detail, explains why the pure depends upon the transcendental, and devotes almost all his later years to the development of a new logic. It is indeed no accident that Fichte and Schelling held his *Logik* in great esteem.[71]

10.9. The Principle of Determinability

Maimon's demand for a reform of logic, his insistence on the priority of transcendental over formal logic, and his allegiance to the Kantian ideal of science (that is, a system organized around a single principle), all imposed a formidable task upon him. He had to find the single, fundamental guiding principle of transcendental logic. Only when such a principle was found would transcendental philosophy be able to organize all the forms of judgment and syllogism into a complete system. Indeed, only then would transcendental philosophy be built on a firm scientific foundation.

In his later writings Maimon claimed that he had indeed found such a principle. This was his so-called principle of determinability *(Satz der Bestimmbarkeit)*, which he considered of the greatest significance. In his *Briefe an Aenesidemus,* for example, he declares that it is nothing less than the first principle of philosophy and thus the successor to Reinhold's proposition of consciousness.[72] This principle certainly does play several important roles in Maimon's thought: it is the key to his deduction of the categories, the criterion by which he appraises synthetic a priori claims to knowledge, and the basis for his construction of an ideal language.

As the first principle of transcendental logic, the main aim of the principle of determinability is to formulate a criterion of cognitive significance to determine which judgments are either true or false of the real world. This criterion therefore has a double task: to determine which judgments are either true or false (for example, 'Water freezes at zero degrees centigrade'), as opposed to those which are neither true nor false ('Virtue is red'); and to determine which judgments can be true of the real world ('Bachelors are timid'), as opposed to those which are only formally true of all possible worlds ('Bachelors are unmarried men'). In other words, the criterion must distinguish material significance (the capacity of a proposition to be either true or false of the real world) from material insignificance, and material significance from purely formal significance.

Using Maimon's own terms, the purpose of the principle of determinability is to formulate a criterion to distinguish 'real thought' from 'formal' and 'arbitrary' thought.[73] 'Real thought' consists in those judgments which are either true or false of reality, or those which can give us knowledge of it. It differs from 'formal thought' in that it is about the real world and not all possible worlds. Examples of 'formal thought', then, would be laws of logic, such as 'A is A', or analytic judgments, such as 'A triangle is an enclosed three-sided figure'. Both real and formal thought consist in cognitively significant or meaningful judgments; but real thought consists in materially significant judgments, and formal thought in purely formally significant ones. In contrast, real thought differs from 'arbitrary' thought in that its judgments are either true or false, whereas those of arbitrary thought are not. Examples of arbitrary thought are 'The triangle is sweet' and 'My ideas are red'. Both real and arbitrary thought are nonformal; but real thought consists in materially significant, and formal thought in materially insignificant, judgments.

According to Maimon, the need to formulate a principle of 'real thought' or of material significance arises from an inadequacy of pure logic.[74] The basic principle of pure logic, the principle of noncontradiction, determines only the formal possibility of a judgment, that is, whether or not it is self-contradictory. But not all formally possible judgments are also materially possible. There are many judgments that are not self-contradictory but still cannot be true or false of reality, for example, 'This triangle is sweet', 'This concept weighs one ounce'. Hence there also must be a criterion to determine the *material* possibility of a judgment, whether its terms are semantically compatible so that they form a true or false judgment. The formulation of such a criterion is the task of the principle of determinability. So what the principle of noncontradiction is to the form of a judgment, the principle of determinability is to its content; and just as the principle of noncontradiction is the first principle of pure logic, so the principle of determinability is the first principle of transcendental logic.

There are two possible readings of the principle of determinability, depending upon the two possible senses in which there can be a criterion for real thought in contrast to arbitrary thought. Although these two versions of the principle are never distinguished by Maimon, his texts give strong support to each of them.[75] There is a weak and a strong reading. According to the weak reading, the purpose of the principle of determinability is to provide a criterion of semantic compatibility to determine which predicates are attributable to which subjects; in other words, the principle has to distinguish materially significant predications, which are true or false, from materially insignificant predications, which are not true or false. For example, it has to determine why the judgment 'The triangle is sweet' is insignificant and why the judgment 'The triangle is isoceles' is significant. According to the stronger reading, though, the aim of the principle is to provide a criterion of objective knowledge in contrast to subjective perception or the mere association of ideas. This task is identical to Kant's in the *Prolegomena,* when he attempts to find a criterion to distinguish 'judgments of experience' ('The sun warms the sand') from 'judgments of perception' ('I feel the sun warming the sand'). On this reading the principle determines not only the semantic compatibility of terms, but also whether or not a judgment is objectively or subjectively true. Thus there are two classes of arbitrary thought, and the reading of the principle of determinability depends upon which class one has in mind. The first class consists in those judgments which cannot be true or false because their terms are semantically incompatible; the second class consists in those judgments which are true or false, and whose terms are semantically compatible, but which are merely subjective and do not succeed in attributing anything to reality itself. The weak reading contrasts real thought with the first class of arbitrary thought, while the strong reading contrasts it with the second.

The central thesis of Maimon's principle of determinability is that if a judgment is to attain the status of real thought, then its terms must be able to stand in a relation of one-sided or nonreciprocal dependence. One term must be independent and conceivable by itself; and the other term must be dependent upon and conceivable only through the other.[76] In the statement form 'A is B', for example, A must be independent of B, so that it is conceivable without B; but B must be dependent on A, so that it is inconceivable without A. Judging from Maimon's examples, the paradigms of such judgments are those where one term is the genus and the other term one of its species: '2 is a number', 'red is a color'. Although the species is not possible without the genus, the genus is possible without the species.

Maimon insists that such one-sided dependence is the distinctive feature of real thought in contrast to formal or arbitrary thought. In other words, only a judgment whose terms can stand in such a relation is either true or false of reality. Suppose the contrary, Maimon asks us. Consider the two cases where there is not such a one-sided dependence. (1) Assume that both terms are independent of one another, so that A is conceivable without B as B is conceivable without A. In this case there is only arbitrary rather than real thought. Arbitrary thought consists in either a mere association of ideas or a semantically nonsensical combination of terms; hence there is no necessary connection between the terms of its judgments. Consider such examples as 'The triangle is sweet' or 'My ideas are two inches long'. Here the former term is always possible without the latter, and the converse is true as well. (2) Assume that both terms are dependent upon one another, so that A is not possible without B as B is not possible without A. Such mutual or reciprocal dependence is the characteristic quality of formal thought in contrast to real. All judgments of formal thought have such interdependent terms since they are all analytic truths, instances of the law of identity 'A = A'.

Maimon sees the principle of determinability as an explication of Leibniz's principle of sufficient reason.[77] He states that when there is a one-sided dependence of A on B, where A is possible without B, but not conversely, then A is the sufficient reason of B. The terms of the principle of determinability, then, have to be understood as ground and consequent, condition and conditioned, where the independent term is the ground and condition, and the dependent term is the consequent and conditioned. In affirming that the principle of determinability is the criterion for knowledge of reality, Maimon is thus agreeing with Leibniz that the principle of sufficient reason is the principle for knowledge of matters of fact. To assume that we have knowledge of the state of affairs 'A is B', is also to assume that A is the sufficient reason of B; but, Maimon adds, this is also to affirm in turn that A and B depend upon each other as formulated by the principle of determinability.

Maimon calls the terms governed by the principle of determinability the 'determinable' *(Bestimmbare)* and the 'determinate' *(Bestimmte)*. The determinable is the more universal term and the determinate is the more specific one. Alternatively, the determinable term is the whole of which the determinate is only a part.[78] According to the principle of determinability, the determinable or universal term is the independent one, the determinate or specific term the dependent one. The determinable and determinate, then, relate to one another as the genus to its species: although a genus is possible without any particular one of its species, each of its species is not possible without the genus.

In both his *Logik* and *Versuch* Maimon argues that his distinction between determinable and determinate terms is also the proper distinction between subject and predicate.[79] The subject is that term which is independent and determinable, whereas the predicate is that term which is dependent and determinate. In attributing a predicate to a subject, Maimon states, we are specifying or making determinate our notion of the subject. All predication therefore consists in specification or determination. Maimon then divides the principle of determinability into two further statements, one about the subject and the other about the predicate of a subject-predicate judgment.[80] The statement about the subject affirms that the subject is the independent term and conceivable by itself. The statement about the predicate affirms that the predicate is the dependent term and conceivable only through the subject. In advancing this distinction between subject and predicate, Maimon is of course only returning to the earlier metaphysical tradition of Descartes and Spinoza. According to Spinoza's *Ethica*, for example, the subject is that which is conceived in and through itself, while the predicate is that which is conceived in and through the subject.[81]

The principle of determinability is likely to be misleading if we take it at face value. Prima facie it appears to mean that the only true or false judgments consist in one independent and one dependent term, where the independent term is the genus and the dependent term the species. Such a criterion would be absurdly narrow, however, since there are obviously many true or false judgments that do not have this form. If, then, we are not to attribute such an absurd criterion to Maimon, it is necessary to come up with a more charitable reading of his principle of determinability. Upon closer inspection, what Maimon means is this: any true or false judgment *presupposes*, though it does not necessarily *state*, that the subject belongs to the genus of which its predicate is only a species. In other words, the attribution of a predicate to a subject is materially significant only if the genus, to which the predicate belongs, is true of the subject.

According to this more generous reading, Maimon's principle of determinability is not about the grammatical, but the logical, form of a judgment. It does not state that every judgment grammatically has to contain one dependent term (the species) and another independent term (the genus), but it does state that it logically presupposes such terms. All true or false judgments, therefore, must be translatable into a logical form where the subject specifies its genus, and the predicate one species of the genus: 'This is red' ought to be translatable into 'This color is red'. Here the predicate will not be possible without the genus of the subject, although the genus of the subject will be possible without this determinate species. Keeping this purely logical point in mind, we may reformulate the principle of determinability in the following way. If the predicate of a judgment cannot be conceived apart from the genus of the subject, and if the genus of the subject can be conceived apart from the species of the predicate, then the judgment is materially significant or either true or false of the real world. If, contrary to the first condition, the predicate is possible apart from the genus of the subject, then the judgment is not true or false, but only an insignificant concoction of words. For example, the judgment 'This triangle is sweet' is materially insignificant because the predicate 'sweet' is possible without the genus triangle, whereas the judgment 'This triangle is isoceles' is significant because the predicate 'isoceles' is not possible without the genus triangle. And if, contrary to the second condition, the genus of the subject is not possible without the predicate, then there is nothing but a formal tautology that cannot be true of reality, for example, 'This triangle is an enclosed three-sided figure'.

After reformulating the principle of determinability in this manner, it is not difficult to appreciate Maimon's philosophical purpose in developing it. His aim is to construct an ideal language of semantic types or categories, a Leibnizian *characteristica universalis*.[82] Using the principle of determinability as its criterion, this language will determine which predicates are predicable of which subjects, so that it will be able to state all the possible types of judgment that can be true or false of reality. Such an ideal language will consist in a number of chains of predication, where a predicate will become the subject of another predicate, and so on. A chain will begin with the most determinable subjects, those which cannot be the predicates of any further subjects, and it will end with the most determinate predicates, those which cannot be the subjects of any further predicates. Progress along a chain of predication will advance in a more specific determination of the nature of the subject. In accord with the principle of determinability, the subject of a chain will be conceivable without each of its predicates, although none of the predicates will be conceivable apart from the subject. The subject will have several possible predicates, but the predicates will have one, and only one, subject. When it is completed, this language will have determined all the possible types of judgment that can be true or false of reality, and every true or false judgment will be assigned a definite place in the hierarchy of predication. The ultimate types of judgment will be determined by those genera of which all predicates are only species and differentia; these genera will then be the Kantian-style categories. After constructing such an ideal language, Maimon will have realized Kant's ideal of a systematic transcendental philosophy. All the categories will be rigorously and systematically derived from a single principle, the principle of determinability. According to Maimon, Kant failed to find the guiding idea for the construction of such a system; but now, thanks to the principle of determinability, such a principle is finally available.

10.10. Maimon's Controversy with Reinhold

In 1791 K. P. Moritz, a mutual friend of Maimon and Reinhold, traveled from Berlin to Jena and Weimar, carrying with him a copy of Maimon's recently published *Wörterbuch der Philosophie*. Moritz's purpose in bringing this book with him was to reveal Maimon to the Weimar and Jena luminaries. At the time, Maimon was still a puzzle to his Berlin friends.[83] They could not understand him; but they also knew that Kant considered him his best critic. Hence Moritz decided to bring Maimon to the attention of the literary scene in Jena, where he knew that at least one person would be able to understand him. That person was Reinhold, who was reputed to be the definitive expositor of Kant. Moritz duly showed the *Wörterbuch* to Reinhold, who responded in the kindest manner. Reinhold not only promised to review the book for the *Allgemeine Literatur Zeitung*, he also indicated that he would like to enter into a correspondence with Maimon. This was a gesture that Maimon could not ignore. Here was a chance to pit his views against the foremost Kantian of the day. Shortly after Moritz's visit, Maimon wrote Reinhold, eager to prove his superior knowledge of Kant. Thus began one of the most vitriolic exchanges in the history of post-Kantian philosophy.

Maimon and Reinhold's acrimonious correspondence ranges over a number of issues, but perhaps the most important concerns the justification of Reinhold's first principle, the proposition of consciousness. In his opening letter Maimon bluntly tells Reinhold that this principle is vulnerable to skepticism. It cannot answer the simple skeptical question 'How do I know this?' he claims. Of course, this principle is supposed to describe 'a fact of consciousness'. "But," Maimon asks Reinhold, "how do you know that it describes a fact? . . . And, indeed, how do you know that it describes a primary and immediate fact rather than a derived and mediate one?"[84]

Reinhold's response to these aggressive and difficult questions did not satisfy Maimon, who quickly insinuated that his correspondent was being deliberately evasive. In his first reply Reinhold proudly states that his first principle could demonstrate the fundamental beliefs of morality and religion.[85] "But that is not the question," Maimon impatiently answers. "The issue is not whether this principle can demonstrate others, but whether it is true."[86] Reinhold seemed to be forgetting that we might deduce true propositions from false premises. After further attempts by Maimon to pin him down, Reinhold finally states his bottom line: "All philosophy must begin with self-evident facts," he writes, "and these are indemonstrable since they are the basis of all demonstration."[87] But this stance only increased Maimon's exasperation. He again protests that this was not the point. "Of course all philosophy must begin with self-evident facts," he concedes, "but the question is how we know the principle of consciousness expresses such a fact."[88] In the end the debate reached a stalemate. Reinhold assured Maimon that it was just a fact that the proposition of consciousness expresses a fact; and he pleaded that it would be self-defeating for him to justify this. But Maimon dug in his heels and refused to accept Reinhold's assurances, which he regarded as dogmatic.

After such an unproductive and intemperate exchange, it should not be surprising that the correspondence degenerated into mutual recrimination. While Maimon accused Reinhold of evasiveness and highmindedness, Reinhold charged Maimon with willfully misunderstanding him. In a fit of pique, and without Reinhold's consent, Maimon eventually decided to publish their correspondence, leaving it to the public to decide who was right and who was wrong.[89]

Although it ended in deadlock and acrimony, Maimon's controversy with Reinhold raises some important philosophical questions: What value is there in appealing to self-evident principles if they are not self-evident to a skeptic? When does allegiance to first principles become dogmatic, and when does doubt about them become absurd? Most important, is the critical philosophy based on self-evident first principles that establish it as neither dogmatic nor skeptical? Maimon's basic aim was precisely to show that there are no such first principles.[90] He wanted to illustrate how any debate about first principles ends either in dogmatism, Reinhold's appeals to self-evidence, or skepticism, his own persistent questioning. In a long footnote Maimon clearly explains his general position on this issue.[91] A truly critical philosophy has to examine all claims to self-evidence, he insists, because it is always possible that they contain hidden and questionable presuppositions.

Maimon then confesses that he cannot understand how Mendelssohn, Kant, and Reinhold could appeal to the self-evidence of common sense, conscience, or the facts of consciousness. These philosophers swear their allegiance to criticism; but the first demand of criticism is to question all claims to knowledge, including claims to self-evidence.

After their correspondence had broken off, Maimon did not stop thinking about his position vis-à-vis Reinhold. In his later works he was able to clarify and refine his position, adding some of his most important criticisms of the *Elementarphilosophie*. The heat of controversy had even faded enough for Maimon to find some broad points of agreement with his old adversary. In his *Briefe an Aenesidemus* he states that he agrees with Reinhold on two fundamental points.[92] First, they both reject dogmatic metaphysics and insist upon the need for criticism. Second, they both think that Kant has not perfected or completed his plan for a critique of pure reason. It is indeed to Reinhold's great credit, Maimon writes in a rare moment of generosity, that he dismisses the whole troop of dogmatic Kantians who believe—uncritically—that the letter of the *Kritik* is the last word on the critical philosophy itself. Reinhold and Maimon are agreed, then, that criticism is necessary, and that the critical philosophy is not completed by Kant. But here their agreement ends.

Maimon's differences with Reinhold begin with the very basics: he cannot accept Reinhold's conception of the task of criticism. Reinhold misconceives this task from the start, Maimon argues, since he thinks that criticism should find the first principles of knowledge.[93] But, in Maimon's more skeptical view, its primary goal is to criticize these principles. What the critical philosopher wants to know first and foremost is not whether a principle organizes our beliefs, but whether it is true. Reinhold thus gives priority to system building over a more basic duty of the philosopher, the inquiry into truth.

Maimon's disagreements with Reinhold concern not only the conception but also the execution or realization of Kant's critical program. In other words, even if he were to accept Reinhold's contention that the critical philosophy should look for a self-evident first principle, he would reject his argument that the proposition of consciousness is that principle. According to Maimon, the proposition of consciousness cannot be the first principle of the critical philosophy because the concept of representation does not describe what Kant regards as an original or fundamental conscious state.[94] "What would the critical analysis of the concept of representation be?" Maimon asks. If we closely examine the transcendental deduction, he says, then we find that a representation is a conscious state which is part of a synthetic unity of such states—it is connected with them according to a rule. A conscious state then 'represents' an object only if it belongs to such a synthetic unity, for its object is in fact nothing more than the rule of the understanding that connects these distinct states together to form the idea of a single object. Now if we are to follow this critical analysis of a representation—and Reinhold certainly pretends to be following Kant's principles—then it is necessary to drop the belief that representation is an original act of consciousness. If it were an original act, then it would be simple, unanalyzable into others, and all others would be analyzable into terms that included it. In fact, the very opposite is the case: it is a complex act composed of others that are more basic. The most basic act is that of synthesis, which must be present before a conscious state can represent anything. In pointing out the fundamental role of synthesis in the transcendental deduction, Maimon draws attention to a concept previously neglected. Beck and Hegel were to follow his precedent in stressing the importance of this concept.

Maimon's final word on Reinhold's *Elementarphilosophie* is to accuse him of 'dogmatism', the worst sin for any Kantian. Rather than being true to the spirit of the critical philosophy, Reinhold engages in transcendent speculation, reintroducing a metaphysics that Kant would only condemn. A clear example of this speculation, in Maimon's view, is Reinhold's argument that the subject and object are the causes of the form and content of a representation.[95] Since Reinhold himself says that the subject and object themselves cannot be given to any representation, his assumption that they are the causes of representation amounts to a transcendental application of the category of causality. Another even more flagrant example of Reinhold's dogmatism, which Maimon highlights, is his deduction of the thing-in-itself.[96] The main premise behind this deduction—that the content of a representation represents an object which exists apart from it—is condemned as thoroughly uncritical. It assumes that we can *per impossibile* get outside our representations to see if they correspond or mirror things-in-themselves. But this assumption is absurd, Maimon says, and it is totally at odds with the transcendental deduction. According to the deduction, a representation acquires its truth not by conforming to a thing-in-itself that exists apart from it, but by conforming to the rules of synthesis of the understanding. We can thus account for the concept of truth by remaining within the realms of consciousness, so that there is no need to talk as Reinhold does about a representation mirroring or resembling things outside it.

10.11. Maimon versus Schulze

It was only later in his career that Maimon discovered his skeptical contemporary Schulze. At the earliest, *Aenesidemus* appeared on the philosophical scene in April 1792, two years after Maimon's *Versuch* and one year after his *Wörterbuch,* texts in which Maimon had already presented many of his mature views. There can be little doubt, however, that Schulze had a positive influence on Maimon. He forced Maimon to explain his position; and he stimulated him to clarify the aims and discourse of transcendental philosophy in general. In his *Briefe Philalethes an Aenesidemus* (1794) Maimon duly paid homage to Schulze, writing a reply to *Aenesidemus*. In this epistolary commentary, Philalethes (Maimon) writes to Aenesidemus (Schulze) to express his agreements and disagreements with Aenesidemus' skepticism.

The historical significance of Maimon's *Briefe* lies in its explanation of the logic of Kant's transcendental discourse. More than any other work of this period it clarifies the second-order nature of Kant's discourse and contrasts it to the first-order concerns of psychology and metaphysics. Many of the early criticisms of Kant rested upon a psychologistic or metaphysical misconception of his project, and Maimon deserves credit for seeing through these misinterpretations.

The fundamental point at issue between Maimon and Schulze concerns the very possibility of a transcendental philosophy. Schulze attacks and Maimon defends this possibility. According to Schulze, transcendental philosophy is a self-defeating enterprise since it cannot escape a vicious circle. In order to determine the origins and conditions of knowledge, it has to apply the principle of causality, which is the very principle it must question.

To Maimon, this objection reveals a misunderstanding of the aims of transcendental philosophy.[97] Its business is not to speculate about the causes or origins of knowledge, but only to analyze and systematize the content of knowledge; it does not examine the causal conditions of experience, but the truth conditions of our judgments about it. A transcendental philosophy is thus a strictly second-order investigation: it is not about things—even if they are the subject and object of knowledge—but about our synthetic a priori knowledge of things. Hence, Maimon concludes, Schulze's circle is escapable: the transcendental philosopher does not have to commit himself to the principle of causality in order to get his inquiry off the ground.

Maimon does not deny that Kant uses psychological language in the *Kritik*. But he interprets it as a metaphor for the logical conditions of synthetic a priori knowledge.[98] According to Maimon, Kant does not see the mind as the cause of knowledge any more than Newton regards gravity as the cause of attraction of bodies. Just as Newton's law of gravity is nothing more than a general concept for more specific laws, so Kant's notion of mind is nothing more than a general concept for the various forms of knowledge. All Kant's talk about faculties is not a literal description of mental powers, but a metaphor to express logical possibilities.

On similar grounds Maimon objects to Schulze's argument against the

Kantian transcendental subject.[99] Schulze's claim that this subject cannot be conceived as the cause of experience—whether it be a noumenon, thing-in-itself, or idea—is beside the point. Kant intends to explain not the origin of experience but the truth conditions of synthetic a priori judgments. Moreover, Schulze falsely restricts Kant's options by assuming that the disjunction 'noumenon, thing-in-itself, or idea' is exhaustive. The transcendental subject is none of these things because it is no entity at all. Rather, it is nothing more than the formal unity of all representations, the necessary condition of having consciousness at all.

To complete his defense of the critical philosophy, Maimon turns to one of the most challenging parts of Schulze's polemic: his critique of the refutation of idealism. His reply is of historical interest as the first defense of Kant's refutation in post-Kantian literature.[100] According to Maimon, Schulze's argument that there is no difference between Kant's and Berkeley's idealism—save the inconsistent postulate of the thing-in-itself—is a non sequitur. Although Kant and Berkeley are both idealists in denying the existence of things independent of consciousness, it does not follow that they share the same idealism. Thus if Kant wants to distinguish his idealism from Berkeley's, he does not have to prove the existence of things apart from consciousness. Rather, he need only point out that there is an important difference between two classes of representation. There are subjective representations, which are private and arbitrary, differing from one perceiver to the next, such as sensations of color, heat, and sound; and there are objective representations, universal and necessary, the conditions for any possible experience for anyone. According to Maimon's interpretation, what Kant is trying to do in his refutation is to show how space and time belong to the second and not the first class of representation. Kant rejects Berkeley's idealism because it conflates the second with the first class, seeing space and time as arbitrary and private as the sensations of color and heat. The difference between Kant's and Berkeley's idealism is now clear: Kant distinguishes, but Berkeley conflates, objective and subjective representations.

Aenesidemus was a great challenge to Maimon largely because it forced him to defend the originality of his own skepticism. Prima facie his skepticism was the same as Schulze's: both were meta-critical and limited knowledge to experience. What, then, was distinctive about Maimon's position? Maimon could confidently answer this question with the claim that his skepticism was more consistent and radical than Schulze's, questioning premises that Schulze presupposed. Thus he called his position 'critical skepticism' to contrast it with Schulze's 'dogmatic skepticism'. There are three respects in which Schulze's skepticism remained 'dogmatic', in Maimon's view. First, Schulze was a naive empiricist who believed in 'facts of consciousness', although the existence of such facts is questionable, since there is no clear borderline between experience and theory, fact and interpretation. Second, Schulze adhered to a correspondence theory of truth without questioning it and without noting Kant's criticism of it in the transcendental deduction. Third, Schulze presupposed a dogmatic concept of the thing-in-itself, as if it denotes a kind of entity. In admitting that we might acquire knowledge of things-in-themselves with the advance of the sciences, Schulze only revealed his naive belief in the reality of the thing-in-itself. On all these grounds Maimon felt justified in concluding that Schulze's skepticism was more dogmatic than his own.

Conclusion

IF WE LOOK BACK over the dramatic philosophical developments of the 1780s and early 1790s, it is difficult to resist the conclusion that the *Aufklärung* faced an insurmountable crisis. There seemed to be no rescue in sight for the tottering authority of reason. No one seemed able to avoid Jacobi's dilemma. Mendelssohn's metaphysics was vulnerable to the objections of Kant's *Kritik;* Kant's practical faith seemed inadequate after all the attacks upon it; and Herder's vitalism, though new and promising, could not provide cogent replies to Kant's weighty objections against teleology. Hence Jacobi's dilemma was just as much a challenge in the 1790s as it was in the summer of 1785, when Jacobi first thrust it upon the philosophical scene. As late as the early 1790s it seemed necessary to choose between a rational nihilism and an irrational fideism.

The fate of reason seemed to be all the more dire in the mid-1790s, after the defeat of Reinhold's *Elementarphilosophie*. Reinhold had drawn attention to the pressing need for reform in epistemology; and he had persuaded all but the most obdurant Kantians that the critical philosophy required a new foundation. Almost everyone had agreed with him that the critical philosophy would have a safe foundation only when it had been built upon a single, self-evident first principle. But if Reinhold had convinced almost everyone that the critical philosophy stood in need of such a foundation, he had convinced almost no one that the *Elementarphilosophie* provided that foundation. The attacks of Schulze and Maimon had shown, at the least, that the proposition of consciousness could not be the first principle of philosophy. More serious, Reinhold's demand for a self-evident first principle, though legitimate, seemed unsatisfiable. Maimon had argued that any first principle would be vulnerable to skeptical questioning; and Schulze had contended that it would be as unknowable as the thing-in-itself. Thus, the demise of the *Elementarphilosophie* had very serious repercussions for the authority of reason. Without a first principle, there seemed to be no middle path between the extremes of dogmatism and skepticism. During the mid-1790s, then, all criticism tended toward a meta-critical skepticism, and no one seemed capable of reversing the trend.

The final blow to the authority of reason came in the early 1790s with the resurgence of Humean skepticism and the disillusionment with the Kantian transcendental deduction. The criticisms of the deduction by Reinhold, Schulze, Maimon, Platner, Ulrich, and Tittel all came to the same disturbing conclusion: Kant had not refuted Hume's doubts about causality. There was no apparent justification for the application of the principle of sufficient reason to experience. Hence the champions of reason had no basis for their proud belief that it could explain everything in nature. In referring to the importance of Hume's problem in the *Prolegomena*, Kant had opened a veritable Pandora's box. No one was willing to lapse into some precritical dogmatic slumber; but at the same time it did not seem as if Kant had any cure for the nightmare that had awakened him. Of course, the *Kritik* had transformed the problem of knowledge; but it had not solved it. The problem was no longer one of showing how such distinct entities as a mental representation and a physical object could correspond with each other. Rather, it was one of showing how such heterogeneous representations as an a priori concept and an a posteriori intuition of sensibility could correspond with each other. This dualism, though new, was no more bridgeable. Thus the grand postulate of the correspondence between thought and being, which was as important for the Enlightenment in the eighteenth century as it was for metaphysical rationalism in the seventeenth century, had been shattered.

Yet if the prospects for reason looked bleak at the end of the eighteenth century, they were not hopeless. While the beginning of the 1790s witnessed a formidable challenge to the authority of reason, at its shakiest point since its assertion by Descartes nearly two centuries before, there were also forces working silently toward its resurrection. These forces were indeed so strong that by the end of the 1790s there was a revival of metaphysics, comparable to the vigorous and widespread metaphysical speculation of the mid-seventeenth century. By the year 1800 there arose the absolute idealism of Hegel and Hölderlin, the *Naturphilosophie* of Schelling and Steffans, the logical realism of Bardili and Reinhold, and the mystical pantheism of Goethe, Novalis, and Schleiermacher. This reinstatement of metaphysics brought with it a daring reassertion of the claims of reason, one so bold that it surpassed the most confident claims of Leibniz, Wolff, Spinoza, and Descartes. Almost all these new metaphysical systems claim that reason is in possession of self-evident first principles, that it gives us knowledge of reality in itself, and that it provides us with a foundation for our essential moral, religious, and political beliefs. They sharply criticize the *Aufklärung* for having misconceived the nature of reason; but they do not depart from its most essential belief: the authority of reason.

How do we explain this Phoenix-like revival of metaphysics, this bewildering reassertion of the claims of reason in the face of its imminent collapse? If the resurrection of metaphysics in the late 1790s seems miraculous, it was also an utter necessity. There was one, and only one, escape from the dangers and difficulties posed by Kant's philosophy, and that was the reawakening of the slumbering but not comatose spirit of metaphysics. This was already clear in a number of ways by the early 1790s. First, Mendelssohn's, Flatt's, Schulze's, and Wizenmann's polemics against Kant's doctrine of practical faith reached the conclusion that the only tenable defense of faith would again have to come from the theoretical reason of metaphysics rather than the practical reason of the moral law. Second, the Wolffian theory of the objectivity of logic, which even Kant did not deny, provided a plausible path out of the mire of Kantian solipsism; for, even if our sense impressions were perceiver-dependent, the laws of logic would still be valid for being in general. Third, Ulrich and Maimon had put forward powerful arguments to the effect that the critical philosophy could solve its internal problems only by incorporating a metaphysics within itself. According to Maimon, only the idea of an infinite understanding could bridge the gap between understanding and sensibility; and according to Ulrich, only a transcendent application of the categories of causality and substance could explain the origin of experience. Fourth and last, Hamann and Jacobi had suggested that there was a higher intuitive form of knowledge that was not subject to all the restrictions which Kant had imposed upon discursive knowledge in the first *Kritik*. All the critical results of the *Kritik* could then be recognized—and circumvented—simply by appealing to this new form of knowledge. Later, Schelling and Hegel elevate this knowledge into the new organon of metaphysics, baptizing it 'intellectual intuition'.

Such were the forces working toward the resurrection of metaphysics in the late 1790s, which served to vindicate reason after the crisis of the early 1790s. But it is important to see that these forces were only contributing factors, which cannot provide a full explanation of the revival of metaphysics at the beginning of the nineteenth century. The mystery still remains: why did metaphysics seem a necessity in 1800 after Kant had declared it an impossibility in 1780? This is an important question, and indeed the central one for understanding the rise of post-Kantian idealism at the beginning of the nineteenth century. But to answer it would require another volume. Here, we have only been witnesses to the crisis of reason at the end of the eighteenth century; how that crisis was eventually resolved is another story.

Notes
Bibliography
Index

Notes

The full title and details of all works are cited in the bibliography. For collected editions, roman numerals refer to volume numbers, arabic numerals to page numbers. Subdivisions within a volume or edition are indicated by an arabic numeral following the volume. Thus I/2 refers to volume I, "Stück" or "Abteilung" 2.

Citations of Kant's first *Kritik* refer to the page numbers of the first or second editions, "A" to the first and "B" to the second. All other citations of Kant's works refer to the Akademie edition. *KrV* stands for *Kritik der reinen Vernunft,* and *KpV* for *Kritik der praktischen Vernunft.*

The following abbreviations are used for eighteenth-century journals:

Allgemeine deutsche Bibliothek	*AdB*
Allgemeine Literatur Zeitung	*ALZ*
Berlinische Monatsschrift	*BM*
Deutsches Museum	*DM*
Gothaische gelehrte Zeitung	*GgZ*
Göttingen gelehrte Anzeige	*GgA*
Hessische Beyträge zur Gelehrsamkeit und Kunst	*HB*
Neue Allgemeine deutsche Bibliothek	*NAdB*
Neue philosophisches Magazin	*NpM*
Philosophisches Archiv	*PA*
Philosophisches Magazin	*PM*
Philosophische Bibliothek	*PB*
Teutsche Merkur	*TM*
Tübinger gelehrte Anzeige	*TgA*

Introduction

1. It would be incorrect to assume that these questions arose as a result of the German reaction to the French revolution. The debates surrounding Kant's and Spinoza's philosophy, which first raised the problem of the authority of reason, took place before the onset of the revolution in July 1789. The pantheism controversy

reached its height in the summer of 1785; and the offensive against Kant's philosophy was well under way by 1788. However, the later reaction against the revolution did intensify the hostile reception of Kant's philosophy.

2. Concerning early attitudes toward Spinoza's philosophy in Germany, see Mauthner, *Atheismus,* III, 170–173; Hettner, *Geschichte,* I, 34–38; and Grunwald, *Spinoza,* pp. 45–48. This interpretation of Spinoza will be further discussed in section 3.4.

3. Kant, *KrV,* A, xx; B, xiii, xviii.

4. Hume, *Treatise,* pp. 263–274.

5. This problem will be discussed in more detail in section 2.4.

6. To quote Nietzsche; see *Werke,* XII, 125. All translations from the German are my own.

7. This will be discussed in more detail in sections 2.1 and 7.3.

8. Thus Heine in his *Geschichte,* Werke, VIII, 201–202.

9. See Gay, *Enlightenment,* I, 130ff.

10. See Kant, *KrV,* A, 12.

11. See, for example, Hamann, *Werke,* III, 189, 277; Herder, *Werke,* XXI, 18; Schlegel, *Werke,* II, 173; Schulze, *Aenesidemus,* p. 34; and Platner, *Aphorismen* (1793), par. 706.

12. Kant, *KrV,* B, 884.

13. Ibid., A, xi.

14. Kant did begin to answer this question in some of the late notes of his *Opus Postumum;* see Kant, *Werke,* XXI, 81–100. But these scattered and inchoate remarks do not amount to an explicit and general meta-critical theory.

15. This point has been well argued by Beck in his "Toward a Meta-Critique of Pure Reason," in *Essays on Kant and Hume,* pp. 20–37.

16. See Hamann, *Werke,* III, 284.

17. See Jacobi, *Werke,* IV/1, 230–253; IV/2, 125–162.

18. Concerning Hamann's thought on sexuality, see O'Flaherty, *Hamann,* pp. 39–42.

19. See Herder, *Werke,* VIII, 179, 185.

20. See Cassirer, *Enlightenment,* p. 22.

21. This is, of course, only one reading, and a very simplified one, of Kant's argument. I have cast Kant's argument in this form only to make the reaction of his contemporaries more intelligible.

22. These arguments will be discussed in more detail in section 10.2.

23. See section 5.3.

1. Kant, Hamann, and the Rise of the *Sturm und Drang*

1. See Goethe, *Werke,* IX, 514ff.

2. Concerning Hamann's influence on Herder, see Dobbek, *Herders Jugendzeit,* pp. 127–136; Adler, *Der junge Herder,* pp. 59–69; and Clark, *Herder,* pp. 2–4, 156–162.

3. Concerning Schelling's reception of Hamann, see Gründer, *Hamann Forschung,* pp. 40–41.

4. See Schlegel, "Hamann als Philosoph," *DM* 3 (1813), 35–52.

5. Hegel, "Hamanns Schriften," in *Werke*, XI, 275.

6. Concerning Hamann's influence on Kierkegaard, see Lowrie, *A Short Life of Kierkegaard*, pp. 108–109, 115–116. Also see Kierkegaard's tribute to Hamann in *Concluding Unscientific Postscript*, p. 224.

7. Concerning Hamann's relation to Luther, see Blanke, "Hamann und Luther," in Wild, *Hamann*, pp. 146–172.

8. The only complete and detailed account of their relationship is Weber, *Hamann und Kant* (1908). But this account is now out of date, having appeared before the critical edition of Hamann's works and correspondence.

9. Concerning Rousseau's influence on the *Sturm und Drang*, see Hettner, *Geschichte*, II, 9ff.

10. The nature of Hamann's mission is still unknown. The accepted explanation is given by Nadler in his *Hamann*, pp. 73–74.

11. See the letters to Senel, January 14 and 24, 1758, in Hamann, *Briefwechsel*, I, 234–241. The case for Hamann's homosexuality has been well documented by Salmony, *Hamanns metakritische Philosophie*, pp. 75–84. But for a dissenting view, see Koep, "Hamann's Londoner Senelaffäre," *Zeitschrift für Theologie und Kirche*, 57 (1960), 92–108; 58 (1961), 68–85.

12. This account is given by Hamann himself in *Gedanken über meinen Lebenslauf*, *Werke*, II, 40–41.

13. See Hamann's *Biblische Betrachtungen*, *Werke*, I, 5, 9.

14. These writings comprise the *Biblische Betrachtungen, Brocken, Gedanken über meinen Lebenslauf*, and *Betrachtungen zu Kirchenliedern*. All written compulsively and in great haste, they were completed in only three months, from March to May 1758. They hold *in nuce* many of the basic themes of Hamann's mature philosophy; and they are indeed indispensable for the interpretation of his later works. Although they were never published in Hamann's lifetime, it is noteworthy that both Herder and Jacobi saw them before Hamann's death. Concerning their circulation, see the "Schlusswort" to vol. I of Nadler's edition of the *Werke*, pp. 323–324.

15. Concerning the importance of naturalism for the philosophy of the Enlightenment, see Cassirer, *Enlightenment*, pp. 37–50.

16. Hamann, *Werke*, I, 308.

17. Concerning the importance of this belief for the Enlightenment, see Hampson, *Enlightenment*, pp. 35ff., and Wolff, *Aufklärung*, pp. 10–11, 36–37, 114–115.

18. Hamann, *Werke*, I, 303.

19. Ibid., I, 14–15.

20. Ibid., I, 301.

21. Ibid., I, 300–301.

22. In his London writings Hamann does not explicitly criticize post-Cartesian epistemology; but the implications of his position became clear to him later on. Thus in his letter of June 2, 1785, to Jacobi, Hamann remarks about Kant's philosophy: "Not *Cogito ergo sum*, but the converse and more hebraic *Est ergo cogito*. With the reversal of such a simple principle perhaps the whole system will get a different language and direction." See Hamann, *Briefwechsel*, V, 448.

23. Hamann, *Werke*, I, 9.

24. Hamann to Lindner, March 21, 1759, in Hamann, *Briefwechsel*, I, 307.

25. "Kant has an excellent head," Hamann wrote his brother, April 28, 1756. He formed this opinion after reading Kant's *Nova Dilucidatio;* see Hamann, *Briefwechsel*, I, 191.

26. Hamann to his brother, July 12, 1759, in Hamann, *Briefwechsel*, I, 362.

27. Hamann to Lindner, August 18, 1759, in Hamann, *Briefwechsel*, I, 398–399.

28. Hamann, *Briefwechsel*, I, 379.

29. Ibid., I, 378.

30. Vorländer maintains that Kant lectured on Hume as early as 1755, and he cites Borowski's biography of Kant as evidence; see his *Kant*, I, 151. But if we take a close look at the biography, Borowski never states, or even implies, that Kant lectured on Hume in 1755. The passage referred to by Vorländer is extremely vague. Borowski merely says: "In den Jahren, da ich zu seinen Schülern gehörte . . . ," leaving it open which years in particular Kant lectured on Hume. The fact that Borowski *began* hearing Kant's lectures in 1755 is obviously not conclusive. In fact, in discussing Kant's 1755 lectures, it is significant that Borowski never refers to Hume. See Borowski, *Darstellung des Lebens und Charakters Kants*, pp. 18, 78.

31. Hamann openly acknowledged the role of Hume in the formation of his thought. See, for example, his letter of April 27, 1787, to Jacobi in Hamann, *Briefwechsel*, VII, 167: "I was full of Hume when I wrote my *Sokratische Denkwürdigkeiten*, and page 49 of my little book refers to him. Our own existence and the existence of things outside us must be believed and cannot in any way be demonstrated." The passage Hamann is referring to is in *Werke*, II, 73.

32. See the "Beylage zu Dangeuil," in Hamann, *Werke*, IV, 225–242.

33. Concerning the significance of this antithesis for early German philosophy, see Wolff, *Aufklärung*, pp. 15–16.

34. See section 2.4.

35. Hamann, *Werke*, II, 68.

36. Ibid., II, 76.

37. Ibid., II, 69–70.

38. Ibid., II, 73.

39. Ibid., II, 74.

40. Ibid., II, 74.

41. Ibid., II, 74.

42. Ibid., II, 74.

43. See section 1.7.

44. Hamann, *Werke*, II, 74.

45. See section 4.2.

46. Thus Hamann is skeptical about Jacobi's faculty of intellectual intuition. See Hamann to Jacobi, November 14, 1784, and January 22, 1785, in Hamann, *Briefwechsel*, V, 265, 328–329.

47. See, for example, *Brocken*, in Hamann, *Werke*, I, 298.

48. This is indeed the position of Jacobi, who advocates a *salto mortale* because reason proves atheism and fatalism. But it is significant that Hamann rejects Jacobi's

position. See his letter of February 3, 1785, to Herder, in Hamann, *Briefwechsel,* V, 351.

49. See Kant's early essay "Gedanken bei dem frühzeitigen Ableben des Herrn Friedrich von Funk," in *Werke,* II, 37–44. In this essay Kant raises the question of what existence would be like without providence and then uses the above metaphor.

50. See Jacobi's *Fliegender Blätter,* in *Werke,* VI, 155.

51. Hamann, *Werke,* I, 147.

52. Hamann, *Briefwechsel,* I, 452. Cf. Hamann to Lindner, October 12, 1759, in Hamann, *Briefwechsel,* I, 425–426.

53. Hamann, *Briefwechsel,* I, 452.

54. Ibid., I, 452. Also cf. *Werke,* I, 10.

55. The original is lost, though its rough contents can be inferred from Hamann's December 1759 letters.

56. These letters were eventually edited and published by Hamann himself in his *Fünf Hirtenbriefe* (1763). See Hamann, *Werke,* II, 371–374.

57. There is a draft of a letter to Kant written after the three December 1759 letters. See Hamann, *Briefwechsel,* I, 453–454. This draft suggests that Kant had written to Hamann, if only not to offend him and to call off the project formally. In any case Hamann was still offended by Kant's late and cool response.

58. The suggestion that Hamann prepared the ground for Kant's later reception of Rousseau is Gulyga's; see his *Kant,* pp. 61–62. Yet Gulyga puts Hamann's stimulus much later on in the *Aesthetica in nuce* of 1762. The arguments of the 1759 letters are more explicitly Rousseauian, however, and a more likely source of this stimulus.

59. This thesis is argued in detail by Unger, *Hamann und die Aufklärung,* I, 233ff.

60. Usually, the primacy of aesthetics in Romantic philosophy is ascribed to the influence of Kant's third *Kritik* and Schiller's *Aesthetische Briefe.* See, for example, Kroner, *Von Kant bis Hegel,* II, 46ff. But neither Kant's nor Schiller's influence is sufficient to explain the importance given to art in Romantic philosophy. Both Kant and Schiller relegate art to the realm of appearance and do not see it as an instrument for acquiring metaphysical knowledge. The Romantics thought art to be important, however, precisely because they saw it as such an instrument. The crucial influence behind their belief in the metaphysical value of art is most probably Hamann.

61. Concerning this trend, see Cassirer, *Enlightenment,* pp. 297ff.

62. Hamann, *Werke,* II, 206.

63. See Hamann, *Werke,* II, 198–199. Elsewhere in the *Aesthetica,* however, Hamann appears to cast scorn on the notion of imitation; see, for example, II, 205–206. Still these passages reject not the notion per se but only Batteau's interpretation of it.

64. Hamann, *Werke,* II, 198–199.

65. Ibid., II, 198, 207.

66. Ibid., II, 207.

67. Ibid., II, 207.

68. At least Hamann says little about Kant in his correspondence during this

period; and it was his habit to report on almost every incident in his life. For further details on Kant and Hamann's relationship at this time, see Weber, *Kant und Hamann,* pp. 46–55.

69. Hamann to Herder, January 26, 1785, in Hamann, *Briefwechsel,* V, 108.

70. Hamann's term 'Metakritik' is significant. It is a play upon the etymology of 'metaphysics'. The essay "Metakritik" is to follow the *Kritik* as Aristotle's *Metaphysics* follows his *Physics.* The term is to serve as a reminder to Kant that the concepts of philosophy stem not from pure reason but from the vagaries of use. See Hamann's comment on this point in *Werke,* III, 125.

71. See Hamann to Jacobi, September 28, 1785, in Hamann, *Briefwechsel,* VI, 75.

72. See, for example, how Hamann turns Kantian criticism against itself in the opening paragraph of his review of the *Kritik,* in *Werke,* III, 277.

73. Hamann, *Werke,* III, 284–285.

74. See Goethe's oft-cited summary of Hamann's philosophy in *Dichtung und Wahrheit, Werke,* IX, 514.

75. Hamann, *Briefwechsel,* IV, 293–294. Also cf. Hamann to Herder, December 9, 1781, in Hamann, *Briefwechsel,* IV, 355.

76. Hamann offers no explanation of this intriguing phrase, either in the "Metakritik" or elsewhere. The precise connection between reason and language was a long-standing problem for him, though he never succeeded in going beyond bald statements of their identity. He admitted that the whole problem was mysterious to him. See his letter of August 8, 1784, to Herder in Hamann, *Briefwechsel,* V, 177.

77. Hamann, *Werke,* III, 285.

78. See Hamann to Jacobi, November 14, 1784, in Hamann, *Briefwechsel,* V, 264: "With me the question is not so much 'What is reason?', but 'What is language?'. And here I suspect the reason for all those paralogisms and antinomies that one attributes to reason; the problem is that one holds words to be concepts and concepts to be things."

79. Hamann, *Werke,* III, 286.

80. Ibid., III, 284–285.

81. Ibid., III, 286, lines 2ff.

82. See, for example, Kant's remarks on the transcendental imagination, in *KrV,* B, 103, 180–181.

83. Hamann, *Werke,* III, 286.

84. *KrV,* A, xvii.

85. Hamann, *Werke,* III, 287.

86. Hamann to Herder, December 9, 1781, in Hamann, *Briefwechsel,* IV, 355.

87. Hamann, *Werke,* III, 289.

88. Ibid., III, 289.

89. Herder articulated these implications of Hamann's critique in his later polemics against Kant. See his *Metakritik* (1799), in Herder, *Werke,* XXI, 88, 197ff.

90. The common view that this search begins with Reinhold is untenable. This not only ignores Hamann, but it also fails to go back far enough in Reinhold's

philosophical development. As will be discussed in section 8.2, Reinhold was under Hamann's influence in searching for the common source of Kant's faculties.

91. Hamann himself was prone to such language. In his later correspondence he often refers to Bruno's *principium coincidentiae oppositorum*, which he regards as the solution to "all contradictions in the elements of the material and intellectual world." See Hamann to Jacobi, January 16, 1785, in Hamann, *Briefwechsel*, V, 327.

2. Jacobi and the Pantheism Controversy

1. This is a misnomer since the main issue behind the controversy did not concern pantheism. I shall continue to use this name, however, because it is so traditional.

2. Setting any single time as the beginning of the dispute is a largely arbitrary matter. Jacobi first told Mendelssohn of Lessing's Spinozism in the summer of 1783. But Jacobi and Mendelssohn did not formally decide to enter into a dispute until the autumn of 1784. The dispute became public only with the publication of Jacobi's *Briefe* in autumn of 1785.

3. In this connection Hermann Timm rightly remarks: "The *Kritik der reinen Vernunft* made no break in the philosophical self-understanding of the age. But it was otherwise with the Spinozistic legacy of Lessing. Its *pro et contra* made contemporaries conscious of the change of epochs." See *Gott und die Freiheit*, I, 6.

4. See Heine, *Werke*, VIII, 175.

5. See Jenisch to Kant, May 14, 1787, in Kant, *Briefwechsel*, p. 315.

6. Goethe, *Werke*, X, 49.

7. Hegel, *Werke*, XX, 316–317.

8. Concerning the influence of Pascal and Rousseau on the young Jacobi, see Heraeus, *Jacobi und der Sturm und Drang*, pp. 117–118.

9. Concerning Pascal's importance for the philosophes, see Cassirer, *Enlightenment*, pp. 144–145.

10. See Jacobi to Hamann, June 16, 1783, in Hamann, *Briefwechsel*, V, 55.

11. See Hamann to Herder, February 3, 1785, in Hamann, *Briefwechsel*, V, 351. Also see Hamann to Jacobi, October 23, 1785, in Hamann, *Briefwechsel*, VI, 107–108, where Hamann is skeptical of Spinoza's metaphysics, which Jacobi thinks proves the necessity of atheism.

12. Ever since its publication in 1916, the standard text on the controversy has been Scholz, *Hauptschriften*. But this work is more an anthology than an analysis of the dispute.

The best treatments of the complicated background to the dispute are given by Altmann, *Mendelssohn*, pp. 593–652, 729–744, and Strauss in the "Einleitung" to vol. III/2 of Mendelssohn's *Schriften*. My own account of the background to the controversy is greatly indebted to Altmann and Strauss. The most thorough and systematic treatment of the views of Lessing, Jacobi, and Mendelssohn is Timm, *Gott und die Freiheit*.

13. See, for example, Hettner, *Geschichte*, I, 761.

14. See, for example, Scholz, *Hauptschriften*, pp. xi–xii.

15. Concerning the early history of Spinozism in Germany, see Mauthner, *Atheismus*, III, 170–173; Hettner, *Geschichte*, I, 34–38; and Grunwald, *Spinoza in Deutschland*, pp. 45–48.

16. See Wolff, *Werke*, VIII/2, 672–730.

17. See Leibniz, *Schriften*, I, 139–150.

18. See Wolff, *Herrn D. Buddens Bedencken*, pp. 9–15, 35–37, 66–76, 134–135.

19. Thus Mauthner points out that most of the first attacks on Spinoza were against the *Tractatus*. The *Ethica* contained a much more obscure message than the *Tractatus*, and was not 'refuted' until 1692, a decade after the first polemics against the *Tractatus*; see Mauthner, *Geschichte*, III, 171.

20. For more detailed information on all these thinkers, see Mauthner, *Geschichte*, III, 170–272, and Grunwald, *Spinoza in Deutschland*, pp. 41–45, 67–83. Concerning Lau and Stosch, see Stiehler, *Materialisten*, pp. 7–35. Also helpful for the early Spinozists is the chapter "Spinoza," in Adler, *Der junge Herder*, pp. 233–270.

21. In adopting the term 'Protestant Counter-Reformation', I follow Beck, *Early German Philosophy*, pp. 148–156.

22. Although the *Ethica* was a rare book in Germany, the *Tractatus* had a considerable clandestine circulation. See Beck, *Early German Philosophy*, p. 353.

23. See Heine, *Geschichte*, *Werke*, VIII/1, 57ff.

24. It is significant that the connection between pantheism and political radicalism had already been firmly established in the German mind long before the arrival of Spinoza in the late seventeenth century. In the early sixteenth century two of the leading thinkers of the Protestant Counter-Reformation, Sebastian Franck and Valentin Weigel, used pantheism in their struggle against the new orthodoxy of the Reformation. Franck and Weigel were also, more than a century before the dawn of the *Aufklärung* in Germany, the advocates of such progressive doctrines as tolerance, biblical criticism, natural religion, equality, and the separation of church and state. All the radical doctrines of Spinoza's *Tractatus* are clearly prefigured in their writings. Weigel and Franck thus laid the ground for the later reception of Spinoza in Germany. Their doctrines exercised a deep influence over the pietist movement—the very movement from which most of the early Spinozists sprang. Concerning Franck's and Weigel's pantheism, see Franck, *Paradoxa*, no. 2, 48–49, and Weigel, *Nosce teipsum*, erster Teil, das ander Buchlein, chapter 13.

25. Thus it is interesting to note that those Lutherans with pietistic backgrounds who rejected pantheism maintained their faith in the Bible. This is true for Hamann, Jacobi, and Wizenmann.

26. The customary view is that Jacobi deserves the credit for resurrecting Spinoza; see, for example, Scholz, *Hauptschriften*, p. xvii. But it is important to be clear about Jacobi's precise role in the revival of Spinozism: though his *Briefe* was the immediate stimulus for the general acceptance of Spinoza, he was by no means the first to demand a reappraisal of his views.

27. Wolff's *Theologicus naturalis* cannot make any such claim to objectivity, although, much too generously, Mendelssohn bestows his own laurels upon Wolff. See Mendelssohn, *Schriften*, I, 15–16.

28. See Lessing to Michealis, October 16, 1754, in Lessing, *Werke*, XVII, 401.

29. The legend is that Mendelssohn, while visiting Edelmann's house in Berlin, refused to drink a glass of wine for orthodox reasons. This irked Edelmann, who felt that Mendelssohn's orthodoxy was nothing but superstition. Edelmann boasted to Mendelssohn: "We strong spirits recognize no such constraints and follow our appetites." Offended, Mendelssohn abruptly took his leave. This story is reported in Mauthner, *Geschichte*, III, 228.

30. See Altmann, *Mendelssohn*, p. 37.

31. Mendelssohn, *Schriften*, I, 15.

32. Ibid., I, 7.

33. Ibid., I, 22.

34. Ibid., I, 17.

35. Mendelssohn's purified pantheism will be discussed in section 3.4.

36. This important passage occurs only in the first edition of *David Hume* (1787), pp. 79–81, and was deleted in the later edition of the *Werke*.

37. See Kant, *Werke*, II, 155–163.

38. Jacobi later gave a different basis for this idea. In the *Briefe* of 1785 he focuses on the principle of sufficient reason rather than the ontological argument to drive home his point that all philosophy ends in Spinozism.

39. See Lessing, *Werke*, XIV, 175–178.

40. See Altmann, *Mendelssohn*, p. 37.

41. See Lessing, *Werke*, XIV, 292–296.

42. See Hettner, *Geschichte*, I, 758.

43. See Lessing's *Anti-Goeze,* in *Werke*, XIII, 143.

44. For a more detailed discussion of Reimarus's work, see Hettner, *Geschichte*, I, 360–372, and Beck, *Early German Philosophy*, pp. 293–296.

45. Hettner, *Geschichte*, I, 364.

46. See *AdB* 90 (1780), 385.

47. See Goeze, *Etwas Vorläufiges.*

48. Lessing, *Werke*, XII, 428.

49. Lessing did not conclude from this, however, that the concept of revelation was useless and should be banished from religion. In his *Erziehung des Menschengeschlechts,* which arose directly from his controversy with Goeze, Lessing saw revelation as God's means of educating mankind. See Lessing, *Werke*, III, 416, 431–432.

50. Thus both Jacobi and Hamann saw the debate with Mendelssohn in just this light. See Hamann's letter of December 5, 1784, to Jacobi, and Jacobi's letter of December 30, 1784, to Hamann, in Hamann, *Briefwechsel*, V, 274, 301.

51. Jacobi, it is important to note, had extremely liberal political views, which he expounded in his *Etwas, das Lessing gesagt hat;* see Jacobi, *Werke*, II, 325–389. Jacobi published this work just before the debate with Mendelssohn, perhaps so as to avoid being tarred with Goeze's brush.

52. Concerning the effect of Ernesti's and Michealis's biblical criticism, see Hettner, *Geschichte*, I, 354–355.

53. In his *Early German Philosophy*, p. 359, Beck notes it is a paradox that Spinoza's influence was on the rise in Germany as that of rationalism was on the

wane. This paradox disappears, however, once we recognize the Lutheran dimension of *Goethezeit* pantheism.

54. Jacobi, *Werke,* IV/1, 38n.

55. Ibid., IV/1, 39–40.

56. According to Jacobi, Lessing had already told him that he never informed Mendelssohn of his latest views; see *Werke,* IV/1, 42.

57. Jacobi, *Werke,* II, 334.

58. Mendelssohn, *Schriften,* VI/1, 103–108.

59. Jacobi, *Werke,* II, 404–405.

60. Mendelssohn, *Schriften,* XIII, 120ff.

61. Ibid., XIII, 123ff.

62. That Mendelssohn wanted to preempt Jacobi and save Lessing's reputation is evident from two later letters of Mendelssohn's. See his letters of October 8, 1785, to Nicolai, and of October 21, 1785, to Reimarus, in *Schriften,* XIII, 309, 320.

63. Jacobi, *Werke,* IV/1, 43–46.

64. Ibid., IV/1, 46–47.

65. This is one part of Jacobi's report that rings slightly untrue. In an early fragment, "Durch Spinoza ist Leibniz nur auf die Spur der vorherbestimmten Harmonie gekommen," Lessing doubts the identity of Leibniz and Spinoza. See Lessing, *Werke,* XIV, 294–296.

66. Mendelssohn, *Schriften,* XIII, 156–160.

67. Ibid., XIII, 157.

68. Ibid., XIII, 165–166.

69. The original is lost. See Altmann's comments on its likely comments in Mendelssohn, *Schriften,* XIII, 398.

70. Mendelssohn, *Schriften,* XIII, 398.

71. See Mendelssohn's "Erinnerungen an Herrn Jacobi," in Mendelssohn, *Schriften,* III/2, 200–207.

72. Mendelssohn, *Schriften,* XIII, 216–217.

73. See Jacobi to Hamann, October 18, 1784, in Hamann, *Briefwechsel,* V, 239–242.

74. Jacobi, *Werke,* IV/1, 210–214.

75. Ibid., IV/1, 167.

76. Mendelssohn, *Schriften,* XIII, 281.

77. That Mendelssohn was acting according to this strategy is evident from his letter of April 29, 1785, to Elise Reimarus; see Mendelssohn, *Schriften,* XIII, 281. Here Mendelssohn insists that Reimarus should not allow Jacobi to see the manuscript of his forthcoming book. Only the published copy was meant for Jacobi's eyes; but by then, of course, it would be too late for Jacobi to take effective action.

78. Mendelssohn, *Schriften,* XIII, 282.

79. Ibid., XIII, 292.

80. Jacobi, *Werke,* IV/1, 226–227.

81. See Mendelssohn to Kant, October 16, 1785, and to Reimarus, October 21, 1785, in Mendelssohn, *Schriften,* XIII, 312–313, 320–321.

82. Jacobi, *Werke,* IV/1, 42.

83. See Mendelssohn to Reimarus, October 21, 1785, in *Schriften*, XIII, 320–321.

84. See, for example, the preface by Engel to *An die Freunde Lessings*, in Mendelssohn, *Schriften*, III/2, 179–184. Engel cited Marcus Herz's report on Mendelssohn's last illness.

85. Karl Phillip Moritz made the charge explicitly in the January 24, 1786, edition of the *Berlinische privilegirte Zeitung*.

86. As cited in Altmann, *Mendelssohn*, p. 745.

87. Concerning this controversy, see Altmann, *Mendelssohn*, pp. 744–745.

88. We have to read a little behind the lines to see this; but it is unmistakably the case. See Jacobi, *Werke*, II, 410–411, and IV/2, 248–249, 272–273. Also see Jacobi to Hamann, June 16, 1783, and Jacobi to Buchholtz, May 19, 1786, in *Jacobi's Nachlass*, I, 55–59, 80.

89. Jacobi, *Werke*, IV/2, 250, 268–270.

90. Ibid., IV/2, 244–246, 272.

91. Ibid., IV/2, 244–246.

92. See Mendelssohn's essay "Was heisst aufklären?" in *Schriften*, VI/1, 115–119.

93. See the "Fünftes Gesprach" to Lessing's *Ernst und Falk*, in Lessing, *Werke*, XIII, 400–410. Jacobi cites this work in *Werke*, IV/2, 182.

94. See Lessing's "Gegensatze des Herausgebers," in Lessing, *Werke*, XII, 431ff. Also see his letters of April 8, 1773, and February 2, 1774, to his brother Karl in Lessing, *Werke*, XIX, 83, 102.

95. It was indeed Lessing's precedent in publishing this heretical work of Reimarus that sanctioned Jacobi's later decision to divulge Lessing's Spinozism to the public. Jacobi accepted Lessing's teaching about one's duty to state the truth, no matter how uncomfortable. See his *Wider Mendelssohns Beschuldigungen*, in *Werke*, IV/2, 181–182.

96. Jacobi, *Werke*, IV/1, 216–223.

97. Mendelssohn, *Schriften*, XIII, 157–158.

98. Ibid., III/2, 194–196.

99. Ibid., XIII, 398.

100. Concerning the details of this controversy, see Altmann, *Mendelssohn*, pp. 201–263.

101. Mendelssohn, *Schriften*, III/2, 205. Mendelssohn defended these views on Judaism and Christianity in his *Jerusalem*. See Mendelssohn, *Schriften zur Aesthetik und Politik*, II, 419–425.

102. Mendelssohn, *Schriften*, III/2, 303.

103. In his more desperate moments in *An die Freunde Lessings*, Mendelssohn does question this. See, for example, *Schriften*, III/2, 191–192. On the whole, however, Mendelssohn's stategy was to accept the reality of Lessing's confession, but then to interpret it in some harmless way.

104. See, for example, *Wider Mendelssohns Beschuldigungen*, in *Werke*, IV/2, 181, where Jacobi virtually rules out Mendelssohn's 'purified pantheism'.

105. In this respect it is interesting to note that, in his *Brief an Fichte* (1799),

Jacobi saw Fichte's philosophy, not Spinoza's, as the paradigm of all speculation. But this, he insists, does not involve any fundamental change in his views since he thinks that Fichte's system is just as fatalistic as Spinoza's. See Jacobi, *Werke*, III, 9–11.

106. Jacobi, *Werke*, IV/1, 59, 70–72.

107. Ibid., III, 49.

108. In 1799 Jacobi uses this term for the first time, in his *Brief an Fichte;* see Jacobi, *Werke*, III, 44.

109. See, for example, the "Beylage" to *David Hume*, *Werke*, II, 310.

110. See the *Brief an Fichte*, *Werke*, III, 22–23, 44.

111. Jacobi, *Werke*, III, 22.

112. Thus Baum, *Die Philosophie Jacobis*, pp. 37ff., rightly stresses the epistemological meaning of 'nihilism' in Jacobi; but he then underplays its ethical significance. I suggest that Jacobi replaced the earlier term 'egoism' with 'nihilism' precisely to stress the ethical consequences of egoism.

113. Jacobi, *Werke*, III, 36–37.

114. Ibid., III, 49.

115. Judging from Jacobi's account of his discovery of Spinoza, he had a different interpretation earlier on, when he did stress Spinoza's rigor as a metaphysician. See the first edition of *David Hume*, pp. 79–81.

116. Jacobi, *Werke*, IV/1, 124–125; IV/2, 133–139.

117. Ibid., IV/2, 145–146, 153–155, 159.

118. Ibid., IV/1, 56.

119. Ibid., IV/1, 125–126.

120. Ibid., IV/2, 149, 154.

121. Ibid., IV/2, 153–157.

122. Ibid., IV/2, 157.

123. Ibid., IV/1, 155.

124. This has been assumed by Beck in his *Early German Philosophy*, p. 335.

125. Kant, *Werke*, VIII, 143n.

126. See Jacobi, *Werke*, IV/2, 149; IV/1, 147–148. Earlier, during his years in Geneva, Jacobi reacted against the atheism and determinism of some of the French encyclopedists. See Levy-Bruhl, *Philosophie Jacobi*, pp. 29–50.

127. See Jacobi, *Werke*, IV/1, 230–253. Jacobi's intention is not perfectly clear from these passages. He does not explicitly state that he intends to criticize this belief of the *Aufklärung*. But see his *Fliegende Blätter*, in *Werke*, VI, 167–168.

128. Jacobi, *Werke*, IV/1, 234–235, 248.

129. See Jacobi, *Werke*, IV/2, 125–162 and *Werke*, II, 222–225.

130. See, for example, Jacobi's *Brief an Fichte*, where he restates this definition of reason with Kant explicitly in mind. *Werke*, III, 3–16.

131. Jacobi, *Werke*, IV/2, 130–131.

132. Ibid., IV/2, 131. Here Jacobi is probably writing under the influence of Herder. See his early essay on Herder's *Ueber den Ursprung der Sprache*, in *Werke*, VI, 243–264.

133. Mendelssohn's belief in the possibility of objective inquiry will be discussed in sections 3.2 and 3.3.

134. See the "Vierter Brief" to Jacobi's *Briefe über Recherches philosophiques* (1773), in *Werke*, VI, 325–344.
135. Jacobi, *Werke*, IV/1, 232.
136. Ibid., IV/1, 212–213, 240–244.
137. Ibid., IV/1, 212–213.
138. Ibid., IV/1, 212.
139. Ibid., IV/1, 237.
140. Ibid., IV/1, 238.
141. Ibid., IV/1, 240.
142. Ibid., IV/1, 210.
143. Ibid., IV/1, 210–211, 223.
144. Ibid., II, 144–146.
145. See Goethe to Jacobi, October 21, 1785, in *Briefwechsel zwischen Goethe und Jacobi*, pp. 94–95. Also see Herder to Jacobi, June 6, 1785, in Herder, *Briefe*, V, 128–129.
146. Jacobi, *Werke*, II, 142ff.
147. Ibid., II, 128–129, 156–157, 164–165.

3. Mendelssohn and the Pantheism Controversy

1. The only figure of comparable stature to Mendelssohn was Spinoza. But Spinoza turned his back on Jewish life, thus abandoning any attempt at reconciliation.
2. Thus Heinrich Heine in his *Zur Geschichte der Religion und Philosophie in Deutschland*. See Heine, *Werke*, VIII, 185.
3. Concerning the influence of *Jerusalem*, see Altmann, *Mendelssohn*, pp. 530–531, 533–535, 550, 593.
4. Concerning the significance of Mendelssohn's translation, see Schoeps, *Mendelssohn*, pp. 131ff.
5. Thus Beck in his *Early German Philosophy*, p. 326.
6. For a useful summary of Mendelssohn's place in the history of aesthetics, see Beck, *Early German Philosophy*, pp. 326–332, and Best, "Einleitung" to Mendelssohn's *Aesthetische Schriften*, pp. 3–24.
7. Concerning Mendelssohn's political theory, see Altmann, *Mendelssohn*, pp. 514ff., and Schoeps, *Mendelssohn*, pp. 126–149.
8. See Kant to C. G. Schütz, late November 1785, in *Briefwechsel*, 280–281. Also compare Kant's tribute to Mendelssohn's style in the *Prolegomena*, *Werke*, IV, 262.
9. Thus Beck writes of Mendelssohn's "Prize Essay": "No other single work gives so perspicuous a presentation of the Leibnizian-Wolffian epistemology; every strength of that tradition is persuasively presented, every fault inadvertently revealed." See his *Early German Philosophy*, pp. 332, 335.
10. See, for example, Hegel's view of Mendelssohn in his *Geschichte der Philosophie*, *Werke*, XX, 264.
11. This theory and Mendelssohn's general epistemology are expounded in the first seven lectures of *Morgenstunden*, the section entitled "Vorerkenntnis." See

Schriften, III/2, 10–67. Mendelssohn's argument here is largely a repeat of his earlier position in the "Prize Essay" (1763). I have therefore read *Morgenstunden* in the light of this earlier work. The relevant passages from the "Prize Essay" are in *Schriften*, II, 273–275, 277–278, 302–303, and 307–308.

12. Jacobi, *Werke*, II, 193–199.

13. See Crusius, *Werke*, II, 52–53, 123–124; and Kant, *Werke*, II, 52–53, 123–124. It is important to note, however, that Kant corrects Crusius's own formulation of the distinction between logical and real connection. See Kant, *Werke*, II, 203.

14. Mendelssohn, *Schriften*, II, 283, 293, 299.

15. Ibid., II, 293–294.

16. See Basedow, "Vorbericht," in *System der gesunden Vernunft*, esp. pp. 5, 76, 144.

17. Although Mendelssohn complained in the preface to *Morgenstunden* that he had not been able to keep up with all the new advances in philosophy, and particularly with the works of "the all-crushing Kant," he had still read the *Kritik* and was well apprised of its contents. See his letter of April 10, 1783, to Kant, in Mendelssohn, *Schriften*, XIII, 99–100. He had also read Garve's review of the first *Kritik* and discussed the critical philosophy with Nicolai. Concerning Mendelssohn's knowledge of the first *Kritik*, see Altmann, *Mendelssohn*, pp. 673–675.

18. Mendelssohn, *Schriften*, III/2, 69–72.

19. Ibid., III/2, 72.

20. Lessing, *Werke*, XIII, 24.

21. See Mendelssohn's *Jerusalem*, in *Schriften zur Aesthetik und Politik*, II, 275ff.

22. Mendelssohn, *Schriften*, III/2, 81ff.

23. Thus Mendelssohn holds that the fundamental beliefs of morality and religion are only common sense. See his *An die Freunde Lessings*, in *Schriften*, III/2, 197ff.

24. See "Vorlesung X," and "Allegorischer Traum," in *Schriften*, III/2, 81ff.

25. Mendelssohn, *Schriften*, III/2, 82.

26. Ibid., III/2, 79–80.

27. Ibid., III/2, 197–198.

28. Ibid., III/2, 198.

29. Ibid., III/2, 82.

30. Ibid., III/2, 104.

31. Ibid., III/2, 105–106.

32. Ibid., III/2, 106–107.

33. See Wolff, *Theologica naturalis*, *Werke*, VIII/2, 686, par. 683.

34. Mendelssohn, *Schriften*, III/2, 107.

35. Ibid., III/2, 107–110.

36. Here Mendelssohn is referring to his three-faculty theory according to which the mind consists in the faculties of thought, desire, and judgment. He expounds this theory in *Morgenstunden*, lecture 7, in *Schriften*, III/2, 61ff.

37. It is sometimes assumed that Mendelssohn accepts a purified pantheism. See, for example, Beck, *Early German Philosophy*, pp. 354, 339. But this assumption

is flatly inconsistent with the text of the latter half of lecture 14, where Mendelssohn refutes Lessing.

38. Mendelssohn, *Schriften*, III/2, 118.

39. It is interesting to note that Mendelssohn explicitly rejects Hegel's and Schelling's later solution to this problem. He denies the possibility of God 'alienating' his nature—of the infinite understanding embodying itself in the finite—because this would be incompatible with God's infinity. See *Morgenstunden*, *Schriften*, III/2, 120.

40. Mendelssohn, *Schriften*, III/2, 3.

41. See, for example, the passages in *Schriften*, III/2, 10, 60ff., 152ff., 170–171.

42. Mendelssohn's image of Kant as a dangerous skeptic was formed long before the appearance of the *Kritik*. In his review of Kant's *Träume eines Geistes-sehers* (1766), Mendelssohn expressed his dismay at the skeptical and derisory tone of Kant's tract. See Mendelssohn's article in *AdB* 4/2 (1767), 281. This image lost none of its power for Mendelssohn. In *Morgenstunden* he refers to the works of *der alles zermalmenden Kants*. The *Popularphilosophen*, from whom Mendelssohn received much of his information about Kant, probably reinforced this image in his mind. Garve, Nicolai, Feder, and Platner all told Mendelssohn their views of Kant; but they all saw him as a skeptic.

43. Mendelssohn, *Schriften*, III/2, 10–67, esp. 35–67.

44. Mendelssohn accepted the interpretation of Kant in Garve's review in the *Allgemeine deutsche Bibliothek*. See Mendelssohn to Reimarus, January 5, 1784, in *Schriften*, XIII, 168–169. After Feder's editing, Garve's review equated Kant's and Berkeley's idealism.

45. Mendelssohn, *Schriften*, III/2, 56–57, 59.

46. Ibid., III/2, 47, 15–17, 53–55.

47. Concerning Kant's plans, see Hamann to Jacobi, September 28 and October 28, 1785, in Hamann, *Briefwechsel*, VI, 77, 107. As it happened, Kant did eventually attack *Morgenstunden*, but in no polemical detail. See his "Bemerkungen" to *Jakobs Prüfung der Mendelsohnischen Morgenstunden*, in *Werke*, VIII, 151–155.

48. See Hume, *Treatise on Human Nature*, bk. I, sec. 2, pp. 187–218.

49. Mendelssohn's exposition of the concept of probability in *Morgenstunden* is based on his earlier *Gedanken von der Wahrscheinlichkeit* (1756). See Mendelssohn, *Schriften*, I, 147–164. But as Beck said of this work: "Mendelssohn completely missed the difficulty of Hume's problem." See his *Early German Philosophy*, p. 321.

50. Mendelssohn, *Schriften*, II, 300.

51. Ibid., III/2, 153.

52. Ibid., III/2, 148–149.

53. Ibid., III/2, 152–153.

4. Kant, Jacobi, and Wizenmann in Battle

1. Concerning the impact of the *Resultate*, see Jenisch to Kant, May 14, 1787, in Kant, *Briefwechsel*, p. 315; and Goltz, *Wizenmann*, II, 158–159, 164, 166–167, 186–187.

2. See Hamann to Jacobi, May 13, 1786, in Hamann, *Briefwechsel*, VI, 390.

3. Wizenmann's attitude toward Spinoza changed in his later years, however. He began to prefer skepticism to Spinozism. See Glotz, *Wizenmann*, II, 169.

4. Wizenmann claims that he wrote the *Resultate* without even telling Jacobi. See his letter of September 8, 1785, to Hausleutner, in Goltz, *Wizenmann*, II, 116–117. In the same letter Wizenmann even criticizes Jacobi's recently published *Briefe*. For his part, Jacobi did not dispute Wizenmann's claim to independence. See the preface to the first edition of *Wider Mendelssohns Beschuldigungen*.

5. Wizenmann's debts were as much to Herder and Hamann as to Jacobi. See his letter of July 4, 1786, to Hamann, in Hamann, *Briefwechsel*, VI, 454–456. Wizenmann says that, of all people, he was most loyal to Herder. But even here he stresses: "I remained, to my knowledge, always free in judgment."

6. See Kant, *Werke*, VIII, 134.

7. See section 4.3, for a detailed discussion of this controversy.

8. Kant, *Werke*, V, 143.

9. Thus Beck in his *Early German Philosophy*, p. 372.

10. Wizenmann, *Resultate*, pp. 35–36, 39ff.

11. Ibid., pp. 35–36.

12. Ibid., pp. 132–134.

13. Ibid., pp. 172–173.

14. Ibid., pp. 162–163, 166.

15. Wizenmann has in mind Jacobi's position as sketched in the *Briefe über Spinoza, Werke*, IV/1, 230ff.

16. Kant, of course, would disagree. He would argue that it is the very province of reason to criticize the demands of action. So, in his view, the inconsistency still holds.

17. Wizenmann was happy to appeal to Kant in the *Resultate* because it was still not clear whether Kant would enter into the dispute on Mendelssohn's side. Indeed, at this time, Jacobi was hoping that Kant would enter on his side. Still, Wizenmann had a critical reaction to Kant from the very beginning, unlike Jacobi. See his letters of June 9 and July 15, 1786, to Hausleutner, in Glotz, *Wizenmann*, II, 156, 169. As early as 1783, long before Jacobi, we find Wizenmann evincing a critical stance toward Kant. See, for example, his letter of August 30, 1783, to Hausleutner, in ibid., I, 347. All this is indicative of Wizenmann's independence from Jacobi.

18. Wizenmann, *Resultate*, 20ff.

19. Ibid., p. 185.

20. Ibid., pp. 196–197.

21. Ibid., pp. 159–160.

22. Cf. Kant's argument against mysticism in *Werke*, VIII, 142.

23. See Wizenmann's letter of September 19, 1785, to Hausleutner, in Glotz, *Wizenmann*, II, 169. Here Wizenmann says that everything in his philosophy rests upon "sensible-historical experience."

24. See Glotz, *Wizenmann*, II, 169.

25. Jacobi, *Werke*, IV/2, 256–257.

26. Hamann, *Briefwechsel*, VI, 119.

27. Mendelssohn, *Schriften*, XIII, 312–313.

28. See Schütz to Kant, February 1786, and Jakob to Kant, March 26, 1786, in Kant, *Briefwechsel*, pp. 282, 287.

29. See Kant to Schütz, November 1785, in *Briefwechsel*, pp. 280ff.

30. See Hamann to Jacobi, April 9, 1786, in Hamann, *Briefwechsel*, VI, 349–350.

31. See Hamann to Jacobi, September 28 and October 28, 1786, in Hamann, *Briefwechsel*, VI, 71, 107.

32. It is important to note this since it is sometimes assumed that Kant was secretly on Jacobi's side. See, for example, Altmann, *Mendelssohn*, p. 707.

33. Kant to Herz, April 7, 1786, in *Briefwechsel*, pp. 292–293.

34. See Kant, *Briefwechsel*, pp. 299–304.

35. See Biester to Kant, November 8, 1785, and March 7, 1786, in *Briefe*, X, 417–418, 433.

36. Significantly, Kant uses this phrase at the close of his essay "Was heisst: Sich im Denken orientiren?" See Kant, *Werke*, VIII, 144.

37. Kant, *Werke*, VIII, 140–141.

38. Precisely how Kant derives these beliefs from the categorical imperative is a complex matter that would take us too far afield here. In "Was heisst . . ." Kant himself does not engage in such a derivation. The reader is referred to Kant's arguments in the second *Kritik*, *Werke*, V, 110–118.

39. Kant, *Werke*, VIII, 143–144.

40. Ibid., VIII, 141.

41. Ibid., VIII, 143–144.

42. Ibid., VIII, 140.

43. Ibid., VIII, 142–143.

44. Ibid., VIII, 144–146.

45. Ibid., VIII, 144f.

46. Ibid., VIII, 144.

47. Wizenmann, "An Kant," in Hausius, *Materialien*, II, 108–109.

48. Wizenmann, *Resultate*, pp. 233–234, 140–141.

49. Wizenmann, "An Kant," in Hausius, *Materialien*, II, 124.

50. Kant, *Werke*, V, 142–146.

51. Wizenmann, "An Kant," in Hausius, *Materialien*, II, 122–130.

52. On Kant's earlier intentions, and on the critics who were a target of the second *Kritik*, see Beck, *Commentary*, pp. 56–61, and Vorländer, "Einleitung" to *Kritik der praktischen Vernunft*, pp. xvff.

53. See Kant, *Werke*, V, 134–146.

54. Ibid., V, 122–124, 134ff.

55. Ibid., V, 134–146.

56. Ibid., V, 110–111.

57. Ibid., V, 125.

58. See Glotz, *Wizenmann*, II, 156–157, 205. In his letter of March 10, 1787, to Jacobi, in *Briefwechsel*, VII, 114ff., Hamann states that Wizenmann was "martyred" by his struggle in the pantheism controversy.

59. Jacobi, *Werke*, IV/2, 256ff.

60. See Hamann to Jacobi, September 28 and October 28, 1785, in Hamann, *Briefwechsel*, VI, 77, 107.

61. Hamann, *Briefwechsel*, VII, 36.

62. The importance that Jacobi confers on Kant's philosophy in his *Brief an Fichte* (1799) marks a definite change in his position as expressed in the *Briefe* (1785). While the *Briefe* sees Spinoza's metaphysics as the paradigm of philosophy, the *Brief an Fichte* regards Kant's philosophy, in its radical and systematic Fichtean form, as the only true system of reason: ". . . a true system of reason is possible only in the Fichtean manner." See Jacobi, *Werke*, III, 19. All the dangers of nihilism that Jacobi once found in Spinoza's atheism and fatalism he now discovers in Fichte's idealism. Since he has come to regard Fichte's system as the *one and only* paradigm of reason, there has been a clear change in Jacobi's views.

Although Jacobi is self-conscious of this change, he does his best to minimize it and to explain it away. In his *Brief an Fichte* he explains that he does not mean that Fichte's philosophy *replaces* Spinoza's as the paradigm of speculation, as if Fichte's philosophy is somehow superior to Spinoza's in consistently drawing out the nihilistic consequences of rationality. Rather, all that he means is that Fichte's *and* Spinoza's philosophy share a single fundamental principle, a principle of which they are complementary formulations. This is nothing less than the first principle of all knowledge and speculation, the so-called principle of 'subject-object identity'. See Jacobi, *Werke*, III, 10–11.

According to Jacobi, all philosophy attempts to demonstrate the identity of subject and object, mind and body, ego and nature. Fichte and Spinoza represent the two complementary methods of demonstrating this identity. Whereas Fichte begins with the ego and deduces the reality of nature, Spinoza starts with nature and derives the reality of the ego. Fichte's philosophy is nothing more than 'inverted Spinozism'. Fichte takes his starting point from Spinoza's principle that the mind and body are only attributes of one and the same substance; except that instead of placing this single substance in the universe outside himself, as Spinoza does, he puts it within the absolute ego inside himself. See Jacobi, *Werke*, III, 10–11.

63. See *KrV*, A, xx; B, xviii, xiii.

64. Jacobi, *Werke*, III, 15ff.

65. See Schelling, *Fernere Darstellung*, in *Werke*, I/2, 405–413, and Hegel, *Phänomenologie*, *Werke*, II, 137f. Fichte also struggles with just this dilemma at the close of his 1794 *Wissenschaftslehre;* see Fichte, *Werke*, I, 280–282.

66. The locus classicus for this argument is the "Beylage" to Jacobi's *David Hume*, *Werke*, II, 291ff. It is worthwhile to note the *ipsissima verba* of Jacobi's argument, which differs from many of its interpretations. As Jacobi originally formulates his argument, he directs it not explicitly against the thing-in-itself, but against things which are the causes of representations, which he identifies with 'transcendental objects'. Jacobi also does not make the criticism, which is often attributed to him, that postulating the thing-in-itself illegitimately extends the categories of existence and causality beyond experience. Never in his "Beylage" does he specifically mention Kant's teaching about the limits of the categories. This criticism is an implication of Jacobi's argument; but it is never explicitly stated by him.

67. Jacobi, *Werke*, II, 304.

68. See Jacobi, "Vorrede zugleich Einleitung," in *Werke*, II, 34–37; *Ueber das Unternehmen des Kriticismus die Vernunft zu Verstande zu bringen*, III, 100–103; and *Brief an Fichte*, III, 40–41.

69. Jacobi, *Werke*, III, 40–41.

5. Herder's Philosophy of Mind

1. See section 2.4.

2. Concerning the importance of Boerhaave and Haller for Herder's philosophy of mind, see Clark, *Herder*, pp. 233ff.; and concerning the importance of Needham's and Maupertuis's criticisms of the preformation theory, see Hampson, *Enlightenment*, pp. 88, 222–223.

3. See the first edition of the *Fragmente* (1767), *Werke*, I, 151ff., and the second edition (1768), *Werke*, II, 1–111. The *Fragmente* had already worked out in rough outline the philosophy of language contained in Herder's later treatise; but the treatise went further than the *Fragmente* in articulating and defending a general philosophical program.

4. Haym, *Herder*, I, 401.

5. Herder, *Werke*, V, 38.

6. At one point in his treatise, Herder forswears all speculation about the origin of reason. See *Werke*, V, 95. But this remark has to be seen in context. It is a renunciation of metaphysical speculation, not of an empirical theory of the origin of reason. The fact remains that the second half of Herder's book does little more than develop an empirical theory of the genesis of reason.

7. Süssmilch, "Einleitung," in *Beweis*, pars. 3, 16.

8. Herder, *Werke*, V, 39–40.

9. Ibid., V, 32–33.

10. See Herder, *Werke*, VI, 299–300.

11. See Süssmilch, "Einleitung" and "Schluss," in *Beweis*.

12. See Rousseau, *Sur l'inégalité parmi les hommes*, in *Oeuvres Complètes*, I, 175ff. Herder also criticizes Maupertuis, whose theory is similar to Rousseau's. See Maupertuis, *Dissertation*, p. 349.

13. Condillac, *Essai sur l'origene des connaissances humaines*, pt. 2, sect. 1, pars. 1–12.

14. Herder, *Werke*, V, 21.

15. Ibid., V, 21.

16. See Locke, *Essay*, bk. 2, chap. 1, par. 4: "By REFLECTION then . . . I understand to mean, that notice which the Mind takes of its own Operations, and the manner of them, by reason whereof, there come to be Ideas of these Operations of the Understanding."

17. See Herder, *Ideen zur Philosophie der Geschichte der Menschheit* (1785), in *Werke*, XIII, 144–145.

18. Herder, *Werke*, V, 28–34.

19. Ibid., V, 35.

20. Indeed, Hamann had already written an essay on language in response to

an earlier competition of the Akademie held in 1759. This is his "Versuch über eine akademische Frage," in Hamann, *Werke,* II, 121–126. The competition centered on the question of "L'influence reciproque du langage sur les opinions & des opinions sur le langage." In this essay Hamann defends the idiomatic qualities of natural languages against the prevailing rationalistic views of Gottsched and Michaelis.

21. Ignorance of Tiedemann's work has led the best commentators astray. Thus Elfriede Büchsel, in her commentary on Hamann's writings concerning language, assumes that (1) Tiedemann remains within the confines of the orthodox rationalism, and that (2) he does not envisage a genetic approach to the problem of language. See *Hamanns Hauptschriften erklärt,* IV, 131. But the first assumption is at odds with Tiedemann's empiricism; and the second is flatly inconsistent with his text. See Tiedemann, *Versuch,* pp. 173–174.

22. Tiedemann, *Versuch,* pp. 163–167.

23. Hamann, *Werke,* III, 16.

24. Concerning Herder's early relationship with Hamann, see Haym, *Herder,* I, 31–51; Dobbek, *Herders Jugendzeit,* pp. 116–137; and Adler, *Der junge Herder,* pp. 59–67.

25. See Hamann to Herder, June 14, 1772, in Hamann, *Briefwechsel,* III, 7–8.

26. Hamann, *Werke,* III, 19.

27. Also important for Hamann's debate with Herder are the following writings: "Au Solomon de Prusse," "Selbstgespräch eines Autors," and "An die Hexe zu Kadmonbor," all in *Werke,* III, 55–60, 67–79, and 81–87.

28. Thus Pascal claims that Hamann simply 'turned back' to the divine origin theory of Süssmilch. See his *Sturm und Drang,* p. 176. Haym adopts a similar attitude in his *Herder,* I, 494–495.

29. Hamann, *Werke,* III, 41ff.

30. It is plausible that Hamann is also attacking Kant here. See "Vorrede," in *Allgemeine Naturgeschichte,* where Kant admits the similarity of his theory to that of Epicurus, in *Werke,* I, 226–227.

31. Hamann, *Werke,* III, 29, 40.

32. Ibid., III, 27.

33. Ibid., III, 27.

34. See Hamann, *Werke,* III, 17, ll. 20–26, where Hamann seems equally disgruntled with Süssmilch's theory.

35. Hamann, *Werke,* III, 20–21.

36. Ibid., III, 32.

37. Ibid., III, 27, ll. 1–14.

38. Ibid., III, 27, ll. 15–21.

39. Ibid., III, 28–29, 39–40.

40. Ibid., III, 38.

41. This is, at any rate, Hamann's reading of Herder's treatise. But such a reading is not entirely accurate or fair. In his "Zweites Naturgesetz," for example, Herder stresses that man is "a creature of society"; see Herder, *Werke,* V, 112. Nevertheless, in his polemic against Condillac's conventionalism, Herder does get carried away and makes the extreme claim that man could develop language in

isolation; see *Werke*, V, 38. This is the passage that determined Hamann's reading of the treatise.

42. Hamann, *Werke*, III, 39.

43. Concerning the influence of the *Ideen*, see Haym, *Herder*, II, 260–264, and *Die romantische Schule*, pp. 582ff.

44. Herder, *Werke*, I, 141–143, 247–250.

45. Ibid., II, 1–110.

46. Concerning the importance of this text for the young Herder, see Adler, *Der junge Herder*, pp. 56–59.

47. Herder, *Werke*, II, 62.

48. Ibid., V, 503.

49. Although Herder does not use this term, it serves as an accurate summary of his position.

50. Concerning Herder's originality on this point, see Berlin, *Vico and Herder*, pp. 209ff.

51. Herder, *Werke*, V, 502–503, 507–508, 509–510.

52. Ibid., V, 509.

53. Ibid., V, 503.

54. Concerning the complicated history behind its composition, and the significant differences between its versions, see Haym, *Herder*, I, 669–670.

55. Haym, *Herder*, I, 671.

56. Hamann had prepared the ground for such an Aristotelian definition of the mind in "Philologische Einfälle und Zweifel." See Hamann, *Werke*, III, 37–41. It is likely that this was one stimulus for Herder's own theory.

57. Herder, *Werke*, VIII, 176–177.

58. Ibid., VIII, 178.

59. See the chapter "Reiz" in the final version, in Herder, *Werke*, VIII, 171ff.

60. Herder, *Werke*, VIII, 171.

61. Ibid., VIII, 177.

62. Ibid., VIII, 171.

63. Concerning Herder's early relationship with Kant, see Haym, *Herder*, I, 31–51; Dobbek, *Herders Jugendzeit*, pp. 96–116; and Adler, *Der junge Herder*, pp. 53–59.

64. See Herder to Hamann, August 1, 1772, and Hamann to Herder, October 6, 1772, in Hamann, *Briefwechsel*, III, 10, 16–17. Also see Herder to Hamann, January 2, 1773, in Hamann, *Briefwechsel*, III, 28–29.

65. See Hamann to Kant, April 1774, and Kant to Hamann, April 6 and 8, 1774, in Kant, *Briefwechsel*, pp. 118–129.

66. See Herder to Hamann, early March 1782, in Herder, *Briefe*, IV, 209.

67. See Caroline Herder, *Erinnerungen, Gesammelte Werke* (Cotta ed.), LIX–LX, 123.

68. This is the plausible explanation for Kant's hostile review of Herder's *Ideen*. The motives for Kant's review have often been the subject of speculation, however. One common explanation is that Kant saw Herder's *Ideen* as a recrudescence of some of his own precritical teachings, which he now wanted to denounce. See, for example, Clark, *Herder*, p. 317, and Haym, *Herder*, II, 246. Yet it is difficult to see

how this theory amounts to an explanation. Why should Kant attack Herder so sharply for adhering to his old doctrines? Such loyalty could only have been flattering, and is more reason for gentle remonstrance than harsh criticism. All the previous speculation concerning Kant's motives suffers from one serious flaw: it ignores the testimony of Caroline Herder. It was she who said that Kant held Herder responsible for the poor reception of the *Kritik*. If this is true—and we have no reason to doubt such testimony—then it easily explains Kant's hostility.

69. Clark, *Herder*, p. 317.

70. This is a common view. See, for example, Beck, *Early German Philosophy*, p. 382.

71. In his *Reisejournal*, for example, Herder expresses the wish to have a metaphysics in "the spirit of a Kant"—a metaphysics that is not "empty speculation" but that "comprehends the results of all the empirical sciences"; see *Werke*, IV, 383–384. The "Prize Essay" is the obvious source of such sentiments.

72. Kant, *Werke*, VIII, 54.

73. Ibid., VIII, 53.

74. Herder, *Werke*, XIII, 119–126.

75. Kant, *Werke*, I, 355–356.

76. Ibid., VIII, 53–54.

77. Kant, *Werke*, I, 250, 255, 306–307, esp. 228.

78. Ibid., VIII, 45.

79. See Herder to Wieland, January 1785, in Herder, *Briefe*, V, 102–103.

80. Kant, *Briefwechsel*, p. 319.

81. Among Herder's allies was Kant's later disciple K. L. Reinhold, whose spirited defense of Herder provoked a sharp riposte from Kant. See Kant, *Werke*, VIII, 56–58.

82. See Leibniz, *Discours de Metaphysique*, pars. x–xi, xix–xxii, in *Schriften*, IV, 434–435, 444–447.

83. Several times in the first *Kritik* Kant does insist upon the regulative status of teleology; see *KrV*, B, 718–721. But, significantly, he still does not consider teleology to be another contender for the explanation of the noumenal realm. Rather, he tends to treat teleological explanations as if they were ultimately reducible to mechanical ones; see *KrV*, B, 720–721. The theory of teleology advanced in the third *Kritik* is by no means anticipated in Kant's earlier writings. In reducing teleological to mechanical explanations, the first *Kritik* is at odds with the third. Furthermore, before the third *Kritik* Kant sometimes treats teleological principles as if they were verifiable in experience; see, for example, the "Achter Satz" of the world history essay, in *Werke*, VIII, 27. This is at variance with the third *Kritik*, however, which gives such principles a strictly regulative status.

84. See *TM* 4 (October–December 1786), 57–86, 150–166.

85. Concerning Forster's significance in late eighteenth-century Germany, see Hettner, *Geschichte*, II, 579–594.

86. One significant exception to the general neglect of this essay is Riedel, "Historizismus und Kritizismus," *Kant-Studien* 72 (1981), 41–57.

87. See Haym, *Herder*, II, 455–456.

88. Referring to Forster's defense of the concept of power, Kant writes: "Per-

haps in this way Hr. Forster also wanted to do a favor for some hypermetaphysician and to give him some material for his fantasy, which he could amuse himself with later on." The "hypermetaphysician" that Kant is referring to here could only be Herder. This passage is from *Werke*, VIII, 180.

89. For further details see Riedel, "Historizismus und Kritizismus," pp. 43–51.

90. Forster, "Menschenrassen," p. 75.

91. See Kant, *Briefwechsel*, pp. 333–334. This is a new structuring of the critical philosophy since, in some of his earlier classifications of the various branches of philosophy, Kant makes no reference to teleology. See, for example, the preface to the *Grundlegung*, *Werke*, IV, 387–388.

92. Kant, *Werke*, VIII, 180–181.

93. See, for example, Cassirer, *Kants Leben*, pp. 294ff.

94. This much is plain from the introduction to the third *Kritik*. See secs. 2 and 9 of the second introduction, in Kant, *Werke*, V, 174–176, 176–179, 195–197.

95. Kant, *Werke*, VIII, 178–179.

96. Ibid., VIII, 178–182.

97. Exactly when Herder began to study Spinoza is disputed. Haym reckons 1775, basing his date on some remarks of Herder. See his *Herder*, II, 269. But Adler argues that there are traces of Herder's study of Spinoza as early as 1767. See his *Der junge Herder*, pp. 164, 272. There is some good evidence for Adler's view in the essay "Grundsätze der Philosophie," in *Werke*, XXXII, 227–231, which shows elements of Spinozism, and which was written around 1767. Concerning the date of this manuscript, see Suphan's note in *Werke*, XIV, 669.

98. See Herder to Jacobi, February 6, 1784, in Herder, *Briefe*, V, 28.

99. Jacobi, *Werke*, IV/1, 246–247.

100. Herder, *Briefe*, V, 27.

101. See Herder to Jacobi, February 6, 1784, in Herder, *Briefe*, V, 28: "I am of the opinion that, since Spinoza's death, no one had done justice to the system of the One and All."

102. See Herder to Jacobi, February 6 and December 20, 1784, in Herder, *Briefe*, V, 29, 90–91.

103. Ibid., V, 90.

104. Herder, *Werke*, XVI, 492–493.

105. Ibid., XVI, 418, 438.

106. See Herder to Jacobi, February 6 and December 20, 1784, in Herder, *Briefe*, V, 28–29, 90.

107. Herder, *Werke*, XVI, 444–445.

108. Ibid., XVI, 474–476.

109. Spinoza, *Ethica*, par. I, app., *Opera*, II, 71.

110. Herder, *Werke*, XVI, 478–481.

111. See Herder, *Werke*, XVI, 495–496. Cf. Herder to Jacobi, December 20, 1784, in Herder, *Briefe*, V, 90.

112. Herder, *Werke*, XVI, 511.

113. Ibid., XVI, 508, 511.

114. See Herder, *Werke*, IV, 383–384.

115. Herder, *Werke*, XVI, 420. Cf. Herder to Jacobi, February 6, 1784, in Herder, *Briefe*, V, 27.

116. Herder, *Werke*, XVI, 447–448.

117. Spinoza, *Ethica*, par. I, prop. XVI, *Opera*, II, 16.

118. Herder, *Werke*, XVI, 451–452.

119. Concerning Herder's influence upon the *Naturphilosophen*, see Haym, *Die romantische Schule*, pp. 582–583, and Hoffmeister, *Goethe und der deutsche Idealismus*, pp. 1–2, 12ff., 33–34, 39–40.

6. The Attack of the Lockeans

1. Concerning the importance of the concept of education for the *Aufklärung*, see Mendelssohn, "Ueber die Frage was heisst aufklaren?" in *Schriften*, VI, 113–121.

2. This objective is stated explicitly and firmly by the young Reinhold in his early essay "Gedanken über Aufklärung," *Deutsche Merkur*, July/August (1784), 5–8.

3. A complete list of the works translated by the *Popularphilosophen* is given in Wundt, *Schulphilosophie*, pp. 270–271.

4. There are other dividing lines. See, for example, Erdmann's classification in *Kants Kriticismus*, pp. 8–9.

5. Concerning the Lockeans' early attitude toward Kant, see Feder, *Leben*, p. 117; Selle to Kant, December 1787, in Kant, *Werke*, X, 516–517; and Garve to Kant, August 7, 1783, in Kant, *Briefwechsel*, p. 225.

6. See, for example, Feder, *Raum und Causalität*, p. 8ff.; Tittel, *Kantische Denkformen*, pp. 51–52, 36–37, 27–28; Weishaupt, *Zweifel*, pp. 6–7; and Tiedemann, *Theäet*, pp. xii, 120–121.

7. See, for example, Feder, *Raum und Causalität*, pp. viii–ix; Tittel, *Kantische Denkformen*, pp. 94ff., and *Kants Moralreform*, pp. 4–6, 20–21; Weishaupt, *Zweifel*, pp. 6–7; and Nicolai, *Beschreibung*, XI, 186, 206, 182.

8. See, for example, Tittel, *Kants Moralreform*, pp. 20–21; Selle, *Grundsätze*, pp. 26–28; and Pistorius, "Ueber den Kantischen Purismus und Sellischen Empirismus," in Hausius, *Materialien*, I, 210–211.

9. See, for example, Tittel, *Kants Moralreform*, pp. 4–6; and Nicolai, *Abhandlungen*, III, 12ff.

10. Although the Wolffians also argued this thesis, they followed in the footsteps of the Lockeans. It was indeed the Lockeans who constantly referred to Berkeley when they accused Kant of solipsism.

11. See, for example, Feder, *Raum und Causalität*, pp. 48–51, 56–57, 107–108; Pistorius, "Kritik der reinen Vernunft," *AdB* 81/2 (1788), 343ff.; and Weishaupt, *Gründe und Gewissheit*, pp. 65–66.

12. The loci classici for the Lockean attack on Kant's theory of space and time are Feder, *Raum und Causalität*, pp. 17–42; Weishaupt, *Zweifel*, passim; Tiedemann, *Theäet*, pp. 59–81; and Pistorius, "Schultz's Erläuterung," in Hausius, *Materialien*, I, 165–166.

13. In general, the "Analytik" did not receive fair attention from Kant's critics until Maimon's *Versuch einer Transcendentalphilosophie* (1790). The "Deduktion" became the center of attention only in 1796 with Beck's *Einzig mögliche Standpunkt*.

14. The loci classici for this criticism are Tittel, *Kantische Denkformen*, pp. 10–17; Garve, "Kritik der reinen Vernunft," *AdB*, supp. to 37–52 (1783), 842ff.; and Weishaupt, *Gründe und Gewissheit*, pp. 48–49.

15. See, for example, Tittel, *Kants Moralreform*, pp. 14–15, 33–36; Pistorius, "Grundlegung zur Metaphysik der Sitten," in Hausius, *Materialien*, III, 221–223; Nicolai, *Abhandlungen*, III, 6ff.; and Garve, *Versuch*, pp. 373–374.

16. Kant to Bernouilli, November 16, 1781, in Kant, *Briefwechsel*, p. 203.

17. See Mendelssohn to Kant, April 10, 1783, in Kant, *Briefwechsel*, pp. 212–213.

18. In his autobiography Feder claims to have received letters from Tetens that reveal his opinion of the *Kritik;* he implies that Tetens's reaction was mainly negative. See Feder, *Leben*, p. 108.

19. Schultz, "Vorrede," in *Erläuterung*.

20. Kant, *Prolegomena, Werke*, IV, 380.

21. See *GgA* 3 (January 19, 1782), 40–48.

22. See "Beilage II" of Vorländer's edition of the *Prolegomena*, p. 167. This is a reprint of the Feder edition of the review. All references will be to this more accessible edition.

23. See, for example, Feder's fulsome review of Reid's *Essays on the Intellectual Powers of Man*, *PB* I, 43ff.

24. Vorländer, p. 169.

25. Ibid., p. 173.

26. The sections of the *Prolegomena* that reply to the Göttingen review are, in addition to the appendix, the following: the second and third "Anmerkung" to the "Erster Hauptfrage," in *Werke*, IV, 288–294; par. 39, in *Werke*, IV, 332; and the "Anmerkung" to pars. 46, 48, and 49, in *Werke*, IV, 333–334. The influence of the review on the general plan of the *Prolegomena* is a matter of dispute. In 1878–79, Erdmann and Arnoldt quarreled over the extent to which the *Prolegomena* was a result of the review. For a useful summary of this debate, see Vorländer, *Prolegomena*, pp. xiv–xix.

27. Kant, *Werke*, IV, 372.

28. Ibid., IV, 377.

29. Ibid., IV, 377.

30. Ibid., IV, 288–290, 374–375.

31. As Kant himself says, Berkeley is an empiricist who reduces all a priori principles to sense impressions. See *Werke*, IV, 375.

32. This was first observed by B. Erdmann in his *Kants Kriticismus*, pp. 91–95.

33. *KrV*, A, 491.

34. Kant, *Werke*, IV, 289.

35. Garve to Kant, July 13, 1783, in Kant, *Briefwechsel*, pp. 219f.

36. See Kant to Herz, November 24, 1776, in Kant, *Briefwechsel*, p. 148.

37. This has been a much disputed question. In his *Beziehung Garves zu Kant,*

Stern argues that Garve is indeed justified in renouncing the review, and that it is Feder who is responsible for its most notorious theses (see pp. 17–26). Stern's thesis has been criticized by Arnoldt in his *Kritische Exkurse, Schriften,* IV, 12–25. Arnoldt argues that Feder only reproduces Garve's original, at least philosophically if not stylistically. The charge of Berkeleyan idealism is simply taken over from Garve, in Arnoldt's view. Thus Stern and Arnoldt represent diametrically opposed views about the authorship of the Göttingen review. Stern argues the case for essential distortion; and Arnoldt puts forward the case for essential fidelity. In what follows I will try to steer a middle course between their positions.

38. See *AdB,* supp. to 37–52 (1783), 838–862. It is possible that Garve changed the original in preparing it for publication; such changes would have the advantage of appeasing Kant and confirming his disclaimers. But Garve claims not to have touched it. See his letter of July 13, 1783, to Kant, in Kant, *Briefwechsel,* 219ff.

39. This is the result of Arnoldt's painstaking analysis and comparison of the texts. See his *Exkurse, Schriften,* IV, 9–11.

40. Erdmann maintains that only these suppressed remarks could have been of some interest to Kant. See *Kants Kriticismus,* p. 99.

41. See Garve, *AdB* review, pp. 850, 860.

42. After his first cursory reading, Kant did have a more favorable opinion of the original. See Kant to Schultz, August 22, 1783, in Kant, *Briefwechsel,* p. 238. According to a later report of Hamann's, however, Kant complained that he had been treated "like an imbecile." See Hamann to Herder, December 8, 1783, in Hamann, *Briefwechsel,* V, 107.

43. See Feder, *Leben,* p. 119. That it was Feder who identified empirical idealism with Berkeley's idealism is the crucial point missed by Stern and Arnoldt. They are both guilty of non sequiturs. Stern is right in thinking that Garve does not equate Kantian and Berkeleyan idealism; but he is wrong in implying that Garve does not accept the general thesis of the identity of transcendental and empirical idealism. Both Garve and Feder adhere to this thesis in a broad sense, even though they have different understandings of 'empirical idealism'. Conversely, Arnoldt is correct in assuming that Garve accepts Feder's general thesis; but he goes astray in concluding that this implies Garve's equation of Kantian and Berkeleyan idealism.

44. See *GgZ* 68 (August 24, 1782). This review was written by Ewald, a minor court official in Gotha. It is a sign of Kant's pessimism that he was pleased with the notice, which did little more than give a rough summary. Concerning Kant's reaction to it, see Hamann to Hartknoch, September 17, 1782, in Hamann, *Briefwechsel,* IV, 425–426.

45. See Kant to Schultz, August 26, 1783, in Kant, *Briefe,* X, 350–351.

46. See *AdB* 59/2 (1784), 332ff. The author of this review was H. A. Pistorius.

47. Concerning Kant's role in the publication of Schultz's *Erläuterung,* see Erdmann, *Untersuchungen,* pp. 102–111.

48. Both Erdmann and Vorländer insist that the *Erläuterung* could not have been widely read. Although it received good reviews, its impact was not felt beyond Berlin and Königsberg. See Erdmann, *Kants Kriticismus,* p. 112, and Vorländer, *Kant,* I, 288.

49. See *GgZ* 12 (February 11, 1784), 95, and *AdB* 59/1 (1784), 322ff.

50. See *HB* I, 113–130, 233–248, 464–474. Although the collected volume

did not appear until 1785, the individual pieces were published separately in 1784.

51. Ibid., I, 115.
52. Ibid., I, 118–120.
53. Ibid., I, 473–474.
54. See Kant to Bering, April 7, 1786, in Kant, *Briefwechsel*, p. 291.
55. See Kant's *Reflexionen*, no. 5649, in *Werke*, XVIII, 296–298.
56. See Kant to Herz, May 1, 1781, in Kant, *Briefwechsel*, pp. 192–193.
57. Kant, *Briefe*, X, 516–517.
58. Selle's article "Versuch eines Beweises," which took issue with Kant without mentioning him by name, appeared in the December 1784 issue of the *Berliner Monatsschrift*, and thus after Tiedemann's *Hessische Beyträge* review. In the August and October 1784 issues of the *Monatsschrift*, two other articles appeared, which are a prelude to Selle's later critique of Kant, "Von den analogischen Schlussart" and "Nähere Bestimmung der analogischen Schlussart." Both articles defend the possibility of induction, which Selle felt Kant had misunderstood.
59. Selle was attacked by Schmid in the appendix to the second edition of his *Wörterbuch*, by Born in his *Versuch*, pp. 64–65 and 98–99, and by Schultz in his *Prüfung*, I, 86, 129. Selle was also criticized by Mendelssohn in "Ueber Selles reine Vernunftbegriffe," in *Schriften*, VI/1, 101–102.
60. See Ouvrier, *Idealismi*, which is a defense of Selle.
61. Pistorius defended Selle in "Ueber den Kantischen Purismus und Selleschen Empirismus," *AdB* 88 (1788), 104ff.
62. See Kant to Selle, February 24, 1792, in Kant, *Briefwechsel*, pp. 558–559.
63. See Selle, *Grundsätze*, pp. 15, 51, 63, 88.
64. See Selle, "Versuch eines Beweises," in Hausius, *Materialien*, I, 99.
65. Selle, "Versuch eines Beweises," in *Materialien*, I, 105; and *Realite et Idealite, PA* I/1, 83–84.
66. This line of argument emerges most clearly in *Idealite et Realite, PA* I/1, 123–125, 119, 83f.
67. Concerning Feder's influential textbooks, see Wundt, *Schulphilosophie*, pp. 290–292, 306–307. Kant himself used Feder's *Grundriss der philosophischen Wissenschaften*, which he preferred because its philosophical content was preceded by a sketch of the history of philosophy.
68. This was an important text for the young Hegel. Concerning its impact on him, see Harris, *Hegel's Development*, pp. 24, 26, 51, 53, 79, 175.
69. Kant to Garve, August 7, 1783, in Kant, *Briefwechsel*, p. 225.
70. Schütz to Kant, July 10, 1784, in Kant, *Briefwechsel*, p. 255.
71. Biester to Kant, June 11, 1786, in Kant, *Briefwechsel*, p. 304.
72. Feder, *Leben*, pp. 123–124.
73. See Feder, *Leben*, p. 190. The effect that Feder has in mind here—the addition of the "Refutation of Idealism" in the second edition of the *Kritik*—is much more likely to have resulted from the Göttingen review alone.
74. Feder himself ascribed his decline to Kant's increasing popularity; see his *Leben*, p. xiv.
75. *Ueber Raum und Causalität* was discussed in Schaumann, *Aesthetik*, pp. 29ff.; and Schultz, *Prufüng*, I, 16ff., 87ff., 99ff., 123.
76. See *KrV*, B, 38–40.

77. Feder, *Ueber Raum und Causalität*, pp. 17–20.

78. Ibid., p. 24.

79. Ibid., pp. 24, 27.

80. Feder says that his main bone of contention with Kant is that space is not an a priori representation or innate idea. See *Raum und Causalität*, pp. 4–5, 16.

81. See *KrV*, B, 34–35. Kant is still guilty of some looseness of language, however, and Feder's misreading is indeed excusable on these grounds. Although Kant calls space 'a form of intuition' to distinguish it from intuition proper, he also goes on to call it 'a pure intuition' as if it were only a special kind of intuition. He also refers to space as a 'representation' *(Vorstellung)* from time to time.

82. Feder, *Raum und Causalität*, pp. 4–5, 16.

83. Ibid., pp. 48–51, 56–57, 107–108.

84. Ibid., p. 64n.

85. Ibid., pp. 66–67, 64n.

86. Concerning the details of Tittel's career, see his "Etwas von meinem Leben," in Tittel, *Dreizig Aufsätze*, pp. viiff.

87. Feder's influence upon Tittel is plain from the contents and title of his *Logik: Nach Herrn Feders Ordnung* (1783).

88. See Biester to Kant, June 11, 1786, in Kant, *Briefwechsel*, p. 304.

89. See Kant to Schütz, June 25, 1787, in Kant, *Briefwechsel*, p. 320.

90. Kant, *Werke*, V, 8.

91. Tittel, *Kants Moralreform*, p. 6.

92. Ibid., pp. 9–10, 90–93.

93. Ibid., pp. 20–21.

94. Ibid., pp. 14–15, 33, 35–36.

95. Ibid., pp. 33–34.

96. Ibid., p. 35.

97. Tittel, *Kantische Denkformen*, pp. 44, 94.

98. Ibid., pp. 10–11.

99. Ibid., pp. 34–35.

100. Concerning Weishaupt's role in the formation of the *Illuminati*, see Epstein, *Genesis*, pp. 87–100.

101. Kant's disciples rushed to his defense in a number of articles and books. See, for example, Born, *Versuch*, pp. 21–55; Schultz, *Prüfung*, I, 85–86, 95–96, 144–145; and the anonymous article in the *ALZ* 3 (1788), 10ff.

102. Weishaupt, *Gründe und Gewissheit*, p. 34.

103. Ibid., pp. 119–120.

104. Ibid., pp. 62–63, 125–126.

105. Ibid., pp. 20–21, 107, 157, 164.

106. Ibid., pp. 171–172.

107. Ibid., pp. 73–74, 158–159, 201–202.

108. *KrV*, A, 105.

109. See Kant's praise of Pistorius in the *Opus Posthumum*, *Werke*, XXI, 416.

110. Kant, *Werke*, V, 8.

111. Ibid., V, 6.

112. See Parthey, *Mitarbeiter*, pp. 20–21.

113. Pistorius did, however, receive some recognition: Jenisch told Kant that he had "many adherents." See Jenisch to Kant, May 14, 1787, in Kant, *Briefwechsel*, p. 316.

114. Pistorius, "Schultz's *Erläuterung*," in Hausius, *Materialien*, I, 158–159.

115. Pistorius, "Kant's *Prolegomena*," in Hausius, *Materialien*, I, 148.

116. It is unclear whether Kant heeded this request. But there are some signs that he did. In the preface to the second *Kritik*, while discussing objections to the first *Kritik*, Kant mentions the need to defend his "strange assertion" that we know ourselves only as appearances (see *Werke*, V, 6). And in the preface to the second edition of the *Kritik*, Kant refers to objections against his theory of time (i.e., inner sense) in the "Aesthetik"; it is indeed possible that the passage concerning "inner affection" added in the second edition (B, 67-8) is a reply to Pistorius. De Vleeschauwer conjectures that Kant wanted to reply to Pistorius in an appendix to the *Metaphysische Anfangsgründe*. Here he appeals to Kant's letter of September 13, 1785, to Schütz; see his *La Deduction transcendentale*, II, 581.

117. See *AdB* 81/2 (1781), 349–352.

118. Pistorius, "Kants *Grundlegung*," in Hausius, *Materialien*, III, 114–115. Cf. the review of the second *Kritik* in Bittner, *Materialien*, pp. 162–163.

119. Kant, *Werke*, V, 9.

120. Ibid., V, 59–65, esp. 63–65.

121. Pistorius, "Kants *Grundlegung*," in Hausius, *Materialien*, III, 230–231.

122. Kant, *Werke*, V, 72–106, esp. 75–76. Although Kant does not say that this section is a reply to Pistorius, it clearly answers the objections in his review of the *Grundlegung*. The theory of incentives is indeed characteristic of the second *Kritik*, not appearing in the *Grundlegung*.

123. Pistorius, "Kants *Grundlegung*," in Hausius, *Materialien*, III, 237.

124. Kant, *Werke*, V, 27–28.

125. Pistorius, "Schultz's *Erläuterung*," in Hausius, *Materialien*, I, 173ff.

126. Kant, *Werke*, V, 50–57.

127. Ibid., V, 31–34.

7. The Revenge of the Wolffians

1. There were two exceptional works: Ulrich's *Institutiones* (1785) and Platner's *Aphorismen* (1784 edition).

2. The *Magazin* gave rise to another pro-Kantian journal, which was designed to counteract it, the *Neues Philosophisches Magazin* (Leipzig, 1789), edited by J. G. Born and J. H. Abicht. After the *Magazin* folded in 1792, it was replaced by the *Philosophisches Archiv* (1792–1795), which was also edited by Eberhard, and which had the same goals as the *Magazin*.

3. See Eberhard, "Vorbericht," *PM* I/1, iii–x and his "Ausführlichere Erklärung," *PM* III/3, 333ff.

4. See, for example, Eberhard, *PM* I/1, 28 and IV/1, 84ff., and *PA* I/2, 37–38. Eberhard is the most vigorous spokesman for this view, and it is in just such terms that he sums up his polemic against Kant in his *Dogmatische Briefe*; see *PA*

I/2, 37ff. But the same view is also represented in J. S. Schwab's *Preisschrift*, pp. 78ff.

5. See, for example, Eberhard, *PM* I/1, 28–29 and I/3, 264–265; Schwab, *Preisschrift*, pp. 121–122, and Flatt, *Beyträge*, pp. 78–79.

6. See Eberhard, *PA* I/2, 80 and *PM* I/1, 26; Flatt, *Beyträge*, pp. 4–7, 64; and Platner, *Aphorismen*, par. 699.

7. See Eberhard, *PM* I/3, 307ff.; II/2, 129ff.; and Maass, *PM* II/2, 186ff. An exception here is Ulrich, whose *Institutiones* accepts Kant's distinction.

8. Concerning the details of this controversy, see Eberstein, *Geschichte*, II, 171ff.

9. See Eberhard, *PM* II/2, 169–170 and II/3, 322ff.; Eberhard, *PA* I/1, 126ff.; Maass, *PA* I/3, 100ff.; Schwab, *PM* III/4, 397ff.; L. David, *PM* IV/3, 271ff. and IV/4, 406ff.; and Kästner, *PM* II/4, 391ff., 403ff., 420ff.

10. Eberhard, *PM* II/2, 129ff. and I/3, 370ff.; Maass, *PM* II/2, 222ff.; and Schwab, *PA* II/1, 117ff.

11. Eberhard, *PM* II/3, 316 and Schwab, *Preisschrift*, pp. 133, 139–140.

12. Eberhard, *PM* I/3, 269–272, 280–281; Flatt, *Beyträge*, pp. 80–81 and Ulrich, *Institutiones*, pars. 177, 309. Platner accepts Kant's criterion, though he has doubts about his ability to justify it; see *Aphorismen*, p. ii.

13. Eberhard, *PA* I/2, 39ff.; Flatt, *Beyträge*, pp. 15ff., 80–81; Platner, *Aphorismen*, par. 701; Ulrich, *Institutiones*, pars. 177, 309; and Schwab, *Preisschrift*, p. 124.

14. Eberhard, *PM* II/4, 468–473; Schwab, *Preisschrift*, pp. 118ff. and *PM* IV/2, 195ff.; and Maass, *PM* II/2, 218ff.

15. Eberhard, *PM* II/3, 244–245 and *PA* I/2, 85–86; Schwab, *PM* IV/2, 200–201; Maass, *PM* II/2, 218; and Flatt, *Beyträge*, pp. 94ff.

16. Eberhard, *PA* I/4, 85ff.

17. See Maass, *Briefe*, pp. 12ff. and passim; Schwab, *Preisschrift*, p. 123; Flatt, *Beyträge*, pp. 162ff.; and Platner, *Aphorismen*, par. 703.

18. Flatt, *Beyträge*, pp. 150–151, 165ff.; Schwab, *PA* II/2, 1ff.; and Ulrich, *Eleutheriologie*, passim.

19. Eberhard, *PA* I/3, 94 and I/4, 76ff.; Platner, *Aphorismen*, par. 704; Schwab, *Preisschrift*, pp. 126ff.; and Flatt, *Briefe*, pp. 13ff. and passim.

20. See, for example, Eberhard's *Dogmatische Briefe* in *PA* I/2, 72–74, where Eberhard admits that his philosophy is not in tune with his age. Also see a similar confession in Schwab, *Preisschrift*, p. 3.

21. For the Wolffian defense of these values, see Eberhard's *Ueber Staatsverfassungen und ihre Verbesserungen*, which is a classic statement of the moderate reaction against the French Revolution. For an appraisal of the historical significance of this work, see Epstein, *Genesis*, pp. 492–493.

22. See Eberhard's encomium to Prussia in *PM* I/2, 235.

23. See Mendelssohn, *Jerusalem, Schriften zur Aesthetik und Politik*, II, 395–396, and Eberhard, *Staatsverfassungen*, I, 130–131, 141.

24. This reaction is particularly clear, and particularly well documented, in the case of the *Tübinger Stift*. Concerning the students' enthusiastic reception of the

revolution, and the ensuing rejection of the old metaphysics, see Fuhrmanns, *Schelling, Briefe und Dokumente,* I, 16ff.

25. See Eberhard, *PA* I/4, 74–76 and I/2, 72–74.

26. Eberhard, *PA* I/4, 40ff., and *Staatsverfassungen,* I, 85–86 and II, 51ff.

27. See the "Vorbericht" to Eberhard, *Staatsverfassungen,* I, 3–6.

28. Hence the *Magazin* was followed by the *Archiv* in 1792; and Maass and Schwab doubled their efforts by publishing additional polemics.

29. It was already clear to Kant's contemporaries that the major source of the popularity of his philosophy in the 1790s was the Revolution. See, for example, Feder, *Leben,* p. 127 and Nicolai, *Abhandlungen,* I, 260–261.

30. This was certainly the case for the young Schelling and Hegel. See, for example, Schelling's letter of February 4, 1795, to Hegel, and Hegel's letter of April 16, 1795, to Schelling in Fuhrmanns, *Briefe und Dokumente,* II, 63–64, 66–67. Also see Hegel's letter of August 30, 1795, to Schelling, where Hegel expresses his *Schadenfreude* at the passing of Eberhard's *Magazin* and *Archiv,* ibid., II, 74.

31. The loci classici for the former theory are Eberhard, *PM* I/3, 307ff. and II/2, 129ff.; Maass, *PM* II/2, 186ff.; and Schwab, *PA* II/1, 117ff. And for the latter theory, see Eberhard, *PM* II/3, 244–245 and *PA* I/2, 85–86; Schwab, *PM* IV/2, 200–201; and Maass, *PM* II/2, 218.

32. This is surprising given the Wolffians' allegiance to Leibniz, who would have reduced all a priori truths to the analytic a priori. See, for example, Leibniz, "Primae Veritates," in Couturat, *Opuscles,* pp. 518–523. The Wolffians were willing to consider reduction to the analytic a priori only in the case of mathematics and not of metaphysics.

33. See, for example, Eberhard, *PM* I/3, 326–327 and II/3, 318.

34. Eberhard, *PM* I/3, 326 and *PA* I/2, 55–56; and Maass, *PM* II/2, 196–197.

35. See, for example, Eberhard, *PM* II/2, 137–138.

36. Eberhard, *PM* II/2, 137–138.

37. Maass, *PM* II/2, 222–224 and Eberhard, *PM* I/2, 328–329.

38. Maass, *PM* II/2, 220; Schwab, *PM* IV/2, 195ff.; and Eberhard, *PM* II/4, 468–473.

39. See section 3.2.

40. Eberhard, to be fair, does acknowledge the point that his eternal truths are only hypothetical. See, for example, *PM* II/2, 138–139 and I/3, 330–331. It is too basic a point for even him to miss. But it is also noteworthy that Eberhard says that logical truth is ipso facto transcendental truth. See, for example, *PM* I/2, 156–157. At the heart of the problem is Eberhard's self-confessed 'Platonism', his tendency to reify all logical truths as eternal truths in the mind of God. See, for example, *PA* I/4, 50–51.

41. See Kant, *Ueber eine Entdeckung, Werke,* VIII, 241–242. Kant's argument here is not fully appreciated or understood by Lovejoy in his classic essay defending Leibniz and Wolff. See Lovejoy, "Kant's Antithesis of Dogmatism and Criticism," *Mind* (1906), 191–214.

42. Eberhard, *PM* I/2, 165–166.

43. Eberhard, *PM* II/2, 157.

44. Eberhard, *PM* II/3, 338.

45. See Ulrich, *Erster Umriss einer Anleitung in den philosophischen Wissenschaften*.

46. See Reinhold to Kant, March 1, 1788, in Kant, *Briefwechsel*, p. 343.

47. See Schütz to Kant, September 20, 1785, in Kant, *Briefwechsel*, pp. 266–267.

48. See Ulrich to Kant, April 21, 1785, in Kant, *Briefwechsel*, p. 263.

49. See Reinhold to Kant, October 12, 1787, and January 19 and March 1, 1788, in Kant, *Briefwechsel*, pp. 328, 339, 343. Also see Bering to Kant, December 5, 1787, in Kant, *Briefe*, X, 507.

50. See Reinhold to Kant, October 12, 1787, in Kant, *Briefwechsel*, p. 328.

51. See Reinhold to Kant, January 19, 1788, in Kant, *Briefwechsel*, p. 339.

52. Ulrich, *Institutiones*, pars. 177, 309.

53. Ibid., par. 317.

54. Ibid., pars. 236, 239.

55. Ibid., pars. 238–239.

56. See *ALZ* 295 (1785), 297–299.

57. See Schütz to Kant, November 13, 1785, in Kant, *Briefwechsel*, p. 274. Prima facie it is surprising that Schultz, such a close disciple of Kant, should write such a critical review. Apparently, the review upset Kant and nearly resulted in a break with Schultz. Hamann wrote Jacobi, April 9, 1786, that the review led to an emergency meeting of Kant and Schultz, whose outcome was acceptable to Kant. See Hamann, *Briefwechsel*, VI, 349.

58. Kant, *Werke*, IV, 474n.

59. Ibid., IV, 475.

60. Ibid., IV, 476. Cf. *KrV*, B, 140–141, par. 19.

61. *KrV*, B, 121.

62. Reinhold to Kant, October 12, 1787, in Kant, *Briefwechsel*, p. 329.

63. Kant, *Werke*, VIII, 183–184.

64. This review is in Kant, *Werke*, VIII, 453–460.

65. Kant's original manuscript is reproduced in *Werke*, XXIII, 79–81. Kant's role in the Kraus review was first explained by Vaihinger in his "Ein bisher unbekannter Aufsatz von Kant über die Freiheit," *Philosophischen Monatshefte* 16 (1880), 193–208.

66. Ulrich, *Eleutheriologie*, 62.

67. Ibid., pp. 8–11.

68. Ibid., pp. 10–11, 31, 37.

69. Ibid., pp. 10–11, 37.

70. Kant, *Werke*, VIII, 457–458.

71. Ibid., VIII, 456.

72. Ulrich, *Eleutheriologie*, pp. 33–35.

73. Concerning Storr's theology and its historical background, see Henrich, "Historische Voraussetzungen von Hegels System," in *Hegel im Kontxt*, pp. 51–61 and Pfleiderer, *The Development of Theology in Germany since Kant*, pp. 85–87.

74. Concerning Storr's tendentious use of Kant's moral theology, see Storr, *Bemerkungen über Kants philosophische Religionslehre*, passim.

75. Concerning Hegel's and Hölderlin's attendance of Flatt's lectures, see Harris, *Hegel's Development*, pp. 72–74, 83–84, 88, 94–95, 74n; and concerning Schelling's attendance, see Fuhrmanns, *Briefe und Dokumente*, I, 19–26.

76. See, for example, Hegel to Schelling, December 24, 1794, Schelling to Hegel, January 6, 1795, and Hegel to Schelling, end of January, 1795, in Fuhrmanns, *Briefe und Dokumente*, II, 54–55, 56–57, 61.

77. Concerning the young Hegel's and Schelling's criticism of Storr's and Flatt's moral theology, see Düsing, "Die Rezeption der kantischen Postulatenlehre," *Hegel-Studien Beiheft* 9 (1973), 53–90.

78. Concerning the contemporary assessment of Flatt, see Eberstein, *Geschichte*, II, 233 and Maass *PM* I/2, 186–187.

79. In his letter of October 27, 1793, to Kant, Flatt indicates the shift from his earlier position when he says that he has learned to value his moral proof of God's existence. See Kant, *Briefe*, XI, 461.

80. See Flatt's article "Etwas über die kantische Kritik des kosmologischen Beweises des Daseyns Gottes," *PM* II/1, 93–106.

81. See Kant's contemptuous reply to Flatt in the "Vorrede" to the *Metaphysik der Sitten*, *Werke*, VI, 207. Also see Hamann to Jacobi, May 13, 1786, in Hamann, *Briefwechsel*, VI, 309, where Hamann reports about Kant's displeasure over "the Tübingen review of his *Moral*."

82. *KpV, Werke*, V, 24.

83. See *TgA*, May 13, 1786 and February 16, 1786.

84. See *KpV*, "Vorrede," *Werke*, V, 4n, 5–6. Kant's reply to this second objection is also a reply to Pistorius.

85. Flatt frequently cites Ulrich in the *Beyträge*. According to Harris, Flatt used the *Institutiones* as a basis for some of his lectures. See *Hegel's Development*, p. 78.

86. *KrV*, B, 301.

87. Flatt, *Beyträge*, p. 12.

88. Flatt, *Briefe*, pp. 18–19.

89. Ibid., p. 13. Cf. Flatt's article in *PM* II/1, 106.

90. Flatt, *Briefe*, pp. 14–15.

91. Ibid., pp. 15–16.

92. Ibid., pp. 30–36.

93. Ibid., pp. 52–54.

94. Ibid., pp. 58–59.

95. *KrV*, B, 837–838.

96. Flatt, *Briefe*, pp. 64–65.

97. Ibid., pp. 72–79. Kant argues against the physicotheological argument that it can infer not the infinity but only the comparative goodness of God.

98. As Düsing, "Rezeption," p. 58n, points out, Schelling's early critique of the "Postulatenlehre" shows similarities with that of Flatt.

99. See Eberstein, *Geschichte*, I, 434.

100. See, for example, the introduction to Mendelssohn's *Morgenstunden* in Mendelssohn, *Schriften*, III/2, 3.

101. See Heydenreich to Reinhold, July 20, 1789, in *Reinholds Leben*, p. 344.

102. Eberstein, *Geschichte,* I, 434.

103. Platner, *Aphorismen* (1784), pars. 855, 866, 873.

104. Ibid., par. 719.

105. Ibid., pars. 792–810.

106. Kant's influence on Platner has been documented by Seligowitz, "Platners Stellung zu Kant," *Vierteljahrschrift für wissenschaftliche Philosophie* 16 (1892), I, 85–86.

107. The first edition of the first part appeared in 1776; the first edition of the second part in 1782; and the second revised edition of the first part in 1784. This 1784 edition makes some interesting criticisms of Kant, but by and large it still represents Platner's old Leibnizian standpoint. The third, completely revised edition of the first part appeared in 1793. This is the most important edition for post-Kantian philosophy. A second, completely revised edition of the second part was published in 1800.

108. Concerning the details of this discussion, see Eberstein, *Geschichte,* II, 386–394.

109. See, for example, Schad, *Geist der Philosophie,* pp. 241ff., in which he quotes Platner at length. Even Adickes, who was by no means generous to Kant's critics, admits that Platner's criticisms are "acute throughout." See his *Bibliography,* pp. 41ff.

110. See Reinhold, "Ausführlichen Darstellung des negativen Dogmatismus," in *Beyträge,* II, 159ff.

111. See Born, *Versuch,* pp. xi–xiv. Cf. Born to Kant, October 6, 1788, in Kant, *Briefe,* X, 547.

112. Concerning the details of Fichte's lectures on Platner, see Lauth and Gliwitsky, "Einleitung" to Fichte, in *Gesamtausgabe,* II/4, v–vi, 23–25.

113. See, for example, Eberstein, *Geschichte,* II, 366ff.

114. Platner, *Aphorismen* (1793), par. 699.

115. Ibid., pars. 694, 696, 705.

116. *KrV,* B, 791, 795–796.

117. Platner, *Aphorismen* (1793), note on p. vi. Cf. Reinhold to Kant, June 14, 1789, in Kant, *Briefwechsel,* p. 405.

118. Platner, *Aphorismen* (1793), p. vi.

119. Nonetheless, Platner is a sharp critic of Kant's moral theology. See, for example, *Aphorismen* (1793), par. 704.

120. Platner, *Aphorismen* (1793), pp. viiiff.

121. See "Platner's Briefwechsel," in Bergmann, *Platner,* p. 324. Cf. Platner to Luise Augusta, May 19, 1792, ibid., pp. 325–327.

122. Platner, *Aphorismen* (1793), pp. xi–xii.

123. Ibid., p. xiii.

124. Ibid., par. 700.

125. Ibid., par. 699.

126. Ibid., pars. 705–706, 710.

127. See Reinhold to Kant, April 9, 1789, in Kant, *Briefwechsel,* p. 375.

128. See Kant to Reinhold, May 19, 1789, in Kant, *Briefwechsel,* p. 393. Here Kant abstains from the struggle against Eberhard for the usual reasons of time and

age. When the third *Kritik* was completed, however, Kant decided to break his resolve and fight. See Kant to Reinhold, September 21, 1789, in Kant, *Briefwechsel*, p. 417.

129. See Kant to Reinhold, May 12 and 19, 1789, in Kant, *Briefwechsel*, pp. 377–393; and Kant to Schultz, June 29 and August 2, 1789, ibid., 465–466.

130. According to Eberstein, all the skirmishes between Kant's friends and foes had produced only one clear result: that the Wolffians were not beaten. See his detailed account of these exchanges in *Geschichte*, II, 165–180.

131. See Rehberg, *ALZ* 90 (1789), 713–716; and Reinhold, *ALZ* 174–175 (1790), 577–597.

132. See Eberhard's reply to Rehberg, *PM* II/1, 29ff.; and his reply to Reinhold, *PM* II/2, 244ff.

133. Rehberg, *ALZ* 90 (1789), 715.

134. Although the third *Kritik* and the *Entdeckung* appeared at the same time, the third *Kritik* was already substantially completed by the time Kant began to work on the *Entdeckung*. See Kant to la Garde, October 2, 1789, in Kant, *Briefwechsel*, p. 417.

135. The later *Fortschritte* also discusses the Leibnizian-Wolffian school; but here Kant abandons polemics, and his perspective is more historical.

136. Concerning the impact of the *Entdeckung*, see Jachmann to Kant, October 14, 1790, in Kant, *Briefwechsel*, p. 484. Also see Vorländer, *Kant*, I, 342 and Eberstein, *Geschichte*, II, 231–232.

137. According to Eberstein, Kant could not afford to ignore Eberhard, who then had "the reputation of a deep-thinking *Weltweisen*." See his *Geschichte*, II, 166.

138. This claim is often misrepresented. Thus Tonelli says that Eberhard "claimed that Kant's views were entirely derived from Leibniz, and that they were a special form of dogmatism." See his article "Eberhard," in the *Encyclopedia of Philosophy*, II, 449. But Eberhard never made such a strong claim and always insisted that there were differences between Kant's and Leibniz's views. Still less was Eberhard accusing Kant of plagiarism, as Adickes implies in his *Bibliography*, p. 87.

139. Eberhard, *PM* I/1, 26.

140. Ibid., I/1, 23.

141. Ibid., I/1, 26.

142. Ibid., I/1, 17.

143. Ibid., I/1, 28 and I/3, 264–265.

144. Ibid., I/1, 19–20.

145. Eberhard, *PM* I/2, 161ff.

146. Wolff, *Werke*, II/1, 17–18, par. 31.

147. Eberhard, *PM* I/2, 163–164.

148. Kant, *Werke*, VIII, 193–198.

149. Ibid., VIII, 207–225, esp. 207ff.

150. Ibid., VIII, 205.

151. See Eberhard, *PM* I/3, 269–272, 280–281.

152. Kant, *Werke*, VIII, 188–189.

153. Ibid., IV, 474n.

154. See Eberhard, *PM* I/3, 307–309, 326.

155. Kant, *Werke*, VIII, 229, 232.

156. Ibid., VIII, 246–251.

157. There are two well-known passages, one where Kant says that appearances are of things-in-themselves, which are their grounds (*Werke*, VIII, 215); and another where Kant categorically rejects innate ideas, insisting that there is only an a priori activity of acquisition (*Werke*, VIII, 221–222). Although these passages are often cited, there is little here that the attentive reader could not have already gleaned from the *Kritik*. Concerning the first point, see *KrV*, B, xxvi, 55, 60; concerning the second, *KrV*, B, 1, 117–119.

158. Thus Nicolai noted that one effect of Eberhard's campaign against Kant was that it dispelled the air of authority surrounding the critical philosophy. See his *Gedächtnisschrift*, p. 41.

159. See, for example, the second part of Schulz's *Prüfung*, which is almost entirely devoted to defending these doctrines against Eberhard.

160. Kant, *Werke*, XX, 260.

161. See Reinhold, *Beyträge*, I, 288–294, 323–326, 329.

162. Thus Bardili dedicates his chief work, *Grundriss der ersten Logik*, to "the rescuers of the scholastic understanding in Germany," among them Herder, Schlosser, Nicolai, and, most striking of all, Eberhard.

163. Concerning Reinhold's move away from the critical philosophy, see Lauth, "Reinhold's Vorwurf," in Lauth, *Philosophie aus einem Prinzip*, pp. 225–276.

8. Reinhold's *Elementarphilosophie*

1. See Fichte, "Ueber den Begriff der Wissenschaftslehre," in *Werke*, I, 38ff., and Schelling, *Ueber die Moglichkeit einer Form der Philosophie ueberhaupt*, *Werke*, I/1, 45–73.

2. See Hegel, *Werke*, II, 35ff.

3. This claim has been put forward by Cassirer, *Erkenntnisproblem*, III, 33ff., and Klemmt, *Elementarphilosophie*, pp. 58–68.

4. See the works by Kossmann, Pirner, Goes, Werdermann, Visbeck, and Abicht in the bibliography.

5. Thus Eberhard's *Archiv* reserved its major articles for Reinhold rather than Kant; and Schulze, in his famous *Aenesidemus*, intentionally spent most of his time and energy attacking Reinhold's *Elementarphilosophie*, which he regarded as the final and systematic form of the critical philosophy.

6. See *TM* 2 (February 1785), 148–173.

7. Schiller, who is usually associated with the circle, became part of it only in the summer of 1787. By that time Reinhold was already a convert to Kant. It was indeed Reinhold who introduced Schiller to Kant. Concerning Reinhold's relation to Schiller, see Abusch, *Schiller*, pp. 128, 141.

8. Reinhold, *TM*, pp. 162ff.

9. Ibid., pp. 161–165.

10. See section 5.7.

11. Some of these early articles are reprinted in Reinhold, *Schriften*.

12. See Reinhold, *Versuch,* pp. 203ff.

13. See Reinhold, *Briefe,* I, 147ff.

14. See Schütz to Kant, February 18, 1785, in Kant, *Briefwechsel,* p. 261.

15. Kant, *Werke,* VIII, 56.

16. Concerning the reaction to Kant's review among Herder and his friends, see Gulyga, *Kant,* p. 170. See also Herder to Wieland, January 1785, in Herder, *Briefe,* V, 102–103.

17. *ALZ* 179 (July 30, 1785), 125–128.

18. See Reinhold, "Schicksale," in *Versuch,* pp. 53ff.

19. See Reinhold to Kant, October 12, 1787, in Kant, *Briefwechsel,* pp. 326–327.

20. Reinhold, *Briefe,* I, 11–13.

21. See Reinhold's early essay "Gedanken über Aufklärung," *TM* 3 (July 1784), 4ff.

22. There were two editions of the *Briefe.* The first appeared in installments in the *Teutsche Merkur,* starting in 1786; the second was published as a separate book but came out in two volumes: the first volume in April 1790, the second in October 1790. There are significant differences between the first and second editions. The second edition not only adds new letters, it also changes passages in the first edition, introducing references to the *Elementarphilosophie.* It is regrettable that there is no critical edition of the *Briefe* which notes these important variations. The reissue of the *Briefe* in 1923 by Schmidt simply reproduces the second edition without noting its differences from the first. Since this edition is still the only easily accessible one, it is cited here. All significant variations from the original 1786 edition will be noted, however.

23. Concerning the details of this dispute and the parties to it, see Hettner, *Geschichte,* I, 349–374, and Beck, *Early German Philosophy,* chap. 12.

24. Reinhold, *Briefe,* I, 83–84, 99–100.

25. In the 1790 edition Reinhold inserted the phrase "through a new theory of representation," thus advocating his *Elementarphilosophie* instead of the *Kritik.*

26. Reinhold, *Briefe,* I, 92–93.

27. Ibid., I, 100–101.

28. Ibid., I, 100–101, 118–119, 132.

29. Ibid., I, 120–121.

30. Ibid., I, 123.

31. See Jenisch to Kant, May 14, 1787, in Kant, *Briefwechsel,* p. 315. Concerning the impact of the *Briefe,* see also Reinhold to Kant, October 12, 1787, in Kant, *Briefwechsel,* p. 327; and Baggesen to Reinhold, December 10, 1790, in Baggesen, *Briefwechsel,* I, 5–6.

32. Kant, *Briefwechsel,* pp. 325–329.

33. Ibid., pp. 333–336.

34. Kant, *Werke,* VIII, 183–184.

35. See Reinhold, "Schicksale," in *Versuch,* pp. 51ff.

36. Ibid., pp. 49–50, 62–65.

37. Ibid., pp. 63–67.

38. Although Reinhold continued to work on the *Elementarphilosophie* until

as late as 1796, all the major writings stop after his departure from Jena in 1794. In 1797 Reinhold formally declared himself a disciple of Fichte.

39. See Reinhold to Kant, June 14, 1789, and January 21, 1793, in Kant, *Briefwechsel*, pp. 403, 622. Another letter, probably written in May 1790, has been lost. See Kant, *Briefe*, XI, 181. But this must have obtained a similar request, judging from Kant's reply to Reinhold, September 21, 1791, in Kant, *Briefwechsel*, p. 525.

40. See Kant to Reinhold, December 1, 1789, September 21, 1791, and December 21, 1792, in Kant, *Briefwechsel*, pp. 425, 525, 615. Concerning the details of this correspondence, see Klemmt, *Reinholds Elementarphilosophie*, pp. 149–167.

41. That Kant wanted Reinhold's support, and was eager to avoid a break, is evident from his letters of March 7, 1788, and September 21, 1791, to Reinhold. See *Briefwechsel*, pp. 349–350, 525–526.

42. See Kant, *Briefwechsel*, pp. 526–527. Also see Kant to Beck, November 2, 1791, in Kant, *Briefwechsel*, p. 537, where Kant complains of the "obscure abstractions" of Reinhold's theory.

43. See "Ueber das Verhältnis der Theorie des Vorstellungsvermögens zur Kritik der reinen Vernunft," in *Beyträge*, I, 263ff.

44. Kant, *KrV*, B, 673, 861–862, ix, xxxv. Cf. *Werke*, IV, 468–469.

45. Reinhold, *Fundament*, pp. 72–75; *Beyträge*, I, 263–264.

46. Reinhold, *Beyträge*, I, 315–316.

47. Reinhold, *Fundament*, p. 76; *Beyträge*, I, 267.

48. Reinhold, *Beyträge*, I, 267–268. Reinhold does not mention the faculty of judgment since the third *Kritik* had not yet appeared.

49. Kant, *KrV*, B, 25–26, 788–789; A, xii.

50. Reinhold, *Beyträge*, I, 281.

51. Ibid., I, 288–294.

52. Ibid., I, 323–326, 329.

53. Here Reinhold has in mind the arguments of Eberhard, Maass, and Schwab. See section 7.1.

54. Reinhold, *Fundament*, pp. 72–75; *Beyträge*, I, 295.

55. Reinhold, *Fundament*, p. 72.

56. Reinhold, *Fundament*, 62–63, 71; *Beyträge*, I, 268–276.

57. Reinhold, *Fundament*, xiv, 72.

58. Reinhold, *Beyträge*, I, 344.

59. Kant, *KrV*, B, 89.

60. The most important pieces on this theme are the second essay of the first volume of the *Beyträge*, "Ueber das Bedurfnis, die Eigenschaften eines allgemeinsten ersten Grundsatzes der Philosophie zu bestimmen," and the fifth essay of the same volume, "Ueber die Möglichkeit der Philosophie als strenge Wissenschaft." Also significant is the first section of the first book of the *Versuch*.

61. Reinhold, *Beyträge*, I, 357–358.

62. Ibid., I, 115–117, 358–362.

63. See *KrV*, B, 337–338.

64. Reinhold, *Fundament*, p. 96.

65. Reinhold, *Beyträge*, I, 115–117.

66. Ibid., I, 358–360.

67. Ibid., I, 134–136.
68. Ibid., I, 143.
69. Ibid., I, 144, 162. Cf. *Versuch*, p. 66.
70. The same seemed to be the case to Hegel in the "Einleitung" to the *Phänomenologie des Geistes*. Hegel's arguments for a phenomenology show many resemblances to Reinhold's.
71. See Reinhold, *Versuch*, bks. I; IV, 1, 2; and II, 6–15.
72. Reinhold, *Beyträge*, I, 357–358; *Versuch*, 189–190.
73. Reinhold, *Versuch*, pp. 177–181, 202–209.
74. Ibid., pp. 179–180.
75. Ibid., pp. 180, 206.
76. Ibid., pp. 157–158.
77. Reinhold, *Fundament*, pp. 90–93.
78. Reinhold, *Versuch*, pp. 195–227. In these passages Reinhold distinguishes between the various senses of the phrase 'faculty of representation'.
79. Ibid., pp. 199–202, 212, 218–219.
80. Ibid., pp. 195–200, esp. 217–220.
81. Ibid., p. 207.
82. Ibid., pp. 200–206, 222.
83. Ibid., pp. 213–214, 221.
84. Ibid., p. 227.
85. Reinhold, *Beyträge*, I, 168ff.
86. Reinhold, *Versuch*, pp. 232–234, 236–237, 256.
87. Ibid., pp. 200–201, 235–238.
88. Reinhold, *Beyträge*, I, 146–147, 168.
89. Ibid., I, 143–144, 168. Cf. *Fundament*, pp. 78–81.
90. *Beyträge*, I, 305–308. *Pace* Reinhold, Kant does formulate his principle so that it holds for any possible representation; see *KrV*, B, 132.
91. *KrV*, B, 132.
92. Reinhold, *Beyträge*, I, 180.
93. Ibid., I, 181–183.
94. Ibid., I, 184–185. Cf.*Versuch*, p. 230.
95. *Beyträge*, I, 183. Cf. *Versuch*, p. 235.
96. Reinhold, *Versuch*, pp. 230–232. Cf. *Beyträge*, I, 183.
97. *Versuch*, pp. 231–232. Cf. *Beyträge*, I, 182.
98. *Versuch*, pp. 240–241.
99. Ibid., pp. 244–255. Cf. *Beyträge*, I, 185–187.
100. *Versuch*, pp. 247–248.
101. Ibid., p. 433.
102. Ibid., pp. 240, 231–232.
103. Ibid., pp. 248–249.
104. Ibid., p. 256. Cf. *Beyträge*, I, 189.
105. *Versuch*, pp. 258–261. Cf. *Beyträge*, I, 190.
106. *Versuch*, p. 257.
107. Ibid., pp. 258–259.
108. Ibid., pp. 262–263.

109. Ibid., pp. 264–265, 267–270, 279–282.

110. Ibid., pp. 277–278.

111. Ibid., pp. 284–285.

112. Ibid., pp. 267–270.

113. Ibid., pp. 293–295.

114. Ibid., pp. 62–63.

115. Ibid., pp. 293–295.

116. Ibid., pp. 295–300.

117. Ibid., pp. 299–302.

118. Ibid., p. 276.

119. See "Grundlinien der Theorie des Begehrungsvermögens," in *Versuch,* 560ff.

120. These difficulties had already been pointed out by Rüdiger and Crusius in their polemic against Wolff's single-faculty theory. See Beck, *Early German Philosophy,* pp. 300, 401.

121. Reinhold, *Briefe,* II, 499–500, 502.

122. Reinhold's distinction here anticipates, and perhaps influences, Schiller's later distinction between a *Formtrieb* and *Stofftrieb* in the *Aesthetische Briefe;* see Schiller, *Werke,* XX, 344–347.

123. See Wolff, *Vernünftige Gedanke, Werke* II/1, 469, 555, pars. 755–756, 894.

124. Concerning the influence of Wolff's theory, and the historical significance of Kant's struggle against it, see Beck, *Early German Philosophy,* pp. 268–269.

9. Schulze's Skepticism

1. See Hausius, *Materialien,* p. xxxix. Hausius was referring to Johann Reimarus, the son of Hermann Reimarus, the author of the notorious *Wolffenbüttel Fragmente.*

2. Concerning Reinhard's influence on Schulze, see Wundt, *Schulphilosophie,* pp. 296, 337–338. According to Wundt, Reinhard is the missing link in the German voluntarist tradition, which leads directly from Crusius to Schopenhauer.

3. See Feder to Reinhold, July 23, 1794, in Reinhold, *Leben,* p. 380.

4. Eberstein, *Geschichte,* II, 385.

5. Hausius, *Materialien,* p. xxxix.

6. Fuelleborn, *Beyträge,* III (1793), 157–158.

7. Fichte, "Briefentwurf an Flatt," dated November/December 1783, in *Gesammtausgabe,* III/2, 19.

8. Abicht, "Vorrede," in *Hermias.*

9. See Reinhold, *Beyträge,* II, 159ff.

10. Hegel, *Werke,* II, 220.

11. Concerning the importance of Hegel's early encounter with skepticism, see Buchner, "Zur Bedeutung," *Hegel-Studien, Beiheft* 4 (1969), 49–56.

12. Schopenhauer, *Werke,* II, 519.

13. Platner and Maimon also developed such a skepticism; but Schulze was the first to do so. His *Aenesidemus* appeared before the 1793 edition of Platner's *Aphorismen* and Maimon's *Briefe Philalethes an Aenesidemus* (1794).

14. Schulze, *Aenesidemus,* p. 18.

15. Schulze's claim to represent the true spirit of ancient skepticism was sharply contested by Hegel. See Hegel's early review of Schulze in *Werke,* II, 222–223.

16. Sextus Empiricus, *Outlines,* bk. I, 180–185, bk. III, 138.

17. See Schulze, *AdB* 100/2 (1792), 419–452. This article is also reprinted in Hausius, *Materialien,* I, 233–234.

18. Schulze, *Aenesidemus,* pp. 72ff.

19. Thus Erdmann, *Versuch,* V, 506, and Kroner, *Von Kant bis Hegel,* I, 325.

20. Cf. Schulze, *Aenesidemus,* p. 36 and Kant, *KrV,* A, xii and B, 766.

21. Schulze, *Aenesidemus,* p. ix.

22. Ibid., pp. 23–24.

23. Thus Erdmann, *Versuch,* V, 506.

24. See Hausius, *Materialien,* I, 233–258. This article has been sadly neglected by scholars and has not even appeared in Liebert's bibliography. Although it appeared anonymously, there can be no doubt that Schulze is the author. It was written under the signature "Ru," which was Schulze's sign; see Parthey, *Mitarbeiter,* pp. 20–21.

25. Schulze, *Aenesidemus,* p. 34.

26. Ibid., p. 15ff.

27. Ibid., p. 19.

28. That this is Schulze's bottom line is evident from a much neglected earlier work, *Ueber den höchsten Zweck des Studiums der Philosophie,* pp. 99–100, 115–116.

29. Schulze, *Aenesidemus,* p. ix.

30. See, for example, Windelband, *Geschichte,* II, 193; Hartmann, *Idealismus,* p. 18; and Kroner, *Von Kant bis Hegel,* I, 325.

31. The most recent and able defender of Reinhold is Klemmt, *Reinholds Elementarphilosophie,* pp. 347ff.

32. A more balanced appraisal of Schulze's merits is to be found in Cassirer, *Erkenntnisproblem,* III, 168, and Erdmann, *Versuch,* V, 501, 506.

33. Schulze, *Aenesidemus,* pp. 41–42.

34. Ibid., p. 34.

35. Ibid., pp. 45–47.

36. Reinhold, *Fundament,* pp. 84–86.

37. Fichte, *Werke,* I, 5.

38. Schulze, *Aenesidemus,* p. 47n.

39. Ibid., pp. 48–52.

40. Ibid., pp. 53–55, 65.

41. Ibid., pp. 56–58, 63–64.

42. Reinhold, *Versuch,* pp. 213–214, 221.

43. Schulze, *Aenesidemus,* pp. 79–80.

44. Ibid., pp. 80–81.

45. Ibid., pp. 81–82.

46. Ibid., pp. 76–78.

47. Ibid., pp. 170–174, 146–153.

48. Ibid., pp. 142–143.

49. Ibid., pp. 143–145.

50. Ibid., pp. 157–158.

51. Ibid., pp. 161–166.

52. Ibid., pp. 305, 319.

53. Ibid., pp. 127–129. Cf. Schulze, *Kritik*, II, 578, 230–233, 563–569, 579–580.

54. Schulze, *Aenesidemus*, pp. 309–312.

55. Ibid., pp. 133–134.

56. Ibid., pp. 94–105.

57. Ibid., pp. 135–136.

58. Ibid., pp. 116–130.

59. Ibid., p. 307.

60. Ibid., pp. 295–296, 202–206.

61. Ibid., pp. 326–331.

62. Ibid., pp. 334–336. Also see Schulze's review of Kant's *Religion innerhalb der Grenzen der blossen Vernunft*, NAdB 16/1 (1794), 127–163.

63. See *KrV*, A, xvii, where Kant states that the subjective deduction, though of great importance, is not essential to his main purpose.

10. Maimon's Critical Philosophy

1. Kant, *Briefwechsel*, pp. 396ff.

2. The importance of Maimon's argument for Fichte and Schelling is apparent from some of their earlier works. See Fichte's "Vergleichung" (1795), in *Werke*, II, 440–441, and Schelling's *Abhandlung* (1798), *Werke*, I, 288–289. Fichte explicitly acknowledged his debt to Maimon. He wrote in a letter to Reinhold: "My respect for Maimon's talent is limitless; I firmly believe, and am willing to prove, that the critical philosophy has been overturned by him"; see Fichte, *Briefwechsel*, III/2, 282.

3. Here I follow Atlas, *Maimon*, 1ff., 331ff.

4. Maimon, *Werke*, I, 557.

5. Thus Kuntze and Erdmann see skepticism as Maimon's final position. See Kuntze, *Die Philosophie Maimons*, p. 41, and Erdmann, *Versuch*, V, 536. Atlas, however, thinks that Maimon's philosophy stops with the dilemma of dogmatism or skepticism; see his *Maimon*, pp. 16–18. Cassirer is alone in thinking that Maimon has, if only *in nuce*, a middle path; see his *Erkenntnisproblem*, III, 103.

6. Maimon, *Werke*, IV, 263–264.

7. Ibid., IV, 79–80.

8. Ibid., IV, 72–73; II, 186–187; V, 477–479; VII, 55–59.

9. Ibid., II, 187–188, 370–373; V, 489–490.

10. Ibid., V, 191–192.

11. Ibid., II, 187–188.

12. Ibid., II, 62–65, 182–183, 362–364.

13. Ibid., V, 426–427.

14. Ibid., IV, 38.

15. Kant himself misses this point. In his reply to Maimon's *Versuch* Kant argues that he can overcome Maimon's objections simply by remaining within the

sphere of consciousness. It is impossible to explain the correspondence between a priori concepts and experience, he says, only if experience is understood as the realm of things-in-themselves. If, however, it is assumed that experience consists in nothing more than appearances, the problem disappears. See Kant's letter of May 26, 1789, to Herz, in Kant, *Briefwechsel*, p. 397. Kant's reply does not explain the correspondence between such distinct kinds of representations as a priori concepts and a posteriori intuitions.

16. Maimon offers little justification for his rejection of empiricism other than his orthodox Kantian belief in the nonreducibility of the synthetic a priori; see his *Versuch*, II, 429–430.

17. Maimon, *Werke*, II, 62–65.

18. Kant himself introduces this idea in the third *Kritik*; see Kant, *Werke*, V, 401–410, secs. 76–77. But Maimon and Kant probably came to this idea independently of each other. The *Versuch* was not in Kant's hands until April 1789, just as the third *Kritik* was nearing completion. See Kant to Reinhold, May 12, 1789, in Kant, *Briefwechsel*, p. 385.

19. Maimon, *Werke*, VII, 131.

20. Ibid., II, 175–179.

21. Ibid., II, 64.

22. Ibid., II, 366.

23. Ibid., III, 186–187, 193. It is possible that this move toward a more regulative reading is due to the influence of Kant's third *Kritik*, which of course insists upon the strictly regulative status of the *intellectus archetypus*. After the completion of the *Versuch* in 1789, and before the publication of the *Wörterbuch* in 1791, Kant sent Maimon a copy of the third *Kritik*. See Maimon to Kant, May 15, 1790, in Kant, *Briefwechsel*, p. 462.

24. Kant, *KrV*, B, 207–211.

25. Maimon, *Werke*, II, 28n; VII, 211–212.

26. Ibid., II, 32.

27. Ibid., II, 33.

28. Wolff, *Werke*, I/1, 148, sec. 48.

29. Maimon, *Werke*, II, 352–353; VII, 215–216.

30. Ibid., II, 28n, 32–33.

31. Ibid., II, 356, Maimon's italics.

32. Ibid., II, 32.

33. Ibid., II, 32.

34. Ibid., II, 34–35.

35. Kant takes exception to Maimon's expansion of the realm of ideas. See his letter of May 26, 1789, to Herz, in Kant, *Briefwechsel*, pp. 399–400.

36. Maimon, *Werke*, 349–350, 75–83.

37. Ibid., II, 76.

38. Ibid., II, 32, 355–356.

39. Ibid., II, 64.

40. Ibid., II, 349–356.

41. Ibid., II, 236–237.

42. Ibid., II, 18; IV, 283; V, 194–195.

43. Ibid., V, 184–186. In a remark to the *Versuch* Maimon criticizes one of Kant's arguments for the a priori status of space and time, and seems to regard space and time as a posteriori; see *Werke*, II, 342. But this passage, which is intended only to point out a weakness in Kant's reasoning, is not characteristic of Maimon's position as a whole.

44. See *KrV*, B, 93, 35–39, 43, and Kant, *Werke*, IV, 285–286. The same arguments apply *mutatis mutandis* for time.

45. Kant, *KrV*, B, 35, 39, 43.
46. See Leibniz, *Schriften*, VII, 372.
47. Maimon, *Werke*, V, 192–193, 196–197.
48. Leibniz, *Schriften*, VII, 356.
49. Maimon, *Werke*, V, 192ff.
50. Ibid., V, 190–191.
51. Ibid., III, 186–187, 193.
52. *KrV*, B, 60–61.
53. Fichte, *Werke*, I, 252ff., 270ff.
54. Maimon, *Werke*, II, 145, 415; V, 429, 177; III, 185.
55. Ibid., II, 372.
56. Ibid., IV, 415; V, 404–406, 412–413.
57. Ibid., IV, 226–227; V, 377–379; III, 472–476.
58. Ibid., V, 176–177; II, 340–341.
59. Ibid., V, 177.
60. Ibid., III, 200–201.
61. Ibid., VII, 193.
62. Kant, *KrV*, B, viii, 90.
63. Maimon, *Werke*, VII, 5; V, 466, 477.
64. Ibid., V, 23; VI, 4.
65. Ibid., VI, 175–178, 163–164; V, 22, 115, 494.
66. In defending the autonomy of infinite judgments, Maimon follows Kant; see *KrV*, B, 97.
67. Maimon, *Werke*, V, 214–215, 462–470; VI, 3–7.
68. Ibid., V, 468; VI, 159–161, 5–6.
69. Ibid., V, 23, 214–216.
70. Reinhold, *Fundament*, pp. 117–121.
71. See Schelling, *Werke*, I/1, 221.
72. Maimon, *Werke*, V, 367–370.
73. Ibid., V, 78–85.
74. Ibid., V, 476, 212–213.
75. On the weak reading see *Werke*, V, 494–495, 88–94; and on the strong reading see ibid., V, 488–489.
76. Maimon, *Werke*, V, 78–86.
77. Ibid., V, 78.
78. Ibid., V, 78–79.
79. Ibid., II, 84ff., 377–378; V, 78.
80. Ibid., V, 78.
81. Spinoza, *Opera*, II, 45, def. III, pt. I.

82. In his *Nachlass* Maimon explicitly revives Leibniz's program; see *Werke*, VII, 649–650.

83. Concerning the attitude of the Berliners to Maimon, see Altmann, *Mendelssohn*, pp. 361ff.

84. Maimon, *Werke*, IV, 213–214.

85. Ibid., IV, 219.

86. Ibid., IV, 224–225.

87. Ibid., IV, 258.

88. Ibid., IV, 263.

89. The correspondence was published in 1793 in Maimon's *Streifereien im Gebiete der Philosophie.*

90. This does not contradict Maimon's own attempt to find a middle path between skepticism and dogmatism. Maimon believes that there is a middle path, but that it is the infinite progress of inquiry and not any self-evident first principle.

91. Maimon, *Werke*, IV, 25–55.

92. Ibid., V, 380–381; cf. IV, 239.

93. Ibid., V, 447–448.

94. Ibid., V, 377–378; IV, 217–218.

95. Ibid., III, 474; V, 391–392.

96. Ibid., IV, 226–227; III, 472, 475–476; V, 377–379.

97. Ibid., V, 404–406, 412–413.

98. Ibid., V, 405; VII, v.

99. Ibid., V, 412–413.

100. Ibid., V, 434–437.

Bibliography

Primary Sources

Abel, J. F. *Plan zu einer systematischen Metaphysik*. Stuttgart, Erhard, 1787.
——*Versuch über die Natur der spekulativen Vernunft*. Frankfurt, 1787.
Abicht, J. F. *Hermias oder Auflösung der die gültige Elementarphilosophie betreffenden Zweifel*. Erlangen, Walther, 1794.
——*Philosophisches Journal*. Erlangen, Walther, 1794–1795.
——*Preisschrift über die Frage: Welche Fortschritte hat die Metaphysik seit Leibnitzens und Wolffs Zeiten in Deutschland gemacht?* Berlin, Maurer, 1796.
Baggesen, J. *Aus Jens Baggesen Briefwechsel mit K. L. Reinhold und F. H. Jacobi*, ed. K. and A. Baggesen. Leipzig, Brockhaus, 1831.
Bardili, C. B. *Briefe über den Ursprung der Metaphysik überhaupt*. Altona, Hammerich, 1798.
——*Grundriss der ersten Logik gereinigt von den Irrthümern bisheriger Logiken überhaupt*. Stuttgart, Loflund, 1800.
——*Bardilis und Reinholds Briefwechsel über das Wesen der Philosophie und Unwesen der Spekulation*, ed. K. L. Reinhold. Munich, Lentner, 1804.
Basedow, J. B. *Philalethie, Neue Aussichten in die Wahrheiten und Religion der Vernunft*. Altona, Iverson, 1764.
——*Theoretisches System der gesunden Vernunft*. Altona, Iverson, 1765.
——*Ausgewählte Schriften*, ed. H. Göring. Langensalza, Beyer, 1880.
Beck, J. S. *Einzig möglicher Standpunkt, aus welchem die kritische Philosophie beurteilt werden muss*. Vol. 3 of *Erläuternden Auszugs aus den kritischen Schriften des Herrn Prof. Kant*. Riga, Hartknoch, 1796.
Bendavid, L. "Deduction der mathematischen Prinzipien aus Begriffen: Von den Principien der Geometrie," *PM* IV/3 (1791), 271–301.
——"Deduction der mathematischen Prinzipien aus Begriffen: Von den Prinzipien der Arithmetik," *PM* IV/4 (1791), 406–423.
Born, F. G. *Versuch über die ersten Gründe der Sinnenlehre*. Leipzig, Klaubarth, 1788.
——"Ueber die Unterscheidung der Urteile in analytische und synthetische," *NpM* 1 (1789), 141–168.

————*Versuch über die ursprünglichen Grundlagen des menschlichen Denkens und die davon abhängigen Schranken unserer Erkenntnis.* Leipzig, Barth, 1791.

Bornträger, J. C. F. *Ueber das Daseyn Gottes, in Beziehung auf Kantische und Mendelssohnischer Philosophie.* Hannover, Schmidt, 1788.

Borowski, L. E. "Darstellung des Lebens und Charakters Immanuel Kants," in *Immanuel Kant, Sein Leben in Darstellungen von Zeitgenossen,* ed. F. Gross. Darmstadt, Wissenschaftliche Buchgesellschaft, 1980.

Brastberger, M. G. U. *Untersuchungen über Kants Critik der reinen Vernunft.* Halle, Gebauer, 1790.

————"Ist die kritische Grenzberichtigung unserer Erkenntnis wahr, und wenn sie ist, ist sie auch neu?" *PA* I/4 (1792), 91–122.

————*Untersuchungen über Kants Critik der praktischen Vernunft.* Tübingen, Cotta, 1792.

Cäser, K. A. *Denkwürdigkeiten aus der philosophischen Welt.* Leipzig Müller, 1786.

Condillac, E. *Essai sur l'origene des connaissances humaines,* ed. J. Derrida. Auversur Oise, Galilee, 1973.

Crusius, C. A. *Die Philosophische Hauptwerke,* ed. A. Tonelli. Hildesheim, Olms, 1964.

Descartes, R. *The Philosophical Works,* ed. and trans. E. S. Haldane and G. R. T. Ross. Cambridge, Cambridge University Press, 1973.

Eberhard, J. A. *Neue Apologie des Sokrates.* Berlin, Voss, 1772.

————"An die Herrn Herausgeber der Berlinerischen Monatsschrift," *PM* I/2 (1788), 235–241.

————"Nachricht von dem Zweck und Einrichtung dieses Magazins," *PM* I/1 (1788), 1–8.

————"Ueber die logische Wahrheit oder die transcendentale Gültigkeit der menschlichen Erkenntnis," *PM* I/3 (1789), 243–262.

————"Ueber die Schranken der menschlichen Erkenntnis," *PM* I/1 (1788), 9–29.

————"Ausführlicher Erklärung über die Absicht dieses Magazins," *PM* I/3 (1789), 333–339.

————"Ueber das Gebiet des reinen Verstandes," *PM* I/3 (1789), 290–306.

————"Ueber den Unterschied der Philosophie und Mathematik in Rücksicht auf ihre Sicherheit," *PM* II/3 (1789), 316–341.

————"Ueber den Ursprung der menschlichen Erkenntnis," *PM* I/4 (1789), 369–405.

————"Ueber den wesentlichen Unterschied der Erkenntnis durch die Sinne und den Verstand," *PM* I/3 (1789), 290–306.

————"Ueber die apodiktischen Gewissheit," *PM* II/2 (1789), 129–185.

————"Ueber die Unterscheidung der Urteile in analytischen und synthetischen," *PM* I/3 (1789), 307–332.

————"Von den Begriffen des Raums und der Zeit in Beziehung auf die Gewissheit der menschlichen Erkenntnis," *PM* II/1 (1789), 53–92.

————"Weitere Anwendung der Theorie von der logischen Wahrheit oder der transcendental Gültigkeit der menschlichen Erkenntnis," *PM* I/3 (1789), 243–262.

————"Die ersten Erkenntnisgründe sind allgemein objektiv gültig," *PM* III/1 (1790), 56–62.

———"Ist die Form der Anschauung zu der apodiktischen Gewissheit nothwendig?" *PM* II/4 (1790), 460–485.

———"Ueber die Categorien, insonderheit über die Categorie der Causalität," *PM* IV/2 (1791), 171–187.

———"Dogmatische Briefe," *PA* I/2 (1792), 37–91; I/4 (1792), 46–90; II/1 (1792), 38–69; II/3 (1792), 44–73.

———"Ueber die Anschauung des inneren Sinnes," *PM* IV/4 (1792), 354–390.

———"Vergleichung des Skepticismus und des kritischen Idealismus," *PM* IV/1 (1792), 84–115.

———*Ueber Staatsverfassungen und ihre Verbesserungen.* Berlin, Voss, 1794.

———*Allgemeine Theorie des Denkens und Empfindens.* Berlin, Voss, 1796.

Ewald, J. L. *Ueber die kantische Philosophie mit Hinsicht auf die Bedürfnisse der Menschheit: Briefe an Emma.* Berlin, Unger, 1790.

Ewald, S. H. "Kritik der reinen Vernunft," *Gothaische gelehrte Zeitungen,* August 24, 1782.

Feder, J. G. H. *Der neue Emil oder von der Erziehung nach bewährter Grundsätzen.* Erlangen, Walther, 1768.

———"F. H. Jacobis David Hume," *PB* 1 (1788), 127–148.

———"Kants *Kritik der praktischen Vernunft,*" *PB* 1 (1788), 182–188.

———"Ueber den Begriff der Substanz," *PB* 1 (1788), 1–40.

———*Ueber Raum und Causalität.* Frankfurt, Dietrich, 1788.

———"Ueber subjektive und objektive Wahrheit," *PB* 2 (1788), 1–42.

———*Logik und Metaphysik.* Göttingen, Dieterich, 1790.

———*J. G. H. Feders Leben, Natur und Grundsätze.* Leipzig Schwickert, 1825.

Fichte, J. G. *Gesammtausgabe der bayerischen Akademie der Wissenschaften,* ed. R. Lauth and H. Jakob. Stuttgart, Fromann, 1970.

———*Werke,* ed. I. Fichte. Berlin, de Gruyter, 1971.

Flatt, J. F. "*Grundlegung zur Metaphysik der Sitten* von Immanuel Kant," *TgA* 14 (February 16, 1786), 105–112.

———*Fragmentarische Beyträge zur Bestimmung und Deduktion des Begriffs und Grundsätze der Causalität.* Leipzig, Crusius, 1788.

———*Briefe über den moralischen Erkenntnisgrund der Religion.* Tübingen, Cotta, 1789.

———"Etwas über die kantische Kritik der kosmologischen Beweises über das Daseins Gottes," *PM* II/1 (1789), 93–106.

———*Beyträge zur christlichen Dogmatik und Moral.* Tübingen, Cotta, 1792.

Forster, G. "Noch etwas über die Menschenrassen, An Herrn Dr. Biester," *TM* (October 1786), 57–86.

———*Werke,* ed. G. Steiner. Frankfurt, Insel, 1967.

Franck, S. *Paradoxa,* ed. S. Wollgast. Berlin, Akademie Verlag, 1966.

Fuelleborn, G. G. *Beyträge zur Geschichte der Philosophie.* Züllichau, Fromann, 1791.

Garve, C. "Kritik der reinen Vernunft von Immanuel Kant," *GgA* 3 (January 19, 1782), 40–48.

———"Kritik der reinen Vernunft von Immanuel Kant," *AdB,* supp. to 37–52 (1783), 838–862.

————*Abhandlung über die Verbindung der Moral mit der Politik*. Breslau, Korn, 1788.

————*Philosophische Anmerkungen und Abhandlungen zu Ciceros Büchern von den Pflichten*. Breslau, Korn, 1792.

————*Versuch über verschiedene Gegenstände der Moral*. Breslau, Korn, 1801.

————*Sämtliche Werke*. Breslau, Korn, 1801–1808.

————*Ueber das Daseyns Gottes, Eine nachgelassene Abhandlung*. Breslau, Korn, 1807.

Goes, G. F. D. *Systematische Dartstellungen der kantische Vernunftkritik*. Nürnberg, Felssecker, 1798.

Goethe, J. W. *Werke, Hamburger Ausgabe*, ed. D. Kühn and R. Wankmüller. Hamburg, Wegner, 1955.

Goeze, H. M. *Etwas Vorläufiges gegen des Herrn Hofraths Lessings feindselige Angriffe auf unser allerheiligste Religion und auf den einigen Lehrgrund derselben, die heiligen Schrift*. Hamburg, Harmsen, 1778.

Goltz, A., ed. *Thomas Wizenmann, der Freund F. H. Jacobi in Mittheilungen aus seinem Briefwechsel und handschriftlichen Nachlässe, wie nach Zeugnissen von Zeitgenossen*. Gotha, Perthes, 1859.

Hamann, J. G. *Sämtliche Werke, Historisch-Kritische Ausgabe*, ed. J. Nadler. Vienna, Herder, 1949–1957.

————*Briefwechsel*, ed. W. Ziesemer and A. Henkel. Wiesbaden, Insel, 1955–1957.

————*Schriften zur Sprache*, ed. J. Simon. Frankfurt, Suhrkamp, 1967.

————*Sokratische Denkwürdigkeiten*, ed. Sven-Aage Jørgensen. Stuttgart, Reclam, 1968.

Hausius, K. G. *Materialien zur Geschichte der critischen Philosophie*. Leipzig, Breitkopf, 1793.

Hegel, G. W. F. *Werke in zwanzig Bänden, Studien Ausgabe*, ed. E. Moldenhauer and K. Michel. Frankfurt, Suhrkamp, 1971.

Herder, C. *Erinnerungen aus dem Leben Johann Gottfried Herders*. Vols. 59 and 60 of *Gesammelte Werke*, ed. J. G. Müller. Stuttgart, Cotta, 1820.

Herder, J. G. *Sämtliche Werke*, ed. B. Suphan. Berlin, Weidmann, 1881–1913.

————*Briefe, Gesammtausgabe*, ed. W. Dobbek and G. Arnold. Weimar, Bohlausnachfolger, 1979.

Heydenreich, K. *Natur und Gott nach Spinoza*. Leipzig, Müller, 1789.

————*Originalideen über die interessantesten Gegenstände der Philosophie*. Leipzig, Baumgartmer, 1793–1796.

Hölderlin, F. *Sämtliche Werke*, ed. F. Beissner. Stuttgart, Cottanachfolger, 1946.

Hufeland, G. *Versuch über den Grundsatz des Naturrechts*. Leipzig, Göschen, 1785.

————*Lehrsätze des Naturrechts und der damit verbundenen Wissenschaften*. Jena, Erben, 1790.

Hume, D. *A Treatise of Human Nature*, ed. L. A. Selby-Bigge. Oxford, Oxford University Press, 1958.

Jacobi, F. H. *David Hume über den Glauben, oder Idealismus und Realismus, ein Gespräch*. Breslau, Loewe, 1785.

————*Wider Mendelssohns Beschuldigungen*. Leipzig, Goeschen, 1786.

———*Werke*, ed. F. H. Jacobi and F. Köppen. Leipzig, Fleischer, 1812.

———*Briefwechsel zwischen Goethe und Jacobi*, ed. M. Jacobi. Leipzig, Weidmann, 1846.

———*Aus F. H. Jacobis Nachlass*, ed. R. Zoeppritz. Leipzig, Engelmann, 1869.

———*Briefwechsel*, ed. M. Brüggen and S. Sudhof. Stuttgart, Holzborg, 1981.

Jakob, L. H. *Prüfung der Mendelssohnischen Morgenstunden oder aller spekulativen Beweise für das Dasein Gottes*. Leipzig, Heinsius, 1786.

Kant, I. *Briefe, Akademie Ausgabe*, ed. R. Reicke. Berlin, Reimer, 1912.

———*Handschriftlicher Nachlass, Akademie Ausgabe*, ed. E. Adickes. Berlin, Reimer, 1912.

———*Grundlegung zur Metaphysik der Sitten*, ed. K. Vorländer. Hamburg, Meiner, 1965.

———*Kritik der Urteilskraft*, ed. K. Vorländer. Hamburg, Meiner, 1968.

———*Prolegomena zu einer jeden künftigen Metaphysik, die als Wissenschaft wird auftreten können*, ed. K. Vorländer. Hamburg, Meiner, 1969.

———*Kritik der reinen Vernunft*, ed. R. Schmidt. Hamburg, Meiner, 1971.

———*Briefwechsel*, ed. K. Vorländer. Hamburg, Meiner, 1972.

———*Kritik der praktischen Vernunft*, ed. K. Vorländer. Hamburg, Meiner, 1974.

———*Werke, Akademie Textausgabe*, ed. W. Dilthey, et al. Berlin, de Gruyter, 1979.

Kästner, A. G. "Ueber den mathematischen Begriff des Raums," *PM* II/4 (1790), 403–419.

———"Ueber die geometrischen Axiome," *PM* II/4 (1790), 420–430.

———"Was heisst in Euklids Geometrie möglich?" *PM* II/4 (1790), 391–402.

Kierkegaard, S. *Concluding Unscientific Postscript*, trans. D. Swenson and W. Lowrie. Princeton, Princeton University Press, 1941.

Kosmann, W. A. *Allgemeines Magazin für kritische und populäre Philosophie*. Breslau, Korn, 1792.

Kraus, J. "Eleutheriologie oder über Freiheit und Nothwendigkeit," *ALZ* 100/2 (April 25, 1788), 177–184.

Leibniz, G. W. *Opuscles et fragments inedits de Leibniz*. Paris, PUF, 1903.

———*Die Philosophische Schriften*, ed. C. Gebhardt. Hildesheim, Olms, 1960.

Lessing, G. E. *Sämtliche Werke, Textausgabe*, ed. K. Lachmann and F. Muncker. Berlin, de Gruyter, 1979.

Locke, J. *An Essay concerning Human Understanding*, ed. P. Nidditch. Oxford, Oxford University Press, 1975.

Lossius, J. C. *Uebersicht der neuesten Litteratur der Philosophie*. Gera, Beckmann, 1784.

Maass, J. G. E. *Briefe über die Antinomie der Vernunft*. Halle, Francke, 1788.

———"Ueber die transcendentale Aesthetik," *PM* I/2 (1788), 117–149.

———"Ueber die höchsten Grundsätze der synthetische Urteile," *PM* II/2 (1789), 186–231.

———"Ueber die Möglichkeit der Vorstellungen von Dingen an sich," *PM* II/2 (1789), 232–243.

———"Vorläufige Erklärung des Verfassers der Briefe über die Antinomie der Vernunft in Rücksicht auf die Recension dieser Briefe in der A.L.Z.," *PM* I/3 (1789), 341–355.

———"Ueber den Beweis des Satzes des zureichende Grundes," *PM* III/2 (1790), 173–194.

———"Beweis, dass die Prinzipien der Geometrie allgemeine Begriffe und der Sätze des Widerspruches sind," *PA* I/1 (1792), 126–140.

———"Neue Bestätigung des Sätzes: Dass die Geometrie aus Begriffen beweise," *PA* I/3 (1792), 96–99.

Maimon, S. *Gesammelte Werke,* ed. V. Verra. Hildesheim, Olms, 1965.

Maupertuis, P. L. M. *Dissertations sur les Differns Moyens dont les hommes se sont servis pour exprimer leurs idees.* In *Oeuvres,* vol. 3, ed. G. Tonelli. Hildesheim, Olms, 1965.

Meiners, C. *Grundriss der Geschichte der Menschheit.* Lemgo, Meyer, 1786.

———*Grundriss der Seelenlehre.* Lemgo, Meyer, 1786.

Mendelssohn, M. *Schriften zur Philosophie, Aesthetik und Politik,* ed. M. Brasch. Hildesheim, Olms, 1968.

———*Gesammelte Schriften, Jubiläumsausgabe,* ed. A. Altmann et al. Stuttgart, Holzborg, 1971.

———*Aesthetische Schriften in Auswahl,* ed. O. Best. Darmstadt, Wissenschaftliche Buchgesellschaft, 1974.

Nicolai, F. *Geschichte eines dicken Mannes.* Berlin, Nicolai, 1794.

———*Beschreibung einer Reise durch Deutschland und die Schweiz im Jahre 1781.* Berlin, Nicolai, 1796.

———*Leben und Meinungen Sempronius Grundiberts, eines deutschen Philosophen.* Berlin, Nicolai, 1798.

———"Vorrede" to J. C. Schwab's *Neun Gespräche.* Berlin, Nicolai, 1798.

———*Ueber meine gelehrte Bildung.* Berlin, Nicolai, 1799.

———*Philosophische Abhandlungen,* 2 vols. Berlin, Nicolai, 1808.

———*Gedächtnisschrift auf J. A. Eberhard.* Berlin, Nicolai, 1810.

Nietzsche, F. *Sämtliche Werke, Kritische Studienausgabe,* ed. G. Colli and M. Montinari. Berlin, de Gruyter, 1980.

Novalis, F. *Werke,* ed. U. Lasson. Hamburg, Hoffmann and Campe, 1966.

Obereit, J. H. *Die verzweifelte Metaphysik zwischen Kant und Wizenmann.* 1787.

———*Die wiederkommende Lebensgeist der verzweifelte Metaphysik.* Berlin, Decker, 1787.

———*Beobachtungen über die Quelle der Metaphysik.* Meiningen, Hanisch, 1791.

Ouvrier, K. S. *Idealismi sic dicti transcendentalis examen accuratius una cum nova demonstrationis genere quo Deum esse docetur.* Leipzig, Crusius, 1789.

Pirner, J. H. *Fragmentarische Versuche über verschiedene Gegenstände.* Berlin, Kunze, 1792.

Pistorius, H. A. "Prolegomena zu einer jeden künftigen Metaphysik," *AdB* 59/2 (1784), 322–356.

———"Ideen zu einer Philosophie der Geschichte der Menschheit," *AdB* 61/2 (1785), 311–333.

———"Erläuterung von Herrn Prof. Kants Critik der reinen Vernunft," *AdB* 66/1 (1786), 92–103.

————"Grundlegung zur Metaphysik der Sitten," *AdB* 66/2 (1786), 447–462.

————"Metaphysische Anfängsgründe der Naturwissenschaften," *AdB* 74/2 (1786), 333–344.

————"Critik der reinen Vernunft im Grundrisse," *AdB* 75/2 (1787), 487–495.

————"Ueber die Quellen menschlichen Vorstellungen," *AdB* 74/1 (1787), 184–196.

————"Grundriss der Seelenlehre," *AdB* 80/2 (1788), 459–474.

————"Prüfung der Mendelssohnischen Morgenstunden," *AdB* 82/2 (1788), 427–470.

————"Critik der reinen Vernunft im Grundrisse: Zweite Auflage," *AdB* 88/1 (1789), 103–122.

————"Eleutheriologie," *AdB* 87/1 (1789), 223–231.

————"Fragmentarische Beyträge zur Bestimmung und Deduktion des Begriffs und Grundsätze der Kausalität," *AdB* 88/2 (1789), 145–154.

————"Gründe der menschlichen Erkenntnis und der natürlichen Religion," *AdB* 85/2 (1789), 445–449.

————"Grundsätze der reinen Philosophie," *AdB* 88 (1789), 191–194.

————"Kants Moralreform," *AdB* 86/1 (1789), 153–158.

————"Plan zu einer systematischen Metaphysik," *AdB* 84/2 (1789), 455–458.

————"Natur und Gott nach Spinoza," *AdB* 94/2 (1790), 455–459.

————"Zweifel über die kantische Begriffe von Raum und Zeit," *AdB* 93/2 (1790), 437–458.

————"Reálité et Ideálité des objets de nos connaissances," *AdB* 107/1 (1792), 191–219.

————"Critik der reinen Vernunft: Zweite Ausgabe," *AdB* 117/2 (1794), 78–105.

————"Versuch über die Transcendentalphilosophie," *AdB* 117/1 (1794), 128–137.

Platner, E. *Philosophische Aphorismen*. Leipzig, Sigwart, 1784. Third completely revised edition, 1794, in *Gesammtausgabe* of Fichte, *Werke,* II/4.

————"Briefwechsel über die kantische Philosophie," in *Ernst Platner und die Kunstphilosophie des 18 Jahrhunderts,* ed. E. Bergmann. Leipzig, Meiner, 1913.

Rehberg, A. W. *Ueber das Verhältnis der Metaphysik zu der Religion.* Berlin, Mylius, 1787.

————"Kritik der praktischen Vernunft," *ALZ* 188/3 (August 6, 1788), 345–352.

————"Philosophisches Magazin, Erste Stück," *ALZ* 10/1 (January 10, 1789), 77–80.

————"Philosophisches Magazin, Zweites Stück," *ALZ* 168/2 (June 5, 1789), 713–716.

Reimarus, J. A. *Ueber die Gründe der menschlichen Erkenntnis und der natürlichen Religion.* Hamburg, Bohn, 1787.

Reinhold, K. L. "Die Wissenschaften vor und nach ihrer Sekulärisation: Ein historisches Gemählde," *TM* (July 1784), 35–42.

————"Gedanken über Aufklärung," *TM* (July 1784), 3–21; *TM* (August 1784), 122–131; *TM* (September 1784), 232–245.

————*Herzenserleichterung zweyer Menschenfreunde in vertrauter Briefe über Johann Caspar Lavaters Glaubensbekenntnis.* Frankfurt, 1785.

————"Schreiben des Pfarrers zu *** an den Herausgeber des T.M. über eine Recension von Herders Ideen zur Philosophie der Geschichte der Menschheit," *TM* (February 1785), 148–173.

———"Ehrenrettung der Reformation gegen zwey Kapitel in des Hofraths und Archivars Herrn M. J. Schmidts Geschichte der Teutschen," *TM* (February 1786), 116–141; *TM* (April 1786), 43–80.

———"Skizze einer Theogonie des blinden Glaubens," *TM* (May 1786), 229–242.

———*Die Hebraischen Mysterien oder die älteste religiöse Freymauerey.* Leipizig, Göschen, 1788.

———*Ueber die bisherigen Schicksale der kantischen Philosophie.* Jena, Mauke, 1788.

———"Philosophisches Magazin, Drittes und Viertes Stück," *ALZ* 168/2 (June 5, 1789), 529–534.

———*Versuch einer neuen Theorie des menschlichen Vorstellungsvermögen.* Prague, Widtmann and Mauke, 1789.

———"Von welchem Skepticismus lässt sich eine Reformation der Philosophie hoffen," *BM* 14 (July 1789), 49–73.

———*Beyträge zur Berichtigung bisheriger Missverständnisse der Philosophen.* Jena, Widtmann and Mauke, 1790–1794.

———*Ueber das Fundament des philosophischen Wissens.* Jena, Widtmann and Mauke, 1791.

———*Preisschrift über die Frage: Welche Fortschritte hat die Metaphysik seit Leibnitzens und Wolffs Zeiten in Deutschland gemacht?* Berlin, Maurer, 1796.

———*Beyträge zur leichtern Uebersicht des Zustandes der Philosophie im Anfange des 19 Jahrhunderts.* Hamburg, Perthes, 1801.

———*Briefe über die kantische Philosophie,* ed. R. Schmidt. Leipzig, Reclam, 1923.

———*Schriften zur Religionskritik und Aufklärung,* ed. Zwi Batscha. Bremen, Jacobi, 1977.

———*Korrespondenz, 1773–1788,* ed. R. Lauth, E. Heller, and K. Hiller. Stuttgart, Fromann, 1983.

Rink, F. T. *Mancherley zur Geschichte der metacriticischen Invasion.* Konigsberg, Nicolovius, 1800.

Rousseau, J. J. *Sur l'inégalité parmi les hommes.* In *Oeuvres complètes,* Vol. 1. Paris, Armand-Aubree, 1832.

Schad, J. B. *Geist der Philosophie unserer Zeit.* Jena, Cröker, 1800.

Schaeffer, W. F. *Auffällende Widersprüche in der kantischen Philosophie.* Dessau, Müller, 1792.

Schaumann, J. G. *Ueber die transcendentalen Aesthetik.* Leipzig, Weidmann, 1789.

Schelling, F. W. J. *Werke,* ed. M. Schröter. Munich, Beck, 1927.

———*Briefe und Dokumente,* ed. H. Fuhrmanns. Bonn, Bouvier, 1962.

Schiller, F. *Werke, Nationalausgabe,* ed. J. Peterson and H. Schneider. Weimar, Bohlau, 1943–.

Schlegel, F. *Werke, Kritische Ausgabe,* ed. E. Behler. Munich, Thomas, 1964.

Schleiermacher, F. D. *Kritische Gesammtausgabe,* ed. H. Birkner and G. Ebeling. Berlin, de Gruyter, 1980–.

Schmid, C. G. E. *Critik der reinen Vernunft im Grundrisse.* Jena, Mauke, 1788.

Schopenhauer, A. *Sämtliche Werke,* ed. A. Hubscher. Wiesbaden, Brockhaus, 1949.

Schultz, J. *Erläuterungen über des Herrn Prof. Kants Kritik der reinen Vernunft.* Königisberg, Dengel, 1784.

——"Institutiones logicae et metaphysicae," *ALZ* 295/4 (December 13, 1785), 297–299.

——*Prüfung der kantischen Critik der reinen Vernunft.* Königsberg, Nicolovius, 1789–1792.

Schulze, G. E. *Grundriss der philosophischen Wissenschaften.* Wittemberg, Zimmermann, 1788–1790.

——*Ueber dem höchsten Zweck des Studiums der Philosophie.* Leipzig, Hertel, 1789.

——"Ueber das philosophische Magazin," *AdB* 100/2 (1792), 419–452.

——"Kritik der Urteilskraft," *AdB* 115/2 (1793), 398–426.

——"Religion innerhalb der Grenzen der blossen Vernunft," *NAdB* XVI/1 (1794), 127–163.

——"Ueber eine Entdeckung nach der alle Kritik der Vernunft entbehrlich gemacht werden soll," *AdB* 116/2 (1794), 445–458.

——*Kritik der theoretischen Philosophie.* Hamburg, Born, 1801.

——*Encyklopädie der philosophischen Wissenschaften.* Göttingen, Bandenhock and Ruprecht, 1824.

——*Aenesidemus oder über die Fundamente der von dem Herrn Professor Reinhold in Jena gelieferten Elementarphilosophie,* ed. A. Liebert. Berlin, Reuther and Reichhard, 1912.

Schwab, J. C. "Prüfung des kantischen Beweises von der blossen Subjektivität der Categorien," *PM* IV/2 (1791), 195–208.

——"Vergleichung zweyer Stellen in Kants Schriften betreffend die Möglichkeit der geometrischen Begriffe," *PM* III/4 (1791), 480–490.

——"Ueber das zweyerley Ich und den Begriff der Freiheit," *PA* I/1 (1792), 69–80.

——"Noch einige Bemerkungen über die synthetischen Grundsätze a prior in der kantischen Philosophie," *PA* II/2 (1794), 117–124.

——"Ueber den intelligibeln Fatalismus in der kritischen Philosophie," *PA* II/2 (1794), 26–33.

——"Wie beweiset die kritische Philosophie, dass wir uns als absolut-frey denken müssen?" *PA* II/2 (1794), 1–9.

——*Preisschrift über die Frage: Welche Fortschritte die Metaphysik set Leibnitzens und Wolffs Zeiten in Deutschland gemacht hat?* Berlin, Maurer, 1796.

——*Neun Gespräche zwischen Christian Wolff und einem Kantianer über Kants metaphysische Anfangsgründe der Rechts und Tugendlehre.* Berlin, Nicolai, 1798.

——*Vergleichung des kantischen Moralprinzips mit dem Leibnitzisch-Wolffischen.* Berlin, Nicolai, 1800.

——*Ueber die Wahrheit der kantischen Philosophie.* Berlin, Nicolai, 1803.

Selle, C. G. "Von der analogischen Schlussart," *BM* 4 (August 1784), 185–187.

——"Nähere Bestimmung der analogischen Schlussart," *BM* 4 (October 1784), 334–337.

————"Versuch eines Beweises, dass es keine reine von der Erfahrung unabhängige Vernunftbegriffe gebe," *BM* 4 (December 1784), 565–576.

————"Ueber Natur und Offenbarung," *BM* 7 (August 1786), 121–141.

————*De la réalité et de l'idéalité des objects de nos connaissances.* Berlin, Realbuchhandlung, 1788.

————*Grundsätze der reinen Philosophie.* Berlin, Himburg, 1788.

————*Philosophische Gespräche.* Berlin, Himburg, 1788.

Sextus Empiricus. *Outlines of Pyrrhonism,* trans. R. G. Bury. London, Heinemann, 1955.

Spinoza, B. *Opera,* ed. C. Gebhardt. Heidelberg, Winters, 1924.

Stattler, B. *Anti-Kant.* Munich, Lentner, 1788.

Stoll, J. G. *Philosophische Unterhaltungen, einige Wahrheiten gegen Zweifel und Ungewissheit in besseres Licht zu setzen, auf Veranlassung von Herrn Prof. Kants Kritik der reinen Vernunft.* Leipzig, Sommer, 1788.

Storr, C. G. *Bemerkungen über Kants philosophische Religionslehre.* Tübingen, Cotta, 1794.

Süssmilch, J. P. *Versuch eines Beweises, dass die erste Sprache ihren Ursprung nicht vom Menschen, sondern allein vom Schöpfer erhalten habe.* Berlin, Realbuchhandlung, 1766.

Tetens, J. *Philosophische Versuche über die menschliche Natur und ihre Entwicklung.* Berlin, Reuther and Reichard, 1912.

Tiedemann, D. "Ueber die Natur der Metaphysik: Zur Prüfung Herrn Professor Kants Grundsätze," *HB* 1 (1785), 113–130, 233–248, 464–474.

————*Geschichte der Philosophie.* Marburg, Akademisches Buchhandlung, 1791–1797.

————*Theätet oder über das menschliche Wissen: Ein Beytrag zur Vernunftkritik.* Frankfurt, Varrentrapp and Wenner, 1794.

————*Idealistische Briefe.* Marburg, Akademisches Buchhandlung, 1798.

Tilling, C. G. *Gedanken zur Prüfung von Kants Grundlegung zur Metaphysik der Sitten.* Leipzig, Büchsel, 1789.

Tittel, G. A. *Ueber Herr Kants Moralreform.* Frankfurt, Pfahler, 1786.

————*Kantische Denkformen oder Kategorien.* Frankfurt, Gebhardt, 1787.

————*Dreizig Aufsätze aus Literatur, Philosophie und Geschichte.* Mannheim, Schwan and Götz, 1790.

————*Erläuterungen der theoretischen und praktischen Philosophie nach Herrn Feders Ordnung.* Frankfurt, Gebhardt and Kurber, 1791.

————*Locke vom menschlichen Verstande.* Mannheim, Schwan and Götz, 1791.

Ulrich, J. A. *Notio certitudinis magnis evoluta.* Jena, Göllner, 1766–1767.

————*Erster Umriss einer Anleitung in den philosophischen Wissenschaften.* Jena, Göllner, 1772.

————*Institutiones logicae et metaphysicae.* Jena, Cröker, 1785.

————*Eleutheriologie oder über Freiheit und Nothwendigkeit.* Jena, Cröker, 1788.

Visbeck, H. *Hauptmomente der Reinholdische Elementarphilosophie in Beziehung auf die Einwendungen des Aenesidemus.* Leipzig, Göschen, 1794.

Weigel, T. *Ausgewählte Werke,* ed. S. Wollgast. Stuttgart, Kohlhammer, 1977.

Weishaupt, A. *Kantische Anschauungen und Erscheinungen.* Nürnberg, Gratenau, 1788.

——*Gründe und Gewissheit des menschlichen Erkennens: Zur Prüfung der kantischen Critik der reinen Vernunft.* Nürnberg, Gratenau, 1788.

——*Ueber Materialismus und Idealismus.* Nürnberg, Gratenau, 1788.

——*Zweifel über die kantische Begriffe von Zeit und Raum.* Nürnberg, Gratenau, 1788.

Werdermann, J. G. K. *Kurze Darstellung der Philosophie in ihrer neusten Gestalt.* Leipzig, Crusius, 1792.

Will, G. A. *Vorlesungen über die kantische Philosophie.* Altdorf, Monat, 1788.

Wizenmann, T. *Die Resultate der Jacobischer und Mendelssohnischer Philosophie von einem Freywilligen.* Leipzig, Göschen, 1786.

——"An Herrn Kant von dem Verfasser der Resultate der Jacobischer und Mendelssohnischer Philosophie," *DM* 2 (February 1787), 116–156.

Wolff, C. *Herrn D. Buddens Bedencken über die Wolffische Philosophie.* Frankfurt, Andreaischen Buchhandlung, 1724.

——*Gesammelte Werke,* ed. H. W. Arndt et al. Hildesheim, Olms, 1965.

Zöllner, J. F. "Ueber eine Stelle in Moses Mendelssohns Schrift an die Freunde Lessings," *BM* 7 (March 1786), 271–275.

Zwanziger, J. C. *Commentar über Herrn Prof. Kants Kritik der reinen Vernunft.* Leipzig, Beer, 1791.

——*Commentar über Herrn Prof. Kants Kritik der praktischen Vernunft.* Leipzig, Hischer, 1794.

Secondary Sources

Abusch, A. *Schiller, Grösse und Tragik eines deutschen Genius.* Berlin, Aufbau, 1980.

Adam, H. *Carl Leonhard Reinholds philosophischer Systemwechsel.* Heidelberg, Winters, 1930.

Adickes, E. *German Kantian Bibliography.* Würzburg, Liebing, 1968.

Adler, E. *Der junge Herder und die deutsche Aufklärung.* Vienna, Europa, 1968.

Alexander, W. M. *Johann Georg Hamann.* The Hague, Nijhoff, 1966.

Allison, H. *The Kant-Eberhard Controversy.* Baltimore, Johns Hopkins University Press, 1973.

Altmann, A. *Moses Mendelssohn: A Bibliographical Study.* London, Routledge and Kegan Paul, 1974.

Arnoldt, E. *Kritische Exkurse im Gebiete der Kant Forschung.* Vol. 4 of *Gesammelte Schriften.* Berlin, Cassirer, 1908.

Atlas, S. *From Critical to Speculative Idealism: The Philosophy of Salomon Maimon.* The Hague, Nijhoff, 1964.

Baudler, G. *Im Worte Sehen, Das Sprachdenken Johann Georg Hamanns.* Bonn, Bouvier, 1970.

Baum, G. *Vernunft und Erkenntnis: Die Philosophie F. H. Jacobis.* Bonn, Bouvier, 1969.

Beck, L. W. *A Commentary on Kant's Critique of Practical Reason.* Chicago, University of Chicago Press, 1960.

——*Early German Philosophy.* Cambridge, Harvard University Press, 1969.

——*Essays on Kant and Hume.* New Haven, Yale University Press, 1978.

Bergmann, E. *Ernst Platner und die Kunstphilosophie des 18 Jahrhundert.* Hamburg, Meiner, 1913.

Berlin, I. *Vico and Herder.* London, Hogarth, 1976.

——"Hume and the Sources of German Anti-Rationalism," in *Against the Current: Essays in the History of Ideas,* pp. 162–187. London, Hogarth Press, 1980.

Best, O. "Einleitung" to *Moses Mendelssohn, Aesthetische Schriften in Auswahl.* Darmstadt, Wissenschatliche Buchgesellschaft, 1974.

Bittner, R., and K. Cramer. *Materialien zu Kants Kritik der praktischen Vernunft.* Frankfurt, Suhrkamp, 1975.

Blanke, F. *Kommentar zu Hamanns Sokratische Denkwürdigkeiten.* Vol. 2 of *Hamanns Hauptschriften erklärt,* ed. F. Blanke et al. Gutersloh, Bertelheim, 1956.

——"Hamann und Luther," in *Johann Georg Hamann, Wege der Forschung,* ed. R. Wild, pp. 146–172. Darmstadt, Wissenschaftliche Buchgesellschaft, 1978.

Bollnow, O. F. *Die Lebensphilosophie F. H. Jacobis.* Munich, Fink, 1969.

Bruford, W. H. *Germany in the Eighteenth Century.* Cambridge, Cambridge University Press, 1935.

——*Germany in the Eighteenth Century: The Social Background of the Literary Revival.* Cambridge, Cambridge University Press, 1965.

Buchner, H. "Zur Bedeutung des Skeptizismus beim jungen Hegel," *Hegel-Studien,* supp. 4 (1969), 49–56.

Büchsel, E. *Ueber den Ursprung der Sprache.* Vol. 4 of *Hamanns Hauptschriften erklärt.* Gutersloh, Mohn, 1963.

Cassirer, E. *Rousseau, Kant and Goethe.* Princeton, Princeton University Press, 1945.

——*The Philosophy of the Enlightenment.* Princeton, Princeton University Press, 1951.

——*Die nachkantische Systeme.* Vol. 3 of *Das Erkenntnisproblem in der Philosophie und Wissenschaft der neueren Zeit.* Darmstadt Wissenschaftliche Buchgesellschaft, 1974.

——*Kants Leben und Lehre.* Darmstadt, Wissenschaftliche Buchgesellschaft, 1977.

Clark, T. *Herder, His Life and Thought.* Berkeley, University of California Press, 1955.

Copleston, F. *Wolff to Kant.* Vol. 6 of *A History of Philosophy.* London, Burns and Oates, 1960.

De Vleeschauwer, H. J. *La Deduction transcendentale dans l'oeuvre de Kant.* Antwerp, de Sikkel, 1934.

——*The Development of Kantian Thought.* London, Nelson, 1962.

Dilthey, W. "Johann Georg Hamann," in *Gesammelte Schriften,* ed. H. Nohl. Leipzig, de Gruyter, 1923, vol. 11, pp. 1–38.

Dobbek, W. *Johann Gottfried Herders Jugendzeit in Mohrungen und Königsberg, 1744–64.* Wurzburg, Holzner, 1961.

Düsing, K. "Die Rezeption der kantischen Postulatenlehre in den frühen philosophischen Entwurfen Schellings und Hegels," *Hegel-Studien*, supp. 9 (1973), 95–128.

Eberstein, W. G. *Versuch einer Geschichte der Logik und Metaphysik bey den Deutschen.* Halle, Ruff, 1799.

Epstein, K. *The Genesis of German Conservatism.* Princeton, Princeton University Press, 1966.

Erdmann, B. *Kants Kriticismus in der ersten und zweiten Auflage der Kritik der reinen Vernunft.* Leipzig, Voss, 1878.

———*Historische Untersuchungen über Kants Prolegomena.* Halle, Niemeyer, 1904.

Erdmann, J. *Die Entwicklung der deutschen Spekulation seit Kant.* Vol. 5 of *Versuch einer wissenschaftlichen Darstellung der Geschichte der Philosophie.* Stuttgart, Holzboorg, 1977.

Fischer, H. *Kritik und Zensur: Die Transcendentalphilosophie zwischen Empirismus und kritischen Rationalismus.* Erlangen, Höfer and Limmert, 1981.

Fischer, K. *J. G. Fichte und seine Vorgänger.* Vol. 5 of *Geschichte der neueren Philosophie.* Heidelberg, Winters, 1900.

Fuhrmanns, H. *Schelling, Briefe und Dokumente.* Bonn, Bouvier, 1962.

Gajek, B., ed. *Johann Georg Hamann, Acta des Internationalen Hamann-Colloquims in Luneberg 1976.* Frankfurt, Klostermann, 1979.

Gay, P. *The Enlightenment, An Interpretation.* New York, Norton, 1977.

German, T. J. *Hamann on Language and Religion.* Oxford, Oxford University Press, 1981 (in the series Oxford Theological Monographs).

Gross, F., ed. *Immanuel Kant, sein Leben in Darstellungen von Zeitgenossen.* Darmstadt, Wissenschaftliche Buchgesellschaft, 1980.

Gründer, K. *Die Hamann Forschung.* Vol. 1 of *Hamanns Hauptschriften erklärt.* Gutersloh, Bertelmann, 1956.

Grunwald, K. *Spinoza in Deutschland.* Berlin, Calvary, 1897.

Gueroult, M. *La Philosophie transcendentale de Salomon Maimon.* Paris, Alcan, 1919.

Gulyga, A. *Herder.* Frankfurt, Rodeberg, 1978.

———*Immanuel Kant.* Frankfurt, Insel, 1981.

Guyer, P. *Kant and the Claims of Taste.* Cambridge, Harvard University Press, 1979.

Hammacher, K., ed. *Friedrich Heinrich Jacobi, Philosoph und Literat der Goethezeit.* Klostermann, Frankfurt, 1971.

Hampson, N. *The Enlightenment.* Harmondsworth, Penguin, 1968.

Harris, H. S. *Hegel's Development, Toward the Sunlight, 1770–1801.* Oxford, Oxford University Press, 1972.

Haym, R. *Die romantische Schule.* Berlin, Weidmann, 1906.

Hazard, P. *La Pensée Européenne au XVIIIeme Siècle.* Paris, Boivin, 1946.

Hebeissen, A. *Friedrich Heinrich Jacobi, Seine Auseindersetzung mit Jacobi,* in the series *Sprache und Dichtung,* ed. W. Heinzen et al. Berne, Haupte, 1961.

Heine, H. *Zur Geschichte der Religion und Philosophie in Deutschland.* Vol. 8 of *Sekulärausgabe,* ed. Renate Francke. Berlin, Akademie Verlag, 1972.

Heizmann, W. *Kants Kritik spekulativer Theologie und Begriff moralischen Ver-*

nunftglaubens im katholischen Denken der späten Aufklärung. Göttingen, Vandenhoeck and Ruprecht, 1976.

Henrich, D. *Hegel im Kontext.* Frankfurt, Suhrkamp, 1967.

Heraeus, O. *Fritz Jacobi und der Sturm und Drang.* Heidelberg, Winters, 1928.

Hettner, H. *Geschichte der deutschen Literatur im 18. Jahrhundert,* 4th ed. Berlin, Aufbau, 1979.

Hinske, N., ed. *Ich handle mit Vernunft: Moses Mendelssohn und die europäische Aufklärung.* Hamburg, Meiner, 1981.

Hoffmeister, J. *Goethe und das deutschen Idealismus.* Leipzig, Meiner, 1932.

Homann, K. F. *H. Jacobis Philosophie der Freiheit.* Munich, Alber, 1973.

Im Hof, U. *Das gesellige Jahrhundert: Gesellschaft und Gesellschaften im Zeitalter der Aufklärung.* Munich, Beck, 1982.

Jørgensen, S. *Johann Georg Hamann.* Stuttgart, Metzler, 1967.

Kayserling, M. *Moses Mendelssohn, Sein Leben und seine Werke.* Leipzig, Mendelssohn, 1862.

Kiesel, H., and P. Munch. *Gesellschaft und Literatur im 18 Jahrhundert.* Munich, Beck, 1977.

Klemmt, A. *Reinholds Elementarphilosophie.* Hamburg, Meiner, 1958.

Knoll, R. *Johann Georg Hamann und Friedrich Heinrich Jacobi.* Heidelberg, Winters, 1963.

Koep, W. "Johann Georg Hamanns Londoner Senel-Affäre, Januar 1758," *Zeitschrift für Theologie und Kirche* 57 (1960), 92–108; 58 (1961), 66–85.

———*Der Magier unter Masken, Versuch eines neuen Hamannbildes.* Göttingen, Vandenhoeck and Ruprecht, 1965.

Kronenberg, M. *Geschichte des deutschen Idealismus.* Munich, Beck, 1909.

Kroner, R. *Von Kant bis Hegel.* Tübingen, Mohr, 1921.

Kuntze, F. *Die Philosophie des Salomon Maimons.* Heidelberg, Winters, 1912.

Lauth, R., ed. *Philosophie aus einem Prinzip: Karl Leonhard Reinhold.* Bonn, Bouvier, 1974.

Lepenies, W. *Das Ende der Naturgeschichte.* Suhrkamp, Frankfurt, 1978.

Levy-Bruhl, L. *La Philosophie de Jacobi.* Paris, Alcan, 1894.

Litt, T. *Kant und Herder als Deuter der geistigen Welt.* Leipzig, Quelle and Meyer, 1930.

Lovejoy, A. "Kant's Antithesis of Dogmatism and Criticism," *Mind* (1906), 191–214.

Löw, R. *Philosophie des Lebendigen, Der Begriff des Organischen bei Kant, sein Grund und seine Aktualität.* Suhrkamp, Frankfurt, 1980.

Lowrie, W. *J. G. Hamann, An Existentialist.* Princeton, Princeton University Press, 1950.

———*A Short Life of Kierkegaard.* Princeton, Princeton University Press, 1970.

Mauthner, F. *Der Atheismus und seine Geschichte im Abendlande.* Stuttgart, Deutsche-Verlag, 1922.

Merker, N. *Die Aufklärung in Deutschland.* Munich, Beck, 1974.

Metzke, E. *J. G. Hamanns Stellung in der Philosophie des 18 Jahrhunderts.* Darmstadt, Wissenschaftliche Buchgesellschaft, 1967.

Meyer, H. M. Z. *Moses Mendelssohn Bibliographie.* Berlin, de Gruyter, 1965.

Minor, J. *Hamann in seiner Bedeutung für die Sturm und Drang.* Frankfurt, Rütten and Loening, 1881.

Nebel, G. *Hamann.* Stuttgart, Klett, 1973.

O'Flaherty, J. C. *Unity and Language: A Study in the Philosophy of Johann Georg Hamann.* New York, AMS Press, 1966.

———*Hamann's Socratic Memorabilia: A Translation and Commentary.* Baltimore, Johns Hopkins University Press, 1967.

———*Johann Georg Hamann.* Boston, Twayne, 1979.

Parthey, G. *Mitarbeiter an Nicolais Allgemeine deutsche Bibliothek.* Berlin, Nicolai, 1842.

Pascal, R. *The German Sturm und Drang.* Manchester, Manchester University Press, 1953.

Pfleiderer, O. *The Development of Theology in Germany since Kant,* trans. J. F. Smith. London, Sonnenschein, 1893.

Reicke, R. *Kantiana, Beiträge zu Immanuel Kants Leben und Schriften.* Königsberg, Theile, 1860.

Reinhold, E. *K. L. Reinholds Leben und literarisches Wirken.* Jena, Fromann, 1825.

Reininger, R. *Kant, Seine Anhänger und seine Gegner.* Reinhardt, Munich, 1923.

Riedel, M. "Historizismus und Kritizismus: Kants Streit mit G. Forster und J. G. Herder," *Kant-Studien* 72 (1981), 41–57.

Roger, J. *Les Sciences de la Vie dans la Pensée Française du XVIIIe Siècle.* Poitiers, Armand Colin, 1963.

Rosenkranz, K. *Geschichte der kantischen Philosophie.* Vol. 12 of *Kants Sämmtliche Werke,* ed. K. Rosenkranz and F. Schubert. Leipzig, Voss, 1840.

Royce, J. *Lectures on Modern Idealism.* New Haven, Yale University Press, 1964.

Salmony, H. A. *Hamanns metakritische Philosophie.* Basel, Evangelischer Verlag, 1958.

Schmid, F. A. *Friedrich Heinrich Jacobi.* Heidelberg, Winters, 1908.

Schoeps, J. H. *Moses Mendelssohn.* Königstein, Athenäum, 1979.

Scholz, H., ed. *Die Hauptschriften zum Pantheismus Streit zwischen Jacobi und Mendelssohn.* Berlin, Reuther and Reichard, 1916.

Schreiner, L. *Johann Georg Hamann, Golgotha und Scheblimini.* Vol. 7 of *Hamanns Hauptschriften erklärt,* ed. F. Blanke et al. Gutersloh, Bertelmann, 1956.

Seligowitz, B. "Ernst Platners wissenschaftliche Stellung zu Kant in Erkenntnistheorie und Moralphilosophie," *Vierteljahrschrift für wissenschaftliche Philosophie* 16 (1892), 76–103, 172–191.

Skinner, Q. *The Foundations of Modern Political Thought.* Cambridge, Cambridge University Press, 1978.

Stern, A. *Ueber die Beziehung Garves zu Kant.* Leipzig, Denicke, 1884.

Stiehler, G. *Materialisten der Leibniz-Zeit.* Berlin, Deutscher Verlag, 1966.

Strauss, L. "Einleitung" to vol. III/2 of *Jubiläumsausgabe* of *Mendelssohns Schriften,* ed. A. Altmann, Stuttgart, Holzborg, 1971.

Taylor, C. *Hegel.* Cambridge, Cambridge University Press, 1975.

Timm, H. "Die Bedeutung der Spinozabriefe Jacobis," in *Die Philosophie F. H. Jacobi,* ed. K. Hammacher. Munich, Fink, 1969.

——*Gott und die Freiheit: Studien zur Religionsphilosophie der Goethezeit.* Frankfurt, Klostermann, 1974.

Tonelli, A. "Eberhard," in *Encyclopedia of Philosophy*, ed. P. Edwards. New York, Macmillan, 1967.

Ueberweg, F. *Die deutsche Philosophie des XIX Jahrhunderts und der Gegenwart.* Berlin, Mittler, 1923.

Unger, R. *Hamanns Sprachtheorie im Zusammenhang seines Denkens.* Munich, Beck, 1905.

——*Hamann und die Aufklärung.* Halle, Niemeyer, 1925.

Vaihinger, E. "Ein bisher unbekannter Aufsatz von Kant über die Freiheit," *Philosophischer Monatsheft* 16 (1880), 193–208.

Verra, V. "Jacobis Kritik am deutschen Idealismus," *Hegel-Studien* 5 (1969), 201–223.

Vorländer, K. *I. Kant, der Mann und das Werk.* Hamburg, Meiner, 1977.

Weber, H. *Hamann und Kant.* Munich, Beck, 1908.

Weischedel, W. *Streit um die göttlichen Dingen: Die Auseinandersetzung zwischen Jacobi und Schelling.* Darmstadt, Wissenschaftliche Buchgesellschaft, 1967.

Wild, R., ed. *Hamann, Wege der Forschung.* Darmstadt, Wissenschaftliche Buchgesellschaft, 1978.

Wilde, N. *Friedrich Heinrich Jacobi: A Study in the Origin of German Realism.* New York, AMS Press, 1966.

Windelband, W. M. *Die Blütezeit der deutschen Philosophie.* Vol. 2 of *Die Geschichte der neueren Philosophie.* Leipzig, Breitkopf, 1904.

Wolff, H. *Die Weltanschauung der deutschen Aufklärung.* Bern, Francke, 1949.

Wrescher, A. *Platners und Kants Erkenntnistheorie mit besonderer Berücksichtigung von Tetens und Aenesidemus.* Leipzig, Pfeffer, 1892.

Wundt, M. *Die deutsche Schulphilosophie im Zeitalter der Aufklärung.* Tübingen, Mohr, 1945.

Zeller, E. *Geschichte der deutschen Philosophie seit Leibniz.* Munich, Oldenburg, 1875.

Zirngiebel, E. *F. H. Jacobis Leben, Dichten und Denken.* Wien, Braumüller, 1867.

Index